News Reporting and Writing will prepare you for a career in journalism in so many ways.

Prepare for the future by learning what's happening now and what's to come. The first unit of the book examines the current news landscape and journalism's role in the twenty-first century. It opens your eyes to the current trends like citizen journalism, the converging media and new forms of journalism that offer exciting career paths.

Key coverage focuses on what's most relevant to your life as a new journalist. Most likely your first job will involve local news reporting and writing. Therefore, we offer you the instruction and tips you need first — covering city and county government, schools, higher education, police and sports in one chapter. The streamlined "Other Types of Local Stories" chapter focuses on reportorial mainstays — crime stories, accident and fire stories, court stories and obituaries.

Success in the news room requires the ability to work collaboratively. Use the activities at the end of each chapter to practice important collaboration skills — from interviewing to investigating — in a team-based environment.

Chapters offer help writing for different media like the Web, radio or television. Chapter 12 ("Writing for the Web") shows you how to structure Web stories, examine online readers' expectations and write effectively for electronic media, while Chapter 13 ("Writing News for Radio and Television") stresses the unique elements of writing for television and radio, as well as how to prepare news copy for these media.

Visual examples *show* you how stories work and how to improve your own writing. Our visually annotated stories walk you through how well-structured articles function. This edition also includes examples that show the best ways to use quotations and attributions; how to write for news websites; see the differences between breaking news stories and follow-up stories; and use verb tenses in television reporting.

Visit *News Central* at bedfordstmartins.com/newscentral to take advantage of the many tools to help you hone your writing and reporting skills and keep you current on each day's events.

News Reporting and Writing

Tenth Edition

The Missouri Group

Brian S. Brooks
George Kennedy
Daryl R. Moen
Don Ranly
School of Journalism
University of Missouri

Bedford/St. Martin's
Boston ▪ New York

For Bedford/St. Martin's

Executive Editor for Communication: Erika Gutierrez
Editor: Karen Schultz Moore
Developmental Editor: Linda Stern
Associate Editor: Ada Fung
Editorial Assistant: Emily Cavedon
Production Associate: Samuel Jones
Senior Marketing Manager: Adrienne Petsick
Project Management: Books By Design, Inc.
Text Design: Books By Design, Inc.
Photo Research: Julie Tesser
Cover Design: Billy Boardman
Composition: Books By Design, Inc.
Printing and Binding: RR Donnelley & Sons Company

President: Joan E. Feinberg
Editorial Director: Denise B. Wydra
Director of Development: Erica T. Appel
Director of Marketing: Karen R. Soeltz
Director of Production: Susan W. Brown
Associate Director of Editorial Production: Elise S. Kaiser
Manager, Publishing Services: Emily Berleth

Library of Congress Control Number: 2010921024

Manufactured in the United States of America.
5 4 3 2 1 0
f e d c b a

For information, write: Bedford/St. Martin's, 75 Arlington Street, Boston, MA 02116 (617-399-4000)

ISBN-10: 0-312-61811-5
ISBN-13: 978-0-312-61811-7

Acknowledgments

Acknowledgments and copyrights appear at the back of the book on pages 521–23, which constitute an extension of the copyright page.

Preface

What does it mean to be a journalist today? Does the image of the hard-bitten print newspaper reporter wielding a trusty pen and notebook still resonate? How often do students read a print newspaper or watch the news on network television? These are important questions in the dramatically changing world of journalism. Traditional newspapers are competing with online news sites, blogs, podcasts and a range of new social media. Similarly, the nightly news broadcasts face off against 24-hour cable news, webcasts and even satiric pseudo-news shows like *The Colbert Report* and *The Daily Show*. What do these changes mean for today's journalism students? How can we best prepare them for a successful career in this evolving industry?

To answer these questions, we visited convergent news rooms in Tampa and Sarasota, we talked with dozens of journalists around the country, and we read scores of articles in every medium to figure out the most important skills new journalists must have to compete in today's job market. Despite the whirlwind of professional change and the development of innovative technologies, one theme consistently emerged: Editors want journalists who can report fully and write clearly, whether for an online news outlet, a professional blog, cable news or a print newspaper. We were pleased to see that even in this convergent world, the keys to being a good journalist are still as fundamental as that.

We have thoroughly revised the 10th edition of *News Reporting and Writing* to reflect both the changing nature of the field and the skills that are essential for success in it today. To this end, we have completely revamped the first unit of the book—including adding an entirely new chapter—to discuss contemporary journalism. While we cannot afford to ignore the challenges the field is experiencing, we also need to remember that along with change come genuinely exciting professional opportunities. Future journalists need to stay up-to-date on the new and evolving careers in their field and need to remember that the work they will do—in its various, evolving forms—is crucial in a free society.

To best support students, we continue to stress essential writing and reporting skills that are the foundations of our profession—past, present and future. We've streamlined coverage to sharpen the focus on interviewing, reporting and writing across media platforms and give special attention to the beat most immediately relevant to new graduates: local news. In addition, we continue to recognize the need to practice what we preach. So, as we've done in all previous editions of this book, we use current examples and issues, and we model in our own writing how journalism students must learn to write—clearly and descriptively. Our emphasis of these topics in the textbook, combined with our robust online support and practice opportunities, ensures that students will have more opportunities than ever before to practice and refine their skills.

Enduring Features of the Text

Users of *News Reporting and Writing* have come to expect that every new edition of our textbook will be readable and current as well as deeply focused on journalistic essentials. We are proud to continue to offer the following features:

- **Comprehensive coverage of all aspects of reporting and writing the news.** *News Reporting and Writing* teaches students the elements of reporting and good writing and provides the basic tools they need to become journalists across various media platforms, including advice on how to conduct interviews and research, employ computer-assisted reporting techniques, and create rich and well-crafted stories for the basic beats.

- **A focus on storytelling.** From life stories to world-news reports, local meetings to national press conferences, good journalism means good writing. We use real-life examples, up-to-the-minute news story samples and a consistent focus on writing essentials to demonstrate how students should craft rich and interesting stories. In addition, Chapter 10, "Writing to Be Read," helps students master coherence, effective language and other techniques central to captivating an audience.

- **Solid coverage of media convergence and online journalism.** *News Reporting and Writing* ensures that students learn how to prepare stories for multiple forms of media effectively. Reflecting current trends, our book's coverage includes the rising role of technology, convergence and the emergence of integrated news rooms, the challenges to legacy media and the future of online journalism.

- **Unparalleled discussion of legal and ethical issues.** Throughout the book, we offer students a framework for critically assessing the ethical questions they will face as journalists. In addition, we dedicate Chapters 21 and 22 to legal and ethical matters respectively.

- **A chapter on math for journalists.** *News Reporting and Writing* includes a chapter on "Reporting with Numbers," which stresses the importance of using and understanding data—a vital skill for business news stories in particular.

- **Coverage of common grammar issues, Associated Press style, and proofreading and copyediting symbols.** The appendixes provide helpful information students need to turn in polished, professionally edited copy. Thousands of accompanying online exercises offer students additional opportunities to improve their grammar and AP style (www.bedfordstmartins.com/newscentral). In addition, the last page and inside back cover offer students an easy-to-find reference of proofreading and copyediting symbols.

New to This Edition

We've made major revisions to the 10th edition of *News Reporting and Writing* to address significant changes in the field and to provide additional opportunities for students to refine their reporting and writing skills. The new edition offers a new chapter that captures the turmoil as the old media try to transform themselves and the new media seek a niche in the market. We look at where the jobs are being lost and where they are being added. We look at what skill sets survive and what new skills students need. We look at how news consumption patterns are changing. In short, this revision is about journalism in the second decade of the 21st century. Specifically, this new edition does the following:

- **Introduces students to journalism today and takes a fresh look at the opportunities ahead.** The first unit of the book examines today's news landscape and the role of journalism in the 21st century, chronicling the evolution of print media, the development of citizen journalism and the convergence of the media. A completely revised Chapter 2, "The Changing Media Landscape," and a new Chapter 3, "The Emerging Media," focus on exciting new forms of journalism and on the challenges and opportunities in the field today.

- **Offers more prominent coverage of writing for the Web, radio and television.** Chapter 12 ("Writing for the Web") describes how Web stories are structured and now offers in-depth coverage of online readers' expectations and tips for effective blogging. This chapter also provides a new annotated model to further illustrate the Web writing process. Chapter 13 ("Writing News for Radio and Television") offers the most up-to-date coverage of the unique elements of writing for and preparing news copy for these media, complete with a new annotated model on verb tenses in television reporting.

- **Spotlights the most relevant content for students: local news.** Local news is most often the first job journalism graduates get. Thus Chapter 14, "Covering a Beat," now gives the instruction and tips students need first; this one chapter covers city and county government, schools, higher education, police and sports. We've also streamlined Chapter 16, "Other Types of Local Stories," which now focuses exclusively on local reportorial mainstays: crime stories, accident and fire stories, court stories and obituaries.

- **Offers even more writing models.** In this edition of *News Reporting and Writing*, we offer four new examples of our popular annotated models. The pedagogically useful annotations in the margins of the stories show students the best ways to use quotations and attributions; how to see the differences between breaking news stories and follow-up stories; and how to use verb tenses in television reporting. An annotated Web story highlights the features that distinguish good Web writing.

- **Offers nine new "On the Job" boxes that prepare students for contemporary careers.** In every chapter, a working journalist illustrates how the skills students learn in class will prepare them for careers across the media and in public relations—even in today's challenging and evolving job market. These journalists have wide-ranging careers, from reporting on the news in Baghdad to running a news museum in Washington, D.C. And while almost all the featured journalists discuss the impact of new technologies on their jobs, several, including Jennifer LaFleur, Sarah Protzman and Brian Storm, chronicle their experiences with new job opportunities created by a field in transition—for example, starting blogs and working in alternative journalism models.

- **Includes new exercises to support group collaboration.** Although our students sometimes struggle with group projects, we know that group work is an essential part of professional success. For this reason, we now offer opportunities at the end of each chapter to practice important collaboration skills—from interviewing to investigating—in a team-based environment. Tips and additional support for these exercises can be found in the Instructor's Manual.

- **Provides the best online tools for today's students.** The *News Central* website gives students the tools they need to become better writers and reporters—from RSS feeds to writing and grammar exercises to instructive videos. For more detailed information, please see "Resources for Students and Instructors" in this preface or visit www.bedfordstmartins.com/newscentral.

Resources for Students and Instructors

As before, *News Reporting and Writing* is supported by a range of effective resources. The following ancillaries are available with this edition:

- **Workbook for *News Reporting and Writing*, 10th Edition.** Supplementing the exercises at the end of each text chapter, the revised workbook gives students extra practice in mastering the principles of journalism.

- **Instructor's Manual to Accompany *News Reporting and Writing*, 10th Edition.** This heavily revised and updated manual contains a sample syllabus; additional teaching resources; and chapter-specific overviews, teaching tips, lecture outlines, classroom activities and discussion questions; as well as answers to the end-of-chapter exercises from the main text and answers to the workbook exercises. The Instructor's Manual is available for immediate download at www.bedfordstmartins.com/newsreporting/catalog.

- ***News Central* website (www.bedfordstmartins.com/newscentral).** Here students can find links to research tools and online exercises, in addition to up-to-the-moment RSS feeds providing students with breaking news all the time. Students can also access *Exercise Central for AP Style* as well as *VideoCentral: Journalism* from the site.

  - *Exercise Central for AP Style.* This free database offers more than 2,500 questions targeting the 20 grammar and usage errors most commonly made by journalism students. In addition, it provides a set of Associated Press style exercises that have been revised to reflect the 2010 AP style updates.

  - *VideoCentral: Journalism.* This brand-new resource offers video clips that introduce students to top journalists like Charles Osgood, Amy Goodman and Clarence Page, who are working in various areas of contemporary media. Additional clips offer practical help with interviewing techniques. Students can learn from watching other students in interview situations with peers. Access to *VideoCentral: Journalism* requires premium access.

Acknowledgments

Our colleagues and students at the University of Missouri have given us invaluable feedback on the book, for which we are grateful.

We especially appreciate the contributions of Dr. Charles Davis, a faculty colleague, who revised the law chapter; Marty Steffens, who holds the Society of American Business Editors and Writers Chair in Business and Financial Journalism, for revising our business chapter, and Jennifer Reeves in our radio-television department for reviewing the chapter on writing for radio and television. We are grateful to Karl Grubaugh of American River College and Granite Bay High School for his superb work on the Instructor's Manual for this edition.

We also thank all of the instructors who thoughtfully reviewed the text: Betsy B. Alderman, University of Tennessee at Chattanooga; Anne Becker, Oakland University; Mark Berkey-Gerard, Rowan University; JoAnne C. Broadwater, Towson University; Betty S. Clapp, Cleveland State University; Jan Barry Crumb, Rutgers University; Helene DeGross, Lake Forest College; Dee Drummond, University of Toledo; Sandra Fish, University of Colorado; Jennifer Follis, University of Illinois; Gwen R. Fowler, Coastal Carolina University; Eddye Gallagher, Tarrant County College; Patrick Harwood, College of Charleston; Ron Hollander, Montclair State University; Amani Ismail, California State University, Northridge; Elena Jarvis, Daytona State College; Kevin R. Kemper, University of Arizona; Laura Krantz, Tyler Junior College; Linda Loomis, State University of New York, Oswego; Therese Lueck, University of Akron; Carole McNall, St. Bonaventure University; Kristi Nies, Peru State College; Carolyn Olson, Maryville University; Debra Patterson, Motlow State Community College; Richard Puffer, Coker College; Cathy Stablein, College of DuPage; Cynthia Thomas, Grand Valley State University; Tracy Warner, Indiana-Purdue, Fort Wayne; Thomas E. Winski, Emporia State University; and Vallorie Wood, Kennesaw State University.

We have worked with editors at Bedford/St. Martin's for 31 years now. With each edition, they have challenged us to improve, and we appreciate their work. We would like to acknowledge the expert work of our developmental editor, Linda Stern, who kept us in line and on time. Thanks are also due to Erika Gutierrez, Karen Schultz Moore, Erica Appel and Ada Fung. We are equally grateful to the production team, which includes Emily Berleth and Nancy Benjamin of Books By Design, as well as our photo researcher, Julie Tesser. We'd like to extend further thanks to our marketing team, Adrienne Petsick and Alexis Smith. Last, but most certainly not least, we want to express our appreciation to our wives—Anne, Robin and Eva Joan—who have been wonderful partners in this undertaking.

As always, we value your comments. You can reach us via e-mail at Brooksbs@missouri.edu; Kennedyg@missouri.edu; Moend@missouri.edu; or Ranlyd @missouri.edu.

Brian S. Brooks
George Kennedy
Daryl R. Moen
Don Ranly

Contents

PART ONE   JOURNALISM AND JOURNALISTS

PART TWO   REPORTING TOOLS

4   Interviewing   60

6   Gathering and Verifying Information   108

7   Finding the News in News Releases   130

8 Reporting with Numbers 148

PART THREE   STORYTELLING

9 The Inverted Pyramid   168

10 Writing to Be Read 194

11 Alternatives to the Inverted Pyramid 220

PART FOUR   WRITING FOR SPECIFIC MEDIA

12   Writing for the Web   244

ANNOTATED MODEL
Figure 12.6 **Anatomy of an Article Page on a News Website** 255

13 Writing News for Radio and Television 268

ANNOTATED MODEL
Figure 13.1   **Use of Verb Tenses in a TV Story**   273

PART FIVE   BASIC STORIES

14   Covering a Beat   290

15 Speeches, News Conferences and Meetings 316

17 Business and Consumer News   368

PART SIX   SPECIALIZED TECHNIQUES

18 Social Science Reporting   390

19 Investigative Reporting   404

20 Working in Public Relations   422

PART SEVEN   **RIGHTS AND RESPONSIBILITIES**

21   Media Law   444

News Reporting and Writing

ALJAZEERA

The Nature of News

1

IN THIS CHAPTER
YOU WILL LEARN:

1. How the forces of technology and economics are reshaping the news.

2. How journalists are finding new tools and how audiences are finding new sources of news.

3. How the unchanging principles of accuracy and fairness will help you meet the challenges of permanent change.

The news today is that journalism is in transition. Audiences for traditional media are shrinking. So is the number of employed journalists. News consumption on the Internet is growing rapidly, but the most popular online news sources, such as Google and Yahoo, provide little original reporting, and the economics of online journalism are highly uncertain.

The 2009 report by the Project for Excellence in Journalism began with these lowlights:

> By our calculations, nearly one out of every five journalists working for newspapers in 2001 is now gone. . . .
>
> In local television, news staffs, already too small to adequately cover their communities, are being cut at unprecedented rates . . . and ratings are now falling or are flat across the schedule.
>
> The number of Americans who regularly go online for news, by one survey, jumped 19 percent in two years. . . . Yet it is now all but settled that advertising revenue—the model that financed journalism for the last century—will be inadequate to do so in this one.

No wonder the authors of this annual report described it as their "bleakest."

Still, behind the gloom we see exciting examples of new possibilities for reporting and receiving the news.

- When young Iranians rose in mass protest of a flawed election, authorities clamped down on traditional news outlets and evicted foreign journalists. Iranians by the thousands made themselves into citizen journalists, using cell phone photographs and Twitter to tell their stories to each other and the outside world.

- When former Republican vice presidential candidate Sarah Palin decided to resign as governor of Alaska, she first announced her decision on Facebook.

- When the staid old *New York Times* received a flood of questions from readers confused about the ongoing conflicts in Iraq and Afghanistan, editors responded by creating a blog on NYTimes.com titled "At War," in which *Times* correspondents explain and expand on their printed reports.

Young—and not so young—entrepreneurs are taking advantage of online technology to provide new forms of journalism to new audiences. Take a look, for example, at http://mediastorm.com, where you'll find fascinating pieces of in-depth reporting using print, still photography and video. (Brian Storm, its creator, even includes a section offering advice for others who want to follow the path he is discovering.) Or visit www.newsy.com, where another journalism school graduate collects video reports from news sources around the world and packages them to provide a variety of perspectives on important issues.

MinnPost.com, voiceofsandiego.org and stlbeacon.org are among the many local news sites that are trying to adapt to the Internet the nonprofit model that National Public Radio and its affiliates use with success. Most of these new sources are staffed by journalists who have been laid off from traditional—often now called "legacy"—media.

So journalism today, like the world it seeks to explain, is in turmoil. It is disturbing but also exciting and promising turmoil.

CONVERGENCE IN JOURNALISM

Convergence is the term that describes efforts to use the different strengths of different media to reach broader audiences and tell the world's stories in new ways. Convergence demands of journalists new skills and new flexibility. Print reporters find themselves summarizing their stories into a television camera. Videographers find themselves selecting images to be published in the partner newspaper. Both print and broadcast journalists look for Web links to connect their stories to the worldwide audience and nearly infinite capacity of the Internet. **Smart phones**, phones capable of surfing the Web, such as iPhones and BlackBerrys, provide new outlets and require new storytelling techniques.

The technological revolution also has exploded traditional definitions of just who is a journalist. Millions of people across the world have launched **blogs**. Although one estimate is that only 5 percent of those sites include original reporting, and although most have tiny audiences, many have become influential voices in the public conversation. In an effort to add personality and encourage interactivity with audience members, traditional news organizations are encouraging staff members to write blogs.

Increasingly, members of the public are being invited to respond to stories that are published or broadcast. Citizens are even being enlisted as amateur reporters. "Crowdsourcing," as it is called, has become a reporting tool at news organizations from North Dakota to Florida. Readers and viewers are invited to submit their own stories, photographs and video. They are sometimes asked to lend their expertise to help solve community problems. In one extreme case, an independent blogger in Missouri announced that he was going to attempt to solve a two-year-old murder and began by asking his readers for their recollections and suggestions.

Even the fundamentals of journalism are evolving as technology speeds up the communication process, provides new sources for both reporters and audiences, and reshapes journalism from a one-way flow of information to a give-and-take with audiences and competitors. One element that hasn't changed, however, is the importance of accuracy and fairness. And the essential role of journalism in a democratic society remains the one assigned to it by James Madison in 1822: "A popular government without popular information or the means of acquiring it is but a prologue to a farce or a tragedy, or perhaps both."

> **"**The old norms of traditional journalism continue to have value. . . .
>
> "The problem facing American journalism is not fundamentally an audience problem or a credibility problem. It is a revenue problem — the decoupling . . . of advertising from news.
>
> "That makes the situation better than it might have been. But audiences now consume news in new ways. They hunt and gather what they want when they want it, use search to comb among destinations and share what they find through a growing network of social media.**"**
>
> — *The State of the News Media, 2009,*
> Project for Excellence in Journalism

The basic skills required of every journalist haven't changed either, despite the revolution in technology. Whatever the medium, the skills of news-gathering and storytelling are essential to good journalism.

WHAT NEWS IS

The criteria that professional reporters and editors use to decide what news is can be summarized in three words:

Relevance

Usefulness

Interest

Relevance, usefulness and interest for a specific audience are the broad guidelines for judging the news value of any event, issue or personality. These criteria apply generally, but each journalist and each news organization uses them in a specific context that gives them particular meaning. That context is supplied by the audience—the reader, listener or viewer. Journalists always determine newsworthiness with a particular audience in mind.

Elements of a Good News Story

Within the broad news standards of relevance, usefulness and interest, journalists look for more specific elements in each potential story. The most important are these:

- **Impact.** The potential impact of a story is another way of measuring its relevance and usefulness. How many people are affected by an event or idea? How seriously does it affect them? The wider and heavier the impact, the better the story. Sometimes, of course, impact isn't immediately obvious. Sometimes it isn't very exciting. The challenge for good journalism is making such dull but important stories lively and interesting. That may require relying on the next three elements.

- **Conflict.** A recurring theme in all storytelling—whether the stories told are journalism, literature or drama—is conflict. Struggles between people, among nations or with natural forces make fascinating reading and viewing. Conflict is such a basic element of life that journalists must resist the temptation to overdramatize or oversimplify it.

- **Novelty.** Novelty is another element common to journalism and other kinds of stories. People or events may be interesting and therefore newsworthy just because they are unusual or bizarre.

- **Prominence.** Names make news. The bigger the name, the bigger the news. Ordinary people have always been intrigued by the doings of the rich and famous. Both prominence and novelty can be, and often are, exaggerated to produce "news" that lacks real relevance and usefulness. For example, in the days following his death, pop star Michael Jackson received more coverage on network television than the wars in Iraq and Afghanistan.

- **Proximity.** Generally, people are more interested in and concerned about what happens close to home. When they read or listen to national or international news, they often want to know how it relates to their own community. Some news organizations are turning to "hyperlocal" coverage as they seek to reconnect with readers by reporting at the neighborhood level, sometimes by soliciting contributions from residents, or citizen journalists. Independent websites devoted to this kind of extremely local coverage are springing up across the country. Increasingly, however, journalists and scholars are recognizing that communities organized around a particular interest—a sport, a hobby or an issue—are at least as important as geographic communities.

- **Timeliness.** News is supposed to be new. With the Internet and cable and satellite television, "new" means instantaneous. Events are reported as they happen, and this poses a challenge for journalists. Speed conflicts with thoughtfulness and thoroughness. Opportunities for error multiply. Perspective and context are needed today more than ever, but both are more difficult to supply with little time for thinking. Despite the drawbacks of 24/7 news coverage, it's clear that for news to be relevant and useful, it must be timely. For example, it is much more useful to write about an issue facing the city council before the issue is decided than afterward. Timely reporting can give people a chance to be participants in public affairs rather than remain mere spectators.

The online age, with its often-confusing multitude of sources, splintering of audiences and growing complaints about negative news, has inspired most journalists to add some new criteria for assessing the value of stories:

- **Engagement.** When news was only broadcast or printed on paper, the flow of information was one-way—from journalists to audiences. No more. Today, a news report is often just the beginning of the conversation. Audience members online respond to, correct and criticize the journalism. Many reporters and commentators maintain blogs to encourage such involvement. Increasingly, a goal of both individual journalists and news organizations is to engage the public with the news and with the news provider.

- **Solutions.** Scholars and audiences alike complain that journalists too often report problems and controversies without offering solutions. The author Richard Saul Wurman and the journalist Al Neuharth have both advocated a "journalism of hope." More and more journalists are seeking out expert sources and inviting audience members not only to explain complex problems but also to suggest solutions.

How Different Media Present the News

Notice that the preceding list suggests two important things about news. First, not all news is serious, life-and-death stuff. The late scholar James Carey described journalism as "a culture's conversation with itself." The conversation that holds a culture together includes talk of crime, politics and world affairs, of course, but it also includes talk of everyday life. It includes humor and gossip. All of that can be news. Second, news is more than a collection of facts. Telling the news usually means telling stories. The narrative, the humanity and the drama of storytelling make up the art of journalism. To gather the facts for their stories, journalists use many of the same techniques used by sociologists, political scientists and historians. But to tell their stories so that those facts can be understood, journalists often use the techniques of other storytellers, such as novelists and screenwriters.

Differences among the news media give different weights to the criteria for assessing the value of news stories and require different approaches to telling those stories. For example, newspapers and magazines are better than television or radio for explaining the impact of an issue or the causes of a conflict. Scholars have learned that, although most people say they get most of their news from television, few can remember very much of what they've seen or heard on a newscast. But print can't compete with television in speed or emotional power. The differing strengths and limitations of each medium make it more likely that you'll find a lengthy explanatory story in a newspaper or magazine, while you're more likely to learn of an event from television, radio or the Internet. A newspaper lets you read the details of a budget or a box score, but television shows you the worker whose job was cut or the player scoring the winning basket. The unique power of online journalism is that it brings together the immediacy of television and the comprehensive authority of print, with endless opportunities for users to pursue their interests through the Web. And they can join the public conversation by posting comments to an existing blog or by launching their own.

The Rise of Citizen Journalism

One important recent development is **citizen journalism**. This is news coverage, usually online, by people who don't work for commercial companies. Some citizen journalists are producing regular reporting for growing audiences. Their focus may be on local communities, as is the case with YourHub.com. Or it may be broader, as with the activist indymedia.org, an international collective with a strongly anti-establishment approach that publishes online editions in a number of major cities.

Few of these citizen journalism outlets are profitable, and many are deliberately nonprofit. Their goal, whether local or international, is to cover communities and issues that even local newspapers and broadcast stations don't reach. Their staffs are a mix of trained journalists and interested amateurs. Their

> **"**If you have any message at all, in any form, that you want to convey to the world, you now have a platform to do so. . . . Your fans and supporters are never more than a click or two away, and they're ready to help you make history — or change it.**"**
>
> — David Mathison, *Be the Media*

audiences are people who don't feel adequately served by the traditional media. Some observers have likened them to the pamphleteers who were the pioneers of American journalism two centuries ago.

Some critics of mainstream, traditional journalism hope that these citizen journalists can fill the gaps left by reduced staffs of professionals or even replace the traditional sources altogether. However, research by two University of Missouri scholars shows that few of the new sites are even close to filling either role. The researchers studied citizen journalism sites and traditional "legacy" sites in 46 randomly selected cities. Their conclusion was that the citizen sites "are much more narrow in their

ON THE JOB

A Career Crosses Media Lines

Look up the term "convergence" on Wikipedia, and you just might find a picture of Scott Norvell. He is currently in New York, where he heads the new content-sharing department of Rupert Murdoch's News Corp. Before that, he was London bureau chief for Fox News. And before Fox . . . well, it's complicated.

After graduating from journalism school as a news-editorial major, Scott began work on a daily paper in Texas. Before long, though, he switched to an alternative weekly. Then came a three-year stint freelancing in Central America. A newspaper job for his wife, Shelley, brought the couple back to the States, where Scott was hired to help launch the website for CNN in Atlanta. Shelley was transferred to Miami, and Scott — despite a total lack of television experience — was hired as Miami bureau chief by the new Fox News network.

Networking of a different sort helped, he recalls, because he had met his new boss years earlier in Guatemala. What also helped his career was Scott's command of Spanish and his experience in the Caribbean.

After three years in Miami, the couple moved to London, where Scott became Fox bureau chief and Shelley continued to work for Cox Newspapers, a national chain headquartered in Atlanta. A year later, they moved again, this time to New York, where Scott took over the Fox website and later became New York bureau chief. In 2003, they returned to London, where he supervised Fox's coverage of Europe.

Scott has learned along the way, he says, the importance of at least a second language, the desirability of technical skills with computers and video, and — above all — the continued centrality of writing. "Arguably, mastery of the written word is even more critical as the amount of information proliferates and competition increases."

In his new job, of course, he'll be looking for and sharing across platforms not only good writing but all forms of storytelling.

content and focus than the legacy media sites in those cities." The citizen sites they studied were predominantly blogs (two-thirds of them) rather than news sites.

THE ROLE OF JOURNALISM

The First Amendment to the U.S. Constitution protects the five freedoms that the nation's founders considered essential to a democracy: the freedom of speech, religion, the press, petition and assembly. In the 1830s, the French aristocrat Alexis de Tocqueville came to study the U.S. and wrote his classic *Democracy in America*. He was struck by the central role played by the only journalism available then, the newspapers. "We should underrate their importance if we thought they just guaranteed liberty; they maintain civilization," he wrote.

Challenges to American Journalism

More than 200 years after they were guaranteed, the First Amendment freedoms are still essential and still under threat. After the terrorist attacks of Sept. 11, 2001, a new emphasis on national and personal security tempted government officials and citizens alike to question just how much freedom is compatible with safety. The role of journalism in guaranteeing liberty and maintaining civilization is challenged by those who make news and those who need it.

American journalism is also under threat from growing public skepticism about how well today's journalists are fulfilling their historic roles. National surveys by the Pew Research Center for the People and the Press show, for example, that more than half the public see bias in the news. About half say that journalists' reports are often inaccurate. Fewer than half say journalism protects democracy, and about one-third say journalism is hurting democracy. In assessing coverage of the 2008 election, voters gave journalists only a grade of C. Views of the press increasingly vary with political affiliation. Republicans are much more critical than Democrats. And those who get their news online rate the major Internet sources—such as Google, Yahoo, AOL and Slate—even lower than the traditional media.

On the other hand, the same surveys show that credibility has improved, at least a little, from historic lows. Comfortable majorities say they believe all or most of what they read in newspapers and see on television news. Most people give higher ratings to the particular newspaper or TV station they use than to the news media in general. Two-thirds rate journalists as highly professional. (For regular samplings of public opinion about journalism, visit http://people-press.org, the website of the Pew Research Center.)

Principles of Good Journalism

What these citizens seem to be saying is that the work journalists do is important, but journalists aren't doing it well enough. The past decade has seen the emergence of several major efforts to improve the performance of American journalism.

One of those efforts has been driven by an informal association called the Committee of Concerned Journalists and the related Project for Excellence in Journalism. The project conducts regular research on journalism and issues reports, which can be accessed on its website, Journalism.org. Among the reports are annual "State of the News Media" assessments, as well as regular reports on the public's news consumption and on journalists' performance. Another product of these reformers is a book that every student and practitioner of journalism should read. Written by two leaders of the committee and the project, Bill Kovach and Tom Rosenstiel, the book is *The Elements of Journalism.*

The book argues that "the purpose of journalism is to provide people with the information they need to be free and self-governing." It proposes 10 principles to achieve this purpose:

1. Journalism's first obligation is to the truth.
2. Its first loyalty is to citizens.
3. Its essence is a discipline of verification.
4. Its practitioners must maintain independence from those they cover.
5. Journalism must serve as an independent monitor of power.
6. It must provide a forum for public criticism and compromise.
7. It must strive to make the significant interesting and relevant.
8. It must keep the news comprehensive and proportional.
9. Its practitioners must be allowed to exercise their personal conscience.
10. Citizens, too, have rights and responsibilities when it comes to the news.

In these principles, you can hear echoes of the Journalist's Creed, written nearly a century before by Walter Williams, founding dean of the world's first journalism school, at the University of Missouri. Williams wrote that "the public journal is a public trust . . . (and) acceptance of a lesser interest than the public interest is a violation of that trust."

Journalists' Responsibilities in a Democracy

The efforts to reform, or restore, journalism recognize these vital functions of journalists in a free society:

- **Journalists report the news.** The first and most obvious function, news-reporting is the foundation of the rest. Reporters cover Congress and council meetings, describe accidents and disasters, show the horrors of war and the highlights of football games. This reporting takes many forms—live television, online bulletins, next-day newspaper analyses and long-form magazine narratives. In 2009, the *Houston Chronicle* was a finalist for journalism's highest honor, the Pulitzer Prize, for its staff coverage of a hurricane threatening the city. Nearly all the reporting, plus blogs by staff and citizens, appeared online rather than on paper. No wonder journalism has been called the first rough draft of history.

- **Journalists monitor power.** Most often, Americans are concerned about the power of government. Lately, private power has become more of a worry and more of a source of news. Alexandra Berzon and her colleagues at the *Las Vegas Sun* won the Pulitzer Prize for public service for their investigation of lax inspections that led to high rates of death and injury among construction workers on the Las Vegas Strip. Monitoring is required even if power is used legitimately—when governments raise taxes or take us to war, for example, or when businesses close plants or cut health care benefits for employees. When the power is used illegally or immorally, another important function comes into play.

- **Journalists uncover injustice.** A television reporter learns that one brand of tires and one model of car are involved in a disproportionate number of fatal accidents. A newspaper discovers that prisoners on death row were convicted unfairly. In those cases and thousands more, journalists bring to light dangerous or illegal abuses that might otherwise go unchecked.

- **Journalists tell compelling stories that delight us and some that dismay us.** For example, the husband-and-wife team of Nicholas Kristof and Sheryl WuDunn told the horrifying and hopeful stories of women struggling to overcome discrimination and abuse in the developing world for *The New York Times* and in a book, *Half the Sky: Turning Oppression into Opportunity for Women Worldwide*. Television's *60 Minutes* and *Frontline* tell the stories of true-life dramas. Bloggers bring firsthand experiences and often great passion to their posts.

- **Journalists sustain communities.** These communities may be small towns, cities or even virtual communities of people connected only by the Internet. Through their reporting, monitoring, revealing and storytelling, journalists serve as the nervous system of the community. They convey information as well as argument.

Scholars use other terms for this combination of vital functions. One is "agenda-setting," the placing of issues on the public agenda for discussion and decision. Another is "gate-keeping," the process by which some events and ideas become news and others do not. Now that the Internet has flooded the world with information, another role is emerging—that of "navigation," guiding readers and viewers through oceans of fact, rumor and fantasy in search of solid meaning. Bloggers such as Matt Drudge and Josh Marshall sometimes serve as agenda-setters for mainstream journalists. Entertainers such as Jon Stewart serve as sources not only of laughs but of information. Even in the Internet age, however, the news you read on Google or some other website probably was first reported in one of the traditional news rooms.

ACCURACY, FAIRNESS AND BIAS

The goal toward which most journalists strive has seldom been expressed any better than in a phrase used by Bob Woodward, a reporter, author and editor at *The Washington Post*. Woodward was defending in court an investigative story published by *The Post*. The story, he said, was "the best obtainable version of the truth."

A grander-sounding goal would be "the truth," unmodified. But Woodward's phrase, while paying homage to the ideal, recognizes the realities of life and the limitations of journalism. Despite centuries of argument, philosophers and theologians are still unable to agree on what truth is. Even if there were agreement on that basic question, how likely is it that the Roman Catholic Church and the Planned Parenthood organization would agree on the "truth" about abortion, or that a president and an opposition presidential candidate would agree on the "truth" about the state of the American economy?

In American daily journalism, that kind of dispute is left to be argued among the partisans on all sides, on the editorial pages and in commentaries. The reporter's usual role is simply to find and write the facts. The trouble is, that task rarely turns out to be simple.

Sometimes it's hard to get the facts. The committee searching for a new university president announces that the field of candidates has been narrowed to five, but the names of the five are not released. Committee members are sworn to secrecy. What can you do to get the names? Should you try?

*II*The new media tools and techniques are wonderful ways to generate information much, much faster. They don't so much take away from the actual reporting as they allow the reporter to know so much more.*II*

— Karen Dillon, reporter, *The Kansas City Star*

Sometimes it's hard to tell what the facts mean. The state Supreme Court refuses to hear a case in which legislators are questioning the constitutionality of a state spending limit. The court says only that there is no "justiciable controversy." What does that mean? Who won? Is the ruling good news or bad news, and for whom?

Sometimes it's even hard to tell what is fact. A presidential commission, after a yearlong study, says there is no widespread hunger in America. Is the conclusion a fact? Or is the fact only what the commission said? And how can you determine whether the commission is correct?

Daily journalism presents still more complications. As a reporter, you usually have only a few hours — or at most a few days — to try to learn as many facts as possible. Then, even in such a limited time, you may accumulate information enough for a story of 2,000 words, only to be told that there is space or time enough for only 1,000 words or fewer. The new media offer more space but no more time for reporting. When you take into account all these realities and limitations, you can see that reaching the best obtainable version of the truth is challenge enough for any journalist.

How can you tell when that goal has been reached? Seldom, if ever, is there a definitive answer. But there are two questions every responsible journalist should ask about every story before being satisfied: Is it accurate? Is it fair?

Accuracy and Fairness

Accuracy is the most important characteristic of any story, great or small, long or short. Every name must be spelled correctly; every quote must be just what was said; every set of numbers must add up. And that still isn't good enough. You can get the details right and still mislead unless you are accurate with context, too. The same statement may have widely different meanings depending on the circumstances in which it was uttered and the tone in which it was spoken. Circumstances and intent affect the meaning of actions as well. You will never have the best obtainable version of the truth unless your version is built on accurate reporting of detail and context.

Nor can you approach the truth without being fair. Accuracy and fairness are related, but they are not the same. Being fair requires asking yourself if you have done enough to uncover all the relevant facts and have delivered those facts in an impartial manner, without favoring one side or another in a story. The relationship between accuracy and fairness—and the differences between them—is shown clearly in this analogy from the world of sports.

The referee in a basketball game is similar, in some ways, to a reporter. Each is supposed to be an impartial observer, calling developments as he or she sees them. (Of course, the referee's job is to make judgments on those developments, while the reporter's job is just to describe them. Rendering judgment is the role of columnists, bloggers and other opinion writers.) Television has brought to sports the instant replay, in which a key play—for example, one in which a player may have been fouled while taking a shot—can be examined again and again, often from an angle different from the referee's view. Sometimes the replay shows an apparent outcome different from the one the official called. Perhaps the players actually didn't make contact. Perhaps what looked like an attempted shot was really a pass. The difference may be due to human error on the official's part, or it may be due to the differences in angle and in viewpoint. Referees recognize this problem. They try to deal with it by obtaining the best possible view of every play and by conferring with their colleagues on some close calls. Still, every official knows that an occasional mistake will be made. That is unavoidable. What can, and must, be avoided is unfairness. Referees must be fair, and both players and fans must believe they are fair. Otherwise, their judgments will not be accepted; they will not be trusted.

With news, too, there are different viewpoints from which every event or issue can be observed. Each viewpoint may yield a different interpretation of what is occurring and of what it means. There is also, in journalism as in sports, the possibility of human error, even by the most careful reporters.

Fairness requires that you as a reporter try to find every viewpoint on a story. Rarely will there be only one; often there are more than two. Fairness requires that you allow ample opportunity for response to anyone who is being attacked or whose integrity is being questioned in a story. However, neither fairness nor objectivity requires that every viewpoint receive the same amount of time or space.

Fairness requires, above all, that you make every effort to avoid following your own biases in your reporting and your writing. (See FIgure 1.1.)

	News Stories	Commentaries
Accuracy	• Make sure facts (events, names, dates, statistics, places, quotes) are correct. • Verify facts with multiple sources. • Use reliable sources for statistics. • Use facts as the substance of the story. • Discover and include all necessary facts.	• Make sure facts (events, names, dates, statistics, places, quotes) are correct. • Include all the facts needed to prove a point of view. • Possibly leave out facts that don't support the argument.
Fairness	• Provide context for facts. • Give all relevant sides of a story. • Strive for balance.	• Provide context for facts. • Use facts and reason to persuade the audience of a point of view. • Appeal to emotion, but not by distorting the facts.
Bias	• Work to leave personal bias out of the story. • Use neutral language.	• Support personal bias with facts and reasoning. • Acknowledge and rebut other points of view. • Use civil language, not highly charged language or personal attacks.

Figure 1.1
Accuracy, fairness and lack of bias are essential in news stories. Writers of commentaries (editorials, blogs, written and spoken essays, reviews and letters to the editor) must also be accurate and fair in order to be credible.

Dealing with Bias

The research summarized earlier in this chapter suggests that citizens don't think journalists do enough to keep bias—conscious or unconscious—out of the news. More than eight out of 10 respondents in a national survey said they see bias at least sometimes. Of those, about twice as many said the bias seemed to be culturally and politically liberal as thought it conservative. A chorus of critics claims that journalists lean to the left. A smaller chorus complains of a rightward tilt. Books and cable television talk shows add heat, if not light, to the criticism. How valid is it?

One answer is that American journalism has many biases built into it. For example, journalists are biased toward conflict. War is a better story than peace. Journalists are biased toward novelty. Airplanes that don't crash are seldom reported. Journalists are biased toward celebrity. The lives and deaths of celebrities are chronicled in detail on the network news as well as in fan magazines.

There's a less obvious but even more important bias, too. This one probably accounts for much of the criticism. It is hidden in the job description of journalism. What do journalists say they do? What are they proudest of? What do they honor?

Journalists describe themselves as the outside agitator, the afflicter of the comfortable and the comforter of the afflicted. They see their job as being the watchdog of the powerful, the voice of the voiceless, the surrogate for the ordinary citizen, the protector of the abused and downtrodden. Journalists expect themselves to be forever skeptical, consistently open-minded, respectful of differences, sensitive to what sociologists call "the other." Neither patriotism nor religion is exempt from their critical examination.

Does that job description seem more "liberal" or more "conservative"? Conservatives generally are respectful of authority and supportive of the status quo. Is it any surprise, then, that the overwhelming majority of conservatives and many liberals see a liberal bias in journalism? Notice that this bias has little or nothing to do with partisan politics.

Now suppose we had a journalism that wasn't questioning, disrespectful of authority, open to new ideas, dogging the powerful and speaking for the weak. Who would benefit, and who would suffer? Would society and democracy be better or worse off?

At a deeper level, however, American journalism is profoundly conservative. Journalists seldom examine critically the foundation stones on which the American way of life is based. Among these are capitalism, the two-party system, the myths of the ethnic melting pot and of social mobility. When was the last time you saw any of those ideas questioned seriously in the mainstream press?

One conclusion suggested by this analysis is that in societies that aren't free—such as America before independence—a free press is a revolutionary instrument. In a society such as 21st-century America, which considers itself free and is overall self-satisfied, the free press becomes, at a fundamental level, conservative.

THE ISSUE OF OBJECTIVITY

The rules that mainstream journalists follow in attempting to arrive at the best obtainable version of the truth—to report accurately, fairly and without bias—are commonly summarized in the concept of objectivity. Objectivity has been and still is accepted as a working credo by most American journalists, as well as by students and teachers of journalism. It has been exalted by leaders of the profession as an essential, if unattainable, ideal. Its critics, by contrast, have attacked objectivity as, in the phrase of sociologist Gaye Tuchman, a "strategic ritual" that conceals a multitude of professional sins while producing superficial and often misleading coverage.

In his classic *Discovering the News*, Michael Schudson traces the rise of objectivity to the post-World War I period, when scholars and journalists alike turned to the methods and the language of science in an attempt to make sense of a world that was being turned upside down by the influence of Sigmund Freud and Karl Marx, the emergence of new economic forces and the erosion of traditional values. Objectivity was a reliance on observable facts, but it was also a methodology for freeing factual reporting from the biases and values of source, writer or reader. It was itself a value, an ideal.

Schudson writes, "Journalists came to believe in objectivity, to the extent that they did, because they wanted to, needed to, were forced by ordinary human aspiration to seek escape from their own deep convictions of doubt and drift."

Objectivity, then, was a way of applying to the art of journalism the methods of science. Those methods emphasized reliance on observable fact. They also included the use of a variety of transparent techniques for pursuing truth and verifying facts. In science, transparency means that the researchers explain their objectives, their methods, their findings and their limitations. In journalism, only part of that methodology is usually followed. Journalists seldom describe their methods or discuss the limits of their findings. If they did, at least some in the public might be less suspicious and less critical.

In *The Elements of Journalism*, Kovach and Rosenstiel worry that a kind of phony objectivity has replaced the original concept. The objectivity of science does not require neutrality or the artificial balance of two sides in a dispute. Scientists are free, and expected, to state their conclusions, as long as they report how they reached those conclusions. However, as usually practiced today, journalistic objectivity employs both neutrality and balance, sometimes instead of the kind of openness that is essential in science. This misunderstanding, or misapplication, of the real principles of objectivity has opened the way for critics to call for its abandonment. Journalists would be more honest, these critics argue, if they were open about their biases. In much of Europe, for example, journalists practice, and audiences expect, openly biased reporting.

The problem with that approach is easy to see in European journalism or, closer to home, in the opinionated journalism of partisan publications, cable television or many blogs. One-sided reports appeal to audiences that share the writer's bias, but they repel those who don't. Fairness and accuracy too often are casualties in this journalism of assertion rather than of verification.

Properly understood, objectivity provides the journalistic method most likely to yield the best obtainable version of the truth. True objectivity, Kovach and Rosenstiel argue, would add scientific rigor to journalistic art. Without that, journalists and audiences alike can be misled.

WHAT IS NOT NEWS

Though there's debate about just how objective a reporter can possibly be, journalists and scholars all agree about one thing: Reporting the news is not the same as expressing an opinion. The primary goal of a news story is to inform. Whether in print, broadcast or online, a reporter's job is to communicate pertinent facts, together with enough background information to help the audience understand those facts. Accuracy and fairness are paramount. By contrast, the primary goal of opinion writers and speakers is to persuade. Accuracy and fairness are still important—though they sometimes get lost in argument. A commentator is expressing a point of view rather than reporting the views of others.

To see for yourself the differences in style and substance, watch Brian Williams deliver the *NBC Nightly News.* Then later in the evening switch to MSNBC, a sister network, and listen to Rachel Maddow discuss the same events. Now move to Fox and Bill O'Reilly. The events of the day, as Williams reported them, haven't changed, but their context and meaning sound very different from the viewpoints of the political left (Maddow) and right (O'Reilly). For another clear example of the differences between reporting and commentary, compare a front-page story in *The New York Times* with an editorial on the same subject on the newspaper's opinion page. The former is seeking to inform you, the latter to persuade you.

Because the aims are different, news stories and commentary approach accuracy, fairness and bias differently.

In 1947 the Hutchins Commission on freedom of the press concluded that what a free society needs from journalists is "a truthful, comprehensive and intelligent account of the day's events in a context which gives them meaning." The goal of this chapter is to show you how the journalists of today and tomorrow understand that need, how they are trying to meet it, and how complex the task is. The rest of the book will help you develop the skills you'll need to take up the challenge. There are few challenges so important or so rewarding.

Suggested Readings

Journalism reviews: Any issue of *Columbia Journalism Review, American Journalism Review, Quill* or *The American Editor,* the bulletin of the American Society of News Editors, offers reports and analyses of the most important issues of contemporary journalism.

Kovach, Bill, and Tom Rosenstiel. *The Elements of Journalism.* New York: Crown, 2001. This little book is packed with practical advice and inspiration, a kind of applied ethics for journalists in any medium.

Schudson, Michael. *Discovering the News: A Social History of American Newspapers.* New York: Basic Books, 1978. This well-written study traces the development of objectivity in American journalism.

Wurman, Richard Saul. *Information Anxiety.* New York: Doubleday, 1990. This guide for consumers of information can also serve as a guide for journalists as they seek to provide understanding.

Suggested Websites

www.asne.org
The American Society of News Editors is the most important of the industry's professional organizations. This website gives you access to the society's landmark credibility project, including the results of a major study of Americans' attitudes toward, and uses of, journalism.

www.cjr.org
Columbia Journalism Review is the oldest of the magazines devoted to critical analysis of journalists' performance. You'll find critiques of major stories and essays on ethics, along with book reviews and trade news. *American Journalism Review* (**www.ajr.org**) offers similar content.

www. journalism.org
The site of the Project for Excellence in Journalism contains relevant research and articles on the current state of journalism. See especially the "State of the News Media" reports for the most comprehensive look at the current performance of all the major news media.

www.people-press.org
The site of the Pew Research Center for the People and the Press is a reliable source for frequent reports on public attitudes toward journalism, as well as on topics in the news.

www.poynter.org
This site is an excellent starting point. The Poynter Institute is the leading center of continuing professional education for journalists. On this site you'll find not only a guide to the services and resources of the institute itself but also links to the sites of every major professional organization and a variety of other useful resources.

Exercises

1. **Team project.** Form a team with two or three other class members. Imagine that you have been asked to collaborate on a series of articles about each of these subjects: (1) the murder of a doctor who performs abortions, (2) a state court case involving the legalization of same-sex marriage, (3) a bill in your legislature raising the drinking age to 25, and (4) an IRS crackdown on people doing jobs for cash payment and not reporting their income for taxation. List and discuss the possible biases you might encounter among people you interview (officials, citizens) and people you work with (publishers, editors, and other reporters). What steps could you take to keep biases out of the stories?

2. The Project for Excellence in Journalism monitors the news flow through dozens of different channels ranging from network television to citizen journalists' blogs. Visit **www.journalism.org**, and examine that flow. Which reports seem most thorough? Which reveal their biases? Which are you most inclined to believe?

3. Spend some time with the citizen journalists at **http://voiceofsandiego.org** and **www.indymedia.org**. Compare what you find with the stories in the mainstream media from those geographic areas. Where do you see overlapping coverage, and what stories are different in each medium? Which sources seem to serve the citizens best?

4. Most Americans say they get most of their news from television. Watch an evening newscast on one of the major networks. Read *The New York Times* or *USA Today* for the same day. Compare the number of stories, the topics covered and the depth of coverage. How well-informed are those television-dependent Americans?

5. Get copies or visit the websites of your local newspaper, a paper from a city at least 50 miles away and a paper of national circulation, such as *USA Today* or *The Wall Street Journal*. Analyze the front page according to the criteria discussed in this chapter.

   a. What does the selection of stories on the front page tell you about the editors' understanding of each paper's audience?

   b. If you find stories on the same topic on two or more front pages, determine whether they were written differently for different audiences.

   c. On the basis of what you've learned in this chapter, do you agree or disagree with the editors' news judgments? Why?

6. As a class project, visit or invite to your class the editor of your local paper and the news director of a local television station. Study their products ahead of time, and then interview them about how they decide the value of news stories, how they assess the reliability of sources and how they try to ensure accuracy.

7. Spend some time sampling sources of information and news on the Internet. Describe briefly at least five sources of information you can use as a journalist and at least five sources of news you can use as a consumer.

The Changing
Media Landscape

2

Read almost any story about the state of the media these days, and the recurring theme is likely to be, "Everyone is tuning out." You've heard it: Young people don't consume news. Newspapers are on their deathbeds. Local television will be the next to die. There's just one thing wrong with that conventional wisdom: It isn't true.

The U.S. population continues to increase rapidly, and the size of the audience for news is growing with it. So, too, is news consumption; people are merely getting the news from a wider range of places. While audiences decline for newspapers and local television, consumers are flocking to cable television and the Internet for news. News consumption on mobile phones is exploding as well. And even those left-for-dead newspaper companies have growing audiences when you combine their print circulations with their online readers.

The problem is not that people are tuning out or using media less frequently. Instead, the problem is **media fragmentation**, which has led to dramatic shifts in media consumption patterns. There are far more places to get news today than there were 25 years ago.

So, there's no lack of interest in news, and the audience is increasing. The problem is a broken business model that might require nothing less than the reconstruction of the media industry. Leonard Downie Jr., a retired executive editor of *The Washington Post*, and Michael Schudson, a professor at Columbia University's School of Journalism, write in *Columbia Journalism Review*:

> Newspapers and television are not going to vanish in the foreseeable future, despite frequent predictions of their imminent extinction. But they will play diminished roles in an emerging and still rapidly changing world of digital journalism, in which the means of news reporting are being re-invented, the character of news is being reconstructed, and reporting is being distributed across a greater variety of news organizations, new and old.
>
> The questions that this transformation raises are simple enough: What is going to take the place of what is being lost, and can the new array of news media report on our nation and our communities as well as—or better than—journalism has until now? More importantly, . . . what should be done to shape this new landscape, to help assure that the essential elements of independent, original, and credible news reporting are preserved?

The broken business model is that of the **legacy media**—companies that specialize in traditional media forms such as newspapers, magazines, radio and broadcast television. Smaller audiences are resulting in less advertising, or reduced prices for it, which has put great financial stress on those legacy media. That's a problem for news consumers because for more than a century the legacy media have funded the extensive news-gathering operation that exists in the U.S. and much of the rest of the world.

Some estimate that even today as much as 85 percent of the news we consume originates at newspapers, even if you read that news online or see it on television. Increasingly, the legacy-media model isn't working as newspapers and television trim the size of their staffs in an effort to survive. A new business model is needed.

What's important to save as we go about this task is not newspapers and television, and not the companies that own them, but the high-quality reporting they produce. In this chapter, we take a look at the impact of all these changes on legacy media and on the people they serve and don't serve. Then, in Chapter 3, we'll consider some promising new ways of financing the news-gathering process.

FINANCIAL CHALLENGES TO LEGACY MEDIA

For the better part of two centuries, owning a newspaper was a license to print money. Great fortunes were made by media barons like William Randolph Hearst, who owned large newspapers, and Donald W. Reynolds, who owned small ones. Their businesses were lucrative: For much of the 20th century, newspapers turned a profit of 20 to 25 cents—sometimes even more—on each dollar that came through the door.

When radio and television came along, they built on this legacy. Both quickly became profitable, and owning television networks and stations eventually became even more lucrative than owning newspapers. Magazines also found a

William Randolph Hearst made a fortune by owning large newspapers.

home in the American media landscape. As advertisers began to covet their ability to deliver targeted audiences, the number of magazines proliferated.

Trouble was brewing, however, and by the end of the 20th century, it became clear that audience fragmentation was becoming a significant problem.

Smaller Audiences as a Result of Media Proliferation

When radio and television came along, they fit into the media landscape with little harm to newspapers and magazines. But by the time the Internet and cable television arrived, it became clear that media outlets were proliferating and that media consumption patterns were shifting. Younger people started turning away from newspapers in favor of the Internet and its thousands of information sources. Cable television took viewers from local stations. In the end, the proliferation of media outlets began to slice audiences into smaller and smaller fragments, taking ad revenue from the traditional legacy media.

Today, it's clear that legacy media—newspapers, magazines, radio and broadcast television—are being damaged severely by newer media forms such as cable television and the Internet. Newspaper revenues have fallen precipitously, and local television stations are now feeling the pinch caused by a proliferation of cable channels. Magazines are still generally healthy, thanks to their ability to target audiences more efficiently than newspapers or local television. But magazines, like newspapers, also suffer from high production and distribution costs. As a result, their long-term prognosis is uncertain.

Lower Advertising Revenues, Higher Debt

Newspapers are costly to produce, and revenue trends are headed in the wrong direction. Classified advertising, long a big moneymaker at newspapers, has been hurt by websites like craigslist.org. Help-wanted advertising, in particular, has plummeted. Newspapers are manufactured products that consume large amounts of expensive paper and ink. They are labor-intensive not only in news-reporting but also in printing and distribution. They are, in effect, an increasingly inefficient—and costly—way to deliver news.

Nevertheless, despite what many would have you believe, most newspapers are *still* profitable. Those that have failed or are suffering mostly fall into two categories: Either they are the second newspaper in a two-newspaper city, or they have been purchased by corporations and have amassed huge debts. Many well-known newspapers have closed, including the *Rocky Mountain News* of Denver and the *Seattle Post-Intelligencer*. Still others—the *Chicago Tribune, Los Angeles Times* and *Boston Globe* among them—were in trouble as this was written because of heavy debt incurred when they were purchased recently for too much money.

More than 1,700 daily newspapers existed as late as 1980, but today the number hovers around 1,400. The Project for Excellence in Journalism estimates that 14,000 news room jobs were lost at newspapers between the start of 2001 and the end of 2009. Newspaper circulation declined almost 5 percent from 2003 to 2008. Ann Arbor, Mich., home to about 115,000 people and a major university, doesn't even have a daily newspaper anymore.

Many forecast a similar pending contraction of local television. No one is predicting that local television stations will disappear, but it's likely that fewer stations will offer local news in the years ahead.

Despite all this, the typical U.S. newspaper still turns a nice profit of about 10 cents on the dollar, and most local television stations are still profitable, too. When you consider that many industries operate quite comfortably on much lower profit margins, newspapers and local television are far from dying.

NEWSPAPERS: THE SOURCE OF MOST NEWS

It's tempting to dismiss newspapers as a product of a bygone era and suggest that we simply move on to newer and better ways of getting news. The problem is that newspapers are the source of most of the news we consume. Indeed, most of the information found on Yahoo or Google News originated with legacy media operations. The same is true with most other Web news sites.

Most of that news is **spot news**—breaking news that occurred today. Replacing that kind of news might not be too tough. After all, if a plane crashes, some blogger or citizen journalist, if no one else, is bound to report it. More problematic is the potential loss of what journalist Alex S. Jones calls "the creation of new awareness provided by either months of investigation or relentlessly regular coverage."

Investigative Reporting

Jones is the Laurence M. Lombard Lecturer in the Press and Public Policy and the director of the Joan Shorenstein Center on the Press, Politics and Public Policy at Harvard University. In his book *Losing the News: The Future of News That Feeds Democracy*, he praises the technological changes that are altering the journalism landscape, but he fears the loss of the "iron core of news that serves as a watchdog over government, holds the powerful accountable, and gives citizens what they need." He's hopeful and optimistic that the "iron core" can be saved.

In a review of Jones' book in *The New York Times*, Harold Evans, former editor of *The Sunday Times of London* and *The Times of London*, points out what happens when this kind of news doesn't get enough attention: "the insufficiently monitored housing bubble; the neglect in New Orleans, leading to the devastation after Katrina; or the formation of Al Qaeda in Afghanistan, leading to 9/11."

Journalistic Independence

Jones and Evans are not alone in their concern about the state of the newspaper industry. Even Congress is showing interest. In a Congressional Research Service report in 2009, analyst Suzanne M. Kirchhoff writes, "Congress has begun debating

The *Orlando Sentinel* is among the many large-market newspapers still doing well.

whether the financial problems of the newspaper industry pose a public policy issue that warrants federal action. . . . Possible policy options might include providing tax breaks, relaxing antitrust policy, tightening copyright law, providing general support for the practice of journalism by increasing funding for the Corporation for Public Broadcasting or similar public programs, or helping newspapers reorganize as nonprofit organizations."

Most journalists are uncomfortable with such talk. Few want a bailout from the people they cover. The problem is that the nation cannot afford to lose its news-gathering apparatus, which for the moment is driven by newspapers. Even as most people claim to get their news today from the Internet and television, Jones estimates that 85 percent of fact-based news originates at newspapers. So if legacy media in general, and newspapers in particular, disappear, who gathers the news, and how is that process financed? Those are the fundamental problems facing the media industry.

JOURNALISM'S ROLE IN A DEMOCRACY

While the overall size of the news audience is growing, not all consumers are embracing the new media. Indeed, some don't consume news at all, and that merely adds to the problems of legacy media.

Decline in News Consumption Among Younger Americans

College student Kendra Logan, 19, is among an increasing number of young people who don't consume news at all. "I don't read newspapers, I don't watch television news, and I rarely look at news on the Internet," she says. She's among the disengaged, and she's not alone. According to a 2008 study by the Pew Research Center for the People and the Press, Logan is among the 34 percent of those younger than 25 who get no news daily, up from 25 percent just 10 years earlier.

It's well-known that people like Logan seldom read newspapers, but they don't consume other news, either. Combine this group with the shifts in news consumption patterns noted earlier, and you get some alarming statistics. According to the Pew survey, those who reported regularly watching local television news declined from 77 percent in 1993 to only 52 percent in 2008. Nightly network news audiences plummeted from 60 percent to 29 percent in the same period. Radio fared only slightly better; audiences dropped from 47 percent in 1993 to 35 percent in 2008.

News Reporting for Informed Decision-Making

That's troubling to those who worry about the foundations of U.S. democracy. Ill-informed members of the public can't make good decisions in the voting booth, if indeed they vote at all. They can't possibly understand the big issues of the day—among them conflicts with extremists, health care, failing schools, illegal immigra-

ON THE JOB

Editing Online News

Sarah Rupp graduated with a degree in newspaper journalism but immediately found herself working at online sites.

Right out of school, she landed an internship at MSNBC.com in Redmond, Wash. She later worked at other online sites, including ABCNews.com, before landing at seattlepi.com, which operates 24/7.

"I usually work a day shift, which means that I have to keep the site fresh with new articles, story updates, breaking news and photos," Rupp says. "Throughout the day we add new wire stories, staff stories, photo galleries and other Web-only features. . . . Besides doing the daily stuff, I also get to work on special projects like producing video and putting together new content channels for the site."

She enjoys the work: "The great thing about working for a news website is you get the chance to do a little of everything — writing, editing, choosing stories, designing graphics, building Web pages, posting photos and editing audio clips.

"There are a lot of exciting things going on in online journalism. . . . No longer are reporters the only people who report the news. That means the very definition of what 'news' is has changed and will continue to change."

tion and poverty. In short, they can't be good citizens. To actively participate in democracy requires knowledge of what's going on in the world, the nation, the state and the community.

Logan is one of millions of uninformed Americans who are tuning out the news as the U.S. experiences the biggest shift in media consumption patterns since colonial times. For more than two centuries, newspapers were the medium of choice in this country. They provided the fuel for public discussion and bound people together with a sense of community. Radio and television helped when they came along. But now, with the proliferation of media choices and the decision of more and more to tune out the news altogether, storm clouds are brewing.

That's bad for the media, but it's also bad for the country, which depends on an informed citizenry to make good decisions in the voting booth. With that in mind, it's important for today's journalist to understand audiences—how and why people decide to consume news and why some choose not to do so.

HOW PEOPLE CONSUME NEWS TODAY

It's clear that legacy media are falling out of favor at an increasing pace. But if there are losers, there also must be winners. Those winners are the Internet and cable television. According to the Pew study, people who reported regular consumption of news on the Internet increased from a minuscule 2 percent in 1996 (just after the creation of the World Wide Web) to 37 percent in 2008. Cable television news consumption grew from 33 percent in 2002 (the first year that cable viewership was measured separately from broadcast television) to 39 percent in 2008. Although cable television has been around for a while, it really took off in the past 20 years. For that reason, we discuss it here as a new media form threatening local broadcast and network television.

ON THE JOB

Journalism for a New Century

Less than five years after he graduated, Adrian Holovaty was invited back to his alma mater to be the graduation speaker. His rapid ascent to the top tier of journalism is directly attributable to these undeniable facts: He's intelligent, and he understands where the media need to go.

After graduation, Holovaty went to the *Lawrence (Kan.) Journal-World*, a recognized leader among newspaper companies trying to figure out how to manage the inevitable transition from print to the Web. He then designed chicagocrime.org, an innovative website that helped the people of Chicago better understand crime in their community. The site won a Batten Award for Innovation in Journalism and captured the attention of the media industry. *The Washington Post* came calling and named Holovaty editor of editorial innovations, a new position.

In his graduation speech, Holovaty urged graduates to follow him:

The fire should be burning under each and every one of you. You should be yearning — aching — to bring this industry into a new age. Your generation — our generation — is going to be the one to do it.

You're going to be the people breaking the rules. You're going to be the people inventing new ones. You'll be the person who says, "Hey, let's try this new way of getting our journalism out to the public.". . .

You'll be the person who asks, "Why are we doing things the way we are?" and when the top editor says, "Because that's the way they've always been done," you'll openly question that. "Because we've always done it that way" doesn't cut it. "Because we've always done it that way" is blatantly unacceptable, blatantly lazy, and you need to call that out.

In his brief time in the industry, Holovaty has been doing just that. He's helping to reinvent journalism for the new century.

Types of News Audiences

The 2008 Pew study places news consumers in one of four audience segments. Understanding those segments helps us understand the shifts in news consumption that affect the future of journalism. They are:

- **Traditionalists.** This group is older, less affluent and not as well-educated as the typical news consumer. Members of this group are heavy consumers of television news at all times of the day and understand news best by seeing pictures rather than reading or hearing. Traditionalists have a strong interest in the weather and relatively low interest in science and tech news. Most have computers, but few of them get news online on a typical day. This group makes up the largest part of the total audience (46 percent) and has an average age of 52.

- **Integrators.** These well-educated, affluent and mostly middle-aged people get news from both legacy media and the Internet. They are more engaged in public affairs than other news consumers, and they are more sophisticated and sought after by advertisers. Television is also a main news source for this group, but most also get news online each day. This group makes up 23 percent of the public.

- **Net-Newsers.** This group is affluent, well-educated and relatively young. Members are more likely to read political blogs than watch network news, and their Web use soars during the day. They are frequent online news viewers and heavy technology users, and they have a strong interest in technology news. Fifty-eight percent of them are men, and the group as a whole makes up 13 percent of the news audience.

- **The Disengaged.** This group stands out for its low levels of news interest and news consumption. This group makes up 14 percent of the public.

These segments account for 96 percent of the U.S. public. Of the remaining 4 percent, Pew reported that 2 percent did not name either a traditional source or the Internet as their main source of news. An additional 2 percent named the Internet as a main source but rarely go online for news.

Can Cable and Internet News Replace Newspaper Reporting?

Perhaps most telling about those numbers is that no single group of consumers leans toward newspapers as a primary source of news. Television—particularly cable television—and the Internet dominate, with the growing Net-Newsers group relying heavily on the Internet. Those who read newspapers or watch network news and local television are older. As that generation starts to die and as younger generations mature into news consumers (or non-news consumers), it's rather obvious that cable television and the Internet stand to be the big winners.

In the view of most journalists, both cable television and the Internet have credibility problems. It's difficult to tell what's news and what's opinion on much of cable television, and determining the veracity of Internet sites is far from easy. Despite that, readers and viewers have spoken. They want to consume news through the new outlets, and as we learned in Chapter 1, some citizen journalists (nonprofessionals who function as journalists) want to participate in the news-gathering process. Still others may not want to report the news but want to engage professional journalists and others in a discussion of that news. Journalists must determine where they fit in that process and adapt.

Most journalists are reluctantly embracing this changing environment, even while they're troubled by what it portends. Almost certainly, there will be fewer jobs in the legacy media. But almost as certainly, there will be new opportunities in the emerging media, which we will discuss in Chapter 3.

This doesn't necessarily mean that newspapers will disappear or that local television will consolidate into one or two stations per market. But the importance of both outlets is declining, and with that comes a major transformation of the American media landscape.

DISTRUST OF THE MEDIA

At least some of the shift in media consumption patterns can be traced to the public's increasing distrust of the legacy media. According to a 2009 Pew study, in July 1985, 55 percent of Americans agreed with the statement that the press gets the facts straight, but by July 2009 only 29 percent agreed. Similarly, in 1985, 72 percent considered the press "highly professional," but by 2009 that number had dropped to 59 percent. A whopping 70 percent agreed that the media try to cover up mistakes in reporting rather than admit them.

Public opinion of the fairness of the media also has suffered. In 1985, 34 percent of the public agreed that the media try to be fair, but by 2009 that had dropped to 18 percent. So, if members of the media believe they are being fair and accurate, the public begs to differ.

Journalists are puzzled about the public's attitude, and there are no clear answers about why distrust of the media is growing. Some likely causes have been suggested:

- People fail to distinguish between reporters (who report, as Bob Woodward says, "the best obtainable version of the truth") and columnists (who offer opinion).
- The decline of profitability of newspapers and local television has led to reduced staffing, which in turn has damaged their ability to ensure accuracy.
- As newspapers have moved away from fact-based writing in the inverted pyramid format (see Chapter 9), they have given reporters greater license to stylize stories with narrative writing. Descriptive writing is often mistaken for opinion-based journalism.

- On cable television, in particular, the lines blur between news programs and talk shows where opinion, not fact, dominates.
- Cable television and talk radio are dominated by right-wing and left-wing talk-show hosts, many of whom, like Rush Limbaugh or Rachel Maddow, make no pretense of objectivity. Many would consider Limbaugh and Maddow journalists, a description that makes most journalists cringe.
- Some people even argue that news coverage itself is tilted leftward or rightward depending on the political slant of the media outlet. Most journalists would deny that, but the public perception remains.

Indeed, a 2009 Pew study of perceptions of press accuracy showed that Democrats have the most favorable view of CNN and MSNBC, while Republicans tilt heavily toward Fox News. That doesn't seem to bother any of the three. Nor does it bother their respective viewers. Some have suggested this marks a return to the partisan press that existed in this country before and just after the American Revolution.

There's also a major disconnect between how the public and those in the media view various news outlets. Most journalists would consider the reporting and accuracy of *The New York Times* and *The Wall Street Journal* to be far superior to that of CNN, Fox News, MSNBC and network television. The public disagrees. Among those media outlets, network television has the highest favorable ratings, followed by CNN, Fox and MSNBC. *The Times* and *The Journal* are last and next to last, respectively. Even widely respected National Public Radio ranks below CNN, Fox and MSNBC.

In recent years, much of the criticism of the press has come from Republicans, particularly those on the far right, who consider most journalists to be left-wing activists who favor Democratic positions. Now, according to Pew, Democrats are almost as critical.

But there is good news in all this, too. Most Americans have favorable views of local television news (73 percent), the daily newspaper they read most often (65 percent) and network television news (64 percent). So while there is great criticism of the press in general, most news consumers have no problem with the media they choose to consume. The prevailing attitude seems to be, "The media in general are lousy and incompetent. But my newspaper or television station is not so bad."

CONVERGENCE AS A RESPONSE TO MEDIA FRAGMENTATION

As shifting media consumption patterns upset the business models of news companies, many are responding by expanding their product offerings and shifting their emphasis away from legacy media and into growth areas, particularly the Internet. If the public wants to read news on the Web, or even on a mobile phone, news companies intend to provide that option.

Journalists call this phenomenon—the coordination of print, broadcast and online reporting in a news operation—**convergence**. It's the transformation of

In the convergent news room of the *Lawrence (Kan.) Journal-World*, journalists write both print and Web stories.

traditional media into something entirely new, a 24/7 news operation where the Web, not the traditional product, comes first. The concept is that consumers should be able to get news on their terms, however and whenever they want it. Radio and television stations put their recorded newscasts online, and some consumers watch on the Web. Sometimes these Web-based newscasts even contain material that didn't make it into the traditional newscast, including, for example, full-length video of the mayor's press conference. Sometimes such material is included even on a newspaper website. And the Web, of course, permits users to interact with data-bases of public information, such as property tax bills, driver's license records and the salaries of public officials and schoolteachers. Neither print nor broadcast out-lets can provide this information as effectively. The *Tampa Tribune*-WFLA-Tampa Bay Online convergence effort of Media General in Florida is one of the oldest experiments in convergence, having started in 2000 (see Figure 2.1).

Enhancing Web Coverage

Increasingly, many news operations—even newspapers—think "Web first." Wrote an editor of *The Philadelphia Inquirer*, "Let's break as much news as we can online, particularly if it's a story, column or review that readers might get from another source, or that benefits from the strengths of the Web."

Many newspapers have become Web-first, 24-hour-a-day operations that embrace citizen journalism. As news breaks, the reporter writes the story first for the Web and mobile devices and posts it for public consumption as soon as it's

Figure 2.1
Tampa Bay Online is a joint venture of *The Tampa Tribune* and WFLA.

ready. Then, when it's time to put together the next morning's newspaper, production efforts shift. If someone in the public comes up with a story before a reporter, so be it.

Without a doubt, more and more media companies are headed in this direction. The Gannett Co. did so with the creation of what it calls Gannett Information Centers. Gannett CEO Craig Dubow described the concept in a letter to Gannett employees:

> The Information Center is a way to gather and disseminate news and information across all platforms, 24/7. The Information Center will let us gather the very local news and information that customers want, then distribute it when, where and how our customers seek it.

In Dubow's opinion, the concept is working:

> Breaking news on the Web and updating for the newspaper draws more people to both those media. Asking the community for help gets it—and delivers the newspaper into the heart of community conversations once again. Rich and deep databases with local, local information gathered efficiently are central to the whole process. The changes impact all media, and the public has approved. Results include stronger newspapers, more popular websites and more opportunities to attract the customers advertisers want.

Synchronized Media Coverage

"Convergence" is the hottest buzzword in the media industry these days, but defining it isn't easy. In the definition of some, convergence occurs when a newspaper or television station starts publishing material on the Internet. According to others, convergence occurs when print reporters start carrying digital voice recorders and produce material for radio as well as the newspaper, or when reporters use a video camera to record a press conference for the newspaper's website.

While those may indeed be forms of convergence, in its most complete sense convergence involves alliances of four communication forms:

- Text.
- Video and audio.
- The Web.
- Mobile phones and other wireless devices.

Take a look at newspaper sites on the Internet, and you will see this happening. Some of the best uses of video anywhere can be found on *The New York Times'* website, something you might not expect. Interactive graphics that help readers visualize processes in new ways also dazzle readers on the *Times'* site. If *The Times* is often seen as gray and stodgy, its website certainly is not. Want news on your iPhone? *The Times* has an app for that. Want breaking news delivered to your phone through instant messaging? The Associated Press has an app for that.

Newspaper companies aren't the only ones doing convergence. British Broadcasting Corp., CNN, CBS, ESPN and others have created stellar websites that not only give users the news but also add to their understanding of it—often in far more detail than they can provide on their traditional newscasts and sportscasts.

EMBRACING CITIZEN JOURNALISM

The best of the legacy media companies are embracing the public's involvement in the news-gathering process and allowing the public to critique stories on the Web. The old "one provider to many consumers" model of newspapers and television is increasingly becoming a thing of the past.

When terrorists planted bombs on a London subway, the first images of the disaster came from survivors who used their mobile phones to take photos and transmit them to the outside world from below ground. When an airplane struck birds during takeoff and subsequently plunged into New York's Hudson River, some of the first images came from nearby apartment dwellers who took photos and video from their windows.

This form of citizen journalism—nonjournalists' gathering and reporting the news—is cropping up on websites around the world, much of it on established sites of the mainstream media. When the BBC asked users around the world to

Figure 2.2
Anyone with a video camera can post observations to a site like CNN's iReport. In order to combat false reports, media outlets are beginning to moderate what gets posted.

snap photos of scheduled anti-war protests and send them in, hundreds of photos were submitted. A citizen in Virginia shot photos of an F-15 military aircraft crash that she sent to a local television station. The photo taken immediately following the impact was used in the newscast along with video footage taken later.

Much of the video and still footage taken by people who happen to be on the scene finds its way to **moblogs**, a form of Internet blogging in which the user publishes blog entries directly to the Web from a cell phone or other mobile device. But when it finds its way onto the sites of mainstream media, as the examples above show, citizen journalists effectively serve as an extension of the media outlet's traditional reporting staff.

A notable example of a community-oriented site with citizen-generated blogs is BlufftonToday.com, an effort of the *Bluffton Today* newspaper in South Carolina. BlufftonToday.com contains community blogs, expert blogs and staff blogs. As a result, everyone is part of the dialogue.

Problems with Citizen Journalism

Sometimes citizen journalism works; sometimes it goes awry. A citizen journalist posted a false report on CNN's iReport.com that Apple CEO Steve Jobs had suffered a heart attack. The erroneous story, which rattled investors, could have had a major impact on Apple's stock if not quickly corrected. iReport is almost completely open and permits users to post "news"—unedited and unvetted—after a minimal registration process. Observed Scott Karp of Publishing 2.0, a blog that reports on the evolution of media, "The problem is—and this is something that advocates of citizen journalism typically overlook—that if a platform is open, and anyone can participate, that means not only can well-intentioned citizens participate but so can bad actors, spammers, liars, cheats and thieves."

That's why most mainstream media outlets are allowing citizens to participate, but they are moderating what goes onto their sites. As a result, back in the news room, journalists often find that their roles have changed. Not only do they perform their traditional roles, but they also edit stories, photos and videos shot by readers and viewers; moderate Internet discussion forums; and write blogs. As a result, news rooms have begun to look different from those of the past, and the Internet sites of traditional media companies are getting more and more attention. That means more and more journalists—even in newspaper news rooms—are being trained in digital audio and video editing. Some find themselves in front of television cameras to create mini-newscasts that will appear on the website.

Forms of Citizen Journalism

While some citizen journalism finds its way onto the sites of legacy media, today's Internet publishing environment makes it easy for citizens to create their own sites and cut out the legacy media entirely. Anyone, it seems, can become a publisher. In an article in *Online Journalism Review*, J. D. Lasica sorted the media forms used in citizen journalism into six types:

- **Audience participation** (user comments attached to news stories, personal blogs, photos or video footage captured from mobile phone cameras, local news written by members of the community). Mainstream media outlets such as MSNBC.com give readers the chance to post comments and other items on their sites.
- **Independent news or information websites** (such as the Drudge Report). These sites are published by those not normally associated with traditional media.
- **Participatory news sites** (*MyMissourian, Northwest Voice*). Here, readers get to write, take photos and publish their work, perhaps even in newspaper format, with the assistance of professional editors. Most have companion websites.
- **Collaborative and contributory news sites** (Slashdot.org, Kuro5hin.org). These sites, often featuring a specific subject-matter area, are based on reader comments and contributions.
- **Thin media** (mailing lists, e-mail newsletters). Through thin media, targeted news content is directed to those with narrowly defined interests.

- **Personal broadcasting sites** (KenRadio.com). On these sites, the operators provide news-based subject matter in a specific area of interest, such as technology. The result is downloadable audio or video in various formats, including Windows Media, QuickTime, podcasts and vodcasts.

Many of these sites seem to be eroding the influence of legacy media. There are more sources of information than ever before, and the public is embracing those alternatives. Many Internet sites target specific groups of readers with great precision. Interested in the latest in football recruiting at your favorite school? There's probably a site for that. Interested in a nontraditional take on local politics? There may well be a blog for that. All of these new alternatives are eating away at the strength of legacy media.

THE FUTURE OF LEGACY MEDIA

If the tone of this chapter sounds discouraging as you plan to enter the media industry, think again. It's true that jobs are being lost as more and more newspapers close. And local television stations, feeling the pinch of declining ad revenues, are laying off reporters and trimming the size of their news staffs.

But the many legacy media companies that remain are hiring young people—often those right out of college—who have the skills the companies need to compete in the emerging media environment. Older workers may not have the skills

Newspaper publishers hope that e-book readers like the Kindle will spark new interest in newspaper reading.

desired for producing and editing audio and video for the Web. Younger people trained in those media do. Blogging and distributing news over mobile phones are new concepts to older workers. Young journalists grew up with them.

Then there is this reality: In almost any city in the U.S., the one newspaper (and usually there is only one) will employ more journalists than all the radio and television stations combined. So while the number of newspapers may be declining, they are far from dead and are still eager to hire young people who can help them make the transition from print to the Web and mobile phones.

So if you're discouraged by what you've read here, don't be. First, not all legacy media will disappear. Some will continue to succeed in their legacy forms, including many newspapers and local television stations, and others will successfully make the transition to the Web and find ways to make it profitable. Still others will create niche sites to create new revenue streams, and others will find totally new models for delivering their content over devices like mobile phones or the Kindle, iPad, tablet computers and other e-book readers. Meanwhile, information-based Internet startups are likely to become increasingly profitable, and foundation-funded, not-for-profit news companies are being tested nationwide (see Chapter 3). With all this comes the need to hire journalists to create the original content consumers demand.

The way journalism is distributed is changing, but the market for good journalism continues to grow.

Suggested Readings

Croteau, David, and William Hoynes. *The Business of Media: Corporate Media and the Public Interest.* Thousand Oaks, Calif.: Pine Forge Press, 2006. A good treatise on the impact of changing economic models on the media industry.

Gillmor, Dan. *We the Media: Grassroots Journalism by the People, for the People.* Sebastopol, Calif.: O'Reilly Media, 2006. A book on the value of citizen journalism by a long-time newspaper reporter and editor.

Hewitt, Hugh. *Blog: Understanding the Information Reformation That's Changing Your World.* Nashville, Tenn.: Thomas Nelson, 2005. A conservative attorney and commentator provides a view of the role of blogs.

Jones, Alex S. *Losing the News: The Future of the News That Feeds Democracy.* New York: Oxford University Press, 2009. A superb review of why legacy media are so critical to democracy.

Madigan, Charles. *-30-: The Collapse of the Great American Newspaper.* Chicago: Ivan R. Dee, 2007. An interesting look at how changes in the media industry have left many in the newspaper business gasping.

Meyer, Philip. *The Vanishing Newspaper: Saving Journalism in the Information Age.* Columbia: University of Missouri Press, 2004. An excellent book on the importance of newspapers in the news-gathering process.

Suggested Websites

http://journalists.org
The site for the Online News Association was organized in 1999.

http://people-press.org
An excellent source that tracks the changing attitudes of the American people toward the press. Pew's research can be found here.

www.grady.uga.edu/annualsurveys
The University of Georgia issues an annual report on the employment patterns of journalism graduates nationwide.

www.magazine.org
Magazine Publishers of America is the professional organization for magazine journalists.

www.naa.org
The Newspaper Association of America, a leading trade association for that industry, tracks trends in newspaper consumption.

www.nab.org
The National Association of Broadcasters is the primary trade organization of the broadcast industry.

www.rtdna.org
The Radio and Television Digital News Association is another leading trade group for broadcast journalists and tracks trends in that field.

Exercises

1. **Team project.** Your instructor will divide the class into groups of three or four. As a team, choose a news aggregator site, such as Google News. On your own, read the top five stories; then read the top five stories on your local newspaper's site. What are the differences and similarities? What does each site do well? What does each do poorly? Discuss your findings in your group, and rate the sites on how well they fulfill the need for news to be relevant, useful and interesting.

2. Find two newspaper websites that carry staff-generated blogs. Compare and contrast them. Are the editors responsive to readers' comments? Is the discussion lively or slow? What role do readers' comments play on these blogs?

3. Analyze a citizen journalism site in your community or in your area. How does the information in the top three stories compare with the information in the top three stories on the local newspaper's website? If there are no citizen journalism sites in your community, find one in a large city nearby.

4. Provide a revised definition of news using the new realities of citizen journalism. Define it for different audiences, including you and your friends, and your parents.

5. The Internet, in addition to being a place to publish, is a useful source of information for journalists. Using the Internet, locate information on the most recent U.S. census, and report the following:
   a. The population of your state.
   b. The population of your city.
   c. The range of income levels and percentages of population that fall within those income levels in your city.
   d. The demographic breakdown of your city by race.

6. Research two legacy media companies. Focus on the history of the companies, especially recent growth or decline. Provide a report on how those companies' incomes have increased or decreased during the past five years. Describe efforts the companies are making to find new revenue streams in emerging media, and compare their strategies.

7. Go to a blog or discussion board, and follow one thread of discussion. Describe how the information you found might be useful to a reporter. Also describe how you would verify the information you found there.

The Emerging Media

3

Jim Spencer saw a new way to approach journalism on the Web. His concept was to create a video-centric website that gives users a look at the news from multiple viewpoints, both foreign and domestic. The result is Newsy.com, a multiperspective website that's growing rapidly.

Newsy takes news from various existing media and repackages it to show how different media are covering a story. A story on Afghanistan, for example, may include a video snippet from Fox News, another from the BBC and yet another from Al Jazeera, the independent television news station headquartered in Qatar and serving the Middle East. And it also may be packaged with links to today's story from *The New York Times* or another from Germany's *Frankfurter Allgemeine Zeitung.*

"We're trying to ride the wave of popularity of Internet video," Spencer says in explaining his marketing concept. Newsy staffers do no original reporting, although they do original research by scouring the Web for background and context. They compile the most interesting and useful perspectives from other media, write a script and then use an anchor to deliver the story in the style of television news. Consumers are finding the concept helpful in understanding complex stories and ensuring that they don't get a one-dimensional perspective.

One thing that makes Newsy unique is its location. It's not based in New York, Washington or even California's Silicon Valley, a common locale for Internet start-ups. Instead, it's based in Columbia, Mo., and has a working relationship with the Missouri School of Journalism at the University of Missouri.

Spencer, a Missouri graduate, knew that Columbia is teeming with hordes of young, would-be journalists eager to enter the media industry. Guided by an experienced professional staff, students craft the stories that appear on Newsy. In the process, they learn a lot about producing compelling content for a website. Still other students help drive traffic to the site, mostly through the use of **viral marketing**—seeding the Internet, especially social networking sites, with information about and links to the site.

"Being in a place like Columbia holds down costs," Spencer says. "Our rent here is a fraction of what it would be in New York or Silicon Valley. At the same time, we have access to a host of talented journalism and advertising students who are excited about the Web. They grew up with it, and they want to be a part of it."

Spencer, who previously worked for MSNBC, America Online and Ask Jeeves, has spent most of his career working in Web-based media. He sees a bright future for the medium: "In the past, it cost a lot of money to start a newspaper or television station. With the Web, the entry costs are much lower. That levels the playing field."

Indeed, that makes it possible for almost anyone to become a media entrepreneur. In this chapter, we'll examine that phenomenon and the many ways people are trying to earn a living—or not—with entirely new kinds of jobs made possible by the growth of the Web.

CHANGES IN THE BUSINESS OF JOURNALISM

Print and broadcast companies understand the shift away from legacy media for consumers of news. Most news companies now see themselves as Web-first operations, and they are embracing the idea of breaking news by transmitting it wirelessly to mobile phones. But it's also true that they still derive the lion's share of their revenue (usually around 93 percent) from their legacy products—primarily newspapers or television—not their websites or mobile phone services. Income from traditional sources is declining, but so far Web and mobile revenue is not increasing rapidly enough to replace it.

It's clear that legacy media companies are embracing the idea of delivering the news whenever, wherever and however consumers want it. What's not clear is how they can prosper doing so. As noted in Chapter 2, newspapers still finance much of the massive news-gathering apparatus needed to cover the news both in this country and around the world. That raises this question: If newspapers continue their downward spiral, can that capacity for news-gathering be replaced using only revenue from newer media operations?

Many believe it's possible. What's clear is that legacy media companies are making a major commitment to the Internet in hopes that they can find a solution to their problems. Newspapers, radio and television stations and even magazines now have substantial news sites online. Often, the news hits there first.

Web Partnerships

Newspaper executives are not the only ones concerned about the problem of how to finance the gathering of news. Eric Schmidt, chief executive officer of Google, insists he's open to helping the newspaper industry make it through the difficult transition it's facing. Some newspaper executives have vilified Google and other **content aggregators** as "newspaper killers," but Schmidt denies that. The problem with newspapers, Schmidt says, is the Internet in general, not just companies like Google and Yahoo. Companies like his have a "moral responsibility" to help newspapers make the transition to the Internet, Schmidt said in an interview with Danny Sullivan of Search Engine Land, a website devoted to covering the search-engine industry.

"We need these content partners to survive," Schmidt said. "We need their content. We are not in the content business.

"Google sees itself as trying to make the world a better place. And our values are that more information is positive—(it results in) transparency. And the historic role of the press was to provide transparency. . . . So we really do have a moral responsibility to help solve this problem."

Schmidt seems to understand that the vast majority of information that appears on Google News comes from legacy media. Without them, he's lost most of Google's news content.

In 2009, Schmidt started putting those words into action. The company introduced an experimental news hub called Fast Flip that allows users to view news

ON THE JOB

Multimedia Journalism

Brian Storm came up with the idea for MediaStorm while still a journalism student in 1994. Upon graduation in 1995, he went to work for MSNBC.com, where he served as director of multimedia until 2002. He then joined Corbis, a digital media agency founded and owned by Microsoft's Bill Gates.

Storm relaunched MediaStorm in March 2005 with a focus on creating cinematic narratives for distribution across a variety of platforms. He now serves as president of the company, which is based in New York and employs a talented team of individuals with backgrounds in journalism and multimedia.

MediaStorm has created award-winning multimedia projects, interactive applications and websites for media companies, foundations and advocacy groups. Its clients include Starbucks, the Council on Foreign Relations and *National Geographic* magazine. MediaStorm projects also have appeared on the websites of MSNBC, Slate, NPR, Reuters and PBS.

"I saw an opportunity for a new kind of company," Storm says. "I worked on the idea for years and then launched the company in 2005."

In November 2005, MediaStorm premiered its award-winning multimedia website, MediaStorm.org. Using animation, audio, video and the power of still photography, MediaStorm specializes in multimedia stories that speak to the heart of the human condition. Since its launch, MediaStorm has won three Emmys (2007, 2008 and 2009) and four Webby Awards.

"Multimedia is a great new way to do stories," Storm says. "It's a powerful way to let people see things they otherwise would never know about."

articles from major publishers and flip through them quickly. Google places ads around the news articles and shares the revenue with publishers. Fast Flip tries to duplicate the browsing experience of thumbing through a newspaper. Flipping through content is fast, so readers can quickly look through a lot of pages until they find something interesting. Fast Flip personalizes the experience for readers by taking cues from selections they make and showing the reader more content from sources, topics and journalists they prefer. There's also a version for delivering news on mobile phones.

Schmidt's willingness to start helping those who provide his content is a step in the right direction. The media industry, too, is seeking solutions. Schemes are being floated to help increase Web revenue, including *micropayment* systems, which make sales involving very small amounts of money possible for highly sought content. Even subscription models are being revisited. The goal is to find new sources of revenue on the Web even as advertising in legacy media shows weakness.

Microsoft's Bill Gates and News Corp.'s Rupert Murdoch also have entered the fray. Microsoft reportedly has had discussions with News Corp., which owns *The Wall Street Journal* and other media companies, about a plan to "de-index"—that is, remove—News Corp.'s news sites from Google. That could result in search engines like Google and Microsoft's competing Bing being forced to pay for news content. This, of course, would be of great benefit to those who originate that content.

Niche Journalism

A 2009 study by the prominent accounting firm PricewaterhouseCoopers points out that there's hope for legacy media. It forecasts that global entertainment and media spending will increase from $1.4 trillion in 2009 to $1.6 trillion in 2013. The U.S. alone will account for $495 billion of that.

Newspapers are expected to benefit. Borrell Associates, a research and consulting firm that has done a good job of tracking newspaper trends, predicted a steady growth in newspaper advertising revenue beginning in 2010, with an eventual increase of 8.7 percent by 2014. Those numbers, while not robust, are hardly numbers that could be associated with a dying industry.

Bill Cobourn of PricewaterhouseCoopers notes that the sharp decline in media revenues experienced in 2008-2009 was not a result of decreasing demand. "In fact, demand . . . appears to be increasing. The challenge is to identify ad models that are able to withstand the downward pressure on ad rates in the digital environment and on subscription models that capture consumers' preferences for premium content."

Most legacy media companies are doing just what Cobourn suggests. They are designing *niche* products—specialized sites that serve a specific audience—to create new revenue streams. Some, particularly those that cover sports, are surviving nicely and even expanding. ESPN is opening localized Internet sites in major cities like Boston, Chicago and Dallas. It is even creating a site devoted to women's high school athletics. All of those operations employ trained journalists.

So do sites that specialize in parenting or cater to young readers. Gannett, which owns more newspapers than any other U.S. company, also owns MomsLikeMe.com, a network of sites connecting mothers in communities nationwide. It also has SparkWeekly.com, a site for young readers connected with the Gannett-owned *News Journal* of Wilmington, Del., as well as similar sites in other cities.

Some Legacy Media Continuing to Thrive

Not all segments of the legacy media are struggling. Many magazines still thrive because of their ability to target audiences that advertisers covet. Indeed, there's a magazine for almost any demographic—*Boating* for boaters, *PC World* for computer aficionados, *The Bridge World* for bridge players. (See Figure 3.1.)

Figure 3.1
There is a magazine for every interest, from knitting to Web design.

Like magazines, small and medium-sized newspapers still do well, too, thanks to their intensely local coverage. They provide content that readers want and are relatively free of competition in smaller communities nationwide.

Another bright spot is National Public Radio, whose audience has grown significantly in the last five years. Local NPR stations also are thriving, and many are expanding staffs to try to fill the vacuum left by other stations that have cut back or abandoned local news. Some are teaming up with Internet startups or even local newspapers.

So, even as some parts of the legacy media struggle to make the difficult transition to the digital economy, other parts thrive. There are still thousands of jobs to be had in legacy media companies. Young people right out of school who are armed with knowledge of the Web are prime candidates for those jobs.

NEW FORMS OF JOURNALISM

Some entrepreneurial journalists are trying to fill the void as legacy media retrench or avoid costly investigative reporting. They seek financing through various means and hope to turn a profit. Still others create sites altruistically with little or no hope

Figure 3.2
Arianna Huffington, co-founder of the news site HuffingtonPost.com, which follows the classic financial model of relying on private investment and advertising.

of turning a profit. Several models for these new forms of Web-based journalism are emerging:

- **Financed by venture capital.** Some sites, like HuffingtonPost.com, received startup financing from private investors and became nationally popular, attracting significant amounts of advertising (see Figure 3.2). Some also charge for subscriptions to premium content.
- **Funded by foundations.** Some sites, like ProPublica.org, which seeks to do investigative reporting nationwide, are financed by grants from foundations and operate as not-for-profit corporations (see Figure 3.3).
- **Financed with hybrid models.** Some sites, like MinnPost.com, are hybrids funded by advertisers and corporate sponsors, as well as individual donors.
- **Financed as an old media/new media hybrid.** Some sites, like Politico.com, sell ads to support their free Web content while publishing traditional products. *Politico* is both a website and a Washington-based political newspaper.
- **Financed by individual entrepreneurs.** Other sites, like WestSeattleBlog.com, were established with spare change and hope to attract enough advertising to survive.

Figure 3.3
ProPublica.org operates as a not-for-profit organization, funded by foundation grants. Other sites may combine corporate funding and individual donations to finance their operations.

- **Not financed at all.** Still other sites, like ColumbiaHeartBeat.blogspot.com, don't even seek to take advertising or make a profit. The publishers of such sites operate them without expectation of profit and often have separate jobs.

Some of the founders of these sites don't even think of themselves as journalists; they're merely filling a perceived void in news coverage in their communities. Others are displaced journalists with formal training and significant experience in news-gathering.

THE NOT-FOR-PROFIT MODEL

For the most part, private citizens, families or publicly traded firms own the legacy media companies in the U.S. As a result, these companies continue to exist only if they earn a profit. Traditionally, most revenue has come from advertising, with some additional revenue from newsstand sales and subscriptions. Many of the new Web-based journalism sites seek to follow the same model by supporting themselves through advertising or subscriptions. Not-for-profit sites, however, seek only to support their operations—pay staff and other costs—not to make a profit for owners or investors.

Financially Successful Not-for-Profit Sites

The not-for-profit models in which foundations are a key source of funding are relatively new, and in some circles they are controversial. Jack Shafer of Slate.com, an online magazine, says, "There's something disconcerting about wanting to divorce the newspaper (or a news website) from market pressures." Others disagree. ProPublica's editors, in explaining how they operate, write:

> Profit-margin expectations and short-term stock market concerns, in particular, are making it increasingly difficult for the public companies that control nearly all of our nation's news organizations to afford—or at least think they can afford—the sort of intensive, extensive and uncertain efforts that produce great investigative journalism.

So, ProPublica relies on grants from foundations, including a major one from the Sandler Foundation, to "support the work of 32 working journalists, all of them dedicated to investigative reporting on stories with significant potential for major impact."

ProPublica typically offers its stories to legacy media operations, free of charge, for publication or broadcast. After a period of exclusivity for the partner organization, the story appears on the ProPublica site. This totally new model works because the credentials of ProPublica's reporters are outstanding. Without that credibility, no legacy media organization would publish or broadcast its stories.

MinnPost.com, formed largely by laid-off journalists in the Minneapolis-St. Paul area, accepts donations from corporations and individuals but also sells advertising. It is professionally staffed and designed, and it operates as a not-for-profit corporation.

Financially Problematic Nonprofit Sites

Still, for every high-quality news site like ProPublica or MinnPost, there are dozens of other civic blogs or websites that are much less professional and that carry little or no advertising. Many are challenging the fundamental principle that media must turn a profit to be viable and long-lasting.

In the first definitive study of such sites, researchers Esther Thorson and Margaret Duffy found that most are more narrow in content and focus than the legacy media sites in the cities where they operate. The citizen sites are predominantly blogs rather than news sites. They contain little advertising.

The site owners they interviewed were not particularly interested in the business side of their operations. Few of them rated making money, or even covering their costs, as a priority. Two-thirds of them had had journalism experience. Their goals for their sites are well-defined—giving citizens a voice, providing fair and accurate information about their communities and enabling residents to decide their own futures.

ON THE JOB

Media Entrepreneur

The media have been rapidly redeploying their resources since Sarah Protzman entered the working world in 2004. That year, her first employer, a newspaper with a circulation of 30,000, made a major push toward Web-only content and blogs.

By contrast, when she moved to New York City a few years later, the weekly trade magazine where she found a job had a lackluster online presence and continued to invest in traditional approaches to covering and distributing the news. It folded 18 months later, and she was transferred to another publication within the company.

Protzman remains anchored in traditional work and freelance, but in response to nascent opportunities available to individual journalists, she began to recount funny stories, missteps and interesting situations on a personal blog. Those essays later became a memoir called *Standing Room Only: Two Years in New York City*, which she self-published in 2009 and continues to sell from her apartment. While documenting her bookjourney on Twitter, she sent press kits, listed the book for Kindle download and granted interviews to blogs, magazines and newspapers.

Her goal in starting her business was to develop maximum flexibility and have additional income to stay afloat should she lose her job. She has little overhead cost, leaving the bulk of revenues going straight to profits. Protzman invested about $300, most of which was profit from book sales, into more books, mailing and printing supplies, and domain names. She autographs and ships every copy herself to add value, improve the buyer's experience and maintain quality.

The positive response to Protzman's book led to the creation of an even more immediate way to share what she'd learned about thriving in New York. In 2009, she shuttered her personal blog and launched NewNewYorkers, a site newcomers rely on for answers to common questions, encouragement, tips on living frugally and humor about making a new life in the city. This kind of entrepreneurial journalism has given Protzman a measure of economic insulation and control in the turbulent industry she loves.

The study, produced for the Knight Foundation and the Pew Charitable Trusts, concluded that while the site owners are clearly dedicated to their work, they operate narrowly and with no clear way of making a business of what they do. Thorson and Duffy conclude, "These results cannot be viewed as encouraging for the power of citizen journalism to replace legacy journalism."

Other forms of startups also are well-intentioned but have little or no commercial viability. Neighborhood newsletters and intensely local websites may have great appeal to small audiences, but they have little hope of becoming profitable. Niche publications that attempt to attract micro audiences also are unlikely to become profitable unless they are extended to much larger geographic areas and therefore are able to attract larger audiences for which advertisers are willing to pay.

Unquestionably, some good publications have emerged on the Web that could best be described as the products of people with a passion for informing their neighbors. Trained journalists produce some; others are less polished and perhaps less professional. Still, all of them employ journalistic techniques in reporting the news. To dismiss any of them would be a mistake.

But whether journalism can be sustained for long periods in the absence of good business models remains to be seen. In the end, as the Thorson-Duffy study showed, profit-based media—or those funded by foundations—are probably the only long-term answer to society's need for top-quality information. Determining how to pay the cost of providing good journalism is problematic.

FOR-PROFIT MEDIA MODELS

Because their costs are high, newspapers and television stations in major markets must have hundreds of thousands of readers or viewers to be profitable for their owners and investors. But with much lower costs on the Web, luring large numbers is not nearly as critical.

Niche Journalism Sites

In his remarkable book, *Be the Media: How to Create and Accelerate Your Message . . . Your Way*, entrepreneur David Mathison outlines dozens of examples of people making money by attracting intensely loyal followers in relatively small numbers. He argues that someone who can attract 1,000 "true fans" can make a profit in almost any business. True fans are those who like your content so much that they are willing to pay for it, not only on the Web but in other forms such as books, music or other merchandise.

Sports Sites

Will that work for news content? Perhaps so. It clearly is working for sports content. Two websites, Rivals.com and Scout.com, compete head-to-head for information on football and basketball recruiting at colleges nationwide. Both do other things, but recruiting coverage, something that legacy media do poorly, is at the heart of their businesses. Discussion boards abound where fans discuss their teams and watch every step in the battle for the nation's best high school players. Users pay premium rates of around $100 a year for access, and they come by the tens of thousands. Advertising boosts profit even more. Most college and university subsidiary sites have independent operators, often trained as journalists, who in turn are connected in the national network. As the sites attract more users, the operators' incomes increase.

While some websites are financed on a shoestring, others have corporate backing. MLB.com was financed with the deep pockets of Major League Baseball, and its team sites employ journalists to give fans an insider's view of what's happening with the Cubs, Marlins, Angels and other teams. Fans outside the local television viewing area can even watch the games on Web-based video.

Then there are the general sports sites on the Web, including ESPN.com, CBSSports.com, Fox Sports on MSNBC (msn.foxsports.com) and dozens of others. Such sites give hope to aspiring sports journalists that there will be jobs for them when they graduate, even if those jobs are not at a newspaper or television station.

Business Sites

Something similar is happening in business journalism. Sites such as Bloomberg .com, various Dow Jones sites and MarketWatch.com are attracting readers—often at premium rates—because of their ability to produce information that readers desire and are willing to pay for. Such sites create increasing numbers of Web-based jobs for journalism graduates. In some cases, related cable television channels create even more jobs for television majors.

General News Sites

Clearly, though, most general news sites are not making money. Some newspaper companies report covering the costs of producing their websites with advertising income, but for the most part the legacy media continue to pay the salaries of those who gather the news.

Some argue that newspapers made a big mistake by giving away their news on websites, but today that's a reality likely never to be reversed. Those who have tried to charge for mainstream news information have largely failed. The only way to reverse this situation would be for all newspapers to agree to start charging for their content, and getting all newspapers to agree is most unlikely. Even then, the companies that participated would probably face antitrust scrutiny from the government.

The key to Internet profitability, then, would seem to come in niche areas like sports and business that attract highly interested readers. Those seeking to provide general news probably will continue to struggle until a feasible economic model is found.

Finding that model is the holy grail of the media industry today, and lots of schemes are under consideration. Among them are these:

- Entrepreneurs and journalists have created entirely new national news websites like Politico.com. These conceivably could fill a significant void in national news coverage if legacy media organizations continue to fail or cut back.
- A few papers, *The Wall Street Journal* and the *Arkansas Democrat-Gazette* of Little Rock among them, charge for most Web content. This seems to work for those publications, but most who have tried it have failed.
- Some companies are considering micropayments. In other words, they would attract readers with some free content, then charge for select news content, much as Apple does with songs on iTunes.

- One small paper, the *Antelope Valley Press* in Palmdale, Calif., offers only head-lines and brief news summaries on its website. The full articles are available only in print.
- Rupert Murdoch's News Corp., which owns *The Wall Street Journal*, the *New York Post* and other newspapers, is talking with other publishers about found-ing a consortium that would collect fees for Web-based news products.

SAN DIEGO: A STUDY IN NEW MEDIA PROTOTYPES

Many not-for-profit as well as for-profit concepts are being tested in San Diego. When a series of budget cuts sliced the size of *The San Diego Union-Tribune* reporting staff in half, a local businessman, Buzz Woolley, financed the startup of an online-only news organization called Voice of San Diego (see Figure 3.4). There, according to *Columbia Journalism Review*, a dozen or so reporters pursue key issues facing the community, including housing, government, the environ-ment and education. Voice of San Diego, a not-for-profit corporation, is financed by donors like Woolley, foundations, advertising, corporate sponsorships and citi-zen "members" who donate to keep the enterprise going, in much the same way that others give to National Public Radio.

Yet another group started the San Diego News Network, a for-profit local news site that aggregates news from its own staff, freelancers, radio and television stations, bloggers and others. It covers much of the same ground as *The Union-Tribune* and does so with a website that resembles the newspaper's.

The Watchdog Institute is perhaps the most unusual of San Diego's startups. It's an independent nonprofit investigative reporting project based on the campus of San Diego State University. Lori Hearn, a former *Union-Tribune* editor, per-suaded her former company's owner to contribute money to the startup. The effort is staffed largely by former *Union-Tribune* reporters, who feed their product back to the newspaper at a much lower cost than if the newspaper had produced the same work for itself. Hearn is seeking other media partners and donations, and she's using San Diego State journalism students to help.

Whether any of these schemes will prove successful in maintaining the watch-dog function of the press in an era of declining profits remains to be seen. In the short term, it appears that the publication of niche products on the Web or foundation-supported media are the most likely ways to underwrite the signifi-cant costs of covering general news.

The primary alternatives to the for-profit model would seem to be either government-financed media, which for the most part is an unpopular and un-welcome idea in the U.S., or foundation-backed media. ProPublica remains the primary example of foundation financing, while National Public Radio and the Public Broadcasting System remain the only good examples of government-financed media.

Figure 3.4
The not-for-profit Voice of San Diego and the online-only San Diego News Network exemplify how news organizations are changing their financing and news-delivery methods.

DOING IT YOURSELF

Jasmine Reese started playing the violin at 14 but felt she was being held back because of her relatively late start with the instrument. She decided there was a need for information on how to improve as a musician even if you got a late start. So she founded LateStarterMusician.com.

Now, at age 21, Reese publishes an *e-zine*, or electronic magazine, and a newsletter for people like her. The site caters not only to late starters but also to disabled and minority musicians—"basically anyone with an impediment that makes access to affordable, convenient and quality music education challenging," she explains.

"I currently run and design the whole website on my own, which sometimes seems like an impossible feat. But thanks to my e-marketing efforts, I have a solid fan base. My networks include Facebook, YouTube, MySpace, Twine, Twitter and LinkedIn," she says.

She's doing all this while enrolled in journalism school. And she's trying to learn as much as she can about how to operate a business, manage accounts, provide security and the like.

Reese is not alone. She and many others like her are following the advice of David Mathison in *Be the Media* and creating businesses around the loyalty of true fans. Others are building news or advertising applications designed for devices like Apple's iPhone or other smart phones—phones capable of surfing the Web.

Developing an Idea

Tony Brown and three other students entered a student competition at the University of Missouri to design iPhone apps for news and advertising. They won with an advertising application called NearBuy, which enables users to find real estate for sale anywhere in the U.S. It gives users the price of the home and details about it, complete with photos of the property.

Brown and his colleagues are forming a company around their creation and plan to charge real estate agents for premium content that will help sell their properties. NearBuy is already one of the most-used free business applications in the iTunes Store, and a companion product for renters is gaining popularity.

Other teams of students created news-oriented applications and also are considering commercializing them. All this reinforces the concept that creating profitable media companies can be just one good idea away. "It's an opportunity to harness the entrepreneurial spirit and technological expertise of students in order to reinvent media content, format and delivery," said Mike McKean, the professor who directed the student competition.

Building Audiences as the Key to Success

People who start news-oriented websites and blogs need to know how to attract audiences. They cannot simply create a site and hope the world flocks to it. As a result, skills that once were never taught to aspiring journalists are being incorporated into courses at many schools of journalism.

Succeeding as an entrepreneurial journalist requires a knowledge of tagging, linking and promotion of sites through viral marketing; the ability to report and edit text, audio and video; an understanding of audiences; knowledge of how to gather reader comments and contributions; and the ability to write headlines, subsidiary decks and text to optimize the chances of being found by search engines.

Search-engine optimization is a key. In newspapers, it's not really important to use the word "baseball" in a headline about the Giants beating the Dodgers. But doing so might well be critical to ensuring that a search engine finds and properly categorizes your story. Understanding **metadata**, key words that don't necessarily appear in the story but help search engines index your story, is just as critical. It's all part of building and maintaining an audience.

The good news is that Internet advertising revenue and Internet subscription revenue both are rising. Much of that revenue today goes to sites unrelated to media companies—often pornography, gambling and shopping sites. But also hugely popular are social media sites such as Facebook.com and MySpace.com.

No one would suggest that journalists use pornography or gambling to promote their products, but using social media sites is an option worth considering. Some media companies are now putting video clips or links to news stories on Facebook, which in turn causes readers to click to their news sites. Increasing traffic is the key to profitability, so viral marketing of this type is increasingly common.

Similarly, texts to smart phones can have embedded links that drive readers to news websites. Many believe that mobile phones will be the next great platform on which people will consume news. With smart phones such as the Palm Pre and Apple's iPhone, the power of telephone-delivered news information is becoming ever more evident.

JOBS IN JOURNALISM

While people like Jasmine Reese and Tony Brown are forming their own companies in the new media economy, others are finding more traditional types of jobs—sometimes at legacy media companies and sometimes elsewhere. (See Figure 3.5 for insight into the range of jobs and salaries available for journalism graduates.)

When Jenifer Langosch went to journalism school, she thought she'd end up working as a newspaper sportswriter. Instead, she found a job covering the Pittsburgh Pirates for MLB.com. Troy Wolverton did end up in a legacy media job, writing a personal technology column for the *San Jose Mercury News*. But he did so only after years in Web-based media, including CNET.com.

"I learned a long time ago that the Web was going to open opportunities . . . that never existed before," says Newsy.com's Jim Spencer. "There's a whole new world out there. Aspiring journalists have all sorts of jobs to lure them that never even existed a decade ago."

Figure 3.5
Median yearly salaries for 2008 bachelor's degree recipients with full-time jobs. *Source:* Lee B. Becker, Tudor Vlad, Devora Olin, Stephanie Hanisak, and Donna Wilcox, "2008 Annual Survey of Journalism and Communication Graduates," chart 35, James M. Cox Jr. Center for International Mass Communication Training and Research, Grady College of Journalism and Mass Communication, University of Georgia, August 5, 2009 (available at http://www.grady.uga.edu/annualsurveys).

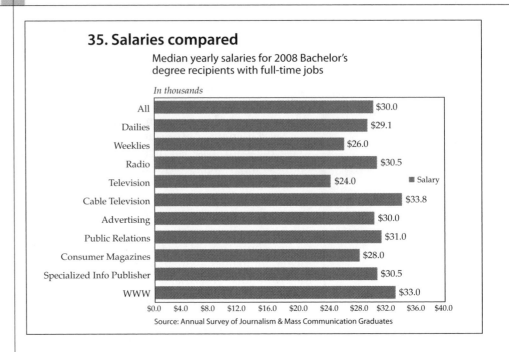

35. Salaries compared

Median yearly salaries for 2008 Bachelor's degree recipients with full-time jobs

In thousands

	Salary
All	$30.0
Dailies	$29.1
Weeklies	$26.0
Radio	$30.5
Television	$24.0
Cable Television	$33.8
Advertising	$30.0
Public Relations	$31.0
Consumer Magazines	$28.0
Specialized Info Publisher	$30.5
WWW	$33.0

Source: Annual Survey of Journalism & Mass Communication Graduates

Training to become a journalist prepares you for many jobs. Some are obvious, some are not. Most jobs, regardless of the medium, fall into one of these categories:

- **Writing and reporting.** Newspaper reporters and magazine writers are examples. At newspapers, most writing jobs are full-time staff positions, but many magazines rely much more heavily on freelance writers who are paid by the story. The skills of reporting and writing go together. No one in journalism can be a good writer without first being a good reporter.

- **Editing.** Great jobs abound for those who can edit well. Newspapers, magazines, radio and television stations and some websites have copy editors, assignment editors and editorial assistants. At newspapers, the entry-level position of copy editor often pays more than the entry-level position of reporter. Copy editors are in greater demand than reporters.

- **Photography and video.** Print publications and websites use lots of photographs and therefore need photographers. At newspapers, most are staff photographers, but at many magazines freelance photography is more common. No longer is video merely the province of television. Video is becoming important for all media operations that run websites.

- **Art and design.** Designers are needed in all media. There are jobs for newspaper and magazine designers and Web designers. Even television stations need Web designers. There also is an increasing demand for information graphics specialists—people who produce maps, charts and graphs.

Jobs in Journalism

Jobs in Legacy Media

Jobs abound for those who seek to enter the legacy media. Here are a few of the possibilities for each medium. Asterisks (*) identify entry-level jobs that beginners are likely to land.

Newspapers (Daily and Weekly)	Magazines	Television	Radio	Online Media	Other Jobs
Reporter*	Writer*	Reporter*	Reporter*	Writer*	Advertising sales*
Copy editor*	Fact checker*	Producer*	Producer*	Producer*	Advertising copy writer*
Page designer*	Editorial assistant*	Desk assistant*	Anchor	Graphics specialist*	Advertising account manager*
Information graphics specialist*	Copy editor*	Videographer*	News director	Executive producer (titles vary)	Public relations practitioner*
Photographer*	Page designer*	Anchor			Account executive
Assignment editor	Senior writer	News director			Art director
News editor	Senior editor	Executive producer			Media critic
Managing editor	Contributing writer				Foreign correspondent
Executive editor	Managing editor				
Columnist	Editor				
	Columnist				

Jobs in Emerging Media

Jobs are rapidly increasing for those who seek work in emerging media. In addition to starting your own website, here are a few of the possibilities for paid jobs in Web-based media. Many jobs listed under "Jobs in Legacy Media" also exist in emerging media. All of the jobs listed below are entry-level jobs that beginners are likely to land.

Websites	Entrepreneurial Activities
Reporter	News software designer
Copy editor	Ad software designer
Designer	E-zine editor
Writer	Multimedia designer
Producer	Newsletter editor
Graphics specialist	
Producer	
Advertising sales	
Advertising design	

- **Production.** Television producers are in high demand. It's quite possible to become a news producer right out of journalism school. Web producers are also in demand, and additional production jobs exist in the print media.
- **Tech support.** Those who combine a knowledge of journalism with computer literacy can find jobs anywhere. Media outlets around the world have a strong interest in computer-literate journalists. To increase their marketability, journalism students should consider a minor or double major in information technology.
- **Advertising and public relations.** Advertising and public relations often are taught within schools and departments of journalism. Jobs in this field abound, and they range from advertising sales and creative design to account management and Internet marketing and promotion.
- **Audience development.** Many websites now have teams of people trained to expand the site's audience. Through the use of viral marketing, audience development specialists place notes on Facebook and Twitter with links to the site. That helps to drive traffic and enhances prospects for advertising revenue.
- **Management.** Many who enter journalism eventually become assignment editors, managing editors or executive editors. Those jobs pay more and are part of a natural progression for reporters and copy editors.

As in any period of transition, there will be losers and winners. Those who position themselves to excel in this environment will find success in journalism — even at legacy media companies.

Suggested Readings

Chaney, Paul. *The Digital Handshake: Seven Proven Strategies to Grow Your Business Using Social Media.* Hoboken, N.J.: John Wiley, 2009. An excellent book on the importance of social media in spreading the word about new websites.

Mathison, David. *Be the Media: How to Create and Accelerate Your Message . . . Your Way.* New Hyde Park, N.Y.: Natural E Creative Group, 2009. An excellent discussion of how to become an entrepreneur and build a circle of "true fans."

Pavlik, John. *Media in the Digital Age.* New York: Columbia University Press, 2008. A thorough treatise on how digital media are transforming society.

Switzer, Janet. *Instant Income: Strategies That Bring in the Cash.* New York: McGraw Hill, 2007. A guide to starting and expanding your own enterprise.

Suggested Websites

www.huffingtonpost.com
The Huffington Post is one of the premier news sites on the Web. It was founded with venture capital and designed to be free of the weight of legacy media.

www.minnpost.com
This hybrid site accepts both advertising and foundation support. It's a not-for-profit designed to provide high-quality journalism for the Minneapolis-St. Paul area.

www.politico.com
Politico.com is an excellent example of a new politically oriented media site that is advertiser-supported. It has a companion newspaper that is traditional in nature.

www.propublica.org
This excellent foundation-supported site brings together some of the nation's top journalists to pursue investigative reporting.

Exercises

1. **Team project.** Your instructor will divide the class into teams of three or four. With the other members of your group, brainstorm a list of ideas for a news website that you could create. Research a few of the ideas on the Web, and then decide together which is the most viable one. Plan your site: What would its purpose be? Who would its audience be? What would the site be like? Would it have video, animation or audio? What text features would you provide? Where would you get your content? How large a staff would you need? How would you support the site? As a team, write a detailed plan for your proposed site, answering these and any other questions you think relevant.

2. Research two companies engaged in producing new forms of media, and provide a report on how they operate. Describe any efforts the companies are making to find new revenue streams.

3. Find a blog or website that tries to cover local news with intensity. Interview the editor about the nature of the site. Does it make money? Does he or she care? Why?

4. Go to **www.minnpost.com**, and do an analysis of the news indexed on the front page. How does this differ from what you see on the front page of **www.startribune.com**, the website of the Minneapolis newspaper?

5. Go to **www.politico.com**. Choose a political story from that site, and contrast how the same story is covered on **www.washingtonpost.com**.

6. Contrast the kinds of stories you see on **www.west seattleblog.com** to those published in *The Seattle Times* or on its website, **http://seattletimes.nwsource.com**. Which seems to provide more government coverage?

7. Think of an idea for creating your own news blog on the Web. What content could you provide that others do not?

Interviewing

4

Journalists get most of their information by asking people questions. Sometimes, though, the hardest part is just getting a source to agree to talk to you. Lane DeGregory, a staff writer for the *St. Petersburg (Fla.) Times*, was writing a story about a Largo, Fla., city manager who was fired when he announced he was going to have a sex-change operation. DeGregory's first hurdle was getting the city manager to talk at length with her. The next hurdle was convincing the manager's wife to talk to her. Says DeGregory, "It came to this: 12 days, 10 phone calls, a two-page letter, a note, two stories, immeasurable groveling and a lot of luck."

Sometimes, journalism is hard work.

Describing to Poynter.org how she obtained the key interviews for the remarkable story, DeGregory said she typed a two-page letter to the wife to explain why she wanted to interview her and added a handwritten note and then delivered it to the house. She finally got the interview one evening when she called the former city manager, who handed the phone to the wife. DeGregory said the wife was at first reluctant. She progressed from yes and no answers to sentences. She started to relax. They talked for four hours.

Not every interview is that difficult, time-consuming or important. But every successful interview begins with establishing trust and ends with telling a story.

Interviewing—having conversations with sources—is the key to most stories you will write. Your ability to make people feel comfortable with you is often the difference between mediocre reporting and good reporting.

Information is the raw material of a journalist. While some of it is gathered from records and some from observation, most of it is gathered in person-to-person conversations. You try first to talk to **primary sources**, those who witnessed the event or have authority over documents. If you can't get to the primary source, you may be forced to go to a **secondary source**, someone who talked to witnesses, such as a public safety official or a lawyer or a next-door neighbor.

Even when you are doing a profile, determine how your source knows your profile subject. Does your source work with the subject? She's probably not much of an authority on his after-hours activities, then. Does he play poker with the person? If so, he probably doesn't know the subject in the workplace. Once you know how your source knows what he or she knows, then you can start the conversation. If you're interviewing for television, broadcast or **webcast** (an audio and/or video report sent over the Internet), your goals and techniques may be different from those of a print reporter, but the basics are the same.

PREPARING FOR THE INTERVIEW

How you prepare for an interview depends in part on what kind of story you intend to write. (Figure 4.1 shows a checklist you can use in doing interviews.) You may be doing a news story, a personality profile or an investigative piece. In each case, you check the newspaper library and search online databases, talk to other reporters and, if there's enough time, read magazine articles and books. Social media sites such as Facebook offer you information on some people you might not

Interviews are best used to solicit reactions and interpretations, not to gather facts. Good reporters do their fact-gathering before interviews.

Figure 4.1
Successful interviews take careful preparation.

otherwise be able to contact. Don't print information off these sites without verification, though.

To prepare for a news story, you pay more attention to clips about the subject of the story than those about the personality of the interviewee. To prepare for a profile, you look for personality quirks and information about the subject's interests, family, friends, travels and habits. To prepare for an investigative piece, you want to know both your subject matter and the person you are interviewing. In all these stories, do not overlook other reporters and editors who know something about the person or subject. Let's look at each of these three types of stories more closely.

Interviewing Checklist

Before the Interview

1. Know the topic.
   - Seek specific information.
   - Research the topic.
   - List the questions.

2. Know the person.
   - Know salient biographical information.
   - Know the person's expertise regarding the topic.

3. Set up the interview.
   - Set the time.
     - Schedule at the interviewee's convenience, but suggest a time.
     - Estimate the length of time needed.
     - Ask about possible return visits.
   - Set the place.
     - Interviewee's turf, or
     - Neutral turf

4. Discuss arrangements.
   - Will you bring a digital recorder?
   - Will you bring a photographer or videographer?
   - Will you let the interviewee check the accuracy of quotes?

During the Interview

1. When you arrive
   - Control the seating arrangement.
   - Place the digital recorder at the optimum spot.
   - Warm up the person briefly with small talk.
   - Set the ground rules: Everything is on the record.

2. The interview itself
   - Use good interviewing techniques.
     - Ask open-ended and closed-ended questions.
     - Allow the person to think and to speak; pause.
     - Don't be threatening in voice or manner.
     - Control the conversational flow, but be flexible.
   - Take good notes.
     - Be unobtrusive.
     - Be thorough.
   - Use the digital recorder.
     - Make sure it's on and working, but take notes too.
     - Note the number on the digital counter at important parts in the interview so you can find quotes easily.

3. Before you leave
   - Ask if there's anything else the interviewee wants to say.
   - Check facts — spellings, dates, statistics — and quotes.
   - Set a time for rechecking facts and quotes.
   - Discuss when and where the interview might appear.
   - For a print publication, ask if the interviewee wants extra copies.

After the Interview

1. Organize your notes — immediately.

2. Craft a proper lead.

3. Write a coherent story.

4. Check accuracy with the interviewee.

The News Story

Usually, reporters don't have much time to prepare to cover a news story. You'll be lucky if you have a few minutes to dig into your news room's files on the event or the issue. With a few more minutes, you can go online to see what other reporters have written on similar topics. Those hurried searches will provide a bit of background and perhaps some context. Then you're out the door. Still, there are some important mental steps you can take while you chase the news.

First, review in your head what you've turned up in your quick background research. If you're off to meet a political candidate, a public official or a celebrity, when was she last in the news? For what? What will your audience (or your boss) most likely want to know now? If you're headed for a crime scene or a disaster, what do you know about the neighborhood? Has anything like this happened lately? With what results?

Second, plan your approach. Who will you seek out at the scene? Who's likely to be in charge? What do you know about that person and her or his attitude toward reporters? Are you alone on this assignment and expected to capture audio or video? If so, double-check your equipment. Will you be reporting live on camera? If so, double-check your appearance.

Finally, plan out your first few questions. Sometimes those are obvious. If the news is a crime or disaster, you'll want to know what happened. Was anybody hurt? What's the damage? If the story is focused on an issue or a person, you'll have some choices to make. Ideally, your backgrounding has gotten you past the most basic "Who are you?" and "Why are you here?" questions. So you may want to start with something like "What are you hoping to accomplish here?" Or "Why do you think this issue is so important?"

Most news interviews aren't adversarial, but if you have tough questions, save them for the end of the conversation. That way, they won't keep you from getting most of what you need.

From there, follow your instincts and your training to find the story.

The Profile

Lane DeGregory, to whom you were introduced at the beginning of the chapter, says writing previous stories on gender issues helped her establish rapport and gain the trust of the city manager who was planning to have a sex-change operation. She knew the language, for one thing. She also knew the issues.

"I knew for most transgendered people, it isn't about who they want to have sex with, but about who they feel they really are. So I didn't have to ask any dumb 'I don't get it' questions, and I could speak with some authority on the subject."

If you don't have the background on your subject that DeGregory had on hers, you will need to research the subject and the person you will be profiling. For most profiles, you will be talking not only to your subject but also to his or her friends, family and co-workers. In many cases, you will get their names from your subject. Ask how your subject knows them: co-worker, social acquaintance, recent

ON THE JOB

Telling Compelling Stories

Bill Reiter is a reporter for *The Kansas City Star*. His first job was in Little Rock, Ark. After that, he reported for *The Des Moines Register*. He shares lessons he has learned about getting information from people:

"My goal was to write a series that would take our readers inside the lives of homeless teenagers. The task seemed daunting. I had to find these young people, build enough trust to enter their world and somehow show the complex problems and dilemmas that kept them on the street.

"So, knowing they were out there but not sure where to go, I followed the first rule of reporting, the one my college professors drilled into me. . . . I left the office. I stopped folks who looked like they might be homeless. I went by a shelter. I talked to a police officer whose beat takes him to poor parts of town. It didn't take long to hear that the man to see about life on the street was a homeless-youth outreach worker named Howard Matalba."

Matalba introduced Reiter to his world and to Gabrielle, a pregnant teenager. Reiter again:

"I spent the next three months with Gabrielle. I wandered town with her, listened for hours to her complaining, filled notebook after notebook with quotes that never made the newspaper. I ate with her at the soup kitchen, followed her when she applied for food stamps and stuck around when she and her boyfriend snuggled up together on a bench or against a building. . . . I was there when Gabrielle applied for an apartment, when she ran out of money and food, and when she took back her boyfriend despite his abusive tendencies. I was there when she gave birth to her daughter. . . .

"My reporting came with costs. I was knocked down by a homeless man. I was punched and scratched by a homeless 19-year-old girl. I conquered my fear of heights because one of my sources, with me right behind him, scuttled over a rickety train bridge on his way to town. I worked nights and weekends, wandered for miles in the cold, and was told in no uncertain terms by a group of homeless men that they'd kill me if I came back. I went back anyway, again and again. . . .

"I looked for moments, dialogue and action that gave life to the issue I was writing about. I didn't rely on quotes that reconstructed something I wanted to write about. Instead, I wrote down what my sources actually said to each other, not what they said to me. I relaxed, acted like myself and remembered the people I was writing about had been through a lot."

His series ran on Page One of *The Register* and set Des Moines talking. For Bill Reiter, that's what counts.

or lifelong friend? Then ask the co-worker or friend how he or she knows your profile subject. With this information, you won't ask inappropriate questions— you don't want to ask about your subject's love for hunting if the interviewee only knows the person from work, for example—and you can properly evaluate the information you are getting.

Another writer, Walt Harrington, specialized in in-depth profiles when he worked for *The Washington Post Magazine.* In his book *Intimate Journalism,* he says he spent one to three months on each profile. For profiles on then-President George H. W. Bush and journalist Carl Bernstein, who had teamed with Bob Woodward to cover the Watergate scandal, he conducted about 80 interviews each. He also accompanied his subjects in their daily routines. Few journalists are afforded the luxury of three months to work on a profile, but whether you do eight or 80 interviews, the lessons are still the same: Be prepared. Be there.

The Investigative Piece

The casual conversations you want to have for profile interviews are not always possible for the investigative reporter. An adversarial relationship determines both the preparation required for an investigative piece and the atmosphere of the interview itself. An investigative reporter is like an attorney in a courtroom. Wise attorneys know in advance what the answers to their questions will be. So do investigative reporters. Preparation is essential.

Lowell Bergman, a veteran investigative reporter who worked in both print and television, advises, "Learn as much about the subject before you get there, regardless of whether you play dumb because you want them to explain it to you, or whether you just want them to know that you're not going to waste their time."

Gathering Information

In the early stages of the investigation, you conduct some fishing-expedition interviews: Because you don't know how much the source knows, you cast around. Start with people on the fringes. Gather as much as you can from them. Study the records. Only after you have most of the evidence should you confront your central character. You start with a large circle and gradually draw it smaller.

Requesting an Interview

DeGregory had difficulty getting her interview because she wanted to ask questions about a personal topic. Investigative reporters frequently have problems getting the interview because the information they seek is often damaging to the person. Sources who believe you are working on a story that will be critical of them or their friends often try to avoid you. Steve Weinberg, author of an unauthorized biography of industrialist Armand Hammer, had to overcome the suspicion of many former Hammer associates. Their former boss had told all of them not to talk to Weinberg. Instead of calling, Weinberg approached them by mail. "I sent letters, examples of my previous work, explained what I wanted to cover and why I was doing it without Hammer's blessing," Weinberg says.

He recommends that you use a letter or an e-mail to share some of what you know about the story that might surprise or impress the source. For instance, a reference such as "And last week, when I was checking all the land records . . ." would indicate the depth of your research.

In his letter to former Hammer assistants, Weinberg talked about how Hammer was one of the most important people in the history of business. The letters opened doors to all seven of Hammer's former executive assistants whom Weinberg contacted.

Weinberg, like DeGregory, has shown former stories as a way of trying to gain the subject's confidence. Weinberg also offers to show the sources relevant portions of his manuscript as an accuracy check. (An *accuracy check* just verifies the facts. It does not give the source the option of choosing what goes in and what stays out of a story.) He makes it clear in writing that he maintains control of the content.

Requesting an interview in writing can allow you to make your best case for getting it. And an offer to allow your sources to review the story assures them that you are serious about accuracy. E-mail makes both the request and the offer simpler and faster.

BROADCAST INTERVIEWS

When you're interviewing someone in front of a camera, the basic rules of preparation and interviewing don't change. For instance, Bob Schieffer, longtime host of *Face the Nation* on CBS, says the most important thing before every interview is to know as much about the story as possible.

Some of your objectives and techniques, however, do change. Television journalists, at least those who appear on camera, are also performers. Sure, they have to report and write, but they also have to be able to tell their stories with both words and body language to people who are watching and listening — not reading. An important part of the television reporter's performance is the interview.

Both print and broadcast reporters often interview to develop information that can be used in further reporting. Interviews on camera usually have a different goal. That goal is the **sound bite**, the few seconds of words with accompanying video that convey not only information but emotion. Print is a medium that mainly provides information. Television is a medium of emotion. The best interviews for television are those that reveal how a situation feels to the participants or witnesses.

Al Tompkins, the Poynter Institute's group leader for broadcast and online journalism, offers what he calls "a new set of interviewing tools" intended to produce better storytelling for television. You can find these and other tools at www.poynter.org. Here are some tips that show both the differences and similarities in print and television interviewing:

- **Ask both objective and subjective questions.** To gather facts, ask objective questions: "When?" "Where?" "How much?" But subjective questions usually produce the best sound bites: "Why?" "Tell me more . . ." "Can you explain . . . ?"

- **Focus on one issue at a time.** Vague, complicated questions produce vague, complicated, hard-to-follow answers. Remember that readers can reread until they understand, but viewers generally can't rewind an interview. (These days, many broadcast organizations, including PBS, are posting interviews online.) Help viewers follow the story by taking your interviewee through it one step at a time.

- **Ask open-ended questions.** For print, you often want a simple yes or no. That kind of answer stops a television interview. Open-ended questions encourage conversation, and conversation makes for a good interview. (For more on this, see "Open-Ended Questions" later in this chapter.)

- **Keep questions short.** Make the interviewee do the talking. Tompkins points out that short questions are more likely to produce focused responses. They also keep the viewer's attention on the person being interviewed and on what she or he has to say.

- **Build to the point.** The best interviews are like the best stories. They don't give away the punch line in the first few words. Ask soft, easy questions to encourage relaxation and trust. Then move to the heart of the issue.

- **Be honest.** As true for television as for print and online, the importance of honesty is too often overlooked by rookie reporters. You do neither your source nor yourself a favor if you lead the source to expect an interview about softball when you have an indictment in mind. Tell the source ahead of time that you'll want to ask some tough questions. Say—and mean it—that you want to get the whole story, to be fair. Then politely but firmly dig in. As Tompkins notes, honesty has the added benefit of helping you defend yourself against any later accusations of malice.

TELEPHONE, E-MAIL AND IM INTERVIEWS

Interviews always are more successful in person. But when you have to interview by phone, there are at least three points to remember. These are more important for feature stories, profiles and investigative work than for standard news stories, though some news stories require more time and effort during interviews than others.

First, just as you do in person, if this is the first time you've spoken to the source, attempt to establish rapport. Don't immediately start firing questions. Express your appreciation for the person's time. Explain why you are calling and how important the interviewee is to the story. If you have talked to others who know this person, mention that to help relax your source.

Second, depending on how much time and how important this interview is, you may want to record it. You must seek the permission of the person you are interviewing: "Is it okay to record this conversation? I want to make sure I get it accurately, and this way, I can concentrate on the content rather than taking notes." Put the request on the recording. In most states, it is illegal to record a phone conversation without the other person's consent. Remember to take notes even if you are recording an interview. If the recorder breaks down, you'll still have material for your story.

Third, just as in any other interview, try to have a conversation rather than a Q&A session. (A *Q&A*—question and answer—story is more or less a verbatim transcript of an interview. The interview material isn't digested and reworked into a story.) React to what is said with affirmations. Laugh when appropriate. Admit when you don't understand, and ask for more explanation.

The phone can be a friend, but it can never replace personal contact. Neither can e-mail, but reporters are using e-mail more frequently because they are facing more deadline pressure than ever as they feed websites, often in addition to another medium.

E-mail interviews have many weaknesses. They don't permit you to establish rapport. And you need to be certain the person with whom you are corresponding is the person you think he or she is. The classic *New Yorker* cartoon shown below explains the risk. Nobody can be absolutely sure who's on the other end of an e-mail.

You can't be sure who's on the other end of an e-mail message, or that other people aren't "helping" the interviewee respond to your questions.

"On the Internet, nobody knows you're a dog."

On the other hand, e-mail is quick and convenient as a follow-up to personal or phone interviews. E-mail can also be effective for a Q&A story. The e-mail captures the original questions and preserves the responses. Once you've made contact and established identity, an e-mail interview can be useful and even surprisingly revealing. Some people will say things at a keyboard they wouldn't say face to face. Some get carried away by the power of their own prose. Some, of course, are cryptic and not forthcoming.

Instant messaging (IM) has the same strengths and weaknesses as e-mail except that it is faster. You can best use it for follow-up questions, clarifications and checking back information to ensure accuracy.

Don't forget that e-mail and IM are permanent. Don't ask or say anything you wouldn't want to see forwarded to others. Do make your questions clear and grammatically correct. The permanence works *for* you, too. The answers are equally permanent. They can't be taken back or denied later. And it's hard to misquote an e-mail.

SETTING UP THE INTERVIEW

All this homework is important, but something as trifling as your appearance may determine whether you will have a successful interview. You would hardly wear cutoff shorts into a university president's suite, and you wouldn't wear a three-piece suit to talk to underground revolutionaries. It is your right to wear your hair however you wish, pierce your body and wear whatever clothes you want, but it is the source's prerogative to refuse to talk to you.

Most interviews are conducted in the source's office. If the story is a profile or a feature, however, it usually is better to get the source away from his or her work. If you are doing a story about a rabbi's hobby of collecting butterflies, seek a setting appropriate to the topic. Suggest meeting where the rabbi keeps the collection.

In some interviews, it would be to your advantage to get the source on neutral territory. If you have some questions for the provost or a public official, suggest meeting in a coffee shop at a quiet time. A person has more power in his or her official surroundings.

It is important, too, to let the source know how much time you need and whether you expect to return for further information. And if you don't already know how the source might react to a recording device, ask when you are making the appointment.

PREPARING QUESTIONS

You have now done the appropriate homework. You are properly attired. You have made an appointment and told the source how much time you need. Before you leave to meet your source, you may want to write down a list of questions to ask.

This reporter dresses to fit in with the marchers he is interviewing; he gains their confidence by being friendly and attentive.

They will guide you through the interview and prevent you from missing important topics altogether. The best way to encourage a spontaneous conversation is to have your questions prepared. You'll be more relaxed. Having questions prepared relieves you of the need to be mentally searching for the next question as the source is answering the last one. If you are trying to think of the next question, you will not be paying close attention to what is being said, and you might miss the most important part of the interview.

Researching Questions

Preparing the questions for an interview is hard work, even for veterans. If you are writing for your campus newspaper, seek suggestions from other staff members. You will find ideas in the newspaper's electronic database. If you anticipate a troublesome interview with the chancellor, you might want to seek advice from faculty members, too. What questions would they ask if they were you? Often, they have more background knowledge, or they might have heard some of the faculty talk around campus. Staff members are also valuable sources of information.

Although you may ask all of your prepared questions in some interviews, in most you probably will use only some of them. Still, you will have benefited from preparing the questions in two important ways. First, even when you don't use many, the work you did thinking of the questions helped prepare you for the interview. Second, sources who see that you have a prepared list often are impressed with your seriousness.

On the basis of the information you have gathered already, you know what you want to ask. Now you must be careful about how you ask the questions.

Phrasing Questions

A young monk who asked his superior if he could smoke while he prayed was rebuked sharply. A friend advised him to rephrase the question. "Ask him if you can pray while you smoke," he said. The young monk was discovering that how questions are structured often determines the answer. Journalists face the same challenge. Reporters have missed many stories because they didn't know how to ask their questions. Quantitative researchers have shown how only a slight wording change affects the results of a survey. If you want to know whether citizens favor a city plan to beautify the downtown area, you can ask the question in several ways:

- Do you favor the city council's plan to beautify the downtown area?
- The city council plans to spend $3 million beautifying the downtown area. Are you in favor of this?
- Do you think the downtown area needs physical changes?
- Which of the following actions do you favor?
  - Prohibiting all automobile traffic in an area bounded by Providence Road, Ash Street, College Avenue and Elm Street.
  - Having all the downtown storefronts remodeled to carry out a single theme and putting in brick streets, shrubbery and benches.
  - None of the above.

How you structure that question may affect the survey results by several percentage points. Similarly, how you ask questions in an interview may affect the response.

By the phrasing of the question, many reporters signal the response they expect or the prejudices they have. For instance, a reporter who says, "Don't you think that the city council should allocate more money to the parks and recreation department?" is not only asking a question but also influencing the source or betraying a bias. Another common way of asking a leading question is this: "Are you going to vote against this amendment like the other legislators I've talked to?" A neutral phrasing would be "Do you think the city council should allocate more money to the parks and recreation department?" To avoid leading or even irritating your source, ask neutral questions.

Also ask the interviewee one question at a time. Listen to journalists at press conferences jump up and ask two or three questions at a time. The source then chooses the one he or she wishes to answer and ignores the rest. That will often happen in one-on-one interviews, too.

In situations where you have to ask embarrassing or awkward questions, Jeff Truesdell of *People* magazine suggests demonstrating empathy. "Say, 'I'm sorry I have to ask this,' or 'I can't believe I'm asking this but here goes,' or 'My editors will want to know'—editors in absentia make for great fall guys—or 'Let me play devil's advocate here,'" Truesdell suggests. "Acknowledge that there are unpleasant questions, apologize for asking, and then ask."

Sometimes a reporter unwittingly blocks a response by the phrasing of the question. A reporter who was investigating possible job discrimination against women conducted several interviews before she told her city editor she didn't think the women with whom she talked were being frank with her. "When I ask them if they have ever been discriminated against, they always tell me no. But three times now during the course of the interviews, they have said things that indicate they have been. How do I get them to tell me about it?" she asked.

"Perhaps it's the way you are asking the question," the city editor replied. "When you ask the women whether they have ever been discriminated against, you are forcing them to answer yes or no. Don't be so blunt. Ask them if others with the same qualifications at work have advanced faster than they have. Ask if they are paid the same amount as men for the same work. Ask them what they think they would be doing today if they were male. Ask them if they know of any qualified women who were denied jobs."

The city editor was giving the reporter examples of both closed- and open-ended questions. Each has its specific strengths.

Open-Ended Questions

Open-ended questions allow the respondent some flexibility. Women may not respond frankly when asked whether they have ever been discriminated against. The question calls for a yes-no response. But an open-ended question such as "What would you be doing today if you were a man?" is not so personal. It does not sound as threatening to the respondent. In response to an open-ended question, the source often reveals more than he or she realizes or intends to.

A sportswriter who was interviewing a pro scout at a college football game wanted to know whom the scout was there to see. When the scout diplomatically declined to be specific, the reporter tried another approach. He asked a series of questions:

- "What kinds of qualities does a pro scout look for in an athlete?"
- "Do you think any of the players here today have those talents?"
- "Who would you put into that category?"

The reporter worked from the general to the specific until he had the information he wanted. Open-ended questions are less direct and less threatening. They are more exploratory and more flexible. However, if you want to know a person's biographical data, don't ask, "Can you tell me about yourself?" That question is too general. Phrase the questions to get information about specific times and places.

Closed-Ended Questions

Eventually, the reporter needs to close in on a subject, to pin down details, to get the respondent to be specific. **Closed-ended questions** are designed to elicit specific responses.

Instead of asking the mayor, "What did you think of the conference in Washington, D.C.?" you ask, "What did you learn in the session 'Funds You May Not Know Are Available'?" Instead of asking a previous employee to appraise the chancellor-designate's managerial abilities, you ask, "How well does she listen to the people who work for her?" "Do the people who work for her have specific job duties?" "Does she explain her decisions?"

A vague question invites a vague answer. By asking a specific question, you are more likely to get a specific answer. You are also communicating to your source that you have done your homework and that you are looking for precise details.

Knowing exactly when to ask a closed-ended question or when to be less specific is not something you can plan ahead of time. The type of information you are seeking and the chemistry between you and the source are the determining factors. You must make on-the-spot decisions. The important thing is to keep rephrasing the question until the source answers it adequately. Sportswriter Gary Smith wrote in *Intimate Journalism*, "A lot of my reporting comes from asking a question three different ways. Sometimes the third go at it is what produces the nugget, but even if the answers aren't wonderful or the quotes usable, they can still confirm or correct my impressions."

Every reporter seeks anecdotes, and closed-ended questions help elicit them. "What is the funniest thing you've ever done?" "The weirdest?" "What's the saddest thing that ever happened to you?" When the source talks in generalities, ask a closed-ended question to get to specifics. "You say Mary is a practical joker. Can you think of an example of a practical joke she played on someone?" The answers to these types of questions yield the anecdotal nuggets that make your story readable.

Closed-Ended Questions	Open-Ended Questions
Do you like the proposal?	What are the strengths of the proposal? What are the weaknesses?
Did you have trouble coping when your child was in the car accident?	How did you cope after your child was in the car accident? Why did you attend counseling sessions?
Did you keep your promises to diet today?	What did you eat today?
Did you give the theater teacher permission to stage that play?	What did you tell the theater teacher when she asked if they could perform the play?
Do you use iChat in your work?	How do you use iChat in your work?

ESTABLISHING RAPPORT

The most basic requirement of any successful interview is a reasonable degree of trust between reporter and source. Usually, as a reporter you have to earn that trust. Wright Thompson, who worked for *The Kansas City Star* when he wrote this story and now works for ESPN, tells about the time he wanted to do a story about a former college football player named Ernest Blackwell, who had gone on a rampage in his neighborhood, shot a child and almost kicked another to death. He'd collapsed on a police gurney afterward and died en route to the hospital. No one could figure out what had happened. Media outlet after media outlet approached the family. All got turned down. Thompson tried a unique approach:

> When I called, I had a line. I told them I was going to talk to the cops and was going to do a story about Ernest. The police, I told them, would give me more than enough detail about the last five minutes of Ernest's life. Then I said, "I think there's a lot more to his life than the last five minutes. I think he deserves to be remembered for how he lived and not just how he died."

Thompson's reasoning won him the interview. His conclusion: "Have a plan. You must give someone a reason why it's better if they talk to you than if they don't."

Because he earned the trust of the family, he was able to develop the insights that allowed him to write this:

> Those who knew him wonder how Blackwell arrived on that day with so much rage in his heart, so much bad intent. Truth is, none of them could peer into the man's soul and see the hate that grew until it reached the breaking point.
>
> On Aug. 11, 2004, Blackwell could take no more.
>
> "Lord, why didn't I see the signs?" says his aunt Joyce Strong, who mostly raised Blackwell. "Why didn't I see he was reaching out for help? He must have been a ticking time bomb waiting to go off."

That's the payoff on the investment in building trust.

You probably won't have many assignments that difficult. It always helps, though, to have a plan. It also helps to have the honesty and empathy that lead strangers to be honest with you. Act like a human being.

Rapport—the relationship between the reporter and the source—is crucial to the success of the interview. The relationship is sometimes relaxed, sometimes strained. Often it is somewhere in between. The type of relationship you try to establish with your source is determined by the kind of story you are doing. Several approaches are possible.

Establishing rapport with interview subjects helps a reporter get better story information.

Interview Approaches

For most news stories and personality profiles, the reporter gains a great deal if the subject is at ease. Often that can be accomplished by starting with small talk. Ask about a trophy, the plants or an engraved pen. Bring up something humorous you have found during your research. Ask about something you know the source will want to talk about. In other interviews, if you think the subject might be skeptical about your knowledge of the field, open with a question that demonstrates your knowledge.

Rapport also depends on where you conduct the interview. Many people, especially those unaccustomed to being interviewed, feel more comfortable in their workplace. Go to them. Talk to the businessperson in the office, to the athlete in the locker room, to the conductor in the concert hall. In some cases, though, you may get a better interview elsewhere if the source cannot relax at the workplace or is frequently interrupted. Reporters have talked to politicians during car rides between campaign appearances. They've gone sailing with businesspeople and hunting with athletes. One student reporter doing a feature on a police chief spent a weekend with the chief, who was painting his home. To do a profile, which requires more than one interview, vary the location. New surroundings can make a difference.

> **"** I need to create what I call accelerated intimacy. We can't write the beautiful narrative stories that we all dream of unless we can get some things from the mouths of our sources. They must be comfortable enough to tell us *anything*. In journalism school, no one called the interactions between journalists and sources *relationships*, but that's what they are. **"**
>
> — Isabel Wilkerson, winner of the Pulitzer Prize in Journalism

There are times when the reporter would rather have the source edgy, nervous or even scared. When you are doing an investigation, you may want the key characters to feel uneasy. You may pretend you know more than you actually do. You want them to know that the material you have is substantive and serious. Seymour Hersh, a Pulitzer Prize-winning investigative reporter, uses this tactic. *Time* magazine once quoted a government official commenting on Hersh: "He wheedles, cajoles, pleads, threatens, asks a leading question, uses little tidbits as if he knew the whole story. When he finishes you feel like a wet rag."

In some cases, however, it is better even in an investigation to take a low-key approach. Let the source relax. Talk around the subject but gradually bring the discussion to the key issues. The surprise element may work in your favor.

So may the sympathetic approach. When the source is speaking, you may nod or punctuate the source's responses with comments such as "That's interesting." Sources who think you are sympathetic are more likely to volunteer information. Researchers have found, for instance, that a simple "mm-hmmm" affects the length of the answer interviewers get.

Other Practical Considerations

Where you sit in relation to the person you are interviewing can be important. Unless you deliberately are trying to make those interviewed feel uncomfortable, do not sit directly in front of them. Permit your sources to establish eye contact if and when they wish.

Some people are even more disturbed by the way a reporter takes notes. A digital recorder ensures accuracy of quotes, but it makes many speakers self-conscious or nervous. If you have permission to use a recorder, place it in an inconspicuous spot and ignore it except to make sure it is working properly. Writing notes longhand may interfere with your ability to digest what is being said. But not taking any notes at all is risky. Only a few reporters can leave an interview and accurately write down what was said. Certainly no one can do it and reproduce direct quotes verbatim. You should learn shorthand or develop a note-taking system of your own.

Be sure that you address the people you are interviewing correctly. If you are unsure how they should be addressed — Mrs., Miss, Ms., Dr., Professor — ask them.

If you are interviewing someone from a culture or race different from your own, recognize and avoid your own stereotypes. Perhaps you are uncomfortable in the presence of an Islamic woman wearing a veil when she attends school in the U.S. Instead of letting your feelings influence your actions, respect her beliefs. As a reporter, take pride in your ability to move among all cultures. This requires that you read about cultural differences. It might help you to know that Chinese are generally uncomfortable with too much eye contact. Many Arabs consider it improper for a man to look into a woman's eyes. No one knows everything about every culture, but you can prepare for some situations, and you can also recognize what you don't know. These days, it is easy enough to do a quick search about specific cultural differences before you conduct an interview.

ENSURING ACCURACY AND FAIRNESS

Accuracy is a major problem in all interviews. Both the question and the answer may be ambiguous. You may not understand what is said. You may write it down incorrectly. You may not remember the context of the remarks. Your biases may interfere with the message.

Knowing the background of your sources, having a comfortable relationship with them and keeping good notes are important elements of accuracy. All those were missing when a journalism student, two weeks into an internship at a major daily, interviewed the public information officer for a sheriff's department about criminal activity in and around a shelter for battered women. The reporter had never met the source. She took notes on her phone interview with the deputy and others in whatever notebook happened to be nearby. She didn't record the time, date or even the source. There were no notes showing context, just fragments of quotes, scrawled in nearly illegible handwriting.

After the story was published, the developer of the shelter sued. Questioned by attorneys, the deputy swore that the reporter misunderstood him and used some of his comments out of context. In several cases, he contended, she completed her fragmentary notes by putting her own words in his mouth. He testified that most reporters come to see him to get acquainted. Many call back to check his quotes on sensitive or complex stories. She did neither.

When the court ordered the reporter to produce and explain her notes, she had trouble reconstructing them. She had to admit on several occasions that she wasn't sure what the fragments meant.

The accuracy of your story is only as good as your notes. David Finkel, whose story on a family's TV-watching habits became a Pulitzer Prize finalist, took extra steps to be certain his material was accurate. Observing what his subjects were watching, he obtained transcripts of the shows so he could quote accurately from them. If he knew transcripts would not be available, he set his recorder near the TV to record the program.

When you finish your interview, go back over the key points in your notes to confirm them. Read back quotes to make sure that you have them right. Realize, too, that you will need to confirm some of the information you get from other, perhaps more authoritative, sources. And if your interview produces allegations against other people or organizations, you will need to talk to those named.

Some possibilities for making errors or introducing bias are unavoidable, but others are not. To ensure the most accurate and complete reporting possible, you should use all the techniques available to obtain a good interview, including observing and asking follow-up questions. Let's examine these and other techniques.

Reporters should do research after an interview to ascertain specific figures when a source provides an estimate. For example, if a restaurant owner says he runs one of 20 pizza parlors in town, check with the city business-license office to get the exact number.

Observing

Some reporters look but do not see. The detail they miss may be the difference between a routine story and one that is a delight to read. Your powers of observation may enable you to discover a story beyond your source's words. Is the subject nervous? What kinds of questions are striking home? The mayor may deny that he is going to fire the police chief, but if you notice the chief's personnel file sitting on an adjacent worktable, you may have reason to continue the investigation.

Wright Thompson says, "It's all about the scenes. Don't just ask questions. Be an observer." Like any good writer, he offers an example to show what he means:

> I was doing a story about former Heisman Trophy winner Eric Crouch. It was almost exactly one year since he'd won the trophy, and that year had been tough for him. He'd quit pro football and had been forced to ask some hard questions about his life. As we sat in an Omaha bar, a clip of him running the football came on the television. One of the women at the table said, "You're on TV, Eric." I remember he looked up at the screen and spat, "That's not me, man." Then he took a shot of liquor. No amount of interviewing could breathe life into the idea that he had changed like that scene.

Asking Follow-Up Questions

If you understand what the source is saying, you can ask meaningful follow-up questions. There is nothing worse than briefing your city editor on the interview and having the editor ask you, "Well, did you ask . . . ?" Having to say no is embarrassing.

Even if you go into an interview armed with a list of questions, the most important questions will probably be the ones you ask in response to an answer. A reporter who was doing a story on bidding procedures was interviewing the mayor. The reporter asked how bid specifications were written. In the course of his reply, the mayor mentioned that the president of a construction firm had assured him the last bid specifications were adequate. The alert reporter picked up on the statement:

> "When did you talk to him?"
> "About three weeks ago," the mayor said.
> "That's before the specifications were published, wasn't it?"
> "Yes, we asked him to look them over for us."
> "Did he find anything wrong with the way they were written?"
> "Oh, he changed a few minor things. Nothing important."
> "Did officials of any other construction firms see the bid specifications before they were advertised?"
> "No, he was the only one."

Gradually, on the basis of one offhand comment by the mayor, the reporter was able to piece together a solid story on the questionable relationship between the city and the construction firm.

There are three questions that are always useful. One is, "What did you mean by that?" The second is, "How do you know that?" and the last is, "Is there anything I haven't asked that I should?"

Other Techniques

Although most questions are designed to get information, some are asked as a delaying tactic. A reporter who is taking notes may fall behind. One good trick for catching up is just to say, "Hold on a second—let me get that" or "Say that again, please." Other questions are intended to encourage a longer response. "Go on with that" or "Tell me more about that" encourages the speaker to add more detail.

You don't have to be stalling for time to say you don't understand. Don't be embarrassed to admit you haven't grasped something. It is better to admit to one person you don't understand something than to advertise your ignorance in newsprint or on the airwaves in front of thousands.

Another device for making the source talk on is not a question at all; it is a pause. You are signaling the source that you expect more. But the lack of a response from you is much more ambiguous than "Tell me more about that." It may indicate that you were skeptical of what was just said, that you didn't understand, that the answer was inadequate or several other possibilities. The source will be forced to react.

Many dull interviews become interesting after they end. There are two things you should always do when you finish your questions: Check key facts, figures and quotes, and then put away your pen but keep your ears open. You are not breaching any ethical rule if you continue to ask questions after you have put away your pen or turned off the recorder. That's when some sources loosen up.

Quickly review your notes and check facts, especially dates, numbers, quotes, spellings and titles. Besides helping you get it right, this shows the source you are careful. If necessary, arrange a time when you can call to check other parts of the story or clear up questions you may have as you are writing. Researchers have found that more than half of direct quotations are inaccurate, even when the interview is recorded. That reflects a sloppiness that is unacceptable. Make sure you are the exception.

As a matter of courtesy, tell the source when the story might appear. You may even offer to send along an extra copy of the article when it's completed.

⟪Today one has the impression that the interviewer is not listening to what you say, nor does he think it important, because he believes that the tape recorder hears everything. But he's wrong, it doesn't hear the beating of the heart, which is the most important part of the interview.⟫

— Gabriel García Márquez, Colombian writer and Nobel laureate

Suggested Readings

Harrington, Walt. *American Profiles: Somebodies and Nobodies Who Matter.* Columbia: University of Missouri Press, 1992. This book contains 15 excellent profiles and the author's explanation of how and why he does what he does.

Kramer, Mark, and Wendy Call, eds. *Telling True Stories.* New York: Plume, 2007. This book contains excellent advice, including how to prepare for and conduct interviews.

Malcolm, Janet. *The Journalist and the Murderer.* New York: Knopf, 1990. Using the Joe McGinnis-Jeffrey MacDonald case, the author accuses all journalists of being "confidence men" who betray their sources.

Paterno, Susan. "The Question Man." *American Journalism Review,* October 2000. http://ajr.org/Article.asp?id=676. The subject of this article, investigative journalist John Sawatsky, specializes in interviewing techniques, particularly in how to phrase questions.

Scanlan, Christopher, ed. *America's Best Newspaper Writing.* St. Petersburg, Fla.: Poynter Institute for Media Studies. Reprints of winners of American Society of News Editors Distinguished Writing Awards and interviews with the authors make this an invaluable resource. It is published annually.

Suggested Websites

www.poewar.com
The Writing Career Center offers advice on a variety of writers' concerns, including interviewing.

www.poynter.org/content/content_print.asp?id=120437
In this interview, *St. Petersburg Times* staff writer Lane DeGregory talks about her story on the city manager who announced he would undergo a sex-change operation. You can also link to the story from this address.

www.poynter.org/content/content_view.asp?id=60848
Bob Schieffer and four print journalists offer tips on how to interview.

Exercises

1. **Team project.** Your instructor will divide you into teams to work on questions in preparation for an interview with a high-ranking official on your campus, such as the provost or chancellor. Brainstorm a list of issues that could be addressed in an interview. Choose an issue. Then prepare three open-ended and three closed-ended questions. As a class, rate the issues the teams have chosen in terms of relevance, timeliness and interest. Evaluate the questions. Which are effective, and why?

2. Learn to gather background on your sources. Write a memo of up to two pages about your state's senior U.S. senator. Concentrate on those details that will allow you to focus on how the senator views the health care issue. Indicate the sources of your information. Do an Internet search on the senator.

3. List five open-ended questions you would ask the senator.
4. List five closed-ended questions you would ask.
5. Interview a student enrolled in your reporting class. Write a two- or three-page story focusing on one aspect of the student's life. Ask your classmate to read the story and to mark errors of fact and perception. The instructor will read your story and the critique.
6. Your instructor will give you a news item. Prepare a list of questions you would ask to do a follow-up interview. As each question is read aloud in class, cross it off your list. See if you can come up with the most original and appropriate questions.

Handling Quotations
and Attributions

5

It was just another Veterans Day celebration. The ceremony featured the usual songs and prayers and a major address. In addition, eight students read excerpts from their winning essays. Reporter Thomas Cullen stayed around to visit with 91-year-old World War II veteran Tony Dolahite, who had served in Austria, Germany and the Philippines.

Cullen listened to many of Dolahite's stories about the service before Dolahite told him about his greatest experience—meeting Gen. George S. Patton, commander of U.S. troops in North Africa, Sicily and Europe during the war.

Cullen wrote: "As he thought about the experience, tears welled up in his eyes. "'I'd go to hell with that man any day,' he said."

These words of Tony Dolahite's are a reporter's dream come true. They are also a perfect way to end a good story. And Cullen did just that in the story he wrote for the *Columbia Missourian.*

Direct **quotes**—the exact words that a source says or writes—add color and credibility to your story. By using a direct quote, Cullen put his readers directly in touch with the speaker in his story. Like a handwritten letter, direct quotes are personal. Quotation marks, which always enclose a direct quote, signal to the reader that something special is coming. Direct quotes provide a story with a change of pace, a breath of fresh air.

As Paula LaRoque, former writing coach and assistant managing editor of *The Dallas Morning News*, says, "The right quotes, carefully selected and presented, enliven and humanize a story and help make it clear, credible, immediate and dramatic. Yet many quotations in journalism are dull, repetitive, ill-phrased, ungrammatical, nonsensical, self-serving or just plain dumb."

Now that's a quotation worth quoting!

Not everything people say is worth quoting. You need to learn what to quote directly, when to use partial quotes and when to paraphrase. You also must learn how and how often to attribute quotations and other information. Remember, though, that attributing a remark or some information does not excuse you from a possible libel suit. And, of course, you want to be fair.

Being fair sometimes is difficult when sources do not want to be quoted. For that reason you also must learn how to deal with off-the-record quotes and background information.

WHAT TO QUOTE DIRECTLY

Crisp, succinct, meaningful quotes spice up any story. But you can overdo a good thing. You need direct quotes in your stories, but you also need to develop your skill in recognizing what is worth quoting. Let's look at the basic guidelines.

Unique Material

A source sometimes tells you information you would not get in any other way. When you can say, "Ah, I never heard *that* before," you can be quite sure your readers would like to know exactly what the speaker said. Sometimes it is something surprising, something neither you nor your readers would have expected that person to say.

When singer Dolly Parton was asked how she felt about dumb-blonde jokes, she replied: "I'm not offended at all because I know I'm not a dumb blonde. I also know I'm not a blonde."

Use Good Judgment in Selecting Quotes

Striking statements like Parton's should be quoted, but not always. The *Arizona Daily Star* did a profile of a chef who writes a weekly column. Describing his food philosophy, the chef said, "I have a food philosophy, but it's a kind of an angry one. I'd eat a baby if you cooked it right. Yeah, that's pretty much it."

The *Star*'s reader advocate wrote that at least a half dozen readers objected. Said one, "Shame on the chef for saying it, and shame on the *Star* for printing it."

Don't Use Direct Quotes for Straight Facts

There is no reason to place simple, factual material inside quotation marks. Here is an extract from a story about similarities in the careers of a father and son that needed no quotes at all:

> "My son was born on campus," says the elder Denney.
>
> "In fact, he was born in the same hospital that I met my wife," he says. Since that time, his son has earned his bachelor's degree "technically in agriculture with a major in biological science and conservation."

Although the quoted material is informative, it contains nothing particularly interesting, surprising, disturbing, new or even different.

Avoid quotes that provide statistics. You can usually make a clearer, more succinct presentation by paraphrasing and attributing the information to your source. Save quotes for reaction and interpretation.

Use Quotes That Move the Story Forward

A direct quotation should say something significant. Also, a direct quotation should not simply repeat what has been said indirectly. It should move the story forward. Here's a passage from a *USA Today* story about a proposed law that would bar health-insurance companies, employers and managed-care plans from discriminating against people because of their genetic makeup:

> Fear of insurance discrimination based on the results of genetic tests has been on the rise for years. "It stops many people cold from getting tested," says Karen Clarke, a genetics counselor at Johns Hopkins University.

The quotation is useful, it is informative, and it moves the story forward.

TIPS

Use direct quotes when

- Someone says something unique.

- Someone says something uniquely.

- Someone important says something important.

Consider Using Dialogue to Tell Part of the Story

Sometimes spoken material is unique not because of individual remarks that are surprising or new but because of extended dialogue that can tell the story more effectively than writers can in their own words. Dialogue is not the same as a quotation. A quotation comes from a source speaking to the reporter. **Dialogue** occurs when two or more sources are speaking to each other.

Here's an example of how dialogue can move the story along and "show" rather than "tell." The story is about the restoration of old cars. A father is passing on a rare technique to his son:

When the lead is smooth and the irregularities filled to his satisfaction, he reaches for his file.

"How long has it been since you've done this?" his son asks.

"It's been at least 20 years."

"How do you tin it so it won't melt and all run off on the floor?"

"Very carefully."

Before the lesson is finished, a customer and two other shop workers have joined the group watching Larry at work. This is a skill few people know.

"I don't like the way this lead melts," he says.

"That's what it does when there's not enough tin?" his son asks.

"Tin helps it stick."

"Why do you pull the file instead of pushing it?"

"So I can see better."

"I would already have the fiberglass on and be done by now."

"I know, but anything worthwhile you have to work for."

Notice the careful instruction and concerned advice from the father. His last sentence contains one of life's lessons: "Anything worthwhile you have to work for."

The Unique Expression

When you can say, "Ah, I've never heard it said *that way* before," you know you have something quotable. Be on the lookout for the clever, the colorful, the colloquial. For example, an elderly man talking about his organic garden said, "It's hard to tell people to watch what they eat. You eat health, you know."

A professor lecturing on graphic design said, "When you think it looks like a mistake, it is." The same professor once explained that elements in a design should not call attention to themselves: "You don't walk up to a beautiful painting in someone's home and say, 'That's a beautiful frame!'"

A computer trainer said to a reporter: "Teaching kids computers is like leading ducks to water. But teaching adults computers is like trying to teach chickens to swim."

Sometimes something said uniquely is a colloquialism. Colloquialisms and regional usages can add color and life to your copy. A person from Louisiana may say, "I was just fixing to leave when the phone rang." In parts of the South you're apt to hear, "I might could do that." A person from around Lancaster, Pa., might "make the light out" when turning off the lights. In some parts of the U.S., people "redd up" the dishes after a meal, meaning that they wash them and put them where they belong.

Important Quotes by Important People

If citizen Joe Smith says, "Something must be done about this teachers' strike," you may or may not consider it worth quoting. But if the mayor says the same words, many journalists would include the quote. Generally, reporters quote public officials or known personalities in their news stories (although not everything the famous say is worth quoting). Remember, prominence is an important property of news.

Quoting sources whom readers are likely to know lends authority, credibility and interest to your story. Presumably, a meteorologist knows something about the weather, a doctor about health, a chemistry professor about chemicals. However, it is unlikely that a television star knows a great deal about cameras, even if he or she makes commercials about cameras. Important, knowledgeable people are good sources for quotes even if what they say is not unique or said uniquely.

ACCURACY AND FAIRNESS IN DIRECT QUOTATIONS

The first obligation of any reporter is to be accurate. You must learn how to get the exact words of the source.

It's not easy.

Scribbled notes from interviews, press conferences and meetings are often difficult to decipher and interpret. A study by Adrienne Lehrer, now professor emerita of linguistics at the University of Arizona, shows only 13 of 98 quotations taken from Arizona newspapers proved to be verbatim when compared to recordings. Only twice, however, were the meanings of the nonverbatim quotes considered inaccurate. Your passion for accuracy should compel you to get and record the exact words of your sources. Only then can you decide which words to put between quotation marks.

> **"**I think of quotes as spices. Spices in themselves have no nutritional value. They make nutritious things taste better, but, like spices, quotes should be used sparingly.**"**
>
> — Isabel Wilkerson, Pulitzer Prize-winning reporter at *The Washington Post*, quoted in *A Writer's Coach*

Be sure to check the policy of your employer. Chances are, it has a policy similar to that of *The Washington Post*: "When we put a source's words inside quotation marks, those exact words should have been uttered in precisely that form."

Nevertheless, Deborah Howell, a former *Post* ombudsman, says: "Be honest with readers. That's what *Post* policy requires. But it doesn't mean reporters need to put every 'huh' or 'ya know' into a quote or to embarrass someone whose English skills are sparse."

Radio and television news editors can cut in and out of quotes, and they can certainly insert them out of context. Doing so is not just inaccurate because it distorts the meaning of what the source has said; it is also unethical.

Verification

When someone important says something important but perhaps false, putting the material in quotes does not relieve you of the responsibility for the inaccura-

Although quotes from experts and public figures are generally used to strengthen a story's authority, quotes from ordinary citizens with unique experience in a newsworthy event may also add credibility.

cies. Citizens, officials and candidates for office often say things that may be partially true or altogether untrue and perhaps even libelous. (See Chapter 21 for more on libel.) Quotations need verification, like any other information you gather.

In the interest of balance, fairness and objectivity, many papers leave out, correct or point out the errors and inconsistencies in quotations. They do this in the article itself or in an accompanying story.

If candidate Joe Harkness says that his opponent, Jim McGown, is a member of the Ku Klux Klan, you should check before you print the charge. Good reporters don't stop looking and checking just because someone gives them some information. Look for yourself. Prisoners may have an altogether different account of a riot from the one the prison officials give you. Your story will not be complete unless you talk to all sides.

Quoting from E-mail, the Internet and Chat Rooms

When you quote from e-mail that you have received personally, you can usually be sure that the sender has written the intended words. If you have doubts, be sure to check with the writer. It's also a good idea to let the readers know that you obtained the quote through e-mail and had no personal contact with the source.

If you quote someone from the Internet, you need to be much more careful. Try to verify the quote with the source, but if you can't do that, at least be sure to tell readers that the quote comes from the Internet, and then cite the URL (Internet address).

Reading what people are saying in chat rooms and blogs can be a useful thing for a reporter to do. However, quoting what people write in these forums is unwise because some statements might be unverified and even libelous. Nevertheless, if you have verified the information—and identified the person who is saying it—and if you specifically state where you obtained the information, you might on occasion use such a quote. Identifying the person might well be impossible because some people use screen names, aliases and pseudonyms on the Internet.

> **"**When you see yourself quoted in print and you're sorry you said it, it suddenly becomes a misquotation.**"**
>
> — Dr. Laurence J. Peter, author of *Peter's Quotations* and *The Peter Principle*

Using Someone Else's Direct Quotations

If you use a direct quotation that you did not personally get from a source, always indicate the source of the quote. Jessica Heslam wrote on BostonHerald.com that a *Boston Herald* review of WBZ-TV political analyst Jon Keller's book *The Bluest State* revealed "almost three dozen instances of direct quotes and other material lifted from numerous newspaper articles without any attribution."

Don't be tempted to use direct quotes you find in news releases. Don't be lazy; get your own quotes. Sources are much less likely to say things that are self-serving if they are talking to a journalist rather than a public relations person.

CAUTIONS IN USING DIRECT QUOTATIONS

By now you realize that although you should use direct quotations, they present many challenges and problems. Though there is no set number you should strive to include, a story with no quotes often lacks life and substance. Still, including lengthy quotes indiscriminately is a sign that you haven't really digested the material for your audience. Instead of quoting someone at length, look for the effective kernel within a long quotation. Let's look at some of the challenges to getting that "kernel."

Paraphrasing Quotes

While some quotations need verification, others need clarification. Do not quote someone unless you are sure of what that person means. The reason (or excuse) "But that's what the man said" is not sufficient to use the quote. It is much better to skip a quotation altogether than to confuse the reader.

The best way to avoid confusing and unclear quotes or needlessly long and wordy quotes is to paraphrase. In a **paraphrase** you use your own words to communicate the speaker's meaning. As a reporter you must have confidence that you will sometimes be able to convey that meaning in fewer words and in better language than the speaker did. Digesting, condensing and clarifying quotes take more effort than simply repeating them word for word. Here is a quote that could be cut drastically:

> "When I first started singing lessons I assumed I would be a public school teacher and maybe, if I was good enough, a voice teacher," he said. "When I graduated from the university, I still thought I would be a teacher, and I wanted to teach."

A paraphrase conveys the meaning more succinctly:

> When he first started singing lessons, and even after he graduated from the university, he wanted to be a public school voice teacher.

Using Partial Quotes

It is much better to paraphrase or to use full quotes than to use fragmentary or partial quotes. Partial quotes often make for choppy, interrupted sentences. Some editors would have you avoid these "orphan quotes" almost altogether. Here is an example of the overuse of partial quotes:

> The mayor said citizens should "turn off" unnecessary lights and "turn down" thermostats "to 65 degrees."

The sentence would be better with no quotation marks at all. Taking out the quotation marks would turn this sentence into an indirect quotation. In an indirect quotation, the reporter uses words and phrases of the speaker's language and includes an attribution but doesn't use quotation marks. Indirect quotations need to meet the same test for accuracy that direct quotations require.

If a particular phrase has special significance or meaning, a partial quote may be justifiable. Sometimes you may want to put a word or phrase in quotation marks to indicate that this was precisely what the speaker said. Look at this use of a one-word quote in a story about genetic engineering in *The Atlantic Monthly*:

> By all but eliminating agricultural erosion and runoff—
> so Brian Noyes, the local conservation-district manager, told me—continuous no-till could "revolutionize"
> the area's water quality.

The writer thought it important that readers know that "revolutionize" was not his word but the word of Brian Noyes. And he was right. "Revolutionize" is a strong word.

When you do use partial quotes, do not put quotation marks around something the speaker could not have said. Suppose a speaker told a student audience at a university, "I am pleased and thrilled with your attendance here tonight." It would be incorrect to write:

The speaker said she was "pleased and thrilled with the students' attendance."

Partial quotes often contain an ellipsis (three spaced periods) to tell the reader that some of the words of the quote are missing. For example:

"I have come here tonight . . . and I have crossed state lines . . . to conspire against the government."

This practice at times may be justifiable, but you should not keep the reader guessing about what is missing. Sometimes the speaker's actual meaning is distorted when certain words are dropped. If a critic writes about a three-act play, "A great hit—except for the first three acts," an ad that picks up only the first part of that quote is guilty of misrepresentation. A journalist who uses the technique to distort the message is no less guilty.

Capturing Dialect or Accent

Using colorful or colloquial expressions helps the writer capture a person in a particular environment. The same can be true when you write the way people talk:

"Are you gonna go?" he asked.
"No, I'm not goin'," she replied.

In everyday speech hardly anyone enunciates perfectly. To do so would sound affected. In fiction, therefore, it is common to use spellings that match speech. But when conversation is written down in newspaper reporting, readers expect correct, full spellings. Not only is correct spelling easier to read, it is also less difficult to write. Capturing dialect consistently is difficult, as these passages from a story about a Hollywood actress illustrate:

"Boy, it's hot out theah," she started. "I could sure use a nice cold beer. How about it, uh? Wanta go get a couple beers?"

If she said "theah," wouldn't she also say "beeah"? Perhaps she said, "How 'bout it, uh?" And if she said "wanta," maybe she also said "geta."

In another passage, the writer has the actress speaking "straight" English:

"Would you believe I used to dress like that all the time? Dates didn't want to be seen with me. I was always being asked to change clothes before going out."

It is unlikely she is that inconsistent in her speech.

The writer of this story tried to show us something of the character of the actress. If he wanted to convey her speech patterns, he should have either been consistent or simply reported that she talked the same off the set as on it.

Sometimes when a newspaper attempts to quote someone saying something uniquely, it betrays a bias. A Southern politician is more likely to have his quote spelled phonetically than an Eastern politician who says "idee-er" and "Cuber."

However, you should not make everyone's speech the same. Barbara King Lord, former director of editorial training for the Associated Press, laments "our frequent inability to write other than insipid speech" and "our tendency to homogenize the day-to-day speech patterns of the heterogeneous people we write about." She acknowledges that writers worry about exposing to ridicule the immigrant's halting or perhaps unconventional speech while the stockbroker's speech appears flawless.

> **The surest way to make a monkey of a man is to quote him.**
>
> — Robert Benchley, humorist

Lord calls the argument specious. Of course, people should not be exposed to ridicule through their speech. "The point here," she says, "is simply that when the writer's intention in writing dialects, quaint expressions, nonconventional grammar, flowery or showy speech, or the Queen's English is to make a person human, that intention is not only acceptable, it's desirable."

The only way you can make people human is to listen to them. Lord says reporters and writers usually hear but rarely listen. She advises reporters to "listen for expressions, turns of phrase, idiosyncratic talk," and to work these into their stories.

J. R. Moehringer of the *Los Angeles Times* did this in his Pulitzer Prize-winning article:

> "No white man gonna tell me not to march," Lucy says,
> jutting her chin. "Only make me march harder."

Here the actual speech makes the speaker's determination and passion all the more evident.

You must be especially careful when quoting people for whom English is a second language. Nearly any attempt to quote them exactly will be looked upon as making fun of their English. Better that you paraphrase their comments, or as some would advise, make them speak good English. Once again, however, if you have audio from baseball star Albert Pujols on your website and have the same quotes in perfect, fluent English in the written text, many would see that as a serious problem. Others would say that you are hurting the uniqueness and character of the great slugger, who was born in the Dominican Republic. These problems are as old as radio and television, but convergence of the media has increased their frequency.

Mix-Matching Questions and Answers

Writers often agonize over whether they may use responses to one question to answer another question. Later on in an interview or in a trial, a person may say something that answers better or more fully a question posed earlier.

The primary questions you must ask yourself are: Am I being fair? Am I distorting the meaning? Am I putting quotes together that change what the speaker intended to say? Sentences that logically go together, that logically enhance one another and that are clearly sequential can and often should be placed together.

Correcting Grammar in Quotes

Perhaps the most perplexing problem tied to the proper handling of direct quotations is this: When do you, or should you, correct grammatical errors in a direct quotation? Should you expect people in news conferences or during informal interviews to speak perfect English?

The Case for Correcting Grammar

Although quotation marks mean you are capturing the exact language of a speaker, it is accepted practice at many newspapers to correct mistakes in grammar and to convey a person's remarks in complete sentences. None of us regularly speaks in perfect, grammatical sentences. But if we were writing down our remarks, presumably we would write in grammatically correct English.

Reporters and editors differ widely on when or even whether to correct quotes. A reporter for the *Rocky Mountain News* quoted an attorney as saying, "Her and John gave each other things they needed and couldn't get anyplace else." The reporter said the quote was accurate but, on second thought, said it might have been better to correct the grammar to "She and John" in the written account.

The Case Against Correcting Grammar

You are most likely to find grammatical errors in direct quotations in the sports pages of daily newspapers. Nevertheless, often you can read an entire newspaper sports section and not find a single grammatical error in a direct quote.

Deborah Howell, former ombudsman for *The Washington Post*, writes about the reporting of two sports writers at the *Post*. One corrected the speaker's grammar; the other did not.

Quoting Clinton Portis from the Washington Redskins, Howard Bryant wrote: "I don't know how anybody feels. I don't know how anybody's thinking. I don't know what anyone else is going through. The only thing I know is what's going on in Clinton Portis's life." Mike Wise quoted Portis in a column: "I don't know how nobody feel, I don't know what nobody think, I don't know what nobody doing, the only thing I know is what's going on in Clinton Portis's life."

Then Howell writes: "To make matters worse, Wise's verbatim quote, caught on tape, was changed to agree with Bryant's."

Bryant, an African-American now working with ESPN, does not agree with the *Post*'s policy of not changing quotes, a policy, which, by the way, he said he never heard of. But Bryant did say, "I am totally convinced—along racial, class and cultural lines—that when it comes to white players from the South, reporters instinctively clean up their language."

Most papers have no written policy on correcting grammatical errors in direct quotations. Because so many variables are involved, these matters are handled on a case-by-case basis. Some argue you should sacrifice a bit of accuracy in the interest of promoting proper English — except for elected officials and public figures.

At times it may be necessary to illustrate a person's flawed use of language. In some cases, you may wish to use "sic" in brackets to note the error, misuse or peculiarity of the quotation. "Sic," Latin for "thus," indicates that a statement was originally spoken or written exactly as quoted. It is particularly important to use "sic" for improper or unusual use of language when you are quoting a written source. However, *The Associated Press Stylebook* says not to use "sic" unless "it is in the matter being quoted." Most book editors avoid it also; some find it appropriate only when confusion may result.

On the subject of correcting grammar in direct quotations, read what AP says under "Quotations in the News":

> Never alter quotations even to correct minor grammatical errors or word usage. Casual minor tongue slips may be removed by using ellipses but even that should be done with extreme caution. If there is a question about a quote, either don't use it or ask the speaker to clarify.

In this age of convergence, print reporters may also have shot video, and even if they haven't, they know someone has. Correcting quotations is even more unwise for radio and television reporters. Writers and editors for print should remember that the quotation they use may have been heard by millions of people on radio or television. Changing the quote even slightly might make viewers and listeners question the credibility of print reports. Readers might also ask why print writers feel the need to act as press agents who strive to make their subjects look good.

That applies to celebrities of all kinds (actors, sports figures), but it might also apply to political candidates and elected officials. At least, some argue, news agencies should have some consistency. If a reporter quotes a farmer using incorrect grammar, then should the same be done for the mayor or for a college professor?

Removing Redundancies

Another question you must deal with as a reporter is whether to remove redundancies and other irrelevant material by using ellipses. Again, there is no agreement in the industry. For most reporters and editors, the answer to the problem of correcting quotes is to take out the quotation marks and to paraphrase. Sometimes you can just remove a phrase or a sentence. However, when you do that, you sometimes lose a lot. The value of quotes often lies in their richness and uniqueness.

When the *Columbia Missourian* quoted University of Missouri basketball star Keon Lawrence after a winning game, it dropped a sentence:

> "'That felt good,' Keon Lawrence said. 'I look forward
> to doing that again.'"

The *Columbia Daily Tribune* wrote it this way:

> "'Oh, that felt good,' Lawrence said a few minutes after the game that hardly anyone thought the Tigers could win. 'I didn't never do that. I look forward to doing that again.'"

Which version do you like better? Which version would you have written?

Deleting Obscenity, Profanity and Vulgarity

Many news organizations never allow some things people say to be printed or broadcast—even if they are said uniquely. Obscenities (words usually referring to sexual parts or functions), profanities (words used irreverently to refer to a deity or to beings people regard as divine) and vulgarities (words referring to excretory matters) are usually deleted or bleeped unless they are essential to the story. Even at major newspapers, policy often demands that an obscenity, for example, be used only with the approval of a top editor.

Of course, there are legitimate reasons to use proper sex-related terms in health stories and in some crime stories, including child molestation stories.

News stories about sexual assaults or accusations sometimes contain words such as these, especially if those involved are noted celebrities or politicians.

Obviously, words such as "God" and "Jesus Christ" used in discussions of religion have always been acceptable to most people.

Nevertheless, the rules are different for what some call "swear" words in direct quotation. Some papers follow *The Associated Press Stylebook* rule: "If a full quote that contains an obscenity, profanity or vulgarity cannot be dropped but there is no compelling reason for the offensive language, replace the letters of the offensive word with hyphens, using only an initial letter."

News is likely to reflect the sensibilities of its audience. Like it or not, language that was once considered vulgar in polite society is now tolerated more widely.

In broadcasting, of course, the Federal Communications Commission, which regulates the broadcast industry, can still fine a broadcaster or suspend a license for indecency. Though that's unlikely, audiences are quick to let a station know that it has gone too far.

At times you may wish to use vulgarities to show the intensity of someone's anger, terror, frustration or bitterness. Few inside the news media condone the casual, gratuitous use of vulgarities, however.

Readers and listeners don't condone it either.

Avoiding Made-Up Quotes

Fabricating a direct quote, even from general things that a source has said or from what the source might say if given the chance, is never a good idea. Even seasoned reporters are sometimes tempted to put quotation marks around words that their sources "meant to say," or to clarify or simplify a quote. The journalist reasons that it's more important to have a clear and concise quote for the reader than to be a slave to the verbose and unclear words of the source. That's bad reasoning. It's better to paraphrase.

An even worse idea is fabricating a quote that makes a source look bad or that is defamatory or perhaps even libelous. Doing so can result in a lawsuit. In 1991, in Masson v. Malcolm, the Supreme Court ruled that suits regarding quotations can proceed to trial if the altered quote "results in a material change in the meaning conveyed by the statement."

Libel or no libel, your credibility as a reporter demands that you be scrupulously exact when you place people's words inside quotation marks. Again, when in doubt, paraphrase.

Practicing Prepublication Review

A decade ago, you would not have had a city editor tell you to check the accuracy of your direct quotations with your source. Today, it is standard practice on many newspapers. Steve Weinberg, a former Missouri School of Journalism professor and former head of the Investigative Reporters and Editors, calls it PPR—prepublication review.

Weinberg states candidly that it is not sensitivity to the feelings of his sources that is his primary motivator for practicing PPR. Rather, he insists that prepublication review loosens the tongues of tight-lipped sources and gets them on the record for making their statements. Prepublication review extends also to checking the facts. Professional journalists insist it does not make them feel compromised or make them surrender control over their stories.

Getting good quotes in a television interview takes skill and practice.

Journalist Philip Weiss offers another reason why more journalists are practicing prepublication review—reporters are often the subjects of stories. "They have had a taste of their own medicine and they don't like it."

Another reason for prepublication review is that it serves as a defense against libel. Jurors are less likely to find "reckless disregard for the truth" in an article that the source reviewed.

But what happens when sources want to change a quote? Weinberg says he makes it clear that the source is checking only for accuracy. He will consider comments about interpretation, phrasing or tone, but he retains the right to change or not change the quotes.

And what happens if someone denies saying something that is in a direct quote? That possibility is why, Weinberg says, you need to have good notes, even if they are in shorthand. Having the interview on tape is even better.

You need to know the policy of your news organization, and someday you may want to help develop a policy that not only allows but also demands prepublication review of the facts and quotations in a story.

ATTRIBUTING DIRECT AND INDIRECT QUOTES

Now that you've learned some of the complexities of using quotations, let's take a look at when and how to attribute them to a source. Figure 5.1, which shows annotated excerpts from a story, may also provide some insight into using quotations and attributions.

When to Attribute

Attribution involves giving the name of, and sometimes other identifying information about, the source of a direct quotation, an indirect quotation or paraphrased material. You should almost always attribute direct quotes—with some exceptions. You would not, for example, attribute a quotation to a 7-year-old who witnessed a gang shooting. You may not wish to attribute a quote to someone who saw a homicide suspect with the victim. To do so in either case could put the source in danger.

You should have a good reason to allow an entire paragraph of direct quotations to stand without an attribution. However, if you are quoting from a speech, an interview or a press conference and only the speaker is mentioned in the story, it may be excessive to put an attribution in every paragraph.

Ordinarily you should attribute indirect quotes. You should usually have a source for the information you write, and when you do, attribute the information to that source. The source can be a person or a written document. However, there are exceptions.

If you are a witness to damages or injuries, do not name yourself as a source in the story. Attribute this information to the police or to other authorities. But if you are on the scene of an accident and can see that three people were involved, you do

Quotations and Attributions

A STIRRING IN ST. ALBANS

Emboldened by '08 Race to Roil Waters at Home

By Anne Barnard
The New York Times, Sept. 4, 2009

Note the quote within the quote, important because these are the words of Dr. Martin Luther King Jr.

Now he [Donald Whitehead] pushed Mr. Simon hard. "He read to me about **'the fierce urgency of now,'**" Mr. Simon **recalled**. Mr. Obama too had quoted the phrase of Dr. King.

The attribution "recalled" is more descriptive here than "said."

The final sentence of this quote gives a unique thought that's uniquely expressed.

Mr. Whitehead recalls saying, "If they could tell you to sit down for four years and be quiet, then you're finished. **If you're not a warrior at 27, when are you going to be a warrior?**"

The attribution "says" is used in both the indirect and the direct quotes. Note that the two quotes are in separate sentences.

The word "toxic" is in quotation marks to indicate that this strong word was spoken by Mr. Simon.

Mr. Simon would not budge. He **says** he never feared retaliation, but thought running [against incumbent Leroy Comrie] would be **"toxic"** and divisive and could deprive the district of an effective legislator. "I put my community first," he **says**.

Again, a well-expressed thought is worthy of quote marks.

Mr. Whitehead reminded him that he had nothing against Mr. Comrie, saying, **"It's not the individual, it's the principle."**

In February, City Comptroller William C. Thompson Jr., running for mayor, spoke in the Whiteheads' basement. The volunteers noted their new clout, and the visit attracted newcomers. One was Clyde Vanel, 35. He wanted to run for City Council.

The lack of attribution tells readers that the reporter witnessed the events herself or that the information and ideas are common knowledge.

Mr. Vanel was the son of Haitian immigrants. A lawyer in Manhattan and an owner of an East Village restaurant, Permanent Brunch, he was not an obvious partner for Donald [Whitehead].

"A hard worker," the highest praise, needed quote marks.

But they talked for hours. Both saw a one-time chance to attract new voters, and Mr. Vanel won Mr. Whitehead's highest praise: **"A hard worker."** . . .

There is no attribution here, and none is necessary. It's clear Mr. Whitehead said it.

This unique quote is rich and colorful. The simile is very expressive.

"It's like if you're sitting on a nail," said Ronald Summers Sr., a transit employee and an Obama volunteer. **"You see an opportunity to get up off that nail, and someone says, I want you to sit back down and wait four years."** . . .

A strong quote is a good way to end. The quote answers the "what's next?" in the story.

The next day, he [Whitehead] **called** Mr. Vanel and said, "Look, let's start work."

"Called" is in the past tense, so "said" must also be in the past tense.

Figure 5.1

In this excerpt from the final paragraphs of a story about local politics in Queens, N.Y., after the election of President Barack Obama, the reporter tells how one activist, Donald Whitehead, encouraged first Brian Simon and then Clyde Vanel to run for City Council.

TIPS

You need not attribute information to a source if you are a witness or if the information:

- Is a matter of public record.

- Is generally known.

- Is available from several sources.

- Is easily verifiable.

- Makes no assumptions.

- Contains no opinions.

- Is noncontroversial.

not have to write, "'Three people were involved in the accident,' Officer Osbord said." If you are unsure of the information or if there are conclusions or generalities involved, your editor probably will want you to attribute the information to an official or a witness. Avoid, however, attributing factual statements to "officials" or "authorities" or "sources." "Such constructions," writes journalist Jack Hart, "suggest that we are controlled by form and that we have forgotten about function."

Hart pleads for common sense regarding attributions. "Let's save them for direct quotations or paraphrased quotes laced with opinion," he writes. "Or for assertions likely to be especially sensitive. Or controversial." He says we should attribute only "if it matters."

This is good advice for the veteran. Nevertheless, although it is possible to attribute too often and although you do not always need to attribute, when you have doubts, include an attribution.

That goes for attributing anonymous sources, too. Even though you should seldom use them, you must attribute them. Try to preserve your credibility by giving as much information as you can about the sources without revealing their names. For example, you may report "a source close to the chancellor said." For the second reference to the same source, use "the anonymous source said."

Whether we like them or not, anonymous sources are common, even in the best of newspapers. Here are a few paragraphs from a story in *The New York Times.* The attributions are highlighted in bold.

> Mrs. Clinton and Ambassador Eikenberry, **senior administration officials said**, wanted to prevent Mr. Karzai or his backers from pre-empting an outside investigation of allegations of irregularities in the Aug. 20 vote.
>
> "We realize that the allegations have reached such a level that we need to be very careful to allow the process to breathe," **said an administration official, who spoke on the condition of anonymity because he was not authorized to speak publicly on the matter**. "The message was, Let's make sure that the electoral bodies do their work, and do it rigorously."
>
> On Tuesday, the United Nations-backed **commission** that is the ultimate arbiter of the vote **said** it found "clear and convincing evidence of fraud" at several polling stations and ordered a partial recount.

Note in the first paragraph "senior administration officials said," and in the third paragraph, the "commission . . . said." In the second paragraph an individual spoke, and here the writer included the reason for anonymous attribution.

Sometimes, as in stories about crime victims, you may have to change someone's name and follow it with "not her real name" in parentheses to protect the source's privacy. At times there is no good reason to put people's lives or their children's in danger.

How to Attribute

In composition and creative writing classes, you may have been told to avoid repeating the same word. You probably picked up your thesaurus to look for a synonym for "to say," a colorless verb. Without much research you may have found

100 or more substitutes. None of them is wrong. Indeed, writers may search long for the exact word they need to convey a particular nuance of meaning. For example:

> The presidential candidate announced the choice of a running mate.

> The arrested man divulged the names of his accomplices.

> The judge pronounced sentence.

At other times, in the interest of precise and lively writing, you may write:

> "I'll get you for that," she whispered.

> "I object!" he shouted.

Nevertheless, reporters and editors prefer forms of "to say" in most instances, even if they are repeated throughout a story. And there are good reasons for this word choice. "Said" is unobtrusive. Rather than appearing tiresome and repetitious, it hides in the news columns and calls no attention to itself. "Said" is also neutral. It has no connotations. To use the word "said" is to be objective.

Some of the synonyms for "said" sound innocent enough—but be careful. If you report that a city official "claimed" or "maintained" or "contended," you are implying that you do not quite believe what the official said. The word "said" is the solution to your problem. If you have evidence that what the official is saying is incorrect, you should include the correct information or evidence in your story.

In some newspaper accounts of labor negotiations, company officials always "ask" and labor leaders always "demand." "Demanding" sounds harsh and unreasonable, but "asking" sounds calm and reasonable. A reporter who uses these words in this context is taking an editorial stand—consciously or unconsciously.

Other words you may be tempted to use as a substitute for "say" are simply unacceptable because they represent improper usage. For example:

> "You don't really mean that," he winked.
> "Of course I do," she grinned.
> "But what if someone heard you say that?" he frowned.
> "Oh, you are a fool," she laughed.

You cannot "wink" a word. Similarly, it is impossible to "grin," "frown" or "laugh" words. But you may want to say this:

> "Not again," he said, moaning.
> "I'm afraid so," she said with a grin.

This usage is correct, but often it is not necessary or even helpful to add words like "moaning" or phrases like "with a grin." Sometimes, though, such words and phrases are needed to convey the speaker's meaning.

Learning the correct words for attribution is the first step. Here are some other guidelines to follow when attributing information:

- **If a direct quote is more than one sentence long, place the attribution at the end of the first sentence.** For example:

"The car overturned at least three times," the police officer said. "None of the four passengers was hurt. Luckily, the car did not explode into flames."

That one attribution is adequate. It would be redundant to write:

"The car overturned at least three times," the police officer said. "None of the four passengers was hurt," he added. "Luckily, the car did not explode into flames," he continued.

Nor should you write:

"The car overturned at least three times. None of the four passengers was hurt. Luckily, the car did not explode into flames," the police officer said.

Although you should not keep the reader wondering who is being quoted, in most cases you should avoid placing the attribution at the beginning of a quote. Do not write:

The police officer said: "The car overturned at least three times. None of the four passengers was hurt. Luckily, the car did not explode into flames."

Place the attribution after the first sentence of the quotation to make the copy flow better:

"The car overturned at least three times," the police officer said. "None of the four passengers was hurt. Luckily the car did not explode into flames."

However, if direct quotes from two different speakers follow one another, you should start the second with the attribution to avoid confusion:

"The driver must not have seen the curve," an eyewitness said. "Once the car left the road, all I saw was a cloud of dust."
    The police officer said: "The car overturned at least three times. None of the four passengers was hurt. Luckily, the car did not explode into flames."

Notice that when an attribution precedes a direct quotation that is more than one sentence long, wire service style requires that a colon follow the attribution.

- **Separate partial quotes and complete quotes.** Avoid constructions like this one:

The mayor said the time had come "to turn off some lights. We all must do something to conserve electricity."

He Said, She Said—Punctuating Direct Quotations

"Always put the comma inside quotation marks," she said. Then she added, "The same goes for the period."

"Does the same rule apply for the question mark?" he asked.

"Only if the entire statement is a question," she replied, "and never add a comma after a question mark. Also, be sure to lowercase the first word of a continuing quote that follows an attribution and a comma.

"However, you must capitalize the first word of a new sentence after an attribution," she continued. "Do not forget to open and close the sentence with quotation marks."

"Why are there no quotation marks after the word 'comma' at the end of the third paragraph?" he asked.

"Because the same person is speaking at the beginning of the next paragraph," she said. "Notice that the new paragraph does open with quotation marks. Note, too, that a quote inside a quotation needs single quotation marks, as around the word 'comma' in the paragraph above."

The correct form is to separate partial quotes and complete quotes:

The time has come "to turn off some lights," the mayor said. "We all must do something to conserve electricity."

- **The first time you attribute a direct or an indirect quote, identify the speaker fully.** How fully depends on how well the speaker is known to the readers. In Springfield, Ill., it is sufficient to identify the mayor simply as Mayor Tim Davlin. But if a story in the *Chicago Tribune* refers to the mayor of Springfield, the first reference should be "Tim Davlin, mayor of Springfield" —unless, of course, the dateline for the story is Springfield.

- **Attribute direct quotes to only one person.** For example, don't do the following:

"Flames were shooting out everywhere," witnesses said.

If indeed any witnesses made statements like this, all you have to do is eliminate the quotation marks to turn this into an indirect quotation. For example:

Several witnesses said that flames were shooting out everywhere.

- **Do not make up a source. Never attribute a statement to "a witness" unless your source is indeed that witness.** At times you may ask a witness to confirm what you have seen, but never invent quotes for anonymous witnesses. Inventing witnesses and making up quotes is dishonest, inaccurate and inexcusable.

ON THE JOB

Off the Record

T. J. Quinn spent 16 years as a news and sports writer — eight at the New York *Daily News* — before moving to ESPN in 2007. As a reporter for the network's investigative/enterprise unit, most of his work is "cross-platform," with versions of the same stories appearing on television, ESPN.com and ESPN radio. His long-form stories appear primarily on the show "Outside the Lines," for which he is a backup anchor. Quinn's work also appears on "SportsCenter" and other ESPN news platforms, and he works as an adjunct professor at the Columbia University Graduate School of Journalism.

He finds that investigative work requires a lot of off-the-record and not-for-attribution interviews. "Be careful," he says. "Don't be too eager to grant sources anonymity unless they truly won't speak to you otherwise." After a not-for-attribution conversation, he usually asks sources whether they would be comfortable saying the same thing on the record. "They often are," Quinn says.

"If you do go off the record, be absolutely clear about what is on and what is off, and if you agree to stay off the record, respect it," Quinn says. "You'll have no credibility if you don't."

- **In stories covering past news events, use the past tense in attributions, and use it throughout the story.** However, features and other stories that do not report on news events may be more effective if the attributions are consistently given in the present tense. In a feature story like a personality profile, when it is safe to assume that what the person once said, he or she would still say, you may use the present tense. For example, when you write, "'I like being mayor,' she says," you are indicating that the mayor still enjoys her job.

- **Ordinarily, place the noun or pronoun before the verb in attributions:**

  "Everything is under control," the sheriff said.

  However, if you must identify a person by including a long title, it is better to begin the attribution with the verb:

  "I enjoy the challenge," says Janet Berry, associate dean for graduate studies and research.

Attributing Written Sources

Do not use the word "says" when quoting from written sources. You may be general at times and write, "As *Time* magazine reported last week . . ." or "According to

Time magazine . . ." When you know the author of the piece, you may wish to include it: "As Katha Pollitt wrote in the Sept. 21, 2009, issue of *The Nation . . .*" For a report, survey or study cited in a news story, it's usually enough to identify the authors, the date of publication and the name of the journal or the issuing agency. (For guidance on avoiding unintentional plagiarism, see Figure 22.2.)

HANDLING ON- AND OFF-THE-RECORD INFORMATION

Your job would be easy if all of your sources wished to be "on the record."

Some sources do not want to be named for sound reasons. You must learn to use professional judgment in handling the material they give you. If you agree to accept their information, you must honor their request to remain off the record. Breaching that confidence destroys trust and credibility and may get you in trouble with the law. But it is your obligation to take the information elsewhere to confirm it and get it on the record.

Anonymous sources helped *The New York Times* report the Bush administration's extralegal bugging of international communications. But another *Times* front-page story based on anonymous sources suggesting presidential candidate John McCain had an extramarital affair with a lobbyist was a great embarrassment.

Problems with Anonymous Sources

Not naming sources is dangerous for three important reasons. First, such information lacks credibility and makes the reporter and the newspaper suspect. Why should readers believe writers who won't cite the sources of their information? Why wouldn't they tend to believe the writers simply made it up to suit their stories?

Second, the source may be lying. He or she may be out to discredit someone or may be floating a trial balloon, that is, testing public reaction on some issue or event. Skilled diplomats and politicians know how to use reporters to take the temperature of public opinion. If the public reacts negatively, the sources will not proceed with whatever plans they leaked to the press. In such cases the press has been used—and it has become less credible.

Finally, once you have promised anonymity to a source, you may not change your mind without risking a breach-of-contract suit. In 1991, the Supreme Court ruled 5-4 in Cohen v. Cowles Media Co. that the First Amendment does not prevent news sources from suing the press for breach of contract when the press makes confidential sources public. That's why papers such as *The Miami Herald* have a policy that only a senior editor has authority to commit the paper to a pledge of confidentiality.

The New York Times' Policy on the Use of Anonymous Sources

*❝*The policy requires that at least one editor know the identity of every source. Anonymous sources cannot be used when on-the-record sources are readily available. They must have direct knowledge of the information they are imparting; they cannot use the cloak of anonymity for personal or partisan attack; they cannot be used for trivial comment or to make an unremarkable comment seem more important than it is.*❞*

—From "Culling the Anonymous Sources" by Clark Hoyt, former public editor, *The New York Times*

TIPS

Three Reasons to Avoid
Anonymous Sources

- You damage your
  credibility.

- Your source may be lying
  or floating a trial balloon.

- You may be sued if you
  later reveal your source.

Disagreement About Terminology

Some reporters make these distinctions regarding sources and attribution:

- **Off the record.** You may not use the information.
- **Not for attribution.** You may use the information but with no reference as to its source.
- **Background.** You may use it with a general title for a source (for example, "a White House aide said").
- **Deep background.** You may use the information, but you may not indicate any source.

By no means is there agreement on these terms. For most people "off the record" means not for attribution. For some it means that you cannot use the information in any way. Some find no difference between "background" and "deep background." Journalists are vague about the meaning of the terms, and so are sources. Your obligation is to make sure you and your sources understand each other. Set the ground rules ahead of time. Clarify your terms.

Be careful not to allow a speaker to suddenly claim something is off the record. Sometimes in the middle of an interview a source will see you taking notes and suddenly try to change the rules: "Oh, I meant to tell you, that last example was off the record." With all the tact you can muster, try, without losing the source altogether, to change the person's mind. At least, tell the person to try to avoid doing that for the rest of the interview.

Background Interviews

If a city manager or police chief wishes to have a background session with you, unless it is against newspaper policy, you should not refuse. Often these officials are trying to be as open as they can under certain circumstances. Without such background sessions the task of reporting complex issues intelligently is nearly impossible. But you must be aware that you are hearing only one point of view and that the information may be self-serving.

Some sources make a habit of saying everything is off the record and of giving commonplace information in background sessions. Although you should not quote a source who asks to remain off the record, you may use the information if one or more of the following is true:

- The information is a matter of public record.
- It is generally known.
- It is available from several sources.
- You are a witness.

So as not to lose credibility with your source, it's a good idea to make it clear that you plan to use the information for one or more of the preceding reasons.

Knowing when and how to attribute background information is an art you will have to give continuing special care and attention to as a reporter. Remember these two important points:

- When possible, set the ground rules with your sources ahead of time.
- Know your newspaper's policy regarding these matters.

Suggested Readings

Brooks, Brian S., James L. Pinson, and Jean Gaddy Wilson. *Working with Words: A Handbook for Media Writers and Editors,* 7th ed. New York: Bedford/St. Martin's, 2009. The section on quotations is excellent and follows Associated Press style.

Callihan, E. L. *Grammar for Journalists,* rev. ed. Radnor, Pa.: Chilton, 1979. This classic text contains a good section on how to punctuate, attribute and handle quotations.

Germer, Fawn. "Are Quotes Sacred?" *American Journalism Review* (Sept. 1995): 34–37. This article presents views from all sides on whether and when to change quotes.

Hart, Jack. "Giving Credit When Credit Isn't Due." *Editor & Publisher* (Sept. 11, 1993): 2. Hart warns against useless attribution.

King, Barbara. "There's Real Power in Common Speech." *Ottaway News Extra,* no. 137 (Winter 1989): 8, 16. The author presents an excellent discussion on using real quotes from real people.

LaRoque, Paula. "People Are Using Quotes More Often — But in Many Cases They Shouldn't Be." *Quill* (March 1, 2004): 32. LaRoque, an excellent writer, writing coach and teacher, provides good advice.

Stein, M. L. "9th Circuit: It's OK to Make Up Quotes." *Editor & Publisher* (Aug. 12, 1989): 16, 30. This article reports reactions from the press and lawyers to the court decision allowing quotes that are not verbatim.

Stimson, William. "Two Schools on Quoting Confuse the Reader." *Journalism Educator* 49, no. 4 (Winter 1995): 69–73. Strong arguments against cleaning up quotes are presented in this article.

Stoltzfus, Duane. "Partial Pre-publication Review Gaining Favor at Newspapers." *Newspaper Research Journal* 27, no. 4 (Fall 2006): 23–37. A practice long thought unconscionable among journalists gains acceptance.

Weinberg, Steve. "So What's Wrong with Pre-publication Review?" *Quill* (May 1990): 26–28. Weinberg answers objections to prepublication review.

Weinberg, Steve. "Thou Shalt Not Concoct Thy Quote." *Fineline* (July/Aug. 1991): 3–4. In this article, Weinberg presents reasons for allowing sources to review quotations before publication.

Weiss, Philip. "Who Gets Quote Approval?" *Columbia Journalism Review* (May/June 1991): 52–54. The growing practice of allowing sources to check quotations before publication is discussed.

Suggested Website

http://journalism.about.com/od/writing/a/attribution.htm
This page provides an excellent discussion of attribution, including on- and off-the-record attribution and deep background.

Exercises

1. **Team project.** With three other classmates, draw up a list of reporters or editors from different news outlets, and divide the list so that each team member interviews at least two people. Develop a series of questions and follow-up questions to ask interviewees about their policies for handling sources regarding the following:

   a. Off the record
   b. Not for attribution
   c. Background
   d. Deep background

   Then compare what the eight interviewees said and prepare a short report that answers these questions: How do different news organizations define the terms listed above? What policies do the organizations follow? How clearly stated are the policies? How much discretion do individual reporters have in guaranteeing sources anonymity? In your conclusion discuss which policy or policies seem the most effective to your team.

2. Rewrite the following story, paying special attention to the use of quotations and attribution. Note the sensitive nature of some of the quotations. Paraphrase when necessary.

   > Christopher O'Reilly is a remarkably happy young man, despite a bout with meningitis eight years ago that has left him paralyzed and brain-damaged.
   >
   > "I am happy," O'Reilly commented, as he puffed a cigarette. He has much to be happy about. Physical therapy has hastened his recovery since the day he awoke from a 10-week-long coma. He has lived to celebrate his 26th birthday.
   >
   > "I had a helluva birthday," he said. "I seen several friends. I had big cake," he added slowly.
   >
   > He lives in a house with his mother and stepfather in the rolling, green countryside near Springfield.
   >
   > O'Reilly's withered legs are curled beneath him now, and his right arm is mostly paralyzed, but he can do pull-ups with his left arm. He can see and hear.
   >
   > "When he came back, he wasn't worth a damn," his mother said. "The hack doctors told me he would be a vegetable all his life," she claimed.
   >
   > "He couldn't talk; he could only blink. And he drooled a lot," she smiled.
   >
   > Now, Chris is able to respond in incomplete sentences to questions and can carry on slow communication. "He don't talk good, but he talks," his mother commented.

   > It all began when he stole a neighbor's Rototiller. His probation was revoked, and he found himself in the medium-security prison in Springfield. Then came "inadequate medical treatment" in the prison system. O'Reilly's family argued that he received punishment beyond what the Eighth Amendment of the U.S. Constitution calls "cruel and unusual."
   >
   > "Those prison officials were vicious," they said.
   >
   > As a result, he was awarded $250,000 from the state, the largest legal settlement in federal court in 10 years. "That sounds like a lot of money. But it really isn't, you know, when you consider what happened and when you consider the worth of a human life, and the way they treated him and all, we thought we should get at least a million," his mother remarked.
   >
   > O'Reilly contracted the infection of the brain after sleeping "on the concrete floor" of a confinement cell, his mother maintained. He had been placed in solitary confinement because he would not clean his cell. The disease went undiagnosed for eight days, leaving him paralyzed and brain-damaged, she said.
   >
   > Now O'Reilly likes watching television. "I like TV," he grinned. "And smoking."
   >
   > His mother said she "never gives up hope" that "one day" her son will "come out of it."

3. Here are some words of writer and artist John Gerstner. Write a brief story covering what Gerstner said, and use three — and only three — direct quotes.

   > I believe a magazine should be everything you would like your mate to be: intelligent, adventurous, stimulating, candid, helpful, spirited, nice to look at and full of surprises. I believe a magazine should feast the eye as well as feed the mind. Leafing through a magazine should be an aesthetic as well as an intellectual experience. Each page should be a synthesis of ideas, concepts, words, photographs, illustrations and graphic design that arrests, intrigues and instantly communicates . . . not only the subject of the article but also some of its nuances as well — no small trick.
   >
   > I believe a magazine should continually evolve and take risks. About the time a winning formula is found is about the time a new one needs formulating. The best magazines stretch themselves in every issue and surprise both readers and staff.
   >
   > I believe a magazine should be a team project. No editor is an island, nor should want to be. The editor's job is to set the course and the standard. After that it's a matter of squeezing every ounce of creativity out of himself or herself and others

and "arguing, procuring, tinkering and sending things back," as one magazine editor put it. And no editor or publisher should ever underestimate the role human chemistry and magic play in putting out a successful magazine.

Finally, I believe the magazine is one of journalism's highest and noblest forms. The magazine format demands not just good reporting and writing but good communicating, which entails visual as well as verbal sophistication. The best magazines move minds, raise sights and spirits, and make waves to break on distant shores. They aspire to—and sometimes achieve—the level of art.

4. Attend a meeting, a press conference or a speech, and record it. While there, write down the quotes you would use if you were writing the story for your local newspaper. Then listen to the recording, and check the accuracy of your written quotations.

5. Read the front-page section of your local daily newspaper. Note every anonymous source that you find used, and decide whether the use of the anonymous source was justified.

6. Engage a classmate in a half-hour interview about his or her life. In your story, use as many direct quotes as you think are fitting. Then check the accuracy of your quotations with your classmate.

7. Listen to a radio news broadcast, and note how the quotations and attributions are used. Write a brief report on what you found.

8. Find a newspaper news story in which the story would have been more alive and engaging had the attributions been in the present tense.

Gathering and Verifying Information

6

Search engines and social media are radically changing the practice of journalism. You probably grew up using Google, as well as other search engines, and Wikipedia, the user-generated online information site, to research school projects. Most professional journalists use them, too. They're among the quickest ways to find background information to help you frame a story in the proper context.

But Google and Wikipedia also can be dangerous. Google can and does lead you almost anywhere on the Web. To make sure the information you find is useful, you need to be able to verify its accuracy (see the box "Evaluating Information on the Web" in this chapter). Similarly, Wikipedia, which is modeled on print encyclopedias, is a terrific resource, but occasionally a contributor adds erroneous information or presents a one-sided view of a topic. Other users typically moderate the content and catch inaccuracies, but what happens if you pick up the bad information while it's still posted?

Social media sites like Twitter, a microblogging service, have already proved their value in breaking news stories. But how accurate is the information sent by people you may not even know? Our advice is to embrace the power of these new technologies while learning to evaluate the accuracy of the information they provide.

When Twitter first appeared, not many journalists thought of it as an enhancement to what they do. Times have changed. Today, *The New York Times* and dozens of other newspapers use Twitter feeds to promote their stories. Perhaps even more important is the papers' use of Twitter to find news sources.

When a building collapsed in Lower Manhattan, for example, Sewell Chan of *The Times* used Twitter to find eyewitnesses. Reporters nationwide are following Chan's lead. When they need knowledgeable sources to comment on a story, a Twitter message to followers or a post on Facebook often leads to those with something useful or insightful to say.

Twitter and Facebook also are sources of breaking news. When the Iranian government cracked down on dissidents following the controversial 2009 elections there, it expelled foreign journalists, cut mobile phone service, blocked instant messaging and censored websites. Bloggers and activists used proxy servers to avoid the censors, and Twitter messages about what was happening began flowing to the outside world.

Similarly, when a jetliner crashed in Amsterdam, some of the first reports of the accident came from citizen journalists using Twitter. Twitter users published the first photos of the crash and beat the BBC with the news by 15 minutes. That led one blogger to label Twitter the world's fastest news source.

These stories illustrate the power of social media — Twitter, Facebook, MySpace and other services — to become significant players in the process of gathering and distributing the news. Professional journalists, as well as citizen journalists, are embracing these new tools.

When a big story breaks and thousands of people start passing the word about it through Facebook, Twitter and other social media sites, what results is **aggregated journalism**. Think of this as the first draft of history. It may include a lot of misinformation and misinterpretation, but ultimately the massive amount of reporting involved leads to a better understanding of the event.

What aggregated journalism does is useful, but what matters even more is sorting through the mass of information and making sense of what happened. That's what professional journalists do. It's their job to separate fact from fiction, the good information from the bad. Call this **explanatory journalism** if you wish. Most journalists simply call it *good* journalism.

In this chapter, we'll explore the process of not only getting information but also getting it right.

ACCURATE INFORMATION: THE BASIS OF A GOOD STORY

Ask any editor whether a reporter can be a good writer without being good at information gathering, and you're likely to hear a resounding, "No!" That's because good writing depends on good reporting. Reporting isn't good unless it is thorough and accurate. To ensure reports are thorough and accurate, journalists employ two main techniques: the discipline of multiple sources and the discipline of verification.

The Discipline of Multiple Sources

Good writing is of course important, as we explore in other chapters, but the quality of writing depends in large part on good fact-gathering, which we call good reporting. It's impossible to write a great story without first doing a great job of reporting. Gathering information requires skilled interviewing, as we discussed in Chapter 4. It also requires knowing how to use the many sources of information readily available. Make no mistake about it: There are hundreds of places to find information.

Good reporters know that the worst kind of news story is one with a single source. Rarely is such a story worth publishing. Even a personality profile should be based on more than just an interview with the subject. To get a fuller perspective, the journalist also needs to talk with individuals who know the subject. Gathering information from multiple sources is one of the keys to good writing and good communication. It's also the best way to ensure accuracy by verifying information. When additional sources are checked and cross-checked, the chances of a story being accurate greatly improve.

Imagine how many sources the reporters for the *Milwaukee Journal Sentinel* used in their award-winning series about how the federal government allowed chemical manufacturers to influence the approval of potentially harmful substances in everyday products:

Chemical Fallout: Bisphenol A Is in You
By Susanne Rust, Cary Spivak and Meg Kissinger

For more than a decade, the federal government and chemical-makers have assured the public that a hormone-mimicking compound found in baby bottles, aluminum cans and hundreds of other household products is safe.

But a *Journal Sentinel* investigation found that these promises are based on outdated, incomplete government studies and research heavily funded by the chemical industry.

In the first analysis of its kind by a newspaper, the *Journal Sentinel* reviewed 258 scientific studies of the chemical bisphenol A, a compound detected in the urine of 93 percent of Americans recently tested. An overwhelming majority of these studies show that the chemical is harmful — causing breast cancer, testicular cancer, diabetes, hyperactivity, obesity, low sperm counts, miscarriage and a host of other reproductive failures in laboratory animals.

Studies paid for by the chemical industry are much less likely to find damaging effects or disease.

U.S. regulators so far have sided with industry by minimizing concern about the compound's safety.

Last week, a panel commissioned by the National Toxicology Program released a report finding bisphenol A to be of some concern for fetuses and small children. It found that adults have almost nothing to worry about.

Its recommendations could be used by the U.S. Environmental Protection Agency and other regulators to assess federal policies on how much bisphenol A is safe and may have huge ramifications for the multibillion-dollar chemical industry.

The panel said it considered more than 700 studies by university scientists, government researchers and industry-funded chemists. It picked the work it felt was best and threw out the rest.

The *Journal Sentinel* found that panel members gave more weight to industry-funded studies and more leeway to industry-funded researchers.

- The panel rejected academic studies that found harm — citing inadequate methods. But the panel accepted industry-funded studies using the same methods that concluded the chemical does not pose risks.

- The panel missed dozens of studies publicly available that the *Journal Sentinel* found online using a medical research Internet search engine. The studies the panel considered were chosen, in part, by a consultant with links to firms that made bisphenol A.

- More and more university researchers and foreign governments are finding that bisphenol A can do serious damage in small doses. But the panel rejected studies mostly submitted by university and international government scientists that looked at the impact at these levels.

- The panel accepted a Korean study translated by the chemical industry's trade group that found bisphenol A to be safe. It also accepted two studies that were not subjected to any peer review — the gold standard of scientific credibility. Both studies were funded by General Electric Co., which made bisphenol A until it sold its plastics division earlier this year.

"This undermines the government's authority," said David Rosner, professor of history and public health at Columbia University. "It makes you think twice about accepting their conclusions."

Panel chairman Robert Chapin, a toxicologist who works for Pfizer Inc., the pharmaceutical giant, defended his group's work.

"We didn't flippin' care who does the study," said Chapin, who worked as a government scientist for 18 years before joining Pfizer.

If the studies followed good laboratory practices and were backed with strong data, they were accepted, Chapin said. . . .

Even in this short excerpt from a multipart series, it's evident that the reporters used dozens of sources, including peer-reviewed research journals that most reporters seldom touch. Such reporting requires analyzing thousands of pages of data, poring over online and paper records, interviewing dozens of people and checking, cross-checking and rechecking. Such reporting is both time-consuming and tedious, but work of this sort is exactly what journalists must do as they act as watchdogs over the actions of government agencies. Getting it right is of paramount importance.

The Discipline of Verification

Journalists, when operating as they should, follow the same investigative system employed by scientists. They develop a hypothesis and then seek facts to support or reject it. In the 20th century, journalists developed the concept of objectivity—an elusive idea that was often interpreted the wrong way.

As Philip Meyer of the University of North Carolina suggests to journalists Bill Kovach and Tom Rosenstiel in *The Elements of Journalism*: "I think [the] connection between journalism and science ought to emphasize objectivity of method. That's what scientific method is—our humanity, our subjective impulses . . . directed toward deciding what to investigate by objective means."

What objectivity isn't, Kovach and Rosenstiel argue, is blind loyalty to the concepts of fairness and balance. Fairness, they argue, can be misunderstood if it is seen as a goal unto itself. Fairness should mean that a journalist is fair to the facts and to the public's understanding of them. It should not mean, "Am I being fair to my sources, so that none of them will be unhappy?" or "Does my story seem fair?" Those are subjective judgments that lead the journalist away from the task of independent verification.

Similarly, balance should not mean that it's necessary to get an equal number of scientists speaking on each side of the global-warming debate, for example, if an overwhelming number of scientists in fact believe that global warming is a reality.

Kovach and Rosenstiel argue that sharpening the meaning of verification and resisting the temptation to simplify it are essential to improving the credibility of what journalists write. So, while citizen journalists rush to get out information quickly without much regard for accuracy, professional journalists seek to get it right—while also producing news as quickly as possible.

The journalistic process of layered editing also helps get facts right. At a good newspaper, magazine, radio or television station, or website, once the reporter writes a story, it may be subject to extensive review by several editors. Each may find facts to correct or language to clarify in the quest for a story that is as compelling—and accurate—as possible. Thus, as a story flows through the editorial process (see Figure 6.1), the goal is to make it as nearly perfect as possible.

Editors talk about the need to look at a story on both the micro and macro levels. *Microediting* is the process of paying attention to detail:

- Are the facts correct?
- Are the names spelled correctly?
- Is the grammar sound?

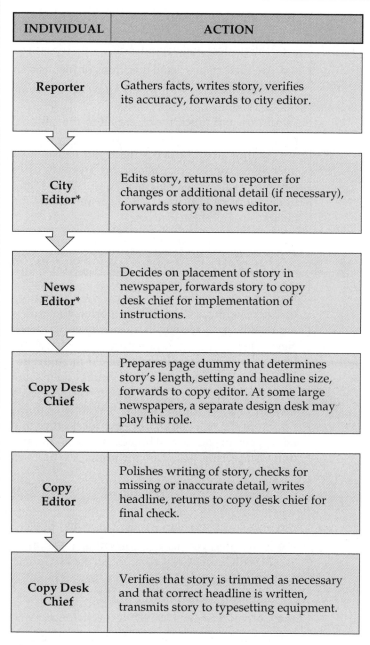

INDIVIDUAL	ACTION
Reporter	Gathers facts, writes story, verifies its accuracy, forwards to city editor.
City Editor*	Edits story, returns to reporter for changes or additional detail (if necessary), forwards story to news editor.
News Editor*	Decides on placement of story in newspaper, forwards story to copy desk chief for implementation of instructions.
Copy Desk Chief	Prepares page dummy that determines story's length, setting and headline size, forwards to copy editor. At some large newspapers, a separate design desk may play this role.
Copy Editor	Polishes writing of story, checks for missing or inaccurate detail, writes headline, returns to copy desk chief for final check.
Copy Desk Chief	Verifies that story is trimmed as necessary and that correct headline is written, transmits story to typesetting equipment.

* Or assistant
Note: At any point in the process, a story may be returned to an earlier editor for clarification, amplification or rewriting.

Figure 6.1
Editing and producing a newspaper is a fast-paced and complex process in which editors at different levels review stories. Shown here is a typical copy-flow pattern for a daily newspaper.

Macroediting, on the other hand, looks at the big picture:

- Will readers understand this?
- Are there unanswered questions or inconsistencies in the story?
- Does this agree with what I know from previous stories on the subject?

All of this, and much more, goes into the editorial process of verification. In the end, the goal is to get the story right.

As they strive to get it right, journalists use all types of sources, including interviews, source documents and a variety of other sources ranging from the obvious, such as a Google search, to online sites, computer databases and traditional sources like printed almanacs and encyclopedias. Good reporters make frequent use of all these sources.

COMPUTERIZED SOURCES OF INFORMATION

Reporters and editors today have a wealth of information available at their fingertips. Researching a story? Most reporters today do what good reporters have always done—check to see what's already been written or broadcast about the subject. Newspaper and magazine reporters do that by checking the publication's news library (archives), traditionally called the **morgue**. Television and radio reporters do that by listening to previous reports their stations have broadcast or checking the newspaper library. After that, most reporters today head for the Web, where they are likely to search Google or Wikipedia to learn about a subject.

From the news library in your local office to national databases of published newspaper, magazine and broadcast stories, the amount of computerized information is staggering. These are the primary sources of computerized information:

- The news library, or morgue, maintained by your own publication or broadcast station.
- Search engines like Google, Yahoo and Bing.
- News sites, portals and content aggregators (USAToday.com, NYTimes.com, MSNBC.com, CNN.com, Yahoo News, Google News).
- Other sites on the World Wide Web. Millions of organizations maintain websites with useful information.
- Commercial database services (Dialog, LexisNexis and others).
- Government databases (city, county, state and federal).
- Special-interest databases (those created by organizations with a cause).
- Custom databases.

Let's explore the usefulness of each.

Your News Library: The Place to Start

News libraries are something most reporters quickly learn to cherish. Before they were computerized, doing research for a story was a laborious process that involved a trip to the newspaper, magazine or broadcast station library to sift through hundreds or even thousands of tattered, yellowed clippings. Too often, clippings had disappeared, were misfiled or were misplaced, which made such research a hit-or-miss proposition. Despite those shortcomings, the library was a valuable asset. Reporters were routinely admonished to check there first.

You will still hear that advice in news rooms today, but many of today's news libraries are computerized, which almost ensures that an item will not disappear and will be easy for you to locate. Typically, you can search the computerized library from your own computer. That makes it easier than ever to do good background work on a story. Your ability to search the library is limited only by your skill with search techniques.

News libraries are what computer experts call **full-text databases**, which means that all words in the database have been indexed and are searchable. Such capability gives you great flexibility in structuring searches using what are known as **Boolean search commands**. Boolean operators like AND, OR and NOT allow you to structure the search to find material most closely related to the subject of your research. For example, if you are interested in finding articles on former South African President Nelson Mandela's visits to the U.S., you might issue this command on the search line:

Mandela AND United ADJ States

The computer would then search for all articles that contain the name "Mandela" and also contain the words "United" and "States" if adjacent to each other. In this example, AND and ADJ (for "adjacent") are the Boolean operators. This search would produce all articles on Mandela and the United States but would exclude articles involving Mandela and, for example, the United Arab Emirates, despite the presence of the word "United" (it's not adjacent to the word "States"). The result of such a search in most cases would be a report from the computer telling you how many articles match your search criteria:

Search found 27 articles. Would you like to see them or further narrow your search?

At that point, you would have the option of further limiting the search (by date, for example) or viewing all 27 articles.

Remember that computers don't really think. In our sample search, an article on Mandela's visit to Miami that did not contain the words "United States" would not have been found. Therefore, it is important to understand the limitations as well as the power of computer-assisted database searching. Good reporters quickly learn to take into account such possibilities and learn to recast their searches in other ways.

There are other limitations. Many news library databases do not allow you to see photos, nor can you see articles as they appeared in the newspaper or magazine. Nor do most current systems permit you to hear how a broadcast story was used on the air. Instead, you have access only to a text-based version of what appeared. That limits your ability to learn how the story was displayed in the newspaper or magazine, or how it was read on the air. If necessary, however, you can always resort to looking up the original in bound volumes or on microfilm. Most newspapers save old editions in one or both of those forms. Many radio and television stations maintain tape libraries of old newscasts. While these older forms of storage may be less convenient to use, taking the time to do so is often worth the effort.

Some newer library computer systems overcome the traditional disadvantages of computerization by allowing you to call graphical reproductions of the printed page to the screen. You can view photographs, charts and maps in the same way. In broadcast applications, more and more libraries permit storage of digital video and sound clips. As such systems proliferate, the shortcomings of present computer libraries will disappear.

Search Engines

For many journalists, the first stop after the morgue is Google. Google or one of the other popular search engines—Yahoo, Bing, Dogpile or Ask—can indeed be helpful to a journalist. The key to their successful use is the ability to recognize whether the information contained on the website to which the search takes you is accurate and therefore usable.

Information from well-known sites may be reliable; information from websites advocating a cause may not be. We discuss how to evaluate such information in the "Evaluating Information on the Web" box in this chapter.

One big advantage of search engines over typical newspaper or magazine library systems is that they index the whole Internet. They also have a less rigorous protocol for searching, which allows you to search using full interrogative sentences:

> Which country produces the most tin?

This query produces "about 3,600,000" results on a Google search. So even when you use search engines, you have to learn how to limit searches to get usable results.

News Sites, Portals and Content Aggregators

You might consider it strange to think of news websites, portals and content aggregators as useful sources of information for reporters. Don't tell that to the reporters who use them. Good reporters don't simply pick up and use material from other news sites. Instead, they use those sites to lead them to the experts they need to interview.

Such sites are accessible to anyone with a computer and an Internet connection. News sites are those published by established media outlets like *The New York Times* (NYTimes.com) and CBS (CBSNews.com), while portals are designed as entry points to the Web, such as AOL.com. Most portals now have news and other information as well as *forums* (electronic bulletin boards) for discussions on topics ranging from genealogy to stamp collecting to sports. Forum participants exchange messages on every conceivable topic. Some even write computer software that facilitates the pursuit of their passion, and they frequently make that software available to others interested in the topic. This makes it simple for reporters to find people knowledgeable about almost any subject.

Online forums provide fertile information to reporters attempting to research a story. For example, if you are assigned to do a story on genealogy and know nothing about the subject, what better way to gauge the pulse of those passionate about the subject than by tapping into their discussions? By logging on to one of these public forums, you can do just that.

If you want to interview those who participated in the U.S. invasion of Cambodia during the Vietnam War, for example, try posting a request for names on one of these services. Chances are you will be inundated with names and telephone numbers of individuals and veterans' groups that would be delighted to help.

The popularity of such services is almost impossible to overstate. What people like about public online forums and blogs is that they do what radio talk shows do — give people a place where they can exchange ideas with those who share similar interests. Writing in *Editor & Publisher*, Barry Hollander, a journalism professor at the University of Georgia, contrasts the skyrocketing popularity of talk radio with the continuing decline of newspaper circulation:

> Newspapers used to be an important part of what bound communities together, a common forum for ideas and discussion. But as communities fragmented along racial and demographic lines, newspapers have done a better job of chronicling the decline than offering ways to offset the trend.
>
> A sense of connection is needed. Newspapers, and [their] electronic editions in particular, offer one opportunity to bring people together in ways similar to talk radio.

Over the years, newspapers, magazines and broadcast stations have attempted to connect with their readers and listeners by doing people-on-the-street interviews. Interviewing people at random seldom produces good results because often those interviewed know nothing about the topic or don't care about it. By tapping into the forums on various online sites or operating your own blogs, you are assured of finding knowledgeable, conversant people to interview.

These services give you a way to reconnect with the public and find expert sources for stories. With their huge amounts of easily accessible material, they also are useful sources of information for reporters and editors.

Evaluating Information on the Web

The Web is a great resource for reporters, but determining the credibility of information on the Web can be problematic. If the source is a respected media organization like *The New York Times*, *The Washington Post* or ABC, chances are the information is solid. But if the information is published by an organization promoting a cause, there is ample reason to be wary.

Stan Ketterer, a journalist and journalism professor, tells reporters to evaluate information on the Web by following the same standard journalistic practices they would use for assessing the credibility and accuracy of any information:

- **Before using information from a website in a story, verify it with a source.** There are exceptions to this rule. They include using information from a highly credible government site like the U.S. Census Bureau. You might also want to use unverified information when you can't contact the source on a breaking story because of time constraints. An editor must clear all exceptions.
- **In most cases, information taken directly from the Web and used in a story must be attributed.** If you have verified the information with a source, you can use the organization in the attribution — for example, "according to the EPA" or "EPA figures show." If you cannot verify the information after trying repeatedly, attribute unverified information to the Web page — for example, "according to the Voice of America's site on the World Wide Web." Consult your editor before using unverified information.
- **If you have doubts about the accuracy of the information and you cannot reach the source, get it from another source, such as a book or another person.** When in doubt, omit the information.

- **Check the extension on the site's Internet address to get clues as to the nature of the organization and the likely slant of the information.** The most common extensions used in the United States are *.gov* (government), *.edu* (education), *.com* (commercial), *.mil* (military), *.org* (not-for-profit organization) and *.net* (Internet administration). Most government and military sites have credible and accurate information. In many cases, you can take the information directly from the site and attribute it to the organization. But consult your editor until you get to know these sites.
- **Treat the sites of colleges and universities as you would other sites.** If college and university sites have source documents, such as the Constitution, attribute the information to the source document. But beware: Personal home pages can have .edu extensions, and the information is not always credible.
- **In almost all cases, *do not* take information directly from the home pages of commercial and not-for-profit organizations and use it without verification.**
- **Check the date when the page was last updated.** The date generally appears at the top or bottom of the first page of the site. Although a recent date does not ensure that the information is current, it does indicate that the organization is paying close attention to the site. If no date appears, if the site has not been updated for a while, or if it was created some time ago, do not use the information unless you verify it with a source.

Then there are the news aggregators — sites like Yahoo News (news.yahoo.com) and Google News (news.google.com), which link to news stories from a plethora of news sites, becoming, in effect, a good place for one-stop news shopping. They will help you find things, but remember that most of what's found there is copyrighted. Don't lift material from such sources for a story you are writing.

Other Sites on the World Wide Web

You probably have been using the Internet for as long as you have had access to a computer. You laugh at the homemade videos on YouTube or watch your favorite TV shows on Hulu. You connect with your friends through Facebook or MySpace. But the Internet is also a valuable source of information for journalists. For the journalist, the Internet serves two primary purposes:

- **It is an increasingly robust source of online information, including federal, state and local government data, and information published by companies on almost any imaginable topic.** Need information on a new drug? Chances are you can find it on the Internet, complete with more detail than you ever wanted to know. Need to know about Estonia? Plenty of websites are available to tell you what you need to know or to give you the latest news from Tallinn, its capital. Further, most North American newspapers, magazines and broadcast stations have a substantial Internet presence, sometimes complete with archives of previously published stories. Some experts, in fact, now refer to the Internet as the world's largest library. That's good stuff for a reporter who needs to do a quick bit of research to provide background material or context for a news story.

- **It is a publishing medium that offers new opportunities for media companies and journalists, and new jobs for journalism and mass communication graduates.** In recent years, media companies large and small alike have rushed to establish a presence on the Web in the belief that this is an exciting new medium of increasing interest to the public and one with enormous commercial potential. Media companies also use the Internet to attract readers and viewers to their more profitable traditional products.

The Internet also serves as an excellent medium for transmitting photos and even audio and video clips. It's possible to tap into the Louvre's website and see paintings from the museum's famous collection in full color, for example, and YouTube is a hot site for posting videos, some of which are quite good.

And then there's Wikipedia, which can be an extremely useful source of information for all sorts of things. Just remember that it's a user-generated encyclopedia, and from time to time a rogue user will insert something in a Wikipedia entry that simply isn't true. Good reporters use Wikipedia often, but they also try to verify the facts they find there with at least one other source.

Commercial Database Services

When newspapers and magazines entered the computer era in the early 1970s, publishers were quick to realize the potential value of saving and reselling previously published information. Newspapers and magazines began selling access to their archives by establishing alliances with companies founded for that purpose.

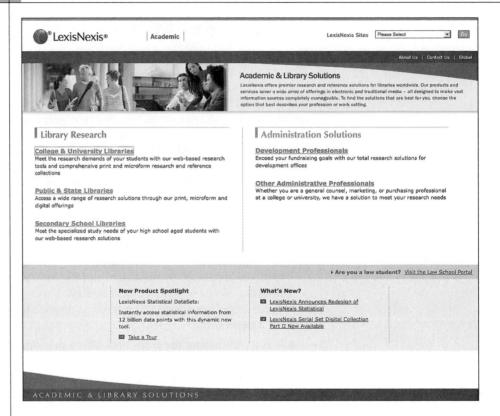

Figure 6.2
LexisNexis is an invaluable resource for reporters researching previous stories written nationwide on a given subject. Check to see if your school library subscribes.

On many topics, searching your own news library will not be sufficient. If U.S. Rep. Barney Frank is making his first appearance in your community and you have been assigned to cover him, your morgue probably won't help; little will have been written about him in your city. It will be much more useful to read recent articles published in Massachusetts, Frank's home state. By doing so, you will be armed with questions to ask about recent events of interest to him. In such situations, the national commercial databases are invaluable.

One of the leading commercial database services is LexisNexis (see Figure 6.2), which provides full-text access to hundreds of newspaper and magazine libraries. It is a rich source of background information for a reporter who wants to see what has already been written on a given subject. LexisNexis and similar commercial databases charge a fee that many organizations are willing to pay so their reporters, students or researchers can access the site.

Government Databases

National, local and state governments all maintain extensive databases of information that are ripe for mining. Need access to the maintenance history of an aircraft that crashed in your area? There's a Federal Aviation Administration database for that. Need to find out who made campaign contributions to your congressman? There's a database for that, too.

In the 1980s, newspapers started to win Pulitzer Prizes for investigative reporting using the technique of database matching. What happens if you match a database of drunken-driving convictions in your state with another listing school bus drivers? You learn how many bus drivers have drunken-driving convictions and who they are. That will make for a great news story after some follow-up interviews.

That reporting technique spurred creation of the National Institute for Computer-Assisted Reporting at the University of Missouri to teach reporters how to use **relational database** programs—those that allow matching of data fields in disparate databases. NICAR conducts regular seminars to train reporters in how to do this. As a result, reporters nationwide have been trained to make better use of existing open-records laws at both the state and federal levels.

Among the reporters who have taken advantage of this technology is Penny Loeb, formerly of *U.S. News & World Report* and *New York Newsday*. At *Newsday*, she used a computer analysis of tax and property records to reveal an astounding story: The City of New York owed $275 million to taxpayers as a result of overpayments on real estate, water and sewer taxes. To get that story, Loeb had to analyze millions of computer records. Doing that by hand would have consumed a lifetime, but with the assistance of a computer, she accomplished the task in a matter of weeks.

Still, Loeb cautions against expecting instant stories:

> Don't just go get a computer [database] and expect a great story. You need a tip that there is a problem that computerized data can confirm. Or you may have seen a problem occur repeatedly, such as sentencing discrimination. The computer can quantify the scope.

After the introduction of this technology, investigative reporters were among the first to use it. But now that such databases are more readily available, you can use them in your day-to-day work just as easily. For example, you might want to tap that FAA airplane maintenance database to produce a story on the safety record of a particular airline. Or, even on deadline, you might use it to check the repair history of an airplane that crashed.

Another common use of computers has been to compare bank records on home mortgages to census data. By tracking how many mortgages are issued to homeowners in predominantly African-American or Hispanic areas, you can document the practice of redlining, through which banks make it difficult or impossible for minorities to obtain loans. Then, using mapping software, you can even demonstrate graphically the areas where loans are tough to get.

Driver's license records, census data, bank records and other forms of data can be used to produce news stories, charts, maps and other graphic devices. Numbers can be useful in helping to tell a story. They can be particularly effective if used to create charts that illustrate the impact of the numbers.

Computer-Assisted Reporting

In this chapter, we describe how some reporters have used computers to produce extraordinary stories. Let's examine one such story from the *Detroit Free Press*:

By Tracy Van Moorlehem
and Heather Newman
Free Press Staff Writers

When it comes to education, the MEAP isn't everything.

It might seem that way, with all the stress in recent years on comparing and improving scores on the MEAP — Michigan Educational Assessment Program — tests, annually given to fourth- and seventh-graders in math and reading and fifth- and eighth-graders in science and writing. School districts use the scores as bragging points; real estate agents for selling points.

The tests, begun in 1969, measure the extent to which each student has learned what the state has defined as basic skills.

By the straight MEAP numbers, schools in affluent areas such as Bloomfield Hills are academic powerhouses while those in relatively poor areas such as Detroit are weaklings.

But consider those MEAP scores in light of other factors beyond the control of the schools, such as poverty, unemployment, the number of single-parent families or parents without a high school diploma in a community.

That's what the *Free Press* did in a computer analysis that produced some surprising results. Detroit schools, for example, are overcoming the odds — doing better than predicted, given the factors working against them.

The analysis shows that students in Bloomfield Hills and some other well-off, high scoring districts could be doing even better.

The study also demonstrates how any straight-up comparison of MEAP scores is inevitably flawed. Consider: Only 49 percent of Detroit fourth-graders pass the MEAP math test, compared with 84 percent of Bloomfield Hills fourth-graders.

Consider: Seventy-one percent of Detroit students are from families poor enough to qualify for a free or reduced-price school lunch; only 2 percent of Bloomfield Hills students qualify.

Yet the test is scored without regard for educational resources, obstacles or opportunity. Educators say MEAP scores brand some schools and entire communities as inferior, creating a cycle that's hard to break.

Mary Anne Bunda, a professor of educational leadership at Western Michigan University, said comparing MEAP scores directly is like rating hospitals based solely on patient death rates: You might think the hospital with the highest numbers gave the worst care.

But what if that hospital specialized in fatal diseases, or was next door to a hospice?

Likewise, schools coping with factors such as severe poverty may be doing a superior job of educating students who start out behind wealthier counterparts. Poor parents, for example, may not be able to afford books, or home computers. Single, working parents may not have as much time to read to children. Parents who dropped out of high school may be too intimidated to approach educators about what's going on with their children in school.

Yet, distorted as MEAP scores may be, they are often used as the sole yardstick of school performance.

Realtors use them to sell one neighborhood over another. Lawyers cite them in child custody battles. State officials use them to accredit schools.

And newspapers, including the *Free Press*, publish them in rank order.

Beginning today, the *Free Press* will take a deeper look at the MEAP, filtering the scores through non-school factors that play a significant role in education.

Researchers and experts say the analysis is a step forward in thinking about the MEAP.

"What you have here is just amazing," said Catherine Taylor, associate professor of educational psychology at the University of Washington in Seattle. She said the "startling" level of correlation between poverty and test scores, especially in urban and suburban districts, illuminates the challenge facing urban educators.

But experts offered a host of cautions, too:

- Poverty and low scores are not inevitably linked.

    "As ammunition for a bigot, it's very, very dangerous," said Harvey Czerwinski, program supervisor in the Office of Research, Evaluation and Testing for Detroit schools.
- Poor schools should not cite adverse circumstances to explain low scores as satisfactory.

    "We are not where we want to be. We are not satisfied with our achievement, even exceeding your model," said Aaron Hedgepeth, also a program supervisor in Detroit's testing department.
- Finally, educators cautioned against making too much of the analyzed MEAP scores, falling into the same trap as with raw scores.

    MEAP tests capture the performance of a small segment of students on one day in a selective curriculum, they said.

"This kind of analysis is better than . . . just looking at the raw numbers, but it's far from ideal," Bloomfield Hills Superintendent Gary Doyle said of the *Free Press* study. "It takes a very limited measure and makes it a little better — but not much."

The *Free Press* story was a complex one that involved taking the raw MEAP test-score data from the Michigan Department of Education and then adjusting the results for factors found to affect school performance. Here's the paper's explanation of the process:

To look at MEAP test scores in light of the different challenges facing schools, the *Free Press* used a statistical analysis method called multiple linear regression.

Here's how it works:

Consider MEAP scores against a factor; for example, poverty within the school district. On a graph, you can see that as poverty goes up, MEAP scores go down.

Multiple linear regression is a way of looking at the possible effect of more than one factor. In addition to poverty, the *Free Press* found an impact from six other factors:

- The percent of single parents in a district.
- The percent of households where no one is a high school graduate.

- The local unemployment rate.
- School funds per pupil.
- The percent of students who speak English as a second language.
- Location, specifically city/suburban, midsize town or rural area.

Among city and suburban school districts, more than 62 percent of the differences in scores can be traced to such nonschool factors.

They accounted for 33 percent of the differences among districts in midsize towns, and almost 16 percent of the differences among rural districts.

By using multiple regression to project test scores based on the makeup of the community, we found some disadvantaged districts that are doing better than expected.

The story went on to show that some districts in the inner city are actually outperforming those in richer suburban districts when variables are factored out. Good reporting such as that helps readers sort out the differences between the rhetoric of political candidates and reality. But doing such stories requires reporters to have a working knowledge of statistical analysis and familiarity with basic math. In this case, the *Free Press* enlisted the help of a nearby university professor to analyze the data. Reporters still had to be able to understand the results and translate them into terms readers could understand.

Reporting such as this is known as computer-assisted reporting, and it has become the heart and soul of investigative reporting in the U.S. Almost all the recent winners in the annual contest of Investigative Reporters and Editors employed this technique. So, too, did recent winners of the Pulitzer Prize for investigative reporting. Organizations like IRE and the National Institute for Computer-Assisted Reporting offer seminars in computer data analysis. Today's best reporters are eager to take advantage of such offerings.

TIPS

Ten Sources of Story Ideas

- Other people

- Other publications

- News releases

- A social services directory

- Government reports

- Stories in your own newspaper

- Advertisements

- Wire copy

- Local news briefs

- You

Special-Interest Databases

Numerous special-interest groups have discovered the usefulness of placing information in computerized databases, and they are eager to make you aware of the existence of that information. Some of that material may be quite useful; indeed, it may be unobtainable from other sources. But just as you must be wary of press releases issued by organizations promoting a cause, you must be equally wary of information in such databases.

It is important to remember that organizations of this type will promote their perspective on a topic, often without any concern for balancing the information with opposing views. The conservative Heritage Foundation, for example, maintains multiple databases of information that appear to be data-driven and seem legitimate enough. Read the context, however, and it's clear that the framing is far from objective, as this excerpt accompanying tables on the national debt shows: "In 2019, interest payments alone on the debt will be $100 billion more than President Obama projects to spend on the whole Department of Defense." It's cast as if Obama were solely responsible for the national debt, when in fact much of it was created by his predecessors. It also compares current dollars to 2019 dollars.

Liberal think tanks such as the Center for American Progress employ similar tactics. Whenever possible, you should avoid using potentially biased sources and instead use government-provided statistics, such as those from the Census Bureau, while seeking comments on the data from experts all along the political spectrum.

Special-interest databases also are provided by organizations without political motivations. Industry advocacy groups, unions and many other organizations try to influence the media and, in turn, public opinion. Good reporters do their own research and rely on data sources that are unlikely to be tainted.

Custom Databases

Journalists Tracy Weber, Charles Ornstein and Maloy Moore had reason to believe the California Board of Registered Nursing was failing in its duty to ensure that nurses are competent, sober and law-abiding. To find out, they had to build their own analysis tool.

Using a database manager, they entered and analyzed all of the accusations filed and disciplinary actions taken by the board between 2002 and 2008. The printouts involved more than 2,000 nurses.

The team, representing the online news organization ProPublica and the *Los Angeles Times*, described the task as an enormous amount of work. But in the end the database enabled the reporters not only to flag the best cases to use as examples but also to highlight a number of weaknesses in the board's oversight. Among the problems they uncovered were nurses involved in multiple disciplinary cases and those with multiple criminal convictions.

The project had immediate impact. The day after the first story ran, California's governor replaced a majority of the nursing board. A day later, the board's longtime executive officer resigned.

ON THE JOB

The Challenges of Editing for the Web

Erik Ulken is among those journalists who have embraced the digital technologies that are changing journalism. After earning bachelor's and master's degrees, Ulken worked as a news producer at NOLA.com, the website of *The (New Orleans) Times-Picayune*, and at *The Columbus Dispatch* before making his way to Los Angeles. He was the managing editor for news at LATimes.com, the website of the *Los Angeles Times*, before leaving the company to become a full-time consultant. He still does work for the *Times*.

Ulken urges would-be journalists to embrace the Web and to think not just about writing jobs but also about editing:

"If you take a newspaper job two or three years from now, chances are much of the work you do won't be for a newspaper at all, but rather for a website. Newsrooms are reorganizing to meet new challenges as their online editions grow in importance. It's still unclear how many duties copy editors ultimately will juggle, but their new responsibilities almost certainly will transcend the traditional role. (Meanwhile, newspaper gigs aren't the only game in town: Broadcast and online-only sites are hiring more copy editors as their Internet operations grow.)

"In addition to learning basic copy-editing skills (which never go out of style), here's how you can prepare yourself:

- **Learn how to use content management systems.** News organizations use a variety of online content platforms, but there are similarities among them. The simplest content management systems are blogging tools such as TypePad and Blogger. Learning how they work will help you pick up more complex systems much faster.
- **Understand how users find news on the Web.** Many come to your site from search engines and aggregator sites such as Google News, which is one reason why Web heads are so important.
- **Understand audio and video.** It's less important to know how to edit in Final Cut Pro than it is to be able to identify what's missing from a multimedia package.
- **Be flexible and make an effort to adapt to new technologies.** Don't assume that the rules as you've learned them are immutable — even when it comes to style and usage: Technology, and indeed language, are constantly evolving.
- **Use the Web constantly.** The best way to learn how to produce great content for the Web is to experience great content on the Web.

"To answer the question I know you're asking: Yes, you'll probably end up doing more work, and doing it faster, than previous generations of copy editors have done. But, on the plus side, the greater variety of tasks should keep the routine from getting old."

Reporters like Weber, Ornstein and Moore who find themselves in the predicament of having data in an inconvenient format sometimes resort to entering it into a database themselves. This is a time-consuming process, but it can be effective. If your knowledge of computer programs is limited, consult with computer experts in your news organization. They will be able to recommend an appropriate tool.

If much of what you are indexing contains textual material, you will need a **free-form database**. A program of this type popular among reporters is askSam, adopted by many of the nation's leading investigative reporters. AskSam makes it easy to construct a database of quotations, notes or similar material. Many database programs do not handle such material so easily.

If you need to create a simple list of names, addresses and telephone numbers, a **flat-file database**, essentially a table of data, might be best. Relational database comparisons require more sophisticated programs such as Microsoft's Visual FoxPro.

Many reporters also are turning to **spreadsheet programs** to help them sort through the complexity of government or corporate financial data. A business reporter might use a spreadsheet program to spot trends in the allocation of resources or changes in sources of income. After data covering several years have been collected, a spreadsheet program, which can easily create graphs from the data, can make it possible to notice trends that otherwise might go undetected. Similarly, a government reporter might use a spreadsheet to spot changes in allocations to various city, county, state or federal departments or agencies.

Today's best reporters keep abreast of technological advances and search for new ways to put computers to work in the news room.

TRADITIONAL SOURCES OF INFORMATION

Accessing information through computerized sources is quick and easy, but don't discount traditional reference sources. Some of the following sources of information, such as the newspaper library, are now computerized; others exist only in printed form.

The Newspaper Library

The newspaper library is usually the first stop for a reporter on any kind of assignment. Covering a speech? Look up background information on the speaker. Covering a sports event? What are the teams' records? Who are the coaches? What's the history of the rivalry? Reporters answer questions such as these, and many others, by checking the newspaper library.

Occasionally, there may be no time for such a check. When a fire or accident occurs, for example, the reporter rushes directly to the scene; there's no time for background preparation. But on any kind of story other than a breaking news event, the reporter's first stop should be the morgue.

Another use for the print or broadcast morgue is to search for photos. There you can find photos of a speaker or coach you haven't met. They will help you recognize that person for a possible one-on-one interview before the speech or game begins.

Other Sources

Traditional sources of information—such as reference books, dictionaries and encyclopedias—still play an important role in the production of the daily news product, as do their modern counterparts. Good reporters and editors make a habit of checking every verifiable fact. Here is a list of 20 commonly used reference sources, some of which may now be found online:

- **City directories.** You can find these directories in most cities. Like telephone books, they list names, addresses and phone numbers, but they may also provide information on the occupations of residents and the owners or managers of businesses. Useful street indexes provide information on the names of next-door neighbors.
- **Telephone books.** Use telephone books for verifying the spelling of names and addresses. They are usually reliable, but they are not infallible. Remember that people move and have similar names. Almost all telephone numbers in North America are now listed on various Internet-based services, including Switchboard (www.switchboard.com).
- **Maps of the city, county, state, nation and world.** Local maps are usually posted in the news room. Look for others in atlases. Online maps show various views of a location, including street views. Google Maps also can be extremely useful if you're headed to a place you've not been before. Google's street views can help you locate a building.
- **State manuals.** Each state government publishes a directory that provides useful information on various government agencies. These directories sometimes list the salaries of all state employees. Increasingly, this information also can be found on state websites.
- ***Bartlett's Familiar Quotations*** (Little, Brown). Always check famous quotations in a reliable published source; online citations can vary widely.
- ***Congressional Directory*** (Government Printing Office). Provides profiles of members of Congress.
- ***Congressional Record*** (Government Printing Office). Contains complete proceedings of the U.S. House and Senate.
- ***Current Biography*** (Wilson). Profiles of prominent people, published monthly.
- ***Dictionary of American Biography*** (Scribner's).
- ***Facts on File*** (Facts on File Inc.). A weekly compilation of news from metropolitan newspapers.

- *Guinness Book of World Records* (Guinness Superlatives). World records listed in countless categories.
- *National Trade and Professional Associations of the United States* (Columbia Books).
- *Readers' Guide to Periodical Literature* (Wilson). An index to magazine articles on a host of subjects.
- *Statistical Abstract of the United States* (Government Printing Office). A digest of data collected and published by all federal agencies.
- *Webster's Biographical Dictionary* (Merriam-Webster).
- *Webster's New World College Dictionary*, Fourth Edition (Wiley). The primary reference dictionary recommended by both the Associated Press and United Press International.
- *Webster's Third New International Dictionary* (Merriam-Webster). The unabridged dictionary is also recommended by AP and UPI.
- *Who's Who* (St. Martin's). World listings.
- *Who's Who in America* (Marquis). A biennial publication.
- *World Almanac and Book of Facts* (Newspaper Enterprise Association). An annual publication.

These useful publications, and many others like them, enable reporters to verify data and to avoid the embarrassment caused by printing or broadcasting errors. Other traditional sources of information include printed government records, documents from businesses, pamphlets published by government and nongovernment agencies, books, newspapers and magazines.

Be careful, though, when using material from a source with which you are not familiar. Some publications come from biased sources promoting a cause. It's the reporter's job to determine whether the information is biased or reliable. A good way to do that is to balance information from one source with information from another source with an opposing viewpoint. It may not always be possible for you to determine who's correct. Ensuring balance between two viewpoints is the next best thing.

Suggested Readings

Brooks, Brian S., James L. Pinson, and Jean Gaddy Wilson. *Working with Words: A Handbook for Media Writers and Editors*, 7th ed. New York: Bedford/St. Martin's, 2010. This handbook is the definitive work on the correct use of language in journalistic writing and editing.

Goldstein, Norm, ed. *Associated Press Stylebook and Briefing on Media Law.* New York: Associated Press, 2010. This is the definitive work on stylistic matters in journalistic writing.

Houston, Brant. *Computer-Assisted Reporting: A Practical Guide.* New York: Bedford/St. Martin's, 2003. Houston, the executive director of Investigative Reporters and Editors, has written an excellent introduction to computer-assisted reporting.

Houston, Brant, and Investigative Reporters and Editors Inc. *The Investigative Reporter's Handbook: A Guide to Documents, Databases, and Techniques.* New York: Bedford/

St. Martin's, 2008. This is the definitive handbook of investigative reporting.

IRE Journal. This monthly magazine is available from Investigative Reporters and Editors of Columbia, Mo. It offers regular articles on the use of computers in the news-gathering process.

Schlein, Alan M. *Find It Online: The Complete Guide to Online Research.* Edited by Peter Weber and J. J. Newby. Tempe, Ariz.: Facts on Demand Press, 2004. This guidebook offers basic information on the use of Web resources.

Suggested Websites

http://reporter.asu.edu
This website, which includes links to a variety of useful sources on the Internet, was compiled by Christopher Callahan, dean of the Walter Cronkite School of Journalism and Mass Communication at Arizona State University.

www.ire.org
Investigative Reporters and Editors maintains an excellent website for anyone interested in investigative reporting.

www.reporter.org
This website provides useful links to a variety of news-support organizations.

Exercises

1. **Team project.** Your instructor will divide the class into teams. With your team, select two print news stories of at least 800 words each on the same subject from different newspapers, magazines or wire services. List all the sources that the reporters used to collect the information and produce the stories. Compare the lists for the two stories. Which seems more comprehensive? Brainstorm a list of additional sources the reporters might have used.

2. Choose any story in your local newspaper, and tell how that story could have been improved with a database search. List databases the reporter could have searched.

3. If you were interested in determining where Apple Inc. is located and needed the name of its chief financial officer, where would you look? What other sources of information about the company might be available?

4. Write a one-page biographical sketch of your congressional representative based on information you retrieve from your library or a database.

5. Using the Internet, find the following information:
   a. The census of Rhode Island in 2000.
   b. The size of Rwanda in land area.
   c. The latest grant awards by the U.S. Department of Education.
   d. The names of universities in Norway that provide outside access via the Internet.
   e. The name of a website that contains the complete works of Shakespeare.
   f. The name of a website that contains federal campaign contribution data.

Finding the News
in News Releases

Big Brothers Big Sisters

Search this site → Search by Topic ▼

find my local agency: Enter Zip Code →

Home > News Archive   print 🖨 email ✉

support us

volunteer

enroll a child

our programs

about us

partners

en español

Join Us!

First Name

Last Name

Email Address

Zip Code →

Sign up for news and updates!

Read back issues »

Big Brothers Big Sisters, Little Brothers Little Sisters Come Together to Thank MetLife Foundation for Hispanic Mentoring Grants Totaling $1 Million

Irving, TX, November 17, 2009 -- Children benefitting from Big Brothers Big Sisters' Hispanic Mentoring Program came together during a celebration held at Gilbert Elementary in Irving, Texas to thank MetLife Foundation for a total of $1 million in grants supporting the organization's nationwide Hispanic mentoring initiatives. The Little Brothers and Sisters (Littles) and Big Brothers and Sisters (Bigs)—who were paired as a result of the efforts of Big Brothers Big Sisters of North Texas – honored MetLife Foundation with testimonials, thank-you cards, and tres leches cake, a dessert served during traditional Latin and Latin American celebrations.

During the program, Paul Torres, Managing Partner of New England Financial, a MetLife company, presented Big Brothers Big Sisters of America with the Foundation's second

"Littles" in the Big Brothers Big Sisters program receive a $500,000 check from the MetLife Foundation to support Hispanic mentoring programs. Back Row - L to R: Big Brothers Big Sisters of America Board Member Frank Bracken, Paul Torres, Managing Partner of New England Financial, a MetLife company, and Irving, Texas Gilbert Elementary School Principal Michael Crotty.

$500,000 grant for the Hispanic Mentoring program. The grant expands upon support begun last year, which enabled Big Brothers Big Sisters of America to develop parent and volunteer outreach materials in English and Spanish, as well as provide funding to 20 local Big Brothers Big Sisters agencies across the country, including North Texas. The new $500,000 grant will enable the 20 agencies to expand their outreach within the Hispanic community, engaging more Hispanic children and adults in mentoring.

7

A 2009 **news release** from Merck & Co. began as follows:

Mistrial Declared in First Federal FOSAMAX® Trial

Top Choice of Plaintiffs' Steering Committee Fails

WHITEHOUSE STATION, N.J., Sept. 11, 2009— Merck & Co., Inc. said today that a mistrial was declared by U.S. District Court Judge John F. Keenan in Boles v. Merck, the first FOSAMAX case to go to trial.

Perhaps you have never heard of Fosamax, or even of Merck & Co., but if your editor hands this news release to you for a story, you had better read on.

You'll learn that Merck & Co. has been marketing Fosamax since 1995 and that millions of postmenopausal women have taken it for the treatment and prevention of osteoporosis. You will also learn that as of June 30, 2009, approximately 899 lawsuits, which include approximately 1,280 plaintiff groups, had been filed and were pending against Merck in either federal or state courts blaming dental and jaw problems on Fosamax.

Consider yourself lucky if your city editor hands you this release. You are sure to find several good stories as a result.

Reporters do not go out and dig up all the stories they write. Many stories come to them. They are mailed, e-mailed, telephoned, sent via Twitter or another social networking service, faxed or hand-delivered by people who want to get something in "the news." They come from people or offices with different titles: public relations departments, public information offices, community relations bureaus, press agents, press secretaries and publicity offices. The people who write them call their stories news releases, **press releases**, or **handouts**.

Because good publicity is so important, private individuals, corporations and government agencies spend a great deal of money to obtain it. Much of the money pays the salaries of skilled and experienced personnel, many of whom have worked in the news business. Part of their job is to write news releases that newspapers, radio and television stations, and syndicated public relations wire services will use and that will appear on websites perhaps throughout the world. PR Newswire, for example, says it issues more than 1,000 news releases every day.

You might very well want to be among the people who write news releases. You might be seeking a career in public relations or advertising, but your journalism department wisely has you begin by studying news and news writing. Only by studying news and how news organizations handle news will you be successful in public relations or in offices of public information. Knowing how reporters are taught to deal with news releases will help you write better releases if that ever is your job. Of course, studying news also helps you enormously in the advertising world.

Skilled public relations or public information practitioners know how to write news stories, and they apply all the principles of good news writing in their news releases. A good news release meets the criteria for a good news story.

Nevertheless, as two of the best PR professionals, Carole Howard, formerly of *Reader's Digest*, and Wilma Mathews, formerly with AT&T and former director of public relations at Arizona State University, tell us, news releases are never intended to take the place of reporters. News releases, they write in *On Deadline: Managing Media Relations*, simply acquaint an editor with the basic facts of potential stories. Those who write news releases accept that their carefully crafted sentences will be checked and rewritten by reporters.

As a reporter, you must recognize that news releases, regardless of how they are delivered, are both a help and a hindrance to news agencies of all kinds. They are a help because without them, news organizations would need many more reporters. They are a hindrance because they sometimes contain incomplete, self-serving or even incorrect information. Because they are intended to promote the interests and favorable reputation of the individuals and organizations that disseminate them, news releases, by their very nature, are not objective.

Nevertheless, wise editors do not discard news releases without reading them. These editors often give them to reporters, often the newest ones, as sources for stories.

When your editor hands you a news release, you are expected to know what to do with it, regardless of which of the media you are employed in. You must be able to recognize the news in the release and apply all that you have learned about news values. The release may lead you to a good story. Your resourcefulness may improve your chances of being assigned to bigger things.

TYPES OF NEWS RELEASES

After you have read a number of news releases, you will notice that generally they fall into three categories:

- Announcements of coming events or of personnel matters — new hires, promotions, retirements and the like.
- Information about a cause.
- Information that is meant to build someone's or some organization's image.

Recognizing the types and purposes of news releases (and recognizing that some are hybrids and serve more than one purpose) will help you know how to rewrite them.

Announcement Releases

Organizations use the news media to tell their members and the public about coming events. For example:

> The Camera Club will have a special meeting at Wyatt's Cafeteria at 7 p.m. on Wednesday, March 20. Marvin Miller will present a slide program on "Yellowstone in Winter." All interested persons are invited to attend.

Although the release promotes the Camera Club, it also serves as a public-service announcement. Community newspapers and websites that offer such announcements are serving their readers. They might choose to present the information in a calendar of coming events.

Here is another example:

The first reception of the new season of the Springfield Art League will be on Sunday, Sept. 8, 3 to 5 p.m. in the Fine Arts Building.

Included in the exhibition will be paintings, serigraphs, sculpture, batiks, weaving, pottery, jewelry, all created by Art League members, who throughout the summer have been preparing works for this opening exhibit of the season.

The event also will feature local member-artists' State Fair entries, thus giving all who could not get to the fair the opportunity to see these works.

The exhibition continues to Friday, Sept. 13. All gallery events and exhibitions are free.

Other news releases concern appointments, promotions, new hires and retirements. The announcement of an appointment may read like this:

James McAlester, internationally known rural sociologist at Springfield University, has been appointed to the board of directors of Bread for the World, according to William Coburn, executive director of the humanitarian organization.

McAlester attended his first board meeting Jan. 22 in New York City. He has been on the university faculty since 1999.

Prior to that, he served as the Ford Foundation representative in India for 17 years.

The 19,000-member Bread for the World organization is a "broad based interdenominational movement of Christian citizens who advocate government policies that address the basic causes of hunger in the world," says Coburn.

The occasion is the appointment of McAlester, but the release also describes the purpose of the Bread for the World organization. By educating readers about the organization's purpose, the writer hoped to publicize its cause.

Companies often send releases when an employee has been promoted. For example:

James B. Withers Jr. was named senior vice president in charge of sales of the J. B. Withers Company, it was announced Tuesday.

Withers, who has been with the company in the sales division for two years, will head a sales force of 23 people.

"We are sure Jim can do the job," James B. Withers Sr., company president, said.

"He brings intelligence and enthusiasm to the job. We're pleased he has decided to stay with the company."

Founded in 1936, the J. B. Withers Company is the country's second-largest manufacturer of dog and cat collars.

A release like this one is an attempt by the company to get its name before the public and to create employee goodwill. Written in the form of an announcement, it is an attempt at free publicity.

ON THE JOB

Reading News Releases: Sweat the Small Print

Lara Jakes is an Associated Press correspondent in Baghdad, Iraq. She formerly served as a military, legal and counterterrorism writer for AP's Washington bureau. Thousands of press releases and transcripts of briefings from around the world cross her desk every week. While it's impossible to scrutinize them all, Jakes files away for future reading those that seem interesting but that don't require a spot — that is, immediate — story.

On a quiet day in her Justice Department press room office in 2008, Jakes went back to a release handed out weeks earlier about new penalties for fraud, waste and abuse in government contracts. Attached to the release was the language of regulations outlining the kinds of abuses that would be prosecuted. And buried within that language was a multibillion-dollar loophole that specifically exempted penalties for overseas government work by private companies — despite U.S. contracts in Iraq and Afghanistan that had cost taxpayers more than $102 billion over five years.

None of the other Justice reporters who got the release had written about the exemption, and at first Jakes assumed she had misread or misunderstood the small print in the rules' language.

"So I called the prosecutor who was in charge of the program," Jakes says. "He somewhat sheepishly agreed there was a major loophole in the regulations and blamed the White House [under President George W. Bush] for the wording of the new rules."

Jakes' stories caught the attention of Congress, sparking House of Representatives hearings and an investigation into how the loophole was quietly slipped into rules that were supposed to punish abusive contractors. One congressman called it an "egregious and flagrant disregard of taxpayer rights." Five months later, Congress passed a law to close the loophole and force stricter oversight of overseas contracts.

According to Jakes, Justice Department prosecutors later jokingly referred to the rules that closed the loophole as "LJ's law." Jakes says it was one of those stories that just seemed too good to be true — especially since it was initially handed over in a press release.

"I would have never found it if I'd not read the text of the regulations," Jakes says. The prosecutor who confirmed that the loophole was in the rules seemed surprised only that she'd found it — not that it was there. "It was almost like they were daring us to not read the release or pay attention to what was going on," Jakes says.

The moral: Sweat the fine print — even in news releases.

Cause-Promoting Releases

News releases in this category seek to further a cause. Some of these releases come from organizations whose worthwhile causes are in need of funds or volunteers. The letter reprinted here is from a county chairman of the American Heart Association to the editor of a newspaper. It is not written in the form of a release, but its effect is meant to be the same:

The alumnae and collegiate members of the Alpha Phi Sorority have just completed their annual Alpha Phi "Helping Hearts" lollipop sale. This year Valerie Knight, project chairwoman, led sorority members to achieve record-breaking sales. The lollipop sale is a national project of the Alpha Phi Sorority.

Sunday, March 5, Valerie Knight presented a check for $1,800 to the American Heart Association, Shelby County Unit. The contribution was presented during a reception at the Alpha Phi house. This contribution is an important part of the annual fund-raising campaign of the American Heart Association.

Heads of organizations attempt to alert the public to their message in any way they can. Any release, notice or letter they can get into the media for free leaves money for the cause that they represent.

Image-Building Releases

Another kind of news release serves to build up some person's or some organization's image. Politicians seeking to be elected or re-elected desire as much free publicity as they can get. For example:

James M. Merlin, honorary chairman of the board and director of Merlin Corporation, has been named honorary chairman of the Finance Committee, which will seek citywide financial support for the campaign to elect Hong Xiang as Springfield's next mayor.

Merlin, a well-known civic leader and philanthropist, termed the election of Xiang "one of the most important and far-reaching decisions the voters of Springfield will make in a long time. The city's financial crisis can only be solved through the kind of economic leadership Xiang has demonstrated the past 10 years as 1st Ward councilperson."

The appointment of Merlin as honorary chairman serves only to promote the image of the candidate. The quote is self-serving.

Organizations and government agencies at all levels often try to build their public image. Many of them persuade local mayors to proclaim a day or a week of recognition for their group, as in the following:

Mayor Juanita Williams has proclaimed Saturday, May 11, as Fire Service Recognition Day. The Springfield Fire Department in conjunction with the University

Fire Service Training Division is sponsoring a demonstration of the fire apparatus and equipment at the Springfield Fire Training Center. The displays are from 10 a.m. to 5 p.m. at 700 Bear Blvd. All citizens are urged to attend the display or visit their neighborhood fire station on May 11.

Our PRODUCT is your SAFETY.

An editor who hands you a release like this has probably decided that it is worth using in some form. The rest is up to you.

HANDLING THE NEWS RELEASE

Regardless of the type of news release, be sure to read the information that appears at the top (see Figure 7.1). All of that information may be useful to you. Even so, many news releases leave unanswered questions. You will probably want to contact people other than the director of information or even the contact person if you have serious doubts about some of the data given. But for routine accuracy checks, the people listed on the release can do the job. They may lead you to other helpful sources, too. Sometimes you may have sources of your own. And sometimes you may uncover the real story only from people who are neither connected to nor recommended by the director of information.

You may have to consult your editor regarding the release date. As a courtesy, most news media honor release dates. However, sometimes waiting would render the information useless. Also, once a release is public knowledge, editors feel justified in releasing whatever information it contains, even prior to the suggested release date. A release date is broken for all when it is broken by one.

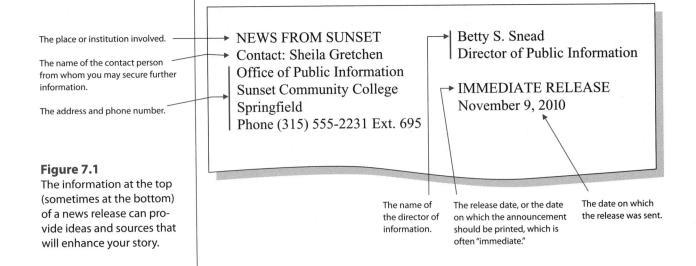

The place or institution involved.

The name of the contact person from whom you may secure further information.

The address and phone number.

Figure 7.1
The information at the top (sometimes at the bottom) of a news release can provide ideas and sources that will enhance your story.

NEWS FROM SUNSET
Contact: Sheila Gretchen
Office of Public Information
Sunset Community College
Springfield
Phone (315) 555-2231 Ext. 695

Betty S. Snead
Director of Public Information

IMMEDIATE RELEASE
November 9, 2010

The name of the director of information.

The release date, or the date on which the announcement should be printed, which is often "immediate."

The date on which the release was sent.

Rewriting the Announcement Release

Sometimes directors of information want nothing more than a listing on the record or calendar page of a newspaper or news site. Here is an example of an announcement release:

FOR THE CALENDAR

Elisabeth Bertke, quiltmaker and designer from Salem, Massachusetts, will discuss her work at 7:00 o'clock P.M. Tues., February 7, in Charters Auditorium, Hampton College. Two quilts designed and constructed by Bertke are included in the exhibit "The New American Quilt," currently on display at the Smith Art Gallery.

"This is an exciting display," Betty Martin, president of the Smith Art Gallery board of directors, said. "You simply can't afford to miss it."

This simple release may go directly to the news desk or to a special calendar editor.

If given to you, rewrite it. Some news organizations insist that you rewrite every news release if for no other reason than to avoid the embarrassment of running the same story as a competing news outlet. For some, it is a matter of integrity and professionalism.

After reading carefully through the release, make sure to check all the facts. Confirm the spelling of Bertke's name, and see if there is an apostrophe in "Charters Auditorium." The Smith Gallery may or may not be on the Hampton campus.

Next, if time allows, do some additional reporting. Call the gallery to ask how long the exhibit will be there. Are quilts made by local people included in the exhibit? Perhaps your questions will lead to a feature story on local quilt-making.

Then do your rewrite. You will drop the quotation of Betty Martin's. It is self-serving and promotional. But you might call Martin, Elisabeth Bertke or someone else connected to the event to try for a better quote. Reread your story to make sure the lead works and the writing is tight and clear.

Finally, correct any violations of AP style. In the preceding example:

- A hyphen should be inserted in "quilt-maker."
- "Massachusetts" should be abbreviated "Mass."
- "7:00 o'clock P.M." should be "7 p.m."
- "Tues." should be spelled out "Tuesday."
- "February" should be abbreviated "Feb."

Avoid relying on the copy desk to do your work if the rewrite is given to you.

Here is another example of an announcement release:

Mr. Richard G. Hernandez has been selected as the Outstanding Biology Teacher of the Year by the National

Association of Biology Teachers. He was previously selected as Nevada Science Educator of the Year.

As an outstanding representative of good high-school biology teaching Hernandez will receive a certificate and a series 50 binocular microscope with an engraved citation. Hernandez has been teaching at Hickman High School since 1980.

The story is far from earthshaking, but the honor is statewide. In large markets the release may not get much play. Smaller markets, however, will use it and perhaps enlarge upon it.

A first reading of the release tells you that it is wordy and leaves many questions unanswered. Hernandez may be an interesting fellow, but the release tells us little about him. You should approach this release in the same way you approach any news release: Finish the reporting, and then rewrite it. News style demands a new lead to the release:

> A Hickman High School science teacher has been named Outstanding Biology Teacher of the Year by the National Association of Biology Teachers.
>
> Richard G. Hernandez, a Hickman teacher since 1980, will receive a certificate and a series 50 binocular microscope with an engraved citation.
>
> Previously selected as Nevada Science Educator of the Year, Hernandez . . .

There the story runs out of information. You need to ask the following questions:

- Age?
- Degrees from where?
- Local address?
- Spouse, family?
- Annual award? One teacher selected from each state?
- Any previous Hickman winners? Any from local high schools?
- Year he received Nevada Science Educator award?
- Nominated for the award by whom?
- Date and place of bestowal? Public ceremony?
- Value of series 50 binocular microscope?

Then call Hernandez, and find out how he feels about the award. Talk to the principal, to fellow teachers and to some of Hernandez's students. Good quotations will spice up your story.

Rewriting the Cause-Promoting Release

News media generally cooperate with causes that are community-oriented. News releases like the following get attention:

A free tax clinic for low-income persons and senior citizens will be held on Feb. 9 and 10 in Springfield.

The clinic is sponsored by the Central State Counties' Human Development Corporation with the Accounting Department of the Springfield University College of Business.

Senior and graduate accounting students under the direct supervision of accounting faculty members will work with each taxpayer to help that taxpayer complete accurately his or her tax return.

The Human Development Corporation encourages persons especially to use the clinic who may be eligible for senior citizens' credits or other credits.

This is the fifth year the clinic has operated in Shelby County. Last year more than 275 persons in the eight counties served were assisted.

For information regarding the location of the clinics and to make an appointment, contact the Shelby County Human Development Corporation, 600 E. Broadway, Room 103, Springfield, 555-8376.

Again, you need more information. To begin with, you need to know more about the Human Development Corporation. A background paragraph on its origins, where it gets its money and its other areas of concern will put the story into context.

The release is unclear about who is eligible. What must an applicant's income be? How old must the person be? Also, you must find out the exact locations of the clinics.

Once you have answers to all your questions, dig for some human interest. Talk to a participating faculty member and to students who helped before and will help again. Then talk to some people who were helped in the past and to some who will come for help. In addition, you must talk to those in charge of the joint effort.

Because activities like these are in the public interest, media outlets will give them some news **play**. They will be more critical with releases that are merely self-serving.

Rewriting the Image-Building Release

The following is a typical release from a politician:

Sen. John Choi said today that nearly $400,000 in grants have been given final approval by two departments of the state government for interlocking improvements in Springfield and Lincoln County.

Choi said, "This is something I have been working on for this past year. It is a chance to show that state agencies are interested in communities. It also demonstrates that two agencies can work together to produce a coordinated, workable solution to improve a blighted area in Springfield."

The grants, Choi said, come from the State Bureau of Outdoor Recreation—$247,000 for purchasing Baltimore and Ohio railroad rights-of-way and developing a strip park—and the Department of Housing and Urban Development—$150,000 for planning the Flat Branch area. The second grant also stipulates that part of the money be used to coordinate the two projects: the B&O strip park and the Flat Branch redevelopment.

"I think residents of Springfield and

> Lincoln County will have a chance to help out in the planning of these two facilities. I hope this means the entire community will express opinions and come to a conclusion that will see these projects become a reality in the next two years."

The first three words of the release show just who is being served by the release. A Springfield reporter might write the lead this way to serve the reader instead:

> Springfield and Lincoln County will receive nearly $400,000 in state grants to fund the B&O strip park and the Flat Branch redevelopment project, Sen. John Choi said today.

The second paragraph of the release is a long quote, with no news value, from the senator. Probably he did not say those words at all; it's likely they were written by his press agent. You should eliminate the paragraph, or if you want a quote from the senator, call him and talk to him yourself.

The second paragraph of your story should indicate the source of the funding. Of course, you will check these figures, as well as all other figures in the news release, with independent sources.

> The grants come from two state agencies. The State Bureau of Outdoor Recreation granted $247,000 for purchasing the Baltimore & Ohio Railroad rights-of-way and for developing a strip park, and the Department of Housing and Urban Development granted $150,000 for planning the Flat Branch area. The second grant also stipulates that part of the money be used to coordinate the two projects.

You could shorten Choi's last quote with a paraphrase, retaining only Choi's essential point:

> Choi said he hoped Springfield and Lincoln County residents would have a chance to help plan the two projects. "I hope this means the entire community will express opinions and come to a conclusion that will see these projects become a reality in the next two years."

Like many news releases of this kind, this announcement would trigger other news stories in the local media. This story would call for local reactions from city and county officials and from local residents. The editor might assign several stories on the matter.

REWRITING A NEWS RELEASE—AN EXAMPLE

Sometimes a news release can lead to an interesting story with broad implications for the community, even if the actual release is self-serving—or misleading. Suppose you were given the following news release.

NEWS RELEASE
Springfield Community Teachers
   Association
Lillian A. Briggs, President
Contact:
   Tom Monnin, SCTA Salary Committee
   Chairman
Phone:
   555-555-6794 (Central High School)
   555-555-2975 (home)

For Immediate Release

Springfield—Police officers and firefighters in Springfield earn a greater starting salary than Springfield teachers, as discovered in a recent survey by the Springfield Community Teachers Association. According to their research, a new teacher in the Springfield public school system makes $40,000, while a firefighter starts at $40,725, $725 more than a new teacher. "This is a shameful situation for an educational community," said Tom Monnin, Springfield SCTA Salary Committee chairman.

The statistics gathered by the Springfield SCTA Salary Committee indicate that police officers with a bachelor's degree make $42,758. A dogcatcher with no college education earns just $6,536 less a year than a beginning teacher. Following is a comparison of starting salaries of some Springfield city employees and of public school teachers for the school year:

Occupation	Starting Salary
Police officer with bachelor's degree	$42,758
Firefighter with bachelor's degree	40,725
Meter reader	32,402
Animal control officer	33,464
Bus operator	32,402
Teacher with bachelor's degree	40,000

"Springfield teachers do not think city employees are overpaid but that teachers are underpaid," Monnin said.

Even though teachers work under a 9¼-month contract, the workweek is not 40 hours. When the hours for preparing and grading, attending sports events, musical concerts, dances, other after-school activities and PTA meetings are considered, a teacher's workweek is much longer than 40 hours. Summer break is used by many teachers for advanced preparation at the university, at their own expense.

The Springfield SCTA Salary Committee will present the salary proposal at the next meeting of the Springfield Board of Education.

The Springfield SCTA represents approximately 523 members in the public school system.

Reading the News Release Carefully

Your first task is to read the release, including the information at the top of the form, closely a couple of times, making notes in the margin about items that stand out for you. For example, the second paragraph cleverly suggests that dogcatchers make nearly as much money as teachers do, but you notice it speaks only of starting salaries. The more you read the release, the more uncomfortable you start to feel with it. No one can blame teachers for wanting more money, but there are other factors to consider.

Checking for Accuracy and Fairness

You should ask yourself what information is missing or what other viewpoints need to be considered. For example, you might wonder, What about working conditions?

Teachers in Springfield's schools certainly don't have to put their lives on the line the way police officers and firefighters do. And most people do not want to spend their lives chasing stray dogs.

Take special care when news releases cite studies, polls or surveys. Check the source of the figures for accuracy and possible bias. If you can't confirm the figures and their reliability, don't use them.

The fact that teachers work for a little more than nine months a year is down in the fourth paragraph. The release fails to mention a two-week break over Christmas and a week off in the spring semester. Most police officers and firefighters get two weeks off per year.

Is the release trying to suggest that because teachers actually spend more than 40 hours a week working, they should not have to work more than $9\frac{1}{4}$ months? Not all teachers spend their summers going to school. You probably know several who have summer jobs or who take long vacations.

Doing Additional Research and Interviews

Before you turn in a rewrite of this release, you have a lot of checking to do. But you also decide to go beyond checking to do some of your own reporting.

You begin by calling the city of Springfield's personnel office. The person answering the phone refers you to the department's website. Here you can gather all of the salary information you need, but you still have some questions. You call the personnel office again. When asked about the $40,725 starting salary of a firefighter, the personnel officer replies: "You wouldn't begin at that salary. Everyone is hired at $39,225 for a trial period of at least six months. If you work out OK, you might jump up to $40,725. Again, there are a lot of considerations besides the college degree."

Now you know you are on to something. Comparing starting salaries is one thing. But how much can a person eventually earn in a position?

You then ask about the starting salary for a police officer. "Yes," the director of personnel says, "$42,758 is the beginning salary for a police officer with a B.S. degree."

You then ask whether anyone with a B.S. degree can get hired at that salary.

"Most people wouldn't stand a chance of being hired," he says. "We have more than 100 applicants for every position, so we can be quite choosy. Unless a person has had some real experience as a police officer, I don't think he or she would make it."

Further questioning reveals that a top salary for a police officer is $54,712 after six years of service.

You also find the website of the Springfield public school system and check its salary schedule for teachers. Then you call a high school teacher. You ask her if she has to put in more than 40 hours a week at her job.

"Oh, yes," she says. "I teach a section of English composition, and I have a lot of papers to grade. I used to spend a lot of evenings preparing for classes, but once you've taught a course, it gets easier. And then I have to go to all those football games and basketball games."

You then find out that she is indeed required to attend, but only because she is in charge of the cheerleaders. When you express sympathy, the teacher replies, "No, I really don't mind. After all, I get $3,500 a year extra for being in charge of the cheerleaders."

You then learn from someone at the Springfield Schools' personnel office that quite a few teachers receive compensation for after-school activities — coaching, directing plays and musical activities, advising the staffs of the school newspaper and senior yearbook, and chaperoning dances. Teachers sponsoring class and club activities can earn from $1,000 to $4,000; a sponsor of the pep squad can earn up to $2,300. The top teacher's salary without any of these extras is $67,214.

Getting Back to the News Release Contact with Questions

Now you are ready to call Tom Monnin, the man whose name is on the release, for additional information. You ask if it is fair to compare a new teacher's salary with a new police officer's salary when the top pay for a police officer is $54,712 and the top teacher's salary is $67,214. Monnin explains that it takes 17 years for a teacher with a master's degree plus 75 hours to reach that top salary. A teacher with a bachelor's degree can make $54,219 after 11 years of teaching. When you ask about summers off and other vacations, Monnin replies, "I figure I work a 60-hour week. That means I work 51 40-hour weeks a year."

Monnin acknowledges that many teachers got paid extra for extracurricular activities. "But not all of them do," he says. "And there are many activities we do feel the responsibility to attend."

When asked about the argument that teachers do not have to put their lives on the line the way police and fire officials and even dogcatchers do, Monnin replies: "It's debatable who has to put their lives on the line. We're not as bad off as some schools, but we often have to restrain students physically. We read about school shootings all of the time, and we can't help but wonder when that will happen here."

Writing the Story

You've checked for accuracy, found out the important facts, and taken all the viewpoints into account. Only now are you ready to write the story. Write a lead that communicates the news, make sure your writing is tight, and check for AP style. Here's what you might write:

> The Springfield Community Teachers Association said Tuesday that new police officers can earn over $2,000 more than new teachers.
>
> What the teachers did not say was that a teacher eventually can earn $12,502 more a year than a police officer can.
>
> The SCTA statement was included with a survey that lists starting teachers' salaries at $40,000. Other figures listed as starting salaries are these: police officer with a bachelor's degree, $42,758; animal control officer, $33,464; meter reader, $32,402; bus operator, $32,402.

TIPS

How to Handle a News Release

- Read the news release, including the information at the top of the release form, carefully.

- Check for accuracy and fairness. Ask questions about missing information. Verify any spellings or information you have doubts about.

- Fill in missing information with your own reporting — research and interviews.

- Call the news release contact person. Watch for self-serving quotations and information.

- Write the story. Make sure your lead is strong, tighten the copy and check for AP style.

- Look for other possible news stories — local angles, reactions and the like — triggered by the release.

"This is a shameful situation for an educational community," said Tom Monnin, the SCTA Salary Committee chairman. "Springfield teachers do not think city employees are overpaid but that teachers are underpaid."

The association officers said that even though teachers work under a nine-month contract, extracurricular activities extend the workweek beyond 40 hours. Summer break, they said, is used for advanced study at the teachers' own expense.

"I figure I work a 60-hour week," Monnin said in an interview. "That means I work 51 40-hour weeks a year."

Some extracurricular activities, such as coaching, directing plays and supervising cheerleaders, earn extra compensation.

Teachers are not compelled to attend after-school functions, but "we do feel the responsibility to attend," Monnin said.

Teachers also feel compelled to continue their education. Top pay for a teacher with only a bachelor's degree is $54,219 after 11 years of teaching. A teacher with a master's degree plus 75 hours of classes can earn $67,214 after 17 years of teaching.

A police officer with a bachelor's degree can reach a top salary of $54,712 after six years of police work. But a person with a bachelor's degree and no police work experience is not likely to be hired, said Phil James, the Springfield director of personnel. James also said all firefighters are hired at $39,225. If a person has a bachelor's degree and stays on, he or she could make $40,725 after a six-month trial period.

Top pay for a dogcatcher is $37,626. "I sure wish I got summers off like those teachers," Tom Merell, an animal control officer, said. "I got nothing against teachers. But most of them make more money than I'll ever make. . . . Besides, students don't bite many teachers."

The SCTA Salary Committee will present its salary proposal at the next meeting of the Springfield Board of Education.

This story does with a news release what you should do with many of them. You should not be satisfied with the way it was written or with the information it contains. By asking some important questions, you can often put together an informative and more accurate story. Without saying that the news release was dishonest or misleading, a good reporter can correct or clarify some of the information contained in it. Here, the plight of the teacher is told clearly and objectively, but it is placed in a much better perspective than that of the news release.

Like many news releases, this one was the basis for a story the news outlet otherwise would not have had. That is why editors pay attention to news releases and why reporters look for the real story.

Suggested Readings

Bivins, Thomas H. *Public Relations Writing: The Essentials of Style and Format*, 4th ed. Lincolnwood, Ill.: NTC/Contemporary Publishing Group, 1999. This book explains how public relations professionals approach a wide variety of writing tasks.

Howard, Carole, and Wilma Mathews. *On Deadline: Managing Media Relations*, 3rd ed. Prospect Heights, Ill.: Waveland Press, 2006. This practical book offers suggestions on how organizations should deal with the news media.

Wilcox, Dennis L., and Lawrence W. Nolte. *Public Relations Writing and Media Techniques*, 6th ed. New York: HarperCollins, 2008. The authors cover the writing, production and distribution of a variety of public relations materials.

Suggested Websites

www.pressflash.com/resources_anatomy.php
On this website for a news release distribution service, you will find a terse description of a good news release.

www.press-release-writing.com/10_essential_tips_for
_writing_press_releases
Note these 10 essential tips for writing news releases. You'll see how serious professionals go about doing them well.

www.prwatch.org
This website is run by the nonprofit Center for Media and Democracy. According to the website, the CMD "strengthens participatory democracy by investigating and exposing public-relations spin and propaganda, and by promoting literacy and citizen journalism, media 'of, by and for the people.'"

Exercises

1. **Team project.** Your professor will place you in groups of three. Read the following release, and divide up the reporting and writing work. One person could explore what kind of power plant your city or community has and where local elected officials might stand on the plan to revise standards. How does anything in the release apply to your community's situation? How would local businesses and individuals be affected by the new standards? Another person could explore what officials in charge of the local plant might have to say about the kinds of changes proposed. What economic or other impact would they anticipate? The third person could explore what local environmentalists might have to say on the subject. Would the revised standards go far enough to be effective? Discuss your findings throughout your reporting. Then decide whether it would be more relevant, useful and interesting for readers to combine your findings into one story or whether to write several stories or a series of stories. Explain your decision in terms of news value for your community.

NEWS RELEASE
Environmental Protection Agency
FOR IMMEDIATE RELEASE
EPA Expects to Revise Rules for Wastewater Discharges from Power Plants
Discharges from power plants can have major adverse effects on water quality and wildlife

WASHINGTON, Sept. 15—The U.S. Environmental Protection Agency plans to revise the existing standards for water discharges from coal-fired power plants to reduce pollution and better protect America's water. Wastewater discharged from coal ash ponds, air pollution control equipment, and other equipment at power plants can contaminate drinking water sources, cause fish and other wildlife to die and create other detrimental environmental effects.

Earlier this year, EPA completed a multi-year study of power plant wastewater discharges and concluded that current regulations, which were issued in 1982, have not kept pace with changes that have occurred in the electric power industry over the last three decades. Air pollution controls installed to remove pollution from smokestacks have made great strides in cleaning the air people breathe, saving lives and reducing respiratory and other illnesses. However, some of the equipment used to clean air emissions does so by "scrubbing" the boiler exhaust with water, and when the water is not properly managed it sends the pollution to rivers and other waterbodies. Treatment technologies are available to remove these pollutants before they are discharged to waterways, but these systems have been installed at only a fraction of the power plants.

As part of the multi-year study, EPA measured the pollutants present in the wastewater and reviewed treatment technologies, focusing mostly on coal-fired power plants. Many of the toxic pollutants discharged from these power plants come from coal ash ponds and the flue gas desulfurization systems used to scrub sulfur dioxide from air emissions.

Once the new rule for electric power plants is finalized, EPA and states would incorporate the new standards into wastewater discharge permits.

More information about EPA's study is provided in an interim report published in August 2008. A final study will be published later this year.

More information on wastewater discharges from power plants: http://www.epa.gov/waterscience/guide/steam

Note: If a link above doesn't work, please copy and paste the URL into a browser.

2. Read each of the following news releases. First, indicate the type of news release it is. Second, list questions you would have if you were to rewrite it, including the facts you would check and the sources you would turn to for the answers. Finally, correct all departures from Associated Press style rules.

a. NEWS RELEASE
   For Further Information Contact:
   Humane Society of Missouri Media Center
   314-802-5712

   Humane Society of Missouri Confirms: Guilty Pleas Entered in Federal Court to Charges from Largest Dog Fighting Raid and Rescue in U.S. History

   Photos and Video of Dogs at Rescue Sites and Emergency Shelter Now Available

St. Louis, MO, September 14, 2009—The Humane Society of Missouri today confirms guilty pleas have been entered in connection to the July 8, 2009 multi-state federal dog fighting raid that resulted in the rescue of more than 500 fighting dogs. Federal agents made 26 arrests and dogs were rescued in 8 states.

This rescue operation is the largest dog fighting raid in U.S. history. The Humane Society of Missouri participated in the 18-month investigation and led the subsequent rescue and shelter operations, working in partnership with the Federal Bureau of Investigation, the Missouri State Highway Patrol, the United States Department of Agriculture's Office of the Inspector General, the U.S. Marshals Service and the United States Attorney.

Four eastern Missouri men, Robert Hackman of Foley, Teddy Kiriakidis of Leasburg, Ronald Creech of Leslie and Michael Morgan of Hannibal pled guilty today in U.S. District Court in St. Louis to charges connected to the dog fighting raid. Another man arrested in connection with the dog fighting raid, Jack Ruppel of Eldon, pled guilty to charges on September 4 in federal court in Jefferson City.

"We can confirm that five of the individuals charged with this gruesome form of animal abuse are being brought to justice," said Kathy Warnick, president of the Humane Society of Missouri. "Today's guilty pleas raise awareness that dog fighting is unacceptable, inhumane and illegal and will not be tolerated. The unprecedented scale of this investigation and rescue operation should alert the entire nation to what a horrible crime dog fighting is and what a dangerous and serious affect it can have on animals and communities."

Warnick continued, "We sincerely hope these guilty pleas will result in sentencing that sends the message that this form of animal abuse will no longer be tolerated. Humane Society of Missouri staff and our many partners have selflessly sacrificed much of their personal lives in the pursuit of this investigation and the care of these dogs. We fervently desire that this historic effort marks the beginning of the end to dog fighting in the United States."

"This was the largest dog fighting raid in U.S. history, but it will not be the last," warned Michael Kaste, Assistant Special Agent in Charge of the FBI in St. Louis. "This case sets precedents for the FBI along with our local, state and federal partners to aggressively root out underground dog fighting rings where people have absolutely no qualms about torturing man's best friend for money and entertainment."

b. NEWS RELEASE
The teaching faculty, administration and staff of The South Shore Country Day School formally began the school year Friday, August 30, with an all day workshop on curriculum planning.

This year, the School will be involved in a year long task of self evaluation. All aspects of the School's curriculum and student life will be considered and a new five year, long range plan for the curriculum will be written. The School's last major plan was constructed in 1994.

The evaluation process is designed to keep curriculum consistent with the School's educational philosophy and statement of mission. It will identify problems, strengths, and opportunities for expansion. At various stages of the process, all constituencies of the School will have an opportunity to express concerns and opinions. By the end of the school year, a new plan will be ready for integration and implementation by the School's administration.

William R. Lopez, Chairman of the School's Board of Trustees, spoke to the faculty about the upcoming project and the need to change. "We will attempt to make the current school better; we will not be creating a new school," he said.

Thomas B. Lang, the School's headmaster, emphasized the importance of total faculty participation in the formulation and execution of the mission statement. "We're all in this together," Lang said. "Curriculum is the sum of all the parts. No one teaches in a vacuum."

Among topics discussed at the workshop were: the importance of academic excellence; student social service; a need for diversity within the student body; the importance of educating the whole child; providing increased opportunity for students to participate in a variety of academic and nonacademic projects; and the ethical considerations in the School.

3. Assume you are a reporter for the Springfield paper. Rewrite the following release. Your instructor will be your news source for any questions you have.

NEWS RELEASE

Nearly 11,000 seat belt violation warnings were issued to motorists by the State Highway Patrol during the first month the new seat belt law was in effect.

Colonel Howard J. Hoffman, Superintendent of the State Highway Patrol, reported today that 10,908 warnings were issued to motorists in passenger vehicles for not wearing their seat belts as required by State Law.

Colonel Hoffman also noted that during this same reporting period, 50 persons were killed in traffic accidents investigated by the Highway Patrol. Only two of the persons killed in these mishaps were found to be wearing seat belts.

"The value of wearing a seat belt cannot be overemphasized," Hoffman said. "We don't know how many of these investigated traffic deaths could have been avoided by the use of seat belts. It is known, however, that seat belts have saved lives and prevented serious injuries to others. We will continue to vigorously enforce the State seat belt law and hopefully more and more motorists will make it a habit to buckle their seat belts."

Reporting with Numbers

8

Brooks Egerton, a *Dallas Morning News* reporter, had written about a wealthy man who shot an unarmed prostitute in the back and got probation for the killing. The sentence seemed so unusual that Egerton wondered how common it was for killers to get probation.

Egerton and his colleague Reese Dunklin started asking people in the legal system about the issue. They learned that probation for murder was rare, but that normally probation would be considered for something like a mercy killing. The story might have been stillborn right there, but the reporters decided to see if they could put some numbers on it.

They obtained a database of everyone on probation in Texas. Then they cross-referenced thousands of police and court records, many of which they obtained by filing about 100 requests under the Texas Public Information Act. Some of the information they gathered the old-fashioned way—they talked people into giving it to them.

What they found was stunning. From 2000 to 2006, Texas judges sentenced 120 convicted killers to probation. Forty-seven of them were in Dallas County, a disproportionate number based on population and number of cases handled. Armed with the numbers, they interviewed more than 200 people and showed their findings to a half dozen legal scholars. The data, Dunklin said, "can liberate you to write with authority."

The numbers were all there, but the reporters put a human face on the stories by talking about specific cases to show the inequities in the system. To illustrate the disparities in sentencing, they told the story of Eddie Mae Dudley, who killed another woman in a fight over a beer. She served seven years. Then she shot and killed one of her housemates, an elderly stroke victim, while he lay drunk in bed. For that murder, she received five years' probation in a plea bargain.

They also told the story of Jacqueline Fox, 17, who had no record. Her ex-boyfriend threatened her at gunpoint. He beat her so hard with a two-by-four that the board broke. Fox stabbed him with a knife and killed him. After waiting in jail four and a half months, she was offered a plea bargain: In exchange for a guilty plea, she would get 10 years' probation, twice that of Dudley, a two-time killer. Fox accepted.

The numbers don't lie. Supported by interviews with law and court officials, with victims' families and even with some of the murderers, the stories were convincing and readable. (Figure 8.1 shows how the series was presented on the Web.) The Dallas County District Attorney's office began reviewing the probation-for-murder plea bargains that its prosecutors had made to see if they should try to revoke probation in any of the cases.

Journalists have a responsibility to understand numbers so that they can report clearly and accurately on everything from courts to schools. This chapter will help you do just that.

Figure 8.1

To write the "Unequal Justice" series, *Dallas Morning News* reporters Brooks Egerton and Reese Dunklin relied on large amounts of statistical information.

PROPORTION

One of the most important services journalists perform for their readers is to give **proportion** to numbers in the news—explaining things relative to the size or the magnitude of the whole. A municipal budget that is going up by $500,000 would be a windfall for a small town in New Hampshire but a minor adjustment for a metropolis such as New York, Chicago or Minneapolis. At the state level in 2009, New York Gov. David A. Paterson proposed cutting $5 billion to try to balance the state budget. That proposed cut would cover the combined state budgets of Alabama, Alaska, Colorado, Indiana and Mississippi.

Other figures might mean a lot or a little, depending on the context. If you know little or nothing about baseball, you might think that Babe Ruth's career batting average of .342—34.2 hits for every 100 times at bat—indicates that Ruth wasn't a good hitter. After all, he failed almost two out of three times at bat. But when you look at the context—other players' averages—you realize that Ruth was exceptional. For instance, in 2009 only two major league players had a higher average and just one tied Ruth—and that was only for the year, not for a career.

Percentages and Percentage Change

Percentages are basic building blocks used to explain proportion. Batting averages explain the percentage of hits compared with the number of times at bat. The political strength of a public official is partly reflected in the percentage of the votes won at the polls. Stories about budgets, taxes, wages, retail sales, schools, health care and the environment all are explained with percentages.

To calculate a percentage, take the portion that you want to measure, divide it by the whole and then move the decimal two places to the right. For example, suppose you want to know what portion of the city's budget is allocated to police services. Divide the police budget by the city budget, move the decimal point two places to the right, and you get the percentage of the budget that pays for police services.

To compute a percentage:

Step 1 Portion (police budget) ÷ whole (city budget) = .xxx
$30,000,000 ÷ $120,000,000 = .25
Step 2 Move the decimal point two places to the right: 25%

Precision in the use of numbers requires that you ask some basic questions. Reporters need to be careful of percentages that might be used in misleading ways or percentages that tell only part of a story.

Populations, Samples and Margins of Error

If someone is giving you percentages, you must ask what **population** the figures are based on. For instance, suppose a juvenile officer tells you that 70 percent of

T I P S

To Calculate a Percentage

● Portion ÷ whole = .xxx

● Move decimal point two places: .xxx = xx.x%.

the juvenile offenders do not have to return to his program. Your first question should be, "What population was used to figure the percentage?" Was it all the juveniles in the program during the last calendar year? If so, perhaps the success rate is high because the period being measured isn't long enough to take less successful years into account. And how has your source counted juveniles who are old enough now to be certified as adults? How does he account for juveniles who may have committed a crime in another jurisdiction?

The officer might explain that the figure is based on a sample of the population in the program over 10 years. A **sample** is a small number of people picked at random so as to be representative of the population as a whole. Using common statistical tables, researchers draw a sample of the names of all juveniles who were in the program over 10 years and contact them. From those contacts, they can determine the success rate of the program. If the figure is based on a scientific sampling like the one just described, there will also be a **margin of error**, which will be expressed as "plus or minus x points." Say that the margin of error for this sample is 4. That means that the success rate is between 66 and 74 percent.

The base on which a percentage is calculated is significant. Say a colleague is making $40,000, and you make $30,000. The salary is the base. Your employer decides to give your colleague a 4 percent increase and to give you a 5 percent increase. Before you begin feeling too good about the honor, consider that your colleague's raise is $1,600, and your raise is $1,500. Your colleague won a bigger raise, and the gap between the two of you grew. Hence, if you have different bases on which to figure the percentages, the comparisons are invalid.

In one investigative report, the *St. Louis Post-Dispatch* recognized it had percentages with different bases, and it handled them correctly. The newspaper examined repeat drunken-driving offenders in seven jurisdictions in its circulation area. In Missouri, drivers convicted two times of driving while intoxicated (DWI) are supposed to be charged with a felony on the third offense. In reporting on the results, the reporters carefully gave the percentages and the base for each jurisdiction. That was important because the base ranged from seven cases in St. Louis city to 120 in St. Louis County. The percentages of cases handled correctly ranged from 29% to 51%.

Percentage Change and Percentage Points

Confusion often occurs when people talk about the difference between two percentage figures. For example, say the mayor won the election with 55 percent of the vote and had only one opponent, who received 45 percent. The mayor won by a margin of 10 **percentage points**. The percentage points, in this case, equal the difference between 55 and 45. However, the mayor won 22 percent more votes (10 divided by 45 equals .22). Because the percentages are based on the same whole number—in this case, the total number of voters—the percentages can be compared. But if you compare the percentage of a city budget devoted to law enforcement in consecutive years, you will need to include the actual dollar amounts with the percentages because total spending probably changed from one year to the next.

TIPS

To Calculate Percentage Change

- (New number) – (old number) = change.

- Change ÷ old number = .xxx.

- Move decimal point two places to right: .xxx = xx.x%.

- Percentage change can be a positive or a negative number.

Another important aspect of percentages is the concept of **percentage change**. This number explains how much something goes up or down. In the city budget summary shown in Table 8.1, for example, look under "Appropriations" and then under "Revised Fiscal Year 2010." Total spending was $18,654,563. The proposed budget for 2011 ("Adopted Fiscal Year 2011") is $19,570,518. What is the percentage increase? You find the percentage change by dividing the increase or decrease by the old budget.

To compute a percentage change:

Step 1   Find the change.
$19,570,518 – $18,654,563 = $915,955 (increase)

Step 2   Change ÷ base amount = .xxx
$915,955 ÷ $18,654,563 = .049

Step 3   Move the decimal point two places to the right: 4.9%

Rounded off, this is a 5 percent increase in spending.

If the 2011 budget is increased 4.9 percent again, that will be a $958,955 increase, or $43,000 more, because of the bigger base.

When changes are large, sometimes it is better to translate the numbers into plain words rather than using a percentage figure. In New York, for instance, that proposed $5 billion cut in the state budget amounts to about $256 per resident of the state.

Averages and Medians

Averages and medians are numbers that can be used to describe a general trend. For any given set of numbers, the average and the median might be quite close, or they might be quite different. Depending on what you are trying to explain, it might be important to use one instead of the other or to use both.

The **average**—more technically called the *arithmetic mean*—is the number you obtain when you add a list of figures and then divide the total by the number of figures in the list. The **median** is the midpoint of the list—half the figures fall above it, and half the figures fall below it.

To compute an average:

Step 1   Add the figures.
Step 2   Divide the total by the number of figures:
Total ÷ number of figures = average.

To find the median:

Step 1   Arrange the figures in rank order.
Step 2   Identify the figure midway between the highest and lowest numbers. That figure is the median.

Note: When you have an even number of figures, the median is the average of the two middle figures.

As a general rule, you are safe using averages when there are no large gaps among the numbers. If you took an average of 1, 4, 12, 22, 31, 89 and 104, you

"Average" Can Mean Different Things to Different People

Although most people understand *average* to refer to "arithmetic mean," the word is sometimes used for other types of statistical results, including "median" and "mode."

In reporting statistics, be certain you know the "average" involved. All of the following are averages.

- **Mean.** The arithmetic average, found by adding all the figures in a set of data and dividing by the number of figures. The mean of 2, 4 and 9 is 5 (2 + 4 + 9 = 15; 15 ÷ 3 = 5).

- **Median.** The middle value in a set of figures. If there is no middle value because there is an even number of figures, average the two middle numbers. The median of 2, 4 and 9 is 4. The medians of 5, 7, 9 and 11 and of 3, 7, 9 and 15 both are 8 (7 + 9 = 16; 16 ÷ 2 = 8).

- **Mode.** The most frequent value in a set of figures. The mode of 2, 5, 5, 5, 15 and 23 is 5.

would get 37.6. The average distorts the numbers because the average is higher than five of the seven numbers. The mean, or midpoint, is 22. On the other hand, if you had numbers ranging from 1 to 104 and the numbers were distributed evenly within that range, the average would be an accurate reading.

Rates

A **rate** is used to make fair comparisons between different populations. One example of a rate comparison is *per capita*, or per person, spending, such as for school funding. Even though a big-city school budget looks incredibly large to someone in a small community, the money has to stretch over more students than it would in a smaller district. As a result, spending per capita provides a better comparison between districts with different enrollments. Suppose your school district (district A) has 1,000 students and spends $2 million. You want to compare spending in

When Averages Distort

Take a set of scores from a final exam in a class of 15 students. The students scored 95, 94, 92, 86, 85, 84, 75, 75, 65, 64, 63, 62, 62, 62 and 62. Both the average (that is, the arithmetic mean) and the median are 75.

The picture can look quite different when the figures bunch at one end of the scale. Consider this example from professional baseball:

In 2009 the Chicago Cubs had a payroll of $134.8 million. With a range of salaries from $400,000 to $18.6 million, the median income was $2.2 million. However, the average, or mean, was $5.4 million ($134,809,000 ÷ 25 players).

your district with spending in district B, which has 1,500 students and a budget of $3 million. You would use the following formula to calculate per capita spending.

To compute per capita spending:

Budget in dollars ÷ number of people = dollar amount per capita
District A: $2,000,000 ÷ 1,000 = $2,000 per capita
District B: $3,000,000 ÷ 1,500 = $2,000 per capita

School district B spends $1 million more a year than district A, but both districts spend the same amount per pupil.

To compare crime incidents or spending amounts among municipalities with varying populations, reporters should use per capita figures.

Remember the "Unequal Justice" series mentioned at the beginning of this chapter? After the series appeared, an attorney in the Dallas County District Attorney's office suggested that the reason Dallas County's numbers were higher was that Dallas County handled more murder and homicide cases than other jurisdictions. Dunklin was able to counter that he and his colleagues had gone beyond the raw numbers and had calculated the rates of homicides. That satisfied the attorney, and he dropped that suggestion. In other words, the reporters used the numbers correctly to reveal facts that even the district attorney's office didn't know.

INTEREST AND COMPOUNDING

Interest is a financial factor in just about everyone's life. Consumers pay interest on home mortgages, car loans and credit card balances. Individuals and businesses earn interest when they deposit money in a financial institution or make a loan. Federal regulations require the interest rates charged by or paid by most institutions to be expressed as an **annual percentage rate (APR)**, so that interest rates are comparable from one institution to another.

There are two types of interest: simple and compound. **Simple interest** is interest to be paid on the **principal**, the amount borrowed. It is calculated by multiplying the amount of the loan by the annual percentage rate.

Suppose a student borrows $1,000 from her grandfather at a 5 percent annual rate to help cover college expenses. She needs only a one-year loan, so the cost is figured as simple interest.

To calculate simple interest:

Multiply the principal by the interest rate.
$1,000 × .05 = $50

To find the amount the student will repay her grandfather at the end of the year, add the principal to the interest. The student will owe $1,050.

If the loan is made over a period longer than a year, the borrower pays **compound interest**. Compound interest is interest paid on the total of the principal and the interest that already has accrued.

TIPS

To Calculate per Capita Spending

- Divide the budget by the number of people:
  Budget ÷ population = per capita spending.

TIPS

To Calculate Simple Interest and Total Amount Owed

- Express the interest rate as a decimal by moving the decimal point two places to the left.

- Multiply the principal by the interest rate:
  $1,000 × .05 = $50

- Add the principal to the interest owed:
  $1,000 + $50 = $1,050

The same result can be obtained another way. Multiply the principal by 1 plus the interest rate expressed as a decimal:
  $1,000 × 1.05 = $1,050

TIPS

To Calculate Compound Interest

● Add 1 to the interest rate expressed as a decimal: 1 + .05 = 1.05

● Using a calculator, multiply the principal by $(1.xx)^n$ (the superscript *n* represents the number of years of the loan).

The result is the total amount owed.

Suppose the student borrows $1,000 at an annual percentage rate of 5 percent and pays her grandfather back four years later, after graduation. She owes 5 percent annual interest for each year of the loan. But because she has the loan for four years, each year she owes not only simple interest on the principal but also interest on the interest that accrues each year.

At the end of year 1, she owes $1,050. To see how much she will owe at the end of year 2, she has to calculate 5 percent interest on $1,050: $1,050 × .05 = $52.50.

Here is how to calculate the interest for all four years. (Note that 1.05 is used instead of .05 to produce a running total. If you multiply 1,000 by 1.05, you get 1,050; if you multiply 1,000 by .05, you get 50, which you then have to add to 1,000 to get the principal and interest.)

$$\$1,000 \times 1.05 \times 1.05 \times 1.05 \times 1.05 = \$1,215.51$$

Because most consumers pay off student loans, car loans, mortgages and credit card debt over a period of time, and because interest is compounded more often than once a year, calculations usually are far more complicated than those in the example. Many financial websites and computer programs offer calculators for computing interest. For instance, you can select from a variety of calculators in the Money section of the *USA Today* website (www.usatoday.com).

Student loans taken out through federal programs administered by banks, credit unions and universities are a prime example of more complicated transactions. Suppose a student has a $5,000 guaranteed student loan with an interest rate of 8 percent per year. After finishing school, the student has 10 years to repay, and each year she pays 8 percent interest on the amount of the original principal that is left unpaid. If the student makes the minimum payment of $65 on time each month for the 10-year life of the loan, she will pay the bank a total of $7,800. She pays $2,800 in interest on top of the original principal of $5,000. If she does not pay the balance down each month, the interest she owes will be even higher.

Consumers get the benefits of compounding when they put money in interest-bearing accounts, because their interest compounds. The same effect takes place when people make good investments in the stock market, where earnings are compounded when they are reinvested.

INFLATION

Inflation is an increase in the cost of living over time. Because prices rise over time, wages and budgets, too, have to increase to keep up with inflation. A worker who receives a 2 percent pay increase each year will have the same buying power each year if inflation rises at 2 percent. Because of inflation, reporters must use a few simple computations to make fair comparisons between dollar amounts from different years.

Let's say the teachers in your local school district are negotiating for a new contract. They claim that their pay is not keeping pace with inflation. You know that the starting salary for a teacher in 1997 was $30,000 and that the starting salary in 2009 was $38,000. To determine whether the teachers' claim is true, you convert 1997 dollars to 2009 dollars, and you find that the starting salary in 2009 would have been $40,368 if the district had been keeping up with inflation. In other words, in constant dollars, first-year teachers earned $2,368 less in 2009 than they earned in 1997. (Numbers that are adjusted for inflation are called *constant*, or *real*, *dollars*. Numbers that are not adjusted for inflation are called *nominal*, or *current*, *dollars*.)

The most common tool used to adjust for inflation is the Consumer Price Index, which is reported each month by the U.S. Bureau of Labor Statistics, a part of the U.S. Department of Labor. You can get current CPI numbers on the Web at www.bls.gov/cpi.

TAXES

Reporters not only pay taxes, but also have to report on them. Governments collect taxes in a variety of ways, but the three major categories are sales taxes, income taxes and property taxes. Tax rates are expressed as percentages.

Sales Taxes

State, county and municipal governments can levy sales taxes on various goods and services. Sales taxes—also known as *excise taxes*—are the simplest to figure out.

To figure a sales tax, multiply the price of an item by the sales tax rate. Add the result to the original price to obtain the total cost.

Take the example of a student buying an $1,800 computer before beginning school at the University of Florida. If he shops in his home state of Delaware, he will pay no state sales tax. If he buys the computer after arriving in Florida, where the state sales tax is 6 percent, he will pay a state sales tax of $108 and another $13.50 in county sales tax, for a total of $1,921.50.

Sales taxes are an excellent way for you to track sales in your city, county or state. The appropriate government unit—a finance or comptroller's office, for instance—will have sales tax revenues, which are a direct reflection of sales and, therefore, an excellent way to use numbers to report on the economy in your area.

Income Taxes

Governments tax a percentage of your income to support such services as building roads, running schools, registering people to vote and encouraging businesses to grow. Income taxes are paid to the federal government, to most state governments, and to some municipalities.

Calculating income taxes can be tricky because many factors affect the amount of income that is subject to the tax. For that reason, the only way to figure

ON THE JOB

Working with Numbers

From city budgets to election results to the economic meltdown, today's important stories frequently involve numbers. Too often, unfortunately, reporters avoid them or leave their interpretation to officials.

But understanding how to interpret and present numbers in a news story can make a big difference. As the computer-assisted reporting editor for three newspapers and as training director for Investigative Reporters and Editors, Jennifer LaFleur saw that reporters who had these skills were able to break important stories. For instance, at *The Dallas Morning News*, math skills led education reporters to uncover millions of dollars in misspending in the Dallas Independent School District. At ProPublica — the nonprofit investigative news room where she now works — many of LaFleur's first stories involved the nation's economic crisis and the nearly $800 billion federal stimulus package. Those math skills have led to uncovering problems in banking and campaign finance.

Over the years, LaFleur has noticed these common problems:

- Love for the superlative leads some reporters to use phrases such as "Texas has the most hunting accidents" or "California has the most cars" without putting them in perspective. Big states have lots of everything, so adjust the numbers for the population.
- Things cost more today than in the past, but too often reporters fail to adjust the figures for inflation. A 1950 dollar was not what it is today.
- In striving for precision, some reporters give readers a false message. A poll of just 400 people can't be that precise, so we shouldn't report that 43.25 percent of respondents said something.

"In a time when every reporter is asked to do more, no reporter should be without the basic skills to interpret the numbers they run across every day," says LaFleur. "They should know how to compute a percent change, percent of total and per capita and know what all those things mean."

a person's income tax is to consult the actual numbers and follow tables published by the Internal Revenue Service (www.irs.gov) or the state department of taxation.

Governments use tax incentives to encourage people to undertake certain types of economic activities, such as buying a home, saving for retirement, and investing in business ventures. By giving people and businesses tax deductions, the government reduces the amount of income that is taxable.

A tax deduction is worth the tax rate times the amount of the tax deduction. The most common tax deduction is for the interest people pay on their home loans. Tax deductions are worth more to people with higher incomes. Take the example of two families who own homes. Both pay $2,500 in interest on their home mortgage in a year, the cost of which is deductible for people who itemize deductions on their income tax forms. The lower-income family is in the lowest federal income tax bracket, in which the tax rate is 10 percent, so that family saves $250 on its tax bill ($2,500 × .10 = $250). The higher-income family, which is in the federal income tax bracket of 33 percent, saves $825 on its tax bill ($2,500 × .33 = $825). In fact, the family in the 33 percent tax bracket probably owns a more expensive home and probably pays much more than $2,500 in mortgage interest a year. The impact is that the family saves even more on its income tax.

Income tax rates are based on your *adjusted gross income*. For example, if you make $8,350 or less after deductions, you will pay a tax of 10 percent ($835). If you make between $8,351 and $33,950 after deductions—enough to move you into the 15 percent bracket—you will pay $835 plus 15 percent of the amount over $8,350.

Property Taxes

City and county governments collect property taxes. When people talk about property taxes, they usually mean taxes on the value of houses, buildings and land. In some places, people also are taxed each year on the value of their cars, boats and other personal property.

The two key factors in property taxes are the assessed value and the millage rate. The **assessed value** is the amount that a government appraiser determines a piece of property is worth. The **millage rate**—the rate per thousand dollars—is the tax rate determined by the government.

To calculate property taxes:

Step 1
Divide the assessed value by 1,000.
$140,000 ÷ 1,000 = 140

Step 2
Multiply the result by the millage rate.
140 × 2.25 = $315 in taxes

Counties and cities hire professional appraisers to assess the values of land and buildings in their jurisdiction, and typically their assessments have been far lower than the actual market value of the property. Because of abuses and public confusion, most states in recent years have ordered revaluations to bring assessments into line with market values, and they have adjusted millage rates accordingly, though assessments can vary widely from appraiser to appraiser.

Appraisals are based on complicated formulas that take into account the size, location and condition of the property. Still, the government may say your house is worth $160,000, even if you know you could sell it for $180,000.

When you are reporting tax rate changes, you should find out how they affect houses in different value brackets to help explain the impact. By talking to the

TIPS

To Calculate Property Tax

- Divide the assessed value by 1,000:
  $140,000 ÷ 1,000 = 140

- Multiply that result by the millage rate:
  140 × 2.25 = $315

assessor or tax collector, you should be able to report, for instance, that the taxes for a house valued at $140,000 would be $315 and that taxes for a house valued at $250,000 would be $562.50.

BUDGETS

The budget is the blueprint that guides the operation of any organization, and a reporter must learn to read a budget just as a carpenter must learn to read a set of blueprints. It's not as difficult as it appears at first glance.

In many cases today, you'll be able to get the budget (and other financial information as well) for your city or school district in an electronic file. You might also be able to view it on a local website, but you probably cannot download that file into a spreadsheet database. However, once you have the budget in an electronic file, you can create your own spreadsheet and perform analyses that not long ago were only in the power of the institution's budget director. This is one of many ways the computer has become an essential news room tool. However, with a computer or without, first you need to know the basics of budgeting.

TIPS

Budget Stories Usually Deal With

● Changes.

● Trends.

● Comparisons.

Budget Basics

Every budget, whether it's your personal budget or the budget of the U.S. government, has two basic parts—*revenues* (income) and *expenditures* (outgo). Commercial enterprises earn their income primarily from sales; not-for-profit organizations depend heavily on contributions from public funding and private donors. Government revenues come from sources such as taxes, fees and service charges, and payments from other agencies (such as state aid to schools). The budget usually shows, in dollar amounts and percentages, the sources of the organization's money. Expenditures go for such items as staff salaries, supplies, utility bills, construction and maintenance of facilities, and insurance. Expenditures usually are listed either by line or by program. The difference is this: A **line-item budget** shows a separate line for each expenditure, such as "Salary of police chief—$150,000." A **program budget** provides less detail but shows more clearly what each activity of the agency costs—for example, "Burglary prevention program—$250,000."

Finding Stories in Budget Changes, Trends and Comparisons

Now let's see what kinds of stories budgets might yield and where to look for those stories. Take a minute to scan Table 8.1, a summary page from the annual budget of a small city. You can apply the skills of reading a city's annual budget to similar accounting documents on other beats—for example, annual reports of businesses and not-for-profit organizations.

The most important budget stories usually deal with changes, trends and comparisons. Budget figures change every year. Generally, as costs increase, so do budgets. But look under "Department Expenditures" in our sample budget (Table 8.1)

Table 8.1
Summary Page of a
Typical City Budget

General Fund—Summary

Purpose

The General Fund is used to finance and account for a large portion of the current operation expenditures and capital outlays of city government. The General Fund is one of the
largest and most important of the city's funds because most governmental programs
(Police, Fire, Public Works, Parks and Recreation, and so on) are generally financed wholly or
partially from it. The General Fund has a greater number and variety of revenue sources
than any other fund, and its resources normally finance a wider range of activities.

APPROPRIATIONS

	Actual Fiscal Year 2010	Budget Fiscal Year 2010	Revised Fiscal Year 2010	Adopted Fiscal Year 2011
Personnel services	$9,500,353	$11,306,619	$11,245,394	$12,212,336
Materials and supplies	1,490,573	1,787,220	1,794,362	1,986,551
Training and schools	93,942	150,517	170,475	219,455
Utilities	606,125	649,606	652,094	722,785
Services	1,618,525	1,865,283	1,933,300	2,254,983
Insurance and miscellaneous	1,792,366	1,556,911	1,783,700	1,614,265
Total operating	15,101,884	17,316,156	17,579,325	19,010,375
Capital additions	561,145	1,123,543	875,238	460,143
Total operating and capital	15,663,029	18,439,699	18,454,563	19,470,518
Contingency	—	200,000	200,000	100,000
Total	**$15,663,029**	**$18,639,699**	**$18,654,563**	**$19,570,518**

DEPARTMENT EXPENDITURES

	Actual Fiscal Year 2010	Budget Fiscal Year 2010	Revised Fiscal Year 2010	Adopted Fiscal Year 2011
City Council	$75,144	$105,207	$90,457	$84,235
City Clerk	61,281	70,778	74,444	91,867
City Manager	155,992	181,219	179,125	192,900
Municipal Court	164,631	196,389	175,019	181,462
Personnel	143,366	197,844	186,247	203,020
Law Department	198,296	266,819	248,170	288,550
Planning and Community Development	295,509	377,126	360,272	405,870
Finance Department	893,344	940,450	983,342	1,212,234
Fire Department	2,837,744	3,421,112	3,257,356	3,694,333
Police Department	3,300,472	4,007,593	4,139,085	4,375,336
Health	1,033,188	1,179,243	1,157,607	1,293,362
Community Services	50,882	74,952	74,758	78,673

(continued)

Table 8.1
Summary Page of a
Typical City Budget
(continued)

TIPS

Some Guidelines for
Reporting Numbers

- Cite sources for all statistics.

- Use numbers judiciously for maximum impact.

- Long lists of figures are difficult to read in paragraph form. Put them in charts and graphs when appropriate.

- Graphs sometimes include estimates. If you use figures from a graph, make sure they are precise.

- Round off large numbers in most cases. For example, use $1.5 million rather than $1,489,789.

- Always double-check your math, and verify any statistics a source gives you.

- Be especially careful with handwritten numbers. It is easy to drop or transpose figures in your notes. Write neatly; when you read your notes, you'll want to be able to tell a 1 from a 7.

- If you don't understand the figures, get an explanation.

DEPARTMENT EXPENDITURES

	Actual Fiscal Year 2010	Budget Fiscal Year 2010	Revised Fiscal Year 2010	Adopted Fiscal Year 2011
Energy Management	—	—	54,925	66,191
Public Works	2,838,605	3,374,152	3,381,044	3,509,979
Parks and Recreation	1,218,221	1,367,143	1,400,334	1,337,682
Communications and Information Services	532,153	730,129	742,835	715,324
City General	1,864,200	1,949,543	1,949,543	1,739,500
Total Department Expenditures	15,663,028	18,439,699	18,454,563	19,470,518
Contingency	—	200,000	200,000	100,000
Total	**$15,663,028**	**$18,639,699**	**$18,654,563**	**$19,570,518**

at the line for the Parks and Recreation Department. There's a decrease between Revised Fiscal Year 2010 and Adopted Fiscal Year 2011. Why? The summary page doesn't tell you, so you'll have to look further. Sometimes that information will be in the detail pages; other times, you'll have to ask the department director. You might discover, as we did, that the drop resulted from a proposal by the city staff to halt funding of a summer employment program for teenagers. That's a story.

Another change that may be newsworthy is the increase in the Police Department budget. In 2010 the budget was $4,007,593, and the budget adopted for 2011 is $4,375,336. In this case, we found that most of the increase was going to pay for an administrative reorganization that would add new positions at the top of the department. The patrol division was actually being reduced. Another story.

Look again at the Police Department line. Follow it back to Actual Fiscal Year 2010, and you'll see that the increase the year before was even bigger. In two years, the expenditures for police increased by nearly one-third, from $3.3 million actually spent in 2010 to nearly $4.4 million budgeted for 2011. That's an interesting trend. The same pattern holds true for the Fire Department. More checking is in order. With copies of previous budgets, you can see how far back the growth trend runs. You can also get statistics on crimes and fires from the individual departments. Are the budget makers responding to a demonstrated need for more protection, or is something else at work behind the scenes?

More generally, you can trace patterns in the growth of city services and city taxes, and you can compare those with changes in population. Are the rates of change comparable? Is population growth outstripping growth in services? Are residents paying more per capita for city services than they paid five or 10 years ago? More good story possibilities.

Another kind of comparison can be useful to your readers, too. How does your city government compare in cost and services with the governments of comparable cities? Some professional organizations have recommended levels of

Lies, Damned Lies and Statistics

Get your facts first, and then you can distort them as much as you please.

— Mark Twain

Sometimes reporters distort the facts without even trying.

The *San Jose Mercury News* reported that women are "10 times more likely to be represented on the Supreme Court of the United States than on the average board of directors for a company in Silicon Valley." The *Mercury News* based that statement on the fact that 22.2 percent of the justices were women, compared with 2.9 percent of Silicon Valley directors.

But there were about 135 million women in the United States; two of them were Supreme Court justices, and 30 of them were Silicon Valley directors. Thus, despite the paucity of women on Silicon Valley boards, the likelihood of a woman being represented there was actually 15 times greater than on the Supreme Court.

In its effort to illustrate a point, the *Mercury News* stumbled into an error that is common in newspapers. It generalized to the entire population of U.S. women from figures that applied only to subpopulations (women on the Supreme Court and Silicon Valley boards). What the *Mercury News* should have said was that the ratio of women to men on the Supreme Court is nearly 10 times greater than on the boards of directors of Silicon Valley companies.

The lesson from the *Mercury News* story is that even when you think you're comparing apples to apples, make sure you don't have some oranges in there. You must have the same base population for a comparison to mean anything.

Here are some of the ways statistics can deceive:

- **Bias can influence the credibility of a survey.** For example, a national survey on sexual behavior indicated that 1 percent of 3,321 men questioned said they were gay, compared with the 10 percent commonly accepted as constituting the gay population. When reporting the survey results, *Time* magazine pointed out that people might be reluctant to discuss their sexual orientation with a "clipboard-bearing stranger."

- **One year does not a trend make.** A large increase in the number of rapes merits a story, but it might represent a fluctuation rather than a trend. Depending on the subject matter, you need to study at least five to 10 years of data to determine whether there is a significant shift.

- **The way organizations compile figures can change, and that can distort comparisons.** The Scripps Howard investigation of sudden infant deaths, for example, found what one expert called a "deeply muddled approach" of wide variations in reporting from one state to the next, distorting real results and making accurate comparisons impossible. Jurisdictions with inadequately trained medical examiners report many times as many "unexplained" deaths as do jurisdictions with more rigorous standards. Inadequately trained journalists unknowingly spread misinformation.

- **Conclusions that sound credible might not hold up under the scrutiny of cause and effect.** Advocacy groups that call for less violence on television say studies show TV violence causes violence in children. They cite research at Yale University showing that prolonged viewing of violent programs is associated with aggressive behavior among children. But the association could be that children who tend to be aggressive watch more violent programming, not the other way around.

service—such as the number of police officers or firefighters per 1,000 inhabitants—that can help you help your readers assess how well they're being governed.

The same guidelines can be applied to the analysis of any budget. The numbers will be different, as will the department names, but the structures will be much the same. Whether you're covering the school board or the statehouse, look for changes, trends and comparisons.

FINANCIAL REPORTS

Another document that is vital to understanding the finances of local government or of any organization is the annual financial report. The report explains the organization's financial status at the end of a fiscal year, which often is not the same as the end of the calendar year. (For example, a fiscal year might end on June 30.) In the report you will find an accounting of all the income the organization received during the year from taxes, fees, state and federal grants, and other sources. You'll also find status reports on all the organization's operating funds, such as its capital improvement fund, its debt-service fund and its general fund.

Making sense of a financial report, like understanding a budget, isn't as hard as it may look. For one thing, the financial officer usually includes a narrative that highlights the most important points, at least from his or her viewpoint. But you should dig beyond the narrative and examine the numbers for yourself. The single most important section of the report is the statement of revenues, expenditures and changes, which provides important measures of the organization's financial health. Depending on the comprehensiveness of the statement, you may have to refer to the budget document as well. You can check:

- Revenue actually received compared with budgeted revenue.
- Actual spending compared with budgeted spending.
- Actual spending compared with actual revenue.
- Changes in balances available for spending in years to come.

The guidelines offered here should help you shape your questions and understand the answers. With financial statements, as with budgets, look for changes, trends and comparisons, and ask for explanations.

CURRENCY EXCHANGE

If you're writing about travel or international business, you need to understand currency exchange. Currency rates change frequently, though not by much unless there is some significant event that makes a particular country's currency more or less valuable. The most popular vacation destination for American travelers overseas is mainland Europe, most of which uses the euro. In late 2009, $1 would buy

.67 of one euro (67 eurocents). Because you get less than one, you know that euros are more expensive than dollars.

Another popular location to visit and study is England, which, unlike most of its European neighbors, uses its own currency, the pound. In late 2009, you could exchange $1 for .61 British pound (61 pence), which means London is even more expensive than mainland Europe. You can find dozens of calculators on the Web that will convert currency for you, and you should use them if you are doing stories about travel or international business. If you are traveling to England, it may be enough to know that one pound costs approximately $1.65.

MIXING NUMBERS AND WORDS

Whatever the story and whatever the subject, you probably can use numbers to clarify issues for readers and viewers. All too often, however, numbers are used in ways that muddy the water. Many journalists have some trepidation about working with numbers, and they create confusion unwittingly when they work with the volatile mixture of numbers and words.

Jennifer LaFleur (see the "On the Job" feature in this chapter) says she has seen numerous reports from government agencies with math errors that a quick double check by a reporter would find. "Reporters background-check sources. They verify anecdotes with documents. But seldom do we double-check numbers," she reminds us.

In *Mathsemantics: Making Numbers Talk Sense*, Edward MacNeal writes that reporters and editors need to be far more careful in applying numbers in the news by questioning the accuracy and meaning of the numbers they gather and report.

For example, consider the following lead: "Each year 65,000 bicyclists go to the emergency room with injuries. Of those, 70–80 percent die because they weren't wearing helmets."

The reporter seems to be saying that more than 45,000 bicyclists, and perhaps as many as 52,000, are dying each year, or about 125 to 140 each day. It's much more likely that the figures mean something else entirely—that 70 to 80 percent of the bicyclists who died of their injuries would have been spared had they been wearing helmets, perhaps. In fact, in 2007, 540,000 bicyclists in the U.S. were injured badly enough to visit an emergency room. In all of that year, 698 bicyclists died, nearly two a day.

Journalists can also encourage misunderstandings by describing large increases in percentage terms. For example, when gasoline prices increased from about $2 to nearly $4 a gallon in 2007–2008, some in the media reported, accurately, that the price had doubled. Others, however, incorrectly called it a 200 percent increase instead of a 100 percent increase: $2 + (100\% \times \$2) = \$4$.

Another trouble spot for mixing numbers and words occurs when reporters calculate how much larger or more expensive something is. For example, a class that grew from 20 students to 100 students is five times bigger than it was ($5 \times 20 = 100$), but it has four times as many students as it had before: $(4 \times 20) + 20 = 100$.

The lesson to be learned from these examples is not to avoid numbers, but rather to use great care to ensure accuracy. Picking the right numbers to use and using them wisely will help your news stories have the biggest impact.

Suggested Readings

Cohen, Sarah. *Numbers in the Newsroom: Using Math and Statistics in News.* Columbia, Mo.: Investigative Reporters and Editors, 2001. This book includes helpful, readable information on how to do basic math, graphs and polls.

Cuzzort, R.P., and James S. Vrettos. *The Elementary Forms of Statistical Reason.* New York: St. Martin's Press, 1996. Non-mathematicians in the humanities and social sciences who must work with statistics will appreciate this basic guide.

Meyer, Philip. *Precision Journalism: A Reporter's Introduction to Social Science Methods*, 4th ed. Lanham, Md.: Rowman and Littlefield, 2002. This step-by-step guide explains how to use social science research methods in news reporting.

Paulos, John Allen. *A Mathematician Reads the Newspaper.* New York: Anchor Books, 1997. Structured like the morning paper, this book investigates the mathematical angles of stories in the news and offers novel perspectives, questions and ideas.

Wickham, Kathleen Woodruff. *Math Tools for Journalists.* Portland, Ore.: Marion Street Press, 1992. This concise guide clearly explains math problems and concepts.

Suggested Websites

www.bls.gov/data/inflation_calculator.htm
The Bureau of Labor Statistics has a calculator that enables you to adjust dollar amounts for inflation. In addition, the website provides Consumer Price Index information for the entire nation, broken down by region and type of spending.

www.dallasnews.com/sharedcontent/dws/spe/2007/unequal/index2.html
Here you can read the *Dallas Morning News* series "Unequal Justice" for yourself. Of particular interest is the interactive graphic that presents the data supporting the series.

www.math.temple.edu/~paulos
John Allen Paulos, a professor at Temple University, is the author of *Innumeracy: Mathematical Illiteracy and Its Consequences.* At this site you can read more from the master of numbers.

www.minneapolisfed.org
The Federal Reserve Bank of Minneapolis maintains a great website that helps you calculate inflation. It also has clear and simple explanations of how inflation is calculated and how to use the Consumer Price Index.

www.robertniles.com/stats
Robert Niles, who worked at newspaper Internet sites in Denver and Los Angeles, is a self-described "math and computer geek." His explanations of statistics are simple and clear.

www.stltoday.com/
Search "DWI felonies" to find the story mentioned in this chapter, "Repeat Drunken Drivers Avoid Felony DWI Charges."

www.usatoday.com/money
USA Today's site offers calculators to figure everything from interest rates to currency conversions.

Exercises

1. **Team project.** Your instructor will divide you into teams to examine crime on your campus and compare it with crime on other campuses. The Clery Act requires colleges and universities to publicly report crimes that occur on campus. Many post the data on their website. One team should get the crime report and student enrollment figures for your campus. A second team should search the Web for crime statistics for comparable campuses and should obtain the student enrollment for each of those campuses. Take the figures for six of the crime categories and report the crimes per capita for each of the schools. As a class, discuss the stories that could grow out of these comparisons.

2. The federal minimum wage began in 1938 at 25 cents. In 1968, it was $1.60. Calculate how much 25 cents in 1938 is worth today and what $1.60 in 1968 is worth today. Compare those numbers with the present minimum wage. Suggest a story idea based on the result. (Consult **www .dol.gov/esa/minwage/america.htm** for the current federal and state minimum wages.)

3. Find out from your campus financial aid office how much the graduating class has borrowed in Stafford Loans, the largest category of student loans. Calculate how much debt the average graduate will have in Stafford Loans. Then calculate how much debt the average indebted graduate will have. (The results will probably be quite different.) Find out what the total amount of payments owed will be for the average graduate with loans.

4. Find out how much your college charged for tuition in 1990, 2000 and today. Adjust those numbers for inflation so they can be compared. (Use an inflation calculator like the one at **www.minneapolisfed.org.**) Write a story about the cost of going to college, and use figures adjusted for inflation.

5. Get a copy of your city or university budget, and come up with five questions that a reporter should ask about the changes, patterns and trends that the budget suggests. The budget may be available on the Internet.

6. If a city budgets $186,247 for personnel one year and $203,020 the next, what is the percentage increase?

7. A city of 219,000 had 103 murders last year. Another city of 88,812 in the same state had 48 murders. How many murders were there per 1,000 residents in each city?

The Inverted Pyramid

9

IN THIS CHAPTER
YOU WILL LEARN:

1. How to translate news values into leads.

2. Five varieties of inverted pyramid leads.

3. How to organize a story using the inverted pyramid.

The **inverted pyramid**—a news story structure that places all the important information in the first paragraph—has been used to write the first draft of history in the United States for generations. Here is the Associated Press lead on the first use of the atomic bomb in 1945:

> An atomic bomb, hailed as the most destructive force in history and as the greatest achievement of organized science, has been loosed upon Japan.

When terrorists attacked the World Trade Center in 2001, the AP informed the world this way:

> In an unprecedented show of terrorist horror, the 110-story World Trade Center towers collapsed in a shower of rubble and dust Tuesday morning after two hijacked airliners carrying scores of passengers slammed into the side of the twin symbols of American capitalism.

The inverted pyramid is used daily for stories historic and routine. Late in 2009, AP reported on a new development in the fight against swine flu:

> ATLANTA (AP)—More than 22 million doses of swine flu vaccine are available now, and most Americans should soon find it easier to get their dose, U.S. health officials said Tuesday.

As these examples show, journalists have been using the inverted pyramid for generations to record the daily history of world events. The form brought you news of Barack Obama's election, bombings in Iraq and increases in college tuition.

Specialized financial news services such as Bloomberg News rely on the inverted pyramid. So do newspapers, despite many editors' emphasis on encouraging new writing forms. So do radio, television, the Internet and newsletters. Businesspeople often use the inverted pyramid in company memos so their bosses don't have to read to the end to find the main point. Public relations professionals use it in news releases to get the attention of news editors.

IMPORTANCE OF THE INVERTED PYRAMID STORY

Frequently misdiagnosed as dying, the inverted pyramid has more lives than a cat—perhaps because the more people try to speed up the dissemination of information, the more valuable the inverted pyramid becomes. In the inverted pyramid, information is arranged from most important to least important. The king in *Alice in Wonderland* would never succeed in the electronic news service business. When asked where to start a story, he replied, "Begin at the beginning and go on till you come to the end; then stop." Reporters, however, often begin a story at its end. Subscribers to financial services such as Reuters, Dow Jones Factiva and Bloomberg, for instance, react instantly to news about the financial markets to get an edge over other investors. They don't want narration; they want news. This is a typical Bloomberg lead:

> (Bloomberg)—The global financial crisis is turning into a bigger drain on the U.S. federal budget than experts estimated two weeks ago, ballooning the deficit toward $2 trillion.

Many newspaper readers, on average, spend 15 to 25 minutes a day reading the paper. Online readers, who skip around sites as if they were walking barefooted on a hot stove, spend even less time. Both prefer short stories with the news on top. If a reporter were to write an account of a car accident by starting when the driver left the house, many readers would never read far enough to learn that the driver and a passenger were killed. Instead, such a story starts with its climax:

> Two people died Thursday when a backhoe fell off a truck's flatbed and sliced the top off an oncoming vehicle near Fairchild Air Force Base.

The inverted pyramid was fairly common by the turn of the 20th century. Before then, reporters were less direct. In 1869, the *New York Herald* sent Henry Morton Stanley to Africa to find the famous explorer-missionary David Livingstone. Stanley's famous account of the meeting begins:

> Only two months gone, and what a change in my feelings! But two months ago, what a peevish, fretful soul was mine! What a hopeless prospect presented itself before your correspondent!

After several similar sentences, the writer reports, "And the only answer to it all is (that) Livingstone, the hero traveler, is alongside of me."

In the inverted pyramid, the lead, which can consist of one or two paragraphs, sits atop other paragraphs arranged in descending order of importance. These paragraphs explain and provide evidence to support the lead. That's why print editors can quickly shorten a story; the paragraphs at the bottom are the least important. On the Internet, as you will learn in Chapter 12, space is not a consideration, but readers' time is. That's why the same inverted pyramid that is used in newspapers is the most common story structure found on such news websites as CNN.com, MSNBC.com, CBSNews.com and ABCNews.com. For instance, CNN used a two-paragraph lead to report the closing of once-popular website GeoCities:

> **❚❚**Because a story is important, it doesn't follow that it must be long.**❚❚**
>
> — Stanley Walker, city editor

> (CNN)—The flashing banner ads, questionable color schemes and omnipresent "Under Construction" signs of GeoCities are no more.
>
> The personal Web-hosting site, launched in 1995 and owned by Yahoo Inc. since 1999, was to be shut down by Tuesday.

T I P S

The Inverted Pyramid

- Puts the most important information first.

- Arranges the paragraphs in descending order of importance.

- Requires the writer to rank the importance of information.

The inverted pyramid does have some shortcomings. Although it delivers the most important news first, it does not encourage people to read the entire story. Stories stop; they don't end. There is no suspense. In a Poynter Institute study, researchers found that half of the 25 percent of readers who started a story dropped out midway through. Interest in an inverted pyramid story diminishes as the story progresses. But the way people use it attests to its value as a quick form of information delivery. Readers can leave whenever their needs are met, not when a writer finishes a story. In an age when time is golden, the inverted pyramid still offers value.

The day when the inverted pyramid is relegated to journalism history is not yet here and probably never will be. Perhaps 80 percent of the stories in today's newspapers and almost 100 percent of the stories on news services for target audiences such as the financial community are written in the inverted pyramid form. The trend is changing, but it's changing slowly. Some of the new media will require other forms. For instance, tailored stories for news-on-demand services that will reach a general audience need not use the inverted pyramid. Nor will those sites devoted to literary journalism (such as www.vanityfair.com). Still, as long as newspaper, electronic and broadcast journalists continue to emphasize the quick, direct, simple approach to communications, the inverted pyramid and its variations will have a role.

There are many other ways to structure a news story. You will learn about some of the options in Chapter 11. Before you get to the alternatives, however, you should master the inverted pyramid. As you do, you will master the art of making news judgments. The inverted pyramid requires you to identify and rank the most newsworthy elements in each story. That is important work. No matter what kinds of stories you write—whether obituaries, accidents, speeches, press conferences, fires or meetings—you will be required to use the skills you learn here.

FINDING THE LEAD

To determine a **lead**—a simple, clear statement consisting of the first paragraph or two of an inverted pyramid story—you must first recognize what goes into one. As you read in Chapter 1, you begin by determining the story's relevance, usefulness and interest for readers. One way to measure these standards is to ask "So what?" or "Who cares?" So what if there's a car accident downtown? If it's one of hundreds a month, it may not be news. Any holdup in a community of 5,000 may be news because the "so what" is that holdups are uncommon and some residents probably know the victim. Neither newspapers nor radio or television stations would report the holdup in a metropolitan area where holdups are common. But if the holdup appears to be part of a pattern or if someone is killed, the story becomes more significant. One holdup may not be news, but a holdup that authorities believe is one of many committed by the same person may be news. The "so what" is that if the police catch this robber, they stop a crime spree. To determine the "so what," you have to answer six basic questions: who, what, when, where, why and how?

TIPS

The Six Basic Questions

1. Who?
2. What?
3. When?
4. Where?
5. Why?
6. How?

More questions:

● So what?

● What's next?

William Caldwell, winner of a Pulitzer Prize in 1971, remembers the best lead he ever heard. He tells the story in an Associated Press Managing Editors "Writing" report:

> One summer afternoon in 1922, I was on my way home from school and my daily stint of work as editor of the village weekly, unhonored and unpaid. Like my father and two uncles, I was a newspaperman.
>
> My little brother came running to meet me at the foot of our street. He was white and crying. A telegram had come to my mother. "Pa drowned this morning in Lake George," he gasped, and I am ashamed to be remembering my inward response to that.
>
> Before I could begin to sense such elements as sorrow, despair, horror, loneliness, anger—before all the desolation of an abandoned kid would well up in me, I found myself observing that the sentence my brother had just uttered was the perfect lead. Noun, verb, predicate, period, and who-what-when-where to boot.

The information from every event you witness and every story you hear can be reduced to answers to who, what, when, where, why and how. If the answers add up to a significant "so what," you have a story. Consider this example of an incoming call at fire headquarters.

> "Fire Department," the dispatcher answers.
>
> "Hello. At about 10 o'clock, I was lying on my bed watching TV and smoking," the voice says. "I must have fallen asleep about 10:30 because that's when the football game was over. Anyway, I woke up just now, and my bedroom is on fire. . . ."

That dialogue isn't informative or convincing. More likely, our sleepy television viewer awoke in a smoke-filled room, grabbed his cell phone and punched in 9-1-1. The conversation would more likely have gone like this:

> "Fire Department."
>
> "FIRE!" a voice at the other end yells.
>
> "Where?" the dispatcher asks.
>
> "At 1705 W. Haven St."

When fire is licking at their heels, even nonjournalists know the lead. How the fire started is not important to the dispatcher; that a house is burning—and where that house is located—is.

The journalist must go through essentially the same process to determine the lead. Whereas the caller served himself and the fire department, reporters must serve their readers. What is most important to them?

After the fire is over, there is much information a reporter must gather. Among the questions a reporter would routinely ask are these:

● When did it start?

● When was it reported?

● Who reported it?

● How was it reported?

- How long did it take the fire department to respond?
- How long did it take to extinguish the fire?
- How many fires this year have been attributed to smoking in bed?
- How does that compare with figures in previous years?
- Were there any injuries or deaths?
- What was the damage?
- Who owned the house?
- Did the occupant or owner have insurance on the house?
- Will charges be filed against the smoker?
- Was there anything unusual about this case?
- Who cares?

With this information in hand, you can begin to write the story.

Writing the Inverted Pyramid Lead

Start by looking over your notes.

Who? The owner, a smoker, Henry Smith, 29. The age is important. Along with other personal information, such as address and occupation, the age differentiates the subject from other Henry Smiths in the readership area.

What? Fire caused damage estimated by the fire chief at $2,500.

Where? 1705 W. Haven St.

When? The call was received at 10:55 p.m., Tuesday. Firefighters from Station 19 arrived at the scene at 11:04. The fire was extinguished by 11:30. Those times are important to gather even if you don't use them. They show whether the fire department responded quickly.

Why? The fire was started by carelessness on the part of Smith, according to Fire Chief Bill Malone.

How? Smith told fire officials that he fell asleep in bed while he was smoking a cigarette.

If you had asked other questions, you might have learned more from the fire department:

- This was the eighth fire this year caused by smoking in bed.
- All last year there were four such fires.
- Smith said he had insurance.
- The fire chief said no charges will be filed against Smith.
- It was the first fire at this house.
- Smith was not injured.

> **"**Writing is easy; all you do is sit staring at a blank sheet of paper until the drops of blood form on your forehead.**"**
>
> — Gene Fowler, author

Have you figured out the "so what"?

Assume your city editor has suggested you hold the story to about four paragraphs. Your first step is to rank the information in descending order of importance. There are lots of fires in this town, but eight this year have been caused by smoking in bed. Perhaps that's the most important thing about this story. You begin to type:

> A fire started by a careless smoker caused an estimated $2,500 in damage to a home.

Only 16 words. You should try to hold every lead to fewer than 25 words unless you use more than one sentence. Maybe it's too brief, though. Have you left anything out? Maybe you should include the time element—to give the story a sense of immediacy. Readers would also want to know where the fire occurred. Is it near their house? Is it someone they know? You rewrite:

> A Tuesday night fire started by a careless smoker caused an estimated $2,500 in damage to a home at 1705 W. Haven St.

Just then the city editor walks by and glances over your shoulder. "Who said it was a careless smoker?" she asks. "Stay out of the story."

You realize you have committed a basic error in news writing: You have allowed an unattributed opinion to slip into the story. You have two choices. You can attribute the "careless smoker" information to the fire chief in the lead, or you can omit it. You choose to rewrite by attributing the opinion. You also revise your sentence to emphasize the cause instead of the damage. You write:

> Fire that caused an estimated $2,500 in damage to a home at 1705 W. Haven St. Tuesday was caused by smoking in bed, Fire Chief Bill Malone said.

Now 28 words have answered the questions "what" (a fire), "where" (1705 W. Haven St.), "when" (Tuesday) and "how" (smoking in bed). And the opinion is attributed. But you have not answered "who" and "why." You continue, still ranking the information in descending order of importance.

> The owner of the home, Henry Smith, 29, said he fell asleep in bed while smoking a cigarette. When he awoke about 30 minutes later, smoke had filled the room.
>
> Firefighters arrived nine minutes after receiving the call. It took them about 26 minutes to extinguish the fire, which was confined to the bedroom of the one-story house.
>
> According to Chief Malone, careless smokers have caused eight fires this year. Smith, who was not injured, said the house was insured.

You take the story to the city editor, who reads through the copy quickly. As you watch, she changes the lead to emphasize the "so what." The lead now reads:

> A smoker who fell asleep in bed ignited a fire that caused minor damage to his home on West Haven Street Tuesday, Fire Chief Bill Malone said. It was the city's eighth fire caused by smokers, twice as many as occurred all last year.

The lead is 44 words, but it is broken into two sentences, which makes it more readable. The importance of the "so what" changed the direction of the story. The fire was minor; there were no injuries. However, the increase in the number of fires smokers caused may force the fire department to start a public safety campaign against careless smoking. The city editor continues:

> The owner of the home, Henry Smith, 29, of 1705 W. Haven St., said he fell asleep in bed while smoking a cigarette. When he awoke about 30 minutes later, smoke had filled the room.

Too many numbers bog down a lead. Focus on the impact of the figures in the lead, and provide details later in the story.

The editor then checks the telephone book and the city directory and uncovers a serious problem. Both the telephone book and the city directory list the man who lives at 1705 W. Haven St. as Henry Smyth: S-m-y-t-h. City directories, telephone books, and other sources can be wrong. But at least they can alert you to possible errors. Confirm spellings by going to the original source, in this case, Mr. Smyth.

Never put a name in a story without checking the spelling, even when the source tells you his name is Smith.

Look at Figure 9.1 to see the completed fire story. There are several lessons you can learn from this example:

- Always check names.
- Keep the lead short, usually fewer than 25 words, unless you use two sentences.
- Attribute opinion. (Smoking in bed is a fact. That it was careless is an opinion.)
- Find out the who, what, where, when, why and how. However, if any of these elements have no bearing on the story, they might not have to be included.
- Write a sentence or paragraph telling readers what the news means to them.
- Report information basic to the story even if it is routine. Not everything you learn is important enough to be reported, but you'll never know unless you gather the information.

When you are learning to write an inverted pyramid story, the process is deliberate. You'll check your notes to be certain you have the six basic questions answered. Eventually, though, you will mentally check through those questions quickly. Of course, you will not always be able to find answers immediately to "how" and "why." Sometimes, experts need time to analyze accidents, crimes, fires, and so on.

TIPS

When Writing the Lead, Remember

- Always check names.
- Keep the lead short, usually fewer than 25 words, unless you use two sentences.
- Attribute opinion.
- Find out the who, what, where, when, why and how. If any of these elements have no bearing on the story, they might not have to be included.
- Write a sentence or a paragraph telling readers what the news means to them.
- Report basic information even if it's routine. Not everything you learn is important enough to be reported, but you'll never know unless you gather the information.

A Sample Inverted Pyramid Story

The identification of "who" is delayed until the next paragraph because the person is not someone readers would recognize and because his name would make the lead unnecessarily long. Also in the lead are the "what," "when," "how" and, most significantly here, the "so what."

The performance of the fire department is monitored.

A smoker who fell asleep in bed ignited a fire that caused minor damage to his home on West Haven Street Tuesday, Fire Chief Bill Malone said. It was the city's eighth fire caused by smokers, twice as many as occurred all last year.

The owner of the home, Henry Smyth, 29, of 1705 West Haven St., said he fell asleep in bed while smoking a cigarette. When he awoke about 30 minutes later, smoke had filled the room.

The "who" is identified. More details on the "how" are given.

The fire department, which received the call at 10:55 p.m., had the fire out by 11:30.

Malone said the damage, estimated at $2,500, was confined to the bedroom. The house was insured.

Details on the "so what" are given. The impact question is answered with the possible campaign.

Careless smokers caused only four fires last year in the city. Malone said that he is considering a public awareness campaign to try to alert smokers to the hazards. Those four fires caused total damage of $43,000. This year, fires started by careless smoking have caused total damages of $102,500, Malone said.

Least important: If someone else had been hurt and charges had been filed, this information would move higher in the story.

No charges will be filed against Smyth because no one other than the smoker was endangered, Malone said.

Figure 9.1
The inverted pyramid structure dictates that the most important information goes in the lead paragraphs. It is the job of the writer and the editor to decide what that information is.

After you've checked your notes, ask yourself, "What else do readers need to know?" Using the news values of relevance, usefulness and interest, decide which answers are the most important so you can put them in the lead. The rest go in the second and third paragraphs.

In the example above, the editor changed the emphasis from the fire, which was minor, to the number of recent fires. She knew that the number of fires was more relevant and more interesting than one minor fire. That angle also answers the question of usefulness by pointing out for readers and public safety officials alike that there is a bigger problem than one minor fire. The angle also answers the "so what" question. There was a minor fire. So what? There are lots of minor fires. Eight fires this year caused by smoking is a "so what" that will grab attention.

Compare the fire story in Figure 9.1 with the accident story in Figure 9.2. In what order are the key questions answered in the fire story? In the accident story? Why is the order different?

The Classic Inverted Pyramid Story

The lead identifies the "what," "where" and "when." The "so what" is that people were killed.

A four-vehicle accident on eastbound I-70 near Stadium Boulevard ended in two deaths on Sunday.

The second paragraph provides details to support the lead and answers "who."

Barbara Jones, 41, of St. Louis died at the scene of the accident, and Juanita Doolan, 73, of St. Joseph died at University Hospital, according to a release from Springfield police. Two other people, William Doolan, 73, of St. Joseph and Theodore Amelung, 43, of Manchester, Mo., were injured in the accident.

This paragraph shows impact beyond deaths.

Both lanes of traffic were closed on the eastbound side and limited to one lane on the westbound side as rescue workers cleared the scene.

Authorities said a westbound late-model Ford Taurus driven by Lan Wang of Springfield was traveling in the right lane, developed a tire problem and swerved into the passing lane. A Toyota pickup truck in the passing lane, driven by Jones, was forced over the grassy median along with the Taurus. The two vehicles entered eastbound traffic where the truck struck an Oldsmobile Delta 88, driven by Juanita Doolan, head on.

The "how" is less important than the "what," "where" and "when," so it appears later in the story.

Wang and the one passenger in his car, Kenneth Kuo, 58, of Springfield, were not injured.

John Paul, a tractor-trailer driver on his way to Tennessee, said he had to swerve to miss the accident.

An eyewitness account adds sensory details that make the scene more vivid.

"I saw the red truck come across the median and hit the blue car," Paul said. "I just pulled over on the median and called 911."

What's next? This would be higher if the driver, rather than a tire, appeared to be the cause of the accident.

Jones, who was wearing a seat belt, died at the scene, Officer Stan Williams said. Amelung, a passenger who had been in the truck, was out of the vehicle when authorities arrived, but it was unknown whether he was thrown from the truck or was pulled out by someone else, Williams said.

No charges have been filed, but the investigation continues.

Figure 9.2
Note how this story, typical of the inverted pyramid structure, delivers the most important news in the lead and provides less essential details toward the end.

Emphasizing Different News Values

In the lead reporting the house fire, the "what" (fire) is of secondary importance to the "how" (how the fire started). A slightly different set of facts would affect the news value of the elements and, consequently, your lead. For instance, if Smyth turned out to have been a convicted arsonist, you would probably emphasize that bizarre twist to the story:

> A convicted arsonist awoke Tuesday to find that his bedroom was filled with smoke. He escaped and later said that he had fallen asleep while smoking.
>   Henry Smyth, 29, who served a three-year term for . . .

That lead emphasizes the news value of novelty. If Smyth were the mayor, you would emphasize prominence:

> Mayor Henry Smyth escaped injury Tuesday when he awoke to find his bedroom filled with smoke. Smyth said he had fallen asleep while smoking in bed.

What, So What and What's Next

You know that the answer to "what" is often the lead. The preceding examples also illustrate the "so what" factor in news. A $2,500 fire is not news to many people in large communities where there are dozens of fires daily. Even if you crafted a tightly written story about it, your editor probably would not want to print or broadcast it.

In small communities, the story would have more impact because there are fewer fires and because a larger proportion of the community is likely to know the victim.

The "so what" factor grows more important as you add other information. If the fire occurred during a fire-safety campaign, the "so what" would be the need for fire safety even in a community where awareness of the problem had already been heightened. If the fire involved a convicted arsonist or the mayor, the "so what" would be stronger. Oddity or well-known people increase the value of a story. If someone had been injured or if the damage had been $250,000 instead of $2,500, the "so what" factor might even push the story into the metropolitan press. As you've seen above, once you have answered all six of the basic questions, it's important to ask yourself what the answers mean to the reader. That answer is your "so what" factor.

In many stories, it is also important to answer the question "What's next?" The City Council had its first reading of its budget bill. What's next? *Members will vote on it next month.* Jones was arrested Monday on a charge of passing bad checks. What's next? *The prosecuting attorney will decide whether there is enough evidence to file charges.*

A reader in a focus group once told researchers that she just wants to be told "what," "so what" and "what's next." That's a good guideline for all journalists to remember.

VARIATIONS ON THE INVERTED PYRAMID LEAD

No journalist relies on formulas to write inverted pyramid leads, but you may find it useful, especially in the beginning, to learn some typical types of leads. The labels in the following sections are arbitrary, but the approaches are not.

A Case Study of Leads

Tina Macias (see the "On the Job" box in this chapter) covered the news of a school bus driver who was charged with driving while intoxicated. Of course, her stories for *The Daily Advertiser* in Lafayette, La., went into detail, but if you read nothing but the leads, you can follow the essential news. She also posted messages on Twitter while at the school board meeting ("The 3-day suspension for bus driver Kenny Mire approved w/out debate. The policy has been pulled and is about to be debated."). The leads from her series of articles appear below. Leads 3 and 4 begin two stories from the same meeting:

Lead from Story 1
The Lafayette Parish School Board at its meeting tonight could approve a new policy that outlines how to discipline bus drivers if they are charged with drunken driving off duty.

Lead from Story 2
The Lafayette Parish School Bus Drivers Association is "behind the superintendent 100 percent" when it comes to a new policy set to be debated tonight.

Lead from Story 3
The Lafayette Parish School Board tonight voted to suspend bus driver Kenny Joseph Mire for three days without pay.

Lead from Story 4
The Lafayette Parish School Board tonight unanimously approved a new policy that addresses how to discipline bus drivers that are arrested for drunken driving off duty.

Lead from Story 5
Bus drivers who are charged with drug- or alcohol-related driving incidents will be suspended with pay until a substance-abuse professional deems them capable of returning to work, according to a policy unanimously approved by the Lafayette Parish School Board on Wednesday.

The new policy puts Lafayette Parish more in line with several other Louisiana school systems.

The "You" Lead

Regardless of which of these leads journalists use, they are trying to emphasize the relevance of the news to the reader. One good way to highlight the relevance is to speak directly to the reader by using "you." This informal, second-person lead—the "you" lead—allows the writer to tell readers why they should care. For instance:

> You will make more money buying Savings Bonds starting tomorrow.
> The Treasury boosted the semiannual interest rate on Series EE Savings Bonds to 5.92 percent from 4.7 percent effective Tuesday.

Readers want to know what's in it for them. The traditional approach is less direct:

> The Treasury boosted Savings Bonds interest Tuesday to the highest rate in three years.

As with any kind of lead, you can overdo the "you" lead. You don't need to write "You have another choice in the student president's race." Just tell readers who filed their candidacy. However, you may use those words in writing for radio or television news as a setup for the story to come.

The Immediate-Identification Lead

In the **immediate-identification lead**, one of the most important facts is "who," or the prominence of the key actor. Reporters often use this approach when someone important or well-known is making news. Consider the following example:

> NEW YORK (AP) —Andre Agassi's upcoming autobi-
> ography contains an admission that he used crystal
> meth in 1997 and lied to tennis authorities when he
> failed a drug test — a result that was thrown out after he
> said he "unwittingly" took the substance.

Names make news.

When writing for your campus newspaper or your local newspaper, you would use names in the lead that are known, not necessarily nationally but locally. The name of your student body president, the chancellor, the city's mayor or an entertainer who has a local following would logically appear in the lead. None of these names would be used in a newspaper 50 miles away.

In any accident, the "who" may be important because it is someone well-known by name or position. If so, the name should be in the lead.

In small communities, names almost always make news. The "who" in an accident is usually in the lead. In larger communities, names are not as recognizable. As a rule, if the name is well-known, it should appear in the lead.

> *"Language is a very difficult thing to put into words."*
>
> — Voltaire, philosopher

The Delayed-Identification Lead

Usually a reporter uses a **delayed-identification lead** because the person, people or organization involved has little name recognition among readers. Thus, in fairly large cities, an accident is usually reported like this:

> MADISON, Wis. — A 39-year-old carpenter was killed
> today in a two-car collision two blocks from his home.
>   William Domonske of 205 W. Oak St. died at the
> scene. Mary Craig, 21, of 204 Maple Ave., and Rebecca
> Roets, 12, of 207 Maple Ave., were taken to Mercy
> Hospital with injuries.

However, in a smaller community, names almost always make news. Unless a name is nationally recognized, it often appears in the second paragraph:

> LOS ANGELES (AP)—An expert witness withdrew testimony Wednesday about one of Anna Nicole Smith's doctors massively increasing her methadone doses, but he still maintained the doctor's actions fed her drug addiction.
>
> Dr. James Gagne, testifying at a preliminary hearing, said he misunderstood records kept by Dr. Sandeep Kapoor and now believes the methadone prescriptions were not a major issue in the drug case against Kapoor and two other defendants.

Few readers would recognize Dr. Gagne, so rather than putting his name and identification in the opening paragraph, the reporter separated them.

In two other situations, reporters may choose to delay identification of the person involved in the story until the second paragraph. One occurs when the person is not well-known but the person's position, occupation, title or achievements are important or interesting. The other occurs when the lead is becoming too wordy.

As Andy Warhol said, people have their 15 minutes of fame, but fame can be fleeting. While Terry Anderson of the AP was being held captive from 1985 to 1992 by the Islamic Jihad in Lebanon, even casual consumers of the news recognized his name because of daily coverage. Years after he was released, when a court ruled that Anderson was entitled to damages, a delayed-identification lead was appropriate.

> WASHINGTON—A former AP newsman was awarded $341 million from Iran on March 24 by a federal judge who said his treatment during his nearly seven years of captivity in Beirut was "savage and cruel by any civilized standards."
>
> U.S. District Judge Thomas Penfield Jackson ordered Iran to pay $24.5 million to Terry Anderson, $10 million to his wife, Madeleine Bassil, and $6.7 million to their daughter, Sulome. The judge also ordered the Iranian Ministry of Information and Security to pay the three $300 million in punitive damages.

A name that would appear in the lead in one city might appear in the second paragraph in another. The mayor of Birmingham, Ala., would be identified by title and name in Birmingham and by title only in Bridgewater, Conn.

The Summary Lead

Reporters dealing with several important elements may choose to sum up what happened in a **summary lead** rather than highlighting a specific action. This is one of the few times when a general statement is preferable to specifics.

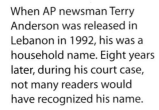

When AP newsman Terry Anderson was released in Lebanon in 1992, his was a household name. Eight years later, during his court case, not many readers would have recognized his name.

When Congress passed a bill giving family members with emergencies the right to unpaid leave from work, the writer had to make a choice: to focus on the main provisions or to write a summary lead. The writer chose the latter:

> A bill requiring employers to give workers up to three months' unpaid leave in family emergencies won Senate approval Thursday evening.

Several other provisions in the bill are explained later in the story:

> The unpaid leave can be for medical reasons or to care for a new child, and employers would have to continue health insurance benefits and restore employees to their previous jobs or equivalent positions.

You can also show the readers the "so what" with the "you" lead:

> The Senate voted Thursday to allow you to take up to three months' unpaid leave in family emergencies without losing your health benefits.

Likewise, if a city council rewrites city ordinances, unless one of the changes is of overriding importance, most reporters will use a summary lead:

> MOLINE, Ill. — The City Council replaced the city's 75-year-old municipal code with a revised version Tuesday night.

ON THE JOB

Inverted Pyramid—A Basic Tool

As an education reporter at *The Daily Advertiser* in Lafayette, La., Tina Macias' time is split between writing human-interest stories and breaking news. She has covered bus wrecks, mold outbreaks and hurricanes.

Despite all the changes in the industry, she believes the inverted pyramid format still is an essential tool, especially in this 24-hour news age.

Macias says the easiest and most efficient way to organize breaking news on the Web is with the inverted pyramid. Only months out of school, she found herself covering hurricanes. Her job was to get information quickly and put it online and then follow with print stories. Most of the information about school closings, food stamps, curfews and power outages appeared on the Web in the inverted pyramid format. This story was put online the Friday before Labor Day when Hurricane Gustav made landfall:

With Hurricane Gustav edging toward the Gulf, and projections showing Acadiana in its path, public and private schools are preparing for the worst.

One day before she arrived at work, a colleague had reported the bare details of a school bus accident that morning. Macias' job was to update the story.

"As I started to make my phone calls, I thought about the vital information and how I could easily organize it," she says. She produced this inverted pyramid lead:

Nine people, including eight children, were transported to a local hospital Monday morning after a black Impala plowed into the side of a Lafayette Parish school bus.

All were transported for minor or moderate injuries and complaints.

Though then a rookie reporter, Macias was able to be productive immediately, in part because of two internships she held while attending journalism school. Now she is used to covering news quickly for both the Web and print.

Summary leads do not appear only in reports of board meetings. A Spokane, Wash., reporter used a summary lead to report a neighborhood dispute:

An Idaho farmer's fence apparently was cut last week. It set off a chain of events Friday night that landed three people in the hospital, killed a cow and totaled a vehicle in the eastern Spokane Valley.

The basic question you must answer is whether the whole of the action is more important than any of its parts. If the answer is yes, use the summary lead.

The Multiple-Element Lead

In some stories, choosing one theme for the lead is too restrictive. In such cases the reporter can choose a **multiple-element lead** to work more information into the first paragraph. But you should write the lead within the confines of a clear, simple sentence or sentences. Consider this example:

> PORTLAND, Ore.—The City Council Tuesday ordered three department heads fired, established an administrative review board and said it would begin to monitor the work habits of administrators.

Notice that not only the actions but also the construction of the verb phrases within the sentence is parallel. Parallel structures also characterize the following news extract, which presents a visual picture of the scene of a tragedy:

> BAY CITY, Mich.—A flash fire that swept through a landmark downtown hotel Saturday killed at least 12 persons, injured 60 more and forced scores of residents to leap from windows and the roof in near-zero cold.

We are told where it happened, what happened, and how many were killed and injured.

Some multiple-element leads consist of two paragraphs. This occurs when the reporter decides that several elements need prominent display. For example:

> The Board of Education Tuesday night voted to lower the tax rate 12 cents per $100 valuation. Members then approved a budget $150,000 less than last year's and instructed the superintendent to decrease the staff by 25 people.
>
> The board also approved a set of student-conduct rules, which include a provision that students with three or more unexcused absences a year will be suspended for a week.

This story, too, could emphasize the "so what" while retaining the multiple elements:

> The Board of Education lowered your real-estate taxes Tuesday. Members also approved a budget $150,000 less than last year's and instructed the superintendent to decrease the staff by 25 people.

Simpler leads are preferable. But a multiple-element lead is one of your options. Use it sparingly.

Many newspapers are using graphic devices to take the place of multiple-element leads. They use summary boxes to list other actions. Because the box appears under the headline in type larger than text, it serves as a graphic summary for the reader who is scanning the page. The box frees the writer from trying to jam too many details into the first few paragraphs (see Figure 9.3).

> ## Other Council Action
>
> In other action, the council:
> - Voted to repave Broadway Ave.
> - Rejected a new sign ordinance.
> - Hired four school crossing guards.
> - Expanded bus hours.

Figure 9.3
A summary box can take the place of a multiple-element lead.

Breaking stories into small segments increases readers' comprehension and retention.

Another approach is to break the coverage of a single event into a main story and a shorter story called a **sidebar**. This approach offers the advantage of presenting the information in short, palatable bites. It also allows the writer to elevate more actions into lead positions. Researchers have found that breaking stories into small segments increases readers' comprehension and retention. For instance, in the example above, the angle about the superintendent's having to decrease staff could be spun off into a short sidebar.

Both methods of presentation have advantages over the more complicated multiple-element lead.

Danger Signals

Here are some leads that understandably raise red flags to editors:

- **Question leads.** Readers don't know the subject, don't know why they are being asked a question and probably couldn't care less. So the next time you are writing a weather story and are tempted to begin with "So, how hot was it yesterday?" lie down until the temptation passes. Either tell readers the temperature or open with an anecdote of a specific roofer sweating on the job. That's showing how hot it is.
- **Leads that say what might happen or what might have happened.** News organizations try to report what happened. Stay away from leads like this: "Springfield residents may be looking forward to warmer weather." Or they may not. Talk to people. Don't speculate.
- **Leads that overreach.** Report what you know. You may think it's harmless to write, "Springfield residents warmly greeted spring yesterday," but you don't know that all Springfield residents were happy about it. Maybe the guy who runs a snow-removal business would rather see winter last longer.

Leads with Flair

Although the inverted pyramid tells readers the news first and fast, not all stories begin with the most important statement. When the news value you want to emphasize is novelty, often the lead is unusual.

When a group of suspected drug dealers was arrested at a wedding, the Associated Press focused on the novelty:

> NARRAGANSETT, R.I. (AP)—The wedding guests included drug suspects, the social coordinator was a narcotics agent, the justice of the peace was a police chief, and 52 officers were party crashers.
>
> For the unsuspecting bride and groom, the ceremony Friday night was truly unforgettable—a sting operation set up by state and local police that led to 30 arrests.

That's not exactly your traditional wedding or your traditional lead. Yet the essential information is contained within the first two paragraphs. A less imaginative writer would have written something like this:

> Thirty suspected drug dealers, including a couple about to be married, were arrested at a wedding Friday night.

> **"The lead should be a promise of great things to come, and the promise should be fulfilled."**
>
> — Stanley Walker, city editor

That approach is like slapping a generic label on a Mercedes-Benz. The inverted pyramid approach is not so rigid that it doesn't permit fun and flair.

What is the difference between the two-paragraph, multiple-element lead on the board of education mentioned earlier and the two-step lead on the wedding story? In the first, the reporter was dealing with several significant actions. In the second, the reporter was dealing with only one, so she used the first paragraph to set up the surprise in the second.

STORY ORGANIZATION

Like a theater marquee, the lead is an attention-getter. Sometimes the movie doesn't fulfill the promises of the marquee; sometimes the story doesn't fulfill the promises of the lead. In either case, the customer is dissatisfied.

The inverted pyramid helps you put information in logical order. It forces you to rank, in order of importance, the information you will present.

The One-Subject Story

As we have seen in this chapter, constructing an inverted pyramid news story involves a series of judgments based on classic news values and the specific news outlet. A fire or an accident in a small community is bigger news than a fire or an accident in another, larger area. Earlier events will also influence how a story is written.

Figure 9.4 shows a story about the arrest of a suspect in an assault case. Police say drugs were involved. If there had been a string of assaults or a pattern of drug-related violence, the writer probably would have emphasized different aspects of

Anatomy of a Single-Subject Inverted Pyramid Story

Man Arrested in Attack, Charged with Child Endangerment

By Elizabeth Phillips
Columbia Missourian

The arrest, not the assault, is the latest development, so it is emphasized.

Police arrested a Columbia man in connection with an attack on his girlfriend Thursday night.

The lead gives "who," "what" and "when."

Details of the charges are in the second paragraph because the list is too long to put in the lead.

Darrell Vanness Johnson, 37, was arrested on suspicion of second-degree domestic assault, unlawful use of a weapon, felony possession of a controlled substance, misdemeanor possession of a controlled substance and endangering the welfare of a child at about 9 p.m. Thursday in the 1500 block of Greensboro Drive.

The name is not in the lead because most readers would not recognize it.

"Where" is identified. "When" is made more specific than in the lead.

The writer adds details, attributed to the police, on how the assault occurred. This information includes the "why."

Johnson and his girlfriend began arguing over drugs Thursday evening, Columbia Police Sgt. Ken Hammond said. Johnson choked her and held a revolver to her head before she was able to escape and call 911 from a neighbor's house, Hammond said. Three children, two 9-year-olds and a 4-year-old, were in the home during the attack, Hammond said.

Information about the children is pertinent because it adds to the "so what" — the children were also endangered.

This paragraph continues the chronology of the assault and capture.

When Columbia police arrived, Johnson was driving away from the Greensboro Drive home with the three children in the car, Hammond said. When police arrested Johnson, they found marijuana and cocaine, Hammond said.

The victim was taken to an area hospital by ambulance for treatment of bruises and scratches to the hands, neck and back, Hammond said. Her injuries were not life threatening.

The writer offers evidence of the injuries and attributes this information.

Now that the basic facts are established, the writer adds background on the suspect, attributed to a public safety website.

According to Missouri Case.net, Johnson has pleaded guilty to third-degree domestic assault three times in the past four years in Boone County Circuit Court, serving close to seven months in jail for those charges. He has also pleaded guilty to theft, first-degree trespass and second-degree property damage in Boone County Circuit Court, serving 75 days in Boone County Jail for the theft charge and receiving two years of unsupervised probation for the trespass and property damage charges.

Johnson violated his probation on the trespass and property damage charges and was scheduled to appear in Boone County Circuit Court for a probation violation hearing in December. He was charged with theft last October in Boone County Circuit Court.

Writer gives the "what's next."

He faces up to 40 years in prison and up to a year in jail in connection with the attack.

Figure 9.4
This typical one-subject story written in the inverted pyramid features a delayed-identification lead.

the story. For instance, the writer could have emphasized the suspect's criminal record with this lead:

> A Columbia man who was convicted of assault three times was arrested again Thursday night for an attack on his girlfriend.

There is almost always more than one way to write a story. The version that is published or broadcast is the result of the judgments of the writer and the editor. If the story in Figure 9.4 had already appeared on the Web or had been broadcast on television or radio, the newspaper probably would have chosen another angle, as in the example highlighting the suspect's criminal record, to make the story different.

The Multiple-Element Story

Multiple-element stories are most commonly used in reporting on the proceedings of councils, boards, commissions, legislatures and courts. These bodies act on numerous subjects in one sitting. Frequently, their actions are unrelated, and more than one action is often important enough to merit attention in the story. You have four options:

1. **You can write more than one story.** That, of course, requires permission from your editor. There may not be enough space.
2. **You can write a summary box.** It would be displayed along with the story. In it you would list the major actions taken by the council or the decisions issued by the court.
3. **You can write a multiple-element lead and story.** Your lead would list all the major actions at the board meeting. The remainder of the story would provide more detail about each action.
4. **You can write a single-element lead and cover the other elements further on in the story.** Your lead would focus on the element you believe readers would find most interesting, relevant and useful.

Let's go back to a multiple-element lead we saw earlier:

> The Board of Education Tuesday night voted to lower the tax rate 12 cents per $100 valuation. Members then approved a budget $150,000 less than last year's and instructed the superintendent to decrease the staff by 25 people.
>
> The board also approved a set of student-conduct rules, which include a provision that students with three or more unexcused absences a year will be suspended for a week.

Four newsworthy actions are mentioned in those two paragraphs: (1) changing the tax rate, (2) approving a budget, (3) cutting staff, (4) adopting conduct rules. In stories that deal with several important elements, the writer usually high-

---

TIPS

Checklist for Assembling the Rest of the Inverted Pyramid

- Introduce additional important information you were not able to include in the lead.

- If possible, indicate the significance or "so what" factor.

- Elaborate on the information presented in the lead.

- Continue introducing new information in the order in which you have ranked it by importance.

- Develop the ideas in the same order in which you have introduced them.

- Generally, use only one new idea in each paragraph.

lights the most important. Sometimes several elements are equally important, as in this example. Most of the time, however, one action stands above the rest. When that is the case, it is important to summarize the other, lesser, actions after the lead.

If you and your editor judge that changing the tax rate was more important than anything else that happened at the school board meeting, you would approach the story like this:

Lead	The Board of Education Tuesday night voted to lower the tax rate 12 cents per $100 valuation.
Support for lead	The new rate is $1.18 per $100 valuation. That means that if your property is assessed at $300,000, your school tax will be $3,540 next year.
Summary of other action	The board also approved a budget that is $150,000 less than last year's, instructed the superintendent to cut the staff by 25 and approved a set of rules governing student conduct.

Notice that the lead is followed by a paragraph that supports and enlarges upon the information in it before the summary paragraph appears. Whether you need a support paragraph before summarizing other action depends on how complete you are able to make the lead.

In every multiple-element story, the first two or three paragraphs determine the order of the rest of the story. To ensure the coherence of your story, you must describe the elements in the order in which you introduced them.

In Figure 9.5, you see a more detailed example of a multiple-element story. Notice the order in which the writer answers the questions who, what, when, where, why and how. Do you agree that the lead contains the most important elements? Could the story be cut from the bottom up, if necessary?

> *"Selecting the quotes isn't so hard; it's presenting them that causes the trouble. And the worst place to present them is at the beginning. Quote leads deserve their terrible reputation. Yet they still appear regularly in both print and broadcast journalism.*
>
> *"We can make three generalizations about quote leads. They're easy, lazy, and lousy. They have no context. The readers don't know who's speaking, why, or why it matters. Without context, even the best quotations are wasted."*
>
> — Paula LaRocque, former assistant managing editor, *The Dallas Morning News*

Writing for the Web

When you are writing for a news website, your challenge is to get people to stop at your site for more than a few seconds. To that end, you have many tools at your disposal.

You have not only photos but often video to attract attention and to help tell the story.

You have more space to write a headline and a deck or subhead than you do in a newspaper. That gives you a better opportunity to summarize and attract attention.

Space is no longer your enemy. You can do pullouts, such as lists that are pulled out from the story, to highlight the main points, and you can use hyperlinks to give the story many layers. Granted, readers in a hurry won't take advantage of these additional features, but others will.

Anatomy of a Multiple-Element Inverted Pyramid Story

U Earns C Average in Student-Access Report

By Norman Draper
Star Tribune

The writer chooses two elements to put in the lead along with "who" and "what." →

The University of Minnesota does better than most of the nation's major public universities in admitting minority students. But it fares poorly in both graduating them within six years and in admitting low-income students.

← Are there any elements in the fifth paragraph that you think should be in the lead?

In order to tell the "what," the writer had to delay revealing the source of the report and the answer to "when." →

Those are among the findings of a report issued Monday by the national Education Trust. The report measured how well the nation's 50 flagship state universities are serving the nation's racial minority and poor students.

← This is the context against which readers can measure the local university's performance.

Having established the most important elements, the writer summarizes the rest of the report. →

Overall, the report's findings described the nation's top state universities as looking "less and less like America—and more and more like gated communities of higher education." Too many, the report stated, aren't pushing hard enough to enroll more minority and poor kids.

Note that the writer offers not only the findings but also the reasons for the findings in this and succeeding paragraphs.

Now the writer summarizes the local details. →

The U of M generally fared relatively well in the report, though it earned only a C average based on six criteria. That's better than many state universities, which got Ds and Fs. Other universities in the survey included the University of Wisconsin-Madison, the University of North Carolina-Chapel, the University of California-Berkeley and the University of Texas-Austin.

Any of these details could have been in the lead. The writer and editor had to make judgments about the most important details. →

The U of M got an A in minority student access because the percentage of black, Hispanic and American Indian students in its fall 2004 freshman class—7.7 percent—was identical to the percentage of those students in the state's spring 2004 high school graduating class. Asian students were not counted as minority students in the report because they are not considered underrepresented.

Notice that the letter grades used in the report give the reader a way to understand the results.

← The terms *black*, *African-American*, *Hispanic*, *American Indian*, and *Asian* are acceptable, according to AP style.

The U got a D in minority student success because of the gap in graduation rates between white students (63.7 percent) and minority students (41.4 percent).

It also got a D in access for low-income students. That's because the number of such students at the U is lower than at all other Minnesota colleges and universities, as measured by the percentage of students who get federal grants.

Here and in the next two paragraphs is the university's response to the report. →

"The University of Minnesota has long been concerned with issues of access for students from all walks of life," U spokesman Daniel Wolter said

(continued)

Figure 9.5
The writer for the Minneapolis *Star Tribune* localized a national study for readers. The study produced multiple findings, so the writer and editor had to rank them from most important to least important.

Figure 9.5
(continued)

in an e-mailed response. "The issue of access for underrepresented minorities has been an important one for the U . . . and our A grade underscores that we're doing a good job on that front." ← Note how the writer handles the e-mail from the spokesman.

Wolter also cited the creation of a new administrative position—vice president for access and diversity—and the U's raising of $150 million in private gifts to support student scholarships as evidence that the U is committed to academic and racial diversity.

In regard to the two Ds, Wolter said, "We recognize those as areas for improvement," but he added that overall U graduation rates have doubled over the past decade.

The background helps readers understand who issued the report. → The Education Trust is a Washington, D.C. nonprofit organization dedicated to improving student achievement, with a special emphasis on low-income and racial minority students.

CNN not only offered all these features in its story on the closing of the San Francisco-Oakland Bay Bridge, but it also invited readers to contribute to the story. About halfway through the story, they asked, in a hyperlinked sentence, "Were you there? Send photos and video." The link took readers to instructions about how to submit photos, video and stories.

As these examples show, the inverted pyramid structure has survived into the Internet age. Whether it is for print or the Internet, the news will always be built around the most important facts arranged in a coherent order.

Suggested Readings

Brooks, Brian S., James L. Pinson and Jean Gaddy Wilson. *Working with Words*, 7th ed. New York: Bedford/St. Martin's, 2009. This book, a must for any journalist, provides excellent coverage of grammar and word usage and has a strong chapter on "isms."

Gillman, Timothy. "The Problem of Long Leads in News and Sports Stories." *Newspaper Research Journal* (Fall 1994): 29–39. The researcher found that sentences in leads were longer than sentences in the rest of the story.

Kennedy, George. "Newspaper Accuracy: A New Approach." *Newspaper Research Journal* (Winter 1994): 55–61. The author suggests that journalists do prepublication accuracy checks with proper safeguards in place.

Maier, Scott R. "Accuracy Matters: A Cross-Market Assessment of Newspaper Error and Credibility." *Journalism and Mass Communications Quarterly* (Autumn 2005): 533–51. This study documents the error rates of journalists and the impact on credibility.

Suggested Websites

www.regrettheerror.com
Regret the Error is a website that chronicles errors made in all media. It is valuable in that it shows that even professional reporters are fallible.

www.stateofthenewsmedia.org
The Pew Project for Excellence in Journalism produces an annual "State of the News Media" report that examines journalistic trends and economic trends.

www.wsu.edu/~brians/errors/index.html
Paul Brians, a professor of English at Washington State University, will answer your questions about the English language.

Exercises

1. **Team project.** Your professor will divide you into teams. Read *The Widget Effect, 2009*, a study done by The Teacher Project, which is an organization, founded by teachers in 1997, "to address the growing issues of teacher shortages and teacher quality throughout the country." The study reports that teachers are not interchangable widgets. It can be downloaded at **http://widgeteffect.org/downloads/TheWidgetEffect.pdf.**

   As you read, annotate your copy of the study with questions and responses, including possible story ideas. Collaborate with your team members to choose four story ideas prompted by the study. Each team member should write a lead for one story idea. As a group, edit the leads to meet the requirements of an inverted pyramid lead. Your teacher may choose to have you report on the best story idea.

2. Identify the who, what, where, when, why and how, if they are present, in the following lead:

   The United Jewish Appeal is sponsoring its first-ever walkathon this morning in Springfield to raise money for The Soup Kitchen, a place where the hungry can eat free.

3. Here are four versions of the same lead. Which of the four answers more of the six questions basic to all stories? Which questions does it answer?

   a. What began 12 years ago with a federal staff investigation and led to hearings and a court fight culminates today with a Federal Trade Commission rule to prevent funeral home rip-offs.
   b. The nation's funeral home directors are required to offer detailed cost statements starting today, a service they say they are now ready to provide despite nearly a dozen years of debate over the idea.
   c. A new disclosure law going into effect today will make it easier for consumers to determine the cost of a funeral.
   d. Twelve years after first being proposed, a federal regulation goes into effect Monday to require funeral homes to provide an itemized list of services and materials they offer, along with the cost of each item, before a person agrees to any arrangements.

4. Rewrite two of the leads in exercise 3 as "you" leads. Which are better, the third-person or second-person leads? Why are they better?

5. From the following facts, write a lead.

Who:	A nuclear weapon with a yield equivalent to 150,000 tons of TNT
What:	Detonated
Where:	40 miles from a meeting of pacifists and 2,000 feet beneath the surface of Pahute Mesa in the Nevada desert
When:	Tuesday
Why:	To test the weapon
How:	Not applicable

   Other information: Department of Energy officials are the source; 450 physicians and peace activists were gathered to protest continued nuclear testing by the United States.

6. From the following facts, write the first two paragraphs of a news article.

Who:	7-year-old boy missing for three years
What:	Found
Where:	In Brick Township, N.J.

When: Monday night

Why: Not applicable

How: A neighbor recognized the child's picture when it was shown after the movie *Adam: The Song Continues* and called police.

Other information: Police arrested the boy's mother, Ellen Lynn Conner, 27; she faces Alabama charges of kidnapping and interference with a custody warrant.

7. From the following facts, write the first two paragraphs of a news article.

Who: 40 passengers

What: Evacuated from a Northwest Airlines jet, Flight 428

Where: At the LaCrosse, Wis., Municipal Airport

When: Monday following a flight from Minneapolis to LaCrosse

Why: A landing tower employee spotted smoke near the wheels.

How: Not applicable

Other information: There was no fire or injuries; the smoke was caused by hydraulic fluids leaking onto hot landing brakes, according to Bob Gibbons, a Northwest spokesman.

8. Describe picture and information-graphic possibilities for the story in exercise 6.

9. Cut out six leads from newspapers. Determine which basic questions are answered and which are not. Identify the kind of lead used.

Writing to Be Read

10

Whether you are writing a newspaper story, a television script, a news release or an article for a website, a good story told well is important to readers and viewers and to the financial success of your company. Many journalists are getting the message. That is why we see stories like this more often:

By Lee Hancock /
The Dallas Morning News
lhancock@dallasnews.com

Editor's note: Facing death can be hardest for a family expecting new life. Perinatal hospice offers choices and resources for parents when an infant's death is imminent. This is one North Texas family's story.

A black gap marred the middle of the computer screen. The void split a cloud of light that ebbed and flowed into the shape of a human fetus.

The sonogram technician turned from her computer screen to Deidrea and T.K. Laux. She told them she saw problems.

T.K. stopped thumbing his BlackBerry. He had just messaged everyone they knew the good news that their child was a boy. Now, he ignored the buzzing of congratulatory responses.

The technician slowly traced a black gap in the center of the screen with a computer arrow. What they were seeing, she told them, was their baby's cleft lip.

OK, Deidrea said to herself as she caught her breath, we can deal with this.

She shifted into planning mode as the technician kept rolling the sonogram wand over her bare belly.

T.K. felt sucker punched. His eyes welled. One of his cousins, born with a cleft lip, still struggled through surgeries at 30.

The technician turned back and focused on the screen for what seemed like hours. The baby's kidneys looked swollen, she finally said, another bad sign. She excused herself to get the Lauxes' obstetrician.

The Lauxes later would recall that their doctor's examining room felt claustrophobic. Reclining on the narrow examining table with her belly still exposed, Deidrea kept telling her husband that pediatric urologists fixed kidneys and plastic surgeons fixed lips.

T.K. squeezed Deidrea's leg and fought tears. How could this be happening, he asked, to their baby boy—to them?

Every question from that moment on would be shattering: What could faith do when medicine offered no hope? What separated surrender and suffering? If survival was only a matter of hours or days, how much life would be enough?

This is the opening to a two-part series. Lee Hancock takes you into the examining room when the couple learn they will have a boy. Minutes later, they learn the baby probably will not live long. You are with them through the five days the baby lived, and through the funeral. The story, however, isn't told until a year later when the couple is again expecting a child.

Readers don't see this type of writing as often as they should. Some are voting with their feet; they are abandoning newspapers and magazines. Those who stay appreciate good stories. One reader who posted a comment on the newspaper's website congratulated the author and photographer "for this beautiful piece." She also thanked the family "for letting us witness their joy and grief at the birth and death of their son."

IN THIS CHAPTER YOU WILL LEARN:

1. How the skills of reporting make good writing possible.

2. Four characteristics of all good writing.

3. Four tools of narration.

There's even some research to support the idea that newspapers are not as easy to read as they should be. Using the Flesch Reading Ease formula, which measures readability, researchers at the University of Texas looked at a century of writing in novels and newspapers. They concluded that novels had become easier to read and newspapers had become harder.

Readability is a function of such elements as the number of words in a sentence, the number of syllables in a word and the number of ideas in a sentence. In general, the more of them there are, the harder a sentence is to understand. Can we blame readers, then, for reeling when they encounter this typical lead?

> WASHINGTON—A 10-year study of an increasingly popular surgical technique used to correct poor distance vision shows that the method is reasonably safe and effective but that it might lead to an accelerated decline in the ability to see things up close, researchers said Wednesday.

That's 45 words. Hidden somewhere in the thicket is the main idea. In case the readers were still standing, the writer followed this with a 47-word sentence.

If you're thinking that science is a complicated subject calling for complicated writing, how do you explain this lead on a story about a celebrity?

> While several of the golden-marquee co-stars Gary Sinise has had throughout the years, like Nicolas Cage, have continued to conduct choruses of box-office *ka-ching* with special effects and eye-candy espionage, and others, like Sharon Stone, have barricaded themselves from paparazzi in makeshift foxholes, Sinise has emerged as a perhaps unlikely great American action hero, having spearheaded a massive movement to support U.S. troops and the children of war they protect.

That's 70 words. The opening dependent clause has 43 words and enough characters to fill two Twitter messages.

Writing to inform and entertain is as important for journalists as it is for novelists. Just because newspapers and broadcast reports are done and gone in a day doesn't mean that we should accept a lower level of skill. Comparing the temporal nature of newspapers to a beach, syndicated columnist James Kilpatrick challenged writers: "If we write upon the sand, let us write as well as we can upon the sand before the waves come in."

If Kilpatrick's challenge to your pride is not enough, then the demands of readers and listeners and of editors and news directors who are hiring should be. Editors are looking for those unusual people who can combine reporting and writing talents. The journalist whose prose jerks around the page like a mouse trapped in a room with a cat has no future in the business. The American Society of News Editors has made improved writing one of its principal long-range goals. Each year, in cooperation with the Poynter Institute of St. Petersburg, Fla., it awards $1,000 to the winners in several categories of the writing competition it sponsors. The winning entries are published annually by the institute in a book series titled *Best Newspaper Writing*. ASNE posts the winning entries and many of its reports on writing at www.asne.org.

Many well-known writers—among them Daniel Defoe, Mark Twain, Stephen Crane, Ernest Hemingway and Alex Haley—began their careers as journalists. A more recent list would include John Hersey, Tom Wolfe and Gay Talese. The bestseller list is peppered with the names of journalists: Bob Woodward, Russell Baker, Ellen Goodman, Anna Quindlen, Richard Ben Cramer, Ron Rosenbaum, Tom Brokaw and Edna Buchanan. At newspapers around the country today, small but growing numbers of journalists are producing literature daily as they deal with everything from traffic accidents to affairs of state. If you have respect for the language, an artist's imagination and the dedication to learn how to combine them, you, too, may produce literature.

We should all attempt to bring quality writing, wit and knowledge to our work. If we succeed, our work will be not only informative but also enjoyable, not only educational but also entertaining, and not only bought but also read.

GOOD WRITING BEGINS WITH GOOD REPORTING

Without the proper ingredients, the best chef is no better than a short-order cook. Without the proper use of participant accounts, personal observation and detail, the best writer's stories land with a thud. Good writing begins with good reporting. You can settle for a dry police report, or you can go to the scene and gather details. In Chapter 9 we introduced you to this lead:

> Two people died Thursday when a backhoe fell off a truck's flatbed and sliced the top off an oncoming vehicle near Fairchild Air Force Base.

Now let's look at some of the detail writer Alison Boggs of *The (Spokane, Wash.) Spokesman-Review* collected by being there:

> The top of the Suburban, from about hood height, was shorn off by the backhoe's bucket. The front seats were forced backward, and the dashboard, roof and steering wheel were torn off.
>
> Parts of the car lay in a heap of crumpled metal and glass under the overpass. The silver Suburban was identifiable only by a 1983 owner's manual lying in the dirt nearby.
>
> Both victims wore seat belts, but in this case, that was irrelevant, (Sgt. Jeff) Sale said. Both suffered severe head injuries.
>
> Sleeping bags, a Coleman cooler and fishing equipment scattered on the highway and in the back of the Suburban suggested a camping trip. Unopened cans of Pepsi were jammed behind the front seat of the car.

Notice that the writer built every sentence on concrete detail. Good reporting makes good writing possible.

ON THE JOB

Setting the Hook in the Opening

Justin Heckert, who is a contract writer for *ESPN The Magazine* and freelances for other national magazines including *Men's Journal* and *Esquire*, believes one of the most important aspects of writing is the first few sentences of a story:

The experience of reading and being hooked can be because of word play, or rhythm, or a particular style or device. I can recite the first sentences to some of my favorite stories. That's just how they stick with me.

"The madness of an autumn prairie cold front coming through." That's Jonathan Franzen. "It was a pleasure to burn. It was a special pleasure to see things eaten, to see things blackened and changed." That's Ray Bradbury. "Aye, that face. There's a story about that face, you know. About what he was willing to do with it." That's Tom Junod. "Sometimes the silence gets inside of you." That's Gary Smith. "They don't count calories at Fausto's Fried Chicken." That's Wright Thompson. These books/stories are nowhere near me as I write this, but I can remember those sentences, and I know I got them right.

This idea has been a huge part of my own writing. I've done it, or tried to, in pretty much every single story I've ever written, be it a success or failure. A recent example: In 2009, I reported and wrote a story for *Men's Journal*. I was sitting on top of amazing material. I could've, honestly, probably just written it out like I was talking to a third grader, and it still would've been an interesting story. But after I talked to my editor and sat down to write it, I sweated forever about how to begin. I sat on the porch and thought about it. I thought about it driving the car. I thought about how to begin while I was watching a football game, before I was going to bed.

The story was about two people who had been pulled out to the sea and had treaded water for hours. The ocean has been written about more than anything since the beginning of time. It was hard to try and think of something new to say about it, to tie it in to the experience of this guy and his son, victims of the ocean, even though they didn't die. How this situation resolved itself is as esoteric as the nature of writing itself: It just came to me.

"The ocean at night is a terrible dream. There is nothing beyond the water except the profound discouragement of the sky, every black wave another singular misfortune." I had stared at the ocean for hours, had thought about how it affected the characters of the story, thought about everything they said about it. I knew it when the words appeared — they came to me the way ideas come to people, inexplicably. I think those are two good sentences. So did my editor. So have a lot of other people who read it. They were that important to me because I wanted them to hook the readers and then keep them with me.

ACCURATE, SPECIFIC DETAILS

Good writing is accurate because it is built on concrete details. When you use language to communicate those details precisely, you inform and entertain your readers.

Use Concrete Examples

For lawyers, the devil may be in the details, but for writers, clarity is in the details. Echoing your bureaucratic sources, you can write of infrastructures or facilities or learning pods. But try actually touching any of these. By contrast, you ride on a highway, sit in an arena and learn in a reading group.

Be specific. You might write that the speaker is big, but compared to what? Abstractions are ambiguous. To someone who is 6 feet tall, someone big may be 6 feet 6 inches tall. To someone who is 5 feet 2 inches tall, 6 feet is huge.

Look at the concrete details in the following lead from *The Boston Globe* about an employee who killed five co-workers:

He was an accountant who had a chip on his shoulder and a bayonet on his kitchen table. He lived with his parents across from a llama farm in a small beige house with a sign informing visitors: "Trespassers will be shot; survivors will be shot again."

As dawn broke over Ledyard yesterday, Matthew Beck, 35, left his folks' home— across town from the casino—got in his car, and drove 1½ hours to his job at Connecticut Lottery headquarters. At some point, he strapped a bandolier of bullets across his chest, over his gray pin-striped shirt but concealed by a brown leather jacket. He carried a 9mm pistol and a knife.

Nearly every sentence contains specific, concrete detail: "accountant," "bayonet," "across from a llama farm," and so on.

Here's a student writer at Indiana University who could have reported simply that several things were missing in the apartment. Instead, she used concrete detail:

When she awoke the next morning, the window was completely open. Random items, including a toaster, a 15-year-old broken VCR, an empty bookbag and the remote control to a stereo, were missing.

To be concrete, you must have facts. And you must describe those facts in a way that makes readers able to touch and examine them. Lazy reporters create puffballs. Poke their stories, and you'll stick your finger clear through them. Instead of saying, "Some council members," say "Five council members." Instead of writing that a business is "downsizing," report that 150 workers will lose their jobs. Avoid abstractions; covet concrete details.

Show, Don't Just Tell

As you chauffeur the reader through the scenes in your story, you can drive down the road or over the green-laced, rolling hills of Kentucky. You can report that a car hit a skunk, or you can convey the nauseating smell. A word here, a phrase there, and you can hear the plane ripping the tin roof off the house, smell the acrid stench of burning tires, feel the boxing glove's leather rasp against the skin. Good writing appeals to one or more of our five senses: sight, hearing, smell, taste and touch.

> *There's a time to sow and a time to reap, but there's never a time for seasonal agricultural activities.*
>
> — Jack Cappon, Associated Press senior writer and writing coach

In addition to years of anecdotal experience, there is also statistical support for the advice to show rather than tell. For instance, researchers constructed 10 sentences telling information and 10 showing information. College students were divided into two groups and asked to read one of the groups of sentences. Then they were asked to rate the sentences on such qualities as interesting-dull, clear-unclear and engaging-unengaging. The authors concluded, "The experiment found strong evidence that, as many experts have implied, show sentences are seen as more interesting and engaging than tell sentences."

Writer Walt Harrington could simply have told readers that detective V.I. Smith picked up his notebook to leave on a call, but he showed us his preparation:

> "Well, here we go," says V.I., in his smooth, lyrical baritone as he palms a radio, unconsciously pats his right breast coat pocket for evidence of his ID wallet, pats his left breast coat pocket for evidence of his notebook and heads out the door in his athlete's saunter, a stylized and liquid stroll, a modern cakewalk.

Readers can see and hear V.I. because the writer is showing, not telling.

A student writer used her sense of touch to gather information: "After 40 years of working outside, his skin is as leathery as an alligator's." Did she actually touch him? "Yes," she says. "I kept looking at his skin. Finally, even though I was embarrassed, I asked him if I could touch his face. He laughed. 'You can tell I don't use no fancy lotions, can't you?'"

The writing is better because the reporters didn't just ask questions and record answers. They looked; they touched; they listened. Readers can see and feel along with the reporters.

Translate Numbers

To many people, numbers are a foreign language. It is our job as journalists to learn the language of numbers and to translate them so that our readers understand.

The most important way to increase comprehension is to compare numbers and sizes. Authorities may announce that forest fires destroyed vegetation over 500 square miles. What does that mean to your readers? One way to make it meaningful is to compare the numbers, the unknown, to something known. Readers in

California can understand how large an area is if they are told the forest fire destroyed an area four times the size of San Francisco. Check your city directory for the size and population of your community.

You can translate large budget numbers on campus by expressing them as spending per student. You can translate a tax increase by expressing it as cost per citizen. You can translate the rate of crime by expressing it as the number of crimes each minute or hour or day in your city or per capita. One newspaper examining the lack of screening for teachers expressed the findings this way:

> Spokane cabbies and Nevada blackjack dealers face tougher screening through background checks than teachers in 42 states.

If every journalist wrote about numbers in plain English, as that one did, more readers would understand.

Use Words Precisely

Words should mean exactly what you intend them to mean. You should never use "uninterested" when you mean "disinterested." Nor should you use "allude" for "refer," "presume" for "assume," "endeavor" for "try," "fewer" for "less," "farther" for "further." If you report that fire destroyed a house, you mean the home needs rebuilding, not repair. If you say firefighters donned oxygen masks to enter a burning building, you are impugning either their intelligence or yours. (Oxygen is dangerous around fire; firefighters use air tanks.) You can make the mayor "say," "declare," "claim" or "growl"—but only one is accurate.

COHERENCE

When you write coherently, your writing is understandable. Coherence is built on a logical structure, by matching the content to the appropriate sentence structure, by using the correct coordinating conjunctions and by guiding readers with transitions.

Decide on the Order of Elements

Chronology is the most easily understood of story structures. You start at the beginning and go to the end. The story that opens this chapter begins when the couple learn their unborn child's heart cannot survive outside the womb and ends a year after they buried their five-day-old baby. (For more on story structure, see Chapter 11.) Journalists, however, often don't have the luxury of readers' time or publication space to use chronology. That's why it is important to outline a story, even if your outline merely lists the three or four points you expect to make. Your outline is your map. If you know where you are going, your readers will be able to follow.

TIPS

**Writing a Coherent
Story**

● Create logical story
   structures.

● Express the relationship
   between ideas properly.

● Use language precisely.

● Use transitions.

Here's a simple outline you might make for a story about a city council meeting:

1. Approved one-way streets.
2. Raised parking fines.
3. Bought snowplows.
4. Will study downtown parking.
5. Hired audit firm.

You rank the actions in order of importance. Then you decide whether to focus on one element or write a summary lead or a multiple-element lead. (See Chapter 9 for more on leads.) Once you have done that, you add detail to your outline:

1. Single-element lead: one-way streets
2. Summary of other actions
   a. Parking fines
   b. Snowplows
   c. Parking facilities
   d. City audit
3. Support for lead
   a. The vote
   b. Jones quote
   c. Opposition
4. Support for other actions in order introduced in second paragraph
   a. Raised parking fines
      (i) Amount; (ii) reason; (iii) no opposition
   b. Bought snowplows
      (i) Cost; (ii) when delivered
   c. Downtown parking
      (i) Define problem; (ii) when study is due; (iii) who will do it;
      (iv) Dehaven quote; (v) Chamber of Commerce request
   d. Audit firm
      (i) Who will do it; (ii) cost; (iii) when due

Although outlining may take five minutes, it will save you much more time. The outline also creates a structure that flows logically from one idea to the next. Here's how you could start the story outlined above:

> The Springfield City Council voted Tuesday to make four streets in the downtown area one-way.
> The council also raised parking fines to $5, voted to buy two snowplows, ordered a study of downtown parking facilities and hired a firm to audit the city.
> Effective March 1, the four streets that will be one-way are . . .

Select the Proper Sentence Structure

Within each sentence, you must express the proper relationships between ideas. One way to do this is to think about your sentence structure. Simple sentences express one idea. Compound sentences express two or more ideas of equal importance. Complex sentences subordinate one idea to another. Here are some examples.

Simple

> The mayor scolded the council.

Compound

> The mayor scolded the council, and she insisted on a vote.

Compound sentences equate two or more ideas without commenting on them. Complex sentences allow you to show sequence and cause and effect, among other things:

Complex

> After the mayor scolded the council, she insisted on a vote. (Shows sequence.)

Complex

> Because the mayor was angry, she insisted on a vote. (Shows cause and effect.)

Both sentences are correct, but the meaning of each is slightly different.

Use the Precise Conjunction

Subordinating conjunctions—such as "if," "since," "while," "after" and "until"— each carry a different and precise meaning. Choose the subordinating conjunction that expresses the idea you want.

Coordinating conjunctions ("and," "or," "but," "for," "nor," "so," "yet") also require careful selection. Observe how the meaning changes with the conjunction in these examples:

> The mayor insisted that the council vote, and the members ignored her.

> The mayor insisted that the council vote, but the members ignored her.

The second example is more coherent because it expresses the council members' reaction more logically.

Use Transitions

Transitions are words, phrases, sentences or paragraphs that show the logical progression of the story structure and the ideas within the structure. Transitions are road signs directing readers through a story. Figure 10.1 shows how transitions can be used in a story.

Using Transitions

The first four paragraphs focus on Billman, which makes the story easy to follow. Billman's name or a pronoun links the paragraphs.

On a Monday afternoon, Dr. Glenn Billman pulled back from the autopsy he was performing on a dead girl and stared at the sight before him.

In his seven years at Children's Hospital, he had never seen anything like it. The girl's colon was severely hemorrhaged, ravaged by bacteria that normally lived in a cow's intestine.

Puzzled and quietly alarmed, Billman notified local health officials. It was the first indication that the lethal strain of bacteria, E. coli 0157:H7, was on the loose.

"But" is a transition that shows the writer is introducing another angle.

But Billman didn't make his discovery at Children's Hospital in Seattle. He made it at Children's Hospital in San Diego, and he made it three weeks before the E. coli epidemic struck the Northwest, killing three children and sickening about 500 people.

In December, San Diego was hit by a small E. coli outbreak that killed the 6-year-old girl and made at least seven other people sick.

Time reference used as a transition: "It is now . . ." links the Northwest outbreak to the earlier San Diego outbreak ("In December . . .").

It is now being linked to the Seattle outbreak, but in its early stages, San Diego health officials were slow to recognize the crisis, and they have been sharply criticized for failing to notify the public about the E. coli death and illnesses.

"I really believe we need to be safe and not sorry, and the fact is, a girl died in San Diego," said San Diego County Supervisor Dianne Jacob. "I was outraged. The only way I found out was by reading it in the newspaper"

Time references ("after the Northwest outbreak" and "When the first . . .") link these paragraphs.

after the Northwest outbreak.

When the first Washington cases were reported in mid-January, authorities there immediately queried neighboring states, including California, but were not told about the E. coli death of the San Diego girl. That information would have alerted them about the bacteria's severity and might have pointed them sooner to the source of the contamination.

The phrase "Like the patients here" links this paragraph to the preceding one.

Like the patients here, the San Diego girl had eaten a hamburger at a Jack in the Box restaurant days before she got sick and died. The seven other E. coli patients had all eaten hamburgers at fast-food restaurants, among them Jack in the Box.

The word "that" is a demonstrative adjective that points to the preceding paragraph.

That information was available in early January, according to Dr. Michele Ginsberg, San Diego County epidemiologist. She would not say how many of the seven patients had eaten at Jack in the Box.

"A variety of restaurants were mentioned," she said. "Naming any one of them would create public reaction and perhaps avoidance of those restaurants."

"That" again creates a transition from the preceding paragraph.

That reticence angers Jacob, the San Diego County supervisor. "I had a follow-up meeting with county health officials, and I have to tell you, very honestly, I was not pleased with their attitude," she said. . . .

Figure 10.1
Transitions, like road signs, help readers understand where they have been and where they are going.

The reference to memory in the next example directs us from the first to the second paragraph:

Mr. and Mrs. Lester Einbender are using their memory
to project life as it might have been.
    That memory centers around a son named Michael,
a rheumatic disease called lupus and a desire to honor
one while conquering the other.

The use of the word "That" at the beginning of the second paragraph is subtle, but its impact is dramatic. If you wrote "A memory," you would not link the reader to the memory already mentioned. If you wrote "The memory," you would be more specific, but by writing "That memory," you point directly to the memory mentioned in the preceding paragraph. Because "a" is good only for general references, "a" is called an *indefinite modifier*. Because "the" is more specific, "the" is called a *definite modifier*. Because "that" is most specific, it is a *demonstrative adjective*; it demonstrates precisely the word or phrase to which you are referring when you couple it with the noun ("memory"). When you move from indefinite to definite modifier, then to demonstrative adjective, you climb the ladder of coherence.

> **❝**But I obsess during writing to the point where I can lose sleep over the right word.**❞**
>
> — Madeleine Blais, writer

Transitions help you achieve coherence, the logical connection of ideas. They guide you from one sentence to the next, from one paragraph to the next. Writers unfamiliar with transitions merely stack paragraphs, like pieces of wood, atop one another. Transitions keep the story, if not the woodpile, from falling apart.

Repeating a word or phrase also helps to keep the story from falling apart. In the preceding example, the writer used a demonstrative adjective and repeated a word. (Other demonstrative adjectives are "this," "these" and "those.")

Parallelism, repetition of a word or grammatical form, is another way to guide readers through a story. Writers frequently use parallelism to achieve coherence.

Writing about the complicated subject of nuclear-waste disposal in America, Donald Barlett and James Steele, then of *The Philadelphia Inquirer*, relied on parallelism for coherence and emphasis. Notice the parallel use of "They said . . ." to start sentences — and the repeated variations of "It cannot":

This assessment may prove overly optimistic. For perhaps in no other area of modern technology have so many experts in the government, industry and science been so wrong so many times over so many years as have those involved in radioactive waste.

They said, repeatedly, that radioactive waste could be handled like any other industrial refuse. It cannot.

They said that science had most of the answers, and was on the verge of getting the few it did not have, for dealing with radioactive waste permanently. It did not, and it does not.

They said that some of it could be buried in the ground, like garbage in a landfill, and that it would pose no health hazard because it would never move. It moved.

They said that liquid radioactive waste could be put in storage tanks, and that rigorous safety systems would immediately detect any leaks. The tanks leaked for weeks and no one noticed.

Barlett and Steele's use of parallelism sets up the story. In the following case, the writer repeated the word "waiting" for emphasis:

> Realized or not, we live in constant anticipation. We're always waiting. Waiting to drive. Waiting to turn 21. Waiting for winter break. Waiting to graduate. Waiting for a significant other to come along.

Chronology and references to time provide other ways to tie a story together. Words and phrases such as "now," "since then" and "two days later" are invaluable in helping readers understand where they have been and where they are going. Chronology is important in everything from reports of automobile accidents (which car entered the intersection first?) to recaps of events that occurred over months, as in Lee Hancock's story at the beginning of the chapter.

CONCISENESS AND SIMPLICITY

Particularly in newspapers and broadcasting where space and time constraints are severe, conciseness is a virtue. However, even when you write for the Web, you have to respect readers' time. No one has unlimited time or attention to give you.

Aim for Conciseness

Being concise means saying what you need to say in as few words as possible. Some subjects require more details than others. Here are four ways to shorten your stories. (See also Figure 10.2.)

1. **Eliminate some subject areas.** Always ask yourself whether all of the subjects need to be included. No doubt, your editor will have a more dispassionate view of what's needed than you will.
2. **Eliminate redundancies.** One way to achieve conciseness is to rid your sentences of cabooses, unneeded words or phrases that hitch themselves, like barnacles, onto other words. Delete the barnacles in italics: remand *back*; gather *together*; consensus *of opinion*; *totally* destroyed; *excess* verbiage; open *up*; fall *down*; my *own personal* favorite; strangled *to death*.
3. **Challenge intensive and qualifying adverbs.** Your job is to select the right word so you don't need two or more. Instead of "really unhappy," perhaps you mean "sad." Instead of "very cold," perhaps you mean "frigid." "Really" and "very" are examples of intensive adverbs. When you say "almost there," you are using a qualifying adverb. Be specific.
4. **Train yourself to value brevity.** Some of the most notable writing in history is brief: Lincoln's Gettysburg Address contains 272 words; the Ten Commandments, 297; and the American Declaration of Independence, 300.

Editing for Conciseness

Bartholow is ~~currently~~ working on other projects, but he ~~has~~ plans to continue ~~with~~ his video game research. ~~In the future,~~ he hopes to recruit female subjects—a difficult task because far fewer women than men play violent video games. He's also interested in examining how ~~a person's prior~~ *people's* gaming history affects ~~his or her~~ *their* response to a single exposure to a violent video game.

Pumpkins are everywhere ~~during the fall season~~ *in fall*. They ~~serve as a way to~~ help families and friends ~~to get closer~~ *bond* during the ~~holiday season~~ *holidays*. Whether you're ~~taking a trip~~ *traveling* to the local pumpkin patch ~~to search for the perfect pumpkin~~, or baking ~~up some delicious~~ treats ~~for people to enjoy~~, pumpkins are a ~~strong~~ reminder that comfort isn't ~~too~~ far away.

"Currently" is usually redundant because the verb tense implies it.

"With" is unnecessary.

The plural form gets around the wordy "his or her."

"Season" isn't required in either sentence in this paragraph.

"Strong" and "too" are unnecessary intensifiers.

Change "has plans" to "plans" to strengthen verb.

"In the future" is already implied in the verb.

No information is lost by eliminating "serve as a way to."

"Traveling" says "taking a trip" in one word.

"Up" is an unnecessary caboose on "baking." Treats are delicious. Whom else do you bake treats for?

Figure 10.2
To be concise, challenge every word or phrase you write. These examples show how to eliminate 36 of the 127 words. (The replacement words are in italics.)

TIPS

Writing Clearly

- Keep sentences short.
- Limit each sentence to one idea.
- Favor subject-verb-object sentences.
- Avoid using more than three prepositional phrases in one sentence.
- Avoid using more than three numbers in one sentence.
- Use plain and simple words instead of jargon, journalese, or clichés.

— Paula LaRocque, writing consultant

You will use fewer words when you figure out what you want to say and then express it positively. Enter the following negatively phrased thicket of verbiage at your own risk:

> The Missouri Gaming Commission has 30 days to appeal a judge's temporary order reversing the commission's decision not to grant a gaming license to a firm that wanted to dock a riverboat casino in Jefferson City.

The writer is lost in a maze of reversals of negative findings. The lead tries to cover too much territory. Express it in the positive and strip it to its essential information:

> The state has 30 days to persuade a judge it should not have to license a firm that wants to open a riverboat casino in Jefferson City.

The writer of this sentence also failed to think clearly:

> Amtrak, formally the National Passenger Railroad Corp., was created in 1970 to preserve declining passenger train service.

Do you suppose the writer meant to write that Amtrak was created to preserve the decline in passenger train service?

Keep It Simple

The readers of one newspaper confronted the following one-sentence paragraph:

> "Paradoxically, cancer-causing mutations often result from the repair of a cell by error-prone enzymes and not the 'carcinogenic' substance's damage to the cell," Abe Eisenstark, director of biological sciences at the university, said at a meeting of the Ad Hoc Council of Environmental Carcinogenesis Wednesday night at the Cancer Research Center.

> *"Short is beautiful. Short and simple is more beautiful. Short, simple and interesting is most beautiful."*
>
> — Don Gibb, educator

If there is a message in those 53 words, it would take a copy editor, a lexicologist and a Nobel Prize-winning scientist to decipher it. The message simply is not clear. Although the sentence is not typical of newspaper writing, it is not unusual either.

The scientist is using the vocabulary of science, which is inappropriate for a general audience. The reporter should say, "I don't understand that exactly. Can you translate it for my readers?" The response may produce an understandable quote, but if it doesn't, paraphrase the statement and check back with your source to be sure you have paraphrased it accurately.

Too much of what is written is mumbo jumbo. For instance:

> Approximately 2 billion tons of sediment from land erosion enters our nation's waters every year. While industrial waste and sewage treatment plants receive a great deal of attention, according to the Department of Agriculture the number one polluter of our waterways is "non-point" pollution.

The writer of that lead contributed some linguistic pollution of his own. The message may have been clear in his mind, but it is not clear in print. Here's another way to approach this story:

> Soil carried into the water by erosion, not industrial waste or sewage from treatment plants, is the number one polluter of U.S. waterways, according to the Department of Agriculture.

One remedy for unclear writing is the short sentence. The following examples introduce the same subject:

> NEW YORK — From measurements with high-precision laser beams bounced off reflectors left at three lunar sites by Apollo astronauts, plus one atop an unmanned Soviet lunar vehicle, scientists believe that the moon is

still wobbling from a colossal meteorite impact 800 years ago.

NEW YORK — The moon may still be wobbling from a colossal meteorite impact 800 years ago.

The writer of the first example drags the reader through some prickly underbrush full of prepositional phrases. The writer of the second has cleared the brush to expose the flowers.

CORRECT AND EFFECTIVE LANGUAGE

Writing to be read is not easy. Reporters become writers by the sweat of their brows. John Kenneth Galbraith, a best-selling author who was able to make economics understandable to the lay reader, commented on the difficulty of writing well. "There are days when the result is so bad that no fewer than five revisions are required," he wrote. "In contrast, when I'm inspired, only four revisions are needed."

Trying the techniques discussed in this chapter is the first step. Mastering them will be the result of repeated practice.

Figures of Speech

Good writers understand how to use literary devices known as figures of speech. Similes and metaphors, two common figures of speech, permit writers to show similarities and contrasts. *Similes* show similarities by comparing one thing to another, often using the word "like" or "as." Describing her roommate's reaction to the news that she was moving, one writer said, "She stared into space for a few moments, scowling, *as if she were squaring large numbers in her head.*" Writing about a high school girls' basketball coach, Madeleine Blais wrote, "At 6 feet 6 inches, Moyer looms over his players. With a thick cap of graying brown hair and bangs that flop down over his forehead, *he resembles a grizzly bear on spindly legs.*"

Metaphor is the first cousin of simile. A simile compares one thing to another, but a metaphor says one thing *is* another: "Michael is a lion with gazelle legs." A metaphor is a stronger analogy than a simile. Describing the radio personality and writer Garrison Keillor, a reporter once wrote, "And there he is. A sequoia in a room full of saplings." The metaphor works on two levels. Keillor is tall enough to tower over most others in the room. Because he is known internationally, his work towers over that of others, too.

With similes and metaphors, writers draw word pictures. These techniques turn the pages of a scrapbook of images in each reader's mind.

> ❙❙The real problem is that misplaced modifiers and similar glitches tend to distract readers. Introduce blunders to an otherwise smoothly flowing story and it's as though a drunk stumbled through a religious procession.
>
> "What's more, while those errors due to carelessness may not permanently damage the language, they can damage a paper's credibility. Botching a small job sows mistrust about the larger enterprise.❙❙
>
> — Jack Cappon, Associated Press

Careful Word Choice

Freedom in word choice is exhilarating when the result is a well-turned phrase. Here's how one student described the weather in fresh terms: "I rushed off the bus into a downpour of beaming sunlight." Here's Julie Sullivan of *The (Spokane, Wash.) Spokesman-Review*: "Hand him a soapbox, he'll hand you a homily."

Freedom in word choice is dangerous when it results in nouns masquerading as verbs (*prioritize, impact, maximize*) or jargon masquerading as respectable English (*input, output, throughput*).

Precision, however, means more than knowing the etymology of a word; it means knowing exactly what you want to say. Instead of saying, "The City Council wants to locate the landfill three blocks from downtown," to be precise, you say, "Some members of the City Council . . ." or, better yet, "Five members of the City Council . . ."

Precision also means using the conditional mood (*could, might, should, would*) when discussing proposals:

Incorrect   The bill will make it illegal . . .

Correct   The bill would make it illegal . . .

The use of "will" is imprecise because the legislation has not been passed. By using "would," you are saying, "If the legislature passes the bill, it would . . ."

Bias-Free Language

Even when used innocently, sexist and racist language, besides being offensive and discriminatory, is imprecise. Doctors aren't always "he," nor are nurses always "she." Much of our language assumes people are male unless it is shown they are female. Precise writers avoid "policeman" ("police officer"), "ad man" ("advertising representative"), "assemblyman" ("assembly member") and "postman" ("postal worker"). In some situations, you can use the plural to eliminate the need for a gender-specific word: "Doctors treat their patients."

Check *The AP Stylebook* to see whether to identify a person's race or ethnicity. Then try to follow the person's own preference and to be as specific as possible: *Asian-American* is acceptable but *Chinese-American* may be preferable. *Black* is acceptable for any nationality, but use *African-American* only for an American of African descent.

Some words, perfectly precise when used correctly, are imprecise when used in the wrong context. "Boy" is not interchangeable with "young man," and "girl" is not interchangeable with "young woman." Not all active retired people are "spry," which implies that the writer is surprised to find that the person is active. "Grandmotherly" fails when you describe people in their 40s who are grandmothers. It also fails when you use it indiscriminately. When Nancy Pelosi became the first female speaker of the U.S. House of Representatives, many accounts identified her as a grandmother. While it is true that she's a grandmother, accounts of new male

TIPS

Avoiding Carelessness in Word Choice

- Know precisely what you want to say.

- Use the conditional mood ("could," "might," "should," "would") when discussing proposals.

- Choose the correct sentence structure to communicate explicitly what you mean.

TIPS

Avoiding Sexism in Language

● Use a generic term ("flight attendant," "firefighter").

● Participate in the movement to drop feminine endings. (Use "comedian," "hero" and "poet" for both sexes.)

● Make the subject plural. ("Reporters must not reveal their opinions.")

● Drop the gender-specific pronoun and replace it with an article. ("A reporter must not form *a* judgment.")

● Rewrite to eliminate the gender-specific pronoun. ("A reporter must not judge.")

● Write the sentence in the second person. ("You should not form *your* judgment.")

leaders seldom mention that they are grandfathers. Pelosi's wardrobe also became a subject of stories, something seldom found in accounts of male leaders.

"Dumb," as in "deaf and dumb," is imprecise and derogatory. Instead, use "speech-impaired." When the terms are used in tandem, use "hearing-impaired and speech-impaired" for parallelism. Because alcoholism is a disease, use "recovering alcoholic" instead of "reformed alcoholic." "Handicapped" is imprecise; "disabled" is preferred.

The Associated Press recommends "gay" and "lesbian" and sometimes allows "homosexual" but does not permit "queer" and other derogatory terms. The battle over abortion extends to the terms used in news. One side wants to be described as "pro-life"; the other wants to be described as "pro-choice." The Associated Press prescribes the terms "anti-abortion" and "abortion rights" in an attempt to be neutral.

Some dismiss this concern for language as overly zealous political correctness. That attitude implies that we are afraid to tell the truth. What is the truth about ethnic slang? The truth is that many words historically applied to groups of people were created in ignorance or hate or fear. During the world wars, American citizens of German descent were called "Krauts" to depersonalize them. Over the years, pejorative terms have been applied to immigrants from Ireland, Poland, China and Africa. We see the same thing happening to more recent immigrants from Latin America, the Caribbean and the Middle East. The adjective "Muslim" is seldom seen or heard in news reports except to modify "terrorists" or "fundamentalists." As writers concerned with precision of the language, we should deal with people, not stereotypes.

Words are powerful. When used negatively, they define cultures, create second-class citizens and reveal stereotypical thinking. They also change the way people think about and treat others. Writers have the freedom to choose precisely the right word. That freedom can be both exhilarating and dangerous.

Correct Grammar and Punctuation

Far too often, grammar and punctuation errors obscure meaning. Consider this example:

> Watching his parents struggle in low-paying jobs, a college education looked desirable to him.

Because the participial phrase ("Watching . . .") is dangling, the sentence seems to mean that the college education did the watching. Write the sentence this way:

> Watching his parents struggle in low-paying jobs, he realized he wanted a college education.

No one who aspires to be a writer will succeed without knowing the rules of grammar. Dangling participles, subject-verb disagreement, pronoun-antecedent disagreement and misplaced modifiers are like enemy troops: They attack sentences and destroy their meaning, as the authors of a survey discovered.

The personnel director of an Inglewood, Calif., aerospace company had to fill out a government survey form that asked, among other things, "How many employees do you have, broken down by sex?" After considering the sentence for a few moments, she wrote, "Liquor is more of a problem with us."

Here are some typical errors and ways to correct them:

Pronoun-antecedent disagreement

Each of the boys brought *their* sleeping bags.

Correct

Each of the boys brought *his* sleeping bag.

Subject-verb disagreement

The *mayor* together with the city council *oppose* collective bargaining by the firefighters.

Correct

The *mayor* together with the city council *opposes* . . .

The *mayor and city council oppose* . . .

Misplaced modifier

Despite his size, the coach said Jones would play forward.

Correct

The coach said that Jones, *despite his size*, would play forward.

Improper punctuation creates ambiguities at best and inaccuracies at worst. For instance:

Giving birth to Cynthia five years earlier had been difficult for Mrs. Davenport and the two parents decided they were content with the family they had.

Without the required comma before "and," a person reading quickly misses the pause and sees this: "Giving birth to Cynthia had been difficult for Mrs. Davenport and the two parents." That's a lot of people in the delivery room. (For more examples of common grammar and punctuation errors, see Appendix 1.)

Most newspapers have two or three people who read each story to catch these and other errors. However, the writer's responsibility is to get it right in the first place.

THE TOOLS OF NARRATION

The tools of narration allow you to build interest in stories. When we use scenes, dialogue and anecdotes, we are using narrative tools that help make our stories as entertaining as they are interesting. In exposition, the writer clearly stands between the reader and the information: Journalists have sources, who tell them things. Journalists then tell the reader what they heard and saw. Scenes, dialogue and anecdotes allow the reader to see the action. If you also learn to tease this good stuff with foreshadowing, readers will be more likely to read it. But more about foreshadowing later.

Scenes

Gene Roberts, former managing editor of *The New York Times*, tells about his first job at a daily newspaper. His publisher, who was blind, had someone read the newspaper to him each morning. One day, the publisher called Roberts into his office and complained, "Roberts, I can't see your stories. Make me see."

We should all try to make readers see, smell, feel, taste and hear. One way to do that is to write using scenes as much as possible. To write a scene, you have to be there. You need to capture the pertinent sights, sounds and smells.

A student reporter at South Dakota State University was there to capture this opening scene:

> Don Sheber's leathery, cracked hands have been sculpted by decades of wresting a living from the earth.
>
> But this year, despite work that often stretches late into the evening, the moisture-starved soil has yielded little for Sheber and his family.
>
> Sheber's hands tugged at the control levers on his John Deere combine last week as rotating blades harvested the thin stands of wheat that have grown to less than a foot high.

The writer allows the reader to visit Sheber on the farm. We can see and feel the farmer's hands. We can touch the John Deere combine and the stunted wheat.

> **"**The most important thing to any writing, and especially profile writing, is the telling detail.**"**
>
> — Jacqui Banaszynski, Pulitzer Prize winner

"Don Sheber's leathery, cracked hands have been sculpted by decades of wresting a living from the earth." Use descriptive language to paint a vivid picture for readers and to bring a story to life.

To create such scenes, you must use all your senses to gather information, and your notebook should reflect that reporting. Along with the results of interviews, your notebook should bulge with details of sights and smells, sounds and textures. David Finkel, winner of the American Society of News Editors Distinguished Writing Award in 1986 and a Pulitzer Prize in 2006, says, "Anything that pertains to any sense I feel at any moment, I write down." Gather details indiscriminately. Later, you can discard those that are not germane. Because you were there, you can write the scene as if you were writing a play.

Because Bartholomew Sullivan of *The (Memphis) Commercial Appeal* was observing and listening closely at a trial, his readers were able to sit in the courtroom with him:

> Helfrich banged an index finger on the rail of the jury box as he recalled Thursday's testimony in which a string of Bowers's Jones County friends testified that he was a solid businessman, a Christian—"a gentleman." One of the witnesses was Nix, who called Bowers a "real, real nice man."
>
> "They talk of gentlemen," Helfrich whispered. Then, shouting, he said: "These people don't have a gentle bone in their bodies. They were nightriders and henchmen. They attacked a sleeping family and destroyed all they owned."

Analyze the detail: the banging of an index finger, the whisper, the shout. We can see and we can hear.

Another scene from another trial was written by Peter St. Onge, then of *The Huntsville (Ala.) Times*. By creating a scene, he allows readers to watch and listen:

> "I not only lost a wife, I lost a best friend, thanks to you two," he said, looking at the boys. "My son looks for his mother to come back. I have to explain to him that his mother's in heaven. I have to explain what you two did."
>
> Johnson rocked back and forth at the words, nodding his head and wiping his eyes. Golden stared blankly, expressionless as he had been all hearing. When Golden's attorney, Val Price, objected and the judge cautioned Wright not to speak directly to the boys, Wright smiled wryly and continued.

In both of these examples, we are transported to the courtrooms because the writers worked in scenes. Neither writer wrote his entire story in scenes, as would be done in a movie script, but both created scenes when possible. The stories were richer as a result.

Dialogue

The use of *dialogue*—conversation between two or more people, not including the reporter—allows the reporter to recede and the characters to take center stage. When you use quotations, you—the writer—are repeating for the reader what the source said, and the reader listens to you relating what was said. But when you use dialogue, the writer disappears, and the reader listens directly to the characters. Dialogue is a key element in creating scenes. Compare these examples:

> During the public hearing, Henry Lathrop accused the council of wasting tax-payers' money. "If you don't stop voting for all this spending, I am going to cir-culate a recall petition and get you all kicked off the council," he said.
>
> Mayor Margorie Gold told Lathrop he was free to do as he wished. "As for us," she said, "we will vote in the best interests of the city."

That is the traditional way of presenting quotations. The reporter is telling readers what was said instead of taking readers to the council chambers and letting them listen. Here is how that account would sound handled as dialogue:

> When Henry Lathrop spoke to the City Council during the public hearing, he pounded on the podium. "You folks are wasting taxpayers' money. If you don't stop voting for all this spending, I am going to circulate a recall petition and get you all kicked off the council."
>
> Mayor Margorie Gold slammed her gavel on her desk.
>
> "Mr. Lathrop," she said as she tried to control the anger in her voice. She looked at him directly. "You are free to do as you wish. As for us, we will vote in the best interests of the city."

At the hearing, Lathrop and Gold were speaking to each other. The second version captures the exchange without the intercession of the writer.

Here's another example of dialogue. This conversation took place between Cindy Martling, a rehabilitation nurse, and Mary Jo, the patient's wife, after Martling scolded the patient for feeling sorry for himself:

> She wandered around a bit, then saw Mary Jo standing in the hallway. The two women went to each other and embraced. "I'm sorry," Martling said through more tears. "I didn't mean to lose control. I hope I didn't offend you."
>
> "What you did was wonderful," Mary Jo said. "He needed to hear that. Dan is going to work through it, and we're all going to be OK."

Anecdotes

The ultimate treats, anecdotes are stories embedded in stories. They can be happy or sad, funny or serious. Whatever their tone, they should illustrate a point. Readers are likely to remember the anecdotes more readily than anything else in a story. You probably remember the stories that your professors tell regardless of whether you remember the rest of the lecture. Long after you've forgotten this chapter, you will probably remember some of the examples from it. Facts inform. Anecdotes inform and entertain.

As befits something so valuable, anecdotes are hard to obtain. You can't get them by asking your source, "Got any good anecdotes?" But you can get them by asking for examples so you can re-create the scene. To do this, be alert to the possibilities that an anecdote may be lurking in the details. One reporter gathered this quote:

> "We had one of those coaching nights where we sat up until I don't know when trying to figure it out," Richardson says. "We refer to that as the red-letter day in Spartan football, and since that day, we are 33-15, with three district titles and a conference championship."

The editor pointed out to the reporter that if it was a red-letter day, the reporter should have asked more questions about that coaching meeting. He did, and he ended up with the scene in the kitchen as the coaches figured out a new offensive philosophy.

Here's another example. Your source says: "Darren is like a one-man entertainment committee. He's always got something going on. And if nothing is going on, he'll hike up his pants really high and dance to the Jonas Brothers."

To turn this from a dry quote to an anecdote, you need to ask, "Can you give me an example of when he acted like an entertainment committee?" or "Tell me about the time he danced to the Jonas Brothers."

Some anecdotes come from phrasing questions in the superlative: "What's the funniest thing that ever happened to you while you were standing in front of an audience?" "What's the worst case you've ever seen come into this emergency room?" "People tell me Rodney is always the first one they call when they need help on a project. Has he ever helped you?" "Can you give me an example?"

When leading bankers were summoned to the Treasury Department during the financial meltdown in the fall of 2008, journalists were not allowed in the meeting. Yet some were able to reconstruct the scene inside. Here's an anecdote set in a scene:

> *When your reporters feel the innovative impulse, suggest that they lie down until it goes away.*
>
> — James Kilpatrick, syndicated columnist

Drama Behind a $250 Billion Banking Deal

By Mark Landler and Eric Dash

WASHINGTON—The chief executives of the nine largest banks in the United States trooped into a gilded conference room at the Treasury Department at 3 p.m. Monday. To their astonishment, they were each handed a one-page document that said they agreed to sell shares to the government, then Treasury Secretary Henry M. Paulson Jr. said they must sign it before they left.

The chairman of JPMorgan Chase, Jamie Dimon, was receptive, saying he thought the deal looked pretty good once he ran the numbers through his head. The chairman of Wells Fargo, Richard M. Kovacevich, protested strongly that, unlike his New York rivals, his bank was not in trouble because of investments in exotic mortgages, and did not need a bailout, according to people briefed on the meeting.

But by 6:30, all nine chief executives had signed—setting in motion the largest government intervention in the American banking system since the Depression and retreating from the rescue plan Mr. Paulson had fought so hard to get through Congress only two weeks earlier.

You use anecdotes to entertain while you are informing. If the relevance of the anecdote to the larger story isn't obvious, tell it going into or coming out of the story.

Foreshadowing

Foreshadowing is the technique of giving hints about what's coming. Moviemakers tease you with the scenes they think will encourage you to buy a ticket. Broadcasters use foreshadowing to keep you from leaving during a commercial: "Coming up, there's a burglar prowling your neighborhood." Every lead foreshadows the story. The leads that not only tell but promise more good stuff to come are the most successful. Tom Koetting, then of *The Wichita Eagle*, spent nine months observing the recovery of a doctor who had nearly lost his life in a farm accident. He produced a story of about 100,000 words. The simple lead promised great things to come: "Daniel Calliendo Jr. had not expected to meet death this calmly."

A student at Florida A&M University used the same technique to invite readers to continue reading the story:

> A North Carolina family thought the worst was behind them when they were robbed Saturday morning at a gas station just off Interstate 95.
> The worst was yet to come.

The worst was yet to come. That's another way of saying, "Read on; the story gets even better."

In the next example, you see a longer opening that is packed with promises of great things to come.

> Deena Borman's relationship with her roommate, Teresa, during her freshman year in college had shattered long before the wine bottle.
> Weeks had gone by with Teresa drawing further and further away from Deena. Finally, after repeatedly hearing Teresa talk about suicide, Deena says, "I kept telling her how silly she was to want to die."
> That made Teresa angry, so she threw a full wine bottle at Deena. It shattered against the wall and broke open the simmering conflict between them. That was when Deena tried to find out what had gone wrong with Teresa's life, and that was when Teresa told Deena that she wanted to do something to get rid of her.
> And that was when Deena began to be scared of her own roommate.

TIPS

Moving Your Story Along

- Create vivid scenes.
- Let the actors speak to each other through dialogue. (When the source tells the reporter who tells the reader, you have a *quotation*. When the reporter records the conversation of two or more people speaking not to the reporter but to each other, you have *dialogue*.)
- Relate memorable anecdotes.
- Foreshadow important events.

The writer is promising a great story. What is wrong with Teresa? Does Teresa really try to hurt Deena? Does Deena really have something to be scared about? There is a promise of great things to come. Would you keep reading?

Suggested Readings

Hart, Jack. *A Writer's Coach: The Complete Guide to Writing Strategies That Work*. New York: Pantheon, 2006. This guide helps you understand the "how" and "why" of sentence, paragraph and story construction.

Kramer, Mark, and Wendy Call, eds. *Telling True Stories*. New York: Plume, 2007. This book offers the collected wisdom of many writers. The advice is gathered in short bits. A reader can jump around easily to pick out applicable parts.

Osborn, Patricia. *How Grammar Works: A Self-Teaching Guide*. New York: John Wiley and Sons, 1999. This book will do for you what it promises: It will guide you, step by step, through the basics of English grammar. Its goal is to make you feel comfortable with grammar and the way words work.

Strunk, William, and E.B. White. *The Elements of Style*, 3rd ed. Boston: Allyn and Bacon, 1995. This little book practices what it preaches. For the beginner, it is a good primer; for the pro, it is a good review of writing rules and word meanings.

Tankard, James, and Laura Hendrickson. "Specificity, Imagery in Writing: Testing the Effects of 'Show, Don't Tell.'" *Newspaper Research Journal* (Winter/Spring 1996): 35–48.

Suggested Websites

http://papyr.com/hypertextbooks/comp1/coherent.htm
Daniel Kies of the Department of English at the College of DuPage explains how to achieve coherence in your writing.

www.nieman.harvard.edu/narrative/home.aspx
The Nieman Foundation at Harvard has a "Narrative Digest" site that offers narrative stories and, often, interviews with writers.

www.poynter.org
Select "Reporting & Writing," and you will enter a world full of advice, most of it from writers. This is a site you should check often.

Exercises

1. **Team project.** Your instructor will divide the class into three groups. On the Internet, find at least three versions of the same news event written on the same day. Each group should compare the sentence lengths. Look for transitions. Find figures of speech and analogies. Which, in your opinion, is the most readable? The least readable? Why?

2. Choose precisely the right word:
   a. We need to (ensure, insure) a victory.
   b. Stop (aggravating, annoying) your friend.
   c. The attorney won because she (refuted, responded to) the allegations.
   d. The prisoner was able to produce (mitigating, militating) evidence.

3. Rewrite Barlett and Steele's story on nuclear-waste disposal (page 205) to take out the parallelism. Which version, the original or yours, is better? Why?

4. Punctuate the following sentences:
   a. Government officials have come under a newly enacted censorship system and several foreign speakers have been denied permission to enter the country.
   b. It was a Monday night and for the next two days he teetered between life and death.

c. The council approved the manager's proposals and rejected a tax increase.

5. Use an analogy to explain the following numbers:

   The student council's budget is $350,000. The university has 19,000 students. The local city budget is $3 million. The city has 70,000 residents.

6. In printed or online newspaper articles, find examples of the following:

   a. Incorrect word usage. (Correct it.)
   b. Ambiguous wording. (Correct it.)
   c. Incorrect grammar. (Correct it.)
   d. Incorrect punctuation. (Correct it.)
   e. A nicely worded sentence or paragraph.
   f. Figures of speech.
   g. Analogies that help translate numbers.

7. Calculate the readability levels of a story you have written and stories from *The New York Times* and the Associated Press. Compare the readability scores, and account for scoring differences and similarities. You can get the calculation at www.standards-schmandards.com/exhibits/rix/.

Alternatives to the
Inverted Pyramid

11

Newspapers, magazines and websites publish some stories that are not suited for the inverted pyramid structure. Here's the opening to a story written as if it were a novel, except that it is all true.

By Jim Sheeler
Rocky Mountain News

Inside a limousine parked on the airport tarmac, Katherine Cathey looked out at the clear night sky and felt a kick.

"He's moving," she said. "Come feel him. He's moving."

Her two best friends leaned forward on the soft leather seats and put their hands on her stomach.

"I felt it," one of them said. "I felt it."

Outside, the whine of jet engines swelled.

"Oh, sweetie," her friend said. "I think this is his plane."

As the three young women peered through the tinted windows, Katherine squeezed a set of dog tags stamped with the same name as her unborn son:

James J. Cathey.

"He wasn't supposed to come home this way," she said, tightening her grip on the tags, which were linked by a necklace to her husband's wedding ring.

The women looked through the back window. Then the 23-year-old placed her hand on her pregnant belly.

"Everything that made me happy is on that plane," she said.

They watched as airport workers rolled a conveyor belt to the rear of the plane, followed by six solemn Marines.

Katherine turned from the window and closed her eyes.

"I don't want it to be dark right now. I wish it was daytime," she said. "I wish it was daytime for the rest of my life. The night is just too hard."

Suddenly, the car door opened. A white-gloved hand reached into the limousine from outside—the same hand that had knocked on Katherine's door in Brighton five days earlier.

The man in the deep blue uniform knelt down to meet her eyes, speaking in a soft, steady voice.

"Katherine," said Maj. Steve Beck, "it's time."

Closer Than Brothers

The American Airlines 757 couldn't have landed much farther from the war.

The plane arrived in Reno on a Friday evening, the beginning of the 2005 "Hot August Nights" festival—one of the city's biggest—filled with flashing lights, fireworks, carefree music and plenty of gambling.

When a young Marine in dress uniform had boarded the plane to Reno, the passengers smiled and nodded politely. None knew he had just come from the plane's cargo hold, after watching his best friend's casket loaded onboard.

At 24 years old, Sgt. Gavin Conley was only seven days younger than the man in the coffin. The two had met as 17-year-olds on another plane—the one to boot camp in California. They had slept in adjoining top bunks, the two youngest recruits in the barracks.

All Marines call each other brother. Conley and Jim Cathey could have been. They finished each other's sentences, had matching infantry tattoos etched on their shoulders, and cracked on each other as if they had grown up together—which, in some ways, they had.

When the airline crew found out about Conley's mission, they bumped him to first-class. He had never flown there before. Neither had Jim Cathey.

On the flight, the woman sitting next to him nodded toward his uniform and asked if he was coming or going. To the war, she meant.

221

He fell back on the words the military had told him to say: "I'm escorting a fallen Marine home to his family from the situation in Iraq."

The woman quietly said she was sorry, Conley said.

Then she began to cry.

When the plane landed in Nevada, the pilot asked the passengers to remain seated while Conley disembarked alone. Then the pilot told them why.

The passengers pressed their faces against the windows. Outside, a procession walked toward the plane. Passengers in window seats leaned back to give others a better view. One held a child up to watch.

From their seats in the plane, they saw a hearse and a Marine extending a white-gloved hand into a limousine, helping a pregnant woman out of the car.

On the tarmac, Katherine Cathey wrapped her arm around the major's, steadying herself. Then her eyes locked on the cargo hold and the flag-draped casket.

Inside the plane, they couldn't hear the screams.

Jim Sheeler uses chronology to follow the journey of a Marine returning his friend's body to his family. In Chapter 9 you learned how to rank information from most important to least important. That inverted pyramid structure serves news, particularly breaking news, well. Other structures support other types of stories better. Like the standard formula for telling fairy tales, chronology works best when characters must encounter complications in bringing the story to a resolution. Writers focus on the people involved in issues to tell important stories—health care, cancer research, prayer in schools—in an interesting and informative way.

If time, detail and space are available, consider the alternative structures we describe in this chapter and summarize in Figure 11.1. Whether you are writing about a car accident, the Boy Scouts jamboree, the campaign for student-government president, corruption in government or the 8-year-old running the corner lemonade stand, writing the story will be easier if you know how to use some of the alternative story forms: chronology, news narrative, focus structure and service journalism formats.

CHRONOLOGY

Stories that work best as a chronology are those that have complications or tension and a resolution worth waiting for. Those elements are present even in events like meetings. When a city council faces a contentious issue, such as a proposed smoking ban in public places, you are presented with controversy (supporters and opponents testifying), tension (weighing health and economic interests) and a resolution (the vote). Time constraints and tradition often dictate an inverted pyramid structure. But you have other options:

- You could summarize the vote in a sidebar and use chronology to tell the story of the meeting.
- You could write an inverted pyramid version of the story for both the website and the newspaper and then write a chronological version for the Web to replace the earlier version.

- You might use news narrative (see the next section) to report the results and then move to chronology.

Where to Start

Oddly enough, when you use chronology, you don't have to begin at the beginning. Instead, you look for a key moment you can use for the lead to engage readers. To get started, writers often jot down a time line. In the case of the council meeting, it might look like this:

7:00 p.m.	Opponents and supporters of the smoking ban begin testifying before the council.
	Jones, an opponent, angrily denounces the proposal.
	Smith, a supporter, relates a story about her cancer.
8:15	Council members begin debate.
	Mayor pounds the gavel to break up an out-of-control argument between two council members.
	Council member Rodriguez is nearly in tears as he urges the council to pass the ordinance.
	Council member Jackson says merchants will face financial ruin.
8:47	Solinski, a member of the audience, interrupts the debate and is escorted out of the chambers by city police. Several in the audience boo, but some cheer.
9:10	During a recess, no council members mingle with the public, which irritates several of those who are attending.
9:30	The council votes 5-4 in favor of the smoking ban. There are both jeers and cheers.

A Sample Outline

You could begin at the beginning of the time line given above, with the chamber filling with members of the public, but this lead would not attract attention. You need a dramatic scene that captures emotion, is short and does not give away the outcome. The removal of a member of the audience has potential; so does the heated argument within the council. Here is a typical outline for a story using chronology:

1. The lead (the scene with Rodriguez).
2. The nut (theme) paragraph.
3. Foreshadowing.
4. A transition back to the beginning of the meeting to pick up the story from that point.
5. The body highlighting key events found in the time line. (As with any news story, much of the action is left out; this is a news story, not a secretary's report.)
6. An ending that highlights the vote and the audience reaction.

News Story Structures

	Inverted Pyramid	Chronology
What is it?	The lead paragraphs have the most important information, and succeeding paragraphs give details in descending order of importance.	Starting at a particular point of interest, the paragraphs tell a story in chronological order.
When should it be used?	It's best used for hard news, where timeliness is essential and the reader wants to know the important facts right away.	It's good for reporting a detailed sequence of events in a story with controversy or tension and resolution, especially as a follow-up to a news story.
How is it structured?	**Traditional news lead** • Give who, what, when, where, why and how. • Frame the story. **Body: support paragraphs in descending order of importance** • Give additional details about the lead. • Summarize other significant actions or elements relevant to the lead. • Give the impact or effect of the event. • Give the "so what" — the story's importance to the reader. • Give background and history. • Describe relevant physical details. • Narrate relevant sequences of events. • Use quotations from relevant sources. • Give sources of additional information, including links to websites. **Ending** • End with the least significant information, *not* with a conclusion, summary or tie-back to the beginning. The story can be cut from the bottom up without compromising its effectiveness.	**Narrative lead** • Describe a dramatic point in the story. • Create narrative suspense with foreshadowing. **Nut paragraph** • Give the theme of the story. **Body: narrative support paragraphs** • Use foreshadowing. • Pick up story with a transition back to the beginning of the narrative. • Tell the story in chronological order, highlighting key events found in the time line. • Describe relevant physical details. • Use narrative techniques like dialogue, flashback and foreshadowing. **Ending** • Give a conclusion to the story. • Resolve the tension or conflict in the story.

Figure 11.1
Different structures are useful for different types of news stories.

News Narrative	Focus Structure
The story combines elements of inverted pyramid and chronology formats, with an emphasis on either news or narrative.	The story follows one individual as a representative of a larger group.
It's useful for stories where timeliness is somewhat important, but the hard news element is not prominent.	It's useful for making complex or abstract stories meaningful to readers.

News Narrative

Narrative lead

- Open with an interesting scene or twist that teases the story.

or

Traditional news lead

- Give who, what, when, where, why and how.

Support paragraphs

- Briefly add whatever helps the reader understand the story summarized in the lead.

Body: narrative support paragraphs

- Go back to the beginning, and tell the story in chronological order.

Ending

- Give a conclusion to the story.
- Resolve the tension or conflict in the story.

Focus Structure

Narrative lead

- Introduce the subject and describe the person's problem.

Transition

- Create a bridge from the subject to the theme of the story.

Nut paragraph

- Give the theme of the story.

Support paragraphs

- Foreshadow.
- Give the "so what" — the story's importance to the reader.
- Give the "to be sure" — opposing perspectives.

Body: narrative and expository support paragraphs

- Interweave narrative about the subject with facts about the theme to tell the story.

Ending

- Conclude the story, with a summary or with a tie-back that refers to the beginning of

The Nut Paragraph, Foreshadowing and the "To Be Sure"

Like the lead in an inverted pyramid story, a **nut paragraph** (or *nut graf*) is a paragraph that gives the theme of the story and summarizes the key facts. Unlike the lead in the inverted pyramid format, however, the nut paragraph is not the first paragraph in the story. For the council story, after the first (or lead) paragraph describing the scene with Rodriguez, the nut paragraph might look like this:

> In a meeting filled with emotional, sometimes angry testimony, citizens and the City Council debated the proposed smoking ban for nearly three hours. Citizens urged — sometimes threatened — council members. The mayor pounded his gavel to bring the council to order several times when some members engaged in heated, personal arguments. In the end, council members voted on the landmark legislation amid jeers and cheers and then left through a back door.
>
> From the beginning, it was clear that emotions were running high. . . .

The nut paragraph both defines the story and foreshadows the heated debate. Even though readers will know the results, many will want to read the blow-by-blow account. It also establishes the "so what": This is a divisive issue, involving landmark legislation, that people care about. Notice that the last line "From the beginning . . ." creates a transition back to the start of the story narrative.

In some stories, you might also need to include a **"to be sure" paragraph**. This paragraph, which gives opposing points of view, is a must when you are focusing on one side of an issue. Before the council vote, you could do a story about a restaurant shift from the perspective of a waiter. You could follow that with a story from the perspective of a smoker at a bar. In both cases, you would include a paragraph acknowledging that others disagree, especially if that opposing viewpoint is not included elsewhere in the story. For instance:

> Not everyone agrees with Megan Addison that smoking should be banned. Others, including smokers and business owners, believe that the proposal infringes on their right to smoke or to run their business as they please. But Addison and her fellow servers at the Sports Grill want to work in a smoke-free environment.

You do not need a "to be sure" paragraph in the council meeting story because all sides are represented in the debate.

The Ending

Stories written chronologically need strong endings. Here's how the four-part story of the Marine who accompanied his fallen friend ends:

As jet engines roared around him, Beck looked at the plane. The Marines marched to the cargo hold, toward the casket.

"See the people in the windows? They'll sit right there in the plane, watching those Marines," Beck said. "You gotta wonder what's going through their minds, knowing that they're on the plane that brought him home."

Commercial airplanes transport caskets every day—including service members killed in action. For the most part, the passengers have no idea what lies below.

Most people will never see the Transportation Security Administration officials standing on the tarmac with their hands over their hearts as a body is unloaded. They won't see the airport police and fire-fighters lined up alongside their cars and engines, lights flashing, saluting the hearse on its way out.

Occasionally, a planeload of passengers is briefly exposed to the hard reality outside the cabin.

"They're going to remember being on that plane for the rest of their lives," Beck said, looking back at the passengers. "They're going to remember bringing that Marine home."

For both the hypothetical council story and the real Marine story, readers want to know the outcome of the narrative. In the council story, how did the meeting end? How heated was it? The Marine story was framed through the eyes of the Marine who accompanied the body home and stayed through the burial. As readers viewed the events through his eyes, they wanted to know, "How does he deal with his emotions? With the emotions of the family and friends?" Readers read a chronology to the end because they want to know the conclusion of the story.

NEWS NARRATIVE

In Chapter 9, you saw examples of inverted pyramid stories that didn't have the news in the first paragraph (see "The 'You' Lead" and "Leads with Flair" in Chapter 9), but as soon as the writer teased the reader, the news lead appeared. Then the writer arranged the rest of the story in the traditional descending order of importance. Further modification, though, offers writers more choices. The **news narrative** structure combines the inverted pyramid and chronology. Here is an outline of its basic elements:

1. An opening with an interesting scene or twist that teases the story.
2. A traditional news lead.
3. Brief paragraphs that add whatever help readers need to understand the story summarized in the traditional lead.
4. A transition back to the beginning to tell the story in chronological order.

The "news" in "news narrative" implies that the story has a time element and that the story is not a feature. **Features**, sometimes called "soft stories," are those that can run nearly any time, such as a profile of a stamp collector, a story on a volunteer at the local food bank or a piece about riding with a police officer for a shift. A story with a time element usually has to be published in the next issue of the newspaper or as soon as possible on the Web. The "narrative" in "news narrative" means that you can use chronology, one of the most important tools of narrative writing. In the news narrative, you will often find other narrative tools, such as those discussed in Chapter 10: scenes, dialogue, anecdotes and foreshadowing.

News Narrative with News Emphasis

When the local sheriff's department broke an unusual burglary ring, Jane Meinhardt of the *St. Petersburg (Fla.) Times* elected to use the news narrative structure. In Figure 11.2, you can read her story, which follows the outline above. Notice that Meinhardt's story is a news narrative with news emphasis. This format works well for news that is significant but not earth-shattering. You probably wouldn't use it to report during the first few hours or perhaps even the first couple of days after an event like the shootings at Fort Hood, Texas. You need to be able to get all the details of how something happened to relate the chronology. Immediately following a disaster or other major event, the authorities don't have all the information, and the reporter might not have access to witnesses or documents.

News Narrative with Narrative Emphasis

When the news is less important, the news narrative structure is also useful, but the emphasis is on narrative rather than news. John Tully, a reporter for the *Columbia Missourian*, was asked to look for a story at a horse-riding competition one Sunday afternoon. Because most of the competitors were not from the newspaper's local area, reporting the results of the competition was not as important as finding a good story.

Tully knew nothing about horse-riding competitions, so he first found people who could explain the judging. He also asked people to suggest interesting competitors. A youth coordinator told him that Cara Walker was competing for the first time since her accident. After gathering more information from the coordinator, Tully found Walker and her mother—and a story that lent itself to news narrative. Through Tully's story (see Figure 11.3), readers learned that Walker, who had been seriously injured in a car accident, was able to recover enough to ride again. What they didn't find out until the end was that she won the competition. Because he had less news to report, Tully was able to go to the chronological format more quickly than Meinhardt. He used the outcome of the competition to reward readers who completed the story.

FOCUS STRUCTURE

For centuries, writers have used the **focus structure** to tell the story of an individual or a group that represents a bigger population. This approach allows the writer to make large institutions, complex issues and seven-digit numbers meaningful. Not many of us can understand—let alone explain—the marketing system for wheat, but we could more easily do so if we followed a crop of wheat from the time it was planted until a consumer bought a loaf of bread.

News Narrative with News Emphasis

The opening paragraphs set the scene with information that informs and is interesting. →

PALM HARBOR—They carried knapsacks and bags to tote loot. They had a screwdriver to pry open doors and windows.

They used latex gloves.

They acted like professional criminals, but officials say they were teenage burglars coached and directed by a Palm Harbor woman whose son and daughter were part of her gang.

A traditional news lead gives "who," "what" and "when." →

Pinellas County Sheriff's deputies arrested Rovana Sipe, two of her children and two other teens Wednesday after a series of home burglaries.

"She was the driver," said Sheriff's Sgt. Greg Tita. "She pointed out the houses. She's the one who said 'Do these.'" ← The writer supports the lead with a quote.

The story continues with the breaking news for the next four paragraphs. →

Sipe, 38, of 2333 State Road 584, was charged with two counts of being a principal in burglary. She was held Thursday in lieu of $20,000 bail.

Her daughter, Jackie Shifflet, 16, was charged with grand theft. Her son, Ryan Shifflet, 15, was charged with two counts of burglary.

Charles Ruhe, 17, of 1600 Ensley Ave., in Safety Harbor, and Charles Taylor, 16, of 348 Jeru Blvd. in Tarpon Springs, also were held on four counts of burglary each.

"They were very well-prepared to do burglaries, especially with the guidance they were given," Tita said. "We recovered thousands of dollars of stolen items. Anything that could be carried out, was."

The burglary ring unraveled Tuesday, Tita said. A Palm Harbor woman saw a large, yellow car driven by a woman drop off three boys, he said. The three went to the back of her house. ← Now that the news has been established, instead of continuing to present the information in order of importance, the writer presents the rest of the story in chronological fashion. Note the important transition from inverted pyramid to chronology: "The burglary ring unraveled Tuesday, Tita said."

They put on gloves and started to pry open a window with a screwdriver, she said. When she tapped on a window, they ran.

She called 911. As she waited for deputies, other neighbors saw the boys walk through a nearby neighborhood carrying bags.

Deputies chased the boys and caught two. The third got into a large yellow car driven by a woman.

The bags contained jewelry, a shotgun and other items deputies say were taken from another house in the neighborhood.

Tita said the boys, later identified as Taylor and Ruhe, told detectives about other burglaries in Dunedin and Clearwater and who else was involved.

At Sipe's house, detectives found stolen VCRs, televisions, camcorders and other valuables. They arrested the other two teens and Sipe.

The story ends with a quote rather than a tie-back or summary. →

"We're very familiar with this family and its criminal history," Tita said. "We have found stolen property at the house in the past and made juvenile arrests."

Figure 11.2
In news narratives with a news emphasis, the writer needs to establish the facts before giving the chronology. This format is associated with breaking news of significance, such as crime.

News Narrative with Narrative Emphasis

The first two paragraphs reveal the news of the injury and the twist that even though doctors were unsure, she recovered enough to compete. The horse show is the news event that generated the story. Note that the second paragraph reveals that she competed but only foreshadows how she did.

About five months ago, Cara Walker, 17, was lying in a hospital recovering from the spinal injury she received when she lost control of her car, rolled the vehicle and was thrown halfway through the side window.

Doctors weren't sure she would ever ride again. On Sunday, in a remarkable turnaround, Walker competed in the Midway Fall Classic Quarter Horse Show at the Midway Expo Center. The results were surprising.

Last July, Walker, a junior at Rock Bridge High School, was taking a lunch break from riding in preparation for the Fort Worth Invitational, where she qualified in five events. Driving with three passengers on a back road near Moberly, she rolled her car at 50 mph where the paved road turned to gravel without warning. Walker was the only one not wearing a seat belt. Her head and upper body smashed through the side window.

"Last July" is the transition to chronology after the news lead.

Fortunately, she was still in her riding boots. Her spurs got caught on the bar under the seat, which Walker says may have saved her life.

At the time of the accident, Walker was nationally ranked in the trail-riding event.

Note that there are no quotes to break the narrative flow. "My spurs got caught on the bar under my seat" and "She first started walking, and going to the mailbox wore her out" (paragraph 8) are paraphrased to stay in storytelling mode.

Doctors fused her neck in surgery. During the next couple of weeks, she was able to shed her full upper-body cast. Walker returned home to her parents and twin sisters two days after surgery, but her mother, Jane Walker, said doctors told her to stay away from her sport for a few months until she healed.

This background helps establish that she isn't just any rider and that she had more to lose in this accident than most riders.

For Walker, the top all-around youth rider in Missouri and the president of the American Quarter Horse Youth Association, the four months following the accident was her first time away from riding.

After returning home she worked to regain strength and mobility from the accident that initially left her right side paralyzed. She walked short distances. Going to the mailbox at the end of the driveway wore her out, her mother recalls.

The story has a surprise ending, which is possible in a chronology. In a straight news story, this would have been the lead.

Walker had to work almost every muscle in her body back into shape. After the accident, the family brought her 10-year-old quarter horse to their barn in Columbia. That motivated Walker to at first walk to the barn and then to start caring for the horse and eventually ride again.

Sunday, the rehabilitation was complete. With ramrod posture and strict horse control, she won first place in the horsemanship class.

Figure 11.3
In news narratives with a narrative emphasis, less space is devoted to the news, and more narrative techniques are used than in the inverted pyramid format. These types of narratives use fewer quotes and save important information for a strong ending. (*Source:* "Horse Power" by John Tully, *Columbia Missourian*, Nov. 27, 2006.)

The Wall Street Journal knew that not many of us would be attracted to a story about the interaction between pesticides and prescription drugs. That's why a reporter focused on one person to tell a story of pesticide poisoning:

> Thomas Latimer used to be a vigorous, athletic man, a successful petroleum engineer with a bright future.
>
> Then he mowed the lawn.

Does this opening make you want to read on?

In a quip attributed to him, the Soviet dictator Joseph Stalin summed up the impact of focusing on a part of the whole: "A single death is a tragedy; a million deaths is a statistic." Think about that the next time you hear that a plane crash killed 300 people. You probably won't be emotionally touched by the crash unless you know someone who was on the plane. However, if you write the story of the crash by focusing on a couple of the victims, you will have a better chance of involving your readers emotionally.

Writing the Lead

Issues like health care, budget deficits and sexual harassment don't have much emotional appeal in the abstract. You make them relevant if you discuss the issue by focusing on someone affected by it. For instance, the college student who wrote the following story spoke to Karen Elliott, who willingly told her story to help others with the same disease. The key word is "story." You write articles about diseases; you write stories about people. The lead paragraphs focus on one person in an anecdote that shows her as a character we can relate to:

> Karen Elliott, 44, remembers the phone call from Dr. Jonathen Roberts, a general surgeon, as if it had happened yesterday. Dr. Roberts' nurse called one afternoon two years ago and told Karen to hold the line. She froze. She had just had a biopsy on her right breast because of a new lump. It's never good news when the doctor calls at home. Dr. Roberts cut to the chase.
>
> "You have atypical hyperplasia," he said.
>
> Being a nurse, Karen knew exactly what he meant. No number of breast self-exams could have detected this. Atypical hyperplasia is a life-long condition characterized by abnormal cells. Affecting only 4 percent of the female population, it puts Karen and others at an increased risk for breast cancer. With her family history of the disease, her risk of breast cancer jumps sky-high.

Reporters working on local stories have just as many opportunities to apply this approach as those writing national and international stories. For example, instead of keeping score on the United Way fund drive, focus on the people who will benefit—or will fail to benefit—from the campaign. If the streets in your city jar your teeth when you drive, write about the problem from the point of view of a driver. If a disease is killing the trees in your city, concentrate on a homeowner who has lost several. The focus structure offers the writer a powerful method of reducing institutions, statistics and cosmic issues to a level that readers can relate to and understand.

TIPS

Applying the Focus Structure

- Focus on the individual.
- Transition to the larger issue.
- Report on the larger issue.
- Return to the opening focus.

Advertising agencies use the technique, too. That's why instead of being solicited for money to help the poor and starving, you are asked to support one child for only pennies a day. The technique gives poverty and hunger a face. A starving population is an abstraction; one starving child is a tragedy.

Writing the Setup

Once you've completed the opening, you must finish the setup to the story. The **setup** consists of the transition to the nut paragraph, the foreshadowing, the "so what" and the "to be sure." Let's look at each of these elements.

The Transition and the Nut Paragraph

When you open with a scene or an anecdote, you must construct a transition that explicitly makes the connection to the nut, or theme, paragraph. "Explicitly" is the key word. If you fail to help readers understand the point of the opening, however interesting it is, you risk losing them. The transition in this example is in italics:

Anita Poore hit the rough pavement of the parking lot with a thud. She had never felt such intense, stabbing pain and could barely lift her heavy head. When she reached for the car door, a police officer stared at her and asked her husband, "Is she drunk?" A wave of nausea swept over her, and she vomited.

"That's it. Get her out of here!" the officer demanded.

Poore was not drunk. She avoided jail, but she faces a life sentence of pain. Now 25, she has suffered migraine headaches since she was in seventh grade.

Not that it is much comfort, but she's not alone. Health officials estimate that Americans miss 157 million workdays a year because of migraines and spend more than $2 million a year on over-the-counter painkillers for migraine, tension and cluster headaches. Researchers haven't found a cure, but they have found methods to lessen the pain.

The italicized transition explicitly places Anita Poore among those who miss work, buy painkillers and are still waiting for a cure. The material that follows the transition is the theme.

Let's return to Karen Elliott, who was diagnosed with atypical hyperplasia. Here is the nut paragraph, the part of the story that states the theme:

What Karen didn't know was that her pleasant life in New Bloomfield would become a roller coaster of ups and downs for the next two years, a ride that nearly destroyed her. Her husband of 19 years, Bob, and their two children, Bethany, 6, and Jordan, 8, could only watch as she struggled with the decision of whether to voluntarily have her breasts removed because Karen, and only Karen, could make that choice.

Types of Journalistic Writing

News Writing

- News stories emphasize facts and current events. Timeliness is especially important.
- Typical news stories cover government, politics, international events, disasters, crime, important breakthroughs in science and medicine, and sports.

Feature (Soft News) Writing

- Feature stories go into depth about a generally newsworthy situation or person. Timeliness is relevant, but not critical.
- Typical feature stories are profiles, day-in-the-life stories, how-to stories, and background stories.

This is where the writer tells readers what the story is about—in this case, Karen's struggle with her decision. There are many other themes the writer could have pursued.

The nut paragraph, says Jacqui Banaszynski, Pulitzer Prize-winning writer, "is like a secret decoder ring—it lets the hapless reader know what your story is about and why they should read it." When you have involved the reader and successfully written the explicit transition to the nut paragraph, you are ready to build the rest of the setup.

Foreshadowing

Foreshadowing can be done in a single line: "The killing started early and ended late." Or you can foreshadow events over several paragraphs. The goal is to assure readers they will be rewarded if they continue reading.

This is what Erik Larson of *The Wall Street Journal* promised readers of his fire investigation story:

> And so began what may well be the most intensive scientific investigation in the history of arson—not a whodunit, exactly, but a whatdunit. So far the inquiry has taken Seattle investigators places arson squads don't typically go, even to the Navy's weapons-testing grounds at China Lake in California. Along the way, the investigation has attracted a team of scientists who, likewise ensnared by the "Twilight Zone" nature of the mystery, volunteered time and equipment. At one point the investigators themselves torched a large building just to test a suspected fuel.

The "So What"

The "so what" tells readers explicitly why they should care. Thomas Latimer was poisoned when he mowed his lawn. Karen Elliott has to decide whether to have surgery. Anita Poore almost got arrested for having a migraine headache. Interesting, but so what? Reporters and editors know the "so what" or they wouldn't spend

ON THE JOB

Tips for Writing

Ken Fuson, a freelance writer living in Des Moines, Iowa, has won several national writing awards, including an ASNE Writing Award and the Ernie Pyle feature-writing award. He offers his top 10 tips for improving your writing:

1. **Write stories.** Write real stories — narrative stories that hook readers from the opening scene and transport them to another world. Stories that make people call out to their spouse or roommate and say, "You have got to read this." Remember: You can find these stories in the courthouse, at city hall and on the police blotter. And they can be done on deadline.
2. **Look for conflict or drama.** Most of the best stories have a conflict and a resolution. Jon Franklin, author of *Writing for Story*, says the more basic the conflict — involving love, hate, death, triumph and travail — the better the story. Pared to its essence, *The Wizard of Oz* consists of two parts. Conflict: Dorothy loses home. Resolution: Dorothy finds home. The plot is what happens in the middle.
3. **Be there.** Put people on the scene. "Make me see," editor Henry Belk told his reporters. "You aren't making me see." Belk was blind. Even spending a half-hour with the subject of a quick-hit profile is better than just conducting a phone interview.
4. **Think scenes.** Use dialogue and descriptions to make readers feel as if they're watching the action unfold as it happens. Move your camera shots — from panning the crowd to close-ups.

time on the story. Too often, however, they fail to tell it to readers. Latimer's story is interesting, but it's much more important because the writer added the "so what" (in italics):

The makers of the pesticide, diazinon, and of Tagamet firmly deny that their products had anything to do with Mr. Latimer's condition. The pesticide maker says he doesn't even believe he was exposed to its product. And in fact, Mr. Latimer lost a lawsuit he filed against the companies. *Even so, the case intrigues scientists and regulators because it illustrates the need for better understanding of the complex interactions between such everyday chemicals as pesticides and prescription drugs.*

Neither the Food and Drug Administration nor the Environmental Protection Agency conducts routine tests for such interactions. Indeed, the EPA doesn't even evaluate the synergy of two or more pesticides commonly used together. "We have not developed ways to test any of that," says an EPA spokesman. "We don't know how to do it." And a new congressional report says the FDA lacks both the resources and the enforcement powers to protect Americans from all kinds of poisons.

5. **Write every sentence.** I'm stealing that advice from Susan Orlean, the wonderful writer for *The New Yorker*. She says we shouldn't distinguish between the "writerly" sentences, which we spend all our time on, and the workman-like sentences that do all the heavy lifting. Think about every sentence. Be the reader's guide through the entire piece, not just the descriptive parts.

6. **Take ownership of a story.** Roy Peter Clark of the Poynter Institute uses music to show that different artists can sing the same song with quite different results. No matter what the assignment — even if it's that hardy perennial, the day-after-Thanksgiving shopping spree story — make it your own.

7. **Search for the universal truth.** The story about a mother who stays by her sick child's bedside isn't about health care; it's a story about devotion. The story of the priest who gives his first sermon isn't about graduating from the seminary; it's a story about faith. The story about the athlete who overcomes childhood arthritis to win an Olympic gold medal isn't about the competition; it's a story about perseverance. Constantly ask yourself: What's this story *really* about?

8. **Look for humor opportunities.** Humor is the most underused tool in our writing kit. Readers love humor almost as much as they love real stories.

9. **Take risks.** I once wrote a one-sentence, one-paragraph weather story that (much to my amazement) has been reprinted several times. It's not just a matter of trying to be clever. It's a matter of doing anything to get read.

10. **Remember Tammy Gaudette.** Tammy is a housewife in Iowa who was invited to appear on a panel of newspaper readers. She was asked what she read. "Oh, I don't like the news," she said. "I like the interesting stories." Always ask yourself: Would I read this?

The "so what" is the impact — the relevance — for people who have no warning that pesticides and prescription drugs may interact to poison them.

In other cases, the "so what" may be included in the theme statement. Let's look at the migraine story again:

> [1] Not that it is much comfort, but she's not alone.

> [2] Health officials estimate that Americans miss 157 million workdays a year because of migraines and spend more than $2 million a year on over-the-counter painkillers for migraine, tension and cluster headaches.

> [3] Researchers haven't found a cure, but they have found methods to lessen the pain.

Sentence 1 is the transition. Sentence 2 is the "so what." The reporter is writing about Anita Poore, but the problem is widespread. Sentence 3 is the theme, which includes foreshadowing. The search for a cure, and the intermediate discovery of ways to lessen the pain, will be the focus of the story. The "so what" establishes the dimensions of the problem. When you define the "so what," you are establishing the story's impact.

The "To Be Sure"

To maintain an evenhanded approach, writers must acknowledge that there are two or more sides to a story. We call this the "to be sure," as in "to be sure, there are other opinions." We've seen in the pesticide story that the drug and pesticide makers "firmly deny that their products had anything to do with Mr. Latimer's condition." We see the technique again in an article about the impact of gambling on Tunica, Miss. Writer Jenny Deam opens with a scene in the mayor's store. The mayor says gambling is the best thing that ever happened to the town. At the front counter, a woman is asking for the $85 back she paid on furniture last week because she lost her grocery money gambling. What comes next is a combination theme and "to be sure" statement, highlighted in italics:

> And so is the paradox of this tiny Mississippi Delta county, now that the casinos have come to call.
>
> On the one hand, unemployment in a place the Rev. Jesse Jackson once called "America's Ethiopia" has dropped from nearly 24 percent to a low last fall of 5 percent. Anyone who wants a job has one with the casinos. There are more jobs than people to fill them. In a county of about 8,100 people, the number of food stamp recipients fell from 4,218 before the casinos to 2,907 now.
>
> *But there is another side. New problems never before seen.*
>
> Since the first casino opened in 1992, the number of DUI arrests has skyrocketed by 400 percent. U.S. Highway 61 leading to Memphis is constantly jammed. On a busy weekend as many as 28,000 cars head toward the nine casinos now open. The criminal court system is just as overloaded. In 1992, there were 1,500 cases filed. A year later, 2,400. As of last month there had already been 6,800 cases filed for this year.
>
> "Well," says the mayor, "it's just like anything else in life: You got to take the evil with the good."

The story of Tunica's economic rebirth had been told before. This story focused on the problems that inevitably follow gambling. To be sure, there are benefits, but this story also examined the costs.

Now that you have constructed the setup, you are ready to enter the body of the story.

Writing the Body

Think of readers as people antsy to do something else. To maintain their interest, offer them frequent examples to support your main points. Use anecdotes, scenes and dialogue to move the story line. Mix *exposition* (the facts) with narration (the story line). Let's return to Karen Elliott, who just learned that she has atypical hyperplasia. The writer, Tina Smithers, has been dealing in exposition for a few paragraphs, so she shares an anecdote set in the following scene to keep the readers' interest:

Karen was walking downstairs to get the beach ball out of the summer box for Bethany's Hawaiian swim party at Kindercare. Suddenly, Karen fainted and fell down the stairs. She knew she had broken something. Coming to, she blindly made her way upstairs and lay on the bed.

"The cat was staring me in the eyes," she mumbled as Bob, fresh from the shower, grabbed ice and a pillow.

Karen noticed Bethany crying in the doorway. At this point, Karen realized she had been shouting, "Call 9-1-1! Call 9-1-1!" She didn't want her daughter to see her lose control. She quieted down and told Bethany to come to her bed.

"It's okay, honey. Mommy broke her arm, but they'll be over soon to fix it." Later, in the ambulance, one of the paramedics tried to cut off her yellow Tommy Hilfiger sweater.

"It's brand new," Karen shouted. "Can't you pull it off?"

They gave one small yank, and Karen immediately changed her mind. Every bump along the way was agonizing. Karen pleaded for more morphine. Her wrist, it turned out, was broken in 20 places.

Writing the Ending

TIPS

Ending the Story

- Use anecdotes, dialogue, scenes and good quotes to end the story.

- Be sure the ending wraps up the whole story, not just the last section of the story.

As in the chronology structure, you need a strong ending in the focus structure. The difference is that in chronology, you end with the resolution or outcome. In the focus structure, one device is the **tie-back**, a reference to something that appears at or near the beginning of the story. Here is a lead in a *Wall Street Journal* story:

ETHEL, Mo.—Kristin Gall can't look at an old tractor without wondering about the lives it's rolled through. "There's a story behind every one if you can find it," says the 36-year-old farmer. In 2000, he began trying to track down one that belonged to his late grandfather.

By then, Leonard Gall had been dead for 11 years and the tractor had been gone from the family for nearly twice that long. But Kristin Gall's memories were stirred after he stumbled across a tattered notebook in which his grandfather had jotted down the vehicle's serial number, along with the dates of each oil change.

The story goes on to detail Gall's successful search. It even mentions, high in the story, that his grandfather sometimes bought his grandchildren pedal-driven toy tractors. The story ends with this tie-back to the lead and that anecdote:

Mr. Gall's hopes are clearer. Aiming to keep his grandfather's tractor in the family for at least one more generation, he revived a tradition his grandfather started: He bought his toddler son a pedal-driven 1206 for Christmas this year.

The goal in the focus structure is to summarize the theme of the story or tie back to the top of the story. Anecdotes, dialogue, scenes and good quotes can all end the story. Don't just stop writing; construct an ending.

SERVICE JOURNALISM

In Chapter 1, you read that one of the criteria for news is usefulness. Many, if not most, of the magazines you find on the racks appeal to readers by presenting information they might find useful. More than that, they attempt to present this useful information in the most usable way. This approach to presenting information has been called **service journalism**. You often see it labeled "news you can use."

A pioneer in service journalism, James Autrey of the Meredith Corporation, liked to call service journalism "action journalism." Its goal is to get readers to use the information. Magazine publishers know that people are more likely to resubscribe to a magazine if they do some of the things the magazine suggests for them to do.

Service journalism strives to present useful information in the most usable way. One way to think of this is "refrigerator journalism," information presented in such a way that people can cut it out and put it on their refrigerator or bulletin board.

Newspapers, too, are doing more service journalism. Some sections, such as travel, food and entertainment, use many techniques of service journalism. Front-page news stories, too, often contain elements of service journalism, even if it's just a box listing a sequence of events or directing readers to more information. Service journalism is even easier on the Web. You can provide links to lists, how-to information, time-date-place of events, and relevant websites.

In this textbook, you see examples of service journalism in the marginal elements that list the learning objectives for each chapter or highlight important points. The techniques of service journalism require that you think about content and presentation even as you are reporting. Ask yourself, "What does the reader need to be able to act on this information?" The answer might range from an address to a phone or fax number to instructions on how to fix a lawnmower or make a loaf of bread. It might include directions on how to travel to a festival or information on where and when to buy tickets. As these examples illustrate, you move from simply talking about something to providing the information the reader needs to act on your story.

Much of the basic service journalism information can be presented as sidebars or lists or boxed material. Figure 11.4 uses common service journalism devices to present more information about this topic.

When snow blanketed Seattle, thousands lost their electricity. Trying to heat their homes and apartments with charcoal or generators inside, six people died from carbon monoxide poisoning and more than 100 others were hospitalized. In response, *The Seattle Times* devoted the top half of its front page to warnings in six languages about the improper use of heating devices. This was service journalism at its finest.

Service Journalism

In today's microwave world, in-a-hurry readers want practical information presented in the most efficient and effective way.

What this means is that you must think not just of a message of words on paper. You also must think of how those words will appear on the page—the presentation.

• •

Basics
Service journalism is:

• **Useful.** You must inform readers, but if you also find ways to demonstrate how the reader can use the information, you will be more successful. Emphasize WIIFM: "What's in it for me?" See how often you can get "you" in the first sentence of your copy.

• **Usable.** Whenever you can, make a list. Lists get more attention and are better understood and more easily retained. You don't have to write sentences. "Tips" is a magical word.

• **Used.** People stop paying attention to information they never use. You should be able to prove that your readers act on information. To get readers to respond, promise them something. Offer a prize; give them something free.

• *Refrigerator Journalism* •
10 tips to serve today's readers

1. **Save them time.**
2. **Help them make more money, save money or get something free.**
3. **Address different levels of news interest.**
4. **Address niche audiences more effectively.**
5. **Become more personally useful.**
6. **Make information more immediately usable.**
7. **Become more accessible.** Give readers your name, phone number, fax number and e-mail address.

8. **Become more user-friendly.** Learn to layer the news, use cross-references, put things in the same place, color-code, tell readers where to find things, use page numbers on contents blurbs—even on covers, use glossaries and show readers where to find more information.
9. **Become more visual and graphic.** Use photos and information graphics.
10. **Become more engaging and interactive.** Use contests, quizzes, crosswords, games—make your readers do things. They remember better if they do something. Give awards to those who send answers to you. Give a coffee mug to the reader with the best tip of the month. Readers involved in your publication are more likely to resubscribe.

Figure 11.4
Employing the common presentation devices of service journalism—such as boxes and sidebars—this example shows how to highlight information so readers can easily find it and use it.

Print is a hot, intense medium. Refrigerator journalism cools off a hot medium and invites access and participation.

Other Devices of Service Journalism

1. Use blurbs. After a title and before the article begins, write a summary/contents/benefit blurb. David Ogilvy says no one will read the small type without knowing the benefit up front. Use the same benefit blurb in a table of contents or menu or briefs column. The best word in a benefit blurb is "how." How to, how you, how I did something. Be personal. Use people in your messages. Also, use internal blurbs, little summaries, pull quotes and tips to tease and coax readers on to the page.

2. Use subheads. Before you write, outline. Put the main points of the outline into the copy. Perhaps a better word than subhead is "entry point." Let readers enter the copy where they find something interesting.

3. Have a question-and-answer column. A Q&A format allows readers to save time by skipping over things they already know or are not interested in.

4. Repeat things in different ways for different people. Don't be afraid to say something in a box or a graphic that you have said elsewhere. Reinforcing a message aids retention.

5. Think more visually. Stop using pictures and graphics that do not contain information. Make them useful. Remember, being effective and efficient is the only thing that matters. We used to write articles and then look for graphics or photos to enhance the message. Now, we put the information in the graphic (where it will get more attention and have more impact) and write a story to enhance the graphic.

"Never be above a gimmick."
—Dave Orman, ARCO

The power of the box

When you can, put some information in a box. Boxes or sidebars, like lists, get more attention, increase comprehension and aid retention.

1. A reference box. "For more information, see, read, call . . ."

2. A note box. Take notes from your articles as if you were studying for an exam. Give them to your readers to complement your message.

3. A glossary box. Put unfamiliar or technical terms in a glossary box. Find a way to indicate which words are defined by putting them in color, setting them in a different typeface or underlining them. Also, teach readers how to pronounce difficult words.

4. A bio box. When you need to say something about where a person lived, went to school, and worked, put this information in a box so that your main story is not interrupted. If you have more than one person in the story, bio boxes are even more useful.

The 4 goals of the service journalist:

In a nutshell

1. Attention
2. Comprehension
3. Retention
4. Action

PR Tip

Newspapers, magazines and newsletters are doing more and more service journalism. "News You Can Use" and "Tips & Tactics" have become familiar heads. Both newspapers and magazines are becoming more visual. Yet most news releases sent out by PR professionals look the same as they did five and 50 years ago. Why not try refrigerator journalism techniques in your next news release?

Suggested Readings

Colon, Aly, and Julie Moos, eds. *Best Newspaper Writing.* Washington, D.C.: CQ Press, 2007. This is a collection of prizewinners from the annual American Society of News Editors prestigious competition. The editors deconstruct the stories to help writing students understand what the writer did and why.

Franklin, Jon. *Writing for Story: Craft Secrets of Dramatic Nonfiction by a Two-Time Pulitzer Prize Winner.* New York: Plume, 1994. If you want to write nonfiction narratives, this book will show you the structure and explain all the elements.

Harrington, Walt H., ed. *The Beholder's Eye: A Collection of America's Finest Personal Journalism.* New York: Grove Press, 2006. Harrington offers this collection of personal narratives to make his point that the first-person perspective is the best way to find truth. He adds an introductory essay to argue that the time has come to cast aside objectivity.

LaRocque, Paula. *The Book on Writing: The Ultimate Guide to Writing Well.* Oak Park, Ill.: Marion Street Press, 2003. This great book for new writers covers three main topics: mechanical and structural guidelines; creative elements of storytelling; and grammar, usage and punctuation.

Stewart, James B. *Follow the Story: How to Write Successful Nonfiction.* New York: Touchstone, 1998. Stewart, formerly of *The Wall Street Journal,* won a Pulitzer Prize in 1988 for his reporting on the stock market crash and insider trading. He uses his work to illustrate how to write narration.

Suggested Websites

www.asne.org
The American Society of News Editors conducts a prestigious writing contest every year. Winners from the past several years are posted on this site. At the home page, select "Resources," then "Old ASNE.org Site," then "Archives" and then "The ASNE Awards" to go to the winning entries.

www.nieman.harvard.edu/narrative
This site, devoted to explaining narrative writing, displays excellent examples from newspapers and magazines.

www.poynter.org
On the home page, select "Reporting & Writing." Frequently updated, this source offers stories, interviews with authors, and writing and reporting tips.

Exercises

1. **Team project.** Your instructor will organize the class into four teams. Each team selects a different story structure to analyze and researches at least three stories in that structure. (The focus structure is often found in *The Wall Street Journal* and *USA Today,* among other places.) Identify the elements of the setup. Find all the anecdotes. Identify any dialogue. Then discuss the impact of the story. How does the story structure suit, or not suit, the subject? Report your findings to the class.

2. Write four to eight paragraphs about how you and your classmates learned to be reporters. Use narrative tools. For instance, re-create a scene from one of your classes. Provide the transition into the body of the story, and then stop.

3. Attend a local school board or city council meeting, and write the story as either news narrative or chronology focusing on a key agenda item.

4. Using a chronology, write about eight paragraphs of a story about some aspect of your experience in your reporting class.

5. Either find a story based on your own reporting or take an inverted pyramid story already published and create a news narrative opening for it.

6. Find two examples in newspapers or magazines of service journalism, and analyze them. Find an example of a story that would have benefited from service journalism techniques. Tell what you would have done to make the information more usable for readers.

7. Write the first two pages of a story describing an event of your life. Try to include as many parts of the setup as you can: scenes, dialogue, foreshadowing and the "so what" statement.

Writing for the Web

12

During his presidential campaign in 2008, Barack Obama recognized that mainstream media were far from the only way of reaching supporters and would-be supporters. Obama's sophisticated website induced people to donate in record numbers and in record amounts. It sold Obama coffee mugs and T-shirts, and it helped supporters send pro-Obama messages to their friends.

It didn't stop there. The website also provided registered volunteers with a detailed script and a list of voters to call in swing states. There was also an Obama-Biden tax calculator to help you determine how much you would gain from the candidates' plans. Elsewhere, there was an Obama YouTube channel; Facebook, MySpace and LinkedIn sites; and even an iPhone application, issued just days after the iPhone 3G upgrade hit the market.

Obama's opponent, John McCain, launched a somewhat less-sophisticated effort in cyberspace but still managed to have his own YouTube channel, a Facebook site and an impressive website.

Clearly, both campaigns were well-aware that the media landscape had changed. No longer were candidates dependent on big media to get out their messages. Nevertheless, although these new channels were important, professional journalists were still essential to the public in making sense of what was happening. And journalists did just that by describing in great detail the shift in direction of the political winds.

There was a big story to tell, and for the most part, the public turned to mainstream journalists to hear it. Journalists responded by writing news for newspapers, magazines, radio, television and the Web. Those who wrote for the Web did so with clarity and purpose and with a newfound sense of what writing for online media is all about.

Like the candidates, journalists also used the Web in innovative ways. In Columbia, Mo., the *Columbia Missourian*; KOMU, the local NBC affiliate; and KBIA Radio, an NPR affiliate, joined forces to produce a four-hour webcast as the election results poured in. Wrapped around it was a "watch party" to which citizens of all political stripes were invited. Other news sites offered election results on demand. For instance, *The New York Times* had a map with voting results broken down to the county level for the entire nation.

All of this demonstrates the increasing importance of the Web in our society's media mix. Although professional journalists work alongside citizen journalists in that arena, to maintain their role as important contributors to the public dialogue, journalists must learn to harness the Web to the best of their ability. In this chapter, we examine the special considerations of writing for online media and see what sets it apart from writing for traditional media.

THE LESSON OF KATRINA

Legacy media really began to understand the power of the Web only when disaster struck in the form of Hurricane Katrina in 2005. Levees along the Mississippi River failed, much of the city was flooded, and thousands were left homeless. No story better illustrates the power of online journalism than that of NOLA.com (see Figure 12.1), the online site of *The (New Orleans) Times-Picayune*, in the wake of Katrina. Floodwaters idled the newspaper's printing plant, making publication impossible, but NOLA.com became a primary source of information. It did so with great distinction.

Mark Glaser writes in *The Online Journalism Review*:

The NOLA.com news blog became *the* source for news on hurricane damage and recovery efforts—including updates from various reporters on the ground and even full columns and news stories.

The blog actually became the paper, and it had to because the newspaper's readership was in diaspora, spread around the country in shelters and homes of families and friends. The newspaper staff was transformed into citizen journalists, with arts reviewers doing disaster coverage and personal stories running alongside hard-hitting journalism. In a time of tragedy and loss, the raw guts of the organization were exposed for us to see.

Glaser writes that NOLA.com editor Jon Donley turned over his blog to his readers, who sent in dozens of calls for help. Most came through Internet text messaging because mobile telephone towers and landlines were downed and inoperable. The calls were relayed onto the blog, which rescuers monitored to know where to go. As a result, NOLA.com not only provided information but also saved lives.

Across the country, newspapers and other media noticed. They began to realize the power of online journalism and set about the task of giving it its own place in the media landscape.

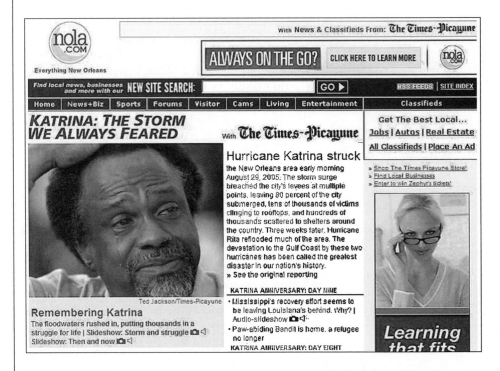

Figure 12.1
NOLA.com, the website of *The (New Orleans) Times-Picayune*, became well-known during Hurricane Katrina.

THE WEB AS ITS OWN MEDIA FORM

Online journalism wasn't always so powerful, and in its infancy few knew how to use it. Indeed, when it first appeared, online journalism followed a familiar pattern—one established when radio began to yield to television. As television arrived as a major medium in the post-World War II era, news reports consisted almost entirely of someone sitting at a desk reading written-for-radio news. Similarly, when the World Wide Web appeared in the mid-1990s, media organizations quickly adopted it but merely regurgitated news written for traditional media—newspapers, magazines, and radio and television stations. Sites operated by traditional media contained little more than the morning's stories, which had already appeared in print or on the air.

As the Internet evolved, that began to change. One reason it changed is that citizen journalism began to flourish—as it did in New Orleans—challenging the dominance of traditional media in the process of disseminating news. Anyone, it seemed, could become a journalist or even a publisher.

Recognizing that the media landscape had changed, traditional publishers began to embrace blogs, instant messaging of news alerts and even citizen journalism itself. Those developments led editors and publishers of traditional media to understand that the Web is an entirely new medium that demands a fresh approach. It's an approach that takes advantage of the Internet's ability to deliver links to other sites, to link people with two-way communication and, with high-speed connections, to provide not only text, photos and graphics but also audio and video on demand.

When the Web first came along, no one knew how to make money with it, an essential ingredient in a country in which the media are not state-supported. All that has changed. By 2012, online advertising revenue is expected to exceed $147 billion worldwide, $62.4 billion of that in the U.S. alone. No other medium was experiencing revenue growth even approaching that from a percentage standpoint, although the base is small. And *Folio:*, the trade publication of the magazine industry, reported that some titles are beginning to use online revenue to make up for lost print revenue, effectively underwriting their older siblings. Clearly, Web businesses based on news are here to stay, and that requires us to study the best ways of producing both advertising and news for them.

Just as writing for television evolved from its early iterations, so, too, is writing for the Web evolving. Most now recognize that writing for the Web is different from writing for television or newspapers. The Web is clearly a unique medium that requires a new approach, but that approach is still evolving as journalists learn new ways to communicate online. Let's take a look at the conventional wisdom on writing for the Web as we know it today. (See Figure 12.2 for a comparison of Web and print writing.)

> **❙❙**Computers can:
>
> - Look things up for us.
> - Navigate for us ('Please turn to page . . .').
> - Link words to other words.
> - Remember where we were and take us back there.
> - Play audio, video and animation.
> - Organize and present information according to a nonlinear structure.**❙❙**
>
> —Andrew Bonime and Ken C. Pohlmann,
> *Writing for New Media*

Comparison of Print and Web News Stories

	Print Stories	Web Stories
Audience	Communication is one-way — from writer to reader. All readers get the same stories.	Communication is two-way: Readers expect to be able to respond online through blogs, forums and so on. Readers customize their reading by using links and specifying preferences.
Structure	Inverted pyramid predominates, but writers use other structures too. All of a news event is covered in one major story.	Inverted pyramid, with the key facts up front, is standard; use of suspense is rare. Coverage is layered so that readers can choose how much of a story to read.
Style	Writers sometimes use literary techniques to enhance stories. Stories are mostly written paragraphs with some breakers.	Readers expect stories to be straightforward, crisp and clear, without much use of literary techniques. Writers use a lot of bullets and lists.
Length	Important stories may be lengthy to accommodate in-depth coverage.	Stories are usually short; additional info is "chunked" into linked sidebar stories that readers can click on if they want to know more.
Sidebars	Writers might add short sidebars on one aspect of a story; newspapers may print the text of a speech.	Stories provide links to past stories that are of possible interest and to information on other sites that readers might want.
Visual appeal	Newspapers use photos, charts, graphs and drawings. Readers expect to see columns of print.	Websites use photos, charts, graphs and drawings, as well as audio, video and animation. Readers expect sites to be colorful, well-designed, interesting and easy to navigate.
Timeliness	Newspapers are published on a regular schedule, and writers have set deadlines for stories.	Websites are continually updated throughout the day, and breaking news is posted immediately.

Figure 12.2
Writing for the Web is different in some respects from writing for newspapers.

WHAT READERS EXPECT FROM THE WEB

Even if you plan to work at a newspaper, magazine, or radio or television station, you will need to know how to write for online media. At a growing number of newspapers, even veteran journalists are being asked to turn in two versions of their stories, one for the newspaper and one for the paper's website. At the *St. Paul Pioneer Press*, all print reporters must file a Web story for the paper's website, TwinCities.com (see Figure 12.3), within 30 minutes after witnessing an event or learning about the news. In the old days, newspapers printed several editions a day and occasionally came out with an "extra." Today, cyberspace has turned newspapers into 24-hour competitive news machines, and "print reporters" are rapidly

Figure 12.3
Reporters for the *St. Paul Pioneer Press* file their first stories for TwinCities.com, the newspaper's website.

becoming a disappearing species. Television reporters, too, post stories to their companies' websites throughout the day.

Of course, online writing isn't just about writing. It's about determining the best way to tell a story and then using all media forms—text, audio, video, photographs and graphics—to deliver it. This requires at least a basic understanding of audio and video production and the use of information graphics. Writing, though, is at the heart of all media, including the Web.

Good online writing has many of the characteristics of other forms of effective writing. Much of what you have read so far about news writing applies to online journalism; what you've learned about news gathering and reporting, either in print or broadcast, applies here. The demand for accurate, simple, clear and concise writing is the same for all the media.

Nevertheless, the online journalist must be aware of some fundamental differences between online and traditional media. These distinctions increasingly result in stories that look quite different from the stories published in print or broadcast. One sure way to drive away online readers is to give them *shovelware*—stories as they appeared in print. Hundreds of publications continue to do that, but it's now clear that most online readers are turned off by shovelware—unless they have a real need for in-depth information.

To be sure, there are readers who want the stories as they appear in the newspaper and not rewritten in some other form. They want shovelware because they want to know what other readers are seeing. Many readers of *The New York Times'* online edition, scattered around the world, undoubtedly want to see what the print readers have read. *The Times* and many other newspapers now produce downloadable versions that look exactly like the newspaper edition. So, there's a market for that. But most readers want stories tailored to take advantage of the Web's considerable power. They want links, and they want graphics, audio and even video to accompany the text.

To write effectively for the Web, you need to learn a unique way of thinking about writing. Let's begin with these three principles about what readers expect:

- The reader rules.
- The writing is nonlinear.
- Structure is everything.

The Reader Rules

Newspaper websites are expanding the reach of their publications in unprecedented ways. According to the Newspaper Association of America, in 2008, unique visitors to newspaper websites rose to 67.3 million over the course of a month. That represented a three-year tripling of newspaper website traffic. This, in turn, was spurring online advertising growth.

Television station websites are at their heels. The Kelsey Group, which monitors media usage, found that a handful of television station websites are now outperforming the newspaper websites in their cities. A few, including six owned by Hearst Corp. stations, outperformed the newspaper sites by a margin of 3 to 1.

Readers Want Multimedia Variety

The most successful sites understand that reading news on the Web is a much different experience from reading it in a newspaper or magazine. The best sites are beginning to learn that the Web excels when it presents news using a full spectrum of assets—not only text but also hyperlinks, photos, graphics, audio and video. Online readers expect more than text, and increasingly that's just what they're getting.

Even a staid publication like *The New York Times* recognizes that and delivers an incredible amount of multimedia on its website. So, too, do ESPN.com (see Figure 12.4), CNN.com and a host of others. And slowly but surely, the way things are written for these websites is changing, too.

Readers Want the News Up Front

On occasion, print journalists writing for newspapers and magazines build a story with a suspenseful ending. Online news writers, on the other hand, should keep no secrets from readers; they should not try to withhold information until later in the story. When writing online, it's important to surrender control of the story's sequence to the reader.

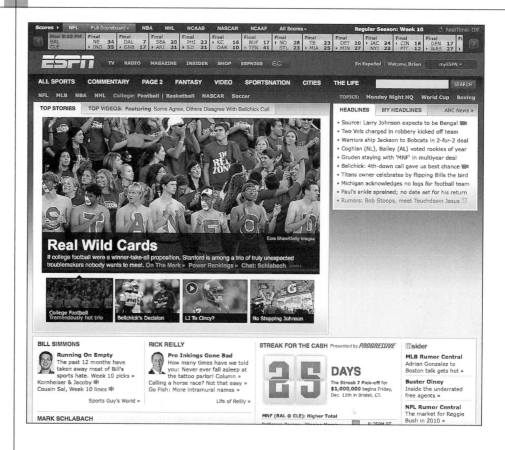

Figure 12.4
ESPN puts lots of effort into its well-read website. Predictably, video complements the text nicely.

In Chapter 9, you were introduced to the most traditional of news writing forms, the inverted pyramid, which places all the important information in the first paragraph. That technique is exactly what's needed for most Web stories because the lead in an online story is even more important than it is in print. It literally may be all that appears on the screen, and readers may have to click to get more of the story. The lead must nail the "what" or the "so what" to get the full attention of the reader. In fact, it is similar to the anchor's introduction to a television news story.

The lead is also important because for most search engines the lead will be the only information provided for the link to the story. It's smart to include keywords such as "Maine" and "governor" in the lead about a story concerning the Maine governor. That way, readers searching for stories about the governor are more likely to find it. In fact, search engines are more likely to rank it higher if those words are repeated in the headline and first couple of paragraphs—something newspaper and magazine editors typically try to avoid.

Sometimes the lead appears like an extended headline, followed by two or three statements that also read as headlines. Readers can often click on the hyperlinked headlines to read the full version of the story on another page within the website.

Readers Want to Customize Content

Online, authors lose their "position of central authority," writes David Weinberger, author and editor of the *Journal of the Hyperlinked Organization*, a newsletter that considers the Web's effect on how business works. Every reader is different; every reader has different needs. Every reader, therefore, not only will select and choose what to read but also will choose a path that best meets those needs.

Think of ways to present different information for different people at different times. Unlike newspapers and magazines, which must decide how long to make a story, online media should present information in such a way that readers can choose the amount they need at any given time. Not many websites have yet mastered this concept, but it's important.

Note also that the reader is active, not passive. Steve Outing writes on PoynterOnline (see Figure 12.5):

If I gave you an assignment to look at the content of 100 news Web sites, you'd probably find that 95 percent of them don't ever go beyond routine presentation of text, images and the occasional audio or video clip. It's still the rare few that craft content in such ways that go beyond what would be possible in print or broadcast.

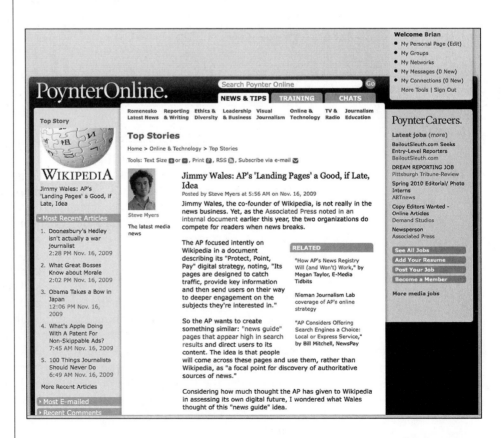

Figure 12.5
PoynterOnline is an excellent website for keeping up with media-industry trends and practices.

Rare is the story that uses online interactive techniques that help the user understand the story best by letting him or her interact with and manipulate elements of the story—to experience it, not just read about it.

Outing writes that good writing for the Web says to the reader, "Don't read—do!" It does this because it plays to the essential nature of the Internet—it is interactive.

The Writing Is Nonlinear

Because most people don't think linearly, writing online is more in line with the way people think. It's even more in line with the way today's readers read. Break the story into short, digestible pieces. Rather than stringing together a long story and trying to get readers to read the whole thing in the order in which you presented it, keep in mind that many readers don't want to read everything you have to tell them. You must give them choices and let them decide what to read and in what order.

Stories that require multiple continuous screens turn off many readers immediately. Many readers hate to scroll on screen. Some exit even before they get to the bottom of the screen. Few will take the time to read a lot of text in one clump. Note, of course, that this is not true of highly motivated readers who crave your information or sites like *Slate* magazine where readers expect long-form stories.

Structure Is Everything

Some who write online forget entirely about structure. That's a huge mistake. Even though an online story takes on an entirely different structure, it still must be organized in a logical, coherent way. The online reader does not revel in chaos. Even though the story may appear on the screen as a mosaic, the way that mosaic is composed will help attract readers, keep them and help them follow what for them is the most logical path.

The online writer should present information in layers. Remember: No two readers are alike. You can present the same information with different degrees of detail and support. It works like this:

Layer 1: Give readers a lead paragraph or several paragraphs—enough to understand the basic story. This first layer is information that is immediately available to readers—no action or effort is demanded of them.

Layer 2: Provide a way for readers to click to continue reading the story. Alternatively, a more substantial read could be reachable easily by moving the cursor or by scrolling.

Layer 3: Provide links to earlier stories on the same subject or to related written material.

Layer 4: Complement the story with video, photos, graphics or audio. Or, alternatively, make the video or photo the centerpiece of the story and subordinate the text. This layer may require readers to click on a link that opens up still more information, perhaps audio, video or a source document.

When you write for print, you need to be concerned with continuity, with themes, with working in all aspects of the story while keeping the writing clear and coherent. When you write online, you need to worry not about the structure or flow of the whole piece but rather about the relationships of the layers and parts. You need to help readers navigate from place to place to get the information they want. That means you must have clear entrances and exits.

Sometimes you have to give clear directions. For example, if you include a hyperlink in your story, more readers will "click here" if you tell them to do so than if you don't. Sometimes you may take readers down one path that branches into several others. Some call this technique "threading." The story of a plane crash can lead to various threads—the airline and its safety record, the plane itself and the record of that type of plane, the place of the accident, the people involved, and so forth.

You need not be concerned about some repetition. Remember, readers choose what parts to read. Besides, a certain amount of repetition or of stating things in different ways, perhaps visually, increases retention. Readers, after all, online or elsewhere, process information differently. (Figure 12.6 shows how the different elements of a Web page work together.)

> **"**Hypertext and hypermedia have the following characteristics:
>
> - They present ideas nonsequentially.
> - They follow the thought process.
> - They allow users to choose individual pathways through the information.
> - They allow information to transcend individual documents.
> - They link text with pictures, audio and video.**"**
>
> — Andrew Bonime and Ken C. Pohlmann,
> *Writing for New Media*

GUIDELINES FOR WRITING FOR THE WEB

Readers online are surfers or scanners, much more so than readers of print, perhaps because it takes 25 percent longer to read online than it does in print. Researchers Jakob Nielsen and John Morkes found that 79 percent of those they tested scanned a new page they came across; only 16 percent read the copy word for word.

Online expert Shel Holtz says you want readers to dive, not to surf. Surfing is what frustrated readers do. Here are 10 ways to make divers out of surfers—or at least to hold their attention long enough to get your message across.

1. Think Immediacy

Although you must of course make sure what you write is accurate, the Internet can deliver news when it is brand-new. Writing online is like writing for the wire services. Everyone on the Internet now consumes information the way a wire-service subscriber does. Keeping readers with you means keeping readers up-to-the-minute. You must expect to update breaking stories quickly and to add depth whenever it is available. But just because you can easily correct your mistakes, that

Anatomy of an Article Page on a News Website

A search box and detailed toolbar enable readers to get right to the news that interests them.

Some datelines give the time a story is posted so readers know how recent the information is.

Buttons at the top enable readers to print or e-mail the story or share it on social networking sites. Readers can adjust the type size for their own comfort.

The Web allows for liberal use of images. Here, readers can click on the photo to see an enlarged version. Some stories also have video and audio.

"Related" links take readers to pages with supporting documents and other articles on the subject. Links may also appear in the story's text.

Readers can navigate to other stories without having to return to the home page first.

Readers can also sign up for the site's RSS feed and receive timely updates automatically.

The "Next Page" buttons at the bottom and top make it easy for interested readers to get the whole story.

The "Comments" function allows readers to give feedback and read others' feedback. Other features, such as reader polls, may also be used for feedback.

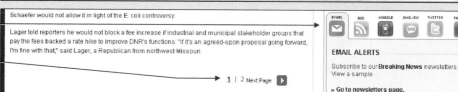

Figure 12.6

The *Springfield (Mo.) News-Leader*'s website uses a number of online-specific elements to complement a story.

ON THE JOB

An Online Career

Since graduating from college, Jenifer Langosch has worked as a beat writer for MLB.com, covering the Pittsburgh Pirates. Though the job revolves heavily around the six-month baseball season, it's a profession that essentially keeps her busy 12 months a year.

Langosch's responsibilities include covering every facet of the ball club. In season, that includes writing game stories and feature stories, covering breaking news and updating fans on roster moves, injuries or implications of certain games or events.

While the demands do lessen a bit during baseball's offseason, she's still responsible for reporting on any news that involves the organization. There are trades and free agent acquisitions to cover, as well as season preview content to put out. She covers baseball's winter meetings every December and races to break news about player movement or personnel changes.

The job sends her to Bradenton, Fla., every winter to cover seven weeks of spring training. She also covers most of the team's road games, which means she lives away from Pittsburgh for much of the baseball season.

Working with MLB.com has afforded Langosch the opportunity to cover other Major League events, too. In her first three seasons with the company, she helped with coverage of two All-Star Games and three playoff series, including a World Series.

"It's hard to narrow down the things I like most about this job," Langosch says. "It's an ongoing challenge to immerse myself so heavily in knowing a team — its players, inner workings, management team, past and future — so that I can bring both a casual baseball fan and a know-it-all type all the information.

does not mean you are allowed to make them. Columnist David Broder of *The Washington Post* warned that posting news quickly could sacrifice quality and damage credibility.

2. Save Readers Time

What most readers do not have is time. Whatever you can do to save readers' time is worth *your* time. It's been said by various people in different ways since the philosopher Blaise Pascal first said it: "Excuse me for this long letter; I don't have time to write a short one." For many stories, if not most, perhaps your chief concern should be this: Have I presented this information in such a way as to cost readers the least amount of time?

"The fact that I get to do so many different types of writing also appeals to me. Writing a game story is quite different than writing an in-depth feature story, which is quite different than writing a hard news article. On a weekly basis, I typically have to do all of these at one time or another. Doing so has really helped me develop different voices in my writing."

The chance to incorporate all forms of new media has also been a plus, further expanding her skill set.

"I run a blog on the site and interact with fans through Twitter. There are times where I take my own digital camera and digital camcorder on site to bring images to fans that way.

"Working with an online company has put me in a position to better weather the storm that the journalism industry finds itself in right now. While I still have a place for newspapers in my heart, my recommendation to anyone wanting to pursue a career in print journalism is to also explore online opportunities. It's the same job, just a different medium."

Langosch also urges would-be journalists to immerse themselves in all forms of journalism.

"Even if you're a writer, learn how to use a camera and camcorder. Find a way to allow social networking sites to help you better reach out and interact with readers. If you're interested in going into sports reporting, know ahead of time that your love of writing, not your love of sports, will sustain your interest in the profession long-term. Expect to work mostly nights and weekends, but also know that sports sometimes allows for the best storytelling."

The best way to save readers' time is to be clear. Choose the simple word; vary the length of sentences, but keep them short; write short paragraphs. Help readers. Emphasize key words by highlighting them or by putting them in color.

Another reason to write simply, using simple words and simple sentences, is to enable the auto-translation programs used by some search engines to translate the page. The simpler the words and sentences, the more likely a foreign-language translation of the story will be accurate and understandable.

3. Provide Information That's Quick and Easy to Get

The overall organization of your story must say to the reader that getting this information is going to be quick and easy. Online readers have zero tolerance for confusion and no time at all to be led astray. It's too easy to click on something else.

Don't get carried away by your own eloquence. Be guided by what your readers want or need to know. Make it easy for them. Write short paragraphs with one idea per paragraph.

4. Think Both Verbally and Visually

In the past, writers for print thought little about how their stories were going to appear. Their job was to write the story—period. The designer's job was to make the story fit on the page in some meaningful way. Writers did not worry about headlines, subheads, summary quotes, photos, illustrations or anything but the story.

Television news writers know that they must write to the pictures. Good television has good video; the visual medium tries to show rather than to tell. Words complement pictures; they say what the pictures do not. Many times, of course, the writer does not make the pictures and is not responsible for getting them. But the writer still must consider the best way to tell the story; sometimes visuals convey the story as no amount of text could possibly do.

As an online journalist, you may not have to do it all by yourself, but you definitely must *think* both verbally and visually. From the outset, you must be concerned about the most effective and efficient way for the information to appear on the screen. You have to think not only about the organization of the page but also about ways to use graphics, to be interactive and to use online tools.

No one doubts that photos and graphics grab readers' attention. That's why you see more icons and information graphics in magazines and newspapers, and that's why you must think, perhaps with the help of graphic designers, of ways to use graphic elements online.

5. Cut Copy in Half

You probably don't have to be told that writing online must be concise. But you do need to be told to cut your copy in half. Years ago, writing expert William Zinsser recommended that writers take their eight pages and cut them to four. Then, he wrote, comes the difficult part—cutting them to three. And that was for print!

Most online readers simply will not read long stories. Even veteran computer users find reading on screen somewhat difficult, even unpleasant, says Jakob Nielsen. Studies contradict each other about people's aversion to scrolling, however. In the not-so-distant past, some experts advised getting the whole story on one screen. Because some screens are small, they advised not writing more than 20 lines of text. Now, because of the proliferation of larger and less-irritating screens, some readers are finding it easier and less frustrating to scroll for more information.

As in broadcast news writing, there's little room online to be cute or even literary. Be crisp and clear.

6. Use Lots of Lists and Bullets

Often you can cut copy by putting information into lists. Whenever possible, make a list. Lists get more attention and allow for better comprehension and more retention than ordinary sentences and paragraphs. Bulleted or numbered lists are scannable. Readers can grasp them immediately. Think of information on the Web as a database. That's how people use their computers, and that's how they use the Web. Besides, it's also quicker for the writer to make lists than to write paragraphs.

Mark Deuze and Christina Dimoudi of the Amsterdam School of Communications Research conclude from their study that online journalism is really a fourth kind of journalism after print, radio and television. Its main characteristic is "empowering audiences as active participants in the daily news." Online journalists have "an interactive relationship with their audience" and a "strong element of audience orientation" and are "more aware of their publics and service function in society than their colleagues elsewhere."

Nielsen tested five versions of the same information for usability. Look first at the longest version, what he calls promotional writing, his control condition:

Nebraska is filled with internationally recognized attractions that draw large crowds of people every year, without fail. In 1996, some of the most popular places were Fort Robinson State Park (355,000 visitors), Scotts Bluff National Monument (132,126 visitors), Arbor Lodge State Historical Park & Museum (100,000), *Carhenge* (85,598), Stuhr Museum of the Prairie Pioneer (60,002), and Buffalo Bill Ranch State Historical Park (28,446).

Now look at this same material in list form:

In 1996, six of the most visited places in Nebraska were:
- Fort Robinson State Park.
- Scotts Bluff National Monument.
- Arbor Lodge State Historical Park & Museum.
- *Carhenge*.
- Stuhr Museum of the Prairie Pioneer.
- Buffalo Bill Ranch State Historical Park.

The list version of the information scored a 124 percent usability improvement over the first version.

7. Write in Chunks

When you can't put material into lists, you can still organize it into chunks of information. Put information into sidebars or boxes. Readers will read more, not less, if you break up the information into small bites. Research has also shown that putting some information in a sidebar can give readers better comprehension of the subject. But the main objective here is to write for diverse readers who want to get only the information they want in the order in which they want to receive it.

Think of your story as having parts. When writing a story for a newspaper, you need to think of ways to join the various parts of the story, you should craft transitions carefully and you may even add subheads. When writing a story online, rather than writing subheads, make each segment of the story a separate story. Be sure that each part can stand on its own enough to be comprehensible and to make your point. Again, remember the importance of a strong lead in the best inverted pyramid form.

8. Use Hyperlinks

To understand the Web, think of a spider web. The Web, says David Weinberger, is a place of connection, a place where we go to connect. Users of the Internet feel connected. If you want them to read your copy and come back for more, you must satisfy and enhance that sense of being connected.

Being connected means being interactive. Web users want to be actively involved in what they are reading. They are not passive observers. Like video-game players, they want to be in control of where they are going and how they get there. Both individual stories and whole pages must be interactive both internally and externally (see Figure 12.7).

Web expert Jakob Nielsen argues that websites must employ scannable text using:

- Highlighted keywords, including hypertext links.
- Meaningful subheads.
- Bulleted lists.
- One idea per paragraph.
- Half the word count of conventional writing.

Figure 12.7
The front page of the *Columbia Missourian* website is rich with links (highlighted in blue) to both wire and local stories.

Internal Connections

The most challenging and necessary aspect of online writing is making the copy interactive. You begin that process by streamlining your copy and not including everything. Create **hyperlinks**, and allow readers to click on information elsewhere on your site.

One of the most perplexing problems writers face is deciding when to include the definition of a word. Will you insult some readers by including the definition? Will you leave others behind if you do not define the term? A similar problem is whether to tell who a person is. Many readers may wonder how stupid you think they are for telling them that actor Arnold Schwarzenegger is the Republican governor of California. Other readers may need or want that information.

The online writer can simply make the word or name a hyperlink to a different "page." Readers need only click on the word to find its meaning or read more about it. No longer do writers have to write, "For more information, see . . ." Academic writers use footnotes. Hypertext and hypermedia, linking readers to audio, video and pictures, are much more convenient.

Writing concisely has never been easier. Rather than defining words, going into long explanations, giving examples or elaborating on the story itself, you can stick to the essentials and make the rest of the story available to readers who need or want it. A story about a homicide can link to a map of where the crime took place, to a chart showing the number of homicides this year as compared with last year, to a piece about friends of the victim, to information about violent crimes nationally, and so forth.

Remember, too, that unlike the newspaper, where you may be short of space, and unlike radio and television, where you may be short of time, online you have unlimited space and time to run photos and aspects of stories that could be of real interest to some readers. Sports fans, for example, would probably enjoy seeing a whole gallery of shots from Saturday's championship game. They would read interviews from all of the stars of the victory—or of the defeat.

> **"**We have derived three main content-oriented conclusions from our four years of Web usability studies:
>
> - Users do not read on the Web; instead they scan the pages, trying to pick out a few sentences or even parts of sentences to get the information they want.
> - Users do not like long, scrolling pages; they prefer the text to be short and to the point.
> - Users detest anything that seems like marketing fluff or overly hyped language ('marketese') and prefer factual information.**"**
>
> — John Morkes and Jakob Nielsen (1997), "Concise, Scannable, and Objective: How to Write for the Web," useit.com

External Connections

Of course, you can do much more. You can hyperlink to different websites. Academic writers include bibliographies. Print journalists often identify sources in their stories. Other writers simply say to readers: That's all I know about the subject, I'm not going to tell you where I obtained my information, and I'm not telling you where you can find more information. Hypertext and hypermedia have changed all that. Not only can you hyperlink online, but readers expect you to do so.

Obviously, you are not expected to draw readers away from your site to a competitor, especially on a breaking story. Nevertheless, readers will come to rely on

Figure 12.8
Google News, a content aggregator, is a leading source of news for millions of Americans.

your site to help them find more information about subjects that interest them greatly. And many news sites post supporting documents to buttress their stories.

To find appropriate external hyperlinks, you need to know how to use search engines like Yahoo (www.yahoo.com) and Google (www.google.com). Google News is a master of providing links galore for readers to peruse (see Figure 12.8).

9. Give Readers a Chance to Talk Back

A big part of being interactive is allowing readers to talk back. The Internet has leveled the playing field. Everyone is an owner or a publisher. Everyone feels the right, and often the need, to write back—if not to the writer of the piece, then to other readers in chat rooms—computer applications that allow users to communicate with one another in real time—or blogs. The wonderful thing about allowing readers to talk back is that they do. When they do, they will revisit the site again and again. Online readers want to be part of the process. Readers love it when newspapers like *The Miami Herald* include the reporter's e-mail address in the byline, and many of them respond.

Never has it been easier to find out what is on the minds of your readers. Print and broadcast have mainly been one-way communication. Now, not only can you get opinions easily and quickly, but you can incorporate them into your story or at least include hyperlinks to them. Letters to the editor have always been among the best-read sections in newspapers and magazines. Many readers, especially those reading online, not only want to express their own opinions but love to read the opinions of others. Be sure, however, that you use the same strict standards for publishing others' remarks on your website that you use for publishing in your newspaper or magazine. Even e-mail polls can and have been flooded by advocacy groups. Reporting their results can be meaningless, misleading and certainly unprofessional unless the polls are monitored carefully.

10. Don't Forget the Human Touch

Veteran correspondent Helen Thomas told a convention of newspaper interactive editors: "I do hope the human touch remains in the robotic scheme of things. Human beings still count." Remember, people make the news. Facts are just facts unless you relate them to people.

The 3-2-2-1 Format

After spending 25 years as a professional newsman, the last four of those as a general manager, Associate Professor Clyde Bentley now teaches classes in online journalism. In one class, students take stories from the newspaper and rewrite them for the online version. Bentley calls students online "producers" rather than reporters.

"I was surprised at the resistance my students had to changing the copy of reporters," Bentley says. "They preferred the 'shovelware' concept so they would not tamper with the prose of their friends."

In frustration, he instituted what he called a "3-2-2-1" format. "It was a way to force my young journalists to take on a new process."

Here's what the numbers mean.

3 Subheads
By inserting three subheads, the producers "chunk" the story into four pieces. "This is easier to read than one long, scrollable piece of text," Bentley says. The subdivisions can be as simple as "who, what, when. . . ."

2 External Links
These links direct readers to further information posted outside the story. "For instance, in a story about the local dog pound, we might have external links to the ASPCA and the American Kennel Club."

2 Internal Links
These explanatory links are tied to text within the story. "In the pound story," Bentley explains, "the word 'Doberman' might be a link that takes one to a breeder's site that explains the Doberman pinscher."

1 Photo or Graphic Not Available in the Print Edition
Print publications limit art primarily because of space limitations. There are no such limits on the Web. "If a photographer shoots 20 shots, we can run more than one," Bentley says. "More commonly, however, the producers insert mug shots of people mentioned in the story. There is no reason not to run mugs of everyone who is mentioned in a story."

A word of caution: Including e-mail addresses on the Web leaves you vulnerable to spammers and others who use a program called an "e-mail siphon" to collect e-mail addresses. Putting your e-mail address in a news story or magazine article can subject you to a deluge of spam. Rather than giving your permanent personal address, include in your stories a different address that you change from time to time.

WRITING WITH SEARCH ENGINES IN MIND

Among other rules for writing online, Ellen Schindler, a senior account executive at Berry Associates, recommends the following:

- Double-space between paragraphs. Leave two spaces after periods.

- Avoid serif type. Serifs get lost on the screen.

- Make the text black. It's easier to read.

- Remember that simple is best.

It's almost impossible to overemphasize one major consideration in writing for online media: If your online story cannot be found, it won't be read. That's why editors of websites place great emphasis on *search-engine optimization*, the process of making sure your story will be found when someone searches for its topic on sites such as Google or Yahoo. Generally, the better job you do getting keywords into the lead, the more likely your story will appear near the top of the search results for that topic.

Newspapers and magazines are notorious for writing baseball stories that never mention the word "baseball" and hockey stories that never use the word "hockey." That's OK if the user searches for the team name, such as Atlanta Braves. She'll find your story even if the word "baseball" is not included. But what if the user searches for "baseball"? Your story will not be found unless it contains metadata—that is, tagging information—that includes that search term. Understanding that requirement is the key to making sure that all possible search terms appear either in the metadata accompanying the story or in the story itself.

Remember, too, that search engines are more likely to rank your story higher if keywords are repeated in the headline and first couple of paragraphs. That's contrary to the practice adopted by most newspapers and magazines of not repeating words in the headline and lead.

Many websites have protocols for ensuring that the proper terms are used, and several companies now offer services that ensure content is maximized for search engines. That can be a wise investment for any site looking to increase readership.

WRITING FOR BLOGS

Blog writing ranges from short, inverted pyramid stories, often written quickly by beat reporters, to essays. Whereas traditional journalism is formal, blogging is informal. Whereas traditional journalism is dispassionate, much of blogging is passionate. Whereas traditional journalism is third person ("he," "she," "they"), much of blogging is first person ("I," "we"). Whereas much of traditional writing is vetted by layers of editors, much of blogging goes straight from the writer to the reader.

Political bloggers capture a disproportionate amount of the attention, but there are respected bloggers, some of them independent, most of them working for startups or the traditional media, who blog on everything from travel to technology. Even some heads of companies are blogging. Public relations professionals are doing it on behalf of their companies or organizations. The best blogs are conversational, based in specifics, full of comparisons, explanations, turns of phrase and links. While some Internet writers do not distinguish between fact and fiction, professional journalists must be meticulous about the facts in their blogs. Here are a few examples of good blogging.

Humor from Loretta Waldman of the *Hartford Courant* (courant.com):

Small Towns Need $ for Websites, But from Where?
By Loretta Waldman on October 30, 2008 12:44 PM

I set out to follow up on the status of Harwinton's town website the other day and out of habit, immediately went looking for it on the Internet.

Then I remembered they don't have a website.

A personal essay from Jeré Longman of *The New York Times* (www.nytimes.com):

EUNICE, La. — The electricity has been out since Hurricane Gustav blew through the Cajun prairie, but I still flick the light switch every time I walk into the kitchen or the bathroom.

My father, who is 76, has been shaving in a pail under the carport and making his coffee on the barbecue pit. "I'd walk a mile for a Camel and a mile for a cup of coffee," he said.

And passion from self-described libertarian Kevin Colby:

Congratulations America! We are part owners of the New Yankee Stadium!

The federal government just gave America's richest sports team another gift.

For the second time in two years, the Internal Revenue Service has approved special rules that allow the Yankees to use additional tax-free bonds to pay the skyrocketing costs of the team's new stadium.

Dan Steinberg, who is a full-time sports blogger for *The Washington Post*, has two gripes about blogs. In an interview with *Gelf* Magazine (GelfMagazine.com), he says bloggers shouldn't steal good stuff from journalists who are doing the reporting. He also chafes at the traditional restrictions of taste imposed upon him by his newspaper. Steinberg, a former beat reporter, spends a lot of time in locker rooms. He would like to reflect some of the off-color talk, but his editors impose the same standards on him as they do the rest of the paper.

Other bloggers have more freedom. Steinberg is one of the few journalists working for the traditional media who are full-time bloggers. Most are beat reporters who drop news tidbits or humorous observations into a blog about their beats. Some are primarily mini-aggregators. They monitor the Web for news of whatever specialty they cover and provide readers the links. From bursts to full-blown essays, bloggers use a variety of writing styles. There may not be rules or even best practices, but there is a worthwhile guideline: Be interesting and be accurate.

A Story Greater Than the Sum of Its Parts

From an interview with Kerry Northrup, former director of publications for Ifra, a global news industry trade organization, in *EPN World Reporter*:

A lot of people who are journalists today simply cannot be journalists tomorrow. They can't grasp the changes in how people get and use news and information. They won't adapt to thinking in terms of multiple media rather than being concerned only about their personal area of specialization. They are media bigots, for want of a better term, insisting past reason that print is print, broadcast is broadcast, Web is Web, and never will they mesh.

The idea of blending formats to create a story greater than the sum of its parts remains foreign to them. Perhaps the kindest and most effective approach for an editorial organization to deal with this situation is to create new jobs that reflect the new requirements, the new skills, the new compensations, the new realities, and then let those that will evolve into them, and those that won't phase out.

If you're writing online, you have to be much more than a wordsmith. You must have a pocketful of other skills. Writing online also demands a great deal of collaboration and not just with other writers. Working closely with those more expert than you in design and photography becomes crucial from the outset.

TOMORROW'S READERS

Print has been around for centuries, and we are still figuring out ways to use it effectively. In contrast, writing for the Web is in its infancy. Like all good writers, online journalists must be students of writing. Both writers and readers are still learning the most effective uses of the newest medium. Writing for the Web is more about showing than telling, about the audience experiencing rather than witnessing, about the audience actively participating rather than being passive, about the audience doing rather than merely reading. Never before have writers been more challenged.

Suggested Readings

Craig, Richard. *Online Journalism: Reporting, Writing, and Editing for New Media.* Stamford, Conn.: Wadsworth-Thomson Learning, 2005. This book is a comprehensive source of information about writing for the Web.

Friend, Cecilia, and Jane Singer. *Online Journalism Ethics: Traditions and Transitions.* Armonk, N.Y.: M. E. Sharpe, 2007. Friend and Singer have written an excellent treatise on the ethics of online sites.

Morkes, John, and Jakob Nielsen. "Concise, Scannable, and Objective: How to Write for the Web." Available from www.useit.com/papers/webwriting/writing.html. This article contains a wonderful summary of the authors' research regarding effective online writing.

Nielsen, Jakob. "How Users Read on the Web." Available from www.useit.com/alertbox/9710a.html. Nielsen offers practical advice, including research, on the usability of online copy.

Rosales, Rey G. *The Elements of Online Journalism.* Lincoln, Neb.: iUniverse, 2006. This is a good book on assembling multimedia news packages.

Suggested Websites

http://espn.go.com
ESPN.com, one of the best sites on the Web, is probably the most extensive Internet site for sports fans. It was an early leader in the use of audio and video.

www.mercurynews.com
MercuryNews.com, one of the first comprehensive local news websites, includes area news courtesy of the *San Jose Mercury News.*

www.miamiherald.com
Like many daily newspapers, *The Miami Herald*'s online edition includes most of the stories from its print edition, along with additional online-only posts.

www.msnbc.msn.com
This companion site to the cable news channel offers a wealth of news resources. Its opinions section includes, among other things, links to top stories; stories from *Slate*, another Microsoft website; and opinion pieces and blogs by pundits and journalists.

www.newsy.com
This innovative, video-heavy site compares how various media around the world covered major stories.

www.useit.com
This is expert Jakob Nielsen's site. You won't find anyone more knowledgeable and up-to-date on the research in the field of online writing than Nielsen.

Exercises

1. **Team project.** Your instructor will divide your class into teams. With your team, select five newspaper or magazine websites. Each team member should read at least three articles on a specific site, evaluating how well the articles illustrate the 10 guidelines covered in this chapter. When the team reassembles, discuss your results. Rank the websites in terms of how good a job they do of using online writing techniques. Share your conclusions with the class.

2. Visit your local newspaper or television station and interview individuals who do the news online. Find out how they were trained and what major challenges they face.

3. Your instructor will assign you a newspaper story. Rewrite it for online use, and indicate any hyperlinks that you might include.

4. Choose a major national story from a recent newspaper or newsmagazine. Then visit two newspaper websites and compare their treatment of the story. Write a 300-word critique of the online writing techniques that the websites used.

5. Find a website that does a good job of linking readers to original source material. Evaluate the use of that technique, and explain why the technique works in this case.

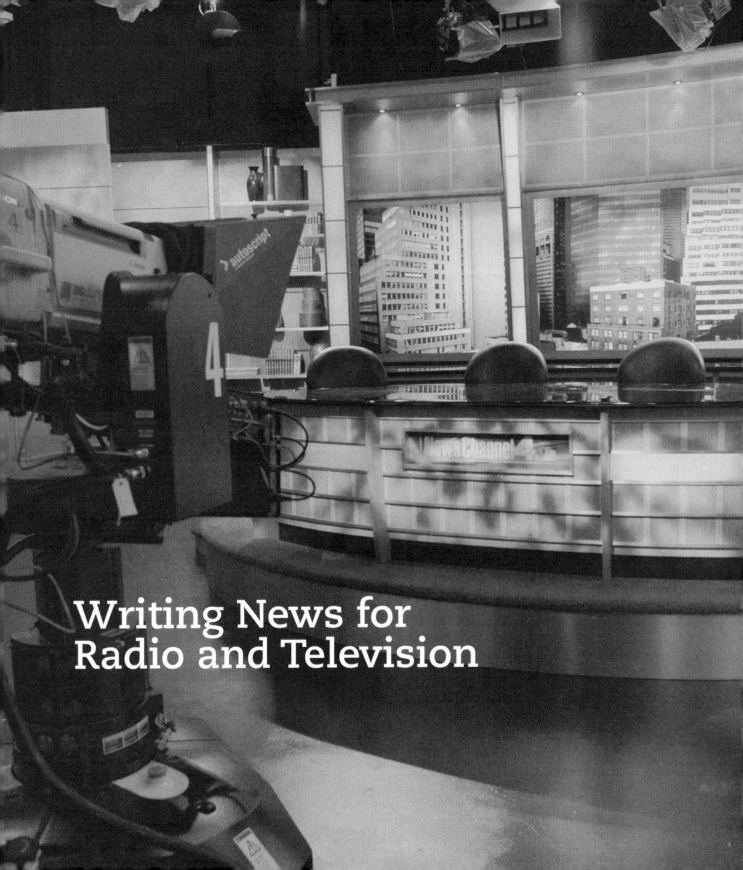

Writing News for
Radio and Television

13

Television can do what no other medium can do. Read what Robert Bianco wrote in *USA Today* on Jan. 21, 2009:

> Yesterday, on a crisp, sun-drenched day that seemed custom-built to showcase a crowd, millions of Americans—possibly more than have ever watched any other televised event—experienced that moment through TV's coverage of the inauguration of Barack Obama. At an event dedicated to a dream no longer deferred, TV did what no other medium, from print to blogs to webcasts, can do as well: It conferred a sense of union and participation, a feeling that you were sharing the experience, not only with those who were there but with everyone who was watching.

Bianco wrote only of the millions in America. He did not mention the millions and millions throughout the world. What he wrote about the "union and participation" of the millions watching the event on television in America was equally true of those in Germany and Kenya.

Bianco's final paragraphs are also worth noting:

> Still, memories of babble will quickly fade. What will remain are those images of an inauguration unlike any other—and yet, in its commemoration of the peaceful, democratic transfer of power, exactly like every other.
>
> And with TV, we all were there.

During Barack Obama's inauguration, television did what it does best: It told the world the details of what happened. During major news events, radio and television newscasters repeat their reports and update their audience as the news develops. If you tune in to CNN, you not only see what's happening and listen to commentary, you also see additional headlines streaming below the picture on a ticker tape. You can pay attention to the news you are most interested in, and you feel as if you are witnessing history. The anchor will remind viewers to go to the network's website, for more information about the story in a written format with more details than the on-air version can offer.

Of course, reporters are not always present to record the news while it is happening. Much of the time, journalists must write and report news after it has occurred. Many, if not most, radio and television stations provide at least some news that is written by journalists working for the wire services, such as the Associated Press or Reuters.

These days, they may also be writing for podcasts, blogs, wikis and online sites such as Twitter, YouTube and Facebook.

The process of selecting and writing news for these online media is different from what's done for print. This chapter, however, explores only the differences between news reporting and writing for print, and news reporting and writing for radio and television. Even if your primary emphasis is not radio or television news, in this day of converging media in news rooms, you may be called upon to work with radio and television reporters and even to prepare copy for their reports. And if you are writing for radio or television news, almost certainly you will be called upon to contribute to the station's website.

269

Radio and television stations have expanded their news operations to give background for stories they don't have time to air. Rather than interrupt programming when new facts arrive on a developing story, they often send listeners and viewers to their websites. CNN and MSNBC, for example, often do that and use instantaneous tools to reach their audiences quickly. Tools such as e-mail, text messaging, Twitter, Facebook and mobile applications offer a "push" method of delivering the news. Audiences do not have to go to the news operation on television or a website to feel informed. The information can go to them. In the new world of convergence, you may well be expected to write radio and television copy, in addition to online copy, for multiple forms of delivery.

CRITERIA FOR SELECTING RADIO AND TELEVISION NEWS

All of the news criteria you have learned so far apply to the selection of news for all media. However, four criteria specifically distinguish radio and television news selection from print news: Radio and television news writers emphasize timeliness above all other news values, information more than explanation, news with audio or visual impact, and people more than concepts.

Timeliness

The radio and television news writer emphasizes one criterion of news value more than any other: timeliness. *When* something happened often determines whether a news item will be used in a newscast. The breaking story receives top priority.

Radio and television news "goes to press" many times a day. If an event is significant enough, regular programming can be interrupted. The sense of immediacy influences everything in radio news, from what is reported to how it is reported. Often this is true of television news as well. Even when radio and television air documentaries or in-depth segments, they typically try to infuse a sense of urgency, a strong feeling of the present, an emphasis on what's happening now.

Information

Timeliness often determines why a news item is broadcast; time, or lack of it, determines how it is reported. Because airtime is so precious, radio and television reporters are generally more concerned with information than with explanation. Most stories must be told in 20 to 30 seconds; rarely does a story run longer than two minutes. A minute of news read aloud is only 15 lines of copy, or about 170 to 180 words. After you subtract time for commercials, a half-hour newscast has only 22 minutes of news, which equates to about one-half of the front page of a newspaper. Although radio and television news writers may never assume that their audience knows anything about a story, they may often have to assume that listeners or viewers will turn to newspapers, newsmagazines or the Internet for further background and details. Often newscasts include time to remind viewers to go to the news outlet's website to expand their view of the story so that viewers can get extra perspective on a story without relying on a different news outlet.

Of course, because of the long success of *60 Minutes* and because of relatively low production costs, newsmagazine formats such as *20/20* and *Dateline NBC* continue to be popular. These programs represent a somewhat different challenge to television news writers, but even in a newsmagazine format, the writing resembles that done for television news.

Audio or Visual Impact

Another difference between radio and television on the one hand and print news on the other results from the technologies involved. Some news is selected for radio because a reporter has recorded an on-the-scene audio report. Some news is selected for television because it is visually appealing or exciting. For this reason, news of an accident or fire that may get attention only in the records column of the newspaper may get important play on a television newscast. If a television crew returns with good pictures of an event, that event often receives prominence in the next newscast.

In today's world of convergence journalism, whether you work for a news organization, for a public relations firm or in organization communications, you may have to decide which of the media will best carry your messages and attract the most attention from your audience. Understanding what kind of information is attractive to a television or radio audience will help encourage coverage by the news outlet.

People

More often than print does, radio and television attempt to tell the news through people. Radio and television writers follow the classic writing formula described by Rudolf Flesch in *The Art of Readable Writing*: Find a problem, find a person who is dealing with the problem, and tell us how he or she is doing. These journalists look for a representative person or family, someone who is affected by the story or who is a chief player. Thus, rather than using abstract concepts with no sound or visuals, television in particular humanizes the story. You can't shoot video of an issue, but you can show visually what impact the issue has on people.

WRITING RADIO AND TELEVISION NEWS

Radio and television news writing emphasizes certain characteristics that newspaper and online news writing do not, and story structure may vary.

Characteristics of Radio and Television News Writing

Because of the emphasis on timeliness, radio and television news writers, like online writers and those who write using social media, must emphasize immediacy

Some all-news radio stations serve their communities with news and commentary 24 hours a day. Many allow listeners to voice their opinions.

and try to write tightly and clearly. Radio and television news writers must work harder at achieving a conversational style.

Immediacy

Radio and television news writers achieve a sense of immediacy in part by using the present tense as much as possible. Note the use of present and present perfect tense verbs (italicized) in this Associated Press story.

WASHINGTON (AP)—More evidence that *there's* room for improvement in urban public schools.

A government study *shows* elementary and middle school children in major cities *perform* worse in science than other students around the country.

Ten urban school districts volunteered to have their students tested and compared with other public school children nationwide. Eighth graders in all ten cities, and fourth graders in all but one, had scores below the national average.

Michael Casserly *heads* a coalition of urban public school districts and *says* more energy *needs* to be devoted to science education. He *says* no one in the country "*has* much bragging rights" when it *comes* to the subject.

The report *underscores* concerns that a lack of scientific achievement could hurt the U.S. economy.

Notice that, for accuracy, the past tense is sometimes necessary, as in the paragraph beginning "Ten urban school districts . . ." But radio and television writers like to use the progressive form of the verb ("is using," "was using," "will be using") to show continuing action and the present perfect tense ("have used") more than the past tense because the present perfect indicates past action that is continuing.

Figure 13.1 shows another example of the use of verb tenses in a television news story. Notice how frequently the present and present perfect tenses are used, compared with the past tense.

Sometimes you stress immediacy by saying, "just minutes ago" or, on a morning newscast, "this morning." If there is no danger of inaccuracy or deceit, though, you can omit references to time. For example, if something happened yesterday, you may report it like this:

> The latest rash of fires in southern California is under control.

But if you use the past tense in a lead, you should include the time element:

> The legislature sent a welfare reform bill to the governor late last night.
> It finished just in time before the spring recess.

Use of Verb Tenses in a TV Story

Present and Present Perfect Tenses

The lead is in the present progressive tense ("are investigating"). The reporter wants to indicate the investigation is continuing.

The attribution "says" is in the present tense to make the report more alive and current. "Getting" is a present participle, again signifying continuing action.

"Reports" and "do not believe" are again in the present tense, even though the event happened in the past.

"Are looking" is present progressive, indicating continuing action. "Is" indicates the man is still a person of interest.

"Do not believe" is a form of the present emphatic, again indicating continuing action.

Police: Jefferson City Couple Found Shot to Death

JEFFERSON CITY, Mo. (AP)—Jefferson City police **are investigating** the shooting deaths of a man and woman.

Jefferson City police Capt. Michael Smith **says** police went to an apartment complex about 3:30 a.m. Monday after **getting** calls from neighbors.

KRCG **reports** that police **do not believe** anyone other than the couple **was** in the apartment.

Police **are looking** for a man who **is** a person of interest in the case.

Authorities **do not believe** the killings **were** drug- or gang-related.

Past Tense

"Was" is simple past tense. No one is presently in the apartment.

"Were" is past tense, indicating that the killings took place in the past.

Figure 13.1
To convey a sense of immediacy, radio and television news writers use the present or present perfect tense whenever possible. (Copyright 2009 by The Associated Press. All Rights Reserved.)

The best way to avoid the past tense is to avoid yesterday's story. You can do that by updating yesterday's story. By leading with a new development or a new fact, you may be able to use the present tense.

Remember, radio and television are "live." Your copy must convey that important characteristic.

Conversational Style

Although "write the way you talk" is questionable advice for most kinds of writing, with some exceptions, it is imperative for radio and television news writing. "Read your copy aloud" is good advice for most kinds of writing; for radio and television news writing, that's what it's all about.

Write so that your copy *sounds* good. Use simple, short sentences, written with transitive verbs in the active voice. Transitive verbs do things *to* things; they demand an object. People rarely use verbs in the passive voice when they talk; it usually sounds cumbersome and awkward. You don't go around saying, "Guess what I was just told by somebody." "Was told" here is in the passive voice; the subject is being acted upon. Note the preposition "by" also tells you the verb is in the passive voice. "Guess what somebody just told me" is active and more natural, less wordy and stronger. "Told" is in the active voice; the subject is doing the acting.

Because casual speech contains contractions, an occasional contraction is OK in radio and television news writing as long as your pronunciation is clear. But remember that the negative "not" is more clearly understood when you use the whole word rather than a contraction. Conversational style also permits the use of occasional fragments. Sentences are sometimes strung together loosely with dashes. They sometimes begin with the conjunction "and" or "but," as in the following example from the Associated Press:

> SPRING LAKE, N.C. (AP)—Aubrey Cox keeps giving police the slip. But he's had lots of practice—he's been doing it for 41 years.

Writing in conversational style does not mean that you may use slang, colloquialisms or incorrect grammar. Nor does it mean that you can use vulgar or off-color expressions. Remember that your audience includes people of all ages, backgrounds and sensitivities.

Tight Phrasing

You must learn to write in a conversational style without being wordy. That means you must condense. Use few adjectives and adverbs. Reduce the use of the passive voice to save a couple of words. Make each word count.

Keeping it short means selecting facts carefully because often you don't have time for the whole story. Radio and television newscasters want good, tight writing

> **"**Good television journalism presents news in the most attractive and lucid form yet devised by man.**"**
>
> — Bill Small, veteran broadcaster, former president of CBS News

that is easy to follow. Let's examine how a wire story written for newspapers can be condensed for radio and television. Look at this newspaper wire story.

ST. CHARLES—The husband of a former St. Charles County prosecutor faces a drug charge after police said he was growing 359 marijuana plants in the basement of their Portage des Sioux home.

Max Conley, 42, of the 900 block of Pawnee Drive, was charged Tuesday with producing a controlled substance, a felony. He is married to Ella Boone Conley, who was put on administrative leave on Aug. 25, pending the results of the investigation. She resigned on Sept. 26 and now works for a law firm in St. Peters.

Her attorney has said she didn't know about the marijuana and was only living there part time because of problems between the couple.

The investigation began after the St. Charles County Regional Drug Task Force got information that Max Conley was growing marijuana. A detective went to the house on Aug. 24 and Conley gave him permission to search the home. The detective found the plants in the basement "in various stages of growth," according to court documents, and he also found lights, wiring, chemicals, potting soil and pots being used to grow the plants.

The court documents said Conley admitted growing the marijuana.

A warrant was issued Tuesday for his arrest, and bail was set at $25,000. At the request of St. Charles County Prosecuting Attorney Jack Banas, a special prosecutor from the St. Louis circuit attorney's office, Jeannette Graviss, headed the investigation.

Graviss said Tuesday that there was not enough evidence to charge Ella Boone Conley and that she was not home when police went to the house. She said Max Conley did not have a job.

Banas did not want to talk about specifics of the case but said it was Boone Conley's decision to resign from his office. He also said the entire situation has been difficult to deal with.

Boone Conley's attorney, Joe Green, said in an interview in September that she resigned to protect the integrity of the St. Charles County prosecuting attorney's office. He also said she was planning to file for divorce. She had filed for divorce in 2002, but the case was later dismissed.

Conley's attorney, Joe McCulloch, said Conley would turn himself in this morning but would not comment further.

Green and Boone Conley could not be reached for comment Tuesday. Conley also could not be reached.

Boone Conley, 44, had worked as an assistant prosecutor in St. Charles County for 13 years and ran unsuccessfully for the Republican nomination for associate circuit judge in the Aug. 8 primary.

Most recently, she had headed the child support enforcement unit.

The print story has 429 words.

Here's how it appeared on the Associated Press *broadcast* wire in its entirety:

ST. CHARLES, Mo. (AP)—The husband of a former St. Charles County prosecutor is accused of growing 359 marijuana plants in the basement of their home.

Forty-two-year-old Max Conley was charged yesterday with felony producing a controlled substance. Conley's attorney says he plans to turn himself in this morning. He is married to Ella Boone Conley, who resigned from the prosecutor's office September 26th amid the investigation.

She ran unsuccessfully for the Republican nomination for associate circuit judge in the August eighth primary and now works for a law firm in St. Peters.

Her attorney says she was unaware of the marijuana and was only living in the home part time because of domestic problems. Ella Boone Conley has not been charged in the case.

The broadcast version has just 128 words. Listeners are given just the bare facts. They must turn to their newspaper or online news source for the details. One newspaper story is often the same length as two or three broadcast stories and perhaps a half dozen online stories.

In radio and television news, tight writing is important even when there is more time. These writers usually strive to waste no words, even in documentaries, which provide in-depth coverage of events.

Clarity

Unlike readers of newspaper and Internet news sources, radio and television news audiences can't go back over the copy. They see or hear it only once, and their attention waxes and wanes. So you must try hard to be clear and precise. All of the emphasis on condensing and writing tightly is useless if the message is not understood.

Clarity demands that you write simply, in short sentences filled with nickel-and-dime words. Don't look for synonyms. Don't be afraid to repeat words or phrases. Oral communication needs reinforcement. Avoid foreign words and phrases. Avoid phrases like "the former" and "the latter." Repeat proper names in the story rather than use pronouns. The listener can easily forget the name of the person to whom the pronoun refers.

When you are tempted to write a dependent clause in a sentence, make it an independent clause instead. Keep the subject close to the verb. Close the gap between the doer and the activity. This version doesn't do that:

> A man flagged down a Highway Patrol officer near Braden, Tennessee, today and told him a convict was hiding in his house. The prisoner, one of five who escaped from the Fort Pillow Prison on Saturday, surrendered peacefully.

The second sentence contains 12 words between the subject, "prisoner," and the main verb, "surrendered." By the time the broadcaster reaches the verb, many listeners will have forgotten what the subject was. The story is easier to understand this way:

> A man flagged down a Highway Patrol officer near Braden, Tennessee, today and told him a convict was hiding in his house. The prisoner surrendered peacefully. He's one of five who escaped from the Fort Pillow Prison on Saturday.

❝Short words are best, and old words, when short, are best of all.❞

— Winston Churchill

The third sentence is still a complex sentence ("who escaped . . ." is the dependent clause), but it is more easily understood. A complex sentence is often just that—complex—only more so in oral communication.

Clarity also requires that you resist a clever turn of phrase. Viewers and listeners are probably intelligent enough to understand it, but a good figure of speech takes time to savor. If listeners pause to savor it (if they grasped it in the first place), they will not hear what follows. For that reason, clever columnists often fail as radio commentators.

Even more dangerous than figures of speech are numbers. Don't barrage the listener or viewer with a series of numbers. If you must use statistics, break them down so that they are understandable. For example, it is better to say that one of every four Americans smokes than to say there are 47 million smokers in the United States. You may be tempted to say how many billion dollars a federal program will cost, but you will help listeners understand if you say that the program will cost the average wage earner $73 for each of the next five years. Television reporters often take advantage of the visual medium to help explain numerical information. An on-air graphic illustrating the data given in the text will help the audience understand the information.

Story Structure

Now that you know the characteristics of radio and television writing, let's examine the story structure. Writers must craft radio and television leads somewhat differently from the way they cast print and online leads. They also must construct special introductions and conclusions to video or audio segments and synchronize their words with taped segments.

Writing the Radio and Television Lead

Like newspaper reporters, radio and television reporters must grab the attention of their audience. Much of what you learned in Chapter 9 applies to radio and television leads. But be aware that people tend to be doing other things when listening to radio or watching television, so when you write for them, you strive to attract their attention in different ways.

One way is by preparing your audience for what is to come. You cue listeners to make sure they are tuned in. You introduce the story with a general statement, something that will pique the interest of the audience; then you go to the specifics. For example:

> **General:** Things are far from settled for Springfield's teacher strike.

> **Specifics:** School officials and union representatives did not agree on a contract yesterday. They will not meet again for at least a week.

Sometimes the opening sentence will cover a number of news items:

> There were several accidents in the Springfield vicinity today.

Christiane Amanpour, anchor of ABC's *This Week*, was formerly CNN's chief international correspondent. Her authoritative reports from around the world informed millions.

"Cuing in" is only one method of opening a radio or television story. Other leads go immediately into the "what" and the "who," the "where" and the "when." In radio or television news, the "what" is most important, followed by "who" did the "what." The time and place may be included in the lead, but seldom is the "why" or the "how." If time permits, the "why" and the "how" may come later in the story, but often they are omitted.

The first words of the lead are the most important. Don't keep the listener guessing as to what the story is about. Don't begin with a dependent clause or with a prepositional phrase as in this example:

> *With the strong endorsement of Governor Bev Perdue,* SANS Technical Fibers LLC will expand its plant in Rockingham County.

The opening words are meaningless without what comes later. The listener may not know what you are talking about. Here is a better way to introduce this story:

> SANS Technical Fibers LLC will expand its plant in Rockingham County — with the strong endorsement of Governor Bev Perdue.

Be sure to "tee up," or identify, an unfamiliar name. By introducing a person, you prepare listeners for the name they otherwise may miss. Do it this way:

> *Veteran Kansas City, Kansas, businessman and civic leader* Kenneth Durban died yesterday in a nursing home at age 83.

Don't mislead. The opening words must set the proper tone and mood for the story. Attract attention; tease a little. Answer questions, but don't ask them. Lead the listener into your story.

Writing Lead-Ins and Wrap-Ups

Radio and television journalists must learn how to write a **lead-in** that introduces a taped excerpt from a news source or from another reporter. The functions of a lead-in are twofold: to set the scene by briefly telling the "where," the "when" and sometimes the "what," and to identify the source or reporter. The lead-in should contain something substantive. Here's an example:

> A grand jury has decided not to charge a Springfield teenager in the killing of his father. Jan Morrow reports the panel believes the death was an accident.

Lead-ins should generate interest. Sometimes several sentences are used to provide background, as in the following:

> We'll all be getting the official word this morning on how much less our dollars bought last month. The consumer price index for March is expected to show another sharp rise in retail prices. The rate of inflation was one percent in January and one-point-two percent in February. Here's more on our inflation woes from Bill McKinney.

Be careful not to include in the lead-in what is in the story. Just as a headline should not steal word-for-word the lead of a newspaper story, the lead-in should not rob the opening words of the correspondent. The writer must know the contents of the audio report in order to write a proper lead-in.

After the recorded report, you may want to wrap up the story before going on to the next item. The **wrap-up** is especially important in radio copy because there are no visuals to identify the person just heard. If the story reported by Evelyn Turner was about a meeting to settle a strike, you might wrap up Turner's report by adding information:

> Turner reports negotiations will resume tomorrow.

A wrap-up like this gives your story an ending and clearly separates it from the next story.

Writing to the Video

Writing for a video report begins with the selection of the subject and deciding how it is to be shot. The writing continues through the editing process and is done with the pictures clearly in mind.

Words and pictures must be complementary, never interfering with each other, never ignoring each other. Your first responsibility is to relate the words to the pictures. If you do not, viewers will not get the message because they will be wondering what the pictures are about.

> **"**Writing a silence is as important as writing words. We don't rely on video enough.**"**
>
> — John Hart, prize-winning TV newsman

You can, however, stick too closely to the pictures by pointing out the obvious in a blow-by-blow account. You need to avoid both extremes and use what Russ Bensley, formerly of CBS News, calls the "hit-and-run technique." This means that at the beginning of a scene or when a scene changes, you must tell the viewer where you are or what is happening. Once you are into the scene, the script may be more general and less closely tied to the pictures.

Suppose the report concerns the continuation of a hospital workers' strike and the opening scene shows picketers outside the hospital. You can explain the tape by saying:

> Union members are still picketing Mercy Hospital today as the hospital workers' strike enters its third week.

Viewers now know two things that are not obvious on the video: who is picketing and where. If the video switches to people sitting around a table negotiating, you must again set the scene for viewers:

> Meanwhile, hospital administrators and union leaders are continuing their meetings — apparently without success.

Once you have related the words to the pictures, you may add other details of the strike. You must not only comment on the video but complete it as well. Part of completing it is giving the report a wrap-up or a strong ending. Don't be cute, and don't be obvious, but give the story an ending. Here's one possible ending for the strike story:

> Strikers, administrators, patients and their families agree on one sure effect of the strike — it's a bad time to be sick.

Now that you know some principles of writing radio and television news, let's learn how to prepare the copy.

PREPARING RADIO AND TELEVISION COPY

Preparing copy to be read by a newscaster has specific challenges. Your goals are to make the copy easy for the newscaster to read and easy for the audience to understand. What follows will help you accomplish these two goals.

Format

Most radio and television news editors want triple-spaced copy. Leave two to three inches on the top of the page and one to two inches on the bottom.

For radio copy, set your computer so that you have 70 characters to a line (see Figure 13.2). Each line will average about 10 words, and the newscaster will average 15 lines per minute. Start each story on a separate piece of paper. That way, the order of the stories can be rearranged, and stories can be added or dropped easily. If a story goes more than one page, write "MORE" in parentheses at the bottom of the page.

Write television copy on the right half of the page in a 40-character line (see Figure 13.3). Each line will average about six words, and the newscaster will average about 25 lines per minute. Use the left side of the copy for audio or video information. This information, which is not to be read by the newscaster, is usually typed in all caps. The copy that is read generally appears in all caps as well.

In television copy, number the stories and the pages, and start each story on a separate page. Do not hyphenate words, and be sure to end a page with a complete sentence or, if possible, with a complete paragraph. Then if the next page should be missing in the middle of a newscast, the newscaster could at least end with a complete sentence or paragraph.

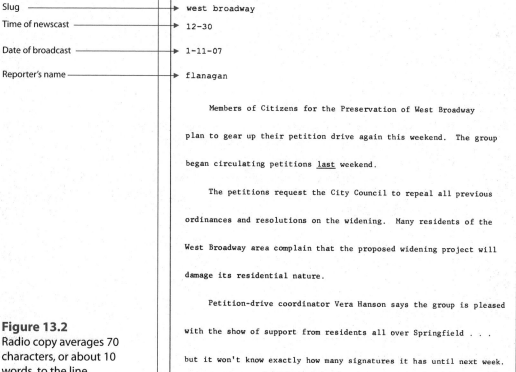

Slug ⟶ west broadway

Time of newscast ⟶ 12-30

Date of broadcast ⟶ 1-11-07

Reporter's name ⟶ flanagan

    Members of Citizens for the Preservation of West Broadway

plan to gear up their petition drive again this weekend. The group

began circulating petitions <u>last</u> weekend.

    The petitions request the City Council to repeal all previous

ordinances and resolutions on the widening. Many residents of the

West Broadway area complain that the proposed widening project will

damage its residential nature.

    Petition-drive coordinator Vera Hanson says the group is pleased

with the show of support from residents all over Springfield . . .

but it won't know exactly how many signatures it has until next week.

Figure 13.2
Radio copy averages 70 characters, or about 10 words, to the line.

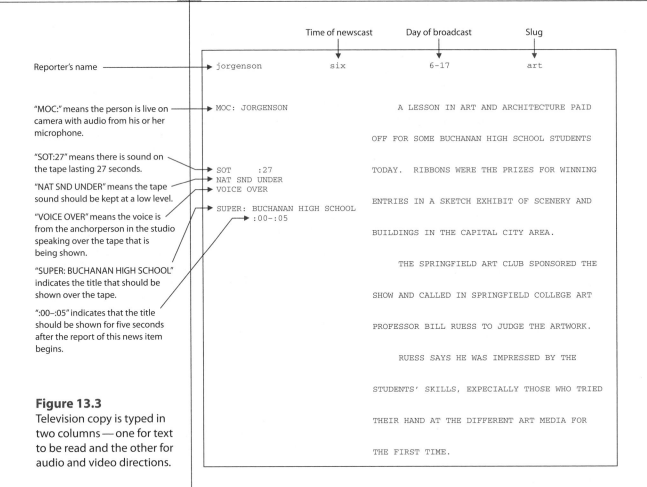

Reporter's name ——————→

Time of newscast   Day of broadcast   Slug

jorgenson   six   6-17   art

"MOC:" means the person is live on camera with audio from his or her microphone.

MOC: JORGENSON   A LESSON IN ART AND ARCHITECTURE PAID

OFF FOR SOME BUCHANAN HIGH SCHOOL STUDENTS

"SOT:27" means there is sound on the tape lasting 27 seconds.

SOT   :27   TODAY.   RIBBONS WERE THE PRIZES FOR WINNING

"NAT SND UNDER" means the tape sound should be kept at a low level.

NAT SND UNDER
VOICE OVER   ENTRIES IN A SKETCH EXHIBIT OF SCENERY AND

"VOICE OVER" means the voice is from the anchorperson in the studio speaking over the tape that is being shown.

SUPER: BUCHANAN HIGH SCHOOL
        :00-:05   BUILDINGS IN THE CAPITAL CITY AREA.

"SUPER: BUCHANAN HIGH SCHOOL" indicates the title that should be shown over the tape.

THE SPRINGFIELD ART CLUB SPONSORED THE

":00-:05" indicates that the title should be shown for five seconds after the report of this news item begins.

SHOW AND CALLED IN SPRINGFIELD COLLEGE ART

PROFESSOR BILL RUESS TO JUDGE THE ARTWORK.

RUESS SAYS HE WAS IMPRESSED BY THE

STUDENTS' SKILLS, EXPECIALLY THOSE WHO TRIED

THEIR HAND AT THE DIFFERENT ART MEDIA FOR

THE FIRST TIME.

Figure 13.3
Television copy is typed in two columns — one for text to be read and the other for audio and video directions.

At most stations, you prepare copy for a teleprompter, an electronic device that projects the copy over the camera lens in the studio so the newscaster can read it while appearing to look straight into the lens.

Date the first page of your script, and type your last name in the upper left-hand corner of every page. Stations vary regarding these directions. The newscast producer determines the slug, or identifying name, for a story and its placement. Some producers insist that the slug contain the time of the broadcast.

Stations with computerized news rooms may use scripting software that alters these formats somewhat. The systems help number the pages for you and can keep track of how long a script might run on the air.

Names and Titles

In radio and television style, unlike that followed by newspapers, well-known names, even on first reference, are not given in full. You may say Senator Snowe of

Maine or Governor Gregoire of Washington. Don't use middle initials unless they are a natural part of someone's name (Edward R. Murrow) or unless they are necessary to distinguish two people with the same first and last names, as with George W. Bush and George H.W. Bush.

Titles should always precede names so that listeners are better prepared to hear the name. When you use titles, omit the first name and middle initial. For example, you would say Federal Reserve Chairman Bernanke and Justice Ginsburg.

Pronunciation

You must help the newscaster pronounce the names of people and places correctly. To do this, write out difficult names phonetically in parentheses. MSNBC has its own reference list, and many individual stations have their own handbooks. The Associated Press offers a pronunciation guide for names that are currently in the news. Also, a growing number of websites offer audio examples on how to pronounce a name or word. Look up difficult names in unabridged dictionaries. If you don't find the name there, call the person's office, or the consulate or embassy. If the name is of a U.S. town, try calling someone in that town. There is no rhyme or reason to the way some people pronounce their names or to the way some names of places are pronounced. Never assume. Never guess. Find out. Here's an example of how you should write out difficult names:

> ZAMBOANGA, Philippines (AP) — There's been another deadly bombing in the Philippines.
>
> A bomb exploded near a Roman Catholic church in the southern city of Zamboanga (zahm-BWAHNG'-gah), killing one person and injuring 12.

Perhaps most people would know how to pronounce Lima (LEE-mah), Peru, but not everyone would correctly pronounce Lima (LIE-mah), Ohio. You must note the difference between NEW-erk, N.J., and new-ARK, Del., both spelled "Newark." And who would guess that Pago Pago is pronounced PAHNG-oh PAHNG-oh?

Abbreviations

Generally, do not use abbreviations in your copy. It is easier to read a word written out than to read its abbreviation. Do not abbreviate the names of states, countries, months, days of the week or military titles. You may use the abbreviations *Dr., Mr., Mrs.* and *Ms.*, and *a.m.* and *p.m.*

When you do abbreviate a name or phrase, use hyphens instead of periods to prevent the newscaster from mistaking the final period in the abbreviation for the period at the end of the sentence. You may abbreviate *United States* when you use it as a noun or adjective— *U-S* would be the correct form. If an abbreviation is well known— *U-N, G-O-P, F-B-I*—you may use it. Hyphens are not used in acronyms like *NATO* and *HUD* that are pronounced as one word.

ON THE JOB

Writing News for Radio and Television

Bernard Choi works as a reporter and fill-in anchor for KING (NBC) in Seattle. He previously worked at KWCH (CBS) in Wichita, Kan. He was the political reporter and also spent two years on the education beat at KWCH. During the summer of his sophomore year in college, he interned at WPSD (NBC) in Paducah, Ky. There he won first place in the Randolph Hearst Journalism Awards in television news. He also won first place in the Education Writers Association's Television Hard News category.

"I was a wide-eyed reporter straight out of college," Choi says. "When my new boss offered me a full-time on-air reporting position, I jumped at the chance. The excitement apparently paralyzed my hearing, as I failed to listen to his one condition: I would have to cover a beat, the education beat.

"I had never covered a beat. I never took a beat-reporting class. I didn't know what covering a beat entailed."

Three years, two beats and countless mistakes later, Choi said, "I realized I was in way over my head. But I'm glad no one caught on and that they gave me the chance to discover the most rewarding type of journalism. It allows you to dig the story up from the ground before it appears in a news release or the news wires.

"When other television reporters in the market scrambled when a story hit the newspaper, I was already on it. It's not because I am a better journalist. It's because I did all the hard work and legwork that led up to it."

Covering a beat involves all the mundane tasks: reading city-council agendas, reading planning reports and zoning regulations, trying to decipher state and district test scores, keeping up with boring school newsletters, reading state laws. You don't always get rewarded with a great story, Choi says, but it's the breadth of knowledge and expertise you develop in an area that pays off in the long run.

The most important lesson Choi learned from covering a beat is you have to talk to people. "I'm generally a shy person with people I don't know. I have had to force myself to walk up to strangers and chat. Stories are about people, and what

Symbols and Numbers

Do not use symbols in your copy because newscasters can read a word more easily than they can interpret a symbol. Never use such symbols as the dollar sign ($) and the percent sign (%). Don't even use the abbreviation for number (*no.*).

Numbers can be a problem for both the announcer and the listener. As in newspaper style, write out numbers *one* through *nine*. Also write out *eleven*, because 11 might not be easily recognized as a number. Use figures for 10 and from 12 to 999. The eye can easily take in a three-digit number, but write out the words *thousand*, *million* and *billion*—for example, 3,800,000 becomes *three million, 800 thousand*.

better way to find a story than to talk to people. More often than not, you will get a story from someone who is plugged in a lot faster than trying to search public records."

A good example came one lazy afternoon. "I already had a story for the day, and I had time to spare at City Hall. I had made a personal resolution to talk more often with the city-council members. Because I had an hour to spare, I went to the council office to hunt a council member down. Once I got there I was told everyone had gone to lunch. Disappointed, I started walking to my car. Then I turned back and headed up to the cafeteria, where I spotted one council member. I hesitated at the door. I had already eaten, and I didn't want to interrupt. After five minutes of internal debate, I bought a lunch and sat next to the council member and started making small talk."

Thirty minutes later, Choi found out the U.S. Attorney's Office was in town covertly investigating former council members for questionable oversight; the city was ready to offer incentives to bring in a major corporation; a top city official was steering business to his wife's firm; and the council member's daughter was headed off to a prestigious college on the East Coast.

"There have been other conversations that netted absolutely nothing," he says. "I've wasted many a precious hour talking with an official and wasted many a night looking through agendas. But I've learned it's that one conversation, it's reading an extra page of a city report, it's that extra phone call that makes the difference. I've learned this because I've also been on the losing end."

The people, the organization and the beat you cover will appreciate the extra work. When you go the extra step to really understand the issue, they know. They can tell when you've done your homework and when you're slacking off. You are dealing with their lives. They don't owe you anything. If you don't take them seriously, they will treat you in kind. It's not just makeup and hairspray. This is a serious enterprise.

Choi's final advice: Journalists should say thanks every now and then.

Write out fractions (two-and-a-half million dollars) and decimal points (three-point-two percent).

Some stations have exceptions. Figures often are used to give the time (3:20 a.m.), sports scores (ahead 5 to 2) and statistics, market reports (an increase in the Dow Jones Industrial Average of 2-point-8 points) and addresses (3-0-0-2 Grand Street; in common speech no one would give an address as "three thousand two").

Ordinarily, you may round off big numbers. Thus, 48.3 percent should be written "nearly half." But when dealing with human beings, don't say "more than one hundred" if 104 people died in an earthquake.

Use *st*, *nd*, *rd* and *th* after dates: August 1st, September 2nd, October 3rd, November 4th. Make the year easy to pronounce by using numerals: June 9th, 1973.

Quotations and Attributions

Rarely use direct quotations and quotation marks. Because it is difficult and awkward to indicate to listeners which words are being quoted, use indirect quotes or a paraphrase instead.

If it is important for listeners to know the exact words of a quotation (as when the quoted words are startling, uncomplimentary or possibly libelous), introduce the quote by saying "in his words," "with these words," "what she called" or "he put it this way." Most writers prefer to avoid the formal "quote" and "unquote," though "quote" is used more often than "unquote." Here's an example:

> In Smith's words, quote, "There is no way to undo the harm done."

When you must use a direct quotation, the attribution should always precede the quotation. Because listeners cannot see the quotation marks, they will have no way of knowing the words are a direct quote. If by chance they did recognize the words as a quote, they would have no idea who was being quoted. For the same reason, the attribution should precede an indirect quote as well.

If you must use a direct quotation, keep it short. If the quote is long and it is important to use it, use a tape of the person saying it. If you are compelled to use a quote of more than one sentence in your copy, break it up with phrases such as "Smith went on to say" or "and still quoting the senator." For television, put a longer or more complicated quote on a full-screen graphic display as you read it.

Punctuation

In radio and television copy, less punctuation is good punctuation. The one exception is the comma. Commas help the newscaster pause at appropriate places. Use commas, for example, after introductory phrases referring to time and place, as in these examples:

> In Paris, three Americans on holiday met their death today when their car overturned and caught fire.

> Last August, beef prices reached an all-time low.

Sometimes three periods are used in place of a comma. Three periods also take the place of parentheses and the semicolon. They signal a pause and are easily visible. The same is true of the dash—typed as two hyphens in most word processing programs. Note the dash in the following example:

But the judge grumbled about the news coverage, and most prospective jurors agreed — saying the news coverage has been prone to overstatement, sensationalism and errors.

The only punctuation marks you need are the period, comma, question mark, dash, hyphen and, rarely, quotation marks. To make the copy easier to read, add the hyphen to some words even when the dictionary does not use it: *anti-discrimination, co-equal, non-aggression.*

Stations vary in writing style and in the preparation of copy. But if you learn what is presented here, you will be well-prepared. Differences will be small, and you will adapt to them easily.

Suggested Readings

Bliss, Edward, Jr., and James L. Hoyt. *Writing News for Broadcast*, 3rd ed. New York: Columbia University Press, 1994. This classic text excels in good writing.

Block, Mervin. *Writing Broadcast News — Shorter, Sharper, Stronger*, 2nd ed. Chicago: Bonus Books, 1997. This excellent book was written by a former network news writer.

Freedman, Wayne. *It Takes More Than Good Looks to Succeed at Television News Reporting.* Chicago: Bonus Books, 2003.

Freedman has been called "the best local TV news feature reporter in the country." His book is packed with practical, down-to-earth advice.

Schultz, Brad. *Broadcast News Producing.* Thousand Oaks, Calif.: Sage, 2004. This text teaches how to put together a newscast.

White, Ted. *Broadcast News Writing, Reporting and Producing*, 3rd ed. Boston: Focal Press, 2001. This is the best book

Suggested Websites

http://writing.umn.edu/docs/publications/Irving%20Fang .pdf
This monograph — "Writing Style Differences in Newspaper, Radio and Television News" by renowned author Professor Irving Fang of the University of Minnesota — offers a clear discussion, along with examples of stories in parallel columns demonstrating the differences in style.

www.nab.org
The National Association of Broadcasters website is a wonderful resource for all kinds of radio- and TV-related information. It includes a career center.

www.newscript.com
This site's purpose is to help radio journalists improve their skills as writers and anchors.

www.rtdna.org
The Radio Television Digital News Association promotes excellence in electronic journalism through research, education and professional training. The site features excellent reports and useful links.

www.tvrundown.com
This site describes the latest successful ideas in local news, programming and promotion.

Exercises

1. **Team project.** Your instructor will divide your class into five groups. Each group will watch a local evening television newscast on either ABC, CBS, NBC, FOX or PBS. With the members of your group, make a simple list of the news stories. Then find those stories in the next morning's newspaper, and compare the coverage. Be prepared for a good class discussion.

2. Check to see if the following AP stories written for broadcast follow acceptable broadcast style. Are they technically correct? Do they emphasize immediacy? Change the copy where you think necessary.

   a. **AZ Judge to Decide If 10-Year-Old Faces Rape Trial**
   By Amanda Lee Myers, Associated Press Writer
   PHOENIX (AP)—A 10-year-old boy charged in the alleged gang-rape of an 8-year-old Liberian girl cried in an Arizona courtroom Monday as his schoolteacher testified that he rarely did his homework and often got into fights with other students.

   Toya Abrams, a second-grade teacher at Camelview Elementary School in Phoenix, says the boy had various behavioral problems.

   The boy eventually put his head down on a table and began sobbing, prompting his attorney to ask for a recess.

   The hearing was aimed at helping Judge Dawn Bergin decide if the boy is competent to stand trial. Two mental-health experts found that he is not.

   The boy is one of four Liberian boys facing charges in the alleged attack. A 14-year-old is charged as an adult, a 13-year-old is undergoing a court-ordered process intended to make him competent for trial, and a 9-year-old has been ruled incompetent.

   b. **Canada's "Prince of Pot" Taken into Custody**
   By Jeremy Hainsworth, Associated Press Writer
   VANCOUVER, British Columbia (AP)—Canada's so-called Prince of Pot is now in jail awaiting extradition to the United States for selling marijuana seeds.

   Marc Emery has sold millions of marijuana seeds around the world by mail over the past decade. In doing so, he has drawn the attention of U.S. drug officials, who want him extradited to Seattle.

   Emery has agreed to plead guilty in Seattle to one count of marijuana distribution in exchange for dismissal of all other counts, and the U.S. District Attorney is pressing for a sentence of five to eight years in a U.S. prison.

   Emery will plead guilty in a Seattle court at a later date. Emery will be extradited after Canada's justice minister signs a surrender order.

   c. **Ecuador's Indian Group Protests Water, Mining Laws**
   QUITO, Ecuador (AP)—Hundreds of Indians have blocked Ecuador's Pan American highway in several provinces with rocks, tree trunks and burning tires to protest new water, mining and oil laws.

   Protesters say the laws threaten their lands and will privatize water resources, a charge leftist President Rafael Correa denies. The ruling party-controlled legislature is expected to approve the laws.

   The powerful Confederation of Indigenous Nationalities of Ecuador split with Correa in 2008 when he refused to grant Indians the right to veto concessions to exploit natural resources on their lands under a constitution approved last year.

   Monday's protests on Ecuador's main highway paled in comparison to protests that ousted presidents in 2000 and 2005.

3. Rewrite the following AP newspaper story in broadcast writing style. Assume that the news is current.

   Scientist Appears in Court in Secrets Case
   By Devlin Barrett and Pete Yost, Associated Press Writers
   WASHINGTON (AP)—A scientist who allegedly tried to sell classified secrets to Israel had worked on the U.S. government's Star Wars missile shield program, and the Justice Department declared Tuesday that he had tried to share some of the nation's most guarded secrets.

   Arrested in an FBI sting operation, Stewart David Nozette was jailed without bond and accused in a criminal complaint of two counts of attempting to communicate, deliver and transmit classified information.

   A former colleague of Nozette says the scientist worked on the Reagan administration's Star Wars missile shield program.

   In an interview, Scott Hubbard said that a scientist arrested in an FBI sting, Stewart David Nozette, was primarily a technical defense expert working on the Reagan-era effort formally named the Strategic Defense Initiative.

   "This was leading edge, Department of Defense national security work," said Hubbard, a professor of aerospace at Stanford University who worked for 20 years at NASA. Hubbard said Nozette worked on the Star Wars project at the Energy Department's Lawrence Livermore National Laboratory.

At Energy, Nozette held a special security clearance equivalent to the Defense Department's top secret and "critical nuclear weapon design information" clearances. DOE clearances apply to access to information specifically relating to atomic or nuclear-related materials.

Nozette more recently developed the Clementine bistatic radar experiment that is credited with discovering water on the south pole of the moon. A leader in recent lunar exploration work, Nozette was arrested Monday and charged in a criminal complaint with attempting to communicate, deliver and transmit classified information, the Justice Department said.

Hubbard said that the Clementine project Nozette worked on in the 1990s was essentially a non-military application of Star Wars technology. Nozette also worked for the White House's National Space Council in 1989 and 1990.

Covering a Beat

14

IN THIS CHAPTER
YOU WILL LEARN:

1. Basic principles for covering any beat.

2. How to apply those principles to some of the most common beats.

Eric Berger covers science for the *Houston Chronicle*. He has had the same beat for several years, but the work itself isn't the same at all. The stories haven't changed that much; he still writes about important discoveries, interesting scientists and threatening weather. It's how he reaches readers, and his relationship with those readers, that's different. He explains:

"I began blogging in June 2005, shortly before hurricanes Katrina and Rita. It seems impossible now, but at the time blogging was relatively rare among newspaper journalists, and the idea of linking to other websites was far from mainstream.

"For the first couple of years, the blog was mostly a sidelight to my regular reporting, as I still thought print first."

No more. Now Eric's work appears first, and sometimes only, online. The change was blown in by a series of hurricanes, beginning with Katrina. "It was a weekend, but I decided to try blogging the storm. A day before landfall, I did more than a dozen entries, and my blog was the most popular link on chron.com."

That was just the beginning. In 2009, the *Chronicle*'s coverage of Hurricane Ike was a finalist for the Pulitzer Prize for Public Service. Most of that coverage was Eric's, and most of it appeared on the paper's website, not in print. He says, "My blog traffic was in the millions during the height of the storm. Reader feedback was incredible."

His conclusion: "Quite simply, the rewards today are for journalists who build a brand." His brand, in print and online, is "the SciGuy."

Not all beat reporters become media stars, but few have escaped the changes brought by technology and economics. Additionally, as you saw in Chapter 1, the definition of news itself is broadening. That change extends the range of beats. Along with such standard beats as local government, police, business and sports, cultural beats reflect the interests and activities of a changing America. Some beat reporters cover shopping malls. Some cover commuting. Some cover spiritual life. Some cover cyberspace.

Covering beats is among the most important work in journalism. Economic pressures have cut the staffs in most news rooms, print and broadcast, leaving fewer reporters to stretch their assignments over multiple beats. Often, today's reporters are trying to do more, on several platforms, with less time. Here's Eric Berger again:

"All of the online work has come at a cost. I write fewer stories for the printed newspaper, and those that I do write are of less depth and have less reporting. . . . There's just not the time, and I am being pulled in so many ways."

Still, he says, his editors give him "a free hand to innovate on the Web and try new things as newspapers try to figure out how to succeed in a digital world."

Increasingly, beat reporters tell their audiences not only what is happening but also how to get involved. Stories include telephone numbers and e-mail addresses along with the names of decision-makers. Much of the most useful reporting is done in advance of public meetings, with the goal of enabling citizens to become participants instead of passive onlookers. Readers are regularly invited to use e-mail or online bulletin boards to speak up on public issues. With all these changes, though, beat reporters remain the eyes and ears of their communities. Surrogates for their readers, they keep track of government, education, police, business and other powerful institutions that shape readers' lives.

The principles of good reporting apply to the coverage of any beat. The same principles also apply to specialized publications, including those aimed at particular ethnic groups, industries or professions. A reporter for *Women's Wear Daily* may cover fashion designers. A reporter for *Diario las Americas* in Miami may cover Cuban exile politics. But each is doing the same job: discovering and writing news that's relevant and useful to the publication's readers.

Editors and audiences expect reporters on these new beats, like those in more traditional assignments, to provide information and understanding that will help readers improve the quality of their lives. That's important work, and it's rewarding work. But it's not easy.

PRINCIPLES FOR REPORTERS ON A BEAT

Whether you cover the public library or the Pentagon, the county courthouse or the White House, the principles of covering a beat are the same. If you want to succeed as a reporter, you must be prepared, alert, persistent and wary. And, on any beat, you must be there.

That checklist will help you win the trust of your sources, keep up with important developments on your beat and avoid the trap of writing for your sources instead of your readers. Let's take a closer look at what each of those rules means in practice.

Be Prepared

Where should preparation begin? For you, it has already begun. To work effectively, any journalist needs a basic understanding of the workings of society and its various governments. You need to know at least the rudiments of psychology, economics and history. That is why the best education for a journalist is a broad-based one, providing exposure to the widest possible sampling of human knowledge. But that exposure will not be enough when you face an important source on your first beat. You will need more specific information, which you can acquire by familiarizing yourself with written accounts or records or by talking to sources.

Reading for Background

In preparing to cover a beat, any beat, your first stop should be the news room library (see Chapter 6). The newspaper library is likely to have computer access not only to material that has appeared in that newspaper but also to worldwide networks of information on nearly any topic. You can often access the contents of major newspapers, magazines, research publications and other reference libraries

TIPS

The Successful Beat Reporter Is

● Prepared

● Alert

● Persistent

● There

● Wary

without regard to physical distance. Use the Internet to acquire background and to understand the context of local events and issues. For example, if your new beat is medicine, you might begin with the website of the Association of Health Care Journalists. Television and Web-only news rooms are less likely to have their own libraries. So you'll need to do this research online, often by accessing the electronic archives of the local newspaper. Your local public and university libraries are also valuable resources, with their online catalogs and generally good collections of recent local periodicals.

In your local research, make notes of continuing issues, questions left dangling in previous stories or ideas for stories to come. Go back several years in your preparation. History may not repeat itself, but knowledge of it helps you assess the significance of current events and provides clues to what you can expect.

Library research is only the start of your preparation. You must become familiar with the laws governing the institution you cover. If a governmental organization is your beat, find the state statutes or the city charter that created the agencies you will be covering. Learn the powers, duties and limitations of each official. You may be surprised to discover that someone is failing to do all that the law requires. Someone else may be doing more than the law allows.

Look at your state's open-meeting and open-records laws, too. Every state has such laws, although they vary widely in scope and effectiveness. Knowing what information is open to the public by law can be a valuable tool for a reporter dealing with officials who may prefer to govern privately.

Talking to Sources

Now you're ready to start talking to people. You should conduct your first interviews in the news room with your predecessor on the beat, your city editor and any veterans who can shed light on the kinds of things that rarely appear in statute books or newspaper stories. Who has been a good source in the past? Who will lie to you? Who drinks to excess? Who seems to be living extravagantly? Whose friends are big land developers? Who wants to run for national office? Who has been hired, fired or promoted? Who has moved to a competing company? Remember that you are hearing gossip, filtered through the biases of those relating it. Be a little skeptical.

Some understanding of the workings of your own news room won't hurt, either. Has your predecessor on the beat been promoted? Has he or she been transferred because of unsatisfactory performance? Will an introduction from your predecessor help you or hurt you with your sources? And what are your city editor's expectations? Is your assignment to report almost every activity of government, or will you have time to do some investigative work and analysis? Living up to your boss's expectations is easier if you know in advance what they are.

Only after gaining as much background as possible are you ready to face the people you will be covering. A quick handshake and a superficial question or two may be all you have time for in the first encounter, but within a week you should arrange for sit-down conversations with your most important sources. These are get-acquainted sessions. You are trying to get to know the sources, but don't forget that they need to know you, too, if they are going to respect and trust you.

You may have noticed that the preparation for covering a beat is similar to the preparation for an interview or for a single-story assignment. The important difference is that preparing for a beat is more detailed and requires more time and work. Instead of just preparing for a short-term task, you are laying the foundation for an important part of your career. A beat assignment nearly always lasts at least six months and often two years or more. Understanding that will help shape your first round of meetings with sources.

A story may emerge from those first interviews, but their purpose is much broader. You are trying to establish a relationship, trying to convert strangers into helpful partners in news-gathering. To do that, you should demonstrate an interest in the sources as people as well as officials. Ask about their families, their interests, their philosophy, their goals. Make it clear with your questions that you are interested rather than ignorant. (Don't ask if the source is married. You should already know. Say, "I understand your daughter is in law school. Is she going into politics, too?" Similarly, don't ask if your source has any hobbies. Find out beforehand. Say, "So you collect pornographic comic books. Sure takes your mind off the budget, doesn't it?")

And be prepared to give something of yourself. If you both like to fish, or you both went to Vassar, or you both have children about the same age, seize on those ties. All of us feel comfortable with people who have something in common with us. This is the time, too, to let your sources know that you know something about their work and that you're interested in it.

Was your source elected as a reformer? Ask about the opposition she is encountering. Has your source complained that he lacks the statutory power to do a satisfactory job? Ask if he's lobbying to change the law. Has the industry become more competitive? Ask about strategies for meeting the challenge. Is it budget time? Let your source know you're aware of the problems with last year's budget. Nothing does so much to create a warm reporter-source relationship as the reporter's demonstrated knowledge of and interest in the beat.

Be Alert

Lisa Arthur learned her way around schools in three years on the education beat for *The Miami Herald*. When she was assigned to cover the shooting of a teacher in Fort Lauderdale, she was ready for any possibility. The shooting had attracted national attention, so a throng of journalists gathered outside the building. School officials announced that only a small group of reporters, called a *pool*, would be allowed inside. Faced with head-to-head competition from a Fort Lauderdale *Sun Sentinel* reporter, Lisa thought fast.

Let her tell the story:

> So I said, I covered schools in Broward for three years, and there are dozens of schools I have still never seen the inside of. Have you ever actually been to this school?

TIPS

Talking to Sources

● Talk to your predecessor on the beat, your city editor and veterans in the news room for background.

● Understand your editor's expectations.

● Establish a relationship with sources — demonstrate interest in them.

She says no. (The mind reels. If there ever was a time to flat-out lie, this was it.)

I said, Look, no offense, but if you knew them that well, they would have just picked you as the pool reporter and not sent you over here to fight it out with us folks they've never seen before. . . . My suggestion is we flip a coin.

She said okay. . . .

I flip. She calls heads. It lands in my palm ever-loving tails side up. . . .

We ended up being in there for about 30 to 40 minutes only. The leash was more like a choke chain. But it was understandable. I got lucky because the guy in there coordinating the mental health team was a psychologist from the Miami-Dade school district. So he was extremely helpful and went as far as he could.

Afterwards I had to give a debriefing to every outlet that wanted it. I literally gave everyone everything in my notebook . . . and all the quotes I used. But nobody could write the inside-the-school story the way we could without giving it a "from pool report" byline. . . .

I could have explained not getting in there to my bosses. No one expected me to. Just getting to the coin toss was a major victory for us. I don't know how she explained it.

Sometimes, being alert means thinking fast and seizing an opportunity. Sometimes, it means recognizing an important story when others don't. Important stories are seldom labeled as such. In many cases, the people involved may not realize the significance of what they are doing. Probably more often they realize it but hope nobody else will. The motivation for secrecy may be dishonesty, the desire to protect an image or a conviction that the public will misunderstand.

If your beat is a government agency, you will find that many public officials and public employees think they know more about what is good for the public than the public does. The theory of democratic government is that an informed citizenry can make decisions or elect representatives to make those decisions in its own best interests. If you are the reporter assigned to city hall, the school board or the courthouse, you carry a heavy responsibility for helping your readers put that theory into practice. To discharge that responsibility, you must probe beneath the surface of events in search of the "whys" and "hows" that lead to understanding.

When you are presented with a news release or hear an announcement or cover a vote, ask yourself these questions before passing the event off in a few paragraphs:

- **Who will benefit from this, and who will be hurt?** If the tentative answer to the first part suggests private interests, or the answer to the second part is the public, some digging is in order.

- **How important is this?** An event that is likely to affect many people for good or ill usually deserves more explanation than one affecting only a handful.

- **Who is for this, and who is against it?** Answers to these questions are often obvious or at least easy to figure out. When you know them, the answers to the first two questions usually become clearer.

- **How much will this activity cost, and who will pay?** An architect's design for renovating downtown may look less attractive when the price tag is attached. The chamber of commerce's drive to lure new industry may require taxpayers to pay for new roads, sewers, fire protection, even schools and other services for an increased population.

The answers to these questions allow you to judge that most important element of news value—impact.

Be Persistent

Persistence means two things to a reporter on a beat. First, it means that when you ask a question, you do not give up until you get an answer. Second, it means that you must keep track of slow-developing projects or problems.

Insisting on a Responsive Answer

One of the most common faults of beginning reporters is that they give up too easily. They settle for answers that are unresponsive to their questions, or they return to the news room not sure they understand what they were told. In either case, the result is an incomplete, confusing story.

"Why is it that our fourth-graders score below average on these reading tests?" you ask the school superintendent.

He may reply, "Let me first conceptualize the parameters of the socioeconomic context for you."

The real answer probably is "I only wish I knew."

Your job is to cut through the jargon and the evasions in search of substance. Often that is not an easy task. Many experts, or people who want to be regarded as experts, are so caught up in the technical language of their special field that they find it almost impossible to communicate clearly. Many others seek refuge in gobbledygook or resort to evasion when they don't know an answer or find the answer embarrassing. Educators and lawyers are particularly adept at such tactics.

Listen politely for a few minutes while the school superintendent conceptualizes his parameters. Then, when he finishes or pauses for breath, lead him back toward where you want to go. One way is to say, "It sounds to me as if you're saying . . ." and rephrase what he has told you in plain English. At those times when you simply are in the dark—and that may be often—just confess your puzzlement and ask for a translation. And keep coming back to the point: "But how does all that affect reading scores?" "How can the problem be solved?" "What are you doing about it?"

All the while, you must ask yourself, "Does that make sense to me?" "Can I make it make sense to my readers?" Don't quit until the answer is yes. You should not be obnoxious, but you do have to be persistent.

Following Up on Slow Developments

Persistence is also required when you are following the course of slow-developing events. Gardeners do not sit and watch a seed germinate. They do, however, check

TIPS

Insisting on a Responsive Answer

● Cut through the jargon and evasions in search of substance.

● Rephrase technical language in plain English.

every few days, looking for the green shoots that indicate that growth is taking place as it should. If the shoots are late, they dig in to investigate.

Beat reporting works much the same way. A downtown redevelopment plan, say, or a revision in a school's curriculum is announced. The story covers the plans and the hoped-for benefits. The seed is planted. If it is planted on your beat, make a note to yourself to check on it in a week or two. And a week or two after that. And a month after that. Start a file of reminders so you won't forget. Such a file often is called a **tickler** because it serves to tickle your memory.

Like seeds, important projects of government or business take time to develop. Often what happens during the long, out-of-public-view development is more important than the announcements at the occasional news conferences or the promises of the promotional brochures. Compromises are made. Original plans turn out to be impractical or politically unpalatable. Consultants are hired. Contracts are signed. Public money is spent. The public interest may be served, or it may not.

Sometimes the story is that nothing is happening. At other times the story may be that the wrong things are happening. Consulting contracts may go to

Skilled reporters are persistent interviewers and insist on responsive answers. Make sure your questions are answered satisfactorily.

cronies of the mayor. Redevelopment may enhance the property values of big downtown landowners. Curriculum revisions may be shaped by some influential pressure groups.

Even if nothing improper is taking place, the persistent reporter will give readers an occasional update. At stake, after all, are the public's money and welfare.

Be There

In beat reporting, there is no substitute for personal contact. Trying to do it all by telephone or e-mail won't work. The only way to cover a beat is to be there—every day, if possible. Joking with the secretaries, talking politics with council members and lawyers, worrying over the budget or trading gossip with the professional staff —you must make yourself a part of the community you are covering.

Remember that the sources who are most important to you probably are in great demand by others, too. They have jobs to do. Maneuver to get as much of their time as you need, but don't demand too much. Do your homework first. Don't expect a school superintendent to explain basic concepts of education. You can learn that information by talking with an aide or by reading. What you need to learn from the superintendent is how he or she intends to apply those concepts, or why they seem to be inapplicable here. Find out what a Class I felony is before asking the police chief why they are increasing. You will get the time you need more readily if busy sources know their time will not be wasted.

There are other simple techniques you can use to build and maintain good relationships with the people on your beat. Here are some of them:

- **Do a favor when you can.** As a reporter, you spend much of your time asking other people to do favors for you—giving you their time, sharing information they need not share, looking up records and figures. If a source needs a favor in return, don't refuse unless it would be unethical. The favors asked are usually small things, like getting a daughter's engagement picture or a club announcement in the paper, procuring a print of a picture taken with the governor to decorate the official's wall, bringing in a few copies of a favorable feature you wrote.

- **Don't shun good news.** One ill-founded but common complaint is that news media report nothing but bad news. Admittedly, there is usually no story when people are doing what they are supposed to do. Sometimes there should be, if they do their duty uncommonly well or have done it for a very long time or do it under the burden of some handicap. Sources like these "good news" stories, and so do readers.

- **Protect your sources.** Many people in government—politicians and bureaucrats alike—are willing to tell a reporter things they are not willing to have their names attached to in print or otherwise. The same is true of people in private business, who may fear reprisals from their employer, co-workers or competitors. Sometimes such would-be anonymous sources are trying to use

ON THE JOB

The Baseball Beat

Derrick Goold's beat is baseball. He covers the Cardinals for the *St. Louis Post-Dispatch*. He loves the work, but that's what it is — work. The demands of covering a beat in the age of convergence require him to be fast and flexible. Here's how he describes his job:

The species of journalist known as beat reporter has two habitats: on deadline and online. For those of us out in the field — working the beats, breaking news and plowing copy — spending the day wired has taken on an entirely new and noncaffeinated meaning. As readers have become increasingly plugged in, reporting has become increasingly real-time and information increasingly available and desired.

My days include a variety of vehicles for reporting. There is the newsletter to write for subscribers in the morning, the blog for the midday traffic, the news update when news needs updating, the radio appearance in the afternoon and the pregame television spot. All sorts of new verbs have been introduced to our inky lexicon: *chat, hit, take, blog* and *tweet.*

Beat writers have become the on-call educated experts, especially in sports and politics. The ability to write and report are still paramount, but the agility to go on the radio, on TV and online and articulate those reports is a benefit to the paper and the writer. That often means breaking from the traditional stoicism of a beat writer and residing in the nebulous place between unbiased and opinionated. Call it assertively analytical. Consider it the future. Nimble beat writers excel.

They also don't forget their roots. Reporters have never been more accessible to their readers. There's interaction, accountability and a 24-hour news cycle. The media is a many-tentacled beast pulling at a beat writer. But a beat writer has to know when it's time to stop writing, stop blogging, stop appearing and get back to the bedrock job of reporting. Step off the hamster wheel and remember that good output requires better input.

As many avenues as these platforms have opened up for our writing, they have also made it possible for our reporting to be deeper, more inventive and more instructive. It is also reporting that sets a beat writer apart. A beat reporter's chats, blogs, hits, updates and tweets have gravity because of reporting.

Content may be the coal of this new media engine. Reporting is still the fire.

you to enhance their own positions. You have to protect yourself and your readers against that possibility. Confer with an editor if you have doubts. Most news organizations are properly wary of relying on unnamed sources. Sometimes, though, the requests for anonymity are valid, necessary to protect the source's career. Once you have agreed to protect a source, you must do it. Don't tell anyone but your editor. An inability to keep your mouth shut can cost you more than a source. It can cost you your reputation. (The protection of sources has legal as well as ethical implications. So-called shield laws in some states offer limited exemptions for journalists from legal requirements to disclose sources; see Chapter 21. But there are no blanket exemptions.)

- **Above all, be accurate.** Inaccurate reporting leads first to loss of respect from sources, then to loss of the sources themselves and finally to loss of the job. If you are a good, tough reporter, not all of the contacts on your beat will love you. But if you are an accurate reporter, they will respect you.

Remember, beat reporting is a lot like gardening. Both require you to be in the field every day, cultivating. And in both, the amount of the harvest is directly proportional to the amount of labor invested.

Be Wary

The point of all this effort—the preparation, alertness, persistence and personal contact—is to keep your readers informed. That is an obvious statement, but it needs to be made because every reporter on a beat is under pressures that can obscure the readers' importance. You must be wary of this problem.

You will have little to do with 99.9 percent of your readers. They will not write you notes when you have done a story they like or call you when they dislike what you have written. They will not offer to buy you a cup of coffee or lunch, or stop you in the hall to urge you to see things their way. But your sources will.

If you write that city council members are thinking about raising the property-tax rate, you will probably hear complaints from council members about premature disclosure. If you write that the police department is wracked by dissension, expect a less-than-friendly reaction from the chief. If you write that the CEO of a major business is looking for a new job, the chances are that he or she will deny it even though the story is true.

All sources have points of view, programs to sell, careers to advance, opponents to undercut. It is likely that they will try to persuade you of the merit of their viewpoint, try to sell their programs through the columns of your newspaper, try to shape the news to help their careers.

Be wary of sources' efforts to use you. You can lose the critical distance a reporter must maintain from those being covered. When that happens, you start thinking like a participant rather than an observer. You begin writing for your sources rather than your audience. This is a real danger. No one can spend as much time as a beat reporter does with sources or devote as much effort to understanding them without becoming sympathetic. You may forget that you are writing for the outsiders when you associate so closely with the insiders.

ONLINE COVERAGE

Before we apply those principles to specific beats, let's look briefly at the opportunities and challenges online journalism presents to beat reporters.

Online reporting offers the opportunity for instant reporting. With cell phones, digital cameras and laptop computers, reporters can and do file short reports and even photographs for posting on the website as the story unfolds. For newspaper reporters, this is a high-tech return to the distant days of multiple editions, when instead of one deadline a day journalists had many. For radio and television reporters, the online opportunities match those of live reporting over the air. Research shows that increasing numbers of online readers rely on websites to stay in touch with news as it happens.

With that opportunity, of course, comes obligation. As you see in the examples of Eric Berger at the beginning of this chapter and Derrick Goold (see the "On the Job" box), beat reporters are expected to use these tools to blog, send Twitter messages and post instant updates to Facebook and other social networking sites throughout the day. All that takes time and energy, often cutting into the reporter's opportunity for in-depth research or even the conversations that are important in developing sources.

Also, reporters are expected to gather and present to readers more information, more detail and more points of view online than either print or broadcast permits. Readers who care enough to follow an issue online want and expect to see the source documents reporters use—and that policy-makers use. They want and expect links to other websites that offer related information or further background.

But what really sets online media apart is interactivity. This term has two practical meanings. First, online journalism permits readers to interact with the information reporters post. Readers can search the website's restaurant reviews, lists of dangerous traffic intersections or any other information that can be tailored to individual needs.

The second type of online interactivity is between journalists and readers. Such conversations give readers a chance to ask follow-up questions and reporters a chance to clarify or personalize the news. Some traditional reporters find this prospect terrifying. They're more comfortable in a world of one-way communication, reporter to reader. That world is quickly disappearing.

COVERING THE MOST IMPORTANT LOCAL BEATS

Your political science courses will introduce you to the structure of government, but from a reporter's viewpoint, function is usually even more important than structure. You must learn who holds the real power, who has the most influence on the power-holders and who are the most likely sources of accurate information. The specifics vary from city to city, but there are some general principles that will help you in covering any type of state or local institution.

- **Information is power.** The holder of information may be a professional administrator (the city manager, school superintendent, police chief or court clerk) or an elected official (the mayor, chair of the county commission or chair of the school board). The job title is unimportant. Find the person who knows in detail how an organization really works, where the money goes and how decisions are made. Get to know that person because he or she will be the most important person on your beat.

- **The budget is the blueprint.** This principle is a corollary of the first. Just as detailed knowledge of how an organization works is the key to controlling that organization, a budget is the blueprint for the organization's activities. The budget tells where the money comes from and where it goes. It tells how many people are on the payroll and how much they are paid. It tells what programs are planned for the year and how much they will cost. Over several years' time, the budget tells where the budget-makers' priorities are, what they see as their organization's role in the community.

  So, find copies of the last two or three years' budgets for your beat. Try to decipher them. Learn all you can from your predecessor and from newspaper clips. Then find the architect who drew up this blueprint—the budget director or the clerk or the assistant superintendent—and get a translation. Ask all the questions you can think of. Write down the answers.

  When budget-making time arrives, follow every step. Attend every public hearing and every private discussion session you can. In those dollar figures are some of the most important stories you will write—stories of how much your readers will be paying for schools and roads and garbage pickup, stories of what they will get for their money.

- **Distributing power and money is politics.** While looking for your beat's power centers and unraveling its budget mysteries, you will be absorbing as well the most interesting part of beat reporting—politics.

  At any level in any type of organization, power and money go hand in hand with politics. Politics provides the mechanisms through which limited resources are allocated among many competing groups. Neither elections nor political parties are necessary for politics. You will have to learn to spot more subtle forms of political maneuvering.

  If you are covering city hall, for example, pay close attention as the city budget is being drafted. You may find the mayor's pet project being written in by the city manager. Nobody elects the city manager, but it is good politics for him or her to keep the mayor happy. Are the builders influential in town? If so, you will probably find plenty of road and sewer projects in the budget. Are the city employees unionized? Look for healthy wage and benefit increases if they are. Is there a vocal retirees' organization? That may account for the proposed senior citizens' center. None of those projects is necessarily bad just because it is political. But you and your readers ought to know who is getting what and why.

  Now suppose an election is coming up, and the builders' campaign contributions will be heavy. A councilman who is running for mayor switches his vote from money for parks to money for new roads. Has a deal been made? Has a vote been sold? That's politics, too. Some digging is in order.

Power, money and politics are the crucial factors to watch in any beat reporting. With this in mind, let's take a closer look at the most important local beats.

City and County Government

Most medium-sized cities have council-manager governments. The mayor and council members hire a professional administrator to manage the day-to-day affairs of the city. The manager, in turn, hires the police and fire chiefs, the public works director and other department heads. Under the city charter, the council is supposed to make policy and leave its implementation to the manager. Council members are usually forbidden to meddle in the affairs of any department.

Some cities, such as New York and Chicago, have governments in which the mayor serves as chief administrator.

Whatever the structure of your city, you will have a range of good sources to draw on:

- **Subordinate administrators.** They know details of budgets, planning and zoning, and personnel matters. They are seldom in the spotlight, so many of them welcome a reporter's attention as long as the reporter does not get them into trouble. Many are bright and ambitious, willing to second-guess their superiors and gossip about politics, again providing you can assure them that the risk is low.

- **Council members.** Politicians, as a rule, love to talk. What they say is not always believable, and you have to be wary of their attempts to use you, but they will talk. Like most of us, politicians are more likely to tell someone else's secret or expose the other guy's deal. So ask one council member about the political forces behind another member's pet project while asking the other about the first's mayoral ambitions. That way you probably will learn all there is to know.

- **Pressure groups.** You can get an expert view of the city's land-use policies from land developers and a different view from conservationists. The manager or the personnel director will tell one side of the labor-management story. The head of the employees' union will tell the other. How about the school board's record in hiring minorities? Get to know the head of the NAACP or of the local Urban League chapter. Public officials respond to pressure. As a reporter, you need to understand those pressures and who applies them.

- **Public citizens.** Consumer advocate Ralph Nader made the term "public citizens" popular, but every town has people—lawyers, homemakers, business executives, retirees—who serve on charter commissions, head bond campaigns, work in elections and advise behind the scenes. Such people can be sources of sound background information and useful assessments of officeholders.

- **Opponents.** The best way to find out the weaknesses of any person or program is to talk with an opponent. Seek out the board member who wants to fire the school superintendent. Look up the police captain demoted by the new chief. Chat with the leader of the opposition to the new hospital. There are at least two sides to every public question and every public figure. Your job is to explore them all.

Once you have found the sources, keep looking, listening and asking for tips, for explanations, for reactions, for stories. The fun is just starting.

Writing for Readers

What does it mean to write for your readers instead of your sources? It means that you must follow several important guidelines.

Translate

The language of bureaucrats, educators, scientists and lawyers is not the same language most people speak. You need to learn the jargon of your sources, but you also need to learn how to translate it into standard English for your readers. The city's planning consultant might say, "Preliminarily, the concept appeared to permit attainment of all our criteria; but, when we cost it out, we have to question its economic viability." Your lead could translate that to:

The proposed plan for downtown redevelopment looks good on paper, but it may cost too much, the city's planning consultant said today.

Make Your Writing Human

In big government and big business, humanity often gets lost in numbers. Your readers want and need to know the impact of those numbers on real people. How many people will be displaced by a new highway? And who are they? Who will be affected by a school closing or a welfare cut? When a police report announced that burglaries were up by 35 percent in the last two months, an enterprising reporter told the story through the eyes of a victim. It began this way:

Viola Patterson picked her way through the shattered glass from her front door, passed the table where her television used to sit, and stopped before the cabinet that had held her family silver.

She wept.

Mrs. Patterson, 72, is one of the more than 75 people victimized by burglars in the last two months.

Think of the Public Pocketbook

If the tax rate is going up 14 cents, how much will it cost the average homeowner? If employees of a firm are seeking a 10 percent raise, how much will that cost the employer? How much of that increase will be passed on to customers? If garbage collection fees are about to be increased, how do they compare to fees in comparable cities?

A city manager proposed "adjusting" the price of electricity to lower the cost to industrial customers and raise rates to private homes. A city hall reporter did a quick survey of comparable cities around the state. Then she wrote:

City residents, who already pay more for their electricity than residents of eight similar-sized cities around the state, would be charged an average of $4 per month more under a proposal announced Tuesday by City Manager Barry Kovac.

Industrial users, whose rate now is about average among the nine cities, would enjoy the second-lowest rate under Kovac's proposal.

Kovac defended his plan as "equitable and necessary to ensure continued economic growth for the city."

Get Out of the Office

City council votes are important, but far more people will have personal contact with government in the form of a police officer, a clerk or a bus driver than with a council member. Go to where government meets its constituents. Ride a bus. Visit a classroom. Patrol with a police officer. Not only will you get a reader's-eye view of your beat, but you may also find some unexpected stories.

Ask the Readers' Questions

Ask "Why?" "How much will it cost me?" "What will I get out of it?" You are the public's ombudsman.

Remember, a good beat reporter has to be prepared, be alert, be persistent and be there. If you always keep in mind the people you are writing *for*, you'll keep the customers — and the editors — satisfied.

Covering a county government is very much like covering a city government. In both cases you deal with politicians, with administrators, with budgets, with problems. The similarities may be obscured by differences in structure and style, however.

Cities are more likely to have professional administrators, for example. The administration of county governments is more likely to be in the hands of elected commissioners, supervisors or judges. Counties, too, are more likely to have a multitude of elected officials, from the sheriff to the recorder of deeds. City governments are more likely to be bureaucracies. One way to generalize about the differences is to say that city governments are often more efficient and county governments are more responsive.

These differences frequently mean, for a reporter, that county government is easier to cover. More elected officials means more politicians. That, in turn, can mean more talkative sources, more open conflict, more points at which constituents and reporters alike can gain access to the governmental structure.

The principles and the problems of reporting are the same. The budget remains the blueprint whether it is drafted by a professional administrator or an elected officeholder. Knowledge is power whether it is the city manager or the elected county clerk who knows where the money goes. Politics is politics.

The Schools

No institution is more important to any community than its schools. None is worse covered. And none is more demanding of or rewarding to a reporter. The issues that arise on the school beat are among the most important in our society. If it is your beat, be prepared to write about racial tensions, drug abuse, obscenity versus free speech, religious conflict, crime, labor-management disputes, politics, sex — and yes, education.

The process of learning and teaching can be obscured by the furor arising from the more dramatic issues. Even when everyone else seems to have forgotten, though, you must not forget that all those are only side issues. The most important part of the school beat is what goes on in the classroom.

Whether those classrooms hold kindergartners or high school students, the principles for covering education remain the same. For the most part, the issues are the same, too. When the schools are private rather than public, you have fewer rights of access.

The classroom is not an easy place to cover. You may have trouble getting into one. Administrators frequently turn down such requests on the grounds that a reporter's presence would be disruptive. It would be, at first. But a good teacher and an unobtrusive reporter can overcome that drawback easily. Many papers, at the start of the school year, assign a reporter to an elementary school classroom. He or she visits frequently, gets to know the teacher and pupils, becomes part of the furniture. And that reporter captures for readers much of the sight and sound and feeling of education.

There are other ways, too, of letting readers in on how well — or how badly — the schools are doing their job. Here are some of them:

- **Examine standardized test scores.** The federal No Child Left Behind law has forced testing to the core of every conversation about school quality. Every school system administers some kind of standardized tests designed to measure how well its students compare either with a set standard or with other students. The results of such tests are or ought to be public information. Insist on learning about them. Test scores are an inadequate measure of school quality, but they are good indicators. When you base a story on them, be sure you understand what is really being compared and what factors outside the schools may affect the scores. Find out what decisions are made on the basis of standardized test scores. For example, do schools with relatively low average scores get additional faculty? Do they get special-education teachers?

- **Be alert to other indicators of school quality.** You can find out how many graduates of your school system go to college, how many win scholarships and what colleges they attend. You can find out how your school system measures up to the standards of the state department of education. Does it hold the highest classification? If not, why not? National organizations of teachers, librarians and administrators also publish standards they think schools should meet. How close do your schools come?

- **In education, as in anything else, you get what you pay for.** How does the pay of teachers in your district compare with pay in similar-sized districts? How does the tax rate compare? What is the turnover among teachers?

- **Get to know as many teachers, administrators and students as possible.** You can learn to pick out the teachers who really care about children and learning. One way to do that is to encourage them to talk about their jobs. A good teacher's warmth will come through.

One reason schools are covered poorly is that the beat often does not produce the obvious, easy stories of politics, personalities and conflict that the city hall and police beats yield. School board meetings usually produce a spark only when a side issue intrudes. Most school board members are more comfortable talking about issues other than education itself, which is often left to the professionals.

The politics and the budgets of schools are very much like those of other institutions. The uniquely important things about the school are the classroom and what happens inside it. Your reporting will suffer if you forget that fact. So will your readers.

Higher Education

Look around you. Relevant and useful stories are everywhere. From the next meeting of the governing board to the classroom of a popular professor, the same principles that apply to coverage of primary schools can be applied on the campus.

Politics, economics and pedagogy — all included as subjects in the course catalog — are also prime prospects for examination. Politics may be partisan, espe-

TIPS

Keeping Up with Issues on the Education Beat

- Subscribe to trade newsletters and magazines.

- Remember the most important part of the beat — what goes on in the classroom.

- Understand what standardized test scores mean.

- Get to know teachers, administrators and students.

cially in public universities with elected or appointed governing boards, or it may be bureaucratic, as individuals or departments compete for power and prestige. The economics of higher education translates to budgets, salaries and tuition costs. Pedagogy, the art and science of teaching, is often overlooked by reporters, but it is really the point of the enterprise.

The Chronicle of Higher Education and campus newsletters are required background reading—the former for insights into national issues and trends, the latter for the nitty-gritty of local developments.

Suppose, for example, that *The Chronicle* reports a slowdown nationally in the skyrocketing rates of tuition. The obvious local story is what's happening on your campus and how that compares with the situation at peer institutions. A less obvious story may be how students are scraping up that tuition money. And an even better, though more difficult, story would be how rising costs affect who can afford to attend, and therefore the composition—by race, ethnicity, social class, even geography—of the student body.

To cover your campus, you'll have to overcome the natural hesitancy of many students to challenge professors, administrators and other authority figures. Try to think of them not as superior beings, but as sources and possible subjects of stories. Then treat them respectfully but not obsequiously, as you would any public official. If your campus is state-supported, they are public officials, after all. That means, among other things, that state laws governing open meetings and records apply.

Here are a few of the issues that should yield good stories on most campuses:

- **Politics.** How are members of the governing board chosen? Who are the members, anyway? What's their agenda? Within the campus, which are the favored departments? How strong is the fraternity and sorority system? How much clout does the athletic department wield with the campus administration or alumni? In an institution founded on free inquiry, just how free is speech for students, faculty and staff?

- **Finances.** How much does the president get paid? The faculty? The janitors? Where does the money to support the institution really come from? The state? Tuition? Alumni giving? Research grants and contracts? Where does that money go? How much is spent on intercollegiate athletics? How much on the English and history departments?

- **Pedagogy.** Who are the best (and worst) teachers on campus? Is good teaching rewarded as much as research is? Among the faculty, who gets tenure and who doesn't? Who does the teaching, anyway? Senior faculty? Graduate students? Part-timers?

You can practice good reporting without leaving your campus.

The Police Beat

The police beat probably produces more good, readable stories per hour of reporter time than any other beat. It also produces some of the worst, laziest reporting and

TIPS

Covering the Police Beat

- Educate yourself in police lore.

- Try to fit in.

- Lend a sympathetic ear.

- Encourage gossip.

- Talk with other police-watchers.

generates many of our most serious legal and ethical problems. It is the beat many cub reporters start on and the beat many veterans stay on until they have become almost part of the force. It offers great frustration and great opportunity. All these contradictions arise from the nature of police work and of reporting.

If you are going to be a police reporter—and nearly every reporter is, at least briefly—the first thing you have to understand is what police officers are and what they do. We hire police officers to protect us from each other. We require them to deal every day with the dregs of society. Abuse and danger are parts of the job, as is boredom. We pay police officers mediocre wages and accord them little status. We ask them to be brave but compassionate, stern but tolerant. Very often what we get is less what we ask for than what we should expect. Police work seldom attracts saints. Police officers are frequently cynical, often prejudiced, occasionally dishonest.

When you walk into a police station as a reporter for the first time, expect to be met with some suspicion, even hostility. Young reporters often are perceived by police as being radical, unkempt, anti-authority. How closely does that description fit you and your classmates?

Police departments are quasi-military organizations, with strict chains of command and strong discipline. Their members are sworn to uphold the status quo. The reasons that police and young reporters are mutually suspicious should be clear by now.

Then how do you cover the police?

- **Educate yourself in police lore.** Take a course in law enforcement, if you can, or take a course in constitutional law. You also might read Joseph Wambaugh's novels for a realistic portrait of the police.

- **Try to fit in.** Keep your hair neat, dress conservatively and learn the language. Remember that police officers, like the rest of us, are usually quicker to trust people who look and act the way they do.

- **Lend a sympathetic ear.** You enjoy talking about yourself to somebody who seems to be interested; so do most police officers. They know they have a tough job, and they like to be appreciated. Open your mind, and try to understand even the points of view with which you may disagree strongly.

- **Encourage gossip.** Police officers may gossip even more than reporters do. Encourage such talk over a cup of coffee at the station, while tagging along in a patrol car or over a beer after the shift. The stories will be one-sided and exaggerated, but you may learn a lot. Those war stories are fascinating, besides. Just don't print anything you haven't verified.

- **Talk with other police-watchers.** Lawyers can be good sources, especially the prosecutors and public defenders who associate every day with the police. Other law enforcement sources are good, too. Sheriff's deputies, for example, may be eager to talk about dishonesty or inefficiency in the city police department, and city police may be eager to reciprocate.

One important reason for all this work is that little of the information you need and want as a police reporter is material you are entitled to under public-records laws. By law, you are entitled to see only the *arrest sheet* (also called the *arrest log* or **blotter**). This record tells you only the identity of the person arrested, the charge and when the arrest took place. You are not entitled by law to see the arrest report or to interview the officers involved.

Writing a story depends on securing more than the bare-bones information. Finding out details depends on the goodwill you have generated with the desk sergeant, the shift commander and the officers on the case.

The dangers—of being unfair, of damaging your reputation and that of your organization—are ever-present. Good reporting requires that you know what the dangers are and how to avoid them.

Sports

A good sports reporter is a good reporter. That's not always obvious, especially to beginners, because the love of sports lures them to the field in the first place. Most sports reporters were sports fans before they were journalists. That's not typical of other specialties. Reporters who cover government seldom attend city council meetings for fun. Medical reporters don't usually spend their days off observing operations. (Instead, they may watch a sports event.)

As a sports reporter and writer, you are likely to find your workplace organized in much the same way as the news department. Typically, in the sports department of a newspaper, there will be reporters, copy editors and an editor. The difference is likely to be the scale. On small papers, the sports editor may double as writer and may even take the photographs, too. On medium-sized papers, the sports reporters usually don't specialize as the news reporters may. One day you may be covering high school swimming; the next, football or a visiting rodeo.

At small and medium-sized broadcasting stations, a "sports department" is likely to consist of one person who serves as writer, photographer and sports anchor at various times of the day or night. The big crews, the "guys in the truck" you hear mentioned on ESPN, are at the network level. At most local stations, you'll be expected to report, to write, to photograph and to deliver your work on camera. Sometimes, when time pressure is great or the game is big, you'll go on the air live, summarizing a game that has just ended or that may even be in progress. Then your skills at ad-libbing will be tested, a challenge print reporters don't face.

One more thing: Don't confuse sports reporters with play-by-play announcers. The latter may be reporters in a literal sense, but they usually aren't journalists. Their skill is in instant description, not the behind-the-scenes digging or the after-the-fact analysis expected of print and broadcast reporters. Often they are hired by the teams they follow or the sponsors they serve instead of by the station carrying their work.

Sports Reporting *Is* Beat Reporting

Before you even thought about sports reporting, chances are good that you were reading, watching and playing sports. In that sense, at least, preparing to be a sports reporter is easier than preparing to cover city hall. But there is more to preparation than immersing yourself in sports. Competition pushes people to their limits, bringing out their best and worst. So you need to know some psychology. Sports has played a major role in the struggles of blacks and women for equality. So you need to know some sociology and history. Sports, professional and amateur, is big business. So you need a background in economics. Some of our greatest writers have portrayed life through sports. So you need to explore literature.

Meet T.J. Quinn, who reports for ESPN: "The myth of the job is that sportswriters sit in the press box, eat hot dogs, live on expense accounts and get to travel all over the country. Mostly true. But covering a beat means keeping track of which players are doing what, who's injured, what a team needs to get better and where they might get it, who wants a contract, who's going to be a free agent, which pitcher is experimenting with a new grip on his slider, which coach is feuding with the owner, which power forward is angry with the point guard because she doesn't pass to the low post enough."

And here's the top of a story that resulted from paying close attention:

Mike Hampton was already a professional athlete the first time he beat his father at basketball.

Until that day, as an 18-year-old minor leaguer, he was oh-for-life against Mike Sr., never walking off the driveway of their Homosassa, Fla., home with so much as a gift win.

When Little Mike was 8 years old, Big Mike blocked his shots. When Little Mike tried to drive the lane, Big Mike would put his body in front of the boy and put him on the ground. The boy bled often but learned to cry less and less. His eyes puffy, his breath short, he would sometimes storm off, but he always came back to play the next day.

"It was gross how tough he was," the new ace of the Mets pitching staff said. "You fall down, get a scratch. 'Get up. It'll stop hurting. Get up; let's go.'"

Big Mike knew it was cruel, and wonders still whether he pushed the boy too hard. But the boy needed to learn that winning meant taking something, not waiting for a handout.

This is a story that entertains while it informs. It shows readers something of the character of an athlete and the meaning of tough love.

Here are a few tips to help you be alert to stories that go beyond the cliché:

- **Look for the losers.** Losing may not—as football coaches and other philosophers like to assert—build character, but it certainly bares character. Winners are likely to be full of confidence, champagne and clichés. Losers are likely to be full of self-doubt, second-guessing and surliness. Winners' dressing rooms are magnets for sportswriters, but you usually can tell your readers more about the game and those who play it by seeking out the losers.

- **Look for the bench warmers.** If you follow the reporting crowd, you'll end up in front of your local version of Alex Rodriguez or Venus Williams every time. Head in the other direction. Talk to the would-be football player who has

To get to the "why" and "how" of a game's outcome, reporters need to dig beneath the mere results. Getting out of the press box to find an interesting story angle or to secure compelling quotes from players and coaches can bring a story to life.

spent four years practicing but never gets into a game. Talk to the woman who dreams of being a professional golfer but is not yet good enough. Talk to the baseball player who is growing old in the minor leagues. If you do, you may find people who both love their sport more and understand it better than do the stars. You may find less press agentry and more humanity.

- **Look beyond the crowds.** Some of the best, and most important, sports stories draw neither crowds of reporters nor crowds of fans. The so-called minor sports and participant sports are largely untapped sources of good stories. More Americans watch birds than play football. More hunt or fish than play basketball. More watch stock-car races than watch track meets. But those and similar sports are usually covered—if at all—by the newest or least talented reporter on the staff. Get out of the press box. Drop by a bowling alley, a skeet-shooting range, the local college's Ultimate Frisbee tournament. Anywhere you find people competing—against each other, against nature, against their own limits—you can find good stories.

Developing Contacts

Being there, of course, is half the fun of sports reporting. You're there at the big games, matches and meets. You're there in the locker rooms, on team buses and planes, with an inside view of athletics and athletes that few fans ever get. If you are to answer your readers' questions, if you are to provide insight and anecdote, you must be there, most of the time.

Sometimes you should try being where the fans are. Plunk down $20 (of your boss's money) for an end-zone seat and write about a football game from the average fan's point of view. Cover a baseball game from the bleachers. Cold hot dogs and warm beer are as much a part of the event as is a double play. Watch one of those weekend sports shows on television and compare the way a track meet or a fishing trip is presented to the way it is experienced in person. Join a city league softball team or a bowling league for a different kind of inside view.

A sports reporter must develop and cherish sources just as a city hall reporter must. You look for the same kinds of sources on both beats. Players, coaches and administrators—like city council members and city managers—are obvious sources. Go beyond them. Trainers and equipment managers have insiders' views and sometimes lack the fierce protectiveness that often keeps players, for example, from talking candidly.

Alumni can be excellent sources for high school and college sports stories. If a coach is about to be fired or a new fund drive is being planned, important alumni are sure to be involved. You can find out who they are by checking with the alumni association or by examining the list of major contributors that every college proudly compiles. The business managers and secretaries who handle the money can be invaluable for much-needed but seldom-done stories about the finances of sport at all levels. Former players sometimes will talk more candidly than those who are still involved in a program. As on any beat, look for people who may be disgruntled—a fired assistant coach, a benched star, a big contributor to a losing team. And when you find good sources, cherish them. Keep in contact, flatter them and protect them. They are your lifeline.

Digging for the Real Story

It is even harder for a sports reporter than it is for a political or police reporter to maintain a critical distance from the beat. The most obvious reason is that most of the people who become sports reporters do so because they are sports fans. To be a fan is precisely the opposite of being a dispassionate, critical observer. In addition, athletics—especially big-time athletics—is glamorous and exciting. The sports reporter associates daily with the stars and the coaches whom others, including cynical city hall reporters and hard-bitten managing editors, pay to admire at a distance. Finally, sports figures ranging from high school coaches to owners of professional baseball teams deliberately and persistently seek to buy the favor of the reporters who cover their sports.

TIPS

Contacts for the Sports Beat

- Players, coaches, administrators
- Trainers
- Equipment managers
- Alumni (for high school and college sports)
- Business managers and secretaries who handle money
- Former players
- People who are disgruntled

TIPS

Digging for the Real Story

- Maintain your distance from the people you cover.

- Keep readers in mind.

- Answer readers' questions about the story behind the story.

- Follow the money.

- Find the real "why."

- Find the real "who."

We are taught from childhood that it is disgraceful to bite the hand that feeds you. Professional teams and many college teams routinely feed reporters. Major-league baseball teams even pay reporters to serve as official scorers for the game. In one embarrassing incident, the reporter-scorer made a controversial decision that preserved a no-hit game for a hometown pitcher. His story of the game made little mention of his official role. The reporter for the opposition paper wrote that if it had been his turn to be scorer, he would have ruled the other way.

Sports journalism used to be even more parasitic toward the teams it covered than is the case now. At one time, reporters routinely traveled with a team at the team's expense. Good news organizations pay their own way today.

Even today, however, many reporters find it rewarding monetarily as well as psychologically to stay in favor with the teams and athletes they cover. Many teams pay reporters to write promotional pieces for game programs. And writing personality profiles or "inside" accounts for the dozens of sports magazines can be a profitable sideline.

Most sports reporters, and the editors who permit such activities, argue that they are not corrupted by what they are given. Most surely are not. But temptation is there for those who would succumb. Beyond that, any writer who takes more than information from those he or she covers is also likely to receive pressure, however subtle, from the givers.

Anywhere athletics is taken seriously, from the high schools of Texas to the stadiums of the National Football League, athletes and coaches are used to being given special treatment. Many think of themselves as being somehow different from and better than ordinary people. Many fans agree. Good reporters, though, regard sports as a beat, not a love affair.

Those sports reporters maintain their distance from the people they cover, just as reporters on other beats do, by keeping their readers in mind. Readers want to know who won, and how. But they also want to know about other sides of sports, sides that may require some digging to expose. Readers' questions about sports financing and the story behind the story too often go unanswered. Accountants have become as essential to sports as athletes and trainers. Talk to them. Readers have a legitimate interest in everything from ticket prices to the impact of money on the actual contests.

When a key player is traded, as much as when a city manager is fired, readers want to know the real "why." When athletes leave school without graduating, find out why. When the public is asked to pay for the expansion of a stadium, tell the public why. One of the attractions of sports is that when the contest is over, the spectators can see who won and how. Often that is not true of struggles in government or business. The whys of sports, however, frequently are as hard to discover as they are in any other area.

Sports figures often appear to their fans, and sometimes to reporters, to be larger than life. In fact, athletics is an intensely human activity. Its participants have greater physical skills, and larger bank accounts, than most other people, but they are people. Sports reporters know that their audience is interested in the real "who" behind the headlines.

Suggested Readings

Houston, Brant, and Investigative Reporters and Editors, Inc. *The Investigative Reporter's Handbook*, 5th ed. New York: Bedford/St. Martin's, 2009. This comprehensive guide to using public records and documents, written by members of Investigative Reporters and Editors, is a must for serious reporters. See also the suggested readings at the end of Chapter 19. They'll be useful in beat reporting, too.

Royko, Mike. *Boss: Richard J. Daley of Chicago*. New York: New American Library, 1971. This is a classic, brilliantly written study of urban machine politics.

Sports Illustrated. This magazine features some of the best examples of how sports should be reported and written.

Suggested Websites

www.espn.com
As every sports fan knows, here you'll find multimedia reporting, commentary, statistics and lots of good story ideas.

www.poynter.org
We list this site repeatedly because it is so useful in so many ways. One feature is its links to nearly every professional journalism organization. See also the bibliography for sources and examples of good current reporting.

www.scout.cs.wisc.edu
The Scout Report is a weekly publication offering a selection of new and newly discovered Internet sources of interest to researchers and educators.

www.stateline.org
This site provides story tips and background information on state government and state-level issues.

Exercises

1. **Team project.** With your classmates, form the class into a news room. Decide on the essential beats to cover. Assign a pool of reporters to each beat. Working with the other members of your group, take the necessary first step toward successful coverage and produce a background memo that identifies key issues and sources for your beat. Present your memo for class discussion. Listen to and comment on other teams' work.

2. Spend some time with any news website. Now compare what you find, and what you can do there, with the content of the newspaper and the television outlet that cover the same area. Which is more useful, more satisfying, more fun?

3. Scout your campus for story ideas. Think of the three broad categories of politics, finances and pedagogy. Write a memo to your editor outlining at least one good idea for each category. What sources would be most useful? What audio or video would you want to accompany your prose?

4. In the library or in a computer database, look up three recent national or international stories about a religious or scientific issue. Write a memo explaining how you would localize each story for your city. Include possible sources.

5. Using LexisNexis or another computer database, examine how two or three major newspapers cover a national beat, such as Congress or a federal agency. What similarities and differences do you see between that work and local coverage? The topics will be different, but what about sources? Do you see any different focus on reader interests?

6. Analyze a local news story about crime. Identify the sources. If you were reporting this story, what other sources would you consult? What specific questions would you try to get answered?

Speeches, News Conferences and Meetings

15

IN THIS CHAPTER
YOU WILL LEARN:

1. How to prepare to cover speeches, news conferences and meetings.

2. What's involved in covering these events.

3. How to structure and write stories about them.

After President Barack Obama reached out to the Muslim world with a major policy speech in Cairo, a Pew Research Center poll showed that the image of the U.S. had improved in 25 countries around the world, sometimes dramatically, and suffered in only one — Israel. In England, France, Germany and Spain, an average of 85.5 percent of respondents said Obama would "do the right thing in world affairs." Only about 15 percent had said the same about former President George W. Bush in 2008.

Speeches and news conferences by world leaders can be powerful and can move polls dramatically, as the Obama speech showed. It's happened many times in the past. Before President Lyndon B. Johnson's televised address on the Gulf of Tonkin incident in 1964, a Harris Survey showed that less than half of the electorate approved of the president's Vietnam policy. After his address, a second poll indicated that 70 percent approved.

Researchers found that voters who listened on radio to the debate between John F. Kennedy and Richard Nixon thought Nixon won it; those who watched on television thought Kennedy won it. Kennedy presented himself better on television and in news conferences. Nixon, in contrast, had little flair for give-and-take and less love for reporters. Consequently, his performance at news conferences added little to his popularity. President Ronald Reagan felt at home in front of cameras, and although he disliked news conferences, his televised speeches helped boost his image tremendously. Town meetings helped President Bill Clinton get to the White House. Former Vice President Al Gore's perceived stiffness on television may have helped put George W. Bush into the White House in 2001.

As a young reporter you probably won't be covering the U.S. president, but your coverage of a speech or news conference by the mayor may have a major impact in your community. So may your coverage of a disputed zoning decision or a meeting of the board of directors of the local animal shelter during a period of controversy. Because the coverage of speeches, news conferences and meetings is similar, we examine all three in this chapter, but you should keep in mind their distinguishing characteristics.

DISTINGUISHING AMONG SPEECHES, NEWS CONFERENCES AND MEETINGS

A *speech* is a public talk. Someone speaks to an audience in person or on radio or television. Regardless of the medium, a speech is a one-way communication. The speaker speaks, and the audience listens, although sometimes a question-and-answer session follows.

Speakers are usually invited and sometimes paid to address an audience. That is not the case with those who hold a *news conference*. People "call" or "hold" news conferences. They do not send invitations to the general public, but they do alert members of the news media. The media respond because of the importance of the person calling the news conference and because the person may have something newsworthy to say. The person holding the news conference often begins with an opening statement and usually accepts questions from reporters. A news conference is meant to be a two-way communication.

Unlike speeches and news conferences, *meetings* are not held with an audience in mind, although an audience may be present and allowed to participate. A meeting is primarily for communication among the members of a group or organization, whether a local parent-teacher association or the U.S. Congress. Reporters who are permitted to witness a meeting tell the public what is of interest and importance. This task of the news media is especially important if the participants are members of a governmental body that spends or allocates taxpayers' money.

PREPARATION

Good reporters know that preparation makes covering a story much easier. In all cases, reporters should do their homework. You prepare for speeches, news conferences and meetings in much the same way. Because these events are usually announced in advance, you often have time for thorough preparation.

Preparing for the Speech Story

Not every speech will demand a great deal of research. Many speakers and speeches will be dry and routine. The person giving the speech will be someone you know or someone you have covered before. At other times you may get an assignment on short notice and be forced to find background information after hearing the speech. In either case, never take the speaker or the topic for granted. Failure to get enough background on the speaker and on the speech almost guarantees failure at writing a comprehensive speech story.

The first step in your research is to identify the speaker correctly. Middle initials are important; sometimes even they are not enough. Sometimes checking the address is not enough. One reporter wrote about the wrong person because he did not know that a father and son with the same name had the same address.

USA Today had to print a "clarification" after reporting that Larry King had made a $1,000 donation to a presidential campaign. The donor was Larry L. King, author and playwright, not Larry King the CNN show host.

Be sure you have the right person. Then, before doing research on the speaker, contact the group sponsoring the speech and ask for the topic. You might find you need to do some reading to prepare yourself to understand the subject. If you are lucky, you may get an advance copy of the speech. Then, check your organization's own library to see what other reporters have written previously about the speaker. If you have access to a national database of newspaper and magazine stories like LexisNexis, use it.

If the speech is important enough, you might want to contact the speaker ahead of time for a brief interview. If he or she is from out of town, you might plan for a meeting at the airport. You might also arrange ahead of time to interview the speaker after the speech. You may have questions and points to clarify.

TIPS

**Preparing for the
Speech Story**

- Be sure you have the right
person.

- Contact the group sponsoring the speech and ask
for the topic.

- Check your newspaper
library for background on
the speaker.

- If the speech is important
enough, contact the
speaker for a brief
interview.

Not every speech will demand that much effort. But even the most routine speech assignment requires preparation. Do not assume, for instance, that Gene Martin, director of the local library, is addressing the state writers' guild to tell members how to use the library to improve their stories. Gene Martin may also be a successful "true confessions" writer, published dozens of times in such magazines as *True Confessions* and *True Romance*. He may be telling guild members how he achieved success.

Sooner or later you may be called on to cover speeches by major political figures, perhaps even the U.S. president. For this task, too, you will need background — lots of it. Doing a good job demands that you read the news and know what is going on. You must keep up with current events.

Preparing for the News Conference Story

Preparing for a news conference is similar to preparing for a speech. You need up-to-date background on the person giving the news conference, and you must learn why the news conference is being held. Often the person holding the news conference has an announcement or an opening statement. Unless that statement is leaked to the press, you will not know its content ahead of time, but you can make some educated guesses. Check out any rumors. Call the person's associates, friends or secretary.

Consult your editor and other staff editors about specific information they want. Then draw up a list of questions to ask at the news conference. Once the news conference begins, you will not have time to think of questions; recording responses to other reporters' questions will keep you too busy. The better prepared you are, the better chance you will have of coming away with a coherent, readable story.

It may be impossible to arrange an interview before or after the news conference. If the person holding the news conference wanted to grant individual reporters interviews, he or she probably would not have called the news conference. But you can always ask — you might end up with some exclusive information.

Preparing for the Meeting Story

You never know what to expect at a meeting, so you must do your best to prepare. Who are the people holding the meeting? What kind of organization is involved? Who are the key figures? Again, the news library is your first stop. Then contact some of the key figures.

See if you can find out what the meeting is about. Perhaps the president or the secretary has a written agenda for the meeting. If you know the main subject to be discussed, you will be able to study and investigate the issues before arriving. Knowing what to expect and being familiar with the issues will make covering the meeting much easier. A reporter with a regular beat — an assigned area of responsibility — usually covers meetings of the most important organizations and groups such as the city council, the school board or the county commission. (Beat reporting is discussed in detail in Chapter 14.) A beat reporter has continuing familiarity with the organization and with the issues involved. Often the meetings of important organizations are preceded by an agenda or an **advance**, a report outlining the subjects and issues to be covered during the upcoming meeting.

COVERING SPEECHES, NEWS CONFERENCES AND MEETINGS

An old story is that of a reporter who prepared well for a speech assignment, contacted the speaker, got a copy of the speech, wrote the story and spent the evening in a bar. Not until after he handed in his story did he find out that the speech had been canceled.

And then there's the yarn about a young reporter assigned to cover a meeting who came back and told the city editor there was no story.

"Why not?" the city editor asked.

"Because the meeting was canceled."

"Why was that?"

"Well," replied the reporter, "when the meeting started, some of the board members got into this big argument. Finally, three of them walked out. The president then canceled the meeting because there was no quorum."

A story about a speech, news conference or meeting often requires direct quotes. Whether you use a recording device or not, be sure to take proficient notes you can use while writing your story, like these reporters interviewing Secretary of State Hillary Clinton.

Of course, the canceled meeting and the circumstances surrounding its cancellation probably were of more interest to readers than the meeting itself would have been.

Preparing to cover an event is only the beginning. Knowing what to do when you get there is equally important. You must cover the entire event—the content of the speech, news conference or meeting; the time, place, circumstances and number of people involved; and the possible consequences of what was said or of the actions taken.

The Medium Matters

What you need to do at a speech, press conference or meeting depends on your final distribution medium. If you're writing a story for print, simply taking good notes, using an audio recorder and getting audience reaction might suffice.

But what if your editor expects a Twitter or mobile phone update from the site of the event or a breaking news item for the website? In that case, you might have to send an instant update, write a brief item for the Web during the meeting—perhaps including a sound bite—and update the story in several forms when the event is complete. You might even be charged with writing a Web story, providing an audio clip and then writing yet another story for the newspaper.

More and more sites are adding video to their websites, which means you may have to learn something about television composition and video editing. That makes reporting today a task more challenging than ever. Print, Web and video coverage require different approaches, and doing all of them at the same time isn't easy. With today's many ways of distributing news information, you need to learn to become a multimedia journalist. Doing so will make you more valuable to your employer.

Getting the Content Correct

You may find a digital audio recorder or video camera useful for covering the content of speeches, news conferences and meetings. Be aware, though, that audio recorders and video cameras often intimidate people who aren't accustomed to being interviewed, so always ask permission to record any interviews you get. Practice using the recorder or video camera. Use it again and again to become familiar with its idiosyncrasies. Make sure you know how sensitive the microphone is. Get to know the camera's operation as best you can.

Some reporters shun even audio recorders because they think that listening to the entire recording takes too long. You may have to listen to a whole speech just to find a certain quote you want to check. But if you have a recorder with a digital counter, you can avoid this problem. At any point in a speech or a meeting when something of importance is said, you need only note the number on the counter. Finding the quotation later will then be easy.

Even if you record an event, take notes in exactly the same way you would if you were not recording. Malfunctions can occur, even with the best machines, at the most inopportune times.

TIPS

Achieving Total Coverage of Content and Event

- Get the content correct. Recorders can be helpful, but always take good notes. Quote people exactly and in context.

- Note the background, personal characteristics and mannerisms of the main participants.

- Cover the event. Look around the edges—at the audience (size, reactions) and sometimes at what is happening outside the building.

- Get there early, position yourself and hang around afterward.

So, with or without a digital recorder, you must become a proficient note-taker. Many veteran reporters wish they had learned shorthand or speed-writing early in their careers. You may find it useful to buy a speed-writing manual and learn a few symbols. Sooner or later every reporter adopts or creates some note-taking shortcuts. You will have to do the same. Learn to abbreviate (*wh* for "which," *th* for "that," *bk* for "book," *st* for "street," *bldg* for "building," etc.). Make up signs (*w/* for "with," *w/o* for "without," *acc/* for "according to"). Whether you're using a notebook or computer, shorthand of this type saves time and allows you to jot down the information accurately.

Taking notes is most crucial when you wish to record direct quotes. As you learned in Chapter 5, putting someone's words in quotation marks means only one thing: You are quoting the person word for word, exactly as the person spoke. Speeches, news conferences and meetings all demand that you be able to record direct quotes. Your stories will be lifeless and lack credibility without them. A speech story, for example, should contain many direct quotes.

Whether covering a speech, news conference or meeting, be careful to quote people in context. For example, if a speaker gives supportive evidence for an argument, you would be unfair not to report it. Quotes can be misleading if you carelessly or deliberately juxtapose them. Combining quotes with no indication that something was said in between them can lead to inaccuracies and to charges of unfairness. Suppose, for example, someone said:

> "Cutting down fuel costs can be an easy thing. If you have easy access to wood, you should invest in a good wood-burning stove. With little effort, you can cut your fuel bills in half."

A reporter who omitted the middle sentence of that quote, even inserting an ellipsis, would make the speaker look ridiculous:

> "Cutting down fuel costs can be an easy thing. . . . With little effort, you can cut your fuel bills in half."

There is more to a speaker than the words he or she is saying. Sometimes, quoting a speaker at length or printing a speech in its entirety may be justified. But when you quote a whole speech, you are recording it, not reporting it. The overall content of the speech may or may not be news. Sometimes the news may be what a speaker left unsaid. You must decide what is newsworthy.

Describing the Participants

In addition to listening to what a speaker says, you must watch for other gestures and expressions. An audio recording does not capture a speaker's facial expressions and gestures. These are sometimes more important than the words themselves.

Simply reporting the words of a speaker (or of the person holding a news conference or participating at a meeting) does not indicate volume and tone of voice,

TIPS

Covering the Event

● Be sure to record what the digital recorder misses — gestures and facial expressions.

● Remember that a person's words often must be measured against his or her background.

● Take note of the tone of questions.

● Note the size of the audience.

inflections, pauses, emphases and reactions to and from those in attendance. You may note that a speaker deliberately winked while reading a sentence. Or you may notice an unmistakable sarcasm in the speaker's voice.

Regardless of who the speaker is or where the speech is taking place, you should always note the speaker's background. A person's words must often be measured against that individual's background. For example, if a former Communist is speaking on communism, this fact may have a bearing on what is said. If a former CIA agent speaks about corruption in the CIA, you would not adequately report the message if you did not mention the person's background.

Sometimes, purely physical facts about the speaker are essential to the story. A blind person pleading for funds to educate the blind, a one-armed veteran speaking about the hell of war, a gray-haired person speaking about care for the elderly —these speakers must be described physically for the story to be complete, accurate and understandable.

You also should note what the person who introduces a speaker says. This may help you understand the significance of the speaker and the importance of what he or she has to say.

Being Observant

Keep an eye on the audience and on what's happening around the edges. You need to measure the mood of the audience by noting the tone of the questions. Are they sharply worded? Is there much laughter or applause? Perhaps members of the audience boo. Does the speaker or the person holding the news conference or the person presiding over the meeting remain calm and in control? Is there casual bantering or joking with the audience? Is the audience stacked with supporters or detractors?

Sometimes the real action takes place outside in the form of a picket line or protest. Sometimes police manage to keep protesters away from the site. Sometimes who is *not* there is news.

Don't overlook the obvious. For example, you should note the size of the audience. Reporting a "full house" means little unless you indicate the house capacity. One way to estimate attendance is to count how many people are sitting in a row or in a typical section. Then you simply multiply that number by the number of rows or sections in the hall. Use good judgment and common sense to adjust for some sections being more crowded than others.

Arriving, Positioning Yourself and Staying On

Most reporters arrive early. At some events they have special seating for reporters, but you should probably not count on that unless you know for sure.

At a speech, sitting in the first row is not necessarily the best thing to do. Perhaps you should be in a location that lets you see the reaction of the audience. If there is a question-and-answer period, you may want to be able to see the questioner. And you certainly want to be in a good position to ask questions yourself.

At a news conference, your location may help you get the attention of the person holding the conference. You should have your questions prepared, but preparing them is not enough. You have seen presidential news conferences on television, and you know how difficult it is to get the president's attention. Indeed, sometimes there is even a list showing the order in which reporters will be recognized. Any news conference presents the reporter with similar difficulties, though on a smaller scale. You have seen how difficult it is for reporters to follow up on their own questions. At some news conferences you will not be called on twice.

But you must do more than try to get your own questions answered. You must listen to others' questions and be able to recognize the making of a good story. Too often a good question is dropped without follow-up because reporters are not listening carefully or are too intent on pursuing their own questions. Listen for what is newsworthy and pursue it. Sticking with an important subject will make the job of writing the story easier. Remember, when the news conference is finished, you will have a story to write. Piecing together notes on dozens of unrelated topics can be difficult, if not impossible.

At a meeting you should be able to see and hear the main participants. Ordinarily, a board or council will sit facing the audience. Before the meeting starts, you should know which members are sitting where. You may want to assign each participant a number so you do not have to write the person's name each time he or she speaks. You also can draw a sketch of where members are sitting. In this way you will be able to quote someone by number and if necessary find out his or her name later. Know who the officers are. The president or the secretary may distribute handouts before the meeting. After a meeting, the secretary may be able to help you fill in missing words or information.

As a general rule, when the speech, news conference or meeting is over, do not rush off unless you are on deadline. Some of the best stories happen afterward. You should have some questions to ask. You may want some clarifications, or you may arrange to interview a key spokesperson. Listen for reactions from those in attendance.

STRUCTURING AND WRITING YOUR STORY

Writing the lead for the speech, news conference or meeting story is no different from writing the lead for any other story. All of the qualities of the inverted pyramid news lead discussed in Chapter 9 are important here as well.

You must be careful not to emphasize something about the event that is of great interest or curiosity but that does not lead into the rest of your story. It's tempting, for example, to lead with a striking quote. But rarely does a speaker or someone holding a news conference highlight the content or the main point in a single, quotable sentence. As always, there are exceptions. As a lead for one of Dr. Martin Luther King Jr.'s most famous addresses, a good reporter might have begun with "I have a dream."

Because of the nature of the inverted pyramid news story, rarely should you follow the chronology of the event you are covering. But the flow of your story may demand *some* attention to chronology (see Chapter 11). If you pay no attention to chronology, you may distort, or cause readers to misinterpret, the meaning of the event.

Writing the Speech Story

Although you may not soon be called upon to cover the speeches of well-known politicians, you can learn a lot from the way the pros handle important political addresses. These speeches can be long and complex, such as President Obama's call for a new era in U.S.-Muslim relations on June 4, 2009. Here is how the Associated Press reported on reaction to the speech:

By Marjorie Olster
CAIRO (AP)—Muslim shopkeepers, students and even radical groups such as Hamas praised President Barack Obama's address Thursday as a positive shift in U.S. attitude and tone. But Arabs and Muslims of all political stripes said they want him to turn his words into action—particularly in standing up to Israel.

Obama impressed Muslims with his humility and respect, and they were thrilled by his citing of Quranic verses. Aiming to repair ties with the Muslim world that had been strained under his predecessor, George W. Bush, he opened with the traditional Arabic greeting "Assalamu Aleikum," which drew enthusiastic applause from his audience at Cairo University.

Even some extremist Web sites, which have carried statements from al-Qaida in the past, gave rare praise for Obama by calling him a "wise enemy." One posting on a chat room expressed admiration for Secretary of State Hillary Rodham Clinton "wearing a head scarf . . . and she and Obama taking off their shoes" during a visit to Cairo's Sultan Hassan mosque.

Mohammed Zakarneh, a 33-year-old former fugitive militant in the West Bank town of Jenin, said Obama's speech "planted seeds of hope in our hearts, as Arabs and Muslims."

Obama's address touched on many themes Muslims wanted to hear. He insisted Palestinians must have a state and said continued Israeli settlement in the West Bank is not legitimate. He assured them the U.S. would pull all its troops out of Iraq by 2012 and promised no permanent U.S. presence in Afghanistan.

But at the top of his priorities, he put the battle against violent extremism. And he was faulted for not apologizing for U.S. wars in Muslim countries.

Notice how Olster used careful writing to convey the thought that while the speech was generally well-received, Muslim nations expect action, not just words, from the Obama administration. The story continued with more reaction:

The Iranian government, which Obama is trying to draw into a dialogue, was silent. But state television described the speech as: "Too many words. Attractive but unbelievable."

Fawzi Barhoum, a Hamas spokesman in Gaza, said there was change in tone. But he complained that Obama did not specifically mention the suffering in Gaza following the

---

TIPS

Technical Concerns for the Television Journalist

Speeches, news conferences and meetings present several technical challenges. Here are three to keep in mind:

- Think visuals. What will your backdrop be? Will there be signs, photos, samples, logos or flip charts to help tell the story?

- Think sound. Will there be one microphone or a multi-box for you to insert your mic, or will you be free to set up your own microphone?

- Think light. Will the event take place outdoors or in a well-lit room, or must you bring your own lighting? How far is the camera throw (the distance from the event to your camera)? Will there be a camera platform or a set space, or will you be free to set up your camera anywhere?

Israeli incursion this year that killed more than 1,000 Palestinians.

"There is a change between the language of President Obama and previous speeches made by George Bush," he said. "So all we can say is that there is a difference in the statements, and the statements of today did not include a mechanism that can translate his wishes and views into actions," said Barhoum, whose group the U.S. considers a terrorist organization.

But Palestinian President Mahmoud Abbas, a moderate who rivals Hamas for leadership of the Palestinians, welcomed Obama's words.

"The part of Obama's speech regarding the Palestinian issue is an important step under new beginnings," his spokesman Nabil Abu Rdeneh said. "It shows there is a new and different American policy toward the Palestinian issue."

You, too, need to get reactions, and, as Olster did, you may want to put them in a story separate from the account of the speech itself. Reaction stories often accompany stories about presidential speeches. Sometimes they work in other contexts, too.

The approach for a video reporter is somewhat different. For television or video on the Web, you'll introduce the subject and the speaker, then cut in video snippets of the speech itself. You may well end the piece with an interview of someone who attended and in the process get reaction.

Writing the News Conference Story

Writing the news conference story may be a bit more challenging than writing the speech story. Because you will go to the conference with different questions in mind than your fellow reporters, you may come away with a different story. Your lead, at least, may be different from the leads of other reporters.

A news conference often covers a gamut of topics. Often it begins with a statement from the person who called the conference.

For example, when the mayor of Springfield holds a news conference to announce her candidacy for a second term, you can be sure that she will begin with a statement to that effect. Although her candidacy might be news to some people, you may want to ask her questions about the location of a new landfill that the city is rumored to be planning. Most citizens will admit the need for landfills, but their location is always controversial. And then there's that tip you heard about the possibility of the city manager resigning to take a job in a large city.

Other reporters will come with other questions. Will there be further cuts in the city budget? Will the cuts mean that some city employees will lose their jobs? What happened to the plans to expand the city jail?

After you come away from a news conference that covered many topics, you have the job of organizing the material in some logical, coherent order. You can choose to write a multiple-element lead (see Chapter 9). But usually you will treat the most newsworthy subject first and deal with the other subjects in the order of their importance. Rarely would you report on them in the chronological order in which they were discussed.

Speeches, such as this one from President Barack Obama, require the reporter to be alert not only to what is said but also to the audience's reaction.

Suppose you decide the location of the landfill is the most important item of the news conference—especially if the mayor revealed the location for the first time. You might begin your story this way:

> The city will construct its new landfill near the intersection of State Route 53 and Route E, four miles north of Springfield, Mayor Juanita Williams said today.
>
> "After nearly a year of discussion and the best advice we could obtain, we are certain the Route E location is best for all concerned," Williams said at a news conference.
>
> The mayor admitted there would be continued opposition to the site by citizens living in the general area, especially those in the Valley High Trailer Court. "No location will please everyone," Williams said.
>
> Williams called the news conference to make the expected announcement of her candidacy for a second term.

Now you have to find a way to treat the other topics of the conference. You might want to list them first in a series of bullet points:

In other matters, Williams said:

- City Manager Diane Lusby will not be resigning to take another post.
- Budget constraints will not permit any new construction on the city jail this year.
- Budget cuts will not cost any city employees their jobs. However, positions vacated by retiring personnel will not be filled.

After this list, you will either come back to your lead, giving more background and quoting citizens or other city officials on the subject, or go on to treat, one at a time, the matters you listed. Pay particular attention to making proper transitions from paragraph to paragraph so your story is coherent. "On other subjects, the mayor said . . . ," "The mayor defended her position on . . . ," "Again she stressed. . . ."

If one of the subjects is of special interest, you may want to write a sidebar, a shorter piece to go with your main story. For this story, you could do a sidebar on the mayor's candidacy, her record, her possible opponents and the like.

With a longer or more complicated story, you may want to make a summary list of all the main topics covered and place the list in a box or sidebar.

Remember, your job is to give readers the news, as simply and clearly as possible. Remember, too, to cover the event as well as the content. Perhaps only three reporters turned up for the news conference, or perhaps some picketers protested the mayor's remarks about a local abortion clinic. Sometimes what happens at a news conference is more newsworthy than anything the person holding the conference says. What happens there might well be the lead of your main story, or you may want to place it in a sidebar.

Writing the Meeting Story

Readers want you to take their place at the meeting you are covering. Let's look at a simple meeting story—in this case, a meeting of a local school board:

The decision of three national corporations to protest a formula used to compute their property taxes is causing more than $264,000 to be withheld from the Walnut School District's operating budget for the 2009-10 school year.

Superintendent Max Schmidt said at Monday's school board meeting that International Business Machines Corp., ACR Corp. and Xerox are arguing that the method used in computing their property taxes was no longer valid. Nine California counties are involved in similar disputes.

The taxes, totaling $264,688, are being held in escrow by the county until the matter is resolved. Some or all of the money eventually may be returned to the district, but the administration cannot determine when or how much.

"If we take a quarter million dollars out of our program at this time, it could have a devastating effect," Schmidt said. "Once you've built that money into your budget and you lost it, you've lost a major source of income."

Mike Harper, the county prosecuting

ON THE JOB

Speeches, News Conferences and Meetings

After receiving a master's in journalism, Barry Murov worked as an associate editor of a Washington, D.C., newsletter, where he covered federal job programs. Then after working for the *St. Louis Business Journal* for six years, first as a reporter, then as managing editor, Murov became editor of *St. Louis Magazine*. Now he's employed by Fleishman-Hillard Inc., an international public relations firm.

Murov has written and edited dozens of stories covering speeches, meetings and news conferences. Here are some tips he has for you.

"Always ask for a copy of the speech ahead of time," Murov says. "Even when you are lucky enough to get a copy, don't assume that the speaker will stick to the text."

As a consultant for Fortune 500 corporations, Murov knows that "many executives tend to tinker with their speeches, even making significant changes, up until the final minute."

Murov says you should follow along in the text to note where the actual presentation differs. "You don't want your story to include a statement from the text that the speaker deleted. Also, you may find the real news nugget buried in the speech."

Don't leave a meeting or news conference immediately. "Go up to the spokesperson or the leader of the meeting and ask a question that hasn't been covered during the actual event.

"That can benefit in two ways: One, you will have something extra for your readers. Two, it helps you build a relationship with the spokesperson that may pay off in the future."

attorney, and Larry Woods, the school district attorney, advised board members to take a "wait-and-see attitude," Schmidt said. He said that one alternative would be to challenge the corporations in court. A final decision will be made later.

The board also delayed action on repayment of $80,000 to IBM in a separate tax dispute. The corporation claims the district owes it for overpaid 2007 property taxes. The county commission has ruled the claim is legitimate and must be repaid.

A possible source of additional income, however, could be House Bill 1002, Schmidt said. If passed, this appropriations bill would provide an additional $46 million for state education, approximately $250,000 of which could go to the Walnut School District.

Charles Campbell, the district architect, said plans for the area's new vocational technical school to be built on the Rock Bridge High School campus will be given to contractors in February. Bids will be presented at the March 15 board meeting.

The board voted to have classes on Presidents Day, Feb. 15, to make up for time missed because of the teachers' strike.

The issue of the meeting was money problems—a subject that concerns every taxpayer. The writer jumped right into the subject in the lead, giving the "what" in the first paragraph, and then in the second paragraph giving us the "who," "when" and "where." The reporter then dealt with specifics, naming names and citing figures, and quoted the key person at the meeting. In the last two paragraphs the writer dealt with other matters discussed in the meeting.

The issues discussed at a meeting are not your only considerations in covering a meeting story. Remember, too, to cover the event. Who was there? Who represented the public? Did anyone have reactions after the meeting was over?

One reporter began her meeting story in this way:

> Even though they are footing the bill, only one of Boone County's residents cared enough to attend a Tuesday night hearing on the county's 2010 budget.
>
> With an audience of one citizen plus two reporters, County Auditor June Pitchford presented her official report on the $21 million budget to the Boone County Commission in a silent City Council chamber.

Even when covering routine, boring events, you are allowed to use your creativity. In addition to getting all the facts, your job is also to be interesting, to get people to read the story. Remember, two of the criteria for news are that it be relevant and useful. Another is that it be interesting.

If you're a video reporter, your approach to a meeting story will be quite different. There's almost nothing as boring as video of a city council meeting, so telling the story creatively is important. If you know the council will be debating increased garbage pickup rates, get some video of garbage trucks to show while you're narrating the gist of the story. Then, of course, interviews with council members or members of the public can be used to complete the story.

No matter which medium you work for, you are always expected to write well—even for a common event like a speech, news conference or meeting.

Suggested Readings

Biography and Genealogy Master Index. Detroit, Mich.: Gale Research Co., 1981 to present. This compilation of biographical directories lists people whose biographies have been written and indicates which date and volume of those reference books to consult for the actual biography.

Biography Index. Bronx, N.Y.: H.W. Wilson Co., 1946 to present. This reference helps you locate biographical articles that have appeared in 2,000 periodicals and journals, as well as in biographical books and chapters from collective biographies.

Current Biography. Bronx, N.Y.: H.W. Wilson Co., 1940 to present. This monthly publication about people in the news includes a photo of each subject. It is an excellent source for people not included in more formal biographical sources.

Suggested Websites

www.notrain-nogain.org/Train/Res/Report/cmeet.asp
This guide to meeting coverage was prepared by people who train journalists for just that kind of work.

www.rcameron.com/journalism/citycouncil
This website takes you step-by-step through the process of covering a city council meeting.

Exercises

1. **Team project.** Your instructor will divide the class into teams of three or four each. Find out when your university's faculty council or similar faculty representative group is having its next meeting. As a team, plan the steps you will take to prepare for the meeting, and share the information you gather as you prepare. Then cover the meeting, taking notes. Discuss your notes with one another, and then write individual stories for the student newspaper. Compare your stories. How similar are the leads and the story structures? How different? Did you make effective use of direct quotations? How could the stories be improved?

2. You learn that actor Robert Redford is holding a news conference before speaking to a local group about environmental issues. You also learn that Redford is personally and actively involved in these issues. In preparation for covering the conference, gather and record background information on Redford from the Web or from commercial databases to which you have access at your school newspaper or library.

3. Journalist Andrea Mitchell is coming to town to speak on the current U.S. president's relationship with the press. Prepare to cover the speech. Record the steps you will take to prepare for the speech and the information you have gathered on Mitchell.

4. Find out when a public figure in your area—a government official or a college administrator, for example—plans to give a speech on a specific topic. Prepare for and cover the speech, using a digital recorder. Then write your news story in two versions—one for immediate posting on a website and one for the print version of a newspaper. For the Web version, what specific links would be useful? Suggest at least one possible sidebar.

5. Figure out when a news conference, preferably of local interest, will be held in your area. Prepare for and cover the news conference. Record or, if possible, videotape the event. Then write your news story in two versions—one for a print newspaper and one for a local television news program. What segment of video would you use for the broadcast story? How else would you supplement the different stories?

6. Prepare for and cover a meeting of a local government agency or committee—the school board, the city council, or a similar group. Try to interview one of the participants before or after the meeting. Then write your story in two versions—one for a website specializing in local events and one for a local radio news broadcast. How do the two stories differ? How do you meet the criteria of usefulness, relevance and interest in each story?

Other Types of Local Stories

16

When a soldier at Fort Hood, Texas, opened fire on his comrades Nov. 5, 2009, journalists across the country called on the newest technology and traditional techniques to tell a horrifying story. The news broke on Twitter. The first reporters on the scene followed up with blog posts. A few hours later came the first fully formed stories.

An editor at the *Austin American-Statesman* told Poynter.org that the newspaper learned of the shootings in a Twitter message from a local television station. The paper immediately got a reporter on the phone with military authorities to confirm. The paper's own Twitter account came next, while reporters rushed 60 miles to the fort. From the scene, those reporters and others from multiple news organizations sent Twitter messages and then, as they gathered more facts, posted blogs on their organizations' websites.

At first, information was fragmentary and public interest was frantic. So the *Statesman, The New York Times, The Huffington Post* and other organizations used a new tool, the Twitter List, which essentially creates groups on Twitter, to share information and allow readers to follow the developing reporting. By the next morning, fuller stories using traditional formats showed up on websites, broadcasts and front pages.

CNN.com, for example, used a personal approach:

> It was the kind of phone call military families dread receiving from Iraq and Afghanistan—not from Texas.
>
> Peggy McCarty's daughter called Thursday afternoon to say she had been wounded by a gunshot in her left shoulder. Keara Bono, 21, assured her mother that she was OK, but McCarty's heart skipped.
>
> She knew she had much to fear when Bono, an Army specialist, arrived at Fort Hood to prepare for an early December deployment to Iraq. But McCarty never thought she would have to worry about her child getting wounded on American soil. . . .

The New York Times, by contrast, stuck to the inverted pyramid for its hard-news version:

> An Army psychiatrist facing deployment to one of America's war zones killed 13 people and wounded 30 others Thursday in a shooting rampage with two handguns at the sprawling Fort Hood Army post in central Texas, military officials said.
>
> It was one of the worst mass shootings ever at a military base in the United States. . . .

Succeeding days were filled, of course, with follow-up stories as reporters learned more about the shooter and his victims and as issues ranging from religion to homeland security stirred the public conversation.

You may never have to cover a tragedy that serious, but nearly all reporters at some time find themselves covering crime, chasing fire trucks or trying to make sense of court proceedings. This chapter will help. You also are likely to be assigned to tell the life story of someone who has died. This chapter will help with that, too.

YOUR PREPARATION

When news breaks, as it did that Thursday in November, you won't have much time to prepare before rushing out the door or picking up the phone. However, there is some instant research you can do, even if you're using your BlackBerry while on your way to the scene (preferably with someone else driving). Begin as you would with any other story—by checking your news room's electronic morgue. There you'll learn whether a similar crime has occurred before, whether accidents are common at the location of the latest one, whether similar suspicious fires have occurred or whether the person charged with the crime has been in trouble before. And don't overlook Google.

Reporters can sometimes use an iPod or similar device to research background on a breaking story before arriving at the scene.

Preparing for the Crime Story

Meetings, news conferences, speeches and court proceedings are usually scheduled events, so on most occasions you should have ample time beforehand to do background research on the individual or topic to be covered. Obituaries also call for a first stop in the television station or newspaper library, but crime reporting may be different. If the police radio reports a murder in your area, you may be dispatched to the scene as the story is breaking. At that point, no one will know who is involved or what happened. There will be no time to check the library, and you will have to do your initial reporting at the scene.

Most information about crimes comes from three sources:

- Police officials and their reports.
- The victim or victims.
- The witness or witnesses.

The circumstances of the crime may determine which of the three is most important, which should be checked first or whether they should be checked at all. If the victim is available, as a reporter you should make every effort to get an interview. But if the victim and witnesses are unavailable, the police and their reports become primary sources.

In the era of convergence, you'll need more than a pencil and notebook to gather information at the scene of a crime. A digital recorder will allow you to record your interviews for publication on your news organization's website, and a digital camera or phone camera might help record what happened at the scene. That's particularly true if you are covering the event alone without the help of a photojournalist or videographer.

The point at which your editor assigns you to a crime story is important. If you are dispatched to the scene of the crime as it happens or soon afterward, you will probably interview the victim and witnesses first. The police report probably hasn't even been written yet. But if you are assigned to write about a crime that occurred the night before, the police report is your starting point.

The timing affects what kinds of material you will be able to gather and which medium might use your information first. A major breaking story might warrant a mobile phone news bulletin or a television report. Something that happened the night before might require more sophisticated work, such as gathering information for a detailed information graphic of a crime scene.

A police officer investigating a crime covers much of the same ground as you. The officer is interested in who was involved, what happened, when, where, why and how. Those details are needed to complete the official report of the incident, and you need them for your story. When you write about crime, always check the police report. It is often the source of basic information, such as:

- A description of what happened.
- The location of the incident.

- The name, age and address of the victim.
- The name, age and address of the suspect, if any.
- The offense police believe the suspect has committed.
- The extent of injuries, if any.
- The names, ages and addresses of witnesses, if any.

If you arrive at the scene of a crime as it takes place or immediately afterward, you have the advantage of being able to gather much of that information firsthand. When timely coverage is impossible, however, the police report allows you to catch up quickly. The names of those with knowledge of the incident usually appear on the report, and the reporter uses that information to learn the story.

Reporters sometimes write crime stories from the police report alone. Good journalists, however, demand more because police reports are frequently inaccurate. Most experienced reporters have read reports in which the names of those involved were misspelled, ages were wrong and other basic information was inaccurate. Sometimes such errors are a result of sloppy reporting by the investigating officer or mistakes in transcribing notes into a formal report. Occasionally, the officer may lie in an attempt to cover up shortcomings in the investigation or misconduct at the scene of the crime. Whatever the reason, you should do your own reporting and not depend solely on a police officer's account. Remember that editors frown on single-source stories of any kind. It's your job to do solid reporting, and you are expected to consult multiple sources.

For crime stories, a background check in the news room's morgue is often done after you return to the office. Once you have the names of those involved, for example, you can see whether the morgue reveals relevant information about them. Was the suspect arrested before? Was the store robbed before? The morgue might help answer those kinds of questions.

Preparing for Accident and Fire Stories

If you are assigned to cover an accident or fire, you can expect some of the same problems you'd encounter if covering a crime. Much depends on whether the police or fire report is available before or after you are assigned to the story. If the accident or fire took place overnight, the official report is the place to start. It will give you most of the basic information you need. It will also lead you to other sources.

If you are sent to the scene of an accident or fire, your job is to collect much of the basic information yourself. As for crimes, the basic information you'll need includes:

- A description of what happened.
- The location of the incident.
- The name, age and address of the victim or victims.

TIPS

What to Do at the Scene of an Accident

- Question the person in charge of the investigation.
- Try to find and interview witnesses.
- Try to find friends or relatives of the victims.
- If possible, interview the victims.
- Talk with others at the scene.
- Be sensitive to victims and their families.

- The extent of injuries, if any.
- The names, ages and addresses of witnesses, if any.

Preparing for the Court Story

Most court stories you are likely to cover will be follow-ups to earlier stories. If a murder suspect is appearing for a preliminary hearing, details of the crime probably were reported earlier, and a check of the news room's morgue may give you ample background information as you prepare for your visit to the courtroom. Otherwise, a chat with the district attorney, the police chief or one of their assistants might provide ample background for writing the story.

Court stories are often difficult for beginners who are unlikely to understand the complex process used in criminal prosecutions. In addition, reporters might be asked to cover civil court proceedings, which are lawsuits that charge an individual or company with harming another. Here's our best advice on how to approach court stories: Ask plenty of questions of the judge and attorneys before or after the court proceeding or during recesses. It's much better to admit your lack of knowledge about the court process than to make a serious error in a story because you didn't understand what was happening.

WRITING THE STORY

Knowing how to organize stories about crime, accidents, fires and court proceedings is essential. It helps to have a model, and the examples that follow are designed to assist you.

The Crime Story

There is no magic formula for writing crime news. Solid reporting techniques pay off just as they do in other types of reporting; then it is a matter of writing the story as the facts demand. Sometimes the events are most effectively told in chronological order, particularly when the story is complex (see Chapter 11). More often, a traditional inverted pyramid style works best. The amount of time the reporter has to file the story also influences the approach. Let's take a look at how the newspaper accounts of two crimes were developed over time and why different writing styles seemed appropriate for each.

Gathering facts from the many sources available and sorting through conflicting information can be time-consuming tasks. Sometimes, especially when you are posting online, you may have to write the story before all the facts are gathered. The result is a bare-bones account. (See two different versions of a news story in Figure 16.1.)

If a number of people witnessed or were affected by a crime, you may supplement the main story with a sidebar that deals with the personal impact of the

Breaking News Story

A short, inverted pyramid story may be posted online immediately after the news breaks.

A Highway Patrol marksman shot and killed a Kansas man in a rural area south of Springfield this morning after the victim threatened to blow off the head of his apparent hostage.

The summary lead captures the action and some of the drama.

A hitchhiker reportedly told police earlier this morning that his "ride" had plans to rob a service station on Interstate 70. That tip apparently followed an earlier report of a van leaving a station at the Millersburg exit of I-70 without paying for gasoline.

An ensuing hour-long chase ended at 9:30 a.m. in an isolated meadow in the Pierpont area when Capt. N.E. Tinnin fired a single shot into the stomach of the suspect, identified as Jim Phipps of Kansas City, Kan.

Phipps, armed with a sawed-off shotgun, and his "hostage," identified as Anthony Curtis Lilly, 17, also of Kansas City, Kan., eluded police by fleeing into a rugged, wooded area at the end of Bennett Lane, a dead-end gravel road off Route 163.

Then comes a chronological reconstruction, but without much detail or background.

Tinnin said he fired the shot with a .253-caliber sniper rifle when it appeared Phipps was going to shoot Lilly. Two troopers' efforts to persuade Phipps to throw down his weapon and surrender were unsuccessful, Tinnin said.

Follow-Up Story

With more time to learn the full story, the reporter can give readers a more complete account, either online or in print.

James Phipps and Anthony Lilly, a pair of 17-year-olds from Kansas City, Kan., were heading west on Interstate 70 at 7:30 a.m. Friday, returning from a trip to Arkansas.

The reporter can use narrative to bring interest to an ongoing story.

Within the next hour and a half, Phipps had used a sawed-off shotgun stolen in Arkansas to take Lilly hostage, and, after holding that shotgun to Lilly's head, was shot and killed by a Highway Patrol captain on the edge of a rugged wooded area south of Springfield.

As the episode ended, local officials had only begun to piece together a bizarre tragedy that involved a high-speed chase, airplane and helicopter surveillance, a march through a wooded ravine and the evacuation of several frightened citizens from their country homes.

After the lead (the first two paragraphs) comes a paragraph of scene-setting and foreshadowing.

One attribution (underlined) allows the reporter to narrate the story without repeating the source.

As police reconstructed the incident, Phipps and Lilly decided to stop for gas at the Millersburg exit east of Springfield at about 7:30 a.m. With them in the van was Robert Paul Hudson Jr., a San Francisco-bound hitchhiker.

Figure 16.1
Comparison of a Breaking News Story and a Follow-Up Story
With breaking news, a reporter might post the basic facts online immediately in an inverted pyramid story. Once the basic news is posted, the reporter has some time to gather additional facts and craft a chronological narrative that gives readers the full story.

Hudson was not present at the shooting. He had fled Lilly's van at the Millersburg exit after he suspected trouble.

The trouble began when Lilly and Phipps openly plotted to steal some gasoline at Millersburg, Hudson told police. He said the pair had agreed to display the shotgun if trouble arose with station attendants.

Here is a necessary bit of explanation.

Hudson said he persuaded Phipps to drop him off before they stopped for gas. He then caught a ride to Springfield and told his driver of the robbery plans he had overheard. After dropping Hudson off near the Providence Road exit, the driver called Springfield police, who picked up Hudson.

Then the narrative begins.

Meanwhile, Phipps and Lilly put $8.90 worth of gas in the van and drove off without paying. The station attendant notified authorities.

As he approached Springfield, Phipps turned onto U.S. 63 South, where he was spotted by Highway Patrol troopers Tom Halford and Greg Overfelt. They began a high-speed chase, which ended on a dead-end gravel road near Pierpont.

Transitions orient the reader and keep the story moving.

During the chase, which included a U-turn near Ashland, Phipps bumped the Highway Patrol car twice, forcing Halford to run into the highway's median.

Upon reaching the dead end, the suspects abandoned the van and ran into a nearby barn. At that point, Phipps, who Highway Patrol officers said was wanted in Kansas for escaping from a detention center, turned the shotgun on Lilly.

The reporter uses a direct quote to add color to the narrative.

When Halford and Overfelt tried to talk with Phipps from outside the barn, they were met with obscenities. Phipps threatened to "blow (Lilly's) head off," and vowed not to be captured alive.

Phipps then left the barn and walked into a wooded area, pressing the gun against Lilly's head. Halford and Overfelt followed at a safe distance but were close enough to speak with Phipps.

While other officers from the Highway Patrol, the Lincoln County Sheriff's Department and Springfield police arrived at the scene, residents in the area were warned to evacuate their homes. A Highway Patrol plane and helicopter flew low over the woods, following the suspects and the troopers through the woods.

The four walked through a deep and densely wooded ravine. Upon seeing a partially constructed house in a nearby clearing, Phipps demanded of officers waiting in the clearing that his van be driven around to the house, at which time he would release his hostage. Halford said, "They disappeared up over the ridge. I heard some shouting (Phipps' demands), and then I heard the shot."

Another direct quote lends authenticity while giving the story a dramatic conclusion.

After entering the clearing from the woods, Phipps apparently had been briefly confused by the officers on either side of him and had lowered his gun for a moment.

The story is wrapped up in the final paragraph.

That was long enough for Highway Patrol Capt. N.E. Tinnin to shoot Phipps in the abdomen with a high-powered rifle. It was about 8:45 a.m. Phipps was taken to Boone County Hospital, where he soon died.

crime—the "so what." The writer of the chronological account shown in Figure 16.1 also decided to write a separate story on nearby residents, who had little to add to the main story but became a part of the situation nonetheless:

In the grass at the edge of a woods near Pierpont Friday afternoon, the only remaining signs of James Phipps were a six-inch circle of blood, a doctor's syringe, a blood-stained button and the imprints in the mud where Phipps fell after he was shot by a Highway Patrol officer. Elsewhere in the area, it was a quiet, sunny, spring day in a countryside dotted by farms and houses. But inside some of those houses, dwellers still were shaken by the morning's events that had forced a police order for them to evacuate their homes.

Mrs. James G. Thorne lives on Cheavens Road across the clearing from where Phipps was shot. Mrs. Thorne had not heard the evacuation notice, so when she saw area officers crouching with guns at the end of her driveway, she decided to investigate.

"I was the surprise they weren't expecting," she told a Highway Patrol officer Friday afternoon. "I walked out just before the excitement."

When the officers saw Mrs. Thorne, "they were obviously very upset and shouted for me to get out of here," she said. "I was here alone and asked them how I was supposed to leave. All they said was, 'Just get out of here!'"

Down the road, Clarence Stallman had been warned of the situation by officers and noticed the circling airplane and helicopter. "I said, 'Are they headed this way soon?' and they said, 'They're here,'" said Stallman.

After Stallman notified his neighbors, he picked up Mrs. Thorne at her home and left the area just before the shooting.

On the next street over, Ronald Nichols had no intention of running.

"I didn't know what was happening," Nichols said. "The wife was scared to death and didn't know what to do. I grabbed my gun and looked for them."

Another neighbor, Mrs. Charles Emmons, first was alerted by the sound of the surveillance plane. "The plane was flying so low I thought it was going to come into the house," she said. "I was frightened. This is something you think will never happen to you."

Then Mrs. Emmons flashed a relieved smile. "It's been quite a morning," she said.

The techniques of writing in chronological order and separating the accounts of witnesses from the main story worked well in the preceding case. More often, however, crime stories are written in the classic inverted pyramid style because of time and space considerations.

Accident and Fire Stories

When you are assigned to cover an accident or a fire, many of the facts and all of the color are gathered at the scene. If the accident has just taken place, a visit to the scene is essential. Being there will give you the best picture of what happened, and you will be able to write a solid story. Too many reporters cover accidents and fires as purely passive observers. Indeed, you must observe. But you must also actively solicit information from those who are present. Many of them, including those directly involved, you may never be able to find again. Keep a digital recorder and digital camera at hand. You may be asked to prepare stories for multiple media.

When you are dispatched to the scene of an accident, move as quickly as possible to collect this information:

- The names, ages, addresses and conditions of the victims.
- Accounts of witnesses or police reconstructions of what happened.
- When the accident occurred.
- Where it occurred.
- Why or how it happened or who was at fault, as determined by officials in charge of the investigation.

If that list sounds familiar, it should. You could simplify it to read "who, what, when, where and why." As in any news story, that information is essential. You must gather it as quickly as possible after being assigned to the story. Just as important is knowing what to do when you arrive on the scene. These suggestions will help:

- **Question the person in charge of the investigation.** This individual will attempt to gather much of the information you want. A police officer, for example, needs to know who was involved, what happened, when it happened and who was at fault. If you are able to establish a good relationship with the investigator, you may be able to secure much of the information you need from this one source, though single-source stories are usually inadequate.

  Remember that the spellings of names, addresses and similar facts must be verified later. Any veteran reporter can tell you that police officers and other public officials are notoriously bad spellers and often make errors in recording the names of victims. To avoid such errors, call relatives of the victims or consult the city directory, telephone book or other sources to check your information.
- **Try to find and interview witnesses.** Police and other investigators may lead you directly to the best witnesses. The most accurate account of what happened usually comes from witnesses, and the investigators will try to find them. You should, too. A good way to do that is to watch the investigators. Listen in as they interview a witness, or approach the witness after they are finished. If there is time, of course, try to find your own witnesses. You cannot and should not always rely on investigators to do your work for you.
- **Try to find friends or relatives of the victims.** These sources are helpful in piecing together information about the victims. Through them you often get tips about even better stories.
- **If possible, interview the victims.** Survivors of an accident may be badly shaken, but if they are able to talk, they can provide firsthand details that an official report never could. Make every attempt to interview those involved.

TIPS

Source Checklist for Accidents, Fires and Disasters

- Civilian witnesses.
- Victims of personal injury, if they can be interviewed.
- People who were involved but escaped injury.
- Victims of property damage, including property owners, tenants and employees.
- Neighbors and passersby.
- Relatives and neighbors of victims.
- Rescue workers (firefighters, police, EMS workers, hospital personnel, etc.).
- Government regulatory agencies (local, state and federal).

- **Talk with others at the scene.** If someone died at the scene of the accident, an ambulance paramedic or the medical examiner may be able to give you some indication of what caused the death. At the least you can learn where the bodies or the injured will be taken. That may help, because later the mortician or hospital officials may be able to provide information you need for your story.
- **Be sensitive to victims and their families.** You have a job to do, and you must do it. That does not mean, however, that you can be insensitive to those involved in an accident or fire.
- **Sketch elements of the scene on a piece of paper.** This sketch may be useful in helping an information graphics artist re-create the scene.
- **Record your interviews.** You might need a recording for your website or to help you make sure the information is correct.

Of course, your deadline will have a major impact on the amount of information you are able to gather. If you must meet a deadline soon after arriving at the scene, you will probably be forced to stick to the basics of who, what, when, where, why and how. Thus it is important to gather that information first. Then, if you have time, you can concentrate on more detailed and vivid information to make the story highly readable.

Accidents and fires present similar problems for the reporter, but at a fire of any size you can expect more confusion than at the scene of an accident. One major difference, then, is that the officer in charge will be busier. At the scene of an accident, the damage has been done and the authorities are usually free to concentrate on their investigation. At a fire, the officer in charge is busy directing firefighters and probably will be unable to talk with you. The investigation will not even begin until the fire is extinguished. In many cases, the cause of the fire will not be known for hours, days or weeks. In some cases, it may never be known. Seldom is that so in an accident, except perhaps for air accidents.

Another problem is that you may not have access to the immediate area of the fire. Barriers often are erected to keep the public—and representatives of the news media—from coming too close to a burning structure. The obvious reason is safety, but such barriers may hamper your reporting. You may not be able to come close enough to firefighters to learn about the problems they are having or to obtain the quotes you need to improve your story.

These problems usually make covering a fire more difficult than covering an accident. Despite the difficulties, you cover a fire in much the same way, interviewing officials and witnesses at the scene. You also should try to interview the property owner. Moreover, because the official investigation will not have begun, you must conduct your own. When covering any fire, you must learn:

- The location of the fire.
- The names, ages and addresses of those killed, injured or missing.
- The name of the building owner or, in the case of a grass fire or forest fire, the landowner.

Hazards at the scene of a disaster, such as this fire resulting from a Los Angeles-area earthquake, can make a reporter's job difficult and dangerous.

- The value of the building and its contents or the value of the land.
- Whether the building and contents were insured for fire damage. (Open land seldom is.)
- When the fire started, who reported it and how many firefighters and pieces of equipment were called to the scene.
- What caused the fire, if that is known.

As in any story, the basics are who, what, when, where, why and how. But the nature of the fire will raise other questions that must be answered. Of primary importance is whether life is endangered. If it is not, the amount of property damage becomes the major emphasis of the story. Was arson involved? Was the building insured for its full value? Was there an earlier fire at the same location? Did the building comply with fire codes? Were any rare or extremely valuable objects inside? Did explosives inside the structure complicate fighting the fire and pose an even greater threat than the fire itself?

Your job is to answer these questions for your readers or viewers. You will be able to obtain some of this information later on from official fire reports if they are ready before your story deadline. But most information will come from interviews that you conduct at the scene with the best available sources. Finding your sources may not be easy, but you can begin by looking for the highest-ranking fire official. Large departments may have a designated press officer whose job is to deal with you and other reporters.

Another important source is the fire marshal, whose job is to determine the cause of the fire and, if arson is involved, to bring charges against the arsonist. You should make every effort to talk with the fire marshal at the scene, if he or she is available.

The Court Story

Criminal justice proceedings can be very complicated, with a case moving through a number of stages, from occurrence of the crime, to police investigation, to actions by prosecutors and defense attorneys, to actual criminal trials, to legal punishments like incarceration and execution.

Throughout this cycle of events, a reporter has numerous opportunities to write stories. The extent to which the reporter does so depends on the importance of the case and the amount of local interest in it. In a major case, the filing of every motion may prompt a story; in other cases, only the verdict may be important. As in any type of reporting, news value is the determining factor.

Avoiding Libelous Statements

Also, as in any form of reporting, accuracy is important. Perhaps no other area of writing requires as much caution as the reporting of crime and court news. The potential for libel is great.

Libel is damage to a person's reputation caused by a written statement that brings the person into hatred, contempt or ridicule or that injures a person's business or occupational pursuits (see Chapter 21). Reporters must be extremely careful about what they write. One of the greatest dangers is the possibility of writing that someone is charged with a crime more serious than is the case. After checking clippings in the news room library, for example, one reporter wrote:

> The rape trial of John L. Duncan, 25, of 3925 Oak St. has been set for Dec. 10 in Jefferson County Circuit Court.
>
> Duncan is charged in connection with the June 6 rape of a Melton High School girl near Fletcher Park.

ON THE JOB

Lessons of the Police Beat

When *The San Diego Union-Tribune* expanded its zoned editions, the paper hired journalism graduate James Grimaldi to cover El Cajon, Calif. His goal was to go from the suburbs to the city desk.

"The fastest way to the front page was police stories," Grimaldi says.

One Sunday, the El Cajon police discovered a quadruple homicide. Grimaldi volunteered to cover the story. By the end of the day, he had scored an exclusive jailhouse interview with the killer. Within six months, Grimaldi was promoted to police reporter.

He combed through hundreds of police reports looking for trend stories while covering the internal policies of the San Diego Police Department. At that time, the force was wracked by a high officer death rate and embarrassed by a sensational, racially divisive trial of a black man acquitted of shooting to death a white police officer in what he said was self-defense.

Once, as coroners removed a charred body from a San Diego Dumpster, Grimaldi was on the scene. He later was the first to report that the death was probably the work of a serial killer. He wrote about police corruption, including the chief's use of city-owned video equipment to tape a TV show on bass fishing.

"There's no better way to learn how to report and write than covering crime," Grimaldi says. "It is the quickest way to explore any community. There's humor and pathos, politics and social issues. Every rookie reporter should spend some time covering crime."

From *The Tribune*, Grimaldi went to *The Orange County Register* as a general-assignment reporter. Crime stories taught Grimaldi reporting techniques he used for an investigation of medical deaths, rapes and drug-dealing at the California Institution for Women in Frontera. The Frontera stories won numerous national prizes.

A few years later, Grimaldi was named *The Register's* bureau chief in Washington. Now at *The Washington Post*, he still relies on the reporting foundation first built on the police beat.

In 2006 Grimaldi, together with Susan Schmidt and R. Jeffrey Smith, two other *Washington Post* journalists, was awarded a Pulitzer Prize for investigative journalism, for a series of articles on congressional corruption involving Washington lobbyist Jack Abramoff.

Duncan had been charged with rape following his arrest. However, the prosecutor later determined that the evidence was insufficient to win a rape conviction, the charge was reduced to assault and the newspaper had to print a correction.

Many courts handle both civil and criminal cases. Media coverage often focuses on criminal cases, although civil actions—lawsuits involving disputes of one type or another—are often excellent sources of stories.

Court Organization and Procedure

When a person is charged with a crime, the reporter's job is only beginning. Because the public wants to know what happens to criminal suspects, the media devote much time and space to court coverage of criminal charges.

To write about criminal cases, reporters need to learn the basics of law, court organization and procedure. The following material will give you some understanding of what is happening. You can, and should, also ask questions of the judge and attorneys involved.

Court Organization

The U.S. has two primary court systems: federal and state. Each state has its own system, but there are many similarities from state to state. The average citizen is most likely to have contact with city or municipal courts, which have jurisdiction over traffic and other minor violations of city ordinances. News from these courts is handled as a matter of record in many newspapers.

Cases involving violations of state statutes usually are handled in the state trial courts found in most counties. These are *courts of general jurisdiction* (often called *circuit* or *superior courts*). "General jurisdiction" is important. It means these courts try more cases, of greater variety, than any other type of court, including federal district (trial) courts. Courts of general jurisdiction handle civil cases, such as contract disputes, as well as the criminal cases that are the primary focus of news reporters.

Federal district courts handle cases involving violations of federal crime statutes, interpretation of the U.S. Constitution, civil rights, election disputes, commerce and antitrust matters, postal regulations, federal tax laws and similar issues. Federal trial courts also have jurisdiction in actions between citizens of different states when the amount in controversy exceeds $50,000.

Court Procedure

Under state statutes, the two primary categories of crimes are misdemeanors and felonies. Most state statutes describe a misdemeanor as an offense punishable by a fine, a county jail term not to exceed one year or both. Felonies are punishable by a fine, a state prison sentence of more than one year or death.

Pretrial Proceedings in Criminal Cases

A person arrested for a crime is usually taken to a police station for fingerprinting, photographs and perhaps a sobriety test or a lineup. Statements may be taken and used in evidence only if the person arrested has been informed of and waives what are called Miranda rights, named after a U.S. Supreme Court case. Those rights include the right to have an attorney (hired by the defendant or appointed by the court if the defendant is indigent) and the right to remain silent. Within a certain time, usually 24 hours, a charge must be filed or the person must be released.

Initial Appearance

If the prosecuting attorney decides to file charges, the defendant is usually brought before a judge, informed of the charges and reminded of the Miranda rights. Bail is usually set at this time.

If the charge is a misdemeanor and the defendant pleads guilty, the case is usually handled immediately: A sentence is imposed or a fine is levied. If the plea is not guilty, a trial date is usually set.

If the crime is a felony, the defendant does not enter a plea. The judge sets a date for a preliminary hearing, unless the defendant waives the right to such a hearing. A defendant who waives this hearing is bound over to the general jurisdiction trial court; that is, the records of the case are sent to the trial court.

Preliminary Hearing

A preliminary hearing in a felony case is usually held before a magistrate or a lower-level judge in state court systems. The prosecutor tries to convince the judge that there is probable cause to believe a crime has been committed by the defendant. The defendant can cross-examine the state's witnesses and present evidence, but this normally is not done. Thus, because preliminary hearings often are one-sided, reporters must be careful to write a story that is well-balanced.

If the judge does find probable cause, the prosecuting attorney must file what is called an "information" within a short period of time (usually 10 days). This information must be based on the judge's findings of probable cause.

Grand Jury Indictment

In most states, a person accused in a felony case can be brought to trial in one of two ways. One is the preliminary hearing; the other is a grand jury indictment. In federal courts, the U.S. Constitution requires indictment by a grand jury in felony cases.

Grand jury hearings are secret in some states, and potential defendants are not allowed to be present when testimony is given concerning them. The prosecuting attorney presents evidence to the grand jury, which must determine whether there is probable cause to prosecute. The prosecutor acts as adviser to the grand jury.

A grand jury returns a "true bill" if it finds probable cause and a "no true bill" if it does not. When a grand jury finds probable cause, an indictment is signed by the grand jury foreperson and the prosecuting attorney. The indictment then is presented in open court to a trial judge.

Arraignment

If the defendant is not already in custody, the judge orders an arrest warrant issued. Arraignment in the trial court follows. This is the first formal presentation of the information or the indictment to the defendant. The arraignment is conducted in open court, and the defendant enters a plea to the charge. Three pleas — guilty, not guilty, and not guilty by reason of mental disease or defect — are possible.

Plea bargaining sometimes occurs at this point. In this process, a defendant changes a plea from not guilty to guilty in return for a lighter sentence than might be imposed if a jury returns a guilty verdict. Typically, the defendant pleads guilty to a lesser charge than the one outstanding. A defendant charged with

premeditated or first-degree murder, for example, may plead guilty to a reduced charge of manslaughter. The prosecutor is often willing to go along with this if the time and expense of a trial can be saved and if justice is served.

If the defendant enters a guilty plea, the judge may impose a sentence immediately, or a *presentencing investigation* of the defendant's background may be ordered to help the judge set punishment. Many jurisdictions require presentencing investigations, at least in felony cases. A sentencing date may be set.

If the defendant enters a not-guilty plea, the judge sets a trial date. Most jurisdictions require speedy trials in criminal cases and limit the amount of time from the date the charge is filed to the date of the trial.

As the prosecutor and defense attorney prepare for trial, they may file motions for disclosure of evidence, suppression of evidence and similar rulings. Journalists will have a special interest if a defense attorney files a motion for a *change of venue*, which allows the trial to be conducted in a county other than the one in which the alleged crime occurred. Such requests often result from pretrial stories in the local media that the attorney feels may prejudice potential jurors.

The Trial

The trial starts at this point with jury selection and continues through opening statements, examination of witnesses, jury deliberation, verdict and sentencing. A basic tenet of criminal law in the U.S. is that the prosecution must prove the defendant guilty. The defendant is not required to prove anything or even to testify.

Jury Selection

A jury, usually of 12 members and at least one alternate, is selected from a group of citizens called for jury duty. During the selection process, called *voir dire* (vwar-DEER), the prosecutor and defense attorney question the prospective jurors to identify jurors they hope will be sympathetic to their positions. In the federal system the judge often asks questions, but the prosecutor and defense attorneys may suggest questions for the judge to ask.

(continued)

Court Organization and Procedure (continued)

Each attorney can eliminate a certain number of people as jurors without having to state a reason. Thus, either attorney can dismiss a prospective juror believed to be prejudiced against the attorney's side. Each attorney is also allowed an unlimited number of challenges *for cause* (if, for example, the prospective juror is related to the accused).

Opening Statements

Once the jurors are chosen and sworn, the prosecutor makes an opening statement that outlines how the prosecutor, acting on behalf of the state, expects to prove each of the elements of the crime. The defense attorney may follow with an outline of the defense or may wait until after the prosecution has introduced its evidence. The defense may also waive an opening statement.

Examination of Witnesses

To establish what happened and to link the defendant to the crime, the state calls witnesses to testify. First, the prosecutor asks questions, and the witness responds. The defense attorney may then *cross-examine* the witness. Frequently, one attorney will object to questions posed by the other, and the judge must rule on the objection. When the defense attorney finishes cross-examination, the prosecutor conducts *re-direct examination* to try to clarify certain points or to bolster a witness's credibility. This process of cross-examination and re-direct examination can continue until both sides have asked the witness all their questions.

After the prosecution witnesses have testified and the state rests its case, the defense almost always makes a motion for acquittal, in which it argues that the state has failed to prove its case beyond a reasonable doubt. Almost always, such motions are denied.

The defense then calls witnesses to support its case, and the prosecutor is allowed to cross-examine them. Finally, when all witnesses have testified, the defense rests.

The prosecutor then calls *rebuttal witnesses* in an attempt to discredit testimony of the defense witnesses. The defense then has the right to present even more witnesses, called *surrebuttal witnesses*. After the various rebuttal witnesses have testified, the judge instructs the jury about possible verdicts and about key points of law. The prosecutor then makes his or her closing argument, usually an impassioned plea for a guilty verdict addressed directly to the jury. The defense attorney's closing argument follows, and the prosecutor is allowed a final rebuttal. In the federal system, closing arguments precede the judge's instructions to the jury. The jury then retires to deliberate.

Jury Deliberation, Verdict and Sentencing

Because unanimous verdicts are required in a criminal trial, deliberations often are protracted. If the jury fails to reach a unanimous verdict (a *hung jury*) after a reasonable period of time, the judge may order a mistrial; then the entire case will be retried from the beginning of jury selection. If a verdict is reached, the jury returns to the courtroom, where the verdict is read. In some states, juries are permitted to recommend sentences in guilty verdicts. Sometimes, in a second stage of the trial, the jury must decide, for example, whether to recommend life imprisonment or death. But the final decision is always made by the judge unless a crime carries a mandatory sentence. Sentencing may be done immediately, but more likely a presentencing report will be ordered and a sentencing date set.

The defense often files a motion asking that a guilty verdict be set aside. Such motions are usually denied. A motion for a new trial usually brings similar results. However, in most jurisdictions a motion for a new trial and a denial are prerequisites to the filing of an appeal. Appeals often follow guilty verdicts, so a verdict seldom is final in that sense. Except in cases involving serious crimes, judges often permit the defendant to be released on bail pending the outcome of appeals.

Any story involving arrests should raise caution flags. You must have a working knowledge of libel law and what you can and cannot write about an incident. Any reporter who writes the following, for example, is asking for trouble:

> John R. Milton, 35, of 206 East St. was arrested Monday on a charge of assaulting a police officer.

It would be safer, and more accurate, to write that he was arrested "on suspicion of" the assault. Only a prosecutor, not a police officer, may file charges. In many cases, a police officer may arrest a person with the intent of asking the prosecutor to file a certain charge, but when the prosecutor examines the evidence, the evidence may warrant only a lesser charge. For that reason, many journalists prefer to release the name of an arrested person only after the charge has been filed.

Reporters who cover court news encounter many such pitfalls. They are not trained as attorneys, and it takes time to develop a working knowledge of legal proceedings. The only recourse is to ask as many questions as necessary when a point of law is not clear. It is far better to display ignorance of the law and ask questions than to commit a serious error that harms the reputation of the accused and exposes the newspaper to costly libel litigation.

However, it is also important to know that anything said in open court is fair game for reporters. If, in an opening statement, a prosecutor says the defendant is "nothing but scum, a smut peddler bent on polluting the mind of every child in the city," then by all means report the comment in context in your story. But if a spectator makes that same statement in the hallway during a recess, you probably would not report it. Courts do not extend the qualified privilege to report court proceedings beyond the context of the official proceeding.

Now let's trace a criminal case from the time of arrest through the trial to show how a reporter might cover each step.

A Typical First Story

The following straightforward account of an arrest was filed on deadline. Later the reporter would interview neighbors about Rivers' personality and write an improved story for other editions. This bare-bones story, however, provides a glimpse of several key points in covering arrest stories:

> An unemployed carpenter was arrested today and charged with the Aug. 6 murder of Springfield resident Anne Compton.
>
> Lester L. Rivers, 32, of 209 E. Dillow Lane was charged with first-degree murder, Prosecuting Attorney Mel Singleton said.
>
> Chief of Detectives E.L. Hall said Rivers was arrested on a warrant after a three-month investigation by a team of three detectives. He declined to comment on what led investigators to Rivers.
>
> Compton's body was found in the Peabody River by two fishermen on the morning of Aug. 7. She had been beaten to death with a blunt instrument, according to Dr. Ronald R. Miller, the county medical examiner.

Notice that the reporter carefully chose the words "arrested and charged with" rather than "arrested for," a phrase that may carry a connotation of guilt.

Another important element of all crime and court coverage is the tie-back sentence. This sentence relates a story to events covered in a previous story—in this case, the report of the crime itself. It is important to state clearly—and near the beginning of the story—which crime is involved and to provide enough information about it so that the reader recognizes it. Clarification of the crime is important even in major stories with ready identification in the community. This story does that by recounting when and where Compton's body was found and by whom. It also tells that she died after being hit with a blunt instrument.

Follow-Up Story: First Court Appearance

The following morning the suspect was taken to Magistrate Court for his initial court appearance. Here is a part of the story that resulted:

Lester L. Rivers appeared in Magistrate Court today charged with first-degree murder in connection with the Aug. 6 beating death of Springfield resident Anne Compton.

Judge Howard D. Robbins scheduled a preliminary hearing for Nov. 10 and set bail at $10,000. Robbins assigned Public Defender Ogden Ball to represent Rivers, 32, of 209 E. Dillow Lane.

Rivers said nothing during the 10-minute session as the judge informed him of his right to remain silent and his right to

an attorney. Ball asked Robbins to set the bail at a "reasonable amount for a man who is unemployed." Rivers is a carpenter who was fired from his last job in June. Despite the seriousness of the charge, it is essential that Rivers be free to help prepare his defense, Ball said.

Police have said nothing about a possible connection between Rivers and Compton, whose body was found in the Peabody River by two fishermen on the morning of Aug. 7. She had been beaten to death.

The reporter clearly outlined the exact charge and reported on key points of the brief hearing. Again, the link to the crime is important to inform the reader about which murder is involved.

Follow-Up Story: Preliminary Hearing

Next came the preliminary hearing, where the first evidence linking the defendant to the crime was revealed:

Lester L. Rivers will be tried in Jefferson County Circuit Court for the Aug. 6 murder of Springfield resident Anne Compton.

Magistrate Judge Howard D. Robbins ruled today that there is probable cause to believe that a crime was committed and probable cause that Rivers did it. Rivers was bound over for trial in Circuit Court.

Rivers, 32, of 209 E. Dillow Lane is being held in Jefferson County Jail. He has been unable to post bail of $10,000.

At today's preliminary hearing, Medical Examiner Ronald R. Miller testified that a tire tool recovered from Rivers' car at the time of his arrest "could have been used in the beating death of Miss Compton." Her body was found floating in the Peabody River Aug. 7.

James L. Mullaney, a lab technician for the FBI crime laboratory in Washington, D.C., testified that "traces of blood on the tire tool matched Miss Compton's blood type."

In reporting such testimony, the reporter was careful to use direct quotes and not to overstate the facts. The medical examiner testified that the tire tool *could have been used* in the murder. If he had said it *had been used*, a stronger lead would have been needed.

Defense attorneys usually use preliminary hearings to learn about the evidence against their clients and do not present any witnesses. This apparently was the motive here because neither the police nor the prosecutor had made a public statement on evidence in the case. They probably were being careful not to release prejudicial information that could be grounds for a new trial.

Follow-Up Story: Arraignment

The prosecutor then filed an information, as state law required. The defendant was arraigned in Circuit Court, and the result was a routine story that began as follows:

> Circuit Judge John L. Lee refused today to reduce the bail of Lester L. Rivers, who is charged with first-degree murder in the Aug. 6 death of Springfield resident Anne Compton. Rivers pleaded not guilty. Repeating a request he made earlier in Magistrate Court, Public Defender Ogden Ball urged that Rivers' bail be reduced from $10,000 so he could be freed to assist in preparing his defense.

The not-guilty plea was expected, so the reporter concentrated on a more interesting aspect of the hearing—the renewed request for reduced bail.

Follow-Up Story: First Day of the Trial

Finally, after a series of motions was reported routinely, the trial began:

> Jury selection began today in the first-degree murder trial of Lester L. Rivers, who is charged with the Aug. 6 beating death of Springfield resident Anne Compton.
>
> Public Defender Ogden Ball, Rivers' attorney, and Prosecuting Attorney Mel Singleton both expect jury selection to be complete by 5 p.m.
>
> The selection process started after court convened at 10 a.m. The only incident occurred just before the lunch break as Singleton was questioning prospective juror Jerome B. Tinker, 33, of 408 Woodland Terrace.
>
> "I went to school with that guy," said Tinker, pointing to Rivers, who was seated in the courtroom. "He wouldn't hurt nobody."
>
> Singleton immediately asked that Tinker be removed from the jury panel, and Circuit Judge John L. Lee agreed.
>
> Rivers smiled as Tinker made his statement, but otherwise sat quietly, occasionally conferring with Ball.

The testimony is about to begin, so the reporter set the stage here, describing the courtroom scene. Jury selection is often routine and becomes newsworthy only in important or interesting cases.

Follow-Up Story: Trial Testimony

Trial coverage can be tedious, but when the case is interesting, the stories are easy to write. The reporter picks the most interesting testimony for leads as the trial progresses:

A service station owner testified today that Lester L. Rivers offered a ride to Springfield resident Anne Compton less than an hour before she was beaten to death Aug. 6.

Ralph R. Eagle, the station owner, was a witness at the first-degree murder trial of Rivers in Jefferson County Circuit Court.

"I told her I'd call a cab," Eagle testified, "but Rivers offered her a ride to her boyfriend's house." Compton had gone to the service station after her car broke down nearby. Under cross-examination, Public Defender Ogden Ball, Rivers' attorney, questioned whether Rivers was the man who offered the ride.

"If it wasn't him, it was his twin brother," Eagle said.

"Then you're not really sure it was Mr. Rivers, are you?" Ball asked.

"I sure am," Eagle replied.

"You think you're sure, Mr. Eagle, but you really didn't get a good look at him, did you?"

"I sold him some gas and got a good look at him when I took the money."

"But it was night, wasn't it, Mr. Eagle?" Ball asked.

"That place doesn't have the best lighting in the world, but I saw him all right."

The reporter focused on the key testimony of the trial by capturing it in the words of the participants.

Follow-Up Story: Verdict

Eventually, there is the verdict story, which is usually one of the easiest to write:

Lester L. Rivers was found guilty of first-degree murder today in the Aug. 6 beating death of Springfield resident Anne Compton.

Rivers stood motionless in Jefferson County Circuit Court as the jury foreman returned the verdict. Judge John L. Lee set sentencing for Dec. 10.

Rivers, 32, of 209 E. Dillow Lane could be sentenced to death in the electric chair or life imprisonment in the State Penitentiary.

Public Defender Ogden Ball, Rivers' attorney, said he will appeal.

After the verdict was announced, Mr. and Mrs. Lilborn O. Compton, the victim's parents, were escorted from the courtroom by friends. Both refused to talk with reporters.

Many other types of stories could have been written about such a trial. Lengthy jury deliberations, for example, might prompt stories about the anxiety of the defendant and attorneys and their speculations about the cause of the delay.

Covering court news requires care and good reporting. As in any kind of reporting, you must be well-prepared. If you understand the language of the courts and how they are organized, your job is simplified.

OTHER ISSUES IN CRIME AND COURT REPORTING

Covering crime and the courts is not a simple matter. While the complexity of court proceedings can be baffling to a beginning reporter, there are other pitfalls as well.

The Free-Press/Fair-Trial Controversy

The 1954 murder trial of Dr. Samuel Sheppard in Cleveland was the landmark case involving the perceived conflict between a defendant's right to a fair trial and the public's right to know. Sheppard was accused of murdering his wife. News coverage in the Cleveland newspapers, which included front-page editorials, was intense. In 1966, the U.S. Supreme Court said the trial judge had not fulfilled his duty to protect the jury from the news coverage that saturated the community and to control disruptive influences in the courtroom.

That case, more than any other, ignited what is known as the **free-press/fair-trial controversy**. This controversy raged during the O.J. Simpson case in the mid-1990s. On numerous occasions, Judge Lance Ito threatened to end television coverage of court proceedings to protect Simpson's rights during his criminal trial.

Lawyers charged that the media ignored the Sixth Amendment right of the accused to an impartial jury. The media countered with charges that lawyers ignored the First Amendment.

> **❚❚**To make inroads into the mind-set that 'if the press reported it, it must be true' is the lawyer's most challenging task.**❚❚**
>
> — Robert Shapiro, attorney

Editors realize that coverage of a crime can make it difficult to impanel an impartial jury, but they argue that courts have available many remedies other than restricting the flow of information. In the Sheppard case, for example, the Supreme Court justices said a **change of venue**, which moves the trial to a location where publicity is not as intense, could have been ordered. Other remedies suggested by the Court in such cases are to "continue" (delay) the trial, to grant a new trial or to head off possible outside influences during the trial by sequestering the jury. Editors also argue that acquittals have been won in some of the most publicized cases in recent years.

Gag Orders and Closed Trials

Despite the remedies the Supreme Court offered in the Sheppard case, trial judges continued to be concerned about impaneling impartial juries. Judges issued hundreds of gag orders in the wake of the Sheppard case. Finally, in 1976, in the landmark case of Nebraska Press Association v. Stuart, the Supreme Court ruled that a gag order was an unconstitutional prior restraint that violated the First Amendment to the Constitution. The justices did not go so far as to rule that all gag orders are invalid. But in each case, the trial judge has to prove that an order restraining publication would protect the rights of the accused and that no other alternatives would be less damaging to First Amendment rights.

That ruling, of course, did not end the concerns of trial judges. Rather than issue gag orders restricting the press from reporting court proceedings, some attempted to close their courtrooms. In the first such case to reach the U.S. Supreme Court, Gannett v. DePasquale, the press and public suffered a severe but temporary blow. On July 2, 1979, in a highly controversial decision, the justices said, "We hold that members of the public have no constitutional right under the Sixth and Fourteenth amendments to attend criminal trials." The case itself had involved only a pretrial hearing.

As a result of the decision and the confusion that followed, the Supreme Court of Virginia sanctioned the closing of an entire criminal trial. The accused was acquitted during the second day of the secret trial. The U.S. Supreme Court agreed to hear the appeal of the trial judge's action in a case known as Richmond Newspapers v. Virginia. On July 2, 1980, the court said that under the First Amendment "the trial of a criminal case must be open to the public." Only a court finding of an "overriding interest," which was not defined, would be grounds for closing a criminal trial.

Covering Sex Crimes

The reporting of sex crimes often causes controversy. Most news executives think of their products as family newspapers or broadcasts and are properly hesitant about reporting the lurid details of sex crimes.

Sex Crime Victims. One problem in reporting on sex crimes is the question of how to handle rape victims. Too often, rapes are not reported to police because victims are unwilling to appear in court to testify against the suspects. Defense attorneys sometimes use such occasions to attack the victim's moral character and imply that she (or he) consented to sexual relations. Many victims decline to press charges because of fear that their names will be made public in the media. Both of these things happened to the woman who accused basketball star Kobe Bryant of rape. There is, after all, still a lingering tendency to attach a social stigma to the rape victim, despite increasing public awareness of the nature of the crime. In some states, "rape shield" statutes prohibit a defendant's attorney from delving into the rape victim's prior sexual activity unless some connection can be shown with the circumstances of the rape charged.

Sex Crime Offenders. In Massachusetts, a judge excluded the public and press from the entire trial of a man accused of raping three teenagers. A Massachusetts law provided for the mandatory closing of trials involving specific sex offenses against minors. The U.S. Supreme Court held in 1982 in Globe Newspaper Co. v. Superior Court that the mandatory closure law violated the First Amendment right of access to criminal trials established in the Richmond Newspapers case. The justices ruled that when a state attempts to deny the right of access in an effort to inhibit the disclosure of sensitive information, it must show that the denial "is necessitated by a compelling governmental interest." The court indicated in the opinion that in some cases *in-camera proceedings* (proceedings that take place in a judge's chambers outside the view of the press and public) for youthful witnesses may be appropriate.

In Press-Enterprise v. Riverside County Superior Court, the U.S. Supreme Court ruled in 1984 that a court order closing the jury-selection process in a rape-murder case was invalid. The court ruled that jury selection has been a public process with exceptions only for good cause. In a second Press-Enterprise v. Riverside County Superior Court case, the U.S. Supreme Court said in 1986 that preliminary hearings should be open to the public unless there is a "substantial probability" that the resulting publicity would prevent a fair trial and there are no "reasonable alternatives to closure." In 1993, the Supreme Court continued its emphasis on the importance of open court proceedings. It struck down a Puerto Rican law that said preliminary hearings "shall be held privately" unless the defendant requests a public preliminary hearing.

Press-Bar Guidelines

These cases appeared to uphold the right of the press and the public to have access to criminal proceedings. Judges, however, have a duty to protect the rights of the accused. The Supreme Court of the State of Washington, in Federated Publications v. Swedberg, held in 1981 that press access to pretrial hearings may be conditioned on the agreement of reporters to abide by voluntary press-bar guidelines that exist in some states. The decision involved a preliminary hearing in a Bellingham, Wash., murder case tied to the "Hillside Strangler" murders in the Los Angeles area. The state Supreme Court ruled that the lower-court order was "a good-faith attempt to accommodate the interests of both defendant and press." The lower court had required reporters covering the hearing to sign a document in which the reporters agreed to abide by press-bar guidelines. The state Supreme Court said the document should be taken as a moral commitment on the part of the reporters, not as a legally enforceable document.

The U.S. Supreme Court in 1982 refused to hear an appeal of that case. Fortunately, many states have statutes to the effect that "the setting of every court shall be public, and every person may freely attend the same." When such statutes are in place, the closed-courtroom controversy appears to be moot. In states that have no such statute, the result seems to be that:

- A criminal trial must be open unless there is an "overriding interest" that requires some part of it to be closed.
- Judges must find some overriding interest before closing pretrial hearings.

One effect of the Washington decision is that many media groups are withdrawing from state press-bar agreements in the few states that have such guidelines. Their reasoning is that the voluntary guidelines in effect could become mandatory.

Cameras in the Courtroom

In 1994, the U.S. Judicial Conference ended its three-year experiment on cameras in federal courts by banning cameras. In 1996, the Judicial Conference agreed to permit cameras in some lower federal courts. And 47 states do allow cameras in at least some state courtrooms. Only Indiana, Mississippi, South Dakota and the District of Columbia ban courtroom cameras.

The fact remains that there are many ways for judges to protect the rights of the accused without trampling on the right of the press and public to attend trials and pretrial hearings. Indeed, most editors are sensitive to the rights of the accused. Most exercise self-restraint when publishing or broadcasting information about a crime. Most have attempted to establish written policy on such matters, although others insist that individual cases must be judged on their merits.

Coverage of Minority Groups

Reporters and editors must share with judges the burden of protecting the rights of the accused. They also must ensure that certain groups within our society are not treated unfairly, either by the courts or in the media. In a study of crime reporting at the Gannett Center for Media Studies, Robert Snyder discovered that minorities tend to be covered by the media mainly in the context of crime news. Crime reporting is a staple of urban news, and urban areas are where minorities are concentrated. In large cities like New York and Los Angeles, some areas of the city often make news only because of crime. As it is reported now, Snyder says, crime is almost always a conversation about race. He concludes that if the media are to change that perception, they must cover minorities more broadly and sympathetically. The real story of crime, Snyder says, should be the "breaking down of communities and the real weakening of the social structure."

Many editors are concerned about the way minorities are portrayed in crime stories. Many newspapers and broadcast stations, in fact, studiously avoid gratuitous mentions of race. Their reporters are allowed to mention the race of a suspect only as part of the complete identification of a fugitive. For many years, it was common to read or hear references to a "six-foot-tall black man" wanted for a crime. Today such a description would be considered unacceptable. Too many men fit that description, and the racial reference merely reinforces the stereotype of blacks as criminals. If, however, a complete description of a fugitive might help lead to an arrest, it is appropriate to mention race as a part of that description. Only when race becomes the central theme of a story should it be emphasized.

Similarly, most editors consider a person's sexual orientation off limits unless the story focuses on heterosexuality or homosexuality. Increasingly, though, gays and lesbians are willing to talk openly about their sexual orientation as a means of advancing the cause of gay rights. Such issues cannot and should not be ignored by the media. But tastefully handling crime news involving homosexual crimes often proves to be difficult. This was never more true than in the sensational murder trial of Milwaukee's Jeffrey Dahmer, convicted of sexually molesting young boys and men, killing them and eating parts of their bodies. In such cases, the press walks a fine line between responsibly informing the public and pandering to its seemingly insatiable appetite for sensational crime news.

Coverage of Terrorism

Since the 2001 attacks on the World Trade Center and the Pentagon, much has been written about the rights of those arrested as alleged terrorists. Suspects have been held for years without charge at the U.S. naval base at Guantánamo Bay, Cuba, and interrogated by U.S. officials in foreign countries. Rights activists and the suspects' attorneys have challenged such actions as unconstitutional, and the courts have agreed. This ongoing battle is likely to be a matter of contention for the foreseeable future.

Issues of Taste and Ethics

News editors ponder a number of major issues involving taste and ethics in crime and court reporting:

- When should the media reveal details of how a murder or another crime was committed?
- When should the media reveal details about sex crimes or print the names of sex-crime victims?
- When should the media reveal a suspect's confession or even the fact that the suspect confessed?
- When should the media reveal a defendant's prior criminal record?
- When should the media reveal the names of juveniles charged with crimes?

None of these questions can be answered to everyone's satisfaction, and it is doubtful whether rules can be established to apply in all such situations.

Reporting Details of a Crime

There have been charges that when the media reveal details of a murder, some people use the techniques described to commit additional murders. This charge is directed most frequently at television, but newspapers have not been immune and online media may also face this issue.

Reporting Confessions and Prior Convictions

Many editors will not publish or broadcast details of a suspect's confession in an effort to protect the suspect's rights. Revealing such information blocks the way for a fair trial perhaps more than anything else the media can do. Some newspapers and broadcast stations, however, continue to reveal assertions by police or prosecutors that a confession was signed. Many critics question whether such information isn't just as prejudicial as the confession statement itself.

Occasionally, journalists question whether to suppress an unsolicited confession. After a youth was charged with a series of robberies and was certified to stand trial as an adult, a newspaper reporter phoned the youthful defendant, who was free on bail, for an interview. The result was interesting. The defendant admitted to two other robberies in what amounted to a confession to the newspaper and its readers. The editor, who would not have printed a simple statement by police that the defendant had confessed to the crimes, printed this one. Why? The editor reasoned that information about a confession to police amounts to secondhand, hearsay information. The confession to a reporter, however, was firsthand information obtained by the newspaper directly from the accused.

Lawyers also view as prejudicial the publication of a defendant's prior criminal record. Even if authorities refuse to divulge that information, much of it may be in the morgue. Should it be reported? Most journalists believe it should be, particularly if a prior conviction was for a similar offense. Most attorneys disagree.

Identifying Juveniles

Whether to use the names of juveniles charged with crimes is a troublesome issue as well. Most states prohibit law enforcement officers and court officials from releasing the names of juveniles. The reasoning of those who oppose releasing juveniles' names is that the publicity marks them for life as criminals. Those who hold this view argue that there is ample opportunity for these individuals to change their ways and become good citizens—if the media do not stamp them as criminals. Others argue that juveniles who commit serious offenses, such as rape and armed robbery, should be treated as adults.

Questions such as these elicit divergent views from editors, some of whom regularly seek the advice of their lawyers. Little guidance for the reporter can be offered here. Because the decision to publish or not to publish is the editor's, not the reporter's, consultation is necessary. Each case must be decided on its merits.

OBITUARIES AND LIFE STORIES

In the online world, obituaries are big business. Newspaper websites sell advertising to funeral homes and auxiliary services because they have found that readers search for obituaries frequently. Even former residents of a city monitor obituaries. Some websites are devoted to obituaries and provide resources for readers and advertisers. One, www.legacy.com, partially owned by a newspaper, provides links and a searchable database to hundreds of newspapers and, in turn, sells advertising to the funeral industry. It also allows readers to post memorials to friends and family members who have died.

Web editors and entrepreneurs are just discovering the drawing power of obituaries, but most newspaper editors have known about it for years. Chuck Ward, publisher of the *Olean (N.Y.) Times Herald*, once told his readers about the time his editor asked whether they should do a special obituary on the father of one of their employees: "My response was that unless the father (or any relative) of the employee met the criteria for a glorified obituary, the obituary should be treated as 99 percent of our obituaries are."

He then recounted that when he went to the visitation that evening, the line extended 50 yards outside the mortuary. He returned in an hour, and the line was still long. That got Ward thinking about his question earlier in the day: "What did he do?"

"All he did, apparently, was live a wonderful, loving life with a splendid family. During the course of that life, he must have touched the lives of countless people in our community. And they all were there to say goodbye."

Ward learned that people don't have to be public figures to deserve well-reported obituaries. Too many obituaries read as if they were written by a computer program—efficient but lifeless. This tendency persists despite readership surveys that show that about 50 percent of readers look at obituaries, about twice as many as those who look at most other features.

And obituaries are read critically. If the deceased was an Odd Fellow, you'd better not say he was an Elk. If the deceased belonged to the Shiloh Baptist Church, count on a phone call if you say she was a member of Bethany Baptist. Reporting and writing obituaries is important work.

Despite this importance, many newspapers do not publish a news obituary unless the person who died was well-known. Television news generally follows the same policy. However, you're more likely to find staff-written obituaries in local publications, in print and online. Jim Nicholson of the Philadelphia *Daily News*, who wrote obituaries full-time and won the American Society of News Editors Distinguished Writing Award, explained why. Readers want to know, he said, "How did someone live a good life? How did they get through this world?"

An obituary is a news story. You should apply the same standards to crafting a lead and building the body of an obituary as you do to other stories.

Crafting a Lead

You begin by answering the same questions you would answer in any news story: who (Michael Kelly, 57, of 1234 West St.), what (died), where (at Regional Hospital), when (Tuesday night), why (heart attack) and how (while jogging). With this information, you are ready to start the story.

The fact that Kelly died of a heart attack suffered while jogging may well be the lead, but the reporter does not know this until the rest of the information essential to every obituary has been gathered. You also must know:

- Time and place of funeral services
- Time and place of burial
- Visitation time (if any)
- Survivors
- Date and place of birth
- Achievements
- Occupation
- Memberships

Any of these items can yield the nugget that will appear in the lead. However, if none of these categories yields notable information, the obituary will probably start like this:

> Michael Kelly, 60, of 1234 West St., died Tuesday night at Regional Hospital.

Another standard approach could be used later in the news cycle:

> Funeral services for Michael Kelly, 60, of 1234 West St., will be at 2 p.m. Thursday at St. Catherine's Roman Catholic Church.

However, good reporters often find distinguishing characteristics of a person's life. It may be volunteer service, an unusual or important job, service in public office or even just having a name of historical significance. Whatever distinguishes a person can be the lead of the obituary.

Building the Story

You will find most of the obituary information on a standard form from the mortuary. When the reporter relies only on the form, this is usually what results:

Michael Kelly, 60, of 1234 West St., died Tuesday night at Regional Hospital.

Kelly collapsed while jogging and died apparently of a heart attack.

Services will be at 2 p.m. Thursday at St. Catherine's Roman Catholic Church. The Rev. Sherman Mitchell will officiate. Burial will be at Glendale Memorial Gardens in Springfield.

Friends may visit at the Fenton Funeral Chapel from 7 to 9 p.m. Wednesday.

Born Dec. 20, 1950, in Boston to Nathan and Sarah Kelly, Kelly was a member of St. Catherine's Roman Catholic Church and a U.S. Navy veteran of the Vietnam War. He had been an independent insurance agent for the last 25 years.

He married Pauline Virginia Hatfield in Boston on May 5, 1970.

Survivors include his wife; a son, Kevin, of Charlotte, N.C.; and a daughter, Mary, who is a student at the University of North Carolina at Chapel Hill.

Also surviving are a brother, John, of Milwaukee, Wis., and a sister, Margaret Carter, of Asheville, N.C.

TIPS

Five Safeguards for Obit Writers

- Confirm spellings of names on the mortuary form.

- Check the addresses. If a telephone book or city directory lists a different address, contact the mortuary about the discrepancy.

- Check the birth date against the age, noting whether the person's birthday was before or after the date of death.

- Verify with the mortuary or family any obituary phoned or faxed to the newspaper.

- Check your newspaper's library for stories about the deceased, but be sure you don't pull stories about someone else with the same name.

Writing Life Stories

The Kelly obituary is a dry biography, not a story of his life. There is no hint of Kelly's impact on friends, family or community. Good reporting produces stories of life, such as this one:

> Frank Martin loved to garden and loved to share.
>
> "When the ground began to thaw, he'd try to figure out how to grow things," friend and co-worker Walter Begley recalled.
>
> Another friend, Caroline Newby, said he would come to her home to help take care of her small vineyard. He made wine from the grapes to share with his family during the holidays. When she had problems with her crop, Mr. Martin would drive over and open the trunk of his old Dodge to reveal a nursery of soil and gardening tools.
>
> On the back of that car was a bumper sticker that read "Practice Random Acts of Kindness and Senseless Acts of Beauty." Newby said Mr. Martin lived by that phrase. . . .

The more traditional biographical information, along with information about visitation and funeral services, appears later in the story.

When writing a life story, you ask people what was important to the deceased and what the evidence for that is. If the subject volunteered, find out where and why and talk to the people served. Your goal is to capture the theme of the person's life. If the family and friends recognize the deceased in your story as the person they knew, you have done your job. Amy Rabideau Silvers, the obituary writer for the *Milwaukee Journal Sentinel*, provides such an example in Figure 16.2.

Sources of Information

Writing an obituary or life story is like writing a feature story. You seek anecdotes that reveal the person. Your sources include the mortuary form, paid funeral notices, your publication's own library, and family and friends of the deceased.

The Mortuary Form

For many reporters, the standard form from the mortuary is the primary source of information. The mortuary can be of further help if you need more information. Does your city editor want a picture of the deceased? Call the mortuary. They can usually obtain one quickly from the family. Is there some conflicting or unclear information on the form? Call the mortuary for clarification.

Writing obituaries from the mortuary's information alone is a clerk's work. As a reporter, you should go beyond the form. You should also confirm every fact on the sheet. Mortuary forms are notoriously inaccurate.

Sometimes, what the mortuary form doesn't tell you is as important as what it does. For the writer of the following obit, the first clue that the death notice was unusual was the age. The deceased was 12. That alone was enough for the reporter

A Life Story

OBITUARY
A Life of Love Was Made Public in End
Couple Came Out, Testified at Capitol

By Amy Rabideau Silvers, Staff
Milwaukee Journal Sentinel

The opening teases, much like a feature story lead.

For nearly 49 years, Richard Taylor and Ray Vahey did not speak openly about their long and loving relationship.

They did not tell family. They did not tell friends at work.

Two short sentences in a separate paragraph bring attention to themselves.

That changed a year ago, after Vahey was asked if they might speak at PrideFest. Together, they wrote a speech. Vahey gave it, Taylor at his side.

This is the "so what." It establishes the impact Vahey and Taylor had on the state debate. This story is a history of an era told through the experience of two men, one of whom died.

They went on to other appearances, including a state hearing last November in Madison, speaking against the proposed amendment that would ban gay marriage and civil unions in Wisconsin. They spoke at area churches. They were asked to speak at PrideFest in June, but Taylor, hospitalized with cancer, was too ill to go.

"We wrote the speech together at his hospital bed," Vahey said. Then Taylor said something Vahey will never forget.

This strong anecdote motivates the reader to keep on reading.

"Ray, remember, I'm standing right beside you," he said.

"And I feel that now," Vahey said.

News peg. This is a variation of the focus structure.

Richard Taylor died Friday. He was 81.

By chance, his name appeared twice in the *Journal Sentinel* on Sunday. The longtime partners were mentioned in a "Crossroads" opinion piece opposing the proposed amendment. His death notice appeared in the same edition.

"We were from the silent generation," Vahey said. "It was an exaggerated version of don't ask, don't tell."

Vahey is the primary source because they lived together for nearly 50 years.

"I was 18 and he was 31" when they met in 1956, Vahey said. Both grew up in Ohio—Taylor in Cleveland and Vahey in Youngstown.

Taylor's service in the Navy becomes important later in the story.

"When Richard was 17, he convinced his father to allow him to join the Navy during World War II," Vahey said.

Taylor served aboard a naval tanker on convoy duty, first in the North Atlantic and then in the Mediterranean. His tanker next moved into the Pacific.

"His tanker fueled a cruiser while it bombarded Mount Suribachi on Iwo Jima, and then they went on to Okinawa, where they came under kamikaze attack," he said.

Figure 16.2
This life story uses the basic focus structure. All it lacks is a tie-back.

Taylor, who had a high school education, was also self-taught, widely read in economics and philosophy, history and politics. As the two men grew older, they came to see history in a new light.

Here is the impact of his Navy service.

"Richard voluntarily put himself into harm's way to protect his country and the rights of all Americans of that day, and all of the generations that have followed. Now there is an attempt to separate Richard from society and take away his right to equality under the law."

Over the years, they lived in Ohio, Illinois, California, New Jersey and Virginia. In 2000 they decided to move to Milwaukee, a city they knew from visits to Taylor's brother.

Finally, they decided to step out of the closet for good.

This anecdote reveals the depth of their cover-up.

"I never told my sister about us until the night we testified in Madison," Vahey said, adding that she took the news without surprise or judgment. "It was like the elephant in the living room. It was there, but no one addressed it."

The official transcripts of hearings and stories in your newspaper library are good sources for quotes.

"Euphemisms like 'partnership' or 'union' set us apart from society," Vahey said at the legislative hearing last fall. "Substitute terms that categorize and separate us become our yellow Star of David badges. . . . Here at home, African-Americans learned long ago that 'separate but equal' is not equal."

Taylor and Vahey planned a wedding ceremony for Sept. 16, the 50th anniversary of their life together. But when Taylor became increasingly ill, they had moved up the date, marrying in a religious ceremony at the hospital on Memorial Day. Invitations now will be sent for a special memorial event Sept. 16, which also will be a fund-raiser for Fair Wisconsin's anti-amendment efforts.

The story concludes with basic obituary information.

Visitation will be from 5 to 7 p.m. today at the Suminski Family Funeral Home, 1901 N. Farwell Ave.

In addition to Vahey, Taylor is survived by brother Robert Morgan, nieces and nephews.

to start asking questions. The result was an obituary that moved from the records column to the front page:

Sandra Ann Hill, 12, lost her lifetime struggle against a mysterious muscle ailment Wednesday night. The day she died was the first day she had ever been admitted as a hospital inpatient.

Although they knew it was coming, the end came suddenly for Sandra's family and school friends, said her father, Lester, of 1912 Jackson St.

Just last Friday, she attended special classes at the Parkdale School. "She loved it there," Hill said. "Like at recess, when

TIPS

Policy Options for Handling Obits

- Run an obituary that ignores any embarrassing information and, if necessary, leave out the cause of death. If circumstances surrounding the death warrant a news story, run it separate from the obituary.

- Include embarrassing details and the cause of death in all obituaries.

- Include embarrassing details and the cause of death in the obituary only for a public figure.

- Put a limit on how far back in the person's life to use derogatory information such as a conviction.

- Print everything thought newsworthy that is learned about public figures but not about private figures.

- Print everything thought newsworthy about public and private figures.

- Decide each case as it comes up.

the sixth graders would come in and read to her. She always wanted to be the center of attention."

"Bright as a silver dollar" was the way one of Sandra's early teachers described her. In fact, no one will ever know. Sandra couldn't talk.

"We didn't know what she knew or didn't know," her father said. Sandra's only communication with the world around her came in the form of smiles and frowns — her symbols for yes and no.

"There were times when I'd come around the corner and kind of stick my head around and say 'boo,'" her father recalled. "She smiled. She liked that."

The care and attention Sandra demanded makes the loss particularly hard for her family to accept, Hill said. "I can't really put it into words. You cope with it the best you can, keep her comfortable and happy. We always took her with us."

Sandra came down with bronchitis Friday. Complications forced her to be admitted Wednesday to Lincoln County Hospital, where she died later that night.

Sandra's fight for life was uphill all the way. It started simply enough when she was 4 months old. Her mother, Bonnie, noticed she "wasn't holding up her head" like her other children.

Although her ailment was never firmly diagnosed, doctors found Sandra's muscles held only half the tissues and fibers in a normal child's body. The diagnosis: a type of cerebral palsy. The prognosis: Sandra had little chance to live past the age of 2. Medical knowledge offered little help.

Sandra was born in Springfield on Jan. 15, 1984. She is survived by her parents; one brother, Michael Eugene Hill; one sister, Terrie Lynn Hill, both of the home; and her grandparents, Gordon Hill of Seale, Ala., and Mrs. Carrie Harris of Phoenix, Ariz.

Services will be at 3:30 p.m. today at the Memorial Funeral Chapel with the Rev. Jack Gleason conducting. Burial will follow at the Memorial Park Cemetery.

The family will receive friends at the Memorial Funeral Home until time for the service.

The reporter who wrote this obituary obviously did a great deal of research beyond what was on the mortuary form. Because the girl was not a public figure, the reporter could not consult a reference work such as *Who's Who in America* or a national publication. But the reporter did have access to the newspaper library and could interview the girl's family and friends.

The News Room Library

In the news room library, you may find an interview with the deceased, an interesting feature story or clips indicating activities not included on the mortuary form. In an interview or feature story the person may have made a statement about a philosophy of life that would be appropriate to include in the obituary. The subject also may have indicated his or her goals in life, against which later accomplishments can be measured. You can find the names of friends and co-workers in the clips as well. These people are often the source of rich anecdotes and comments about the deceased.

Your news room files are not the only source for information on people who have state or national reputations. You or your librarian should also search electronic databases for stories that have appeared in other publications.

Interviews with Family and Friends

Journalists treat public figures in more detail than private citizens not only because they are newsworthy but also because reporters know more about them. Even though private citizens are usually less newsworthy, many good stories about them are never written because the reporter did not—or was afraid to—do the reporting. The fear is usually unfounded.

Cause of Death

If the person who died was not a public figure and the family does not wish to divulge the cause of death, some news organizations will comply. That is questionable news judgment. The reader wants to know what caused the death. A reporter should call the mortuary, the family, the attending physician and the appropriate medical officer. Only if none of these sources will talk should you leave out the cause of death.

A death certificate must be filed for each death, but obtaining it often takes days, and some states do not make the cause of death part of the public record. Even if the state lists the cause of death and the reporter has timely access to the death certificate, the information is often vague.

If the deceased was a public figure or a young person, most newspapers insist on the cause of death. If the death is the result of suicide or foul play, reporters can obtain the information from the police or the medical examiner. Some newspapers include suicide as the cause of death in the obituary, others print it in a separate news story, and still others ignore it altogether. This is one way to report a suicide:

> Services for Gary O'Neal, 34, a local carpenters' union officer, will be at 9 a.m. Thursday in the First Baptist Church. Coroner Mike Pardee ruled that Mr. O'Neal died Tuesday of a self-inflicted gunshot wound.

Embarrassing Information

Another newspaper policy affecting obituaries concerns embarrassing information. When the *St. Louis Post-Dispatch* reported in an obituary that the deceased had been disbarred and that he had been a key witness in a bribery scandal involving a well-known politician 13 years earlier, several callers complained. The paper's reader's advocate defended the decision to include that history in the obituary:

> One who called to complain about the obit told me it reminded her of the quotation from Shakespeare's *Julius Caesar*, about how the good a man does is often buried with him and forgotten.
> Yes, I said, and the first part of that quotation could be paraphrased to say that the news a man makes often lives after him.

✒ I don't write about death, I write about life. ✒

— Michael Best, *The Detroit News*

TIPS

Sources for Obits

- Mortuary forms.
- Paid funeral notices.
- The news room's library.
- Interviews with family and friends of the deceased.

When author W. Somerset Maugham died, *The New York Times* reported that he was a homosexual, even though the subject generally had not been discussed in public before. Yet many years later, when Susan Sontag died, few publications included the fact that she had acknowledged her bisexuality in a newspaper interview, even though Sontag herself clearly wasn't embarrassed by this information. When Bill Mauldin, a Pulitzer Prize-winning editorial cartoonist, died in 2003, the *Chicago Sun-Times*, where he had worked for years, wrote, "In his last years, Mr. Mauldin battled alcoholism and Alzheimer's."

The crucial factor in determining the extent to which you should report details of an individual's private life is whether the deceased was a public or private person. A public figure is someone who has been in the public eye. A participant in civic or social activities, a person who spoke out at public meetings or through the mass media, a performer, an author, a speaker—these all may be public figures. A public official, an individual who has been elected or appointed to public office, is generally treated like a public figure.

Whether the subject is a public figure or a private citizen, the decisions newspapers must make when dealing with the obituary are sensitive and complicated. It is your obligation to be aware of your organization's policy. In the absence of a clear policy statement, consult an editor.

Suggested Readings

Center on Crime, Communities and Culture and *Columbia Journalism Review. Covering Criminal Justice.* New York: Graduate School of Journalism, Columbia University, 2000. This manual lists resources to help reporters cover crime and the courts.

Giles, Robert H., and Robert W. Snyder, eds. *Covering the Courts: Free Press, Fair Trials and Journalistic Performance.* Piscataway, N.J.: Transaction, 1998. This book provides useful guidance from professional journalists.

Pulitzer, Lisa Beth. *Crime on Deadline: Police Reporters Tell Their Most Unforgettable Stories.* New York: Boulevard, 1996.

Real stories from nine of the nation's top crime reporters are featured in this book.

Siegel, Marvin, ed. *The Last Word:* The New York Times *Book of Obituaries and Farewells: A Celebration of Unusual Lives.* New York: Quill, 1998. Examples abound of well-written and compelling obituaries from *The New York Times.*

Singer, Eleanor, and Phyllis M. Endreny. *Reporting on Risk: How the Mass Media Portray Accidents, Diseases, Disasters and Other Hazards.* New York: Russell Sage Foundation, 1993. The authors take a critical look at media reporting of accidents and disasters.

Suggested Websites

www.fbi.gov
The FBI website provides useful information about crime.

www.fema.gov
The Federal Emergency Management Agency, part of the U.S. Department of Homeland Security, provides assistance during major emergencies. This site provides useful background information and contacts.

www.ntsb.gov
The National Transportation Safety Board website is an excellent source of accident information.

www.ojr.org
The site for *The Online Journalism Review* has useful tips, articles and information about tools and techniques for reporting and storytelling online.

www.supremecourtus.gov
The Supreme Court of the United States is the nation's highest court. The Court's website outlines its operation.

Exercises

1. **Team project.** Working in teams, analyze the coverage of a major national crime, accident or fire story. Each team member should scrutinize the coverage of the story by a different news organization—print, online or broadcast. Then meet with the other members of your team to compare notes and discuss which stories are most satisfactory and why.

2. Find an accident story in a local newspaper. List all the sources the reporter used in obtaining information for the story. List additional sources you would have checked.

3. Talk with a firefighter in your local fire department about the department's media policy at fire scenes. Using what you learn, write instructions for your fellow reporters on what to expect at fires in your city or town.

4. Cover a session of your local circuit court. Write a story based on the most interesting case of the day.

5. Research the coverage of constitutional rights as they pertain to terrorism suspects. Evaluate whether the media have done an adequate job of covering this issue. If you find fault with the coverage, describe what you would have done differently.

6. Research and write the life story of a resident of your city.

Business and Consumer News

17

The Wall Street meltdown of 2008 sunk the country into what is being called the Long Recession. Mortgage foreclosures, job losses and a rollercoaster stock market have Americans glued to the latest news on the economy.

Business news is now big news. Turn on satellite or cable television in any country around the world, and you'll find 24-hour channels like CNBC or Bloomberg devoted to following the world stock markets, broadcasting that information in English, Chinese, Arabic, Spanish, Portuguese and German. And the speed of the Internet and TV adds complications to an already hard-to-understand topic. Print newspapers and specialized magazines—the legacy media—provide the foundation of information on which the electronic media elaborate.

Many young business journalists soon find themselves at the center of the world's most important stories. On a Sunday night in September 2008, a mere 14 months after graduating from journalism school, FoxBusiness.com reporter Ken Sweet found himself collaborating with editor Kathryn Vasel to piece together a story that would change the financial world. The investment bank Lehman Brothers had collapsed. "It was a Sunday night, and there were so many moving parts—we had Lehman collapsing and then the news broke that Bank of America was buying Merrill Lynch—any other day it would have been a huge story, but it was sidelined by Lehman, and then the problems at AIG came into the mix," says Vasel.

"First you have to get the straight news story out, but it doesn't end there—you have to add in company statements, reaction and what this means for the average consumer and other companies. You have to constantly massage the story to make sure it still flows with the latest add-ins while making sure the latest news is still in the lead," she says. On a major story, Vasel knew she had to get details precisely right, making sure she didn't overstate or mislead. "It was hard to swallow such a big story, but I also had to make sure to do the mundane tasks of double-checking names and titles to get it right."

Despite woes in many parts of journalism, business news has seen growth, and knowledgeable young journalists have attractive job prospects. Sean Sposito, a 2009 graduate, was able to choose from three job offers before taking the real estate beat for *The (Newark) Star-Ledger.* Joanna Schneider, who graduated in 2008, has found that college training in business reporting helped her continue her freelance career in Kansas City.

So, how do you get started covering business news? First, you need to understand basic business terminology and basic math. You also need to learn how to read financial statements, which is surprisingly easy. Beyond that, you need the skills of any journalist: perseverance, curiosity and an ability to ask questions and get answers.

THE GROWING IMPORTANCE OF BUSINESS JOURNALISM

With government taking an active role in industry, like the government supervision of General Motors, it's especially important for political reporters to learn the basics of business. The declining state of the U.S. economy was the key issue in the

2008 presidential election campaign. Health issues, as well, are becoming increasingly related to economics, and reporters covering health care reform need to understand the business side of health care in order to explain these new changes to citizens. Influenza epidemics, like the one involving the H1N1 virus, have profound financial effects on the workforce and tourism.

All stories have some sort of business angle. A quick glance at an edition of *The Wall Street Journal* shows the breadth of news with an economic angle — from admissions policies at Ivy League schools to the latest technology employed by Procter & Gamble scientists in the $1.3 billion home hair-coloring industry.

Yet many news directors and editors still struggle with the focus of their business news. Who is their audience? Is it consumers, investors, local business executives or people looking for work? When gasoline prices rise in Texas, should reporters in Dallas emphasize how high prices hurt consumers or how they increase the costs of goods shipped by highway? Or should they write about how higher oil profits will spur more oil exploration off the Texas Gulf Coast? Or should they focus on the potential loss of jobs at refineries hurt by a decline in gasoline consumption? This array of ways to focus business stories provides both a crisis and an opportunity in the field of business journalism.

Business news is changing rapidly. Financial news, including up-to-the-second stock prices, is now available on mobile devices. Business executives use Twitter to send messages directly to customers, and the number of business-related Facebook sites is growing.

The increasing number of business news outlets is just one reason why business-trained journalists are in high demand. Even in a troubled newspaper industry, these specially trained journalists often command a 20 percent premium in salary, according to Detroit-based recruiter Joe Grimm, who blogs for the Poynter Institute.

Business journalism training is also important for those who seek jobs in corporate communications. With more than 60 percent of Americans owning stock, mostly through 401K retirement plans, corporate communications divisions employ journalists to write about investor and consumer issues.

Specialized Business News

Local newspapers are shedding business staff members as part of a major employment decline, but those reporters are finding some job opportunities at weekly journals that have grown and expanded in all major U.S. cities — from Fresno to Louisville to Hartford. American City Business Journals, based in Charlotte, N.C., publishes profitably in multiple cities.

Pick an industry and there is a magazine, Internet news site, newsletter or newspaper that specializes in covering it. Far from sleepy operations, these publications often find themselves in the midst of breaking news. *CFO* magazine — whose audience is chief financial officers in a wide range of industries — doesn't shy away from covering the scandals that have rocked the finance industry. A weekly trade newspaper, *The Packer*, based in Lenexa, Kan., covered the recall of bacteria-infected fresh spinach, which resulted in several deaths. Matt Jarzemsky covers the skyscraper office rental market, and Libby Sallaberry covers debt issues for Institutional Investor newsletters—a New York-based premium subscription product that covers industry sectors.

Global Reach

Business journalism is a growing global industry. Business newspapers are now prevalent in China's major cities. The *Shanghai Securities News*, founded in 1991, focuses on covering the Shanghai and Hong Kong Stock Exchanges as well as Asian economic news. American business media outlets have bureaus in major Asian cities and often employ multilingual reporters. It was a team of Chinese and American reporters for Dow Jones Newswires, the fee-based industry wire service, that broke the China copper-trading scandal in 2005. Those stories won several distinguished journalism prizes.

Business journalists who work for mainstream organizations must acknowledge the often-conflicting outcomes of economic events. A story about an outbreak of mad cow disease in Washington state could have multiple effects—depressing the earnings of McDonald's but boosting the price of Brazilian beef and leading to trade restrictions from a nervous Taiwan.

And business journalists must be able to see the big picture. While many Americans have lost jobs that went to workers in India or Mexico, an increasing number of Americans now work for global employers. Workers in South Carolina make small refrigerators for Chinese-owned Haier Inc. Autoworkers in southern Indiana learn Japanese manufacturing techniques while building SUVs for Toyota. The 2008-2009 foreclosure crisis in many U.S. states caused ripples throughout the world because of bonds sold around the globe.

Wide Range of Topics

The range of business stories can be as broad as the range of business itself. Business stories may be about a company's promotions and retirements. Or they may concentrate on company profits, which are of interest to investors and potential investors in that company. Other business stories can cover personal finance issues that are of interest to lay readers rather than investment community insiders. Such stories explore issues such as these: Which is a better choice, a 15- or 30-year mortgage? Is art a good investment? Which mutual funds are high performers? Personal finance news is so popular that there are scores of websites devoted to this topic, like CNN's Money.com. A business story might also be about new products, like a new mobile device. The story would interest not just shareholders of the company but potential buyers as well.

Many stories are both global and local. A story about a decision by the Federal Reserve Board's Open Market Committee to expand or tighten the money supply may seem far removed from your audience. But that decision can affect the rate your readers pay for a car or mortgage loan. A sizable trade deficit for the United

States may weaken the value of the dollar and increase the price of a Sony TV, a Volkswagen car or a bottle of Cutty Sark Scotch whiskey. It takes skill, but a good business journalist can make these seemingly esoteric stories clear and relevant to the audience.

Many major corporate and economic decisions that affect us all are made in Washington, New York, Chicago and a few other major metropolitan centers. But those cities do not have a monopoly on the creation and coverage of business news. Even in towns of a few thousand residents, businesses will be opening or closing, and manufacturing plants will be increasing or decreasing production, hiring or firing employees. Local residents will be spending money for houses, cars, ski trips or new laptop computers, or socking it away in the town's banks or savings and loan associations. There is a business story in every such development.

Increasingly, economics has a strong role in disaster coverage. Hurricane Katrina caused at least $125 billion in economic damage when it swamped coastal areas in Louisiana, Mississippi, Alabama and Florida in 2005. Only half of that was covered by insurance, and recovery is still ongoing. The region will be hampered by the economic effects of the damage long after the cleanup and rebuilding effort ends.

In fact, the economic risk of natural disaster is of paramount interest to investment professionals, who abide by the investing wisdom "Buy on rumor and sell on news." Two days before Katrina hit, financial news outlets like Bloomberg News were already reporting the potential impact on oil drilling and gasoline refineries in the Gulf.

HOW TO REPORT BUSINESS STORIES

Business stories use the same story structures as other types of stories—inverted pyramid, chronology, news narrative and focus. So the preparation is the same as for any other beat. But business writers also have some unique challenges.

Avoiding Jargon and Finding the "So What"

What separates a business story from a soccer story—or, for that matter, a soccer story from a story about atomic particles—is the knowledge and language required to ask the right questions, to recognize the newsworthy answers and to write the story in a way that the reader without specialized knowledge will understand. A reporter who understands the subject can explain what the jargon means.

Business reporters must use understandable language. But oversimplification can turn readers off. *The Wall Street Journal* avoids both traps by shunning jargon as much as possible and explaining any technical terms essential to the story. In one story, for example, *The Journal* explained the terms "Federal Open Market Committee," "federal funds rate," "M1," "M2" and "free-reserve position." Sophisticated readers might know what those terms mean, but many of the paper's readers would not.

TIPS

Reporting Business Stories

- Use language readers will understand, but don't oversimplify.

- Always be fair. You will win the trust and confidence of business-people — or at least their grudging respect.

- Appearances count. It may help you to dress as businesspeople do.

- The more you can demonstrate that you understand a business, the more likely you are to generate trust that will draw out the information you seek.

- There are many sides to business stories — and you need to understand the viewpoint of shareholders, customers, competitors, suppliers and workers.

- Always remember that a company, government agency or pressure group may be using you to plant stories that serve some special interest.

For example, if banks change their lending rates, the personal finance reporter might be the person to write the story explaining that an increase of one percentage point could result in higher interest rates for car or home loans.

If West Coast longshoremen go on strike, one reporter covering local corporations might explore the impact on the supplies for a local manufacturer, while a retail reporter might talk to store owners about whether they'll have a popular toy on their shelves in time for Christmas. With terrorism continuing to affect the airline and travel markets, labor and transportation reporters at the *Orlando Sentinel* often work together on a story about how security alert levels affect local employment.

Putting Sources at Ease

Sourcing presents a major challenge for business reporters: How do you get information from someone who does not legally have to tell you anything? It often takes more creative reporting skills to coax a story from a business source than from a government official. Almost all government information is public. Many business records are not.

The mistrust that many businesspeople have of the press can make it difficult to cover stories adequately, even when it would be in the business's interest to see that the story is told. Even if executives are willing to talk, they may become angry if the reporter quotes an opposing point of view or points out a wart on the corporate visage.

The best antidote a reporter can use against this animosity is to report fairly and accurately what a business is doing and saying. By always being fair, you can win the trust and confidence of businesspeople—or at least their grudging respect.

Because business executives tend to be cautious when talking with reporters, it may help you to dress more like a business manager than a concert reviewer. Appearances count, and businesspeople, like reporters, plumbers, generals and linebackers, feel more comfortable with their own kind. The more you demonstrate that you understand their business, the more likely you are to generate the trust that will draw out the information you seek. Public relations people are often helpful in providing background information and directing you to executives who can provide other comments and information, but you should try to get to know as many company executives as you can. Sometimes you can do this best through a background interview, one not generated by a crisis but intended simply to provide information about what the company is doing. Perhaps you can arrange to have lunch to see what the managers are thinking about and to give them a chance to see that you are probably not the demon that they may have thought you were.

Watching Out for Biases and Conflicts of Interest

Always remember that a company, government agency or pressure group may be trying to use you to plant stories that serve some special interest. Companies want a story to make them look promising to investors with the hope of driving up the price of the stock or to make them appear to be attractive merger partners. If you

ON THE JOB

are suspicious, do some digging; talk to competitors and analysts, and ask detailed questions. Just because a company or some other group is pushing a story does not mean you have to write it.

Conflict-of-interest issues challenge business journalists because they often write stories, some of which are unfavorable, about advertisers. Business editors across the country have become increasingly concerned as advertisers threaten to pull advertising over unfavorable coverage. For instance, a 2003 story in the *Orlando Sentinel* on the shoddy practices of homebuilders cost the newspaper $700,000 in canceled advertisements. Because business news can affect market prices, business journalists must adhere to a strong code of ethics to make sure that there is no appearance that stories are being influenced. In addition, business journalists violate U.S. securities laws and face jail time if they trade stocks based on inside information uncovered during the reporting process.

WHERE TO FIND BUSINESS STORIES

The starting point in writing a business story is similar to the first step in reporting any story—understanding the subject you're writing about. For the business reporter, that almost always means some basic research into the subject. For openers,

TIPS

Where to Find Business Stories

● Conduct some basic research into the subject. Check the electronic and paper archives to learn what's been written locally about the topic or company.

● Turn to your computer. From a broad spectrum of databases you can obtain lists and summaries of stories published on a wide range of subjects.

● Read print sources to find stories about your business or industry.

check your organization's archives to learn what's been written locally about your topic or company.

There is a broad spectrum of Internet-accessible databases that provide lists and summaries of stories published on a wide range of subjects. The truly adept can plumb raw data, including stock market transactions, to track the impact of announcements, mergers and personnel changes on stock prices. But everyone can use simple Internet searches to access annual reports, stock analyses, press releases and other announcements.

Of growing importance are databases that provide lists and summaries of stories published on a range of topics. Standard & Poor's, Dow Jones Factiva and Disclosure Inc. are some of the companies providing these data. Reuters, Dow Jones Factiva and Bloomberg Business News also provide background information on companies and securities, historical prices and real-time news on business and economic issues. Likewise, Business Wire, PR Newswire, all major newspapers and magazines, and the Associated Press all provide online business information.

Journalists also use websites focused on investors, such as Yahoo Finance, which compiles news on companies and provides links to government-required SEC filings and historical stock-price charts.

Records and Reports

Here are some good sources of information that you will find invaluable when writing business stories. Remember, many of these can be accessed through various online databases. That means you can decide on a question, log on and have the information you need right away.

Corporate Data

Basic information on corporations can be found online, either on the company's own website or through government filings. Independent sources include *Dun & Bradstreet's Million Dollar Directory*, a list of U.S. companies worth $1 million or more. The *Middle Market Directory* profiles companies worth $500,000 to $999,999. The three-volume *Standard & Poor's Register of Corporations, Directors and Executives* provides similar information for about 36,000 U.S. and Canadian companies. Volume 2 provides brief biographies of executives and directors. Other directories are the *Thomas Register of American Manufacturers* and the *Thomas Register Catalog File*.

Investment Data

To get specific information about the financial performance of a company or an industry, check reports prepared by Standard & Poor's (especially valuable is S&P's Compustat Services Inc.), Moody's, Dun & Bradstreet, Thomson First Call and Value Line Investment Survey. These reports also discuss company prospects and major trends. Also helpful are annual corporate scoreboards prepared by *Fortune*, *Business Week* and *Forbes* magazines.

Financial Ratios

To assess a company's financial picture and management, you should compare your subject's financial ratios with the averages for other firms in the same industry. Industry ratios and averages can be found in reports prepared by Dun & Bradstreet, Moody's, and S&P's Compustat and in a number of trade journals.

Company Filings

For years, the Securities and Exchange Commission operated under the guiding principle that companies should make available a maximum amount of information so that stockholders could make the most informed decisions regarding management's performance. The SEC preferred to keep out of corporate affairs and to let the stockholders provide the necessary discipline. Much of the information companies provide to stockholders is made public through SEC filings.

You should start with the annual report, which will give you an attractively packaged overview of the company's operations and finances. The 10-K, a more detailed version of the annual report required by the SEC, also will give you the number of employees, a list of major real estate and equipment holdings, and information on any significant legal proceedings. Many other important documents, such as labor contracts, are listed by reference and can be acquired through the company, a Freedom of Information Act request or a private service such as Disclosure Inc. Annual reports often show up on the nightstands of business reporters. Carol Loomis, a prize-winning reporter for *Forbes* magazine, read 50 years' worth of company annual reports while researching a story on Bethlehem Steel.

Most filings are available free of charge through the SEC's online EDGAR system, but journalists often use the pay service Morningstar Document Research, which alerts them electronically to SEC filings by the companies they cover. Other outlets, such as MarketWatch and Yahoo Finance, will let you set up "alerts" to news and filings on companies of interest.

Another SEC filing, the *proxy statement*, which goes to shareholders before the annual meeting or other important meetings, provides an outline of issues to be voted on, as well as executive salaries and information on the company's board of directors. The proxy also sometimes contains leads about the company's business dealings. Interesting nuggets are found under mundane headings such as "Other Matters" or "Legal Proceedings." For example, now-bankrupt Enron Corp. disclosed some hints about its offshore partnerships in the footnotes of the Houston company's SEC filings. Those footnotes generated some stories, but company officials did not disclose the true extent of the company's financial problems. In any filing, always read anything pertaining to lawsuits. That, in turn, can lead you to public documents regarding a particular suit.

Many companies are quite willing to send you their annual report, 10-K and proxy statement. They may even send you the other documents outlined above. To keep up with SEC filings, you may want to follow the *SEC News Digest* at your local library or use the SEC's EDGAR service.

Trade Press

Beyond the newspapers and magazines you already know and read is another segment of journalism known as the *trade press*. In these journals and house organs you will find grocers talking with grocers, undertakers talking with undertakers and bankers talking with bankers. You will learn the important issues in a field, how an industry markets its products and services, and what legislation it fears and favors. Interested in health care and physicians? Try *Medical Economics*, where investigative reporter Jessica Mitford predicts you will find "many a crass and wonderfully quotable appeal to the avarice of the practitioners of the healing arts."

A number of trade publications are independent and objective. Among them are *Advertising Age, Aviation Week & Space Technology, Institutional Investor, American Banker, Medical World News* and *Variety,* the last of which covers the entertainment industry. Many more, however, are practically industry public relations organs. But even these can be valuable for learning about current issues, marketing and lobbying strategies, and even market shares. To find trade publications, consult the *Standard Periodical Directory, Ulrich's International Periodicals Directory, Standard Rate & Data Service: Business Publication Rates and Data* and *Gale Directory of Publications and Broadcast Media.* Many trade publications offer online versions, like www.ogj.com, the online version of the comprehensive trade publication *Oil & Gas Journal.*

Newsletters

Newsletters have become an important source of inside information in recent years. Some are purely ideological, but others can be valuable. Among the best are *The Energy Daily, Nucleonics Week* and *Education Daily.* Peter Zollman, a former reporter for United Press International, runs a subscription-only print and online newsletter, *Classified Intelligence,* which covers the $7 billion online classified industry, which includes such companies as Monster.com and Craigslist.

Directories

Directories, many of them online, can be an invaluable tool for locating information on companies, organizations or individuals. You can use them to learn who makes a certain product, to identify company officers or directors or to find an expert source for an interview. Basic directories include *Who's Who, Directory of Directories, Guide to American Directories, Consultants and Consulting Organizations Directory, Directory of Special Libraries and Information Centers, Research Centers Directory, Consumer Sourcebook, Statistical Sources* and *Directory of Industrial Data Sources.*

Court Records

Most companies disclose only information required by the SEC. But when a corporation sues or is sued, an extensive amount of material becomes available. Likewise, criminal action against principals in a firm can provide the lead to a good story. It is important to check court testimony and records at all levels, including those of bankruptcy and divorce courts. Information about the pay package and executive perks of former General Electric CEO Jack Welch were found by journalists in Welch's divorce filing.

Local Regulators

Frequently, businesses want to enlarge their facilities or expand into new markets. To do so, a business may seek funds from an industrial bond authority, which helps the company obtain large sums of money at below-market rates. Or when an institution such as a hospital wants to expand its services, often it must make a case for the expansion before a regional or local agency. In either case, documents filed to support the requests may be revealing and may put into the public record information that previously was unobtainable. Local reporters who know how to find business plan filings in the county or city planning commission office gain insight into their area's economic development. These records are public but are often underutilized by reporters.

Other Sources

The preceding lists are certainly not exhaustive. Other relevant materials may be found at local tax and record-keeping offices, as well as in filings with the Federal Trade Commission, the Federal Communications Commission, the Food and Drug Administration, the Interstate Commerce Commission, the Bureau of Labor

Publicly Held Companies' SEC Filings

The following is a list of places to look for publicly held companies' SEC filings:

- **13-D.** Lists owners of more than 5 percent of the voting stock. Filed within 10 business days. Must report increases and decreases of holdings.
- **13-F.** Quarterly report of ownership by institutional investors. Includes holders of less than 5 percent of the company.
- **8-K.** Report of a significant incident.
- **10-Q.** Quarterly financial statement.
- **10-K.** Annual financial statement. Includes number of employees, major real estate and equipment holdings, significant legal proceedings. Many other important documents, such as labor contracts, are listed by reference and can be acquired through the company, a Freedom of Information Act request or a private service.
- **Proxy statement.** Contains executive salaries, director information and shareholder voting issues.
- **Annual report to shareholders.** May lack much of the data found in the 10-K.
- **Securities registration statement/prospectus.** Submitted when new stock is to be issued. Usually contains same information as 10-K and proxy but is more up-to-date.

Statistics and various state agencies, such as the secretary of state's office, which compiles information on businesses registered in each state.

Don't overlook the Federal Reserve—the central bank of the U.S.—which employs scores of economic analysts at each of its 12 regional banks. Eight times a year, the Fed publishes a comprehensive book of regional statistics and analysis, nicknamed the "Beige Book," which is available online at www.federalreserve.gov. The Consumer Confidence Index, a survey of 5,000 sample households by the Conference Board, gauges consumer sentiment on the U.S. economy. This is an important monthly index, followed by market watchers as well as the Federal Reserve in setting interest rates.

The Department of Commerce's Bureau of Economic Analysis (www.bea.gov) now allows reporters to generate economic data by county, region or state. The BEA uses data from agencies that don't issue public reports, such as the Internal Revenue Service. The Census Bureau has launched an interactive database that allows you to look at an area's employment statistics and population and income demographics. The "dynamic" mapping tool on the site allows journalists to analyze data within specific points on the electronic map. You can find the Longitudinal Employer-Household Dynamics information at http://lehd.did.census.gov/led.

Human Sources

Who are the people you should talk to on the business beat? Here are some who are important sources of information.

Company Executives

Although many public relations people can be helpful, the most valuable information will probably come from the head of the corporation or corporate division. Chief executive officers are powerful people, either out front or behind the scenes, in your community. They are often interesting and usually well informed. Not all of them will be glad to see you, although many executives value open communication with the press. In 2000, in an effort to tighten up information that could lead to illegal stock trading based on inside information, the SEC adopted Regulation FD (Fair Disclosure). It governs how corporate executives release information about corporate finances and other material information. Though Regulation FD has an exemption for journalists, it has caused executives to be more cautious in releasing information. As a result of Reg FD and the 2002 Sarbanes-Oxley Act, companies now release quarterly financial information via electronic news services like PR Newswire and Business Wire and discuss those results in Web-based conference calls in which journalists can participate.

Public Relations Sources

Don't automatically assume the public relations person is trying to block your path. Many people working in corporate communications are truly professional, and providing information to journalists is part of their job. Remember, though, that they are paid to make the company look good, so they are likely to point you in the direction of the company's viewpoint. Public relations professionals aren't objective, but that doesn't mean that the information they provide is untrue. Instead, you should assume that it is being packaged to show the company in its best light.

Academic Experts

Your college or university has faculty members with training and experience in business and economics. Often they are good sources of local reaction to national developments or analysis of economic trends.

Trade Associations

Although trade associations clearly represent the interests of their members, they can provide expert commentary on current issues or give explanations from the perspective of the industry. When *The New York Times* reported on the revival of the moving industry, the Household Goods Carriers Bureau, a major trade group, proved to be an important source. To find trade associations, look in the *Encyclopedia of Associations* or the *National Trade and Professional Associations of the United States.*

Chamber of Commerce Officials

Chamber of commerce officials are clearly pro-business. They will seldom make an on-the-record negative comment about business, but they usually know who is who and what is what in the business community. The chamber may be involved in such projects as downtown revitalization and industry recruiting. State and regional areas all have economic development agencies that receive tax funds and are required to file reports of their recruitment activities.

Former Employees

Many business reporters say that their most valuable sources are former employees of the company they're profiling. Business reporter and analyst Chris Welles writes, "Nobody knows more about a corporation than someone who has actually worked there." He warns, "Many, probably most, have axes to grind, especially if they were fired; indeed, the more willing they are to talk, the more biased they are likely to be." The good reporter will exercise care in using information obtained from former employees.

Labor Leaders

For the other side of many business stories and for pieces on working conditions, contracts and politics, get to know local union officials. The workings, legal and otherwise, of unions make good stories, too.

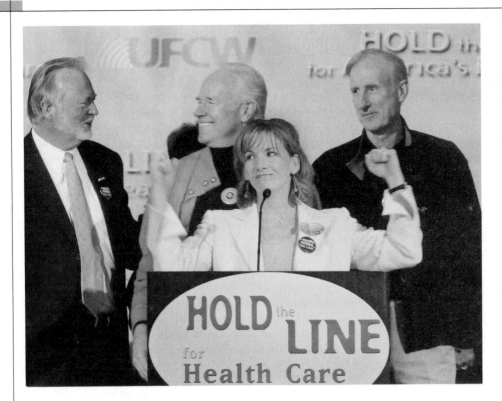

Union meetings, such as this one of the United Food and Commercial Workers in Los Angeles, can be an excellent source of labor stories.

Other Sources

Don't overlook the value of a company's customers, suppliers and competitors. You may also want to consult with local bankers, legislators, legislative staff members, law enforcement agencies and regulators, board members, oversight committee members and the like. Don't forget those ubiquitous consultants, who are usually well informed and often willing to talk, if only for background.

Announcements and Meetings

The source of much business news, and the starting point for many good stories, is an announcement by a company of a new product or the firm's reaction to some action by a government agency. News conferences can take many forms—in person or via a webcast. Companies also send out news releases via electronic outlets like PR Newswire or Business Wire, or news might be sent directly by e-mail to a reporter from a company public relations person.

   If you work in a city where one or more corporations are based, you may have the opportunity to cover an annual meeting, which invariably produces some news. Although some meetings are more lively and more newsworthy than others, all say something about the state of the company's business and provide an opportunity for shareholders to ask management questions about the company's performance.

The time leading up to the annual meeting also can produce drama, as key players jockey for position.

Reporter Enterprise

As in other areas of journalism, often the best business news stories are generated by a reporter's initiative, sparked by a hunch or a tip passed along by an editor, a shareholder or a disgruntled employee or customer. Sometimes a self-promoting source can lead to a good story. When the president of a new commodity options firm called *The Boston Globe* to suggest a story on her company, reporter Susan Trausch was dispatched. The reporter quickly became suspicious of some things she saw and was told. The investigation that followed produced a series on abuses in an unregulated industry and won several national prizes. The original caller got her name in the paper all right, but hardly as she had expected.

In other cases, a news release may raise questions that turn into stories. For example, a routine announcement of an executive appointment may lead a curious reporter to a story about the financial problems that produced the change in leadership. A stockholder's question may result in a story about a new trend in corporate financing or a shift in emphasis on operations within the company. Or a former employee's call that a company is quietly laying off workers may produce a story about the firm's declining fortunes.

LOOKING AT THE NUMBERS

An understanding of the numbers that a business generates is essential to any intelligent analysis of a company or an industry. The most complete summary of the financial picture of a business is found in its annual report and 10-K.

More than 100 million copies of annual reports are pumped out each year, and almost all can be downloaded from the Internet, as can recordings of "conference calls"—or the conversation that company executives have with investment analysts.

Annual reports can often be complicated, and new journalists should look first at Microsoft's reports, which feature easy-to-read financial statements. A typical table of contents of an annual report includes:

- Opening letter from the CEO
- Key financial data
- Results of continuing operations
- Market segment information
- New product plans
- Subsidiary activities
- Research and development activities on future programs
- Summarized disclosures from the 10-K report

Consumer activist organizations can be a good source of background information on an issue. Remember to take the group's mission into consideration, though.

Most veteran reporters, like Diana Henriques, investigative business reporter for *The New York Times*, start with the auditor's statement, which is generally located near the back of the annual report, together with basic financial data, footnotes and supplementary financial information. The basic auditor's report, ranging from one long paragraph to three or four paragraphs, states that the material conforms to generally accepted auditing standards and that it fairly presents the financial condition of the company. But read the report closely. Sometimes auditors hint at trouble by deviating from the standard language.

Next, move on to the footnotes, where the seeds of many fascinating stories may be germinating among the innocuous prose and numbers that follow and supplement the company's basic financial data. Then, turn to the front of the annual report and find the report from the chairman or chairwoman. It is usually addressed "To our shareholders" and should give an overview of the company's performance.

After that you're ready to look at the numbers. Here are a few things to watch for:

- **Balance sheet.** This report is a snapshot of the company on one day, generally the last day of the fiscal year. The left side of the balance sheet lists the *assets*, or what the company owns. On the right side are the *liabilities*, or what the company owes, and the *shareholders' equity*, or the dollar value of what stockholders own. The two sides must balance, so the balance sheet can be summarized with the following equation: assets equal liabilities plus shareholders' equity. The balance sheet shows how the year in question compares with the previous year. Reporters should note any significant changes worth exploring for a possible story.

- **Income statement.** This report, also referred to as an *earnings statement* or *statement of profit and loss*, answers this key question: How much money did the company make for the year? Look first at *net sales* or *operating revenues* and determine if they went up or down. If they increased, did they increase faster than they did last year and faster than the rate of inflation? If sales lagged behind inflation, the company could have serious problems.

- **Return on sales.** Company management and financial analysts calculate a number of ratios to gain better insights into the financial health of an organization. One important test of earnings is the relation of net income to sales, which is obtained by dividing net income by sales. This will tell you how much profit after taxes was produced by each dollar of sales. Reporters should remember that average percentages can vary widely by industry.

- **Return on equity.** This ratio, which shows how effectively a company's invested capital is working, is obtained by dividing net income minus preferred dividends by the common stockholders' equity for the previous year. Every year since 1997, Standard & Poor's Equity Research staff has compiled a list of the best returns on equity by U.S. companies of various sizes.

- **Dividends.** These payments to shareholders are declared quarterly and generally are prominently noted in the annual report. Dividends are an inducement to shareholders to invest in the company. Because companies want to see dividends rise each quarter, they sometimes go so far as to change their accounting or pension assumptions so enough funds will be available to increase dividends. Other companies, such as Berkshire Hathaway Inc., declare no dividends because they prefer to reinvest profits internally. Shareholders of Microsoft Corporation complained for years that the software giant was holding on to too much cash and urged the board to return more money to its investors through higher dividends.

Now that you have an idea of how to examine an annual report and its numbers, it is time for some important words of caution. First, the numbers in an annual report, though certified by an auditor and presented in accordance with SEC regulations, are not definite because they are a function of the accounting assumptions used in their preparation. That leads to the second and third points: Look at a company's numbers both in the context of its industry and compared with several years' performance. To understand how well a firm is performing, examine the numbers along with those of other firms in the same industry. Look at how the company has performed for the last five to 10 years. Then you will discern trends instead of basing your conclusions on one year's performance, which may be atypical.

PREPARING TO COVER CONSUMER NEWS

The phrase "consumer news" is in its broadest sense arbitrary and redundant. All news is, directly or indirectly, about consumers. A story about the stock market may affect or be of interest to "consumers" of stocks and bonds even though those items aren't consumed in the same sense as cornflakes. A story about the price of crude oil affects consumers of gasoline and many other products refined from crude oil. A story about a drought that may drive up the price of wheat has an impact on consumers of hamburger buns.

Many news outlets, especially local and network television, run "consumer target" features that respond to consumer complaints of alleged fraud or unfair treatment by merchants or landlords.

Where to Find Consumer News

Sources of consumer news fall into three general categories: government agencies, consumer groups and private businesses. Let's consider each of these groups.

Government Agencies

Many municipalities, especially large cities, have a consumer advocate who calls public attention to problems that affect consumers. Most county prosecuting attorneys' offices also have someone — or even a whole department — to challenge business practices of questionable legality. Cases of consumer fraud — in which people pay for something they do not receive or pay for something of a certain quality and receive something less — are handled by these offices.

At the state level, most states have a consumer affairs office to investigate consumer problems and to order or recommend solutions. In addition, state attorneys general investigate and prosecute cases of consumer fraud. Most states also have regulatory commissions that represent the public in a variety of areas. The most common commissions regulate rates and practices of insurance companies, rates and levels of service of utilities and transportation companies, and practices of banks and savings and loan associations. Another source is your state auditor's office, which may also uncover fraud and wrongdoing within government or government contracts.

At the federal level, government regulatory agencies involved in consumer affairs have the power to make rules and to enforce them:

- The Federal Trade Commission oversees matters related to advertising and product safety.
- The Food and Drug Administration watches over prices and safety rules for food, drugs and a variety of other health-related items.
- The Securities and Exchange Commission oversees the registration of securities for corporations and regulates the exchange, or trading, of those securities.
- The Interstate Commerce Commission regulates prices and levels of service provided by surface-transportation companies in interstate commerce.
- The Federal Energy Regulatory Commission regulates the rates and levels of service provided by interstate energy companies.
- The Occupational Safety and Health Administration has inspectors who routinely visit and report on safety in workplaces and factories and who investigate workplace accidents.

Consumer Groups

Nongovernment consumer groups are composed of private citizens who have organized to represent the consumer's interest. They, too, are often good sources of background information or comment.

Common Cause, which lobbies for federal and state legislation, and Consumers Union, which publishes the popular *Consumer Reports*, are general in nature. Many states have public-interest research groups. Other organizations are advocates, such as the Sierra Club, which concentrates on environmental matters. Still other groups may be more local in scope. They may try to enact legislation that promotes recycling or to fight what they perceive as discrimination in the way banks and savings and loan associations make housing loans.

Private Businesses

Almost all large corporations and many smaller ones have public relations departments. They try to present their company in the most favorable light and to mask the scars as much as possible when the company is attacked from the outside, whether by the press, the government or a consumer group.

Because of the successes of the consumer movement, a number of companies have taken the offensive and have instituted programs they deem to be in the public interest. Oil companies tell drivers how to economize on gasoline, electric utilities tell homeowners how to keep their electric bills at a minimum, and credit card companies suggest ways to manage money better.

How to Report Consumer Stories

Consumer stories may be exposés, bringing to light a practice relating to consumers that is dangerous or that increases the price of a product or service. Research for such stories can be simple and inexpensive to conduct, and the findings may arouse intense reader interest. The project can be something as simple as buying hamburger meat at every supermarket in town to see if all purchases weigh what they are marked. Some college newspaper reporters have compared the interest rates and fees of credit cards offered to students. Databases offer ideas for such consumer-focused project stories.

Susan Lundine, a reporter for the *Orlando Business Journal*, scoured Florida state insurance records to detail claims from the hurricanes that crisscrossed the state in 2004—Charley, Frances, Ivan and Jeanne. Lundine found, for example, that homeowners who lived in 12 counties on Florida's east coast, 370 miles from where Ivan made landfall, claimed more than $65 million in damages from that storm. The *Business Journal* ran a county-by-county map of claims for each of the four storms, which starkly showed how ludicrous some of the claims were. The state reacted, investigating additional cases of potential insurance fraud.

Consumer stories may also be informational, intended to help readers make wiser or less expensive purchases. Other consumer stories can be cautionary,

A Business Mini-Glossary

Bonds

Governments and corporations issue bonds to raise money (capital). The bonds pay interest at a stated rate and are redeemable on a predetermined maturity date.

Constant Dollars

Because of inflation, $10 doesn't buy in 2011 what it did in 1991. Constant dollars take inflation into account by figuring their value compared with a base period. See Chapter 8 for more on writing about inflation.

Consumer Price Index

A measure of the relative price of goods and services, the CPI is based on the net change compared with a base period. An index of 115 means the price has increased 15 percent since the base period. Thus, to report the significance of a rise or drop in the CPI, you need to know the base year.

Dow Jones Industrial Average

The DJIA is the principal daily benchmark of U.S. stock prices. It is based on the combined value of 30 major stocks, which are changed on a regular basis. Those stocks, despite the name, are no longer purely industrial, and they represent some companies listed on the

NASDAQ and not the New York Stock Exchange. The DJIA exceeded 12,000 for the first time in 2006 but fell sharply in the 2008 Wall Street meltdown.

Individual Retirement Accounts

IRAs are savings accounts whose earnings (as well as some contributions) are tax-free until withdrawal. A person generally cannot take out the funds until retirement.

Mutual Funds

These funds are collections of bonds, stocks and other securities managed by investment companies. Individuals buy shares in them much as they buy shares of stock, but mutual funds provide more diversity.

Stocks

A share of stock represents a piece of a company. The price varies from day to day. "Blue chip" stocks are generally less volatile stocks that are meant for long-term investing. The price per share of blue chip stocks does not generally increase at any sort of going rate, but these stocks can give decent or large returns in the long term.

warning readers of impending price increases, quality problems with products or questionable practices of business or consumer groups. Such stories can have great impact. A Houston television station's reports about Firestone tire deficiencies led to a massive recall. Dozens of magazines and books focus on consumer news, from stories on what to look for when building a new house to how to select a good nursing home.

Consumer stories can put news organizations at odds with advertisers. It was a consumer story that led to a lawsuit against *The Denver Post* when it published a story about a dry cleaner that consistently lost customers' clothes.

Suggested Readings

Houston, Brant, and Investigative Reporters and Editors. *The Investigative Reporter's Handbook: A Guide to Documents, Databases and Techniques*, 5th ed. New York: Bedford/St. Martin's, 2009. See the chapter on business.

Morgenson, Gretchen. *The Capitalist's Bible: The Essential Guide to Free Markets—and Why They Matter to You.* New York: HarperCollins, 2009. This guide offers a good discussion of business terms and concepts.

Smith, Rebecca, and John R. Emshwiller. *24 Days: How Two Wall Street Journal Reporters Uncovered the Lies That Destroyed Faith in Corporate America.* New York: Harper-Collins, 2003. This is an inside-the-news-room account of the Enron scandal, the biggest bankruptcy in recent business history.

Sorkin, Andrew Ross. *Too Big to Fail: The Inside Story of How Wall Street and Washington Fought to Save the Financial System—and Themselves.* New York: Viking Adult, 2009. This is an excellent chronicle of the Wall Street collapse in 2008.

Taparia, Jay. *Understanding Financial Statements: A Journalist's Guide.* Chicago: Marion Street Press, 2004. Taparia, a popular trainer in business journalism, walks journalists through complicated financial statements.

Suggested Websites

http://businessjournalism.org
This website, funded by the Donald W. Reynolds Institute, offers tips and tutorials for business journalism professionals and students.

http://data.nicar.org
The National Institute for Computer-Assisted Reporting provides access to databases and training in how to use them to analyze business, economic and regulatory information.

http://finance.yahoo.com
This portal is an accessible and free index of corporate financial filings, stock prices and corporate news.

www.bea.gov and **www.bls.gov**
These sites, from the U.S. Department of Commerce and the U.S. Department of Labor, respectively, offer overviews of the U.S. economy and exhaustive studies about each segment of the economy.

www.business.com
This directory of business websites offers information about individual companies and industries.

www.investorwords.com
This is one of many commercial sites with reliable definitions of words used in finance.

www.sabew.org
The Society of American Business Editors and Writers can be a good source for contacts, story ideas and student training opportunities. Students can join the organization.

Exercises

1. **Team project.** The foreclosure crisis that began in 2008 has created many stories about the impact of foreclosures on communities, from rampant homelessness to the influx of illnesses caused by mosquitoes that breed unchecked in abandoned pools. Your instructor will divide the class into teams. Each team should choose an area of the country and research effects of the foreclosure crisis. How many families were affected? Why did families lose their homes? What kinds of mortgages were involved? How did state and local governments handle the crisis? Divide the research tasks among team members. Then meet to discuss and plan a series of stories you might write. If time permits, assemble your results into stories.

2. Find newspaper, television and Internet stories on the same business topic, such as the latest federal employment statistics. Compare their detail and sources. Which is the most informative? Which is the most interesting?

3. Identify a local business reporter. Study her or his work, and then interview the reporter. Ask about sources, story ideas and career opportunities.

4. Download or send away for a prospectus on a mutual fund, and study its investment rationale. Or read a prospectus on a stock offering, and study its price-earnings ratio, yield on dividends and other value indicators. Look up commentary on the fund or stock on the Web, and explain the fund's or stock's performance.

5. Use LexisNexis or the SEC's EDGAR database and EDGAROnline.com to find the 10-K report on a publicly traded company with a local operation.

Social Science Reporting

18

Journalists don't usually regard themselves as scientists. Many would resist the very suggestion. But the best reporting has a great deal in common with the work of political scientists, historians and sociologists. Like these social scientists, reporters frame research questions or hypotheses. They seek answers to their questions through the careful accumulation of reliable data and the use of scientific formulas and statistics to analyze the information they've gathered. They double-check their findings for reliability. Then they report clearly and carefully what they have learned.

Consider, as just one example, a project of the Scripps Howard news service called "Saving Babies: Exposing Sudden Infant Death." Reporters Thomas Hargrove, Lee Bowman and Lisa Hoffman analyzed more than 40,000 cases of unexplained infant death nationwide. They found that sloppy procedures, manipulated statistics and poorly trained coroners have hindered rather than advanced the search for causes of thousands of those deaths. They even created a searchable database at ScrippsNews.com that allows readers to make their own comparisons of diagnoses from state to state.

That work won the Philip Meyer Journalism Award, which is named after the pioneer of social science reporting and the author of *Precision Journalism*. The national Centers for Disease Control and Prevention posted the project on its website. A few months later, then-Sen. Barack Obama introduced legislation requiring medical examiners to investigate all cases of sudden infant death.

This wasn't just reporting what somebody said, or even what a reporter had observed. This was new knowledge, developed by the reporters and presented to readers who had no way, on their own, of learning what they, and policy-makers, needed to know. And that is the essence of social science reporting.

Led by Hargrove, who directs computer-assisted reporting in Scripps Howard's Washington bureau, the team used sophisticated statistical analysis. However, the social science tool journalists use most often is the public opinion survey. It is also the tool they misuse most often. Here's an example from McClatchy Newspapers:

WASHINGTON—Democrats are slightly ahead of Republicans in three election battleground states that will help determine control of the Senate, a series of polls released today showed.

In Montana, Democrat Jon Tester had the support of 47 percent of registered voters while incumbent Republican Sen. Conrad Burns had the support of 40 percent.

In Ohio, Democrat Rep. Sherrod Brown was the choice of 45 percent of registered voters, while incumbent Republican Sen. Mike DeWine had 43 percent.

In Tennessee, Democratic Rep. Harold Ford Jr. got the nod from 43 percent of voters and former Chattanooga mayor Bob Corker, the Republican Senate nominee, had 42 percent.

A few paragraphs later, the story reported that the polls had "an error margin of plus or minus four percentage points." See the problem? Many readers wouldn't. That last phrase—"an error margin of plus or minus four percentage points"—means that the first paragraph is just plain wrong. Any scientist would tell you that a 4 percent margin of error, also called a *sampling error*, means that the poll really shows that, for example, Tester's support was somewhere in the range of 43 percent to 51 percent and Burns' support was between 36 and 44 percent. Brown was in the range of 41 to 49 percent, and DeWine was in the range of 39 to 47 percent. So the story really should have said that all three races were too close to call.

These examples show both the power and the pitfalls of using the research tools of social science in reporting. The increasing complexity of the world around us requires the journalists of today and tomorrow to learn to use tools adequate to the task of understanding and explaining that world. Often the most useful tools turn out to be those developed and regularly used by social scientists. In unskilled hands, however, such tools can be dangerous.

COMPUTER-ASSISTED REPORTING

American journalism—print, broadcast and online—relies on computers. Reporters write on computers. Photographers edit and transmit their pictures by computer. The almost unlimited storage capacity of computers and the flexibility of digital technology enable online journalists to combine text and video with links to original documents and to related information stored anywhere in the world. Increasingly, journalists are also using computers to analyze data, to do what the Scripps Howard team did and create knowledge that nobody had before.

Computers assist reporting in two main ways:

- Journalists can access digital information from databases on the Internet. (You learned about these resources and how to tap them in Chapter 6.)
- Journalists can become knowledge creators by compiling and analyzing information that was previously not collected or not examined.

David Herzog, director of the National Institute of Computer-Assisted Reporting, teaches University of Missouri students and hundreds of practicing journalists from all over the world how to use their computers as more than word processors. His students learn how to acquire data from government agencies, nonprofit organizations and other researchers. Then they place the information into a searchable database, such as an Excel spreadsheet, so they can analyze the data. Often they match information from two or more databases to find something even policy-makers didn't know.

Take, for instance, the topic of guns. Jo Craven McGinty was a graduate student at Missouri who mastered analytical techniques and worked part-time for NICAR, helping professional journalists tell statistics-based stories. She came across an FBI database on the use of weapons by police officers. When she took an internship at *The Washington Post*, she took with her that knowledge and a story idea. Months later, as part of the *Post*'s investigative team, she helped tell the story that Washington, D.C., police used their guns to shoot civilians more often than police in any other city. The story won a Pulitzer Prize for *The Post*. Later she moved to *The New York Times*, where she is on the computer-assisted reporting team.

Not all computer-assisted reporting leads to Pulitzers, but much of it reveals important information that otherwise would remain hidden in bureaucratic files. Sometimes those stories are hidden in plain sight, and the data must just be arranged to be understood. Herzog is an expert in computer mapping, which is the use of special software programs to display information in maps to reveal significant patterns. Instances of crime, for example, can be mapped to show the truly dangerous areas of a city. Outbreaks of disease can be mapped to help identify sources of infection. Patterns of immigration or unemployment or voting can be demonstrated more clearly by electronic maps than words alone could describe.

To learn more, or to get help with your own reporting, go to http://data .nicar.org. There you can benefit from computer-assisted learning.

PARTICIPANT OBSERVATION

Audiences around the world watched in real time as America's wars in Iraq and Afghanistan unfolded. Viewers saw desert terrain spread out across their screens as cameras mounted on military vehicles captured the progress of American and British troops toward Baghdad. From Afghanistan came timeless images of Special Forces soldiers on horseback riding into battle. Correspondents wearing camouflage uniforms often slipped into the first-person plural as they described the experiences of the soldiers they were accompanying. In military jargon, those reporters were "embedded" with their units. A social scientist would say that they were engaged in participant observation.

Participant observation is a tool long used by anthropologists and sociologists to learn about unknown societies by becoming part of the scene they are studying. War correspondents have used it for just as long to provide firsthand accounts of campaigns. Other journalists have employed participant observation for **undercover reporting,** to expose crimes or social ills from the inside. All participant observers get close-up views of their subjects, insights not obtainable from studying statistics or formal interviewing. Facts and feelings can be captured that otherwise would remain unknown.

Along with its unique advantages, participant observation also poses some unique problems. These problems may have no clear solutions, but you and your editors need at least to consider them before you set out to become an ambulance attendant or a migrant worker. (Be aware that it's illegal to pretend to be a licensed professional, such as a cop or a physician.)

The Problem of Invasion of Privacy

Unless you identify yourself as a reporter, you are, in effect, spying on people—an ethically questionable activity. But if you do identify yourself, some of the advantages of participant observation are lost. In either case, sensitivity is essential, especially when the people you write about may be embarrassed by your reporting or have their jobs placed in jeopardy.

TIPS

Cautions About
Participant Observation

● Sensitivity is essential; people don't always feel as you do. What you write about others may embarrass them or jeopardize their jobs.

● Don't become so involved that you change the course of the events you're observing.

● Participant observation usually works best as a supplement to interviewing and examining documents.

The Problem of Involvement

There are two things to watch out for. First, do not become so involved that you change the course of the events you are observing. You may be on stage, but you are not the star performer. Second, do not assume that the people you are observing feel the same way you do. No matter how hard you work at fitting in, you remain an outsider, a visitor. The view from inside a migrant workers' camp or a psychiatric hospital is different when you know you will be there for two weeks instead of two years or a lifetime.

The first of these was the issue that drew the most criticism of the embedded reporters in Iraq. Reporters' perspective on the war was necessarily that of the units to which they were attached. One reporter for *USA Today* even wrote a column in which he described how, during a battle, he was asked to help a medic who was treating a wounded soldier. The reporter told how he put his "objectivity" aside to save the life of a man who might have saved the reporter's life if the fight had turned out differently.

The Problem of Generalizing

Scientists know well the danger of generalizing from limited observations. Reporters don't always recognize that danger, or sometimes they forget it. Keep in mind that although participant observation yields a detailed picture of a specific situation, it tells you nothing reliable about any other situation. Participant observation is a good tool, but it is a limited one. It usually works best as a supplement to the standard techniques of interviewing and examining documents. This, too, was true of the war reporting. As the embedded journalists pointed out, theirs was not the only angle from which the war was reported. Other reporters at military headquarters, back home or even in besieged Baghdad all contributed to the overall account. That's a lesson to keep in mind.

SYSTEMATIC STUDY OF RECORDS

The Scripps Howard example at the beginning of this chapter relied on the systematic study of records. Kathleen Kerr and Russ Buettner of *Newsday* used the same technique to analyze a different situation. Their goal was to discover whether New York City's criminal justice system discriminated against the poor. Their method was to acquire computer databases of city and state records on 27,810 prisoners and then to use their own computer to sort those cases by race and other criteria. They found that the poor, especially minorities, were often denied bail and forced to wait in jail for trials that often found them not guilty. No amount of traditional interviewing and observing could have produced such credible stories.

Scholars have long used the systematic study of records in their research. Its use by reporters is still limited but growing. The advantage of the detailed analysis

TIPS

Once You Begin a
Study . . .

● Make sure it is systematic.
Either examine all the pertinent records or choose
the ones you examine in
such a way that they are
truly representative of
the rest.

● Be sure to ask the right
questions and record the
information necessary to
answer them.

● Remember that a com-
puter can perform com-
plicated analyses very
quickly but cannot ana-
lyze facts that have not
been input.

of court records, budgets, voting records and other documents is that it permits reporters and readers to draw conclusions based on solid information. The wide-spread availability of powerful personal computers and easy-to-use analytical programs brings the systematic study of records within the reach of any news organization.

The main obstacles to such study are shortages of time and money. Major projects for a large metropolitan daily often require months of work by one or more reporters. On small papers, especially, you may have trouble freeing yourself for even several days. And reporters' time and computer time both cost money. Editors and publishers must be convinced that the return will be worth the invest-ment before they will approve the project. You probably should have at least some clues that wrongdoing, injustice or inefficiency exists before launching your study.

Once you have begun a study, make sure that it is systematic. Either examine all the pertinent records or choose the ones you examine in such a way that they will be truly representative of the rest. Be sure to ask the right questions, and record the information necessary to answer them. A computer can perform com-plicated analyses quickly, but it cannot analyze facts that have not been input. People who use computers have a term for that problem — GIGO, the acronym for "garbage in, garbage out."

Don't set out on a systematic study without assurances of time and money, a clear idea of what you're looking for and expert technical advice. If the expertise is unavailable at your newspaper, look for it at the nearest college.

FIELD EXPERIMENTS

Reporters may not think of themselves as scientists, but they conduct a great many experiments. A common one is to examine the honesty of auto mechanics by tak-ing a car in perfect condition to several shops and reporting what "defects" each finds. Consumer reporters also commonly check weights and measures: Does a "pound" of hamburger really weigh a pound? And they test for discrimination by having a black reporter and a white reporter apply for the same insurance policy or mortgage.

Here's a test you can do. Say you want to find out whether landlords in your town discriminate against nonwhite would-be renters. Send out teams of different races to visit the same rental agencies or to respond to the same advertisements. Then compare the results. Did the all-white teams receive more welcoming treat-ment than others? A scientist conducting that kind of test would call it a **field experiment**. In all such experiments, researchers take some action in order to observe the effects.

If reporters' field experiments are to be successful, they must follow the same guidelines — and avoid the same pitfalls — that scientists' experiments must. A little scientific terminology is necessary here. It is fairly straightforward, though, and it will be useful if you ever have the opportunity to set up an experiment.

ON THE JOB

State the Hypothesis and Identify the Variables

Your field experiment must have a **hypothesis**, a statement of what you expect to find. Your hypothesis must be stated clearly and simply. When it is, it will help focus your attention on the two elements of the experiment: the independent variable and the dependent variable. The **variables**, just as their name implies, are the things that change during the experiment. The *independent variable* is what you think may be a cause. You change it and observe what happens to the *dependent variable*, the effect.

Let's look again at the search for bias in renting. As a social scientist, you would state the hypothesis you're testing: "Landlords in our town discriminate against renters of color." The independent variable is race. The dependent variables are the forms of security, the kinds of identification and the rents charged to each team. You're looking to see how differences in the variable of race affect the dependent variables.

Control the Experiment and Choose Subjects Randomly

There are two other steps you must take to ensure a successful experiment. First, you must **control** the experiment. Every aspect of the experiment must be carefully structured to make sure that any change you observe is caused only by the independent variable you want to test. For example, your teams of would-be "renters" must be as much alike as possible in the financial details they provide, the way they dress, their gender and their age. Otherwise, any differences in the responses by the landlords might be due to something other than race, the variable you are interested in. Also, the applicants should visit the same landlords and speak to the same officials. Without careful control of the experiment, you may end up being unable to say whether the results support your hypothesis or not. Then you've got no story.

The other step is called **randomization**, or random selection. In a small town you could run your experiment with every landlord. But in a big city that would be impossible. So if you want to be reasonably sure that the results of the experiment apply to all the landlords in town, you must choose at random the ones to approach. Randomization allows you to assume that what you select — 10 landlords, for instance — is representative of the whole (the total number of landlords in the city).

Choosing anything at random simply means that you employ a method for choosing that gives every person or thing an equal chance of being picked. The procedure for making a random selection is beyond the scope of an introductory reporting text. The Suggested Readings at the end of the chapter include books in which you can find material relating to the concepts introduced here. Much of that material deals with statistics. Many experiments require statistical analysis to ensure that what you have found is significant. Most polls and surveys require some statistical analysis, too. Explanations of the fairly simple math involved also can be found in the books listed in the Suggested Readings.

PUBLIC OPINION POLLS

Surveying is a powerful journalistic tool. At the beginning of the chapter, we examined an example of its misuse. Despite such problems, more journalists, politicians, businesses and scholars today are using poll results because they show more reliably than anecdotes or ordinary interviews what the public thinks about important issues. Many news organizations now go beyond reporting the findings of national polling firms such as Gallup and Harris Interactive and conduct or commission their own surveys. Several journalism schools — including those at the universities of Alabama, Florida, North Carolina and Missouri — have developed scientific polling operations staffed by faculty and students to serve newspapers and broadcasters.

MAKING SENSE OF NUMBERS FROM POLLS

Every day, new poll results illustrate what people think about various topics in the news. And just about every day, journalists confuse readers when they try to interpret the results.

The Margin of Error

The most important thing to keep in mind about polls and surveys is that they are based on samples of a population. Because a survey reflects the responses of a small number of people within a population, every survey has a margin of error. The results must be presented with the understanding that scientific sampling is not a perfect predictor for the entire population.

Suppose your news organization buys polling services that show that Candidate Hernandez has support from 58 percent of the people surveyed, Candidate Jones has support from 32 percent, and 10 percent are undecided. The polling service indicates that the margin of error of the poll is plus or minus five percentage points. The margins separating the candidates—53 to 63 percent for Hernandez, 27 to 37 percent for Jones and 5 to 15 percent undecided—are well beyond the margin of error, so you can write that Hernandez is leading in the poll.

Now suppose Hernandez has 50 percent support and Jones has 45 percent. The difference between them is within the margin of error, less than plus or minus five percentage points. Thus you should report that the race is too close to call, though you may say that Hernandez "appears to be leading."

Polling voters on Election Day is an excellent way to forecast election results. However, polls must be conducted properly and interpreted carefully to produce reliable information.

Journalists faced a race that was too close to call in the presidential elections in 2008. For weeks, the difference in the polls between Senators Barack Obama and John McCain often fell within the margin of error, yet many in the media inaccurately reported each little change as an advantage for one candidate or the other.

Most of the media reported more carefully on the 2008 Minnesota Senate race, which was eventually decided only after a recount and a lengthy legal battle. This excerpt is from *The Washington Post*:

> In Minnesota, Sen. Norm Coleman (R) has slipped into a dead heat with his Democratic opponent Al Franken; Franken stands at 38 percent to 36 percent for Coleman and 18 percent for independent candidate Dean Barkley.

Note that while Franken had a two-point lead, the writer said the contest was a dead heat because it was within the margin of error of three points. The poll turned out to be accurate; the race was so close that there was a recount.

Lesson number one is not to write that one candidate is ahead of another unless the difference between them is larger than the margin of error for both candidates combined. Lesson two is that if you look at smaller groups within your polling group, the margin of error will be even larger. Subgroups within a sample are subject to a larger margin of error because fewer people are in the subgroup. Fewer respondents means less accuracy. If you wanted to write about how many women supported Franken or Coleman in 2008 according to the survey quoted by *The Post*, you would have to use the margin of error based on the smaller number of women surveyed. Suppose you wanted to know how women in the survey were going to vote. If women were half the sample, the margin of error would approximately double. Being honest about figures that are so unreliable can be difficult, but doing so is the only way to keep your reporting accurate and fair.

When polls are conducted properly and reported carefully, they can tell people something they could not know otherwise and perhaps even help to produce wiser public policies. But when they are badly done or sloppily reported, polls can be bad news for journalists and readers alike.

The chances are good that sometime in your reporting career you will want to conduct an opinion poll or at least help with one your newspaper is conducting. The Suggested Readings listed at the end of the chapter will tell you much of what you need to know for that. Even if you never work a poll, you almost certainly will be called on to write about polling results. What follows will help you understand what you are given and will help you make sure your readers understand it, too.

Sound Polling

The Associated Press Managing Editors Association prepared a checklist of the information you should share with your audience about any poll on which you are reporting. Several of their points require some explanation:

- **Identity of the sponsor.** The identity of the survey's sponsor is important to you and your readers because it hints at possible bias. Most people would put more trust in a Gallup or Harris poll's report that, for instance, Smith is far ahead of Jones in the presidential campaign than they would in a poll sponsored by the Smith for President organization.

- **Exact wording of the questions.** The wording of the questions is important because the answer received often depends at least in part on how the question was asked (see Chapter 4 on interviewing for more detail). The answer might well be different, for example, if a pollster asked, "Whom do you favor for president, Jones or Smith?" rather than "Wouldn't Jones make a better president than Smith?"

- **Population.** In science, the *population* is the total number of people — or documents or milkweed plants or giraffes — in the group being studied. For an opinion survey, the population might be, for example, all registered voters in the state, black males under 25 or female cigarette smokers. To understand what the results of a poll mean, you must know what population was studied. The word *sampled* refers to the procedure in which a small number — or sample — of people is picked at random so as to be representative of the population.

- **Sample size and response rate.** The sample size is important because — all other things being equal — the larger the sample, the more reliable the survey results should be. The response rate is especially important in surveys conducted by mail, in which a low rate of response may invalidate the poll.

- **Margin of error.** The margin of error, or sampling error, of any survey is the allowance that must be made for the possibility that the opinion of the sample may not be exactly the same as the opinion of the whole population. The margin of error depends mainly on the size of the sample. For instance, all other things being equal, a sample of 400 would have a margin of error of 5 percent, and a sample of 1,500 would have a margin of error of 3 percent. If, with a sample of 1,500, the poll shows Jones with 60 percent of the votes and Smith with 40 percent, you can be confident that Jones actually has between 57 and 63 percent and Smith actually has between 37 and 43 percent. The laws of probability say that the chances are 19 to 1 that the actual percentages fall within that range. Those odds make the information good enough to publish.

- **Which results are based on part of the sample.** The problem of sampling error helps explain why it is important to know which results may be based on only part of the sample. The smaller that part is, the greater the margin of error. In political polls, it is always important to know whether the results include responses from all eligible voters or only from individuals *likely* to vote. The opinions of the likely voters are more important than others' opinions.

- **When the interviews were collected.** When the interviews were collected may be of critical importance in interpreting the poll. During campaigns, for example, the candidates themselves and other events may cause preferences to

TIPS

Cautions About Using Poll Data

- The people interviewed must be selected in a truly random fashion if you want to generalize from their responses to the whole population.

- The closer the results, the harder it is to say anything definitive.

- Beware of polls that claim to measure opinion on sensitive, complicated issues.

"*Next question: I believe that life is a constant striving for balance, requiring frequent tradeoffs between morality and necessity, within a cyclic pattern of joy and sadness, forging a trail of bittersweet memories until one slips, inevitably, into the jaws of death. Agree or disagree?*"

Some pollsters' questions seem designed to elicit a desired response.

change significantly within a few days. Think of presidential primaries. As candidates join or drop out of the race, support for each of the other candidates changes. A week-old poll may be meaningless if something dramatic happened after it was taken. Candidates have been known to use such outdated results to make themselves appear to be doing better than they really are, or their opponents worse. Be on guard.

Caution in Interpreting Polls

Whether you are helping to conduct a survey or only reporting on one produced by someone else, you must exercise caution. Be on guard for the following potential problems:

● **The people interviewed must be selected in a truly random fashion if you want to generalize from their responses to the whole population.** If the selection wasn't randomized, you have no assurance that the interview subjects are really representative. The old-fashioned people-in-the-street interview is practically worthless as an indicator of public opinion for this reason. The man or woman in the street probably differs in important ways from all those men and women who are not in the street when the questioner is.

Also invalid are the questionnaires members of Congress mail to their constituents. Only strongly opinionated—and therefore unrepresentative—people are likely to return them. For the same reason, the "question-of-the-day" feature that some newspapers and broadcast stations ask you to respond to online tells you nothing about the opinions of the great mass of people who do not respond. Even worse are the TV polls that require respondents to call or send a text message to a number to register their opinions. Because there is a charge for such calls, these pseudopolls produce not only misleading results but profits that encourage their use.

- **The closer the results, the harder it is to say anything definitive.** Look again at the example of the Smith-Jones campaign. Suppose the poll showed Smith with 52 percent and Jones with 48 percent of the vote. Smith may or may not be ahead. With the 3 percent margin of error, Smith could actually have only 49 percent, and Jones could have 51 percent. All that you could report safely about those results is that the race is too close to call. Many reporters—and pollsters—are simply not careful enough when the outcome is unclear.

- **Beware of polls that claim to measure opinion on sensitive, complicated issues.** Many questions of morality, or social issues such as race relations, do not lend themselves to simple answers. Opinions on such matters can be measured, but only by highly skilled researchers using carefully designed questions. Anything less can be dangerously oversimplified and highly misleading.

Polling—like field experiments, systematic analysis and participant observation—can help you as a reporter solve problems you could not handle as well with other techniques. But these are only tools. How effectively they are used—or how clumsily they are misused—depends on you.

Suggested Readings

Campbell, Donald, and Julian Stanley. *Experimental and Quasi-Experimental Designs for Research.* Skokie, Ill.: Rand McNally, 1966. This classic guide to field experimentation is also useful in providing a better understanding of scientific research.

Demers, David Pearce, and Suzanne Nichols. *Precision Journalism: A Practical Guide.* Newbury Park, Calif.: Sage, 1987. A primer for students and journalists, this book is simply written and complete with examples.

Houston, Brant. *Computer-Assisted Reporting,* 3rd ed. New York: Bedford/St. Martin's, 2004. Houston has written a practical introduction to data analysis and field reporting.

McCombs, Maxwell, Donald L. Shaw, and David Grey. *Handbook of Reporting Methods.* Boston: Houghton Mifflin, 1976. The authors offer examples of real-life uses of social science methods in journalism but do not provide enough on statistics to serve as a guide in employing the methods.

Meyer, Philip. *Precision Journalism*, 4th ed. Lanham, Md.: Rowman and Littlefield, 2002. This detailed introduction to surveying, conducting field experiments and using statistics to analyze the results was written by a reporter who pioneered the use of these methods in journalism. A theoretical justification of the techniques is included as well.

Seltzer, Richard A. *Mistakes That Social Scientists Make: Error and Redemption in the Research Process.* New York: St. Martin's Press, 1996. Seltzer has written a useful book about the kinds of errors often made by social scientists during their research.

Suggested Websites

http://data.nicar.org

At the website of the National Institute for Computer-Assisted Reporting, you'll find many stories reported using CAR techniques, plus tips for doing this kind of reporting yourself.

http://people-press.org

This is the site of the Pew Research Center for the People and the Press. Here you'll find not only the results of polls but also explanations of their methodology and limitations.

www.aejmc.org

The Association for Education in Journalism and Mass Communication is the professional organization of journalism teachers and researchers. For a journalist or journalism student, perhaps the most useful feature of this site is the links to the organization's research publications. Many of the reports in those publications use, and explain, the techniques discussed in this chapter.

www.gallup.com

The Gallup organization is one of the most reputable of the national polling companies. This site contains the results of a wide variety of public polls and explains their methodology.

Exercises

1. **Team project.** Your instructor will divide your class into teams of four or five. Working as a team, design a field experiment: Brainstorm ideas for an experiment that could yield results for news stories. Develop and state a hypothesis, identify the dependent and independent variables, and describe the controls that you would use. Write up your plan, and present your experiment idea to the class for discussion.

2. As a class, choose from among the experiments the teams designed in exercise 1. Assign tasks, and carry out the chosen field experiment. Pool all the results, and write individual stories using the field experiment data.

3. Go to www.ire.org or http://data.nicar.org, and find at least one story that uses one or more of the social science techniques discussed in this chapter. Analyze the reporting and writing. How do the stories you found differ from stories that rely on interviewing? What possible sources of practical or ethical problems can you identify?

4. Find a newspaper story that reports on the results of a public opinion poll. Analyze the story using the guidelines discussed in this chapter.

5. As a class, transform yourselves into survey researchers. Design a simple survey using the technique described by Philip Meyer in *Precision Journalism* (see the Suggested Readings). Then carry out the experiment, and report your results.

Investigative Reporting

This is 21st-century investigative reporting:

A team of 14 reporters from 10 countries exposed the billion-dollar racket of tobacco smuggling, which has tentacles stretching from Russia and China to Western Europe, Canada and New York. Articles ran in 10 languages and prompted tougher controls on trafficking. This was a project of the nonprofit International Consortium of Investigative Journalists.

This also is investigative reporting:

A team at *The Indianapolis Star* uncovered the abuse of official parking passes that clogged downtown streets with illegally parked but unticketed cars. City officials immediately acted to reform a broken system. This work was done between other assignments by a reporter from the business beat and one from general assignment.

As these examples illustrate, the forces of technology and economics are reshaping the form of reporting that is most difficult, most rewarding and most expensive.

James Grimaldi, a past president of Investigative Reporters and Editors, is gloomy about the state of his craft today in the United States. At *The Washington Post*, he says, "I am one of the few who is still allowed to do what we used to call long-form investigative reporting."

He adds, "There's pressure for reporters to produce more often for a variety of instant and online media (Web stories, blogs, audio, video, social networking pages, Twitter, etc.). This has caused a domino effect in the news room beginning with traditional beat reporting, which is suffering. That in turn leads to investigative reporters being tapped to contribute more often to the daily report the kind of enterprise (not necessarily investigative) stories that beat reporters don't have time to produce."

Looking ahead, though, Grimaldi remains optimistic. "I'm certain that substantive investigative reporting will survive. We might need to learn new tools for new media, but the goal is no different. No matter the medium, there will be a public hunger for exposing truths and righting wrongs.

"Student journalists should have every reason to aspire to a job in investigative journalism. It might be a cliché, but it is still true that investigative reporting is where you can really make a difference in the world."

INVESTIGATIVE REPORTING: AN AMERICAN TRADITION

Investigative reporting has a rich tradition in American journalism. The fiercely partisan editors of the Revolutionary era dug for facts as well as the mud they hurled at their opponents. In the early 20th century, investigative reporting flowered with the "muckrakers," a title bestowed angrily by Theodore Roosevelt and worn proudly by journalists. Lincoln Steffens explored the undersides of American cities, one by one, laying bare the corrupt combinations of businessmen and politicians that ran them. Ida Tarbell exposed the economic stranglehold of the oil monopoly. Theodore Dreiser, Upton Sinclair and Frank Norris revealed the horrors of working life in factories and meatpacking plants.

Ida Tarbell, one of the original muckrakers, helped set the pattern for investigative reporting with her exposé of Standard Oil.

Just as the work of the muckrakers appeared in magazines, nonfiction books and even novels, today the work of investigative reporters is produced beyond traditional news rooms. The most prominent example of 21st-century muckraking is a new nonprofit called ProPublica. Funded initially by foundation grants and led by a former editor of *The Wall Street Journal*, ProPublica's staff of experienced journalists tackles major investigations of national significance, often in partnership with traditional news organizations.

As economic pressures force staff cuts in those traditional news rooms, other investigative innovations are emerging at local and regional levels, too. For example, reporter Andy Hall, who decided to leave his newspaper when the staff was reduced, has launched the Wisconsin Center for Investigative Journalism (WisconsinWatch.org), a nonprofit cooperative that seeks to pick up where diminished news rooms are leaving off. Another pair of veteran journalists have formed the New England Center for Investigative Reporting (http://necir-bu.org/wp/), another nonprofit funded by start-up grants and staffed by experienced reporters. Similar efforts are under way across the country.

These professional heirs of the original muckrakers today bring to the work the same commitment to exposure and reform. They use refinements of many of the same techniques: in-depth interviews, personal observation, analysis of documents.

But modern muckrakers have a powerful tool their predecessors didn't dream of. The computer allows reporters today to compile and analyze masses of data, to perform complicated statistical tests, and to create charts and graphs to enhance understanding. This tool, in turn, requires of reporters numeracy as well as literacy. It requires the addition of another set of skills to every serious journalist's repertoire.

Computer-assisted reporting gives young reporters the opportunity to be admitted to the major league of journalism. If you develop your computer-research skills and acquire the techniques taught in this chapter, you will be equipped for the 21st century.

THE PROCESS

Most investigations start with a hunch or a tip that something or someone deserves a close look. If a preliminary search bears out that expectation, a serious investigation begins. When enough information has been uncovered to prove or modify the reporter's initial hunch, it's time to analyze, organize and write the story.

Beginning the Investigation

No good reporter sets out on an investigation unless there is some basis for suspicion. That basis may be a grand jury report that leaves something untold or a tip that some public official is on the take. It may be a sudden upsurge in drug overdoses, or it may be long-festering problems in the schools. If you don't have some idea of what to look for, an investigation is too likely to turn into a wild-goose chase.

Acting on the tip or suspicion, together with whatever background material you have, you form a hypothesis. Reporters hardly ever use that term, but it is a useful one because it shows the similarity between the processes of investigative reporting and scientific investigation (see Chapter 18). In both, the hypothesis is the statement of what you think is true. Your informal hypothesis might be "The mayor is a crook" or "The school system is being run incompetently." It is a good idea to clearly state your hypothesis when you begin your investigation. By doing so, you focus on the heart of the problem and lessen the possibility of any misunderstanding with your editor or other reporters who may be working with you.

Once the hypothesis is stated, the reporter—like the scientist—sets out to support it or show that it is not supportable. You should be open to the possibility that your first assumption was wrong. Reporters—like scientists—are not advocates. They are seekers of truth. No good reporter ignores or downplays evidence just because it contradicts his or her assumptions. In journalism, as in science, the truth about a situation is often sharply different from what is expected. Open-mindedness is an essential quality of a good investigative reporter. Remember, too, that you may have a good story even if your hypothesis is not supported.

TIPS

Carrying Out the Investigation

● Be organized. Careful organization keeps you on the right track and prevents you from overlooking anything important.

● Draw up a plan of action. Write out a plan; then go over it with your editor.

● Carry out your plan, allowing flexibility for the unexpected twists that most investigations take.

● Be methodical. The method you use isn't important as long as you understand it.

Carrying Out the Investigation

The actual investigative work usually proceeds in two stages. The first is what Robert W. Greene, a legendary reporter and Pulitzer Prize-winning editor for *Newsday*, named the **sniff**. After you form a hypothesis, you nose around in search of a trail worth following. If you find one, the second stage, serious investigation, begins.

Preliminary checking should take no more than a day or two. Its purpose is not to prove the hypothesis but to find out the chances of proving it. You make that effort by talking with the most promising source or sources, skimming the most available records and consulting knowledgeable people in your news room. The two questions you are trying to answer at this stage are these: (1) "Is there a story here?" and (2) "Am I going to be able to get it?" If the answer to either question is no, there is little point in pursuing the investigation.

When the answer to both questions is yes, the real work begins. It begins with organization. Your hypothesis tells you where you want to go. Now you must figure out how to get there. Careful organization keeps you on the right track and prevents you from overlooking anything important as you go. Many reporters take a kind of perverse pride in their illegible notebooks and cluttered desks. As an investigative reporter, you may have a messy desk, but you should arrange your files of information clearly and coherently. Begin organizing by asking yourself these questions:

● Who are my most promising sources? Who is likely to give me trouble? Whom should I go to first? Second? Last?

● What records do I need? Where are they? Which are public? How can I get to the ones that are not readily accessible?

● What is the most I can hope to prove? What is the least that will still yield a story?

● How long should the investigation take?

Then draw up a plan of action, such as the one shown in Figure 19.1. Experienced reporters often do this mentally. But when you are a beginner, it's a good idea to write out a plan and go over it with your editor. The editor may spot some holes in your planning or have something to add. And an editor is more likely to give you enough time if he or she has a clear idea of what has to be done.

Allowing flexibility for the unexpected twists that most investigations take, carry out your plan. During your first round of interviews, keep asking who else you should talk to. While you are checking records, look for references to other files or other people.

Be methodical. Many investigative reporters spend an hour or so at the end of every day adding up the score, going through their notes and searching their memories to analyze what they have learned and what they need next. Some develop elaborate, cross-indexed files of names, organizations and incidents. Others are

2/26/10   Plan for Mayor Jane Jones story

Hypothesis: Mayor Jones accepted improper campaign contributions from Top Construction as a council member, and as mayor she later awarded the company a contract to build a new high school.

Initial source: During the course of a conversation, XX casually suggested info about the campaign contribution.

Draft: Due 3/7.

Questions
--How much of this hypothesis can I prove?
--Is XX trustworthy? What does XX have to gain? Will XX go on the record?
--Will documents support the hypothesis? What records are important?
--What other people should I interview—on both sides?
--Will I have at least two credible sources for each fact?
--How can I make sure the story is relevant, useful and interesting?
--Is this one story or a series?
--What extras (documents, audio, video) can I get for the online version?

Plan
Request and review relevant documents:
--Any docs from XX.
--Campaign contribution records; get Stacy to help w/this.
--Contract bids for HS; ask Manuel how to compare.

Interview major people:
--XX, to follow up on initial info.
--Schools chancellor about bids.
--Mayor's campaign manager (Roberts?) about contributions.
--Pres. of Top Construction (Smythe?) about contributions.
--Mayor.

Write outline:
--What's the lead?
--Story structure: inverted pyramid?
--Enough facts? details? anecdotes? quotes?
--Don't forget those online elements.

Write draft:
--Is the story complete? easy to follow? convincing? compelling?

Next steps:
--Editor? legal department?
--Need more facts? details?
--Revise and finalize draft?
--With editors, decide what to post online and when.

Figure 19.1
A plan of action lists the hypothesis and the steps the journalist will take to gather information and draft a story.

less formal. Nearly all, however, use a code to disguise the names of confidential sources so that those sources will remain secret even if the files are subpoenaed. The method you use isn't important as long as you understand it. What is vitally important is that you have a method and use it consistently. If you fail to keep careful track of where you're going, you may go in the wrong direction, or in circles.

Getting It Right

The importance of accuracy in investigative reporting cannot be overstated. It is the essential element in good journalism of any kind. But in investigative reporting especially, inaccuracy leads to embarrassment, to ruined reputations and, sometimes, to lawsuits. The reputations ruined are often those of the careless reporter and the newspaper. Most investigative stories have the effect of accusing somebody of wrongdoing or incompetence. Even if the subject is a public official whose chances of suing successfully for libel are slim (see Chapter 21), fairness and decency require that you be sure of your facts before you put them in print.

Many experienced investigators require verification from two independent sources before they include an allegation in a story. That is a good rule to follow. People make mistakes. They lie. Their memories fail. Documents can be misleading or confusing. Check and double-check. There is no good excuse for an error.

Writing the Story

Most investigative stories require consultation with the newspaper's lawyer before publication. As a reporter, you will have little or nothing to say about the choice of your paper's lawyer. That lawyer, though, will be an important part of your investigative career. The lawyer advises on what you can print safely and what you cannot. Most editors heed their lawyer's advice. If you are lucky, your paper's lawyer will understand and sympathize with good, aggressive journalism. If he or she does not, you may find yourself forced to argue for your story. You will be better equipped for such an argument — few reporters go through a career without several — if you understand at least the basics of the laws of libel and privacy. Chapter 21 outlines those laws, and several good books on law for journalists are listed in the Suggested Readings at the end of that chapter.

> **"**Go to the scene of the disaster and don't let the breaking story stop you from thinking ahead. There, you will find almost all of the sources to tell you what went wrong in responding to the disaster. Though you will have to get your proof through public-record requests, you will get your leads at the scene.**"**
>
> — James Grimaldi, *The Washington Post*

The last step before your investigation goes public is the writing and rewriting. After days or weeks of intense reporting effort, the actual writing strikes some investigative reporters as a chore — necessary but unimportant. That attitude is disastrous. The best reporting in the world is wasted unless it is read. Your hard-won exposé or painstaking analysis will disappear without a trace unless your writing attracts readers and maintains their interest. Most reporters and newspapers that are serious about investigative reporting recognize this. They stress good writing almost as much as solid reporting.

Selecting an Effective Story Structure and Lead

How do you write the results of a complicated investigation? The general rule is, as simply as you can. One approach is to use a **hard lead** (an inverted pyramid lead that reports newly discovered facts), displaying your key findings in the first few paragraphs. Another option is to adopt one of the alternative approaches to story-telling explained in Chapter 11.

Mei-ling Hopgood helped report and write a *Dayton Daily News* investigation of the dangers of the Peace Corps. Here's how that series began:

> AGUA FRIA, El Salvador—On a clear Christmas night near a moonlit stretch of Pacific beach, a man with a pistol came from the darkness and forced Diana Gilmour to watch two of her fellow Peace Corps volunteers being gang-raped while a male volunteer was pinned helpless on the ground.
>
> One of the men—his breath reeking of alcohol—raped Gilmour, too. Then the attackers herded the volunteers at gunpoint to a field of high grass where they feared they would be executed.
>
> "I was constantly waiting to hear a shot in the dark," Gilmour said.
>
> Suddenly another volunteer approached with a flashlight, and the attackers fled.

The best stories are usually about people, and this one is no exception. The drama of one case introduces readers to the bigger story. A few paragraphs later Hopgood and colleague Russell Carollo show that big picture:

> Records from a never-before-released computer database show that reported assault cases involving Peace Corps volunteers increased 125 percent from 1991 to 2002, while the number of volunteers increased by 29 percent, according to the Peace Corps. Last year, the number of assaults and robberies averaged one every 23 hours.
>
> The *Dayton Daily News* spent 20 months examining thousands of records on assaults on Peace Corps volunteers occurring around the world during the past four decades. . . .

Moving from the particular to the general is both a logical progression and an effective way to show readers both the humanity and the full scope of the investigation.

Including Proof of the Story's Credibility

Notice that the last paragraph quoted above also lets readers know something about how the information was developed. That's important, too, if you want to be believed. In this case, the paper's editor also wrote a column explaining both the motivation and the methods of the investigation. That's another good idea. You owe it to your audience to be as open as possible about not only what you know but how you know it. In this era of diminished credibility, it's especially important to do everything you can to be honest and open about your work.

ON THE JOB

Using New Tools to Do a Traditional Job

Karen Dillon entered journalism through the back door — literally. She began in the back shop of a small paper in Iowa. After working her way into the news room, she decided to go to college, where she earned degrees in political science and journalism. After school, she got a job covering the police in Florida. Now she works on the special projects desk at *The Kansas City Star*.

She is eager to get to work every day.

"Despite the financial gloom, it really is an exciting new age in media," she says. "*The Star*, like the rest of the media, has its 24/7 website that is updated continuously. And blogs are like bellybuttons — everyone's got one. Other social networking tools such as Facebook and Twitter keep up a constant chatter, too.

"Quick news has its advantages. After I obtained a confidential report that showed a local utility with coal-fired plants probably violated federal clean air laws, we put up a short story on our website with plans to update the story as I continued to get responses.

"But within an hour the utility petitioned a judge to bar the newspaper from publishing the story, and the judge ordered us to take the story down from the website. But by then, the story had been picked up and published by bloggers and websites around the world, including in Europe and Australia. . . .

"Even more exciting than the many ways a reader can receive the news are the changes in the way that news is gathered. It's much faster and easier. Every reporter is wired. (I confess I'd be lost without my BlackBerry.)

"Just think what that means. I'm closer now to officials and sources than ever before because I can have daily contact with them by e-mail, which is obviously

Striving for Clear, Simple Explanations

Writing an investigative story so that it will be read takes the same attention to organization and to detail as does any good writing. Here are a few tips that apply to all types of writing but especially to investigative stories:

- **Get people into the story.** Any investigation worth doing involves people in some way. Make them come alive with descriptive detail, the kind we were given in the Peace Corps story.

- **Keep it simple.** Look for ways to clarify and explain complicated situations. When you have a mass of information, consider spreading it over more than one story — in a series or in a main story with a sidebar. Think about how charts, graphs or lists can be used to present key facts clearly. Don't try to print everything you know. Enough to support your conclusions is sufficient; more than that is too much.

quicker than calling, leaving voicemails and getting a return call a couple days later.

"Have a question about a person, place or thing? Google it.

"Have an open records request for documents? E-mail it.

"Even in these wired times, traditional beats still must be covered. The new age has made it so much easier."

Dillon offers a few helpful hints for beginning reporters:

- **"First, know the community, the issues and the government agencies involved.** One of the best ways to spend your first days on the job is to read articles on the newspaper and television news websites. Look at stories going back five or 10 years. The easiest way to do that is to go to LexisNexis.
- **Become well versed in using still cameras and video cameras.** You don't have to be an expert, but you never know when this skill will come in handy.
- **Buy a digital recorder, and learn how to use it.** Audio is easy to post to the Web, and everyone likes a good sound bite. Besides, recording will also help you clarify quotes for your print story, online or on paper.
- **Know how to blog.** Most news organizations have blogs, especially for police and political news, that reporters are expected to feed frequently. You will often have to write and post a couple of paragraphs summarizing a developing story.
- **Know how to use Google for information.** Google is a reporter's best friend. I'm never far from Google on my computer and on my BlackBerry. I use it to find all sorts of information, to verify names and facts, find people, check numerous types of documents such as inspection records or court cases, find studies, review city and state laws and check political campaign expenditures. My advice is, if you don't know where it is, what it is or how to spell it, look it up on Google."

- **Tell the reader what your research means.** A great temptation in investigative reporting is to lay out the facts and let the reader draw the conclusions. That is unfair to you and your reader. Lay out the facts, of course, but tell the reader what they add up to. A reporter who had spent weeks investigating the deplorable conditions in his state's juvenile corrections facilities wrote this lead: "Florida treats her delinquent children as if she hated them." Then he went on to show the reality that led to that summary. If the facts are there, drawing the obvious conclusions is not editorializing. It is good and helpful writing.

- **Organize.** Careful organization is as important in writing the investigative story as it is in reporting it. The job will be easier if you have been organized all along. When you are ready to write, examine your notes again. Make an outline. Pick out your best quotes and anecdotes. Some reporters, if they are writing more than one story, separate their material into individual folders, one for each story. However you do it, know what you are going to say before you start to write.

- **Suggest solutions.** Polls have shown that readers prefer investigative stories that show how to correct the problems described in the stories. Many of today's best newspapers are satisfying readers' demands by going beyond exposure in search of solutions. Are new laws needed? Better enforcement of present laws? More resources? Better training? Remember that the early-20th-century Progressive movement (of which the original muckrakers were a part) produced reforms, not just good stories.

- **Use the Web to support your story.** Readers are skeptical. They want to be shown, not just told. So use the expanded capacity of your organization's website to post supporting documents, photographs, audio or transcripts of key interviews. And make sure to include any responses or defenses offered by the people or institution you're examining. Fairness is essential.

Think of writing as the climax of a process that begins with a hypothesis, tests that hypothesis through careful investigation, checks and double-checks every fact, and satisfies the concerns of newspaper editors and lawyers. Every step in that process is vital to the success of any investigative story.

THE SOURCES

Investigative reporters—like other reporters—get their information from people or documents. The perfect source would be a person who has the pertinent documents and is eager to tell you what those documents mean. Don't count on finding the perfect source. Instead, count on having to piece together the information you need from a variety of people and records—some of the people not at all eager to talk to you and some of the records difficult to obtain and, if you do gain access to them, difficult to understand. Let's consider human sources first.

Human Sources

Suppose you get a tip that the mayor received campaign contributions under the table from the engineering firm that just got a big city contract. Who might talk?

- **Enemies.** When you are trying to find out anything bad about a person, his or her enemies are usually the best sources. More often than not, the enemies of a prominent person will have made it their business to find out as much as possible about that person's misdeeds and shortcomings. Frequently, they are happy to share what they know with a friendly reporter.

- **Friends.** Friends are sometimes nearly as revealing as enemies. In trying to explain and defend their friend's actions, they may tell you more than you knew before. Occasionally, you may find that someone your subject regards as a friend is not much of a friend after all.

- **Losers.** Like enemies, losers often carry a grudge. Seek out the loser in the last election, the losing contender for the contract, the loser in a power struggle. Bad losers make good sources.

- **Victims.** If you are investigating a failing school system, talk with students and their parents. If your story is about nursing home abuses, talk with patients and their relatives. The honest and hardworking employees caught in a corrupt or incompetent system are victims, too. They can give you specific examples and anecdotes. Their case histories can help you write the story. Be wary, though. One thing enemies, losers and victims have in common is that they have an ax to grind about your subject. Be sure to confirm every allegation they make.

- **Experts.** Early in many investigations, there may be a great deal that you don't understand. You may need someone to explain how the campaign finance laws could be circumvented, someone to interpret a contract, someone to decipher a set of bid specifications. Lawyers, accountants, engineers or professors can help you understand technical jargon or complicated transactions. If they refuse to comment on your specific case, fit the facts you have into a hypothetical situation.

- **Police.** Investigative reporters and law enforcement agents often work the same territory. If you are wise, you will make friends with carefully selected agents. They can — and frequently will — be of great help. Their files may not be gold mines, but they have investigative tools and contacts you lack. When they get to know and trust you, they will share. Most police like seeing their own and their organization's names in the paper. They know, too, that you can do some things they cannot. It takes less proof for you to be able to print that the mayor is a crook than it may take to convince a jury. Most police investigators want to corner wrongdoers any way they can. You can use that attitude to your advantage.

- **People in trouble.** Police use this source and so can you, although you cannot promise immunity or a lesser charge, as prosecutors can. A classic case is the Watergate affair, in which members of President Richard Nixon's administration recruited five men to break into the headquarters of the Democratic National Committee to wiretap phones illegally. Once the Nixon administration started to unravel, officials trying to save their careers and images began falling all over each other to give their self-serving versions of events. People will react similarly in lesser cases.

As an investigative reporter, you cultivate sources in the same ways a reporter on a beat does. You just do it more quickly. One excellent tactic is to play on their self-interest. Losers and enemies want to get the so-and-so, and thus you have a common aim. (But don't go overboard. Your words could come back to haunt you.) Friends want their buddy's side of the story to be explained. So do you. If you keep in mind that no matter how corrupt your subject may be, he or she is still a human being, it may be easier to deal sympathetically with that person's friends. That attitude may also help ensure that you treat the subject fairly.

Experts just want to explain the problem as you present it. And you just want to understand. People in trouble want sympathy and some assurance that they still merit respect. No reporter should have trouble conveying either attitude.

One newspaper exposed the ugly truth about pollution in Puget Sound.

Reporter: Robert McClure
Reporter: Lisa Stiffler
Photographer: Paul Joseph Brown

For 150 years, Puget Sound has provided the Seattle area with food, jobs and commerce as well as recreation and inspiration. In return, the region has treated the sparkling blue waters of the Sound like a sewer. Until recently, nobody paid much attention to the consequences of that destructive pattern. Then, in November, the Seattle Post-Intelligencer published a five-part series called "Our Troubled Sound."

For the first time, area residents became aware of the size and severity of the crisis. The series led to a public outcry for the government to take action. As a result, state and federal officeholders have vowed to stop the pollution and begin clean-up programs. This time, the eyes of the region will be on them.

Making waves when public health and natural resources are at risk is another way Hearst Newspapers make a positive contribution to their communities . . . and that's what excellence in journalism is all about.

To read more on this series go to www.seattlepi.com/specials/sound

Hearst Newspapers

Investigative reporters have uncovered scandals and illegal activity and have raised public awareness of issues such as water pollution.

Another way to win and keep sources is to protect them. Occasionally a reporter faces jail unless he or she reveals a source. Even jail is not too great a price to pay to keep a promise of confidentiality. More often, the threats to confidentiality are less dramatic. Other sources, or the subject of the investigation, may casually ask, "Where'd you hear that?" Other reporters, over coffee or a beer, may ask the same question. Hold your tongue. The only person to whom a confidential source should ever be revealed is your editor.

Human sources pose problems as well as solve them. To hurt an enemy or protect a friend, to make themselves look better or someone else look worse—and sometimes simply for fun—people lie to reporters. No reporter is safe, and no source is above suspicion. They may use you, too, just as you are using them. The only reason most people involved on any side of a suspicious situation will talk about it is to enhance their own position. That is neither illegal nor immoral, but it can trip up a reporter who fails to take every self-serving statement with the appropriate grain of salt.

Sources may change their stories as well. People forget. Recollections and situations change. Pressure is applied. Fear or love or ambition or greed intrudes. A source may deny tomorrow—or in court—what he or she told you today.

Finally, sources will seldom want to be identified. Even the enemies of a powerful person are often reluctant to see their names attached to their criticisms in print. Even friends may be reluctant to be identified. Experts, while willing to provide background information, often cite their codes of ethics when you ask them to go on the record. Stories without identifiable sources have less credibility with readers, with editors, even with colleagues.

Written Sources

Fortunately, not all sources are human. Records and documents neither lie nor change their stories, they have no axes to grind at your expense, and they can be identified in print. Many useful documents are public records, available to you or any other citizen on request. Others are nonpublic but still may be available through your human sources.

Remember that most, if not all, of the relevant documents—especially the public records kept by government agencies—are likely to be accessible online. Google and other search engines shouldn't be your only tools, but they are powerful ones. Use them early and often. And don't overlook the revelations, some of them unintentional, that turn up on Web-based networking sites like LinkedIn and Facebook.

Public Records

As the examples earlier show, a great deal can be learned about individuals and organizations through records that are available for the asking, if you know where to ask. Let's take a look at some of the most valuable public records and where they can be found:

- **Property records.** Many investigations center on land—who owns it, who buys it, how it is zoned, how it is taxed. You can find out all that information and more from public records. Your county recorder's office (or its equivalent) has on file the ownership of every piece of land in the county as well as the history of past owners. In most offices, the files are cross-indexed so you can find the owner of the land if you know its location, or the location and size of the property if you know the owner. Those files also will tell you who holds a mortgage on the land. The city or county tax assessor's office has on file the assessed valuation of the land, which is the basis for property taxes. Either the assessor or the local zoning agency can tell you for what use the property is zoned. All requests for rezoning are public information, too.

- **Corporation records.** Every corporation must file a document showing the officers and principal agent of the company. This document must be filed with the state in which the corporation is formed and with every state in which it does business. The officers listed may be only "dummies"—stand-ins for the real owners—but you can find out at least who the stand-ins are. But that is only the beginning.

Publicly held corporations must file annual reports with the Securities and Exchange Commission in Washington. The reports list officers, major stockholders, financial statements and business dealings with other companies owned by the corporation. Nonprofit corporations—such as foundations and charities—must file with the Internal Revenue Service an even more revealing statement, Form 990, showing how much money came in and where it went. Similar statements must be filed with the attorneys general of many states.

Corporations often are regulated by state or federal agencies as well. They file regular reports with the regulating agency. Insurance companies, for instance, are regulated by state insurance commissioners. Nursing homes are regulated by various state agencies. Broadcasters are overseen by the Federal Communications Commission, truckers by the Interstate Commerce Commission. Labor unions must file with the U.S. Department of Labor detailed statements called *5500 forms* showing assets, officers' salaries, loans and other financial information.

Once you have corporation records, you must interpret them. Your public library has books that tell you how. Your news organization's own business experts may be willing to help.

- **Court records.** Few people active in politics or business go through life without becoming involved in court actions of some sort. Check the offices of the state and federal court clerks for records of lawsuits. The written arguments, sworn statements and answers to questions (*interrogatories*) may contain valuable details or provide leads to follow. Has your target been divorced? Legal struggles over assets can be revealing. Probate court files of your subject's deceased associates may tell you something you need to know.

- **Campaign and conflict-of-interest reports.** Federal—and most state—campaign laws now require political candidates to disclose, during and after each campaign, lists of who gave what to whom. Those filings can yield stories on who is supporting the candidates. They also can be used later for comparing who gets what from which officeholder. Many states require officeholders to file statements of their business and stock holdings. These can be checked for possible conflicts of interest or used as background for profile stories.

- **Loan records.** Commercial lenders usually file statements showing property that has been used as security for loans. Known as Uniform Commercial Code filings, these can be found in the offices of state secretaries of state and, sometimes, in local recorders' offices.

- **Minutes and transcripts.** Most elected and appointed governing bodies, ranging from local planning and zoning commissions to the U.S. Congress, are required by law to keep minutes or transcripts of their meetings.

Using and Securing Public Records

The states and the federal government have laws designed to ensure access to public records. Many of these laws—including the federal **Freedom of Information Act**, which was passed to improve access to government records—have gaping loopholes and time-consuming review procedures. Still, they have been and can be useful tools when all else fails. Learn the details of the law in your state. You can get information on access laws and their interpretations by contacting the Freedom of Information Center at the University of Missouri, 127 Neff Annex, Columbia, MO 65211.

Nonpublic Records

Nonpublic records are more difficult, but often not impossible, to obtain. To get them, you must know that they exist, where they are and how to gain access. Finding out about those things requires good human sources. You should know about a few of the most valuable nonpublic records:

- **Investigative files.** The investigative files of law enforcement agencies can be rich in information. You are likely to see them only if you have a good source in a particular agency or one affiliated with it. If you do obtain such files, treat them cautiously. They will be full of unsubstantiated allegations, rumor and misinformation. Be wary of accepting as fact anything you have not confirmed yourself.

- **Past arrests and convictions.** Records of past arrests and convictions increasingly are being removed from public scrutiny. Usually these are easier than investigative files to obtain from a friendly police or prosecuting official. And usually they are more trustworthy than raw investigative files.

- **Bank records.** Bank records would be helpful in many investigations, but they are among the most difficult types of records to get. Bankers are trained to keep secrets. The government agencies that regulate banks are secretive as well. A friend in a bank is an investigative reporter's friend indeed.

- **Income tax records.** Except for those made public by officeholders, income tax records are guarded carefully by their custodians. Leaks are rare.

- **Credit checks.** Sometimes you can get otherwise unavailable information on a target's financial situation by arranging through your newspaper's business office for a credit check. Credit reports may reveal outstanding debts, a big bank account, major assets and business affiliations. Use that information with care. It is unofficial, and companies that provide it intend it to be confidential.

Problems with Written Sources

Even when you can obtain them, records and other written sources present problems. They are usually dull. Records give you names and numbers, not anecdotes or sparkling quotes. They are bare bones, not flesh and blood. They can be misleading and confusing. Many highly skilled lawyers and accountants spend careers interpreting the kinds of records you may find yourself pondering without their training. Misinterpreting a document is no less serious an error than misquoting a person. And it's easier to do.

Documents usually describe without explaining. You need to know the "why" of a land transaction or a loan. Records tell you only the "what."

Most investigative reporters use both human and documentary sources. People can explain what documents cannot. Documents prove what good quotes cannot. You need people to lead you to documents and people to interpret what the documents mean. And you need documents to substantiate what people tell you. The best investigative stories combine both types of sources.

NEW TOOLS, TRADITIONAL GOALS

As you've seen, the computer is the most important new tool of investigative reporting. Once you know how to use it, the computer allows you to obtain, analyze and present information in ways that would have been impossible 20 years ago, let alone in the era of the original muckrakers. But useful as it is, the computer is only a tool. Many modern investigative reporters are guided by goals that their predecessors of a century ago would easily recognize.

Today's investigators, like the original muckrakers, are not satisfied with uncovering individual instances of wrongdoing. They look at organizations as a whole, at entire systems. They seek not only to expose but to explain. In many cases, they also seek to change the problems and abuses they reveal. Many, perhaps most, investigative reporters think of themselves as more than chroniclers of fact or analysts. They also see themselves as reformers. This, too, was true of the muckrakers.

The drive to expose abuses is something the public welcomes and expects from journalists. Studies have shown that the consumers of journalism support investigative reporting when it leads to reforms. There's no conflict between investigative reporting and the journalistic standard of objectivity, either. You'll remember from Chapter 1 that objectivity doesn't have to mean neutrality. In journalism, as in science, objectivity is the method of searching for the truth. Just as scientists are not expected to be neutral between disease and cure, journalists don't have to be neutral between good and evil. What objectivity requires of both scientists and journalists is honest, open-minded investigation and truthful reporting of the results of that investigation.

Suggested Readings

Houston, Brant. *Computer-Assisted Reporting: A Practical Guide*, 3rd ed. New York: Bedford/St. Martin's, 2003. Houston, the executive director of Investigative Reporters and Editors, has written an invaluable how-to guide for using the newest and most powerful reporting tool.

Houston, Brant, and Investigative Reporters and Editors. *The Investigative Reporters' Handbook: A Guide to Documents, Databases and Techniques*, 5th ed. New York: Bedford/St. Martin's, 2009. This handbook tells you how to get and how to use the most important records and documents.

The IRE Journal. Publication of Investigative Reporters and Editors Inc., 138 Neff Annex, Missouri School of Journalism, University of Missouri, Columbia, MO 65211. Every issue has articles on investigations, guides to sources and documents, and a roundup of legal developments. Edited transcripts of IRE conferences are also available.

Suggested Websites

http://data.nicar.org
The National Institute for Computer-Assisted Reporting, a partnership of IRE and the Missouri School of Journalism, teaches the skills and provides the consulting you'll need to get and analyze the data for richer, more revealing stories.

www.ire.org
Begin here. Investigative Reporters and Editors, headquartered at the University of Missouri, is the world's leading source of expertise, story ideas and professional and personal support for investigative reporters.

www.opensecrets.org
The Center for Responsive Politics specializes in collecting, analyzing and making available information on money and politics. The center's handbook, *Follow the Money*, is an invaluable resource for any reporter interested in the impact of money on self-government.

www.publicintegrity.org/investigations/icij
This site takes you to the work of the International Consortium of Investigative Journalists, which did the tobacco smuggling project and other groundbreaking pieces of cross-border digging.

Exercises

1. **Team project.** Much of the best investigative reporting is done in teams. You'll find plenty of examples at the IRE website. Your instructor will divide your class into three- or four-person teams. With your team, pick a topic to investigate and then design your project. Use the format shown in Figure 19.1 as a guide. Then assign responsibilities and devise a system for coordinating your findings. If there's time, dig in. Otherwise, submit the complete plan for class discussion.

2. Go to www.ire.org, and find the stories that have won recent IRE awards. Choose one story from each of at least three categories. Compare the sources and techniques used. What similarities and differences do you find in different media? Which stories seem to you most complete and most satisfying? Why?

3. School board member Doris Hart reported at last week's meeting of the board that major flaws, including basement flooding and electrical short circuits, have shown up in the new elementary school. She noted that this is the third straight project designed by consulting architect Louis Doolittle in which serious problems have occurred. School Superintendent Margaret Smith defended Doolittle vigorously. Later, Hart told you privately that she suspects Doolittle may be paying Smith off to keep the consulting contract, which has earned the architect more than $100,000 per year for the past five years.

   Describe how you will investigate:
   a. The sniff.
   b. Human sources. Who might talk? Where should you start? Whom will you save for last?
   c. What records might help? Where are they? What will you be looking for?
   d. What is the most you can hope to prove? What is the least that will yield a story?

4. Choose a public official in your city or town, and compile the most complete profile you can, using only public records.

5. Use one or more of the computer databases described in Chapter 6 to learn as much as you can about your representative in Congress. Write the most complete investigative profile you can from the databases. In a memo, explain what additional information you'd need to complete your story and where it might be found.

Working in Public Relations

This is not a dinosaur.
Or an extinct species.
Or something your kids will only read about.
But never see.
This is not the last of its kind.
This is worth fighting for.
And it's got a fighting chance.

Earthjustice is using the courts
to protect polar bear habitat
from unsound oil and gas
development. It's just one of the
ways we're preserving our natural
heritage, safeguarding health, and
promoting a clean energy future.
Join us at **earthjustice.org**.

EARTHJUSTICE
Because the earth needs a good lawyer

20

IN THIS CHAPTER
YOU WILL LEARN:

1. Various types of
public relations writing.

2. Guidelines for
persuasive writing.

3. Different approaches
to writing news
releases.

The video was posted on YouTube on a Monday. *USA Today* reported that by Wednesday, it had been viewed 550,000 times. But Ragan.com, a site that specializes in corporate communications, said that by Tuesday more than 700,000 people had already seen it. By Wednesday, according to *The New York Times*, the video had more than a million viewers.

The one thing everyone agreed on: It was a horrific public relations nightmare.

Two Domino's Pizza employees just grossing out—one picking his nose and putting what he found there in a submarine sandwich, sticking pieces of cheese up his nose and passing gas on the salami. The other employee says, while laughing, that the sandwich will be delivered to a customer in five minutes.

USA Today quoted Domino's spokesman Tim McIntyre as saying, "Nothing is local anymore. That's the challenge of the Web world. Any two idiots with a video camera and a dumb idea can damage the reputation of a 50-year-old brand."

Opinions varied about Domino's initial response to the situation. According to Ragan.com, McIntyre said he "doesn't want to put the candle out with a fire hose." The fear was, of course, that almost anything Domino's did would call more attention to the YouTube piece.

Social media experts such as Shel Holtz disagreed completely. He did not think Domino's should have restricted its response to a blog post. "People on Twitter," he said on Ragan.com, "might not know about their response and wonder why Domino's isn't paying attention or saying anything. The communication landscape has changed. You want to stay visible and engaged."

The communications landscape for public relations has indeed changed. Not only must companies and organizations use Twitter, YouTube, Facebook and other social media, but they must constantly monitor these media and be ready to respond immediately. Moreover, at least some expertise in social media is not just for management. Internal public relations and corporate communicators must work hard to get employees trained at least to watch for potential public relations crises and to report them to the proper people immediately.

You might never confront a situation like this early in your career. However, if you are planning to work in this field, don't anticipate that the job will be all fun and games.

Regardless of the situation you are in, professionals agree that the skill most required of public relations people is good writing. Your writing skills should include news writing, and you should be familiar with the way news operations work. That's why journalism schools traditionally require a course in news writing for students interested in public relations, and that's why many public relations professionals like to hire people with some news experience. Only by studying news and how news organizations handle the news will you be successful in public relations or in offices of public information. Knowing how reporters are taught to deal with news releases will help you write better releases. Of course, studying the news also helps you enormously in the advertising world and in what is now frequently called strategic marketing or strategic communication.

PUBLIC RELATIONS TASKS

Dennis L. Wilcox and Glen T. Cameron, writing in *Public Relations: Strategies and Tactics*, list the following activities as common to those who work in public relations. Notice how many involve writing, either directly or indirectly.

Advise management on policy

Plan and conduct meetings

Participate in policy decisions

Prepare publicity items

Plan public relations programs

Talk to editors and reporters

Sell programs to top management

Hold press conferences

Get cooperation from middle management

Write feature articles

Get cooperation from other employees

Research public opinion

Listen to speeches

Plan and manage events

Make speeches

Conduct tours

Write speeches for others

Write letters

Obtain speakers for organizational meetings

Plan and write booklets, leaflets, reports and bulletins

Attend meetings

Design posters

Plan films and videotapes

Greet visitors

Plan and prepare slide presentations

Screen charity requests

Plan and produce exhibits

Evaluate public relations programs

Take pictures or supervise photographers

Conduct fund-raising drives

Give awards

Skilled public relations or public information practitioners know how to write news, and they apply all the principles of good news writing in their news releases. Thus, a good news release meets the criteria of a good news story. Like a good story, it should have some staying power, as organizations often keep recent news releases available on their websites (see Figure 20.1).

These same professionals know that working for an organization and doing internal and external communications demands a different perspective and, in many cases, a different kind of writing. In many ways, of course, good writing is good writing, and what you have learned so far applies to public relations writing. But you also will be called upon to do writing that is different from the kinds of writing done by those who work for news organizations.

STAFFINGINDUSTRY ANALYSTS

For Immediate Release

Temporary Staffing Firms See Improvement in Employment

Staffing Industry Analysts Releases Pulse Survey Data

LOS ALTOS, Calif. – September 28, 2009 – Temporary staffing can be viewed as an early indicator of overall employment. According to Staffing Industry Analysts' latest *Pulse Survey*, a recovering trend is evident. On a monthly basis Staffing Industry Analysts, the nation's premier provider of marketing intelligence and advisory services about the contingent (temporary) workforce, survey's temporary staffing companies about revenue trends.

This month the survey says:

1. There is widespread improvement in sequential revenue trend in August versus July. This is the second month in a row that sequential improvement was commonly noted.
2. Direct hire sequential trends remain flat, however on a weighted-average basis, this sector continues to suffer year-over-year declines in the 35%-45% range.
3. Within temporary staffing, industrial and IT segments are seeing the strongest recovery.
4. Travel nursing and legal temporary staffing are reporting year-over-year declines approaching 50% with no sequential relief.

Figure 20.1
In addition to distributing news releases, organizations may make their recent releases available on their websites. This Staffing Industry Analysts' news release is archived as a printable PDF on the company's site.

PUBLIC RELATIONS WRITING: A DIFFERENT APPROACH

Rex Harlow, called by some the "father of public relations research" and perhaps the first full-time public relations educator, claimed to have found 472 definitions of public relations. The 1978 World Assembly of Public Relations in Mexico came up with this definition: "Public relations is the art and social science of analyzing trends, predicting their consequences, counseling organization leaders and implementing planned programs of action which will serve both the organization's and public interest."

In *Public Relations: Strategies and Tactics*, Wilcox and Cameron claim these key terms are found in all the definitions of public relations:

- **Deliberate:** The "activity is intentional . . . designed to influence, gain understanding, provide feedback, and obtain feedback."
- **Planned:** "organized . . . systematic, requiring research and analysis."
- **Performance:** "based on actual policies."
- **Public interest:** "mutually beneficial to the organization and to the public."
- **Two-way communication:** "equally important to solicit feedback."
- **Management function:** "an integral part of decision-making by top management."

Public relations, then, is not just publicity, which seeks to get the media to respond to an organization's interests. Nor is it advertising, which pays to get the attention of the public, or marketing, which combines a whole host of activities to sell a product, service or idea. Advertising and marketing are concerned with sales.

A Range of Interests

If you wish to write in the field of public relations, you have many areas from which to choose. Here are some of the specialties:

- **Media relations:** seeking publicity and answering questions posed by the media.
- **Government affairs:** spending time with legislatures and regulatory agencies and doing some lobbying.
- **Public affairs:** engaging in matters of public policy.
- **Industry relations:** relating to other firms within the industry and to trade associations.
- **Investor, financial or shareholder relations:** working to maintain investor confidence and good relationships with the financial world.

And the list goes on. Whoever said public relations writing was dull knew nothing of the various worlds these professionals inhabit.

More and more today the term **strategic communication** is replacing *public relations*. Some say that one simple reason for this change is that the term *public relations* has always suffered a "PR problem." But of course the reasons are much more serious than that.

The demands made of public relations professionals are greater today than they were a generation ago. As Ronald Smith explains in *Strategic Planning for Public Relations*,

> No longer is it enough merely to know *how* to do things. Now the effective communicator needs to know *what* to do, *why* and how to *evaluate* its effectiveness. Public relations professionals used to be called upon mainly for tasks such as writing news releases, making speeches, producing videos, publishing newsletters, organizing displays and so on. Now the profession demands competency in conducting research, making decisions and solving problems. The call now is for strategic communicators.

In short, the strategic communicator must take a more scientific approach, do some research, make careful choices, and when finished, evaluate the effectiveness of the completed program. Such a communicator would certainly be expected to write clearly and precisely, but differently from reporters.

Objectivity and Public Relations Writing

Journalists will debate forever whether anyone can be truly objective when writing a story. Most settle the argument by saying what is demanded is fairness. Nevertheless, in traditional reporting, writers strive *not* to have a point of view. Reporters should not set out to prove something. Certainly, they should not be an advocate for a point of view. They should get the facts, and let the facts speak for themselves.

By contrast, columnists have a point of view, and good ones find ways to support it convincingly. Editorial writers use facts to persuade people to change their minds, or to confirm their opinions, or to get people to do something or to stop doing something. (See Figure 1.1 in Chapter 1 for a comparison of how reporters and commentators approach accuracy, fairness and bias in writing.)

That's also what public relations writers do. Though sometimes they wish only to inform their audiences, they most often want to do what editorial writers do—persuade the audience to accept a particular position.

However, there's one major difference. News commentators serve the public. Public relations writers work for an organization or for a client other than a news operation. Their job is to make that organization or client appear in the best possible light. Effective public relations writers do not ignore facts, even when the facts are harmful or detrimental to the cause they are promoting. But they are promoting a cause or looking out for the best interests of the people for whom they are working. As a result, they will interpret all news, even bad news, in the most favorable light.

Public relations writers work much the way attorneys work for clients—as advocates. They don't lie or distort, but perhaps they play down certain facts and emphasize others. In its "official statement of public relations," the Public Relations Society of America says:

> Public relations helps our complex, pluralistic society to reach decisions and function more effectively by contributing to mutual understanding among groups and institutions. It serves to bring private and public policies into harmony. . . . The public relations practitioner acts as a counselor to management and as a mediator, helping to translate private aims into reasonable, publicly acceptable policy and action.

For a good discussion of what public relations is, check the website of the Public Relations Student Society of America at www.prssa.org.

The Public Relations Society of America has a code of ethics for the practice of public relations. The code, given in full on its website (www.prsa.org), requires members to "adhere to the highest standard of accuracy and truth," avoiding extravagant claims or unfair comparisons and giving credit for ideas and words borrowed from others. It also requires members not to "knowingly disseminate false or misleading information."

PUBLIC RELATIONS WRITING: THE MAIN FOCUS

Public relations personnel are concerned with three things: the message, the audience and the media to deliver the message.

The Message

To be an effective public relations professional, you must know the message your organization wants to send. That message may be a product, a program or the organization itself. For every message you work on, you must first know what you hope to accomplish, even if your purpose is just to inform.

That's why it is so important for you to be a reporter first, to know how to gather information and to do so quickly. Like any reporter, you may be called on in an instant to deal with a crisis in the company for which you work. When contaminated meat from a Toronto-based company killed 12 people and sickened dozens more all over Canada, there was work to do. Naturally, the price of the company's stock dropped. The recall cost the firm more than $20 million. Nevertheless, Maple Leaf Food, which employs nearly 23,000 people, is surviving—mainly because of excellent communications.

From the beginning of the crisis, company president Michael McCain took the full blame and regularly apologized to all victims. In a Sept. 5, 2008, news release, for example, he said, "We deeply regret this incident and the impact it has had on people's lives." The release clearly outlined four immediate steps the company had taken. It assured readers that the company was doing everything possible to determine the cause of the contamination and to prevent it from ever happening again.

Ways to Get Noticed

Journalists, especially television journalists, are sometimes accused of creating stories by their very presence, or at least of fanning the flames. While creating news is not in the journalist's job description, a large part of public relations is doing exactly that. Here's a list of how to create news from Dennis L. Wilcox and Glen T. Cameron:

1. Tie in with news events of the day.
2. Cooperate with another organization on a joint project.
3. Tie in with a newspaper or broadcast station on a mutual project.
4. Conduct a poll or survey.
5. Issue a report.
6. Arrange an interview with a celebrity.
7. Take part in a controversy.
8. Arrange for a testimonial.
9. Arrange for a speech.
10. Make an analysis or prediction.
11. Form and announce names for committees.
12. Hold an election.
13. Announce an appointment.
14. Celebrate an anniversary.
15. Issue a summary of facts.
16. Tie in with a holiday.
17. Make a trip.
18. Give an award.
19. Hold a contest.
20. Pass a resolution.
21. Appear before a public body.
22. Stage a special event.
23. Write a letter.
24. Release a letter you received (with permission).
25. Adapt national reports and surveys for local use.
26. Stage a debate.
27. Tie in to a well-known week or day.
28. Honor an institution.
29. Organize a tour.
30. Inspect a project.
31. Issue a commendation.
32. Issue a protest.

You might not have a boss as enlightened as Michael McCain, but as the public relations person, it is your job to try to be candid and truthful with the press and the public. In this case, an editorial in the *Calgary Herald* praised Maple Leaf Foods for its "show of openness and accountability."

This same openness and accountability gained high marks from public relations experts for President Barack Obama when he apologized on NBC for picking Sen. Tom Daschle as his Health and Human Services Secretary without vetting him properly. "I'm here on television saying I screwed up, and that's part of the era of responsibility, . . . not never making mistakes; it's owning up to them and trying to make sure you never repeat them, and that's what we intend to do."

The Audience

Almost as important as knowing all you can about the message is knowing the audience to whom you are directing it. The better you target your audience, the more effective you will be. As in advertising, the demographics and psychographics of your target audience determine the way you write your message, the language you choose, and the simplicity or complexity of the piece you create.

Who are these people, what are their attitudes, what do they do for work and recreation? You will answer these questions somewhat differently if you write for internal audiences (employees or the managers of those employees) or external audiences (the media, shareholders, constituents, volunteers, consumers or donors).

On Valentine's Day in 2007, JetBlue Airways mishandled a snowstorm that caused the cancellation of 1,100 flights, affecting approximately 130,000 people. In the ensuing public relations crisis, Todd Burke, JetBlue's vice president of corporate communications, found himself dealing more with employees than with the public. He told Kevin J. Allen of Ragan.com: "An interesting thing happened. I now found myself having to manage internal audience almost as much as I did external."

Not that the external audience was ignored. The communications team put together a "Passenger Bill of Rights," and they persuaded then-CEO David Neeleman to do a YouTube video in which he apologized to customers. "We are sorry and embarrassed," he said. "But most of all, we are deeply sorry."

The Media

Once you have mastered the message or product and targeted the audience, you then have to choose the best medium through which to deliver the message to the audience.

Television, Radio and Newsstand Publications

For a message that nearly everyone wants or needs to know, television may be your best medium. Procter & Gamble spends millions advertising soap on television because everyone needs soap. Television offers color and motion; television can show rather than tell.

For PR Pros, Nine Rules Taken Directly from Kindergarten

1. Say please.
2. Say I'm sorry.
3. Be friendly.
4. Share.
5. Play fair.
6. Don't litter.
7. Never hurt others.
8. Say excuse me.
9. Listen to others.

— Richie Escovedo, Ragan.com

Radio listeners usually are loyal to one radio station. They will listen to your message over and over. The more often they hear it, the more likely they are to retain it.

Print media such as newspapers and magazines are better for complicated messages and sometimes for delicate messages. Some argue that print still has more credibility than other media and that people can come back again and again to a print message.

The Internet: An All-in-One Medium

Perhaps the best place to do public relations today is online. More and more people are getting the information and products they need online. Here you have the advantages of all the media—print, video and audio—in one medium. Remember, people who are online generally are better educated and more affluent than those who are not. They love the control they have over the messages they find online. They can click on only the information they want, and they can do so in any order they choose. They can be involved and engaged and can respond to one another.

What is so challenging about "new" media is the high degree of individualization; you are in the world of "mass customization." You must present the message at different levels to different people so that they feel they have choices, so that everyone feels as if you are writing only to him or her. It's all about individual choices and involving your readers so they will interact with you. As Web usability expert Jakob Nielsen puts it, online readers are "selfish, lazy and ruthless." For more about writing online, review Chapter 12. Just remember, communicating online means ideally making use of video and audio, as well as print, to get your story across.

Social Networking Media

JetBlue's use of YouTube is just one example of using online resources to reach an audience. When the rising Mississippi continued to flood and wreak havoc on thousands of victims in June 2008, American Red Cross public affairs team member Jeffery Biggs used only a Twitter feed—a social networking service that sends messages in real time—to keep people informed.

Wendy Harman, the American Red Cross's director of new media integration, had been training her team "on how to use the social media for some time." As reported in *O'Dwyer's PR Report* by Darby C. Doll, "Harman established what she calls 'the online newsroom,' consisting of a WordPress blog, Google Maps, Facebook page, YouTube channel and Flickr album, in addition to the Twitter Feed."

In his article, Doll goes on to talk about other forms of microblogging that can be of enormous help to public relations professionals:

- **Jaiku** (jaiku.com): Share photos and music; text "Jaikus" from your smart phone.

- **Plurk** (plurk.com): "Share your life easily with friends, family and fans."
- **Tumblr** (tumblr.com): "Post anything: Customize everything."
- **Identi.ca** (identi.ca): Calls itself a "public timeline."

The huge social media giants Facebook and MySpace have microblogging features. LinkedIn has become enormously popular among corporate and other business users.

All of this has developed rapidly, and most experts believe that we've seen only the beginning. Print will not disappear, but the arrival of the microblog may change the way we write nearly everything.

Internal Publications, Brochures and Billboards

If you work in internal communications, you may decide to publish a newsletter or magazine for employees. A large number of corporations are now communicating with employees throughout the day via an intranet, an internal online service accessible only to them. They are also using social media. As a result, a surprisingly large number of organizations have abandoned their regularly published, internal print publications.

For messages that need more explanation, such as health care matters, perhaps a printed brochure will do the job best. Externally, for matters that may concern the community, you may want to use billboards in addition to paid print ads or radio and television ads. Or you may choose to write news releases and leave it to others to interpret your message. (See Figure 20.2 for a sample news release.)

Sometimes, however, there's no quick fix. What took a long time to build can come tumbling down quickly, and then a long rebuilding process is necessary.

THE MEDIA CAMPAIGN

Research shows that the more media you use, the better chance you have to succeed. That's why effective public relations people, like those in advertising, think in terms of campaigns and strategies. A campaign assumes that you can't just tell an audience once what you want them to learn, retain and act on. You need a strategy to reach a goal that may take days, weeks, months or even years to attain. Which media do you use to introduce the subject? Which media will you engage for follow-up and details? Which aspects of the message are best suited for which media? You accomplish little by sending out the message once and in only one medium. It's far more effective to send the message in a mix of media in a carefully timed or orchestrated way.

Public relations writers adapt messages to the whole spectrum of media available. To do this, you must learn what each medium does best. Perhaps the cultural critic Marshall McLuhan was exaggerating when he wrote that the medium *is* the

Contact: Mary Ann Beahon
Director of University Relations
(573) 592-1127
mbeahon@williamwoods.edu
www.thewoods.edu

December 3, 2008
FOR IMMEDIATE RELEASE

William Woods Senior Art Students Showcase Work

FULTON, Mo. — Demonstrating what they've learned during the past four years, three William Woods University seniors are displaying their talents at the annual Senior Art Show. The show runs through Dec. 12 in the Mildred Cox Gallery of the Gladys Woods Kemper Center for the Arts.

The exhibit features the work of Hillary Reed of Castle Rock, Colo.; Adam Dresden of Granite City, Ill., and Kelly Trustee of Huntsville, Mo. Included in the show are examples of ceramics, oil painting, charcoal, pencil, watercolor and graphic design.

The Mildred Cox Gallery is open 9-4 p.m. Monday through Friday, and 1-4 p.m. Saturday and Sunday. Admission is free and open to the public. For more information about the exhibit, call (573) 592-4245.

Figure 20.2
A traditional news release is double-spaced and follows AP style. Note that this release includes the line "For Immediate Release," the date and the name of the contact. It also gives the contact's title, phone number and e-mail address and the school's website address.

message, but no one doubts there is a great deal of truth to his statement. Think of what this means now that you have all of the new media and social media available to you. The public relations campaign, as practiced by the American Red Cross, takes on a whole new meaning.

You may be hired as a speechwriter or to do something as specialized as writing an organization's annual report. Corporations and institutions such as hospitals and universities hire thousands of communicators to get their messages out to the public. Or you may work for a public relations agency that is hired to do this work for organizations.

Regardless of the means or media you choose to use, your job is to have good relations with the public. You do that best by trying to establish mutually beneficial relationships and situations. All of this is best achieved when you make it possible for two-way communications. You must allow and encourage your various publics to have a voice in what you are trying to accomplish. If you involve your audience in what you are trying to achieve, your chances of achieving it increase. Establishing a website is an excellent way to get people's ideas and reactions. Of course, you must find ways (notices on bulletin boards, brochures, newsletters, blogs and so on) to make your website known.

PUBLIC RELATIONS WRITING: A MATTER OF PERSUASION

Most of the time, your writing will attempt to persuade people. You need to study the techniques of persuasion and to use them carefully.

Your Attitude

To persuade people, you need to believe three things:

1. **People are essentially good.** You need to be convinced of this and to appeal to people's basic goodness and fairness.
2. **People are intelligent or at least educable.** Don't talk down to people; don't assume that you can trick or fool them. Of course, don't assume that just because they are intelligent and educated, they know the subject matter as well as you do. A good rule: Never underestimate the intelligence of your audience; never overestimate what they know. A college professor with a Ph.D. in philosophy may be brilliant in that area but might know nothing about the financial markets.
3. **People are changeable.** You must believe not only that people are changeable but also that you can change them.

Credibility and Trust

More than anything else, you need to establish and maintain your credibility and the credibility of the organization you represent. Aristotle wrote that the character of the speaker is the most essential and powerful component of persuasion. Without a doubt, character is the most important attribute public relations people need to have and to develop. A sterling reputation takes a long time to build—and can be lost in an instant.

> **"**If you don't understand good journalistic style and format (who, what, when, where and why) for writing a press release, you harm your company and yourself.**"**
>
> — G.A. Marken, president of Marken Communications, *Public Relations Quarterly*

In addition, you must assume good will on the part of your audience. You cannot persuade people by beating up on them, by calling them names. What did the spokesman for Domino's accomplish by calling two of its employees "idiots"? You are foolish to look at a client or the public as your enemies. This is particularly true regarding your attitude toward the press. Too many public relations professionals consider the press the enemy, not to be trusted with the truth, to be stonewalled at every opportunity.

In *O'Dwyer's PR Report*, Bill Huey, president of Strategic Communications in Atlanta, writes: "The next time you become incensed about something the media has done—or you want to go on a crusade—call your travel agent and go on a golfing vacation instead."

Consider this example of working with the media. Americans care about what their pets eat. Congress knows what people care about, and sometimes congressional leaders act on that knowledge. In 2007, after a recall of pet foods, Congress called Duane Ekedahl, president of the Pet Food Institute, to testify. That's scary. But the Pet Food Institute was ready. Gene Grabowski reported in *O'Dwyer's PR Report* that staffers "were in daily communication with officials of the FDA and in frequent contact with key congressional aides."

By having the staff do some groundwork before he testified before Congress, Ekedahl ensured that his message was heard around the world, and people became less concerned about the biggest recall in pet-food history. The Institute also established the National Pet Food Commission and advertised it that morning in *The New York Times* and *The Washington Post*. This helped to ease pet owners' concerns.

That's how public relations can, should and sometimes does work.

WRITING NEWS RELEASES THAT GET ATTENTION

Earlier in this chapter you read that good writing is the most important skill for a public relations professional. You also read about all of the various positions you can hold as a public relations person. Each demands a great variety of writing skills directed at different audiences. Remember, whatever you write reflects not only on you but also on those for whom you work.

Perhaps nothing that you will be called on to write is more important than news releases. Even the smallest newspaper or radio or television station gets dozens of news releases daily, most of them now sent electronically and through public-relations wire services. Publications such as those in the American Business Media or of the Specialized Information Publishers Association and myriads of other print and electronic publications also receive dozens of public relations releases daily. How do you break through the clutter and attract the attention of the gatekeepers at these publications? Regardless of how you send your news, your problem is still the same.

Here are some guidelines to help you get your message to your intended audience.

> **❏❏**Employers want people who can write and communicate ideas — who can pull complex or fragmented ideas together into coherent messages. This requires not only technical skill but also intelligence. It also requires a love of writing.**❏❏**
>
> — Thomas H. Bivins, *Public Relations Writing*

Know What News Is and How to Write It

If you are planning on a career in public relations or public information, you're probably taking this news writing course to help you understand the principles of news. The news media will not pay attention to copy that is laced with opinion or self-serving quotations. Worse, they will ridicule your work and discard it immediately. Avoid statements such as this: "Monroe College is recognized as the foremost and most prestigious college of liberal arts in the entire Midwest." Who says?

To write for most publications, certainly for news media and the majority of print and electronic publications, you need to know Associated Press style. (See Appendix 2 for a summary of the style followed by most news publications.)

Correct spelling, usage and grammar are essential, of course, but adhering to AP style is just as important. Why should news editors take you seriously if you don't bother to write in the style of their publications? Some newspapers and magazines have their own stylebooks. Quite a few magazines follow *The Chicago Manual of Style*. Be sure you know what you're doing.

News releases are notoriously inaccurate and inconsistent in style and grammar. How ironic that people so concerned with image can be so careless in the way they present themselves to the public.

Know the Structure and Operations of News Rooms

If you do not get actual experience in a television, radio, newspaper or convergence news room in college, find ways to spend some time in at least one of these. Use your public relations skills to get inside and to experience what goes on there.

The simplest and most important thing you can learn about news rooms is that they have deadlines. Learn the deadlines of the media in your area, and respect those deadlines. This means you cannot call in a story to a television news station a half-hour before airtime. Not only will the station not use your story, but station employees will resent you and not forget the interruption at a critical time. News organizations will tell you what time you must submit a story to make the news that day.

Know the People in the News Media and the Jobs They Hold

It's especially important to know people and their jobs in newspapers you contact. Sending a release addressed simply to a newspaper can be a waste of time and make you look as if you do not know what you are doing. Sending a release to the business editor or to the features editor makes more sense. Addressing by name the editor of the section in which you wish the release to appear works best.

Read what Chris Anderson, editor in chief of *Wired* magazine, has to say on this subject in his blog:

> Sorry, PR people: you're blocked.
>
> I've had it. I get more than 300 e-mails a day and my problem isn't spam . . . it's PR people. Lazy flacks send press releases to the Editor in Chief of *Wired* because they can't be bothered to find out who on my staff, if anyone, might actually be interested in what they're pitching. . . . So fair warning: I only want two kinds of e-mail: those from people I know, and those from people who have taken the time to find out what I'm interested in and composed a note meant to appeal to that (I love those e-mails; indeed, that's why my e-mail address is public).

If the people to whom you send news releases know and trust you, they are more likely to pay attention to your releases. Sometimes you can call them with a story idea and let them write their own stories. There's nothing writers like more than to get wind of good stories. Remember, your job is to help reporters write good stories. If you can help them do that and at the same time serve your client's interests, you will be a successful public relations practitioner.

News Releases That Get Used

Fraser P. Seitel, author, communications consultant and teacher, identifies the following as the eight news-release topics that are most likely to be used:

1. New products or projects
2. Personnel promotions — at least of important people
3. Trends
4. Conflict
5. Topicality — "relating your news to pressing issues of the day"
6. Local heritage — tying news to community roots or history
7. Human interest
8. Insanity — the truly bizarre or unusual

Know the Style of Writing That Fits the Medium

Do not make the mistake of sending to a radio or television station the same news release that you send to a newspaper. Do not expect busy newspeople to translate your newspaper release into broadcast copy. If you can write radio or television copy (see Chapter 13), you have a much better chance of getting the copy read over the air. Remember, too, that writing online copy differs from writing for print (see Chapter 12).

Also, be aware that just as some newspapers will use your news releases almost verbatim — some have sections of verbatim releases about events, promotions, and so on — some radio and television stations will use your audio and video without editing it. The Center for Media and Democracy's 2006 report of a six-month investigation revealed that 46 stations in 22 states inserted video news releases into their newscasts. Moreover, nearly 90 percent did not give the slightest hint to viewers that these were VNRs, even though some of them dealt with controversial subjects such as global warming.

Know How to Distribute Information Online

Of course, not even the largest newspapers or radio or television networks can reach as many people as online media can. For millions of websites, there are practically no limits to the audiences that can be reached. First, you must establish your own credible, up-to-date, interactive website. Second, you must be thoroughly familiar with websites such as Online-PR.com, PRNewswire.com and SynapticDigital.com so that you can distribute your releases online and keep up with what's happening in public relations. Third, you yourself must become expert at using the new media to get across your organization's messages (see Chapter 12).

APPROACHES TO WRITING NEWS RELEASES

To be effective in their jobs, writers of news releases need to learn all the techniques that journalists use in writing news stories.

The Inverted Pyramid

The straight, no-nonsense inverted pyramid news release remains the staple of the public relations professional. Many believe that any other approach will not be taken seriously by news professionals. (See Chapter 9 for more on the inverted pyramid.)

Here's an example. Notice that the release begins with the name, address and phone number of the organization putting out the release and the name of a contact person. If the news is for immediate release, say so. Otherwise, indicate a release date. (To see how a release is formatted, see Figure 20.2.)

NEWS
Missouri Department of Natural Resources
P.O. Box 176, Jefferson City,
Missouri 65102

For further information contact:
Mary Schwartz (573-751-3443)
(For immediate release)

JEFFERSON CITY, Mo., Feb. 25, 2008—The winter solitude of Roaring River, Bennett Spring and Montauk state parks will be shattered by about 8,000 fishing enthusiasts expected to participate in the annual trout opening March 1 in Missouri State Parks.

The start of trout-fishing season in these parks marks the beginning of the vacation season in Missouri State Parks, which are administered by the Missouri Department of Natural Resources. The Department also administers 30 other state parks and 22 historic sites, which officially open on April 15.

"Trout opening is definitely a big event for fishermen in Missouri," said John Karel, director of state parks. "But, it's also a big day for state parks since it traditionally marks the beginning of the upcoming vacation season."

Karel notes that park visitors to Montauk, Roaring River and Bennett Spring state parks will be greeted by a number of new construction and major renovation projects. . . .

The release goes on to talk about the projects and about how many trout tags were sold. It's a traditional approach, although the lead attempts to be a bit creative with "winter solitude" being "shattered." The lead jumps to a quote from an authority, John Karel, the director of the state parks, and uses him as the source throughout.

Going Beyond the Inverted Pyramid

Let's look now at a different approach; some would call it a feature approach. (See Chapter 11 for more on variations in story structure.) In the following example, the information heading at the top of the release shown earlier stays the same.

When the siren sounds at 6:30 a.m. March 1 in Bennett Spring State Park near Lebanon, Bill Brooks will be there. He'll be standing knee-deep in icy water as he's done every March 1 since 1990.

Brooks, known in fishing circles as Big Trout, will join an expected 8,000 other Missouri fishing enthusiasts for the opening of trout-fishing season in Missouri State Parks. Missouri's other trout-fishing state parks are Roaring River, near Cassville, and Montauk, near Salem.

Brooks can't imagine anything, short of a death in the family, that would keep him away. "This is just a tradition for me. I'm already making wagers and getting together my equipment."

As an extra measure, Brooks has made a special trip from his Marshfield home to the park just to check stream conditions.

After 18 years of opening days, Brooks has seen some changes. "I guess you could say they've gotten stricter on us. Things used to be a lot wilder down there in the old days, until they stopped us from gambling and stopped selling beer. . . ."

The release then introduces fishing expert Jim Rogers, who runs concessions at both Bennett Spring and Roaring River. Rogers tells with specific numbers how he has sold more than double the number of trout tags that he sold just eight years ago.

In this approach, the writer uses a "real person," a longtime fisherman, to introduce the story—rather than a person in authority. By using Brooks and Rogers, the writer tells a story and still gives important information, but in an interesting and appealing way. This approach is described in Chapter 11 as the focus structure.

Now suppose the writer accompanied this story with a photo from the year before of Big Trout standing knee-deep in icy water. Public relations professionals

This photo, provided by the Missouri State Department of Conservation, could accompany a news release promoting trout fishing in Missouri.

Guidelines for Writers of News Releases

In *On Deadline: Managing Media Relations*, Carole Howard and Wilma Mathews offer these practical guidelines for writing news releases:

1. Follow an accepted journalistic style of writing. Use AP style.
2. Go easy on length. Hold it to two double-spaced, typewritten pages.
3. Avoid breaks. Don't hyphenate words at the ends of lines, and don't split a sentence at the bottom of a page.
4. Write clearly. Avoid corporate jargon, legalese or other alien language.
5. Remember the pyramid. But don't put all the *w*'s in the lead.
6. Beware of adjectives. Especially avoid superlatives.
7. Make it local.
8. Attribute news to a person — not to a company or organization.
9. Indent the paragraphs.

know that releases accompanied by photos or art of some kind get more attention and more play.

Some professionals have also begun to place attention-grabbing headlines on top of their releases. Others accompany the head with a *summary-contents-benefit blurb* so that the editor or the intended audience does not have to read the entire release to find out what it's about.

In the summary-contents-benefit blurb, try to use a verb in the imperative (command) mood, and be sure to insert the pronoun "you" at least once. For example:

Get ready now. You don't want to miss out on opening day of trout fishing. Here's help.

You might want to go a step further. Why not do some service journalism? Put the parks, their locations and the opening dates in a separate box. How about a map of the area to show people how to get there? Perhaps you could make a list of the top-10 things to remember on opening day. Maybe you could create an infographic indicating where to get trout tags. Sending these items electronically makes it really easy for editors to use them. Some news organizations will use just one sidebar or graphic of what you send. But the important thing is that if you give them choices, you have a better chance of having some of your information used.

In the past, some public relations professionals shied away from what they thought of as gimmicks, for fear that editors would not take them seriously. But the changes in newspapers, especially in special sections, and the ubiquitous presence of online media have altered that perception.

Why not experiment? Attention is harder and harder to get. Don't be afraid to try a "you" lead or even a question. For example, "Are you ready for opening day at

ON THE JOB

Public Relations Writing

After Brad Whitworth received his journalism degree, he joined the staff of a small magazine covering Illinois politics. When the magazine folded abruptly six months later, he moved into corporate communications, where he worked first for a small association and then for a large insurance company.

Whitworth has spent the past 25 years doing public relations, speechwriting and internal communications for Silicon Valley companies, including high-tech giants Hewlett-Packard and Cisco. For 10 of those years his work took him to Asia Pacific, Canada, Latin America and Europe.

"For global audiences, it's important to keep your words and sentences as simple as possible," says Whitworth. "In fact, the more complex or technical your subject matter, the simpler your words need to be.

"It's a good thing the language for doing business around the world is English. But for many audiences, it's their second language. Everything I learned in journalism school about making writing clear, concise, consistent and complete is even more critical when communicating with co-workers or customers halfway around the world."

Throughout his career, Whitworth has relied on the International Association of Business Communicators for his professional development and networking.

"I landed my job at Hewlett-Packard through IABC's job bank and have hired dozens more through the network." He's given back to IABC, too, serving as president of two local chapters and as the youngest-ever chairman of the 16,000-member not-for-profit organization.

"It's really important to stay connected with others who are doing the same kind of work," he says. "You can share best practices, learn about job opportunities and take part in seminars, conferences and workshops. Your learning shouldn't stop when you leave campus."

Bennett Spring?" Remember to get to the "so what" quickly—not the "so what" of your organization but rather the "so what" of the audience. What's in it for the reader or listener? Most readers don't care whether AT&T has announced the purchase of another cell phone company. (Some companies seem never to do anything but "announce" things in news releases.) Readers do care about how this purchase might affect them and their phone bills, however.

Remember, too, that a film clip of Big Trout in action is more likely to be used by a television or Web news producer than a written release is, and a recorded interview might get played on your local radio station or on the Web. A film clip or a slide presentation might enhance an online message or a website enormously. If you are doing a release about a new lodge, you can take your audience on a tour of the facilities.

Even if none of these media uses your material as you presented it, perhaps you will succeed in grabbing the attention of an editor or reporter. If that person is inspired to pursue the story, you'll still get your information to the public.

Be sure that you make yourself available—by phone, e-mail, fax, website, or in person—24 hours a day. Nothing is more important for a public relations practitioner. A reporter on deadline will write the story with or without you. It's *always* best that you talk to the reporter.

In addition to writing news releases, public relations professionals are involved with many other important functions that increase the value of public relations, planning and carrying out successful press conferences and dealing with the foreign press. No wonder public relations demands that you never stop developing your skills and continuing your education.

Suggested Readings

Bivins, Thomas H. *Public Relations Writing: The Essentials of Style and Format*, 6th ed. New York: McGraw-Hill, 2007. Bivens covers the wide variety of writing expected of public relations professionals.

Brown, Rob. *Public Relations and the Social Web: How to Use Social Media and Web 2.0 in Communications*. London and Philadelphia: Kogan Page, 2009. This book discusses the whole range of social media, including social media releases, Twitter sites and wikis.

Cutlip, Scott M., Allen H. Center, and Glen M. Broom. *Effective Public Relations*, 9th ed. Upper Saddle River, NJ: Prentice Hall, 2006. Many professionals say this basic book is the best in the field.

Holtz, Shel. *Public Relations on the Net*, 2nd ed. New York: AMACOM, 1999. Anything Shel Holtz says or writes about online subjects is worth paying attention to. See also http://blog.holtz.com.

Horton, James L. *Online Public Relations: A Handbook for Practitioners*. Westport, CT: Quorum Books, 2001. A superb primer and more, it begins by explaining terminology and ends with 85 industry and general information topics about placing news and gathering information.

Howard, Carole, and Wilma Mathews. *On Deadline: Managing Media Relations*, 4th ed. Prospect Heights, IL: Waveland Press, 2006. This practical book shows how organizations should deal with the news media.

Newsom, Doug, and Jim Haynes. *Public Relations Writing: Form and Style*, 9th ed. Belmont, CA: Wadsworth, 2010. A truly thorough classic, it even has a section on grammar, spelling and punctuation.

Phillips, David, and Philip Young. *Online Public Relations: A Practical Guide to Developing an Online Strategy in the World of Social Media*, 2nd ed. London and Philadelphia: Kogan Page, 2009. The authors discuss many new ways for creative people to reach large audiences.

Seitel, Fraser P. *The Practice of Public Relations*, 10th ed. New York: Prentice Hall, 2006. You can tell Seitel has been a teacher. He writes simply, clearly and engagingly.

Seitel, Fraser P. "'Used' News Releases." *O'Dwyer's PR Report* (September 2006): 31, 42. Seitel's columns on professional development appear regularly in this publication.

Wilcox, Dennis L. *Public Relations Writing and Media Techniques*, 6th ed. New York: Longman, 2008. Filled with practical tips in all areas of public relations writing, this book includes handy boxes and sidebars.

Suggested Websites

www.instituteforpr.com
This website offers information about public relations research, measurement, programs, seminars, publications, scholarship, and so on, from the Institute for Public Relations, which explores "the science beneath the art of public relations."

www.odwyerpr.com
You must subscribe to this website, but when you do, you also receive *O'Dwyer's PR Report*, an excellent monthly publication that devotes each issue to a public relations specialty field.

www.online-pr.com
Amazingly helpful for anyone interested in public relations, this site includes links to loads of websites.

www.prsa.org
The website of the Public Relations Society of America has general information about the society, lists its chapters and sections, and offers information on publications, membership and accreditation, recognition and awards, conferences, and seminars.

www.prwatch.org
This website, from the Center for Media and Democracy, investigates "public relations spin and propaganda." It sends out more than 1,000 news releases each day.

Exercises

1. **Team project.** Your instructor will organize the class into teams. Imagine that a classmate is killed in a car accident. A few thousand dollars were raised to set up a scholarship to honor his memory, but much more money is needed to endow the scholarship. Several students in the class have been training to run in the Chicago Marathon. A group of students decides to solicit money for each mile the runners complete. Organize a campaign on your campus to get people to pledge or donate money. Answer these questions:

   a. Who are your target audiences? Each team should take a different target audience if possible.
   b. Which media will be most effective in reaching your audience? Discuss the pros and cons for each media choice within your team, and make a group selection.
   c. How much will the campaign cost, and how long will it take? Work as a team to project a budget and time schedule for completing the campaign.

   When the teams are finished, the entire class will work together to compile a report that details how to proceed with the campaign.

2. Visit the public relations or public affairs department of a local college, hospital, corporation or association, and investigate thoroughly its public relations program. Interview people in various positions about their jobs and experience, and write a 1,000-word report summarizing what you learned.

3. Read the following news release, and note any deviations from AP style. Also note any content that news organizations might object to.

   NEWS RELEASE
   "Chest Pains", an excellent film in the HEALTHCARE series produced by the American College of Physicians, will be shown from 7:00-8:30 P.M., Wednesday, October 22, at St. Mary's Health Center. Springfield internist, Dr. Harold Kanagawa, will host a question-and-answer period following the film.

   Although most people assume that chest pains signify a heart attack, the public is less aware that other conditions—hiatal hernia, ulcers, viral infections of the heart's membranes—can also cause pains that require prompt diagnosis and appropriate medical treatment. Designed to help increase awareness of the symptoms and their possible significance, "Chest Pains" features an internist and actual patients as they work together to resolve underlying medical problems.

   Through a warm and engaging human-interest style of presentation, each twenty-five-minute documentary encourages people to take an increased responsibility for their own well-being by establishing healthy habits and assuming a more active role in disease prevention.

   The HEALTHCARE series is produced under an educational grant from the Elsworth Company of Midland, Michigan. Other films in this superb, highly acclaimed series cover "Aches, Pains and Arthritis", "Diabetes", and "Abdominal Discomfort".

Doctor Kanagawa, a renowned specialist in internal medicine, is 1 of fifty-thousand members of the American College of Physicians. Founded in 1915, the College is the largest medical specialty society in the U.S. and one of the most prestigious. It represents doctors of internal medicine, related non-surgical specialists, and physicians-in-training.

To register or for more information, contact the Women's Life Center.

4. Interview a student from a small town. Then write a news release about his or her life and activities at the university, and send it to the town's newspaper.

Media Law

21

The First Amendment states:

> Congress shall make no law respecting an establishment of religion, or prohibiting the free exercise thereof; or abridging the freedom of speech, or of the press; or the right of the people peaceably to assemble, and to petition the Government for a redress of grievances.

Read that again: "Congress shall make no law . . . abridging the freedom of . . . the press." No other business in the United States enjoys that specific constitutional protection, unless you consider religion a business.

Why should there be such protection for the press? The Supreme Court gave an eloquent answer to that question in a 1957 obscenity decision. The press is protected, the court ruled, to ensure the "unfettered interchange of ideas for bringing about the political and social changes desired by the people." As the court said in Whitney v. California:

> Those who won our independence believed . . . that public discussion is a political duty; and that this should be a fundamental principle of the American government. They recognized the risks to which all human institutions are subject. But they knew that order cannot be secured merely through fear of punishment for its infraction; that it is hazardous to discourage thought, hope and imagination; that fear breeds repression; that repression breeds hate; that hate menaces stable government; that the path of safety lies in the opportunity to discuss freely supposed grievances and proposed remedies; and that the fitting remedy for evil counsels is good ones. Believing in the power of reason as applied through public discussion, they eschewed silence coerced by law—the argument of force in its worst form. Recognizing the occasional tyrannies of governing majorities, they amended the Constitution so that free speech and assembly should be guaranteed.

The free flow of ideas is necessary in a democracy because people who govern themselves need to know about their government and about those who run it, as well as about the social and economic institutions that greatly affect their day-to-day lives. Most people get that information through newspapers, the Internet, radio and television. Increasingly, citizen journalists are communicating through blogs. While professional journalists debate whether blogs should be considered "real" journalism, the legal system is grappling with the issue of how to apply constitutional precedents to them.

In 1966, Congress passed the Freedom of Information Act to assist anyone in finding out what is happening in federal agencies. This act—which was amended in 1996 by the Electronic Freedom of Information Act to improve access to computerized government records and was amended again in 2008 to ease the process of making requests—makes it easier for you to know about government business. All 50 states have similar **open-records laws**. Though of great assistance to the press, these laws are also used by individuals and businesses to gain information previously kept secret by the government. There are other laws ensuring access to government transactions. The federal government and all the states have open-meeting laws—often called "sunshine laws"—requiring the public's business to be conducted in public. However, all of these access laws contain exemptions that keep some meetings private.

The First Amendment, the Freedom of Information Act and the sunshine laws demonstrate America's basic concern for citizen access to information needed for the "unfettered interchange of ideas." Nevertheless, there are laws that reduce the scope of freedom of the press.

LIBEL

Traditionally, most of the laws limiting the absolute principle of freedom of the press have dealt with libel. These laws result from the desire of legislatures and courts to help individuals protect their reputations. Their importance was explained by U.S. Supreme Court Justice Potter Stewart in a 1966 libel case:

> The right of a man (or woman) to the protection of his (or her) own reputation from unjustified invasion and wrongful hurt reflects no more than our basic concept of the essential dignity and worth of every human being—a concept at the root of any decent system of ordered liberty.

Protection for reputations dates back centuries. In 17th-century England, individuals were imprisoned and even disfigured for making libelous statements. One objective was to prevent criticism of the government. Another was to maintain the peace by avoiding duels. Duels are rare today, and government is freely criticized, but the desire to protect an individual's reputation is just as strong.

A case concerning Gen. Ariel Sharon is helpful in understanding libel. The extensively covered trial was held in the winter of 1984-1985 in the federal courthouse in Manhattan. The case was based on a 1983 *Time* magazine cover story, "Verdict on the Massacre," about Israel's 1982 judicial inquiry into the massacre of several hundred civilians in two Palestinian refugee camps in Lebanon.

> **"The government's power to censor the press was abolished so the press would remain forever free to censure the government."**
>
> — Hugo Black, U.S. Supreme Court Justice

The *Time* article suggested that Ariel Sharon, then Israel's defense minister and later its prime minister, had ordered the massacre. The general sued *Time*. His attorneys knew they would have to show that their client had suffered hatred, contempt or ridicule because these statements were serious attacks on his reputation and not just unpleasant comments.

The jury's decision was in three parts. The first part of the verdict was in answer to this question: Was the paragraph concerning Sharon defamatory? The jury said it was. This meant the *Time* article had damaged Sharon's reputation and exposed him to hatred, contempt or ridicule.

The second question for the jury was this: Was the paragraph concerning Sharon false? Again the jury answered affirmatively. If the answer had been no, the case would have ended there. Truth is a complete defense for libel.

The third question for the jury concerned whether the paragraph was published with "actual malice"—with knowledge that it was false or with reckless disregard of whether it was false ("serious doubt" that it was true). The jury answered no. Thus the trial ended in favor of *Time* magazine, despite the jury's ruling that the article was defamatory.

Courts use four categories to help jurors like those in the Sharon case decide if someone's reputation has been damaged because he or she has been brought into hatred, contempt or ridicule:

1. **Accusing someone of a crime.** This may have been the basis for the Sharon suit.
2. **Damaging a person in his or her public office, profession or occupation.** If the statements by *Time* against Sharon did not accuse him of crimes, they did damage him in his profession as a military man.
3. **Accusing a person of serious immorality.** The example lawyers often use is accusing a woman of being unchaste. Many states have statutes that make an accusation of unchastity a cause of action in a libel suit.
4. **Accusing someone of having a loathsome (that is, contagious) disease.** This category was fading as a source of defamation until the AIDS epidemic gave it new life.

This does not mean you can never say a person committed a crime, was unethical in business, was adulterous or had a loathsome disease. It does mean you must be certain that what you write is true.

Libel Suit Defenses

There are three traditional defenses against libel: truth, privilege, and fair comment and criticism. Two other constitutional standards—the actual malice and negligence tests—also help libel defendants. The court case clarifying these standards involved traditional media, but the principles are now being applied to the Internet, including blogs. In 2006, a blogger in Georgia lost the first of these electronic libel cases. He was ordered to pay $50,000 to a lawyer he had criticized. The diagram in Figure 21.1 shows the various defenses to a libel suit, which are also discussed below.

Truth

Truth is the best defense against libel. In libel cases involving matters of public concern, the burden of proof is on the plaintiff. This placement of the burden, however, does not change the reporter's responsibility to seek the truth in every possible way.

You cannot be certain, for example, whether a person charged with arson actually started the fire. Who told you that Joe Jones started the fire? The first source to check is the police or fire report. If a police officer or fire marshal says

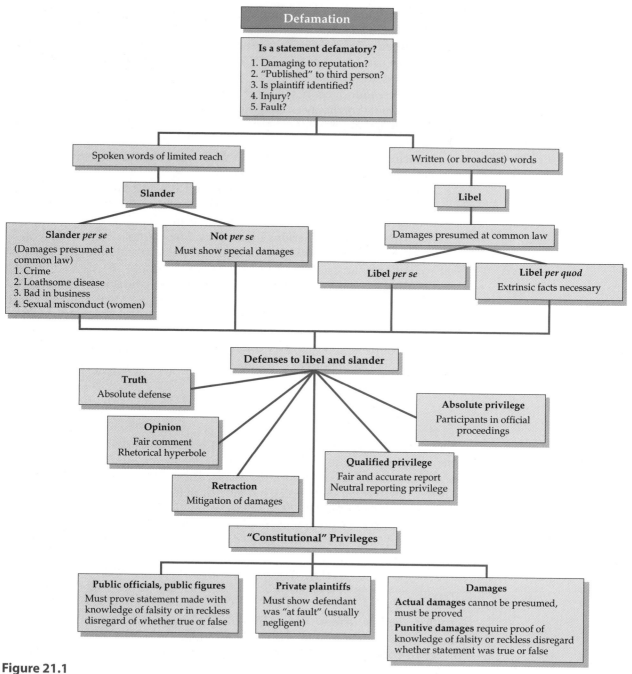

Figure 21.1
An understanding of libel
and related concepts is
essential for journalists.

© Dr. Sandra Davidson

that Jones started a fire, you can report not that Jones did it but that he has been accused of doing it. Unless you have information you would be willing to present in court, you should go no further. Be sure you report no more than what you know is true. And if you have a document in your hands that proves what you write, you're in even better shape.

When a newspaper in Oklahoma reported that a wrestling coach had been accused of requiring a sixth-grader, who wanted to rejoin the team, to submit to a whipping by his fellow students while crawling naked through the legs of team members, the coach sued. He claimed damage to his reputation.

In cases like this, the reporter has to be certain not just that one or more participants told of the incident but also that the statements were true. In court, some participants might testify to an occurrence, and others might testify the incident never took place. A jury would have to decide on the credibility of the participants.

Although you must always strive for absolute truth in all of your stories, the courts will settle for what is known as **substantial truth** in most cases. This means that you must be able to prove the essential elements of all you write.

The Georgia case and others show that the courts are holding bloggers to the same standard established for traditional media. In the Georgia case, a disappointed client accused his former attorney, in a blog, of bribing judges. The lawyer sued and won when the blogger couldn't show that his charge was true.

> *Journalists don't believe . . . the Freedom of Information Act was created to be turned on us as an excuse to hide information.*
>
> — Sarah Overstreet, columnist

Privilege

In addition to truth, the courts traditionally have allowed another defense against libel: **privilege**. This defense applies when you are covering any of the three branches of government. The courts allow legislators, judges and government executives the **absolute privilege** to say anything — true or false — when acting in their official capacities. The rationale is that the public interest is served when an official is allowed to speak freely and fearlessly about making laws, carrying them out or punishing those who do not obey them. Similarly, a participant in a judicial proceeding, such as an attorney, court clerk or judge, is absolutely privileged to make false and even defamatory statements about another person during that proceeding.

In the executive branch it isn't always clear whose statements are privileged and when. The head of state and the major officers of executive departments of the federal and state governments are covered. However, minor officials might not enjoy the protection of absolute privilege.

As a reporter, you have a **qualified privilege**, sometimes called *neutral reporting* or *conditional privilege*, at the federal level and in some states, to report what public officials say. Your privilege is conditioned on your report's providing full, fair and accurate coverage of the court session, the legislative session or the president's press conference, even if any one of the participants made defamatory statements. You can quote anything the president of the United States says without fear of losing a libel suit, even if the president is not acting in an official capacity. Reporters have a qualified privilege to report unofficial statements. But there are many other levels of executives in federal, state and local governments. Mayors of small towns, for instance, often hold part-time positions. Although you are conditionally privileged to report on what those officials say when they are acting in their official capacities, a problem can arise when the part-time mayor says something defamatory when not acting in an official capacity. Courts in some jurisdictions might grant a qualified privilege; some might not.

Fair Comment and Criticism

In some types of writing, you may be commenting or criticizing rather than reporting. The courts have protected writers who comment on and criticize the public offerings of anyone in the public eye. Included in this category are actors and actresses, sports figures, public officials and other newsworthy people. Most often, such writing occurs in reviews of plays, books or movies, or in commentary on service received in hotels and restaurants.

The courts call this **fair comment and criticism**. You are protected as long as you do not misstate any of the facts on which you base your comments or criticism and as long as you do not wrongly imply that you possess undisclosed, damaging information that forms the basis of your opinion. Merely labeling a fact as an opinion will not result in opinion protection, the U.S. Supreme Court ruled in 1990.

The Actual Malice Test and Public Officials

It was a small but momentous step from fair comment and criticism to the case of *The New York Times* v. Sullivan. In 1964, the U.S. Supreme Court decided that First Amendment protection was broader than just the traditional defenses of truth and privilege and that the press needed even greater freedom in its coverage of public officials.

The case started with an advertisement for funds in *The New York Times* of March 29, 1960, by the Committee to Defend Martin Luther King Jr. and the Struggle for Freedom in the South. The advertisement contained small, inconsequential factual errors concerning the police, according to Montgomery, Ala., Commissioner L.B. Sullivan. He thought the errors damaged his reputation, and he won a half-million-dollar judgment against *The New York Times* in an Alabama trial court.

The Supreme Court said it was considering the case "against the background of a profound national commitment to the principle that debate on public issues should be uninhibited, robust and wide open." Thus Justice William Brennan wrote that the Constitution requires a federal rule prohibiting a public official from recovering damages from the press for a defamatory falsehood relating to his or her official conduct, unless the public official can prove the press had knowledge that what was printed was false or that the story was printed with reckless disregard of whether it was true or not. The justices called this the **actual malice test**.

The actual malice test was applied later in a case involving a story on CBS's *60 Minutes* about a retired Army officer. Col. Anthony Herbert contended the broadcast falsely portrayed him as a liar. He tried to prove that producer Barry Lando recklessly disregarded whether or not it was a false broadcast. Herbert asked some questions that Lando claimed were protected by the First Amendment because they inquired into his state of mind and into the editorial processes during the production of the program. Eventually, the U.S. Supreme Court decided the "state of mind" case in Col. Herbert's favor.

The decision in the Sharon case discussed earlier in the chapter is an example of the burden of proving actual malice against the press. The jury decided that *Time* did not know when the article in question was printed that its statement about Gen. Sharon was false.

In 1991, the Supreme Court decided Masson v. *The New Yorker*, the so-called fabricated quotes case. Jeffrey Masson, a psychologist, had sued the magazine and journalist Janet Malcolm, accusing them of making up quotes he never said. Overruling a lower court's decision that journalists could fictionalize quotations by making rational interpretations of speakers' remarks, the Supreme Court protected the sanctity of quotation marks. But the court also made clear that not every deliberate change in a quotation is libelous. Only a "material change in the meaning conveyed by a statement" poses a problem.

Although Masson won the right to try his case, he lost against all defendants in 1994.

The Actual Malice Test and Public Figures

The actual malice protection was expanded in two cases in 1967 to include not only public officials but also *public figures*—people in the public eye but not in public office.

The first case stemmed from a *Saturday Evening Post* article that accused Coach Wally Butts of conspiring to fix a 1962 college football game between Georgia and Alabama. At the time of the article, Butts was the athletic director of the University of Georgia. The article, titled "The Story of a College Football Fix," was prefaced by a note from the editors of *The Post* stating:

> Not since the Chicago White Sox threw the 1919 World Series has there been a sports story as shocking as this one. . . . Before the University of Georgia played the University of Alabama . . . Wally Butts . . . gave (to Alabama's coach) . . . Georgia's plays, defensive patterns, all the significant secrets Georgia's football team possessed.

The Post reported that, because of an electronic error about a week before the game, George Burnett, an Atlanta insurance salesman, accidentally had overheard a telephone conversation between Butts and the head coach of Alabama, Paul Bryant.

ON THE JOB

The Keys to Avoiding Libel

Ken Paulson earned a law degree after graduating from journalism school. He then practiced journalism for 18 years. After serving as senior vice president of the Freedom Forum in Arlington, Va., and executive director of the First Amendment Center at Vanderbilt University, he returned to the news room as editor of *USA Today*. Now he has moved again, to head the Newseum in Washington, D.C.

"Having a law degree has been helpful as a journalist," he says, "but the key to avoiding libel suits really boils down to a few fundamentals."

The keys to avoiding a libel suit are rooted in professionalism and common sense. He suggests that journalists ask themselves these questions:

- Have I reported fully?
- Have I reported factually?
- Have I reported fairly?
- Have I reported in good faith?

"If you can answer those four questions in the affirmative, the law will take care of itself," he says.

Paulson joined the Gannett Co. in 1978. He was executive editor of *Florida Today* in Melbourne, Fla.; editor of the *Green Bay (Wis.) Press-Gazette*; managing editor of the Bridgewater, N.J., *Courier News*; and executive editor of Gannett Suburban Newspapers in the New York counties of Westchester, Rockland and Putnam.

Coach Butts sued Curtis Publishing, publishers of *The Post*, and won a verdict for $60,000 in general damages and $3 million in punitive, or punishment, damages. Curtis Publishing appealed the case to the Supreme Court and lost. The trial judge reduced the amount of the damages to $460,000.

The second case was decided the same day. Gen. Edwin Walker sued the Associated Press for distributing a news dispatch giving an eyewitness account by an AP staffer on the campus of the University of Mississippi in the fall of 1962. The AP reported that Gen. Walker personally had led a student charge against federal marshals during a riot on the Mississippi campus. The marshals were attempting to enforce a court decree ordering the enrollment of a black student.

Walker was a retired general at the time of the publication. He had won a $2 million libel suit in a trial court. However, the Supreme Court ruled against him.

In both cases, the stories were wrong. In both, the actual malice test was applied. What was the difference between the Butts and Walker cases?

The justices said the football story was in no sense "hot news." They noted that the person who said he had heard the conversation was on probation in connection with bad-check charges and that *Post* personnel had not viewed his notes before publication. The court also said, as evidence of actual malice on the part of *The Post*, that no one looked at the game films to see if the information was accurate; that a regular staffer, instead of a football expert, was assigned to the story; and that no check was made with someone knowledgeable in the sport. In short, *The Post* had not done an adequate job of reporting.

The evidence in the Walker case was considerably different. The court said the news in the Walker case required immediate dissemination because of the riot on campus. The justices noted that the AP received the information from a correspondent who was present on the campus and gave every indication of being trustworthy and competent.

In the Butts and Walker cases, the court used two definitions of public figure. The first is a person like Butts who has assumed a role of special prominence in the affairs of society—someone who has pervasive power and influence in a community. The second is a person like Walker who has thrust himself or herself into the forefront of a particular public controversy in order to influence the resolution of the issues involved.

In the 1970s, the Supreme Court decided three cases that help journalists determine who is and is not a public figure. The first case involved Mrs. Russell A. Firestone, who sued for libel after *Time* magazine reported that her husband's divorce petition had been granted on grounds of extreme cruelty and adultery. Mrs. Firestone, who had married into the Firestone Tire and Rubber Co. family, claimed that those were not the grounds for the divorce. She also insisted that she was not a public figure with the burden of proving actual malice.

The Supreme Court agreed. Even though she had held press conferences and had hired a clipping service, the court ruled that she had not thrust herself into the forefront of a public controversy in an attempt to influence the resolution of the issues involved. The court admitted that marital difficulties of extremely wealthy individuals may be of some interest to some portion of the reading public but added that Mrs. Firestone had not freely chosen to publicize private matters about her married life. The justices said she was compelled to go to court to "obtain legal release from the bonds of matrimony." They said she assumed no "special prominence in the resolution of public questions." The case was sent back to Florida for a finding of fault, and a new trial was ordered. Eventually, the case was settled out of court.

The second case involved Sen. William Proxmire of Wisconsin, who had started what he called the Golden Fleece Award. Each month he announced a winner who, in his opinion, had wasted government money. One such winner was Ronald Hutchinson, a behavioral scientist who had received federal funding for research designed to determine why animals clench their teeth. Hutchinson had published articles about his research in professional publications. In deciding that Hutchinson was not a public figure, the court ruled that he "did not thrust himself or his views into public controversy to influence others." The court admitted there may have been legitimate concerns about the way public funds were being spent but said this was not enough to make Hutchinson a public figure.

The third case concerned an individual found guilty of contempt of court in 1958 for his failure to appear before a grand jury investigating Soviet espionage in the United States. Ilya Wolston's name had been included in a list of people indicted for serving as Soviet agents in a 1974 book published by the Reader's Digest Association. Wolston had not been indicted on that charge, and he sued.

The Supreme Court, in deciding that he was not a public figure, found that Wolston had played only a minor role in whatever public controversy there may have been concerning the investigation of Soviet espionage. The court added that a private individual is not automatically transformed into a public figure merely by becoming involved in or being associated with a matter that attracts public attention.

As a journalist, do you have the same protection from a libel action when you write about a person somewhat connected with a news event as you do when you are certain a person is a public figure or public official? A 1974 Supreme Court decision says the answer is usually no. In the landmark Gertz v. Welch case, the justices said states may give more protection to private individuals if a newspaper or radio or television station damages their reputations than if the reputations of either public officials or public figures are damaged. Generally, you have protection from a libel action when you write about people who have thrust themselves into the forefront of a controversy or event. More recent cases have cemented this rule, as the courts tend to look broadly at those involved in newsworthy events as public figures.

The Negligence Test and Private Citizens

Private citizens who sue for punitive damages must meet the same actual malice test as public officials and public figures do. Because of the Gertz case, states have been allowed to set their own standards for libel cases involving private citizens who sue only for actual damages. A majority of states and the District of Columbia have adopted a **negligence test**, which requires you to use the same care in gathering facts and writing your story as any reasonable reporter would use under the same or similar circumstances. If you make every effort to be fair and answer all the questions a reasonable person may ask, you probably would pass the negligence test.

One state, New York, has adopted a gross irresponsibility test. A few states have established a more stringent standard that requires private citizens to prove actual malice. Some states simply require a jury to find "fault."

Libel Remains a Danger

Despite all the available defenses, libel remains a serious risk to journalists' financial health, as the following example demonstrates: In 1997, a Texas jury awarded a record $222.7 million to a defunct bond-brokerage firm against Dow Jones & Co., which owns *The Wall Street Journal*. The judge threw out $200 million in punitive damages but let stand the $22.7 million in actual damages for a *Journal* story about "bond daddies."

For citizen journalists, such as bloggers, even awards that are much smaller could be devastating. If you blog, you should meet the same standards of fairness and accuracy that are expected of traditional media.

Libel and the Internet

As we have seen, individuals who libel others over the Internet can be held responsible. But the Internet raises the interesting question of whether an online service provider like AOL or MSN can be held responsible for the libelous messages of their users.

In 1991, CompuServe successfully defended itself against a libel suit in a New York federal trial court. CompuServe had made a contract with another company to provide an electronic bulletin board in the form of a newsletter about journalism. The second company then used a third company to create the newsletter. Because CompuServe did not try to exercise any editorial control over the newsletter, the court let CompuServe off the hook for libel. The court also reasoned that no library can be held responsible if a book that the librarian has not reviewed contains libel. CompuServe, the court said, was providing an "electronic, for-profit library."

In 1995, however, Prodigy lost a libel case. In order to promote itself as a family-oriented Internet service provider, Prodigy controlled the content of its computer bulletin boards by using screening software to look for forbidden words, and its editorial staff blocked allegedly offensive posts. Unfortunately for Prodigy, no screening software could identify libelous material. A New York trial court said that by holding itself out as exercising editorial control, Prodigy was "expressly differentiating itself from its competition and expressly likening itself to a newspaper." Thus the court treated Prodigy like a newspaper and held it liable for libel posted on one of its bulletin boards.

Congress did not agree with the Prodigy decision, however, and effectively overruled the case in 1996 by passing "protection for 'Good Samaritan' blocking and screening of offensive material." Congress obviously did not support the idea that the failure to screen meant protection from libel but that limited screening could lead to liability. Federal courts have uniformly upheld the rule.

INVASION OF PRIVACY

Libel is damage to an individual's reputation. **Invasion of privacy** is a violation of a person's right to be left alone.

As a reporter, you may be risking an invasion of privacy suit under any of these circumstances:

- You physically intrude into a private area to get a story or picture—an act closely related to trespass.
- You publish a story or photograph about someone that is misleading, and thus you portray that person in a "false light."
- You disclose something about an individual's private affairs that is true but that is also offensive to individuals of ordinary sensibilities.

Invasion of privacy may also be claimed if someone's name or picture is used in an advertisement or for similar purposes of trade. Called *appropriation*, this does not affect you when you are performing your reporting duties.

Consent is a basic defense in invasion of privacy suits. Make sure, however, that your use of the material does not exceed the consent given.

Another basic defense in an invasion of privacy suit is that you're a reporter covering a newsworthy situation. The courts usually protect members of the press against invasion of privacy suits when they are reporting matters of legitimate public interest. There are three exceptions, however.

Trespassing

The first exception arises when you enter private property without permission to get a story. You cannot trespass on private property to get a story or to take a picture, even if it is newsworthy. The courts will not protect you when you are a trespasser.

Two *Life* magazine staffers lost an invasion of privacy suit because, posing as patients, they went into a man's home to get a story about a faith healer. They lost the case even though they were working with the district attorney and the state board of health.

You may enter private property only when you are invited by the owner or renter. And you should never use deception to gain entry to property you otherwise have no legal right of access to.

You may be committing invasion of privacy by:

- Trespassing on private property.

- Portraying someone in a "false light."

- Causing unwanted publicity that is offensive to a person of ordinary sensibilities.

Portraying in a "False Light"

The courts also will not protect you if you invade someone's privacy by publishing misleading information about that person. For example, a legal problem arises if a photograph or information from a true story about a careful pedestrian struck by a careless driver is used again in connection with a story about, say, careless pedestrians. The pedestrian who was hit could file a lawsuit charging libel, "false light" invasion of privacy or even both in some states.

Some states do not recognize "false light" invasion of privacy and insist that libel is the appropriate form of suit. But "false light" suits can cover situations where a picture or story is misleading but not defamatory. Even flattering material can place a person in an unwanted, false light.

Causing Unwanted Publicity Offensive to a Person of Ordinary Sensibilities

The third type of invasion of privacy that the courts recognize—unwanted publicity—arises from stories about incidents that, because they are true, are not defamatory but can be offensive to a person of ordinary sensibilities. The courts say that in order for privacy to be invaded, there must be a morbid and sensational prying into private lives. Merely being the subject of an unflattering or uncomfortable article is not enough. An example is a picture published by *Sports Illustrated* in which a football fan's pants zipper was open. The fan sued for invasion of privacy but lost.

Also in the area of unwanted publicity, the Supreme Court held in 1975 and again in 1989 that truthfully reporting the name of a rape victim is permitted. In 1976 and in 1979 the justices upheld the right of the press to publish the names of juveniles involved with the law because the information was truthful and of public significance.

PROTECTION OF SOURCES AND NOTES

Another area you must know about is your ability—or inability—to protect your sources and notes. The problem may arise in various situations. A grand jury that is investigating a murder may ask you to reveal the source of a story you wrote about the murder. Or you may be asked to testify at a criminal or civil trial.

> **"**(The media) seek to maintain a balance on the constantly shifting tightrope of personal privacy, access to information and government accountability.**"**
>
> — John R. Finnegan Sr., former newspaper editor

The conflict that arises is between a reporter's need to protect sources of information and the duty of every citizen to testify to help the courts determine justice. Your work as a reporter will take you to events that are important and newsworthy. Anyone wanting the facts about an event can subpoena you to bring in all the details. Journalists usually resist. They work for their newspaper or radio or television station, not a law enforcement agency. Their ability to gather information would be compromised if sources knew that their identities or their information could go to the police.

By 2009, some protection against testifying—shield laws—had been adopted by these 35 states and the District of Columbia:

Alabama	Indiana	New York
Alaska	Kentucky	North Carolina
Arizona	Louisiana	North Dakota
Arkansas	Maine	Ohio
California	Maryland	Oklahoma
Colorado	Michigan	Oregon
Connecticut	Minnesota	Pennsylvania
Delaware	Montana	Rhode Island
Florida	Nebraska	South Carolina
Georgia	Nevada	Tennessee
Hawaii	New Jersey	Washington
Illinois	New Mexico	

Shield law protection is important because without it, journalists do go to jail. In 2001-2002, Vanessa Leggett, a freelance journalist in Houston, spent a record

168 days in jail for refusing to hand over notes and interview tapes she had made while writing a book about the murder of a Houston socialite. Texas has no shield law. In 2004-2005, Jim Taricani, a broadcast reporter in Providence, R.I., spent four months under house arrest for refusing to tell who gave him an FBI videotape that showed a Providence official taking a bribe from an undercover FBI agent. A federal judge had ordered Taricani to reveal his source. Although Rhode Island has a shield law, the federal government does not.

Perhaps *New York Times* reporter Judith Miller has garnered the most publicity for being jailed. Her saga started when conservative columnist Robert Novak revealed the name of a CIA undercover agent, Valerie Plame. Plame's husband, retired diplomat Joseph Wilson, had said the Bush administration misrepresented the facts when it claimed that Saddam Hussein had tried to buy depleted uranium from Niger. The disclosure about Plame came after Wilson's assertions.

Miller did not write about Plame, but she went to jail on July 6, 2005, for refusing to reveal the source who had provided her with information about the agent. Because it is a violation of federal law for an official to reveal the identity of an undercover CIA agent, a special prosecutor was assigned to investigate that leak. Several other journalists did testify after receiving permission from their sources. Miller and her bosses at *The Times* took the position that her promise to hold confidential her sources' names was not one she could break. The U.S. Supreme Court refused to hear her appeal. Although her imprisonment inspired bills in Congress calling for a federal shield law, Congress has not yet passed such a law.

Miller was released after serving 85 days in jail. Her source gave her permission to reveal his identity. The only criminal charge to result from the investigation

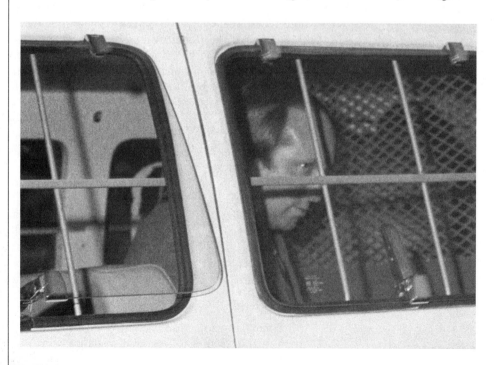

After refusing to disclose to a judge his source for a 1971 article about the trial of mass murderer Charles Manson, reporter William Farr was taken to jail in a police van.

was a charge against Lewis "Scooter" Libby, assistant to Vice President Dick Cheney, of lying to investigators. Libby was convicted in federal court.

In 1980, Congress did pass the Privacy Protection Act. Under that act, federal, state and local law enforcement officers generally may not use a search warrant to search news rooms. Instead, they must get a subpoena for documents, which instructs reporters and editors to hand over the material. Officers may use a warrant to search news rooms only if they suspect a reporter of being involved in a crime or if immediate action is needed to prevent bodily harm, loss of life or destruction of the material.

The difference between a search warrant and a subpoena is great. Officers with a search warrant can knock on the door, enter the news room and search on their own. A subpoena does not permit officers to search the news room. A subpoena for specific documents requires reporters to turn over the material to authorities at a predetermined time and place. In addition, it gives reporters time to challenge in court the necessity of surrendering the material.

Even in states with shield laws, judges in most criminal cases involving grand juries will not allow you to keep your sources secret. In other criminal cases, courts may allow confidentiality if a three-part test is met. Supreme Court Justice Potter Stewart suggested this test in his dissent in Branzburg v. Hayes, decided in 1972:

> Government officials must, therefore, demonstrate that the information sought is clearly relevant to a precisely defined subject of government inquiry. . . . They must demonstrate that it is reasonable to think the witness in question has that information. . . . And they must show that there is not any means of obtaining the information less destructive of First Amendment liberties.

In civil litigation you may be permitted to keep sources confidential in most cases unless the court finds that the information sought is unavailable from other sources and highly relevant to the underlying litigation or of such critical importance to the lawsuit that it goes to the heart of the plaintiff's claim.

If you are sued for libel, you will find it difficult both to protect your sources and to win the lawsuit. The court might well rule against you on whether a statement is true or false if it came from a source you refuse to name.

The best way to avoid such confrontation with the courts is not to promise a source you will keep his or her name confidential. Only for the most compelling reason should you promise confidentiality.

In 1991, the U.S. Supreme Court ruled in Cohen v. Cowles Media Co. that the First Amendment does not prevent a source from suing a news organization if a reporter has promised the source confidentiality but the newspaper publishes the source's name anyway.

ACCESS TO COURTS

The Supreme Court held in 1979 that "members of the public have no constitutional right" under the Sixth Amendment to attend criminal trials. In a reversal exactly one year later, the justices held that the public and the press have a First

Amendment right to attend criminal trials. The justices said the right was not absolute but trial judges could close criminal trials only when there was an "overriding interest" to justify such closure. The basic concern of judges when they close trials is to protect the accused person's Sixth Amendment right to an "impartial jury"—often translated by attorneys as "a fair trial."

In addition, the First Amendment prevents the government from conducting business—even trials—in secret. In the Richmond Newspapers case in 1980, Chief Justice Warren Burger traced the unbroken and uncontradicted history of open judicial proceedings in England and the United States. He concluded that there is a "presumption of openness" in criminal trials and pointed out the important role of the news media as representatives of the public.

By 1984, the Supreme Court had decided that openness in criminal trials "enhances both the basic fairness of the criminal trial and the appearance of fairness so essential to public confidence in the system." Public proceedings vindicate the concerns of victims and the community in knowing that offenders are being brought to account for their criminal conduct "by jurors fairly and openly selected." Proceedings of jury selection could be closed, the chief justice said, only when a trial judge finds that closure preserves an "overriding interest" and is narrowly tailored to serve that interest.

Judges are using that option. For instance, when John Gotti was convicted of organized crime activities in New York, the jurors' names were kept secret. Gotti's attorneys unsuccessfully challenged their anonymity. Jurors' names in the Rodney King case, which resulted in riots in Los Angeles in 1992, also were withheld.

In 1986, the Supreme Court said that only an overriding interest found by a trial judge can overcome the presumption of openness of criminal proceedings. Today, 47 states allow cameras in at least some state courtrooms. Cameras are permitted in some lower federal courts but are excluded from the U.S. Supreme Court.

COPYRIGHT AND FAIR USE

The purpose of copyright law is to ensure compensation to authors for contributing to the common good by publishing their works. The Constitution provides for this in Article 1, Section 8, by giving Congress the power to secure "for limited times to authors and inventors the exclusive right to their respective writing and discoveries." The same section indicates that this provision is intended "to promote the progress of science and useful arts" for the benefit of the public. Copyright laws both protect your work and prohibit you from using significant amounts of others' writings without permission and, in some cases, a fee.

Key elements of copyright law include the following:

- Copyrightable works are protected from the moment they are fixed in tangible form, whether published or unpublished.
- Copyright protection begins with a work's "creation and . . . endures for a term consisting of the life of the author and 70 years after the author's death."

- Works for hire and anonymous and pseudonymous works are protected for 95 years from publication or 100 years from creation, whichever is shorter.
- There is a "fair use" limitation on the exclusive rights of copyright owners. In other words, it may be permissible to quote small excerpts from a copyrighted work without permission. According to the Supreme Court, these factors govern fair use:
  1. The purpose and character of the use.
  2. The nature of the copyrighted work.
  3. The size and significance of the portion used in relationship to the copyrighted work as a whole.
  4. The effect on the potential market for or value of the copyrighted work.

Although a work is copyrighted from the moment it is fixed in tangible form, the copyright statute says certain steps are necessary for the work to receive statutory protection. The author or publisher must:

- Publish or reproduce the work with the word "copyright" or the symbol ©, the name of the copyright owner and the year of publication.
- Deposit two copies of the work with the Library of Congress within three months of publication. Failure to do so will not affect the copyright but could lead to the imposition of fines.
- Register the work at the Library of Congress by filling out a form supplied by the Copyright Office and sending the form, the specified number of copies (usually one copy of an unpublished work and two copies of a published work), and a $30 fee to the Copyright Office. The copies and registration fee may be sent together and usually are.

Copyright law has a special provision for broadcasters of live programs. Broadcasters need only make a simultaneous tape of their live broadcasts in order to receive copyright protection. The tape fulfills the requirement that a work be in a "fixed" form for copyright protection. Because a digital form is a "fixed" form, editors of online newspapers already meet that copyright requirement.

Some aspects of U.S. copyright law changed in 1989, when the United States finally joined the 100-year-old Berne Convention, an international copyright treaty, primarily to prevent the pirating of American film productions in other countries. The changes include the following:

- Placing a copyright notice on a work is no longer necessary to protect a copyright after publication. This is in line with the Berne Convention principle that copyright protection should not be subject to formalities. The copyright notice, however, is still widely used because it acts as a bar to an infringer's claim of innocent infringement.
- Copyright registration is no longer a prerequisite for access to the federal courts for an infringement action. But registration is required for a copyright

owner to recover statutory damages. (Without registration, the copyright owner can recover only the damages he or she can prove, plus court costs and "reasonable" attorney's fees.) The amount of statutory damages, generally between $750 and $30,000, is determined by the judge. If the infringer was not aware he or she was infringing a copyright, the court may award as little as $200. If the infringement was willful, the court can award up to $150,000. Thus, like the copyright notice, copyright registration remains highly advisable.

Online journalism has created new copyright concerns. Using online content from others without permission can raise significant copyright issues, as the courts are still wrestling with the extent of the fair use doctrine when it comes to online usage. The safe route, and the ethical choice, is to seek permission before using the work of others, and to link to other news sites if you wish to direct readers to other content online.

The digital media also have changed the rules of the game for freelancers and other content providers. In 2001, the U.S. Supreme Court, ruling against media companies, said freelance writers have the power to decide whether the articles they sold to print publications may be reproduced in an electronic form. In a 7-2 decision, the justices ruled that *The New York Times* must either pay its freelance authors when redistributing their articles online or negotiate other conditions for republication.

Suggested Readings

Carter, T. Barton, Marc A. Franklin, and Jay B. Wright. *The First Amendment and the Fourth Estate*, 8th ed. Westbury, NY: Foundation Press, 2000. This text focuses on the relationship between the First Amendment and the press itself.

Middleton, Kent R., Robert Trager, and Bill F. Chamberlin. *The Law of Public Communication*, 6th ed. Boston: Allyn & Bacon, 2003. This is a valuable and authoritative treatment of free speech and free press issues.

Overbeck, Wayne. *Major Principles of Media Law*. Toronto: Thomson Wadsworth, 2004. This is a standard text that covers all important aspects of law as it applies to the mass media.

Suggested Websites

www.firstamendmentcenter.org
At this Freedom Forum site you'll find the "State of the First Amendment" report by Donna Demas, which discusses the public's ambivalence about First Amendment issues.

www.medialaw.org
This is the site of the Media Law Resource Center, "a nonprofit information clearinghouse" organized in 1980 by leading media groups "to monitor developments and promote First Amendment rights in the libel, privacy and related legal fields." The site features a 50-state survey of media libel law.

www.rcfp.org
The Reporters Committee for Freedom of the Press maintains online publications and guides on First Amendment and freedom of information issues. Here you'll find current hot stories, plus archives and much more.

Exercises

1. **Team project.** Your instructor will divide your class into teams of four or five. Select one situation from the following list.

   a. A reporter is on an assignment with a photographer who enters a house without permission and photographs the sale of illegal drugs. Should the reporter publish the photos?

   b. A reporter is covering a sexual assault trial in which the victim is a young man. The arresting officer tells the reporter that the crime is not surprising because the victim "is queer." Should the reporter use the officer's quotation?

   c. A team of reporters is working on a series of articles about possible corruption in the city agency responsible for zoning. One reporter gets an anonymous call from a senior official offering to give information about wrongdoing, but only on condition of anonymity. Should the reporter agree to anonymity for the source?

   d. A journalist comes into possession of a private e-mail sent by a well-known person to an apparent lover and considers quoting the e-mail and the recipient's name in a blog. Should the reporter use the e-mail and the recipient's name?

   Discuss within your team the issues raised in the situation you've chosen. Brainstorm possible actions a journalist could take. Come up with a list of pros and cons for each action. Agree among yourselves what a responsible action—journalistically and legally—would be.

2. In a two-page essay, discuss which defense against libel discussed in this chapter you would have used to defend *Time* magazine in the lawsuit filed by Gen. Ariel Sharon. Why?

3. *The New York Times* v. Sullivan, 376 U.S. 254 (1964), was a landmark decision in favor of the press. Discuss, in a short essay, what the consequences for the press might have been if the decision had been different.

4. Using the LexisNexis database, determine how the U.S. Supreme Court has used Richmond Newspapers v. Virginia, 448 U.S. 555 (1980), in later cases dealing with openness in criminal proceedings.

Ethics

The two were proclaimed as heroes by journalists and nonjournalists alike. James O'Keefe, 25, and Hannah Giles, 20, had thoroughly disgraced ACORN, the Association of Community Organizations for Reform Now. ACORN had been repeatedly accused of voter fraud, but according to a study by Peter Dreier and Christopher Martin published by Occidental College, when ACORN officials learned they had registered false names, they immediately notified election officials.

Now, however, O'Keefe and Giles had hidden-camera video of ACORN employees advising a fake prostitute and her bogus pimp how to set up a business in prostitution and avoid paying taxes.

What a coup! Linda Turley-Hansen, a syndicated columnist for the *East Valley-Scottsdale Tribune* and a former veteran Phoenix television news anchor, wrote:

> Most old media have all but ignored these scallywags, which for some reason receive multiples of millions in taxpayer dollars. So, in reflection, it's no surprise that the young showed the way in light of the media's abdication of its own investigative doctrine.
>
> And good news for reporter wannabes. You too can grab your recorders and cameras and journalistic ethics (emphasis on ethics) and go earn your names. Old news operations have lost all rights to claim the industry that is absolutely critical to keeping this nation free. Humongous and entrenched in their egos, they've become sin-city; little more than high-priced billboards, hawking paid-for messages.

Later in her column, Turley-Hansen reports, "Polls show at least two-thirds do not trust the news media."

Turley-Hansen apparently thinks that trust in the media will rise if reporters "grab" their journalistic ethics and secretly videotape people—even when doing so is illegal, as in this case, where the two violated a Maryland law. Also, she and others cheered the videotapers without mentioning that they had been turned away by ACORN workers at seven other ACORN offices.

Few of the 647 news stories in 2007 and 2008 that Dreier and Martin examined in their study, "Manipulating the Public Agenda: Why ACORN Was in the News and What the News Got Wrong," provided any chance for ACORN to respond to the charges of fraud leveled against it. Fewer still spoke of ACORN's history of providing help to the poor and minorities, of registering more than a million people to vote, of helping Americans buy and keep their homes. And even fewer spoke about the people and organizations that sponsored Giles and O'Keefe and continue to operate "to bring balance to the media."

The headline on the article by Linda Turley-Hansen read: "ACORN Story Shows Decline of True Journalism." A headline on a column in the *Columbia Missourian* on the same topic read: "ACORN: A Nice Scoop, but Pseudo-Journalism."

What is the difference between "true journalism" and "pseudo-journalism"?

Ethics. And people's understanding of what is ethical and what is not.

Often people who accuse the news media of being unethical have no clear notion of what journalism and journalism ethics are all about. Yet it's safe to say that most of these people will declare they have no trust in the press because they

IN THIS CHAPTER YOU WILL LEARN

1. Philosophical approaches that can provide answers to ethical questions.

2. A means of ethical reasoning.

3. Ethical questions of special importance to journalists.

consider journalism ethics an oxymoron, a contradiction in terms. Despite this public perception, journalists are arguably more concerned with ethics than ever before. In this chapter we'll explore the practice of ethics in journalism today.

THE PUBLIC PERCEPTION OF JOURNALISM ETHICS

The reasons for the public's negative perception of journalism and journalism ethics are many. Yet contrary to what its critics say, journalism has never been practiced in a more ethical way in this country and in a host of other countries around the globe. How can that be? Let's look at a few factors influencing the theory and practice of journalism today.

Journalism Versus Entertainment

People often lump together mainstream journalism with all other kinds of media. No one denies the existence of wildly sensational tabloids, websites, blogs, radio commentaries, television specials, and so on. When some people condemn

People magazine reportedly paid Brad Pitt and Angelina Jolie $4 million for pictures of their baby. Did the deal include a guarantee for an interview for CNN with Anderson Cooper? Not according to CNN. Both *People* and CNN are a part of Time Warner.

journalism, though, they are often including all television, movies, music and every form of entertainment together with journalism.

You can, of course, find journalism on blogs, in Twitter messages and in every form of social media. And the principles and guidelines for being ethical apply to all media that can correctly be categorized as journalism. But journalism ethics do not necessarily apply to shows featuring political satirists, activist TV commentators, and celebrity watchers, for example. Such shows may have the veneer of journalism, but they are really engaged in using current events for entertainment purposes or have a strong point of view.

Bloggers as Watchdogs

Some of the credit for the increased ethical behavior of journalists belongs to bloggers who are serving as watchdogs of the press and to many other citizens on the Internet who are calling attention to every irregularity they see in journalism. As a result, journalists have responded by becoming much more transparent, by discussing their mistakes and failings. It's safe to say that, unlike in the past, nearly every practicing journalist is concerned about ethics. You need to be, too.

A Journalism Code of Ethics?

In some professions, enforcing a code means a professional association must have the power to keep people from practicing unless they have membership or a license to practice. That also means that the profession must be able to censure practitioners in a meaningful way, perhaps even keeping members from practicing, if they violate the code of the profession.

Despite journalists' increased accountability, journalism as a profession has not established a mandatory and enforced code. Although there are voluntary societies in journalism, no association has the authority to enforce restrictions on journalists' behavior. That's because of a fear that such an association and such a code might in some way infringe upon freedom of the press.

"Ethics is a system of principles, a morality or code of conduct. It is the values and rules of life recognized by an individual, group or culture seeking guidelines to human conduct and what is good or bad, right or wrong.**"**

— Conrad C. Fink, media ethics professor

Associations of journalists such as the Society of Professional Journalists, the Public Relations Society of America, the International Association of Business Communicators, the American Society of Business Publication Editors, the American Society of Magazine Editors, the American Business Media and dozens of others all have codes of ethics. CyberJournalist.net has a model bloggers' code of ethics that is similar to the code of the Society of Professional Journalists. However, journalists do not *have* to belong to such organizations to practice their profession.

Some critics condemn codes of ethics either for being hopelessly general and therefore ineffective or for being too restrictive. Some argue that strict codes help improve journalists' credibility; others say they merely make journalists easy targets for libel suits.

In a vote in favor of codes of ethics, individual news organizations have established codes that have restricted employees in their work. Indeed, a majority of newspapers and television stations now have written codes of ethics, with larger news organizations most likely to have them. These codes of ethics are enforced. Journalists who have plagiarized, for example, have been suspended or fired from their news organizations.

Your organization may or may not have a code of ethics. Either way, you should devise your own ethical values and principles. Your upbringing, your education, and perhaps your religious training have already helped prepare you to do this.

Journalists too often and too easily justify all of their actions by citing the First Amendment. Because of the wide range of the First Amendment and the relatively few legal restraints on journalism, journalists, perhaps more than members of any other profession, need to discuss proper conduct. As the famous Commission on Freedom of the Press concluded in 1947, unless journalists set their own limits on what is acceptable and responsible, government will eventually and inevitably do it for them.

The Problem with Licensing Journalists

For some professions, state governments require a license to practice. Usually, the practitioner must meet certain educational requirements, pass a qualifying exam, or both. Because journalists are not licensed by states, it is difficult to determine who is a journalist. But it is likewise impossible for the state to control who becomes a journalist and what that journalist—or any other person—can write. Only the public, by patronizing specific news outlets, decides whose writing is valuable.

Yet states do recognize that journalists, though unlicensed, need some protection to be able to do their jobs. At this point, 35 states have formally created shield laws—laws that protect journalists and their sources from government pressure (see Chapter 21). To do so, they have had to come up with various definitions of who is protected. According to the Reporters Committee for Freedom of the Press, Sen. Arlen Specter and Sen. Charles Schumer have been pushing for a federal Free Flow of Information Act that will apply to "salaried employees" and independent contractors for established news organizations and also to freelancers and online journalists. Of course, the protection will not be absolute. There will be a public interest balancing test for criminal, civil and leak cases. A judge will weigh the public interest in confidentiality against the public interest served by compelled disclosure.

This much is certain: The U.S. government does not keep anyone from practicing journalism.

THREE ETHICAL PHILOSOPHIES

Your personal ethics may derive from the way you answer one fundamental question: Does the end justify the means? In other words, should you ever do something that is not good in itself in order to achieve a goal that you think is good?

If you answer no to that question, you are in some sense at least an absolutist or a legalist, and you would most likely subscribe to *deontological ethics*. If you answer yes to that question, you are more of a relativist and would subscribe to *teleological ethics*. If you answer maybe or sometimes, you would subscribe to a form of *situation ethics*.

Don't be put off by the jargon of philosophers. To understand ethical thinking, to be able to discuss ethics and to solve ethical problems that arise on the job, you need to learn the vocabulary of ethicists.

Deontological Ethics: The Ethics of Duty

According to the philosophy of deontological ethics, we have a duty to do what is right. Deontologists believe that some actions are always right and some always wrong; that is, there exists in nature (or, for those with religious faith, in divine revelation) a fixed set of principles or laws from which we should not deviate. For a deontologist, the end never justifies the means. That belief is why some refer to this ethical philosophy as **absolutism** or *legalism*. An absolutist or legalist sees one clear duty—to discover the rules and to follow them. For example:

- Suppose you believe that it's always wrong to lie. If you learn that a friend cheated on an exam and you are asked about your friend's actions by a college administrator, you would answer truthfully. You might be torn by loyalty to your friend, but you would not lie.

- Suppose you believe that it's wrong to keep someone else's property without permission. If you find a wallet with $500 in it, you would make every effort to return the wallet and money to its rightful owner.

- Suppose you believe it's right to help people who are worse off than you. Regardless of your income or busy schedule, you would make a point of contributing money or time to charitable causes.

One such absolutist was Immanuel Kant (1724-1804). Kant proposed the "categorical imperative," a moral law that obliges you to do only those things that you would be willing to have everyone do as a matter of universal law. Once you make that decision, you must regard your decision as unconditional and without exception, and you must do what you decide.

Many people draw support for their absolutism or legalism from their religious beliefs. They cite the Bible, the Quran or another religious source. If they themselves cannot resolve an ethical problem, they may turn to a minister, priest, rabbi, imam or guru for the answer. The absolutist is concerned only with doing what is right and needs only to discover what the right action is.

The absolutist journalist is concerned only with whether an event is newsworthy. If an event is interesting, timely, significant or important, it is to be reported, regardless of the consequences. The duty of the journalist is to report the news.

Making Good Ethical Decisions

Ask these 10 questions to make good ethical decisions:

1. What do I know? What do I need to know?
2. What is my journalistic purpose?
3. What are my ethical concerns?
4. What organizational policies and professional guidelines should I consider?
5. How can I include other people, with different perspectives and diverse ideas, in the decision-making process?
6. Who are the stakeholders — those affected by my decision? What are their motivations? Which are legitimate?
7. What if the roles were reversed? How would I feel if I were in the shoes of one of the stakeholders?
8. What are the possible consequences of my actions? Short term? Long term?
9. What are my alternatives to maximize my truth-telling responsibility and minimize harm?
10. Can I clearly and fully justify my thinking and my decision? To my colleagues? To the stakeholders? To the public?

— Daniel Steele, Poynter Online

Period. Newscaster Walter Cronkite once said that if journalists worried about all the possible consequences of reporting something, they would never report anything.

People rely on the news media to keep them informed. That is why journalists enjoy First Amendment privileges. Charles A. Dana, who in 1868 began a 29-year career as editor of *The New York Sun*, said, "Whatever God in his infinite wisdom has allowed to happen, I am not too proud to print."

Absolutists discount any criticism of the press for any stories it delivers to the public. Stop blaming the messenger, they say. We don't make events happen; we just report them.

Teleological Ethics: The Ethics of Final Ends

According to the philosophy of **teleological ethics**, what makes an act ethical is not the act itself but the consequences of the act. Teleologists believe that the end can and often does justify the means. Actions that have "right consequences" are ethical actions. In this philosophy, ethics are more *relativistic* than absolutist.

- Suppose your sister tells you that her husband is abusing her and she is moving to a shelter for battered women. If the husband asked you where your sister went, you would be justified, as a teleologist, in lying to protect her from him.
- Suppose a friend swears you to secrecy before telling you that he is feeling suicidal. As a teleologist, you would be justified in breaking your promise and seeking the advice of a counselor or the friend's family to help your friend.

An important consideration in teleological ethics is the intention of the person performing the act. What one person would declare unethical, another person would do for a good purpose or a good reason. For example, police often work undercover, concealing their identity in order to apprehend criminals. In the course of this work, if they must lie or even get involved in criminal activity, the teleological response would be, so be it. Their purpose is to protect the public; their intention is to work for the good of society. The end justifies the means.

Some journalists would not hesitate to do the same. Some might require that some conditions be in place before they would steal or use deceit, but then they would proceed. They believe their purpose is to be the watchdog of government, to protect the common good, to keep the public fully informed. Whatever they must do to accomplish these goals, they argue, is clearly ethical.

Situation Ethics: The Ethics of Specific Acts

When asked whether the end justifies the means, a person subscribing to situation ethics would reply, "It all depends." Here are five philosophies that make use of some form of situation ethics.

Antinomianism

Antinomianism is the belief that there are no moral absolutes and that there is only one operative principle: Every person or every situation is unique, and to resolve an ethical problem by applying principles held by others or principles that apply in other cases is unethical. An antinomian believes that because each situation is unique, each ethical problem must be judged entirely on its own merits.

Love of Neighbor

Joseph Fletcher has described another type of situation ethics. Fletcher bases his philosophy on love of neighbor as articulated in the Golden Rule and the maxim "You shall love your neighbor as yourself." He presents his ethic from a Christian perspective with roots in Judaic teaching, but one need not profess Christianity to share the conviction that all principles are relative to one absolute—love of neighbor. Indeed, most religions, as well as secular humanism, hold human values as the highest good.

Although people who subscribe to this belief understand and accept other ethical maxims and weigh them carefully when facing an ethical decision, they must be prepared to set those aside completely if love of neighbor demands it. In the broad sense, followers of Fletcher's form of situation ethics always place people first. In every ethical situation, they always do what is best for people. Sometimes they must choose between love for one person and love for a larger community of people.

Utilitarianism

The thinking that Fletcher advocates leads to another form of situation ethics: utilitarianism. From the utilitarian perspective, your choices are ethical if you always choose the action that is likely to bring the most happiness to the greatest number of people.

This theory, formulated by John Stuart Mill (1806-1873) and Jeremy Bentham (1748-1832), was later modified to emphasize the greatest *good* rather than the greatest happiness. Some utilitarians also add the words "over a long period of time" because some actions may seem wrong if one looks merely at the present situation.

Most journalists probably subscribe to a utilitarian philosophy. They know, for example, that publishing a story about the infidelities of a public official may destroy the person's reputation, hurt his or her family and perhaps even lead to suicide, but, taking a utilitarian view, they decide that for the greater good, the public should have this information. The decision to publish would seem even more justifiable if the public official were involved in embezzlement or bribery.

Aristotle's Golden Mean

Another form of situation ethics derives from Aristotle's notion of the Golden Mean, a moderate moral position that avoids either of two extremes. Aristotle

Ethical Guidelines from ASNE

"The primary function of newspapers is to communicate to the human race what its members do, feel and think," stated the American Society of Newspaper Editors in 1923. To ensure the success of this function, the ASNE issued the following ethical guidelines for newspapers:

- **Responsibility.** The right of a newspaper to attract and hold readers is restricted by nothing but considerations of public welfare.
- **Freedom of the press.** Freedom of the press is to be guarded as a vital right of mankind.
- **Independence.** Freedom from all obligations except that of fidelity to the public interest is vital.
- **Sincerity, truthfulness, accuracy.** Good faith with the reader is the foundation of all journalism worthy of the name.
- **Impartiality.** Sound practice makes clear distinction between reports and expressions of opinion. News reports should be free from opinion or bias of any kind.
- **Fair play.** A newspaper should not publish unofficial charges affecting reputation or moral character without opportunity given to the accused to be heard; right practice demands the giving of such opportunity in all cases of serious accusation outside judicial proceedings.
- **Decency.** A newspaper cannot escape conviction of insincerity if, while professing high moral purpose, it supplies incentives to base conduct, such as are to be found in details of crime and vice, publication of which is not demonstrably for the general good.

Source: Quoted from Robert I. Berkman and Christopher A. Shumway, *Digital Dilemmas: Ethical Issues for Online Media Professionals* (Ames: Iowa State University Press, 2003).

states that after considering the extremes, a person is likely to find a rational and moral position somewhere in between—though not necessarily in the middle.

Journalists make choices ranging from refusing to publish photographs of a crime to publishing the most graphic images of a violent death. A person who subscribes to the ethics of the Golden Mean would try to run a photo that indicates the horror of the tragedy without offending the sensibilities of the audience or of the family involved.

Ayn Rand's Rational Self-Interest

Ayn Rand's ethical philosophy of rational self-interest is the opposite of utilitarianism and certainly of Christianity or any form of altruism. Someone subscribing to her notion of *ethical egoism* would never sacrifice himself or herself for the good of others. An ethical egoist always looks out for his or her own self-interest first, believing that if everyone acted in this manner, everyone would be better off.

Journalists who are ethical egoists would not mind using people for stories, even if the people they use have no idea how embarrassing the story may be to them. Photographers would take pictures of dying or dead children and of their grieving parents. Broadcasters would not hesitate to telecast people committing suicide. In their opinion, whatever helps them get good stories and thus advance in the profession is ethical.

Some critics accuse journalists of embracing rational self-interest merely to sell newspapers or to increase ratings. However, on many occasions journalists report stories that anger both their readers and their advertisers.

RESOLVING ETHICAL ISSUES

Unless you are an absolutist, ethical reasoning can take many forms. You may adopt one or more ethical stances, and they will guide your day-to-day ethical decision-making. What is paramount is that you engage in principled reasoning. You must deliberate by reflecting on ethical principles—principles that will help you decide on proper or moral ways to act.

> **❚❚** I tell the honest truth in my paper, and I leave the consequences to God. **❚❚**
>
> — James Gordon Bennett, newspaper publisher, 1836

Principled reasoning assumes that you are not acting ethically if you do something simply because you have been told to do it or because that's what everyone else does. You are not ethical if you report a story just to beat the competition.

To help journalists and others make ethical decisions, ethicists Clifford Christians, Kim Rotzoll and Mark Fackler have adapted a model of moral reasoning devised by Dr. Ralph Potter of Harvard Divinity School. Called the Potter Box (Figure 22.1), the model has four elements:

- **Appraising the situation.** Making a good ethical decision begins with good reporting. You cannot make an ethical decision unless you know all the facts.

  When an anonymous source, identified only as Johntw, posted a story on CNN's iReport that Apple CEO Steve Jobs had suffered a heart attack, Apple's stock fell by more than 10 percent in a short time. Although the letters "CNN" give the site credibility, a disclaimer at the top of the page reads, "Unedited. Unfiltered. News." As Al Tompkins of the Poynter Institute points out, saying that what is on the site is unedited and unfiltered is clearly saying that it is not news because it has not been verified.

- **Identifying values.** What are your personal values, your news organization's values, your community's values, the nation's values? For example, you may place high value on your personal credibility and that of your news organization. Certainly, freedom of the press is a value prized by many in this nation.

  One of the highest values of a news organization is its total independence. In what was called an "ethical lapse of monumental proportions" and a "disastrous decision," *The Washington Post* invited lobbyists to pay $25,000 to attend off-the-record salons at the home of *Post* publisher Katharine Weymouth. There, the lobbyists would have access to top people in the administration, legislators, and even *Post* editors and reporters. In the end, *The Post* canceled the plans, and freedom of the press survived another day at the paper. However, the embarrassment remains.

- **Appealing to ethical principles.** You need to look at the various ethical principles discussed previously. Contrary to what many believe, it's not always

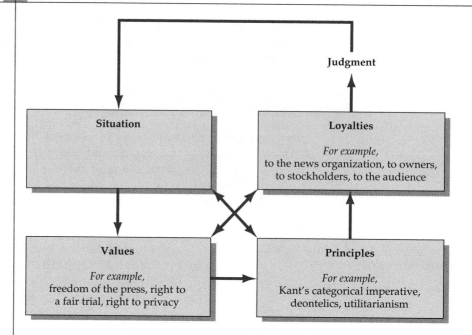

Figure 22.1
The Potter Box can help journalists analyze and resolve ethical problems.

sufficient to follow your gut. If that were true, the world would have only ethical people in it. Nor are the principles meant to be a shopping list from which you choose items that serve your personal interest. To be ethical, you may have to choose a principle or principles that are far from expedient.

When someone discovered that David Pratt, a longtime journalist, used almost identical phrases from an old piece in *Sports Illustrated* for his column in *The Vancouver Province*, Pratt said, "It was Saturday, and I wanted to get out of (the office) before noon." Quite an expedient reason for plagiarism.

- **Choosing loyalties.** You owe a certain loyalty to your news organization, yes, but you must be loyal to your own principles and values and to your readers, listeners or viewers. And what about loyalty to your sources and to the people about whom you are reporting? Finally, some would argue that you also must consider your loyalty to your station's owners and stockholders. If your news agency is not profitable, it will cease to exist.

For some time no one knew that Prince Harry, the third in line to the British throne, was flying missions in Afghanistan. That was because Bob Satchwell, the executive director of the Society of Editors in Britain, had brokered a deal to keep the prince's military exploits out of the papers. *The New York Times* reported: "Today's media are widely perceived to be cutthroat, sensationalistic and anti-authoritarian, yet hundreds of journalists, including those in London's rabid tabloid culture, kept the deployment secret for close to three months." *The Times* quoted Tony Maddox, the executive vice president and managing editor of CNN International, which observed the blackout: "Newspapers and broadcasts can behave themselves better than people think they can when a security situation is involved."

It was a matter of choosing loyalties.

Where did the news of the prince's service in Afghanistan first appear? In the Feb. 28, 2008, edition of the *Drudge Report*. The headline read: "Prince Harry Fights on Frontlines in Afghanistan; 3 Months Tour." It was accompanied by a photo of the prince in pilot's gear sitting in the pilot's seat of a plane.

Was Matt Drudge loyal to his readers? Did he unnecessarily endanger the life of the prince? If the enemies in Afghanistan had known Prince Harry was a pilot, they might have made a special effort to harm him because of the publicity that would result.

One thing is certain about making ethical decisions. Doing so assumes that people are absolutely free to choose. As Sir Harold Evans, the British-born journalist and former editor of *The Sunday Times* and of *The Times*, has written, "The whole of ethics is based on the presumption of free will and the freedom to make choices." Nevertheless, and perhaps for that reason, there is no one clear answer to an ethical problem. Seldom do the most reasonable and experienced news veterans agree completely. But principled reasoning at least makes an ethical decision possible.

> **"** Journalists demean themselves and damage their credibility when they misrepresent themselves and their work to news sources and, in turn, to the public at large. **"**
>
> — Everette E. Dennis, professor and head of the Center for Communication at Fordham University

The four elements in the Potter Box need not be considered in any particular order. Also, don't stop reasoning after you have touched upon the four elements. Principled reasoning should continue, even to another discussion of another ethical problem.

This continuing ethical dialectic or dialogue helps create ethical journalism and ethical journalists. Journalists should not simply reflect society. They should present a reasoned reflection. Journalism should be done by people who make informed, intelligent and prudent choices.

The main objection to the Potter Box is that using it takes too much time and is impractical in the deadline business of journalism. However, as you become better acquainted with ethical principles and more practiced at principled reasoning, you will be able to make ethical decisions much more quickly and reasonably.

Although each case is different and you always must know the situation, you need not always start from the beginning. After a while you will know what your values are, where your loyalties lie and which principles will most likely apply.

ETHICAL PROBLEMS FOR JOURNALISTS

Because of the First Amendment, American society has relatively few "rules" for journalists despite the special problems they face. In this section, we discuss some of these problems.

The Spokesman-Review employed a forensic computer expert to pose as an 18-year-old man on a gay chat room. Spokane Mayor Jim West responded. West had been accused of using his office to offer jobs and gifts to young men. He lost his office in a recall election on Dec. 6, 2005. West died on July 22, 2006, after cancer surgery.

Deceit

Perhaps the most bothersome ethical problem facing journalists involves using deceit to get a story. Deceit covers a wide range of practices. When is it permissible to lie, misrepresent yourself or use a hidden audio recorder or camera? When may you steal documents? For absolutists, the answer is simple: Never! For others, the answer is not easy.

The Spokesman-Review of Spokane, Wash., reported that it used a forensic computer expert posing as an 18-year-old man to ascertain whether Mayor Jim West was using his public position to proposition young men on a gay website. A continuing investigation by *The Spokesman-Review* revealed that the mayor had been involved in sexual abuse as far back as the 1970s and that his whole political career was tainted with allegations. Many praised the newspaper for its actions and investigation; others, of course, did not approve of the deceptive means the newspaper used.

It's particularly easy to conceal your identity as a reporter on the Web. At times, as in the *Spokesman-Review* story, you may be doing undercover investigative reporting, but usually the time to reveal yourself as a reporter is when you begin to question people online, not after you have gotten to a certain point in your story.

A group of journalists in an ethical decision-making seminar at the Poynter Institute for Media Studies devised a list of criteria to justify the use of deceit. The box "Conditions Justifying the Use of Deceit by Journalists" synthesizes their conclusions. All the conditions listed there must be present to justify deceit.

Conditions Justifying the Use of Deceit by Journalists

- An issue of profound public importance:
  - of vital public interest, revealing system failure at high levels
  - a preventive measure against profound harm to individuals
- All other alternatives exhausted.
- Eventual full disclosure of the deception and the reason for it.
- Full commitment to the story by everyone involved.
- The harm prevented outweighs any harm caused.

- A meaningful, collaborative and deliberative decision-making process that takes into account:
  - short- and long-term consequences of the deception
  - the impact on credibility
  - motivations for actions
  - congruence between the deceptive act and the organization's editorial mission
  - legal implications
  - consistency of reasoning and action

Conflicts of Interest

It is generally assumed that reporters start out with no point of view, that they are not out to get someone or to get something from the story. This basic assumption is the foundation of all credibility. Most news media codes of ethics devote the bulk of their substance to determining what constitutes a conflict of interest. And well they should.

The *Columbia Journalism Review* questioned whether veteran NBC News correspondent Andrea Mitchell should be on the air at all during a time of great financial crises. Mitchell, who is married to former chairman of the Federal Reserve Alan Greenspan, apparently never mentions his name in her reporting. *The New York Times* reported that the president of NBC News, Steve Capus, called the *Review*'s article "simplistic," but the network did not allow Mitchell to take the lead in covering congressional hearings about the economy.

Friendship

Perhaps the most obvious, most frequent, yet most overlooked conflict of interest confronting journalists is friendship. Friendship may be the greatest obstacle to the flow of information. No one knows whether friendship causes more stories to be reported or more stories to be killed. Either way, it sets up a powerful conflict of interest. If you ever find yourself covering a story that involves a personal acquaintance, ask your supervisor to assign the story to someone else.

Many readers thought that Jessica McBride's profile of Milwaukee Police Chief Edward A. Flynn in *Milwaukee Magazine* was overly kind to the chief. They did not know that earlier in the year, the two had begun having an affair. McBride, a former reporter for the *Journal-Sentinel* and a lecturer at the University of Wisconsin-Milwaukee, has taught journalism ethics. The Society of Professional Journalists' Code of Ethics says reporters should "remain free of associations and activities that may compromise integrity or damage credibility."

Ethical Problems Faced by Journalists

- Deceit

- Conflicts of interest
  - Friendship
  - Payola
  - Freebies
  - Checkbook journalism
  - Participation in the news

- Advertising pressure

- Invasion of privacy

- Withholding information

- Incorrect and incomplete information

- Plagiarism

ON THE JOB

A Healthy Ethical Process

"Every journalist must 'do ethics' in every story," says Kelly McBride. "Young journalists make a common mistake when they fail to identify everyday decisions as ethical choices. Journalists of all experience levels make an even bigger mistake: They assume they should know the answer to every ethical question. Both mistakes undermine a healthy ethical process."

As a teacher of ethics at the Poynter Institute, McBride spends most of her time fostering "a healthy ethical process." McBride has an undergraduate degree in journalism (1984) and a master's degree in religion from Gonzaga University (2000). She spent 14 years as a reporter at *The Spokesman-Review* in Spokane, Wash.

"Young journalists have more power than they imagine in this process," McBride says. "As a newcomer to the profession, or to a particular news room, you are expected to figure out how things get done."

The best tool to accomplish this? "Curiosity," McBride says. "Use your reporting skills to understand the ethical climate of your news room. Observe the signs. Where do the important conversations occur, and who is involved?

"Test your observations. Ask colleagues involved in a specific decision to describe the process. In your own work, bounce your decisions off your supervisor and your peers. Invite key editors to tell you what they like about the best stories in the paper or on the air.

"Ask this question over and over again: Why do we do it this way? This simple question will force your co-workers to articulate their news rooms' values. It may

Payola

Journalists may not accept payment for a story other than from their employer. Also, news organizations frown upon reporters doing promotional work for people they cover. Economist Ben Stein was fired as a *New York Times* columnist because he was paid to be in advertisements for a company charging people to get their "free credit scores." Stein denied a conflict of interest because he never wrote about credit scores. But he was perceived to be an economist, and therefore, to the editors of *The Times*, there was a clear perception of a conflict of interest.

Other conflicts of interest are perhaps not so obvious. Should news organizations prohibit their business news reporters and editors from owning stock in local companies? Should news agencies prohibit journalists from accepting speakers' fees? Should Congress attempt to legislate full disclosure of journalists' income and associations?

help some people see the gaps between the way things are and the way they ought to be."

These are the things McBride did while a reporter. She observed. "From my desk in the back corner of the news room," she says, "I could see decisions being made. In fact, I could see through the decisions to the very structure, the skeleton if you will, that supported the decision-making process."

She learned that in a healthy news room, reporters constantly turn to one another for exchanges, McBride says. The pathways between the editors' and reporters' desks are busy, two-way streets. At the intersections, journalists cluster in conversation. The most encouraging sign of all occurs when a huddle briefly loosens up and more people are invited into a discussion.

"When the news room is sick, decisions are made in secret, behind closed doors," McBride says. "Surprises show up in the paper or on the air without explanation, and no one knows how the decisions were made. People are afraid to ask questions. There is very little talking."

Now from her desk at the Poynter Institute, McBride gets a larger view. "I get to peer into news rooms around the country," she says. "Part of my job is to offer counseling to journalists trying to make better decisions."

The phone calls and visits reinforce what she first learned about ethical decision-making by sitting in the back of the news room and watching the process. "There are three components to any decision in the news room: the individual, the institutional values and the culture," McBride says. People call her when one of these components is out of kilter.

You can e-mail questions to her at kmcbride@poynter.com and sign up for her regular columns at www.poynter.org.

Freebies

When journalists accept free gifts from people they cover, the gifts always come with a price:

- Can reporters remain objective?
- Do reporters write stories they otherwise would not write?
- Does the public perceive the reporter who accepted or is suspected of accepting freebies as objective?

Again, the perception of conflict of interest is what bothers most news organizations. Some argue that the least reporters must do is disclose prominently in their stories any freebies they accepted. As in any case of deceit, reporters must disclose how they were able to get the story and why accepting freebies was necessary.

For example, travel writers are offered free trips, free cruises, free hotel accommodations and other freebies by companies that expect them to write about what they experience. Many small news outlets cannot afford to send their travel writers on expensive tours. Travel writers who accept freebies should mention doing so in their stories and should let readers decide whether to trust the reporting.

> **"Conflict of interest is practically the only place in ethics where perceptions matter almost as much as what is the case."**
>
> — Lee Wilkins, professor of journalism at the University of Missouri and editor of the *Journal of Mass Media Ethics*

Most news organizations have rules against accepting freebies. The Scripps-Howard newspaper group says, "When the gifts exceed the limits of propriety, they should be returned." The Society of Professional Journalists says, "Nothing of value shall be accepted." Is a cup of coffee something of value? The Associated Press expects its staff members to return gifts of "nominal value." Is a baseball cap of nominal value?

You must learn the ethics code of your news organization. If your personal code is more stringent than the code of your organization, follow your own code. Remember, you may not think a freebie will influence your reporting. But does your audience think that it might?

If you choose a career in public relations, remember that the code of the Public Relations Society of America states that you are to do nothing that tempts news professionals to violate their codes.

Checkbook Journalism

Is it ethical to pay a source for an exclusive story? Should you always report that you had a paid source? Should newspeople be in the business of keeping other newspeople from getting a story? Are paid sources likely to have an ax to grind? Do they come forward only for financial gain? Will the audience believe your story if you paid your source for it?

> **"But I don't believe that paying sources is unethical, as long as it's disclosed to the reader; in some cases I think it makes for better journalism. It gives a fair share of the profits to sources who spend time and take risks."**
>
> — John Tierney, from "Newsworthy," reprinted from the New York Times Company

The terrible consequence of checkbook journalism is that even legitimate news professionals may be cut off from sources who want and expect pay. Some sources have begun asking for a fee even for good news. The increase in tabloid journalism, both in print and in broadcast, has brought the opportunists out in droves. The networks say that they do not pay for interviews, but the tabloids say payments are disguised as consultant fees, writes Richard Zoglin in *Time* magazine. Should sources be paid for contributing to a commercial product?

Surely, good reporting demands that you pay sources only when necessary and only if you can get other sources to corroborate your findings. You'd also better be sure that your bosses know that you're doing it.

Many bloggers are their own boss. Nick Denton, who writes the blog Gawker, regularly pays sources for stories and doesn't apologize for doing so. Peter Kafka reported in his All Things Digital blog that Denton didn't hesitate to pay a student for his story about his involvement, though "unwittingly," in the notorious Balloon Boy case, in which parents falsely told police their child had accidentally been carried aloft in a hot-air balloon. Denton e-mailed Kafka about his practice: "A story is a story. We're not squeamish about the means. And the paroxysms of the j-school ethicists add to the satisfactions."

Participation in the News

At times, doing what seems to be the right, most humane thing might cost you your job as a journalist. When television reporter Alysia Sofios invited the survivors of the slaughter of the Wesson family in Fresno, Calif., to move into a room in her apartment, she did a good deed, but she also lost her job — at least as a news reporter. Even though she was covering the story, Sofios said she never regretted her decision. She later did feature reporting and wrote a book about the mass murder.

> **❞**If you're not involved in the community at all and you're totally neutralized, you end up not knowing enough about the community, not being able to get enough leads and so on in order to do your job.**❞**
>
> — Tony Case, quoting ethicist Louis W. Hodges
> in *Editor & Publisher*

Participation in the news can take other forms. *The Washington Post* issued a memo to staffers that barred any reporters who had participated in a pro-abortion rights march in Washington "from any future participation in coverage of the abortion issue." Don Kowet reported in *The Washington Times* that the same memo prohibited any "news room professional" from participating in such a protest.

But what about participating in a political campaign? And must a religion reporter be an atheist? According to Kowet, Richard Harwood, *Washington Post* ombudsman at the time, told a conference of journalists: "You have every right in the world to run for office, or participate in a political activity or lobbying activity. You don't have the 'right' to work for *The Washington Post*."

Nevertheless, some worry that uninvolved journalists will be uninformed journalists, an unconnected group of elitists. The problem is compounded when editors and even news organizations are involved in community projects. May the editor join the yacht club? May the station support the United Way? Is *New York Times* coverage of the Metropolitan Museum of Art influenced by the newspaper's generous support of that institution? May an HIV-positive journalist report on AIDS?

Finally, should journalists demand of themselves what they demand of politicians — full disclosure of their financial investments and memberships, as well as public knowledge of their personal tastes, preferences and lifestyles?

Advertising Pressure

It's likely you won't work long at a news organization before you realize some subjects are taboo to write about and others are highly encouraged. If you are lucky, you will work for a paper, station or magazine with a solid wall of separation between editorial and advertising, sometimes referred to as the separation of "church" and "state."

The Influence of Advertisers

However, in some places, advertising salespeople are allowed to peek over that wall and see what stories the publication or station is planning to run. That information might help sell some advertising. Some say, what could be wrong with that?

The next step is for the advertising department to climb over the wall and suggest that editorial do a story on some subject so that advertising can be sold.

And then the next step isn't too far away. Advertising begins to suggest or even to dictate what must and must not be printed in a newspaper or said on radio or shown on television or even displayed on a website. In print media, advertising may want the layout, design and type of their ads or sections to look like the publication's normal layout and design. Advertisers may also insist that the word "advertising" appear in small print or at the bottom of the page or be dropped altogether. Some advertisers prefer the term "sponsored by" as softening the pure sales pitch of their message.

Some newspapers have returned to an earlier practice of placing ads on their front pages. When the *Los Angeles Times* ran a front-page ad, some thought it could easily have been mistaken for a news story. Natalie Pompilio wrote in *American Journalism Review* that editor Russ Stanton was not happy and that a circulated petition called the ad deceptive and claimed it made "a mockery of our integrity and our journalistic standards."

"I long ago gave up the idea of front-page ads as sin," says Geneva Overholser, director of the School of Journalism at the USC Annenberg School for Communication & Journalism. Pompilio continues to quote her: "Now, when newspapers are desperately trying to figure out what their future is, it's time to figure out what the principles are. The rule is you don't try to deceive or fool readers. That's deeply offensive and breaks the bond with readers. That's not about the wall breaking down. That's about principles. It's about credibility."

Conflicts and Policies in Print Media

The Washington Post stopped short of holding salons giving politicians and other notables access to journalists in an "intimate and informal dinner and discussion 'entirely' off the record." But the practice is not uncommon. *The Atlantic Monthly* has brought journalists and policymakers together for off-the-record conversations for years, each meeting sponsored by a different corporation. Eric Alterman, a senior fellow at the Center for American Progress, quotes *Atlantic Monthly* Media Chairman David Bradley as saying such meetings are necessary because "the economic foundation beneath journalism is falling away." The article quotes Bradley further: "The imperative, as I see it, is to rebuild journalism on different financial pillars. One of them, and not inconsequential to us, is events—of all types."

The dangers in these practices are twofold. Those involved in these friendly chats are more likely to get friendly stories or, worse, no stories at all. Nonetheless, you would do well to get to know business executives and to have them get to know you. As Chapter 17 points out, sometimes a business lunch can help build trust.

Conflicts and Policies in Other Media

Radio newscasters generally separate themselves from the commercials. Yet many local radio newspeople also read commercials or at least do lead-ins for commercials. Television suffers the same advertising pressures as print, with the added problem that there are only so many minutes in a newscast. Is it ethical to cut a complicated international story to 90 seconds in order to make time for one more commercial?

In online publications, ads regularly break up the copy of news stories or pop up over news stories. There is no separation of ads from editorial content and no attempt to make any separation. Why don't the guidelines generally followed in print apply online? Note what the code of the American Society of Magazine Editors says:

> The same ASME principles that mandate distinct treatment of editorial content, advertisements, and special advertisements, and special advertising sections ("advertorials") in print publications also apply to online editorial projects bearing the names of print magazines or offering themselves as electronic magazines. The dynamic technology of electronic pages and hypertext links creates a high potential for reader confusion. Permitting such confusion betrays reader trust and undermines the credibility not only of the offending online publication or editorial product, but also of the publisher itself. It is therefore the responsibility of each online publication to make clear to its readers which online content is editorial and which is advertising, and to prevent any juxtaposition that gives the impression that editorial material was created for— or influenced by—advertisers.

The ASME code then goes on to spell out 10 specific ways to carry out these general guidelines.

The code of the American Society of Business Press Editors says simply:

> On all such papers, editors should ensure that a clear distinction is made between advertising and editorial content. This may involve type faces, layout/design, labeling and juxtaposition of the editorial materials and the advertisement.

The ASBPE code adds this important sentence: "Editors should directly supervise and control all links that appear with the editorial portion of the site."

Invasion of Privacy

Most journalists would cry out against an invasion of their own privacy. Yet many of them argue for a vague "right to know" when they report on others, especially if those others are public officials or public figures. The head-on collision of the right to know and the right to privacy will confront you every day of your reporting life. The Constitution mentions neither "right."

Crime Victims and Suspects

The most obvious and talked-about issue related to the right to privacy is naming crime survivors, especially rape and abuse survivors. The state of Florida legislated against publishing rape survivors' names, only to have the law struck down by a Florida district court. The U.S. Supreme Court has held that news agencies cannot be punished for publishing lawfully obtained information or information from a public record. Meanwhile, legislators in many states are looking for ways to close the records on rape and to punish police, hospitals, court clerks and other officials for releasing survivors' names.

So the issue comes down to a matter of ethics, and as usual, there is no complete agreement. Not publishing the name continues the stigma that somehow the rape was the survivor's fault. Publishing the survivor's name is heaping more suffering upon that person. Few news outlets would publish a rape survivor's name without the survivor's approval.

Juvenile Offenders

A similar problem arises with publishing the names of juvenile offenders. News agencies traditionally have not published them because they have held that juveniles are entitled to make juvenile mistakes, even if those mistakes are crimes. After all, juvenile court records are sealed. Again, the courts have upheld the right to publish juvenile offenders' names that are on the public record.

Some media critics, such as *The Fresno Bee*'s former editor and ombudsman Lynne Enders Glaser, have applauded the publication of the names of juvenile offenders. Glaser wrote: "It doesn't take a rocket scientist to figure out that more and more violent crimes are being committed by young people. And in increasing numbers, *Bee* readers have challenged the law and the media to stop protecting the identity of criminals because of their age."

However, in addition to the stigma forever attached to the juvenile offender's name and the embarrassment to his or her parents and family, some worry that in some groups a youth's notoriety will encourage other young people to violate the law. Others argue that shame will stop other juveniles from committing crimes.

Public Figures

Reporting on crime victims and juvenile offenders raises just two of the myriad privacy issues you will face. Journalists are still protected when writing about public officials and public figures—most of the time. But what about the children of politicians or celebrities?

For example, someone tried to sell the *New York Post* a videotape of a young woman snorting cocaine for $2 million. Why? She bore a resemblance to social worker Ashley Biden, the daughter of Vice President Joe Biden. Later the price dropped to a mere $400,000.

Websites exist that have files on nearly everyone. Some allow you to see what anyone has ever posted in a chat room. What may journalists use? Most everyone agrees that private e-mail is off-limits. But what about material sent to corporate intranets?

Photos and Video

Photographers and videographers must be especially concerned with privacy. How often and under what circumstances should they stick cameras into people's grieving and anxious faces?

With permission of the family, you may now photograph coffins containing deceased soldiers from the wars in Iraq and Afghanistan. However, when the Associated Press released a photo of a mortally wounded Marine in Afghanistan against the wishes of his parents, few newspapers carried it. The photo was part of a package of photos and articles that, according to AP, "offered vivid insights into how the battle was fought, and into (the Marine's) character and background."

Defense Secretary Robert M. Gates begged AP to defer to the wishes of the family. When they did not, he said, "Your lack of compassion and common sense in choosing to put this image . . . on the front page of multiple American newspapers is appalling."

Another issue is the manipulation of photos and video for greater effect. Neither print nor online publications have dealt well with this problem. *New York Times* photographer Fred Ritchin proposed using an icon to identify a digitally altered photo. But how will readers know how much the image has been altered? Will readers trust what they see?

Withholding Information

Is it ever permissible to withhold information from the news organization for which you work? If you are writing what you hope to be a best-selling book, may you save some "news" until after the book is published?

If you work as a journalist, are you ever off-duty? A doctor isn't. Doctors take an oath to treat the sick. If you, as a reporter, witness something newsworthy at a friend's house or at a party, do you tell your news director about it?

One reporter was fired when his boss discovered that he had attended a rock band's post-concert party where lines of cocaine were openly available. The reporter did not include this information in his coverage of the band. His defense was that if he reported the drug abuse, he would never get interviews or get close to other rock groups, and he would be finished as a music critic. His defense didn't work.

Is it ever permissible to withhold information from the public? If you learn that a political candidate is "sleeping around," would you withhold that information? Would you do so if you knew that if the information became public, the candidate would not be elected? Suppose after the election it became clear that you had had the information before the election but did not publish it?

When should you withhold information because the police ask you to or because it may jeopardize a case? Poynter Institute columnist Kelly McBride says, "Cutting deals to withhold information is dangerous. It should be done with great caution, much forethought and only in rare circumstances." She also warns that "we too readily agree with police and keep information from the public."

Incorrect and Incomplete Information

One situation in which some media organizations withhold information is when they have published incorrect information. Print publications that get the news wrong customarily inform readers of these mistakes in a corrections column. Some online news sites, however, act as if they never make mistakes. They simply post new stories with updated information. Surely journalists owe it to readers to tell them that the story has changed or has been updated with new information and how that was done. Such notice of correction or updating will not be done unless the news site has a clear policy requiring it.

A special problem for online journalists is the use of hyperlinks to external sites. Is raw data journalism? How much and how often may you use raw data, and with what warnings or interpretations? There's little doubt that readers appreciate links to source data so they can make judgments for themselves. At the same time, good websites help readers navigate that information. Journalists are still trying to find the right balance between the two.

PLAGIARISM

No one wants you to use his or her work as your own. No one condones **plagiarism**. The problem is defining exactly what constitutes plagiarism. Most of the time you know when you plagiarize even if no one else does.

If you read Jim Romenesko's blog on the Poynter website (www.poynter.org/medianews) — and you should — it seems that nearly every other day there is a story about some reporter admitting to plagiarism. Perhaps the greatest temptation is to plagiarize material published online. But you also might be tempted to lift words from your own newspaper's stories in the library or to take words out of a wire story. Some reporters have felt justified taking quotes and verbatim sentences from news releases and inserting them into their stories. You always serve your readers better when you get your own quotations. Don't even use your own material or stories or columns again without letting your readers know what you are doing.

Beware of Plagiarism!

Roy Peter Clark of the Poynter Institute gives these cautions about plagiarism:

- **Taking material verbatim (word for word) from the newspaper library.** Even when the material is from your own newspaper, it is still someone else's work. Put the idea in your own words or attribute it.
- **Using material verbatim from the wire services.** Sometimes writers take Associated Press material, add a few paragraphs to give some local flavor, and publish it as their own work. Even though this is a common practice, it is not right.
- **Using material from other publications.** Some blame electronic databases for a whole new explosion of plagiarism. Sometimes writers steal the research of others without attribution. And sometimes they use others' work without realizing it.
- **Using news releases verbatim.** The publicists are delighted, but you should be ashamed — especially if you put your name on the article. Rewrite it, except perhaps for the direct quotations, and use them sparingly. If you use a whole release, cite its source.
- **Using the work of fellow reporters.** If more than one reporter works on a story and you use a byline on top, put the other names at the end of the story.
- **Using old stories over again.** Columnists, beware! Your readers have a right to know when you are recycling your material. Some of them might catch you at it, and there goes your credibility.

Three Final Guidelines

- Be free of obligations to anyone or to any interest except the truth. The primary obligation of the journalist is to be free.

- Be fair. Even children know when you treat them unfairly or when they are being unfair. So do you.

- Remember good taste. Some actions and stories may be ethical, but they may be in bad taste.

Though many believe it is impossible, others believe sometimes writers plagiarize and have absolutely no idea they are doing so. Apparently, sometimes something one has read becomes so familiar that the reader later considers it his or her own. At times it might be a matter of sloppy note-taking. Note the cautions in the box on "Beware of Plagiarism!" by Roy Peter Clark of the Poynter Institute. See also Figure 22.2, which gives some guidelines on handling quotations and paraphrases so as to avoid unintentional plagiarism.

New York Times columnist Maureen Dowd admitted to lifting a paragraph from *Talking Points Memo* editor Josh Marshall's blog. Dowd said she never read the blog but was told the line by a friend of hers who didn't mention its source. It was actually two lines, and the wording was almost exactly the same.

Of course, many reporters say that nothing whatsoever excuses plagiarism. Columnist Lizette Rabe wrote, "Of all our journalistic sins, plagiarism might be the most unforgivable."

You must fight every impulse, question and check any doubts, and avoid any hint of plagiarism. And just as certainly you must resist temptations to make up people, to fabricate events and to invent quotations.

Online journalists have the same ethical concerns about plagiarism as other journalists. Plagiarism is still plagiarism, whether it happens in print or online. Just because you are not "in print" doesn't mean you can distort the truth. You also must always be aware that what is on the Internet is not yours, even though the

Plagiarism, Quotation and Paraphrase

Using an Attributed Quotation — Acceptable
The journalist fully identifies the source of the quotation and puts the source's exact words in quotation marks.

As William A. Henry III writes in *Time* magazine, reporters have a "First Amendment bond" with their readers. "Plagiarism," he writes, "imperils that bond, not because it involves theft of a wry phrase or piquant quote, but because it devalues meticulous, independent verification of fact — the bedrock of a press worth reading."

Paraphrasing a Quotation — Acceptable
The journalist identifies the source and restates the source's original idea in the journalist's own words.

William A. Henry III writes about the destructive effect on journalism that plagiarism can have, suggesting that it compromises the integrity of the reportorial research process.

Plagiarizing — Unacceptable
Even though the source is identified, the journalist errs by using the source's original words (in bold) without putting them in quotation marks. Simply using distinctive words and phrases without quotation marks can constitute plagiarism.

In writing about how plagiarism **imperils** a reporter's **bond** with readers, William A. Henry III says the practice goes beyond stealing **a wry phrase or piquant quote**. It **devalues the meticulous, independent verification of fact** that journalism depends on.

Plagiarizing — Unacceptable
The journalist has not identified the source and has not put the source's original words (in bold) in quotation marks. Changing the occasional word (for example, "striking" rather than "piquant") or the structure of a sentence is not sufficient to avoid plagiarism.

Plagiarism damages the reporter's **bond** with his or her readers. It goes beyond the **theft of a wry phrase or** striking **quote** and diminishes the foundation of journalism — **the meticulous, independent verification of facts**.

Figure 22.2
Writers sometimes misunderstand the nature of paraphrase. Simply altering a few words of a quotation, with or without attribution, often results in plagiarism rather than paraphrase.

very design of it allows you to download words and images. If you use someone else's words, put quotation marks around them and cite the source.

Although the Internet makes it easier to find and steal someone else's work, it also makes it easier to get caught doing so. Already there have been several cases

(Left) Mitch Albom, a popular author and columnist for the now defunct *Detroit Free Press*, wrote that two former Michigan State basketball players flew to St. Louis to see their team play in the NCAA Final Four and sat next to each other at the game. Albom wrote his column on Friday; the game was on Sunday. The two players never made it to St. Louis.

(Right) New York Times columnist Maureen Dowd admitted lifting a paragraph from a blog but said she never read the blog. She said she heard the words from a friend who didn't tell her the source.

where Web readers of local columnists or reviewers have turned in a writer for plagiarism.

It's hard to say what's worse—making up material or stealing it. Don't do either. Ever.

Suggested Readings

Christians, Clifford G., Mark Fackler, Peggy J. Kreshel, Robert H. Woods Jr., and Kathy Brittain McKee. *Media Ethics: Cases and Moral Reasoning*, 8th ed. Boston: Allyn & Bacon, 2008. The authors apply the Potter Box method of principled reasoning to dozens of journalism, advertising and public relations cases.

Christians, Clifford G., and Lee Wilkins. *Handbook of Media Ethics*. New York: Lawrence Erlbaum, 2008. Various scholars look at the intellectual history of mass media ethics over the past 25 years and summarize past and possible future research.

Day, Louis Alvin. *Ethics in Media Communications: Cases and Controversies*, 5th ed. Belmont, CA: Wadsworth, 2005. The book begins with a superb discussion of ethics and moral development, ethics and society, and ethics and moral reasoning, and goes on to discuss nearly every problem facing journalists, accompanied by actual cases.

Fletcher, Joseph. *Situation Ethics: The New Morality*. Louisville: Westminster John Knox Press, 1997. First published in 1966, this classic work on Christian situation ethics is for some a breath of fresh air, for others pure heresy.

Lambeth, Edmund B. *Committed Journalism: An Ethic for the Professional*, 2nd ed. Bloomington: Indiana University Press, 1992. Lambeth creates an ethics framework specific to the practice of journalism.

Wilkins, Lee, and Philip Patterson. *Media Ethics, Issues and Cases*, 6th ed. Burr Ridge: McGraw-Hill Humanities, Social Sciences & World Languages, 2010. This book offers an excellent discussion of journalism ethics with up-to-date cases.

Suggested Websites

www.ijnet.org
This is the website of the International Journalists' Network. Here you can find the codes of ethics of nearly every country or press association that has one. It also reports on the state of media around the world and contains media directories.

www.journalism.indiana.edu/resources/ethics
This site of the School of Journalism of Indiana University contains a large set of cases to help you explore ethical issues in journalism. The initial cases were published in "FineLine," a newsletter by Barry Bingham Jr.

www.ojr.org
This Web-based journal, produced at the Annenberg School for Communication & Journalism at the University of Southern California, contains a worthwhile section on ethics as well as links to other articles about journalism ethics.

www.spj.org/ethics.asp
The ethics site of the Society of Professional Journalists provides the SPJ code of ethics, ethics news, an ethics hotline, an SPJ ethics listserv and other ethics sources. It also provides ethics case studies.

Exercises

1. **Team project.** Your instructor will divide your class into three groups. The groups will do a computer search of articles discussing whether journalists should publish the names of (a) juvenile criminal suspects and defendants and (b) victims of rape and other sex crimes. One group will search for articles written six years ago; another group, for articles written three years ago; and the last group, for articles written one year ago.

   Share the articles within your group, where you identify and discuss the guidelines and attitudes suggested in the articles. As a group, write a summary of the attitudes you discovered and submit it to the instructor. The class will then meet to compare the groups' findings. Have attitudes on the subjects changed in the last six years? If so, how? Do you think attitudes have changed for the better? Explain.

2. You've learned that the daughter of a local bank president has been kidnapped. The kidnappers have not contacted the family, and police officials ask you to keep the matter secret for fear the abductors might panic and injure the child. Describe how a deontologist, a teleologist and a situation ethicist would make their decisions about how to handle the situation.

3. You're assigned to write a piece on a new bus service from your town to Chicago. Your editor tells you to ask the bus company for a free round-trip ticket. What would you do, and why?

4. For at least a year, on four or five occasions, reporters on your paper have heard rumors that a retirement home is negligent in its care of the elderly. Your editor asks you to get a job there as a janitor and report what you find. What would be your response, and why?

APPENDIX 1

Twenty Common Errors of Grammar and Punctuation

Grammar provides our language's rules of the road. When you see a green light, you proceed on faith that other drivers will not go through the red light. That's because drivers have a shared understanding of the rules of the road. Similarly, writers have a shared understanding of the grammar rules that ensure we understand what we are reading. Occasionally, as on the road, there is a wreck. We dangle participles, misplace modifiers and omit commas. If we write "Running down the street, his pants fell off," we are saying a pair of pants ran down a street. If we write "He hit Harry and John stopped him," the missing comma changes the meaning to "He hit Harry and John."

To say what you mean—to avoid syntactic wrecks—you must know the rules of grammar. We have compiled a list of 20 common errors that we find in our students' stories and in the stories of many professionals. Avoid them, and you'll write safely.

To take quizzes based on this list of 20 common errors of grammar and punctuation, go to Exercise Central for AP Style at http://bcs.bedfordstmartins.com/apexercises2. There you will find advice and activities that go beyond grammar; Exercise Central offers exercises on Associated Press style—the style that makes news writing distinctly journalistic.

1. Incorrect comma in a series in Associated Press style

Use commas to separate the items in a series, but do not put a comma before *and* or *or* at the end of the series unless the meaning would be unclear without a comma.

INCORRECT
COMMA BEFORE *AND*
The film was fast-paced, sophisticated, and funny.

CLEAR
WITHOUT COMMA
The film was fast-paced, sophisticated and funny.

UNCLEAR
WITHOUT COMMA
He demanded cheese, salsa with jalapeños and onions on his taco.

A comma before *and* would prevent readers from wondering if he demanded salsa containing both jalapeños and onions or if he wanted the salsa and the onions as two separate toppings.

COMMA NEEDED
BEFORE *AND*
He demanded cheese, salsa with jalapeños, and onions on his taco.

NO COMMA WITH
AND BEFORE *SALSA*
He demanded cheese and salsa with jalapeños and onions on his taco.

No comma with an *and* before *salsa* would mean salsa with both jalapeños and onions.

2. Run-on sentence

An independent clause contains a subject and a predicate and makes sense by itself. A run-on sentence—also known as a *comma splice*—occurs when two or more independent clauses are joined incorrectly with a comma.

RUN-ON   **John Rogers left the family law practice, he decided to become a teacher.**

You can correct a run-on sentence in several ways. Join the clauses with a comma and one of the coordinating conjunctions—*and, but, for, nor, or, yet* or *so*—or join the clauses with a semicolon if they are closely related. Use a subordinating conjunction such as *after, because, if* or *when* to turn one of the clauses into a dependent clause. Or rewrite the run-on as two separate sentences.

CORRECTING A RUN-ON WITH A COMMA AND A COORDINATING CONJUNCTION

John Rogers left the family law practice, for he decided to become a teacher.

CORRECTING A RUN-ON WITH A SEMICOLON

John Rogers left the family law practice; he decided to become a teacher.

CORRECTING A RUN-ON BY MAKING ONE INDEPENDENT CLAUSE A DEPENDENT CLAUSE

John Rogers left the family law practice when he decided to become a teacher.

CORRECTING A RUN-ON BY WRITING TWO SEPARATE SENTENCES

John Rogers left the family law practice. He decided to become a teacher.

3. Fragment

A fragment is a word group that lacks a subject, a verb or both, yet is punctuated as though it were a complete sentence. Another type of fragment is a word group that begins with a subordinating conjunction such as *because* or *when*, yet is punctuated as though it were a complete sentence.

FRAGMENTS   **After she had placed her watch and an extra pencil on the table.**

Without feeling especially sorry about it.

Correct a fragment by joining it to the sentence before or after it or by adding the missing elements so that the fragment contains a subject and a verb and can stand alone.

CORRECTING A FRAGMENT BY JOINING IT TO ANOTHER SENTENCE

After she had placed her watch and an extra pencil on the table, the student opened the exam booklet.

CORRECTING A FRAGMENT BY TURNING IT INTO A SENTENCE

She apologized to her boss for the outburst without feeling especially sorry about it.

4. Missing comma(s) with a nonrestrictive element

A nonrestrictive element is a word, phrase or clause that gives information about the preceding part of the sentence but does not restrict or limit the meaning of that part. A nonrestrictive element is not essential to the meaning of the sentence; you can delete it and still understand clearly what the sentence is saying. Place commas before and (if necessary) after a nonrestrictive element.

UNCLEAR	**The mayor asked to meet Alva Johnson a highly decorated police officer.**
CLEAR	**The mayor asked to meet Alva Johnson, a highly decorated police officer.**
UNCLEAR	**His wife Mary was there.**
CLEAR	**His wife, Mary, was there.**

5. Confusion of *that* and *which*

The pronoun *that* always introduces restrictive information, which is essential to the meaning of the sentence; do not set off a *that* clause with commas. The pronoun *which* introduces nonrestrictive, or nonessential, information; set off a nonrestrictive *which* clause with commas.

INCORRECT	**The oldest store in town, Miller and Co., that has been on Main Street for almost a century, will close this summer.**
CORRECT	**The oldest store in town, Miller and Co., which has been on Main Street for almost a century, will close this summer.**
INCORRECT	**The creature, which has been frightening residents of North First Street for the past week, has turned out to be a screech owl.**
CORRECT	**The creature that has been frightening residents of North First Street for the past week has turned out to be a screech owl.**

6. Missing comma after an introductory element

A sentence may begin with a dependent clause (a word group that contains a subject and a verb and begins with a subordinating conjunction such as *because* or *when*), a prepositional phrase (a word group that begins with a preposition such as *in* or *on* and ends with a noun or pronoun), an adverb such as *next* that modifies the whole sentence, or a participial phrase (a word group that contains a past or present participle, such as *determined* or *hoping*, that acts as an adjective). Use a comma to separate these introductory elements from the main clause of the sentence.

DEPENDENT CLAUSE	**After the applause had died down, the conductor raised his baton again.**
PREPOSITIONAL PHRASE	**Without a second thought, the chicken crossed the road.**
ADVERB	**Furthermore, the unemployment rate continues to rise.**

| PARTICIPIAL PHRASES | **Waiting in the bar, José grew restless.** |
| | **Saddened by the news from home, she stopped reading the letter.** |

Although it is always correct to use a comma after an introductory element, the comma may be omitted after some adverbs and short prepositional phrases if the meaning is clear:

Suddenly it's spring.

In Chicago it rained yesterday.

Always place a comma after two or more introductory prepositional phrases.

In May of last year in Toronto, Tom attended three conventions.

Here are more examples of prepositional phrases:

INCORRECT	**Shaking her head at the latest budget information the library administrator wondered where to find the money for new books.**
CORRECT	**Shaking her head at the latest budget information, the library administrator wondered where to find the money for new books.**
INCORRECT	**After a week of foggy, rainy mornings had passed he left Seattle.**
CORRECT	**After a week of foggy, rainy mornings had passed, he left Seattle.**

7. Missing comma(s) between coordinate adjectives

Adjectives are coordinate if they make sense when you insert *and* between them or place them in reverse order.

| COORDINATE ADJECTIVES | **The frightened, angry citizens protested the new policy.** |
| | **The frightened and angry citizens protested the new policy.** |

The adjectives make sense with *and* between them, so they are coordinate.

The angry, frightened citizens protested the new policy.

The adjectives make sense in reverse order, so they are coordinate. Separate coordinate adjectives with commas.

| INCORRECT | **The gaunt lonely creature was also afraid.** |
| CORRECT | **The gaunt, lonely creature was also afraid.** |

8. Missing comma(s) in a compound sentence

Two or more independent clauses—word groups containing a subject and a verb and expressing a complete thought—joined with a coordinating conjunction (*and, but, for, nor, or, yet* or *so*) form a compound sentence. Place a comma before the conjunction in a compound sentence to avoid confusion.

UNCLEAR	**She works as a pharmacist now and later she plans to go to medical school.**
CLEAR	**She works as a pharmacist now, <u>and</u> later she plans to go to medical school.**

9. Misused semicolon

In a compound sentence that has a coordinating conjunction joining the clauses, place a comma before the conjunction, not a semicolon.

INCORRECT	**The Chicago Cubs did not play in the World Series<u>; but</u> they did win their division.**
CORRECT	**The Chicago Cubs did not play in the World Series<u>, but</u> they did win their division.**

10. Misplaced or dangling modifier

Modifiers are words or phrases that change or clarify the meaning of another word or word group in a sentence. Place modifiers immediately before or directly after the word or words they modify. A *misplaced modifier* appears too far from the word or words it is supposed to modify in the sentence. A *dangling modifier* appears in a sentence that does not contain the word or words it is supposed to modify. A modifier at the beginning of a sentence should refer to the grammatical subject of the sentence.

MISPLACED MODIFIER	*subject* **<u>Having predicted a sunny morning,</u> the downpour surprised the meteorologist.**
CORRECT	*subject* **Having predicted a sunny morning, <u>the meteorologist</u> did not expect the downpour.**
DANGLING MODIFIER	*subject* **<u>Working in the yard,</u> the sun burned her badly.**
CORRECT	*subject* **Working in the yard, <u>she</u> became badly sunburned.**

11. Missing or misused hyphen(s) in a compound modifier

A compound modifier consists of two or more adjectives or an adjective-adverb combination used to modify a single noun. When a compound modifier precedes a noun, you should hyphenate the parts of the compound unless the compound consists of an adverb ending in *-ly* followed by an adjective.

INCORRECT	**His <u>over the top</u> performance made the whole film unbelievable.**
	The <u>freshly-printed</u> counterfeit bills felt like genuine dollars.
	The local chapter of Parents Without Partners will sponsor a <u>come as you are</u> party on Saturday.
CORRECT	**His <u>over-the-top</u> performance made the whole film unbelievable.**

The freshly printed counterfeit bills felt like genuine dollars.

The local chapter of Parents Without Partners will sponsor a come-as-you-are party on Saturday.

12. Missing or misused apostrophe

Do not confuse the pronoun *its*, meaning "belonging to it," with the contraction *it's*, meaning "it is" or "it has." Although the possessive form of a noun uses an apostrophe (*Tom's*), possessive pronouns never take apostrophes.

INCORRECT	**The car is lying on it's side in the ditch.**
	Its a blue 2009 Ford Taurus.
	That new car of her's rides very smoothly.
CORRECT	**The car is lying on its side in the ditch.**
	It's a blue 2009 Ford Taurus.
	That new car of hers rides very smoothly.

For clarity, avoid using the contraction ending in -*'s* to mean "has" instead of "is."

UNCLEAR	**She's held many offices in student government.**
CLEAR	**She has held many offices in student government.**

13. Incorrect pronoun case

A pronoun that is the subject of a sentence or clause must be in the subjective case (*I, he, she, we, they*). A pronoun that is the direct object of a verb, the indirect object of a verb, or the object of a preposition must be in the objective case (*me, him, her, us, them*). To decide whether a pronoun in a compound construction—two or more nouns or pronouns joined with *and* or *or*—should be subjective or objective, omit everything in the compound except the pronoun and see whether the subjective or objective case sounds correct.

INCORRECT	**He took my wife and I to dinner.**

Try that sentence without the first part of the compound, *my wife and*. It sounds incorrect.

CORRECT	**He took my wife and me to dinner.**
INCORRECT	**Her and her family donated the prize money.**

Try that sentence without the second part of the compound, *and her family*.

CORRECT	**She and her family donated the prize money.**

The pronouns *who* and *whom* often cause confusion. *Who* (or *whoever*) is subjective; *whom* (or *whomever*) is objective. If the pronoun appears in a question, answer the question using a pronoun (such as *I* or *me*) to determine whether to use the subjective or objective form.

INCORRECT	**Who does Howard want to see?**

Answering the question—*Howard wants to see me*—reveals that the pronoun should be objective.

CORRECT	**Whom does Howard want to see?**

When *who* or *whom* is not part of a question, it introduces a dependent clause. Determine the case of the pronoun in the clause by removing the clause from the sentence and replacing *who* or *whom* with *I* and *me* to see which form is correct.

INCORRECT	**She welcomed whomever knocked on her door.**

The dependent clause is *whomever knocked on her door*. Replacing *whomever* with *I* and *me* —*I knocked on her door; me knocked on her door*—reveals that the subjective form, *whoever*, is correct.

CORRECT	**She welcomed whoever knocked on her door.**

14. Lack of agreement between pronoun and antecedent

Pronouns must agree in number (singular or plural) and person (first, second or third) with their *antecedents*—the nouns or pronouns to which they refer. Do not shift, for example, from a singular antecedent to a plural pronoun, or from a third-person antecedent to a first- or second-person pronoun.

INCORRECT	**The class meets on Thursdays to check their work.**
CORRECT	**The class meets on Thursdays to check its work.**
	Class members meet on Thursdays to check their work.

15. Biased language

Avoid stereotypes and biased language. Take special care to avoid gender-specific pronouns.

BIASED	**A reporter must always check his work.**
ACCEPTABLE	**Reporters must always check their work.**
	If you are a reporter, you must always check your work.
BIASED	**Local politicians and their wives attended a dinner in honor of the visiting diplomat.**
ACCEPTABLE	**Local politicians and their spouses attended a dinner in honor of the visiting diplomat.**
BIASED	**Dr. Jones, a deaf-mute, spoke about the challenges she faced in medical school.**
ACCEPTABLE	**Dr. Jones, who is hearing-impaired, spoke about the challenges she faced in medical school.**

16. Lack of agreement between subject and verb

Subject and verb must agree in number. Use the form of the verb that agrees with a singular or plural subject. Be especially careful to identify the subject correctly when words separate subject from verb.

| INCORRECT | **The bag with the green stripes <u>belong</u> to her.** |
| CORRECT | **The <u>bag</u> with the green stripes <u>belongs</u> to her.** |

A compound subject with parts joined by *and* is always plural. When parts of a compound subject are joined by *or*, make the verb agree with the part of the compound closest to the verb.

INCORRECT	**A mystery writer and her daughter <u>lives</u> in the house by the river.**
CORRECT	**A mystery writer and her daughter <u>live</u> in the house by the river.**
INCORRECT	**Either Mike or his sisters <u>has</u> the spare key.**
CORRECT	**Either Mike or <u>his sisters</u> <u>have</u> the spare key.**

17. Incorrect complement with linking verb

A linking verb such as *be*, *appear*, *feel* or *become* links a subject with a word or words that identify or describe the subject. When the identifying word—called a *subject complement*—is a pronoun, use the subjective case for the pronoun.

| INCORRECT | **That was <u>him</u> on the telephone five minutes ago.** |
| CORRECT | **That was <u>he</u> on the telephone five minutes ago.** |

A word or words that describe the subject and follow a linking verb must be adjectives.

| INCORRECT | **She feels <u>terribly</u> about the things she said.** |
| CORRECT | **She feels <u>terrible</u> about the things she said.** |

18. Incorrect use of subjunctive mood

Conditions contrary to fact require a verb to be in the subjunctive mood. Apply this rule in stories about all pending legislation at all levels of government. Use the subjunctive mood in "that" clauses after verbs of wishing, suggesting and requiring; in other words, use the subjunctive in clauses, dependent or independent, that do not state a fact.

INCORRECT	**The bylaws require that he <u>declares</u> his candidacy by April 10.**
CORRECT	**The bylaws require that he <u>declare</u> his candidacy by April 10.**
INCORRECT	**The bill <u>will</u> require everyone to register for the draft at age 18.**
CORRECT	**The bill <u>would</u> require everyone to register for the draft at age 18.**

19. Wrong word

Wrong-word errors include using a word that sounds similar to, or the same as, the word you need but means something different (such as writing *affect* when you mean *effect*) and using a word that has a shade of meaning that is not what you intend (such as writing *slender* when you want to suggest *scrawny*). Check the dictionary if you are not sure whether you are using a word correctly.

INCORRECT	**Merchants who appear <u>disinterested</u> in their customers may lose business.**
CORRECT	**Merchants who appear <u>uninterested</u> in their customers may lose business.**
INCORRECT	**The guests gasped and applauded when they saw the <u>excessive</u> display of food.**
CORRECT	**The guests gasped and applauded when they saw the <u>lavish</u> display of food.**

20. Incorrect verb form

Every verb has five forms: a base form (*talk; see*), a present-tense form (*talks; sees*), a past-tense form (*talked; saw*), a present-participle form used for forming the progressive tenses (*is talking; is seeing*), and a past-participle form used for forming the passive voice or one of the perfect tenses (*has talked; has seen*).

Dropping the ending from present-tense forms and regular past-tense forms is a common error.

INCORRECT	**The police are <u>suppose</u> to protect the public.**
CORRECT	**The police are <u>supposed</u> to protect the public.**
INCORRECT	**The city <u>use</u> to tax all clothing sales.**
CORRECT	**The city <u>used</u> to tax all clothing sales.**

Regular verbs end in -*ed* in the past tense and past participle, but irregular verbs do not follow a set pattern for forming the past tense and past participle (for example, *saw, seen*), so those forms of irregular verbs are frequently used incorrectly. Look up irregular verbs if you are uncertain of the correct form.

INCORRECT	**The manager was not in the restaurant when it was robbed because he had <u>went</u> home early.**
CORRECT	**The manager was not in the restaurant when it was robbed because he had <u>gone</u> home early.**
INCORRECT	**The thieves <u>taked</u> everything in the safe.**
CORRECT	**The thieves <u>took</u> everything in the safe.**

Wire-Service Style Summary

Most publications adhere to rules of style to avoid annoying inconsistencies. Without a stylebook to provide guidance in such matters, writers would not know whether the word *president* should be capitalized when preceding or following a name, whether the correct spelling is *employee* or *employe* (dictionaries list both), or whether a street name should be *Twelfth* or *12th*.

Newspapers use the wire-service stylebooks to provide such guidance. For consistency, most newspapers follow rules in *The Associated Press Stylebook*. Many also list their own exceptions to AP style in a separate style sheet. There often are good reasons for local exceptions. For example, AP style calls for spelling out *First Street* through *Ninth Street* but using numerals for *10th Street* and above. But if a city has only 10 numbered streets, for consistency it might make sense to use *Tenth Street*.

This appendix is an abbreviated summary of the primary rules of wire-service style. This summary should be helpful even for those without a stylebook, but we provide it assuming that most users of this book have one. Why? Because this section includes only the rules used most frequently, arranged by topic to make them easier to learn. Only about 10 percent of the rules in a stylebook account for 90 percent of the wire-service style you will use regularly. You will use the rest of the rules about 10 percent of the time. It makes sense, therefore, to learn first those rules you will use most often.

ABBREVIATIONS AND ACRONYMS

Punctuation of Abbreviations

- Generally speaking, abbreviations of two letters or fewer have periods:
  600 B.C., A.D. 1066
  8 a.m., 7 p.m.
  U.N., U.S., R.I., N.Y.
  8151 Yosemite St.
  EXCEPTIONS: *AM radio, FM radio, 35 mm camera, the AP Stylebook, "LA smog,"*
  D-Mass., R-Kan., IQ, TV, EU
- Most abbreviations of three letters or more do not have periods:
  CIA, FBI, NATO
  mpg, mph
  EXCEPTION: *c.o.d.* for *cash on delivery* or *collect on delivery*

Symbols

- Always write out *%* as *percent* in a story, but you may use the symbol in a headline.
- Always write out *&* as *and* unless it is part of a company's formal name.
- Always write out *¢* as *cent* or *cents*.

- Always use the symbol *$* rather than the word *dollar* with any actual figure, and put the symbol before the figure. Write out *dollar* only if you are speaking of, say, the value of the dollar on the world market.

Dates

- Never abbreviate days of the week except in a table.
- Don't abbreviate a month unless it has a date of the month with it: *August 2011*; *Aug. 17*; *Aug. 17, 2011*.
- The five months spelled with five letters or fewer are never abbreviated: *March*; *April 20*; *May 13, 2011*; *June 1956*; *July of that year*.
- Never abbreviate *Christmas* as *Xmas*, even in a headline.
- *Fourth of July* is written out.

People and Titles

- Some publications still use courtesy titles (*Mr., Mrs., Ms., Miss*) on second reference in stories, although most seem to have moved away from them as sexist. Many publications use them only in quotations from sources. Others use them only in obituaries and editorials, or on second reference in stories mentioning a husband and wife. In the last case, some newspapers prefer to repeat the person's whole name or, especially in features, use the person's first name. The Associated Press suggests using a courtesy title when someone requests it, but most journalists don't bother to ask.
- Use the abbreviations *Dr.* (for a medical doctor, not someone with a Ph.D. degree), *Gov., Lt. Gov., Rep., Sen.* and *the Rev.*, as well as abbreviations of military titles, on first reference; then drop the title on subsequent references. Some titles you might expect to see abbreviated before a name are not abbreviated in AP style: *Attorney General, District Attorney, President, Professor, Superintendent.*
- Use the abbreviations *Jr.* and *Sr.* after a name on first reference if appropriate, but do *not* set them off by commas as you learned to do in English class.

Organizations

- Write out the first reference to most organizations in full rather than using an acronym: *National Organization for Women*. For *CIA* and *FBI*, however, the acronym may be used on the first reference.
- You may use well-known abbreviations such as *FCC* and *NOW* in a headline even though they would not be acceptable on first reference in the story.
- Do not put the abbreviation of an organization in parentheses after the full name on first reference. If an abbreviation is that confusing, don't use it at all but rather call the organization something like "the gay rights group" or "the bureau" on second reference.
- Use the abbreviations *Co., Cos., Corp., Inc.* and *Ltd.* at the end of a company's name even if the company spells out the word; do not abbreviate these words if followed by other words such as "of America." The abbreviations *Co., Cos.* and *Corp.* are used, however, if followed by *Inc.* or *Ltd.* (These latter two abbreviations are not set off by commas even if the company uses commas.)

- Abbreviate political affiliations after a name in the following way:
  Sen. Claire McCaskill, D-Mo., said . . .

Note the use of a single letter without a period for the party and the use of commas around the party and state.

- Never abbreviate the word *association*, even as part of a name.

Places

- Don't abbreviate a state name unless it follows the name of a city in that state:
  Nevada; Brown City, Mich.
- Never abbreviate the six states spelled with five or fewer letters or the two noncontiguous states:
  Alaska, Hawaii, Idaho, Iowa, Maine, Ohio, Texas, Utah
- Use the traditional state abbreviations, not the Postal Service's two-letter ones:
  Miss., not *MS*

  EXCEPTION: Use the two-letter postal abbreviations when a full address is given that includes a ZIP code.

  Here are the abbreviations used in normal copy:

Ala.	Fla.	Md.	Neb.	N.D.	Tenn.
Ariz.	Ga.	Mass.	Nev.	Okla.	Vt.
Ark.	Ill.	Mich.	N.H.	Ore.	Va.
Calif.	Ind.	Minn.	N.J.	Pa.	Wash.
Colo.	Kan.	Miss.	N.M.	R.I.	W. Va.
Conn.	Ky.	Mo.	N.Y.	S.C.	Wis.
Del.	La.	Mont.	N.C.	S.D.	Wyo.

- Use state abbreviations with domestic towns and cities unless they appear in the wire-service dateline list of cities that stand alone. Many publications add to the wire-service list their own list of towns well-known in the state or region. Use a nation's full name with foreign towns and cities unless they appear in the wire-service dateline list of cities that stand alone. Once a state or nation has been identified in a story, it is unnecessary to repeat the name unless clarity demands it. The lists of cities in the U.S. and the rest of the world that the wire services say may stand alone without a state abbreviation or nation are too lengthy to include here. Consult the appropriate stylebook. A handy rule of thumb is if it's an American city that has a major sports franchise, it probably stands alone. Likewise, if it's a foreign city most people have heard of, it probably stands alone.
- Don't abbreviate the names of thoroughfares if there is no street address with them:
  Main Street, Century Boulevard West.
- If the thoroughfare's name has the word *avenue, boulevard, street* or any of the directions on a map, such as *north* or *southeast*, abbreviate those words with a street address:
  1044 W. Maple St., 1424 Lee Blvd. S., 999 Jackson Ave.
- In a highway's name, always abbreviate *U.S.* but never abbreviate a state's name. In the case of an interstate highway, the name is written in full on first reference, abbreviated on subsequent ones:

U.S. 63 or *U.S. Highway 63, Massachusetts 2*
Interstate 70 (first reference), *I-70* (second reference)
- Never abbreviate *Fort* or *Mount.*
- Always use the abbreviation *St.* for *Saint* in place names. Exceptions: *Saint John* in New Brunswick, *Ste. Genevieve* in Missouri, *Sault Ste. Marie* in Michigan and Ontario.
- Abbreviate *U.S., U.K.* and *U.N.* as both nouns and adjectives.

Miscellaneous

- Use the abbreviation *IQ* (no periods) in all references to *intelligence quotient.*
- Abbreviate and capitalize the word *number* when followed by a numeral: *No. 1.*
- Use the abbreviation *TV* (no periods) as an adjective or noun as an abbreviated form of *television.*
- Use the abbreviation *UFO* in all references to an *unidentified flying object.*
- Spell out *versus,* except in court cases, which use *v* followed by a period.

CAPITALIZATION

- Proper nouns are capitalized; common nouns are not. Unfortunately, this rule is not always easy to apply when the noun is the name of an animal, food or plant or when it is a trademark that has become so well-known that people mistakenly use it generically.
- Regions are capitalized; directions are not:
We drove east two miles to catch the interstate out West.
- Adjectives and nouns pertaining to a region are capitalized: *Southern accent, a Southerner, a Western.*
- A region combined with a country's name is not capitalized unless the region is part of the name of a divided country: *eastern U.S., North Korea.*
- A region combined with a state name is capitalized only if it is famous: *Southern California, southern Colorado.*
- When two or more compound proper nouns are combined to share a word in common made plural, the shared plural is lowercased:
Missouri and Mississippi rivers, Chrisman and Truman high schools
- Government and college terms are not always consistent.
  - *College departments* follow the animal, food and plant rule: Capitalize only words that are already proper nouns in themselves: *Spanish department, sociology department.* By contrast, always capitalize *a specific government department,* even without the city, state or federal designator, and even if it's turned around with *of* deleted: *Police Department, Fire Department, State Department, Department of Commerce.*
  - *College and government committees* are capitalized if the formal name is given rather than a shorter, descriptive designation: *Special Senate Select Committee to Investigate Improper Labor-Management Practices; rackets committee.*
  - *Academic degrees* are spelled out and lowercased: *bachelor of arts degree, master's degree.* Avoid the abbreviations *Ph.D., M.A., B.A.,* etc., except in lists.
  - Always capitalize (unless plural or generic) *City Council* and *County Commission* (but alone, *council* and *commission* are lowercased). *Cabinet* is capitalized when

referring to advisers. *Legislature* is capitalized if the state's body is formally named that. *Capitol*, the building, is capitalized, but *capital*, the city, is not. Capitalize *City Hall* even without the city name but not *county courthouse* without the name of the county.

- Never capitalize *board of directors* or *board of trustees* (but formal governing bodies, such as *Board of Curators* and *Board of Education*, are capitalized). *Federal*, *government* and *administration* are not capitalized. *President* and *vice president* are capitalized only before a name and only when not set off with a comma:
  President Barack Obama
  Vice President Joe Biden
  the president, Barack Obama,
- *Military titles* (*Sgt., Maj., Gen.*) are capitalized before a name, as are *Air Force, Army, Marines* and *Navy* if referring to U.S. forces.
- *Political parties* are capitalized, including the word *party*: *Democratic Party, Socialist Party*. Be sure, however, to capitalize words such as *communist, democratic, fascist* and *socialist* only if they refer to a formal party rather than a philosophy.

● Some Internet and electronics terms are capitalized; some are not:
  - *Internet* and the *Net* (acceptable in later references) are capitalized.
  - *World Wide Web, the Web* and *Web page* are capitalized. But *website, webcam, webcast* and *webmaster* are lowercased.
  - *E-mail* and other similar terms (*e-book, e-commerce, e-business*) are lowercased.

● Some religious terms are capitalized; some are not:
  - *Pope* is lowercased except before a name: *the pope, Pope Benedict XIV.*
  - *Mass* is always capitalized.
  - Pronouns for *God* and *Jesus* are lowercased.

● Names of religious figures are capitalized: *Prophet Muhammad, Buddha.*
  - Names of holy books are capitalized: *Talmud, Quran* (preferred to *Koran*); *Bible* is capitalized when meaning the Holy Scriptures and lowercased when referring to another book: *a hunter's bible.*
  - Sacraments are capitalized if they commemorate events in the life of Jesus or signify his presence: *Holy Communion* but *baptism, communion.*

● Actual names of races and nationalities are capitalized, but color descriptions are not: *African-American* or *black* (for a black person of African descent who is from the U.S.), *American Indian* or *Native American* (but using the name of a specific tribe is preferable), *Arab, Asian* (preferred to *Oriental* for nations and people), *Caucasian, Cherokee, Chinese* (singular and plural), *French Canadian, Negro* (used only in names of organizations and quotations), *Japanese* (singular and plural), *white.*

● Formal titles of people are capitalized before a name, but occupational names are not: *President Barack Obama, Mayor Laura Miller, Coach Roy Williams, Dean Jaime Lopez, astronaut Ellen Ochoa, journalist Fred Francis, plumber Phil Sanders, pharmacist Roger Wheaton.*

Some titles are not easy to recognize: *managing editor, chief executive officer*. When in doubt, put the title behind the name, set off with commas, and use lowercase.

● Formal titles that are capitalized before a name are lowercased after a name:
  Barack Obama, president of the U.S.; Tom Leppert, mayor of Dallas
  Roy Williams, coach of the North Carolina Tar Heels; Fred Wilson, dean of students

- Formal titles that are abbreviated before a name are written out and lowercased if they follow a name:
  Gov. David Paterson; David Paterson, governor of New York
  Sen. Lindsey Graham of South Carolina; Lindsey Graham, senator from South Carolina
- The first word in a direct quotation is capitalized only if the quote meets both of these criteria:
  - It is a complete sentence. Don't capitalize a partial quote.
  - It stands alone as a separate sentence or paragraph, or it is set off from its source by a comma or colon.
- A question within a sentence is capitalized:
  My only question is, When do we start?

NUMBERS

- Cardinal numbers (numerals) are used in:
  - Addresses. Always use numerals for street addresses: *1322 N. 17th St.*
  - Ages. Always use numerals, even for days or months: *3 days old; John Burnside, 56.*
  - Aircraft and spacecraft: *F-4, DC-10, Apollo 11.* Exception: *Air Force One.*
  - Clothes sizes: *size 6.*
  - Dates. Always use the numeral alone—no *st, nd, rd* or *th* after it: *March 20.*
  - Decades: *the 1980s, the '80s.*
  - Dimensions: *5-foot-6-inch guard* (but no hyphen when the word modified is one associated with size: *3 feet tall, 10 feet long*).
  - Highways: *U.S. 63.*
  - Millions, billions and trillions: *1.2 billion, 6 million.*
  - Money. Always use numerals, but starting with a million, write like this: *$1.4 million.*
  - Numbers: *No. 1, No. 2.*
  - Percentages. Always use numerals except at the beginning of a sentence: *4 percent.*
  - Recipes. All numbers for amounts take numerals: *2 teaspoons.*
  - Speeds: *55 mph, 4 knots.*
  - Sports. Use numerals for just about everything: *8-6 score, 2 yards, 3-under-par, 2 strokes.*
  - Temperatures. Use numerals for all except *zero.* Below zero, spell out *minus: minus 6,* not *-6* (except in tabular data).
  - Times: *4 a.m., 6:32 p.m., noon, midnight, five minutes, three hours.*
  - Weights: *7 pounds, 11 ounces.*
  - Years: Use numerals without commas. A year is the only numeral that can start a sentence: *1988 was a good year.*
- Numerals with the suffixes *st, nd, rd* and *th* are used for:
  - Political divisions (precincts, wards, districts): *3rd Congressional District.*
  - Military sequences: *1st Lt., 2nd Division, 7th Fleet.*
  - Courts: *2nd District Court; 10th Circuit Court of Appeals.*
  - Streets after *Ninth.* For *First* through *Ninth,* use words: *Fifth Avenue, 13th Street.*
  - Amendments to the Constitution after *Ninth.* For *First* through *Ninth,* use words: *First Amendment, 16th Amendment.*

- Words are used for:
  - Numbers less than 10, with the exceptions noted above: *five people, four rules.*
  - Any number at the start of a sentence except for a year: *Sixteen years ago . . .*
  - Casual numbers: *about a hundred or so.*
  - Fractions less than one: *one-half.*
- Mixed numerals are used for fractions greater than one: *1½.*
- Roman numerals are used for a man who is the third or later in his family to bear a name and for a king, queen, pope or world war:
  John D. Rockefeller III, Queen Elizabeth II, Pope John Paul II, World War I

Suggested Website

http://apstylebook.com
The Associated Press provides its stylebook in several formats, including as a traditional printed book and as an iPhone application.

Society of Professional Journalists' Code of Ethics

PREAMBLE

Members of the Society of Professional Journalists believe that public enlightenment is the forerunner of justice and the foundation of democracy. The duty of the journalist is to further those ends by seeking truth and providing a fair and comprehensive account of events and issues. Conscientious journalists from all media and specialties strive to serve the public with thoroughness and honesty. Professional integrity is the cornerstone of a journalist's credibility. Members of the society share a dedication to ethical behavior and adopt this code to declare the society's principles and standards of practice.

SEEK TRUTH AND REPORT IT

Journalists should be honest, fair and courageous in gathering, reporting and interpreting information.

Journalists should:

- Test the accuracy of information from all sources and exercise care to avoid inadvertent error. Deliberate distortion is never permissible.
- Diligently seek out subjects of news stories to give them the opportunity to respond to allegations of wrongdoing.
- Identify sources whenever feasible. The public is entitled to as much information as possible on sources' reliability.
- Always question sources' motives before promising anonymity. Clarify conditions attached to any promise made in exchange for information. Keep promises.
- Make certain that headlines, news teases and promotional material, photos, video, audio, graphics, sound bites and quotations do not misrepresent. They should not oversimplify or highlight incidents out of context.
- Never distort the content of news photos or video. Image enhancement for technical clarity is always permissible. Label montages and photo illustrations.
- Avoid misleading re-enactments or staged news events. If re-enactment is necessary to tell a story, label it.

Sigma Delta Chi's first Code of Ethics was borrowed from the American Society of Newspaper Editors in 1926. In 1973, Sigma Delta Chi wrote its own code, which was revised in 1984 and 1987. The present version of the Society of Professional Journalists' Code of Ethics was adopted in September 1996.

- Avoid undercover or other surreptitious methods of gathering information except when traditional open methods will not yield information vital to the public. Use of such methods should be explained as part of the story.
- Never plagiarize.
- Tell the story of the diversity and magnitude of the human experience boldly, even when it is unpopular to do so.
- Examine their own cultural values and avoid imposing those values on others.
- Avoid stereotyping by race, gender, age, religion, ethnicity, geography, sexual orientation, disability, physical appearance or social status.
- Support the open exchange of views, even views they find repugnant.
- Give voice to the voiceless; official and unofficial sources of information can be equally valid.
- Distinguish between advocacy and news reporting. Analysis and commentary should be labeled and not misrepresent fact or context.
- Distinguish news from advertising and shun hybrids that blur the lines between the two.
- Recognize a special obligation to ensure that the public's business is conducted in the open and that government records are open to inspection.

MINIMIZE HARM

Ethical journalists treat sources, subjects and colleagues as human beings deserving of respect.

Journalists should:

- Show compassion for those who may be affected adversely by news coverage. Use special sensitivity when dealing with children and inexperienced sources or subjects.
- Be sensitive when seeking or using interviews or photographs of those affected by tragedy or grief.
- Recognize that gathering and reporting information may cause harm or discomfort. Pursuit of the news is not a license for arrogance.
- Recognize that private people have a greater right to control information about themselves than do public officials and others who seek power, influence or attention. Only an overriding public need can justify intrusion into anyone's privacy.
- Show good taste. Avoid pandering to lurid curiosity.
- Be cautious about identifying juvenile suspects or victims of sex crimes.
- Be judicious about naming criminal suspects before the formal filing of charges.
- Balance a criminal suspect's fair trial rights with the public's right to be informed.

ACT INDEPENDENTLY

Journalists should be free of obligation to any interest other than the public's right to know.

Journalists should:

- Avoid conflicts of interest, real or perceived.
- Remain free of associations and activities that may compromise integrity or damage credibility.

- Refuse gifts, favors, fees, free travel and special treatment, and shun secondary employment, political involvement, public office and service in community organizations if they compromise journalistic integrity.
- Disclose unavoidable conflicts.
- Be vigilant and courageous about holding those with power accountable.
- Deny favored treatment to advertisers and special interests and resist their pressure to influence news coverage.
- Be wary of sources offering information for favors or money; avoid bidding for news.

BE ACCOUNTABLE

Journalists are accountable to their readers, listeners, viewers and each other.
Journalists should:

- Clarify and explain news coverage and invite dialogue with the public over journalistic conduct.
- Encourage the public to voice grievances against the news media.
- Admit mistakes and correct them promptly.
- Expose unethical practices of journalists and the news media.
- Abide by the same high standards to which they hold others.

GLOSSARY

absolute privilege The right of legislators, judges and government executives to speak without threat of libel when acting in their official capacities.

absolutism The ethical philosophy that there is a fixed set of principles or laws from which there is no deviation. To the absolutist journalist, the end never justifies the means.

actual malice Reckless disregard for the truth. Actual malice is a condition in libel cases.

actual malice test Protection for reporters to write anything about an officeholder or candidate unless they know that the material is false or they recklessly disregard the truth.

add A printed page of copy following the first page. "First add" would be the second page of printed copy.

advance A report covering the subjects and issues to be dealt with in an upcoming meeting or event.

advertising department The newspaper department responsible for advertisements. Most advertising departments have classified and display ad sections.

aggregated journalism The viral dissemination of the news by members of the public, who often use social media for this purpose.

anchor A person in a television studio who ties together a newscast by reading the news and providing transitions from one story to the next.

anecdote An informative and entertaining story within a story.

angle The focus of, or approach to, a story. The latest development in a continuing controversy, the key play in a football game or the tragedy of a particular death in a mass disaster may serve as an angle.

annual percentage rate (APR) The annual cost of a loan expressed as a percentage. The basic method for computing this figure is set forth in the Truth in Lending Act of 1968.

antinomianism The ethical philosophy that recognizes no rules. An antinomian journalist judges each ethical situation on its own merits. Unlike the situation ethicist, the antinomian does not use love of neighbor as an absolute.

AP The Associated Press, a worldwide news-gathering cooperative owned by its subscribers.

APME Associated Press Managing Editors, an organization of managing editors and other editors whose papers are members of the Associated Press.

arithmetic mean See *average*.

assessed value The amount that a government appraiser determines a property is worth.

assistant news director The second in command in a television station news room.

attribution Identification of the source of the information or quotation.

average (1) A term used to describe typical or representative members of a group. (2) In mathematics, the result obtained when a set of numbers is added together and then divided by the number of items in the set.

background Information that may be attributed to a source by title but not by name; for example, "a White House aide said."

backgrounder A story that explains and updates the news.

beat A reporter's assigned area of responsibility. A beat may be an institution, such as a courthouse; a geographical area, such as a small town; or a subject, such as science. The term also refers to an exclusive story.

blog Short for *Web log*. A Web-based publication in which articles or diarylike entries, issued periodically, appear in reverse chronological order.

blotter   An old-fashioned term for the arrest sheet that summarizes the bare facts of an arrest. Today this information is almost always stored on a computer.

book   Assembled sheets of paper, usually newsprint, and carbon paper on which reporters once prepared stories. Books are not used with modern computerized processes.

Boolean search command   The language of searching computer databases in which the search is narrowed through the use of operators such as AND, OR or NOT.

bureau   A news-gathering office maintained by a newspaper somewhere other than its central location. Papers may have bureaus in the next county; in the state capital; in Washington, D.C.; or in foreign countries.

byline   A line identifying the author of a story.

calendar year   The 12-month period from January through December.

change of venue   The transfer of a court proceeding to another jurisdiction for prosecution. This often occurs when a party in a case claims that local media coverage has prejudiced prospective jurors.

chat room   An online site for meeting and communicating by text and sometimes by webcam (a video camera connected to a computer).

circulation department   The department responsible for distribution of the newspaper.

citizen journalism   A new form of media in which citizens actively participate in gathering and writing information, often in the form of news. Also called *participatory journalism.*

city editor   The individual (also known as the *metropolitan,* or *metro, editor*) in charge of the city desk, which coordinates local news-gathering operations. At some papers the desk also handles regional and state news from its own reporters.

clip   A story clipped from a newspaper.

closed-ended question   A direct question designed to draw a specific response; for example, "Will you be a candidate?"

community portal   A website designed as a general entry point for Internet users in a city and its nearby suburbs.

compound interest   Interest paid on the total of the principal (the amount borrowed) and the interest that has already accrued.

conditional privilege   See *qualified privilege.*

constant dollars   Money numbers adjusted for inflation.

Consumer Price Index   A tool used by the government to measure the rate of inflation. CPI figures, reported monthly by the Bureau of Labor Statistics of the U.S. Department of Labor, compare the net change in prices between the current period and a specified base period. Reporters should use these data to accurately reflect the actual costs of goods and services.

content aggregator   A company that collects and distributes news from traditional media sources but does little or no independent news-gathering.

contextual advertising   Advertising on a website directed to likely users of that site according to demographic profiles.

contributing editor   A magazine columnist who works under contract and not as an employee of the magazine.

control   The process of structuring an experiment so that the only forces affecting the outcome are the variables you are observing.

convergence   A term defined in different ways by different people in the media industry but generally used to describe the coordination of print, broadcast and online reporting in a news operation.

copy   What reporters write. A story is a piece of copy.

copy desk   The desk at which final editing of stories is done, headlines are written and pages are designed.

copy editor   A person who checks, polishes and corrects stories written by reporters. Usually copy editors write headlines for these stories; sometimes they decide how to arrange stories and pictures on a page.

cover   To keep abreast of significant developments on a beat or to report on a specific event. The reporter covering the police beat may be assigned to cover a murder.

cutline   The caption that accompanies a newspaper or magazine photograph. The term dates from the days when photos were reproduced with etched zinc plates called *cuts*.

deadline   The time by which a reporter, editor or desk must have completed scheduled work.

deep background   Information that may be used but that cannot be attributed to either a person or a position.

delayed-identification lead   The opening paragraph of a story in which the "who" is identified by occupation, city, office or any means other than by name.

deontelics   Ethical thinking that considers both duties and ends.

deontological ethics   The ethics of duty.

desk   A term used by reporters to refer to the city editor's or copy editor's position, as in "The desk wants this story by noon."

desk assistant   An entry-level position in television news rooms. Desk assistants handle routine news assignments, such as monitoring wire services and listening to police scanners.

developing story   A story in which newsworthy events occur over several days or weeks.

dialogue   A conversation between two or more people, neither of whom normally is the reporter.

direct quote   A quote inside quotation marks that captures the exact words of the speaker.

documentary   In-depth coverage of an issue or event, especially in broadcasting.

e-book reader   An electronic device whose primary function is the digital storage of books, though most e-book readers also offer other features.

editor   The top-ranking individual in the news department of a newspaper, also known as the *editor in chief*. The term may refer as well to those at any level who edit copy.

editorial department   The news department of a newspaper, responsible for all content of the newspaper except advertising. At some papers this term refers to the department responsible for the editorial page only.

editorialize   To inject the reporter's or the newspaper's opinion into a news story or headline. Most newspapers restrict opinion to analysis stories, columns and editorials.

editorial page editor   The individual in charge of the editorial page and, at larger newspapers, the op-ed page. See also *op-ed page*.

executive producer   The television executive with overall responsibility for the look of the television newscast.

explanatory journalism   Journalism that explains not only what happened but how. The use of this technique often distinguishes professional journalism from citizen journalism.

e-zine   Magazines and newsletters distributed by e-mail.

fair comment and criticism   Opinion delivered on the performance of someone in the public eye. Such opinion is legally protected as long as reporters do not misstate any of the facts on which they base their comments or criticism, and it is not malicious.

feature   A story that includes little or no breaking news.

field experiment   A research technique in which the reporter deliberately takes some action to observe the effects. For example, a perfectly tuned automobile could be taken to several repair shops to find out if the mechanics would invent problems that required fixing.

field producer   A behind-the-scenes television reporter who often does much of the field work for a network's on-camera correspondents.

fiscal year   Any 12-month period used to calculate annual revenues and expenditures.

flat-file database   A simple database program that allows users to keep track of almost any type of data. A simple address book is an example.

focus structure   A story organization that begins with the story of an individual person, broadens to include a trend or issue, and then brings the issue back to the person featured at the beginning of the story.

follow   A story supplying further information about an item that has already been published; *folo* is an alternate spelling.

foreshadowing   A technique that teases readers with material coming later in the story as a way of encouraging them to keep reading.

Freedom of Information Act   A law passed in 1966 to make it easier to obtain information from federal agencies. The law was amended in 1974 to improve access to government records.

free-form database   A database that is not limited in structure and allows almost any type of content to be included.

free-press/fair-trial controversy   The conflict between a defendant's right to an impartial jury and a reporter's responsibility to inform the public.

full-text database   A database that permits searches of any text in an article.

futures file   A collection—filed according to date—of newspaper stories, letters, notes and other information to remind editors of stories to assign. See also *tickler*.

gatekeepers   Editors who determine what readers or viewers read, hear and see.

Golden Mean   A moral position, derived from Aristotle, that avoids extremes.

graf   A shortened form of *paragraph*, as in "Give me two grafs on that fire."

graphics editor   Usually, the editor responsible for all nonphotographic illustrations in a newspaper, including information graphics, maps and illustrations.

handout   See *news release*.

hard lead   A lead that reports a new development or newly discovered fact. See also *soft lead*.

hard news   Coverage of the actions of government or business; or the reporting of an event, such as a crime, an accident or a speech. The time element often is important. See also *soft news*.

HTML   The abbreviation for *hypertext markup language*, the coding language used to create text on the Web.

hyperlink   A connection between two places on the Web.

hyperlocal   Information that is intensely local in its emphasis.

hypermedia   Web links among audio, video and pictures.

hypertext   A Web document coded in HTML.

hypothesis   In investigative reporting, the statement a reporter expects to be able to prove, as in, "The mayor took a bribe from that massage parlor." In an experiment, the statement of what a researcher hopes to find.

immediate-identification lead   The opening paragraph of a story in which the "who" is reported by name.

income tax An annual tax on an individual's income or a business's profit. It is levied by the federal government and in some cases by state and local governments. It is calculated as a percentage.

indirect quotation A paraphrase of the speaker's words. Because it is a paraphrase, the words are not in quotation marks.

inflation A term that describes the rising cost of living as time goes by. See also *Consumer Price Index.*

infomedium Short for *information medium,* a term coined to represent the merger of the Internet, television, wireless and other technologies as the medium of the future.

information graphic A visual representation of data.

interest (1) A measure of the cumulative effect of all the news values. The more elements of each of the six news values that appear in the story, the more interesting that story will be to readers. (2) Money earned or paid on a base amount and calculated as a percentage.

Internet The vast network that links computers around the world.

interviewing Having conversations with sources.

invasion of privacy Violation of a person's right to be left alone.

inverted pyramid The organization of a news story in which information is arranged in descending order of importance.

investigative piece A story intended to reveal material not generally known.

investigative reporting The pursuit of information that has been concealed, such as evidence of wrongdoing.

IRE Investigative Reporters and Editors, a group created to exchange information and investigative reporting techniques. IRE has its headquarters at the University of Missouri School of Journalism.

lay out (v.) To prepare page drawings to indicate where stories and pictures are to be placed in the newspaper.

layout (n.) The completed page drawing, or page dummy.

lead (1) The first paragraph or first several paragraphs of a newspaper story (sometimes spelled *lede*). (2) The story given the best display on Page One. (3) A tip.

lead-in An introduction to a filmed or recorded excerpt from a news source or from another reporter.

legacy media Traditional media outlets such as newspapers, magazines, broadcast television and the like.

libel Damage to a person's reputation caused by a false written statement that brings the person into hatred, contempt or ridicule or injures his or her business or occupational pursuit.

line-item budget A budget showing each expenditure on a separate line.

macroediting Editing for the big picture, such as whether the story is missing anything and whether it is organized properly.

maestro The leader of a news-gathering team. Reporters, copy editors, editors and graphic designers work with a maestro to create special reports.

managing editor The individual with primary responsibility for the day-to-day operation of the news department.

margin of error The difference between results from the entire population (all registered voters in your county, for example) and a random sample of the population. It is usually expressed as plus or minus x points. The x depends on the size of the sample. The larger the sample, the smaller the margin of error.

media fragmentation A proliferation of media outlets leading to smaller audiences for traditional media and a resulting decline in the ability to target audiences.

median The middle number in a series arranged in order of magnitude; it is often used when an average would be misleading. (If the series has an even number of items, the median is the average of the two "middle" numbers.) See also *average*.

metadata Keywords attached to an online story, but not necessarily within it, that help search engines index material for display. See also *search-engine optimization*.

microediting Editing for details such as grammar, punctuation and spelling.

micropayment A small payment for reading an article on the Web.

millage rate The tax rate on property, determined by the government.

moblog A type of Internet blog in which the user publishes blog entries directly to the Web from a mobile phone or other mobile device.

more A designation used at the end of a page of copy to indicate that one or more pages follow.

morgue The news room library, where published stories, photographs and resource material are stored for reference.

multimedia assignment desk The news desk in a converged news room where the efforts of print, broadcast and online reporters are coordinated. See also *convergence*.

multimedia editor An editor responsible for coordinating or producing news content for various media.

multimedia journalist A journalist capable of producing content in more than one medium, such as radio and newspapers.

multiple-element lead The opening paragraph of a story that reports two or more news-worthy elements.

narration The telling of a story, usually in chronological order.

negligence test The legal standard that requires reporters gathering facts and writing a story to use the same degree of care that any reasonable individual would use in similar circumstances.

network correspondent A television reporter who delivers the news on-camera. Network correspondents do not necessarily do the actual news-gathering for their stories.

new media Emerging forms of computer-delivered news.

news conference An interview session, also called a *press conference*, in which someone submits to questions from reporters.

news director The top news executive of a local television station.

news editor The supervisor of the copy desk. At some newspapers, this title is used for the person in charge of local news-gathering operations.

news narrative A story that sums up the news in the first paragraph or two and then describes events chronologically rather than ranking them in descending order of importance.

news release An item that is sent out by a group or individual seeking publicity. Also called a *handout* or *press release*.

news story A story, often written in inverted pyramid style, that emphasizes the facts.

news value The measure of how important or interesting a story is.

niche A specific subset of a part of a general audience. A magazine or website directed at weavers or bow hunters would be a niche publication.

nominal dollars Money numbers not adjusted for inflation.

not for attribution An expression indicating that information may not be ascribed to its source.

nut paragraph   A paragraph that summarizes the key element or elements of a story. Nut paragraphs usually are found in stories not written in inverted pyramid form. Also called a *nut graf.*

off-camera reporter   A reporter who gathers news for television but does not report on the air.

off the record   An expression that usually means "Don't quote me." Some sources and reporters use it to mean "Don't print this." Phrases with similar, and equally ambiguous, meanings are "not for attribution" and "for background only."

online editor   The editor of a website for a newspaper or television station.

online media   See *new media.*

op-ed page   The page opposite the editorial page in a printed newspaper, or the corresponding opinion pages in an online publication, frequently reserved for columns, letters to the editor and personality profiles.

open-ended question   A question that permits the respondent some latitude in the answer; for example, "How did you get involved in politics?"

open-meetings law   A state or federal law, often called a *sunshine law,* guaranteeing public access to meetings of public officials.

open-records law   A state or federal law guaranteeing public access to many—but not all—kinds of government records.

parallelism   A technique of presenting ideas in similar grammatical forms.

paraphrase   A technique that digests, condenses or clarifies a quotation to convey the meaning more precisely or succinctly than the speaker's words do; an indirect quotation. Quotation marks are not used with paraphrases.

participant observation   A research technique in which the reporter joins in the activity he or she wants to write about.

payola   Money or gifts given in the expectation of favors from journalists.

per capita   A Latin term meaning "by heads." A per capita amount is determined by dividing a total figure—such as a budget—by the number of people to which it applies.

percentage   A mathematical way to express the portion of a whole; literally, a given part of every hundred. A percentage is determined by taking the number of the portion, dividing by the number of the whole and moving the decimal point right two places. For example, 15 divided by 30 equals .50, or 50 percent.

percentage change   A number that explains by how much something goes up or down.

percentage point   A unit of measure used to express the difference between two percentages. For example, the difference between 25 percent and 40 percent is 15 percentage points.

photo editor   The individual who advises editors on the use of photographs in the newspaper. The photo editor also may supervise the photography department.

piece   See *story.*

plagiarism   Using any part of another person's writing and passing it off as your own.

play   A shortened form of *display.* A good story may be played at the top of Page One; a weak one may be played inside.

podcasting   A method of distributing multimedia files, usually audio or video, to mobile devices or personal computers so that consumers can listen or watch on demand. The term is derived from Apple Computer's iPod, but podcasts may be received by almost any music player or computer.

population   In scientific language, the whole group being studied. Depending on the study, the population may be, for example, voters in St. Louis, physicians in California or all residents of the U.S.

press   (1) The machine that prints newspapers. (2) Also a synonym for *journalism*, as in the phrase "freedom of the press." Sometimes used to denote print journalism, as distinguished from broadcast journalism.

press box   The section of a stadium or arena set aside for reporters.

press conference   See *news conference*.

press release   See *news release*.

primary source   A person who witnesses or participates in an event, or an authentic document from an event.

principal   The amount of money borrowed.

principled reasoning   Reasoning that reflects ethical principles.

Privacy Protection Act   A law passed in 1980 that requires federal, state and local enforcement officers to get a subpoena to obtain documents from reporters and news rooms, rather than a search warrant—unless the reporter is involved in a crime or immediate action is needed to prevent bodily harm, loss of life or destruction of the material.

privilege   A defense against libel that claims journalists have the right to repeat what government officials say or do in their official capacities.

production department   The department of a newspaper that transforms the work of the news and advertising departments into the finished product. The composing room and pressroom are key sections of this department.

profile   A story intended to reveal the personality or character of an institution or person.

program budget   A budget that clearly shows what each agency's activities cost.

property tax   An annual tax, figured as a percentage, on the value of houses, buildings and land that is usually levied by a local or state government.

proportion   An explanation that relates one specific number to another or to the quantity or magnitude of a whole.

public figure   A person who has assumed a role of prominence in the affairs of society and who has persuasive power and influence in a community or who has thrust himself or herself to the forefront of a public controversy. Courts have given journalists more latitude in reporting on public figures than on private citizens.

public information utility   A commercial online service such as CompuServe.

public journalism   The new (or rediscovered) approach to journalism that emphasizes connections with the community rather than separation from it. Among the newspapers best known for practicing public journalism are *The Wichita (Kan.) Eagle* and *The Charlotte (N.C.) Observer*.

publisher   The top-ranking executive of a newspaper. This title often is assumed by the owner, although chains sometimes designate the top local executive as publisher.

Pulitzer Prize   The most prestigious of journalism awards. It was established by Joseph Pulitzer and is administered by Columbia University.

qualified privilege   The right of journalists to report what government officials say or do in their official capacities if the report is full, fair and accurate. Also called *conditional privilege*.

quote   As a noun, a source's exact words, as in "I have a great quote here." As a verb, to report a source's exact words inside quotation marks.

randomization The mathematical process used to ensure that every member of a population being studied has an equal chance of being chosen for questioning or observation. See also *poll.*

rate The amount or degree of something measured in relation to a unit of something else or to a specified scale. In statistics, rate often expresses the incidence of a condition per 100,000 people, such as a murder or suicide rate. Rate also can reflect the speed at which something is changing, such as inflation or the percentage increase in a budget each year.

records column A regular newspaper feature that contains such information as routine police and fire news, births, obituaries, marriages and divorces.

relational database A database program that permits users to determine relationships between two or more dissimilar databases. For example, a relational database program would enable a reporter to compare one database of people convicted of drunken driving with another database of school-bus drivers. The result would show how many bus drivers had drunken-driving convictions.

relevance The impact of a story as measured by the number of readers it affects and how seriously it affects them.

reporter A person whose job is to gather and write the news for a publication or a broadcast outlet.

roundup A story that includes a number of related events. After a storm, for example, a reporter might do a roundup of accidents, power outages and other consequences of the storm.

RSS Short for *really simple syndication*, a form of content distribution over the Internet that relies on a common markup language, XML (extensible markup language).

sales tax A tax, figured as a percentage, on the price of goods. It is usually levied by a local or state government and is paid by the consumer to the retailer at the time of purchase.

sample A portion of a group, or population, chosen for study as representative of the entire group.

search-engine optimization The practice of writing stories and headlines to increase the likelihood that search engines such as Google will index them. Behind-the-scenes metadata also influence search-engine optimization.

secondary source A source who talked to a witness, such as a public safety official investigating a crime. The witness would be a primary source.

second-cycle story A second version of a story already published, also called a *second-day story*. It usually has new information or a new angle.

senior editor A person who edits a section of a major magazine.

senior writer A title reserved for a magazine's best and most experienced reporters.

series Two or more stories on the same or related subjects, published on a predetermined schedule.

service journalism An aspect or type of journalism that recognizes usefulness as one of the criteria of news. Taking into consideration content and presentation, service journalism presents useful information in a usable way—for instance, by placing key information in a list or graphic box.

setup In broadcasting, an introductory statement to pique the interest of listeners or viewers. In written accounts, the material between the opening of a narrative story and the body. It generally consists of the transition to the theme paragraph, the nut paragraph, and, when appropriate, the "so what" and "to be sure" statements and foreshadowing.

shield law   Legislation giving journalists the right to protect the identity of sources.

shovelware   Stories posted on the Web exactly as they appeared in print.

show producer   A television news specialist who produces individual newscasts and who reports to the executive producer.

sidebar   A secondary story intended to be run with a major story on the same topic. A story about a disaster, for example, may have a sidebar that tells what happened to a single victim.

simple interest   Interest paid on the principal (the amount borrowed).

situation ethics   The philosophy that recognizes that a set of rules can be broken if circumstances indicate that the community would be served better by breaking them. For example, a journalist who generally believes that deceiving a news source is unethical may nevertheless be willing to conceal his or her identity to infiltrate a group operating illegally.

slug   A word that identifies a story as it is processed through the newspaper plant or at a broadcast news station. A slug is usually placed in the upper left-hand corner of each take of a newspaper story. See also *take.*

smart phone   A mobile phone with an operating system that expands the uses from just talking and texting to connecting to the Web and using a variety of applications.

sniff   The preliminary phase of an investigation.

social networking   The practice of connecting with others for business or social purposes. Social networking sites make it easy for individuals to connect with others who have similar interests or goals.

soft lead   A lead that uses a quote, anecdote or other literary device to attract the reader. See also *hard lead.*

soft news   Stories about trends, personalities or lifestyles. The time element usually is not important. See also *hard news.*

sound bite   An audio recording that accompanies a story in radio or television news or, more recently, that is available even on newspaper websites as a supplement to the printed product.

sources   People or records from which a reporter gets information. The term often is used to describe people, as opposed to documents.

spot news   A timely report of an event that is unfolding at the moment.

spreadsheet program   A computer program used for analyzing numbers. It is often used to track changes in budgets and expenditures.

story   The term most journalists use for a newspaper article. Another synonym is *piece,* as in "I saw your piece on the mayor." A long story may be called a *takeout* or a *blockbuster.*

strategic communication   A "new" name for public relations (sometimes including advertising) that emphasizes the stronger role of professionals in these fields in conducting research, solving problems and making decisions.

stylebook   A book of rules on grammar, punctuation, capitalization and abbreviation in newspaper text. The AP and UPI publish similar stylebooks that are used by most papers.

substantial truth   The correctness of the essential elements of a story.

summary lead   The first paragraph of a news story in which the writer presents a synopsis of two or more events rather than focusing on any one of them.

sunshine law   See *open-meetings law.*

take   A page of printed copy for newspaper use.

teleological ethics   The ethics of final ends.

teleprompter   A mechanical or electronic device that projects broadcast copy next to the television camera lens so that a newscaster can read it while appearing to look straight into the lens.

30   A designation used to mark the end of a newspaper story. The symbol # is an alternate designation.

tickler   A file of upcoming events kept on paper or stored electronically at the assignment desks of most news organizations. See also *futures file*.

tie-back   (1) The sentence or sentences relating a story to events covered in a previous story. Tie-backs are used in follow-up or continuing stories or in parts of a series. (2) The technique of referring to the opening of a story in the story's ending.

"to be sure" paragraph   In stories focusing on one person or perspective, a statement reflecting the opinions of those who disagree with the person featured, as in "To be sure, not everyone agrees."

truth   Actuality or reality. Truth is the best defense against libel.

undercover reporting   A technique in which a reporter pretends to be someone else in order to gain access to otherwise unobtainable information.

universal desk   A copy desk that edits material for all editorial departments of a newspaper.

update   A type of follow that reports on a development related to an earlier story. See also *follow*.

UPI   United Press International, a worldwide news-gathering organization that is privately owned.

URL   Short for *uniform resource locator*, the address of an Internet site.

usefulness   A quality of news that increases the impact of the story. The story has information that readers can use to act on, such as notification of a meeting before it occurs.

variable   In an experiment, one of the elements being observed. The *independent variable* is what is thought to be a cause; the *dependent variable* is the effect of that cause.

videographer   A television camera operator.

videoprompter   See *teleprompter*.

viral marketing   The practice of using social networking media such as Facebook or MySpace to seed links to a more traditional media form, thus increasing traffic to the other medium.

webcast   A video report available on a website.

website   A location on the World Wide Web, the Internet service that connects hypertext data.

wiki   A type of website that allows users to add or alter content. Wikipedia, for example, is a user-written and user-updated encyclopedia.

Wikinews   A wiki on which users can post or update information in news format.

wrap-up   (1) The completion of commentary that comes at the end of a taped segment in broadcasting. (2) A strong ending to a report.

"you" lead   The first paragraph of a story, written using the informal, second-person pronoun "you."

Acknowledgments

Associated Press. Narragansett, RI (AP) — June 9, 2006. Excerpt from "The wedding guests in-cluded drug suspects. . . ." Washington (AP) — November 15, 2006. Excerpt from "Urban students do worse than nation in science." Jefferson City, MO (AP) — September 28, 2009. Excerpt from "Couple found shot dead in Jefferson City." Quito, Ecuador (AP) — September 28, 2009. Excerpt from "Ecuador's Indian Group Protests Water, Mining Laws." *The Associated Press.* Reprinted with permission. All rights reserved.

Anne Barnard, *New York Times* Staff Writer. "A Stirring in St. Albans: Emboldened by '08 Race to Roil Waters at Home" from *The New York Times*, Metro Section, September 4, 2009 issue, Section A, Page 1. Copyright © 2009 The New York Times. All rights reserved. Used by permission and protected by the Copyright Laws of the United States. The printing, copying, redistribution, or retransmission of the Material without express written permission is prohibited.

Devlin Barrett and Pete Yost. Washington (AP) — October 20, 2009. "Scientist appears in court in secrets case." Copyright © 2009 The Associated Press. Reprinted by permission. All rights reserved.

Robert Bianco, *USA Today.* Excerpt from "TV coverage gives everyone a seat on the Mall" from *USA Today*, Life Section, January 20, 2009, Page B1. Copyright © 2009. USA Today. January 20, 2009. Reprinted with permission.

Roy Peter Clark. "Beware of Plagiarism!" Reprinted with permission of The Poynter Institute.

Committee of Concerned Journalists. "Statement of Shared Purpose." www.concernedjournalists.org. August 8, 2006. Copyright © 2006. Reprinted by permission of Committee of Concerned Journalists.

Norman Draper. "U Earns C Average in Student-Access Report" from *Minneapolis Star Tribune*, updated on website November 20, 2006. Reprinted with permission of *Star Tribune*, Minneapolis, MN.

Richie Escovedo. Excerpt from "For PR pros, 9 rules taken directly from Kindergarten," October 29, 2009, www.ragan.com. Copyright © 2009. Reprinted by permission of Ragan Communications.

Valerie Schremp Hahn. "Ex-prosecutor's husband charged. Accused of growing marijuana plants in his home" from *St. Louis Post-Dispatch*, November 15, 2006. Copyright © 2006 The Associated Press. Reprinted with permission. All rights reserved.

Jeremy Hainsworth. Vancouver, British Columbia (AP) — September 28, 2009. "Canada's 'Prince of Pot' Taken into Custody." Copyright © 2009 The Associated Press. Reprinted with permission. All rights reserved.

Lee Hancock. Excerpt "Facing death can be hardest for a family . . ." from *The Dallas Morning News*, August 30, 2009. Copyright © 2009. Reprinted with permission of *The Dallas Morning News*.

Humane Society of Missouri. "Humane Society of Missouri Confirms: Guilty Pleas Entered in Federal Court to Charges from Largest Dog Fighting Raid and Rescue in U.S. History," news release September 14, 2009. Copyright © 2009. Reprinted by permission of Humane Society of Missouri.

Stan Ketterer, journalist and journalism professor. "Guidelines for Evaluating Information on the Web." Reprinted by permission of the author.

Mark Landler and Helene Cooper, *New York Times* Staff Writers. "Marred Afghan Vote Leaves U.S. in a Delicate Spot" from *The New York Times*, World Section, September 8, 2009 issue. Copyright © 2009, The New York Times. All rights reserved. Used by permission and protected by the Copyright Laws of the United States. The printing, copying, redistribution, or retransmission of the Material without express written permission is prohibited.

Mark Landler and Eric Dash, *New York Times* Staff Writers. "Drama Behind a $250 Billion Banking Deal" from *The New York Times*, Business Section, October 15, 2008 Issue, Section A, Page 1. Copyright © 2008 The New York Times. All rights reserved. Used by permission and protected by the Copyright Laws of the United States. The printing, copying, redistribution, or retransmission of the Material without express written permission is prohibited.

J. D. Lasica. "Six Types of Citizen Journalism" from "What Is Participatory Journalism?", *Online Journalism Review*, August 7, 2003. J. D. Lasica/Socialmedia.biz. Reprinted by permission of the author.

Jeré Longman. "Waiting for Power in the Cajun Prairie" from *The New York Times*, Blog section, September 3, 2008. Copyright © 2008 The New York Times. All rights reserved. Used by permission and protected by the Copyright Laws of the United States. The printing, copying, redistribution, or retransmission of the Material without express written permission is prohibited.

Tina Macias, education reporter. "A Case Study of Leads." Reprinted by permission of the author.

Larry McShane. (AP) — September 11, 2001. Excerpt from "In an unprecedented show of terrorist horror, the 110-story World Trade Center. . . ." Copyright © 2001 The Associated Press. Reprinted with permission. All rights reserved.

Jane Meinhardt. "Mother Accused of Being Criminal Ringleader" from *St. Petersburg Times*, October 21, 1994. Copyright © 1994 by St. Petersburg Times. Reprinted by permission of *St. Petersburg Times*.

MSNBC Interactive News LLC. Los Angeles (AP) — "Smith case expert retracts some drug testimony" from MSNBC, October 28, 2009. MSNBC.com [Online] [Only staff-produced materials may be used] by Associated Press. Copyright © 2009 by MSNBC Interactive News, LLC. Reproduced with permission of MSNBC Interactive News, LLC in the format Textbook via Copyright Clearance Center.

Amanda Lee Myers. Phoenix (AP) — September 28 2009. "AZ Judge to Decide if 10-Year-Old Faces Rape Trial." Copyright © 2009 The Associated Press. Reprinted by permission. All rights reserved.

Marjorie Olster. Cairo (AP) — June 4, 2009. Excerpt from "Obama Arab World Speech: Extremists Call Him 'Wise Enemy.'" Copyright © 2009 The Associated Press. Reprinted by permission. All rights reserved.

Elizabeth Phillips. "Man Arrested in Attack, Charged with Child Endangerment," *Columbia Missourian*, November 17, 2006. Copyright © 2006 Columbia Missourian. Reprinted by permission.

INDEX

Copy Editing and Proofreading Symbols

Writing and editing for today's media are done almost exclusively on computers. Only in the book industry are most manuscripts still prepared on paper. Nevertheless, at some small newspapers and magazines, editors prefer to edit on paper. For that reason, failure to learn the copy editing symbols used in manuscript preparation is a mistake. There is a good chance you will need to use those symbols at some point in your career, if only to satisfy the occasional editor who prefers doing things the old-fashioned way.

You are even more likely to use proofreading symbols, which are used on galley proofs and page proofs to correct typeset copy. While there are some similarities in the two sets of symbols, there also are differences. The chart on the inside back cover shows the most common copy editing symbols (used in manuscript preparation) and the chart below illustrates the most common proofreading symbols (used to correct typeset copy).

Proofreading Symbols

Symbol	Meaning	Symbol	Meaning
∧	Insert at this point.	⌄⌄	Space evenly.
⊥	Push down space.	◡	Close up entirely.
ℓ	Take out letter, letters or words.	⊏	Move to left.
ᓑ	Turn inverted letter.	⊐	Move to right.
(lc)	Set lowercase.	⊔	Lower letter or word.
(wf)	Wrong font letter.	⊓	Raise letter or word.
(ital)	Reset in italic type.	(out, see copy)	Words are left out.
(rom)	Reset in roman (regular) type.	//=	Straighten lines.
(bf)	Reset in boldface type.	¶	Start new paragraph.
⊙	Insert period.	(no ¶)	No paragraph. Run together.
⋏	Insert comma.	(tr)	Transpose letters or words.
⋏	Insert semicolon.	?	Query; is copy right?
H	Insert hyphen.	⊢⊣	Insert dash.
∨	Insert apostrophe.	□	Indent 1 em.
ᵛᵛ	Enclose in quotation marks.	□□	Indent 2 ems.
≡	Replace with a capital letter.	□□□	Indent 3 ems.
#	Insert space.	(stet)	Let it stand.